AF788885

Financial Management

Financial Management

Edited by Nylah Erickson

Clanrye International
www.clanryeinternational.com

Clanrye International,
750 Third Avenue, 9th Floor,
New York, NY 10017, USA

Copyright © 2019 Clanrye International

This book contains information obtained from authentic and highly regarded sources. Copyright for all individual chapters remain with the respective authors as indicated. All chapters are published with permission under the Creative Commons Attribution License or equivalent. A wide variety of references are listed. Permission and sources are indicated; for detailed attributions, please refer to the permissions page and list of contributors. Reasonable efforts have been made to publish reliable data and information, but the authors, editors and publisher cannot assume any responsibility for the validity of all materials or the consequences of their use.

Trademark Notice: Registered trademark of products or corporate names are used only for explanation and identification without intent to infringe.

ISBN: 978-1-63240-833-4

Cataloging-in-Publication Data

Financial management / edited by Nylah Erickson.
p. cm.
Includes bibliographical references and index.
ISBN 978-1-63240-833-4
1. Finance--Management. 2. Business enterprises--Finance. 2. Corporations--Finance.
I. Erickson, Nylah.
HG4026 .F56 2019
658.15--dc23

For information on all Clanrye International publications
visit our website at www.clanryeinternational.com

CLANRYE INTERNATIONAL

Printed in China.

Contents

Preface

Every book is a source of knowledge and this one is no exception. The idea that led to the conceptualization of this book was the fact that the world is advancing rapidly; which makes it crucial to document the progress in every field. I am aware that a lot of data is already available, yet, there is a lot more to learn. Hence, I accepted the responsibility of editing this book and contributing my knowledge to the community.

The efficient and effective management of funds in order to accomplish the goals and objectives of an organization is referred to as financial management. Raising and allocation of capital, for long and short-term budgeting, forms an important focus of this discipline. The most important goal of financial management is the maximization of profit. There are several kinds of profits, such as profits before interest, depreciation and taxes, cash profit, etc. The other objectives of financial management are ensuring the survival of the company, maximizing the shareholders' wealth, maintaining the cash flow and minimizing capital cost. Financial management also encompasses the estimation of the requirement of funds, determination of the capital structure, deliverance of significant returns for the business using a good investment plan, etc. This book elucidates the concepts and innovative models around prospective developments with respect to financial management. It unfolds the innovative aspects of financial management, which will be crucial for the progress of this field in the future. The extensive content of this book provides the readers with a thorough understanding of the subject.

While editing this book, I had multiple visions for it. Then I finally narrowed down to make every chapter a sole standing text explaining a particular topic, so that they can be used independently. However, the umbrella subject sinews them into a common theme. This makes the book a unique platform of knowledge.

I would like to give the major credit of this book to the experts from every corner of the world, who took the time to share their expertise with us. Also, I owe the completion of this book to the never-ending support of my family, who supported me throughout the project.

Editor

Mathematical Integration of the EVA and RI Approach

Preuss B*
Department of International Management and Economics, Copenhagen Business School, Denmark

Abstract

This paper aims to show the connection between the added value and residual value approaches in management accounting and corporate finance. The research project was carried out at the Copenhagen Business School. The research is located in the field of management and finance research. The outcome will be to see whether and to which extent the Lucke-theory can be applied on the residual and the added value metrics. Furthermore it aims to answer whether these metrics give decision makers the same decision direction.

Keywords: Finance; Lucke-theory; EVA; RI; Management; Accounting

Introduction

The concepts of cost and investment calculation developed in the younger past more and more similarities [1]. This makes it necessary to ask the question why the cost accounting focusses less on cash flows throughout modern IT systems in organizations it is possible to perform high complex calculations within a realistic amount of time and costs [2]. The question regarding the combinability of the profit, capital value and added value calculations and models creates the possibility to use these systems in an integrated model. Those integration aspects can be already found in current research [3]. As a base for this paper, the theory of Ga-briel Preinreich is used [4]. This theory was further developed by Wolfgang Lucke [3]. The theory represents an approach that can be seen in comparison to the investment calculations [4].

The target of this paper is to show the relationship between the capital models and the added value models. The core of the paper answers whether and with which limitations can the Preinreich-Lucke theory is applied on the added value models [4]. Here for uses the paper beside the residual income the Economic value added (EVA) to show this relationship in theoretical mathematical equilibrium. Possible limitations of the equilibrium will be stated in the paper [5].

Beside the study of current research the paper will use mathematical equilibriums to show the relation between the residual income model and the EVA model. The analysis may show that both models are inter exchangeable with each other when some facts are fulfilled.

Theoretical Concepts

Preinreich lucke theory

Investments of a corporation are related to all parts of this organization and can affect multiple parts of it. The related tasks can therefore be seen as a core function in an organization and can be seen as highly relevant for the strategic development of a company [6]. In order to make suitable investment decisions a plan for this is necessary A central part of this is the investment calculation which is a way for a rational decision support. Beside the decision support and other important function of the investment calculation is the integration function. The separation of some of the accounting actions in a company raised the integration function of the investment calculation in order to show the overall connection to the other accounting parts in an organization [1]. This integration function leads to an integration of the different parts of the accounting with that the company in its whole can be described from a financial perspective. One solution to achieve this integration function is when the investment calculation will be used as basis for the accounting in an organization [1,7]. In his papers Lucke differentiates between direct and indirect integration. According to Lucke is it possible to explain the connections between Investment, Financial, Cost and Cash-Flow calculation with direct integration. For tax calculations and special KPIs the indirect integration is suitable. But this last way of explanation will not be covered by this paper.

The integration gets possible throughout the concept of discounting. It is crucial to mention that the discounting needs to be made over the whole time a company exists. Based on this calculation it is possible to calculate all balance sheets of the different years with the equilibrium for each period *t*.

This follows the approach that cash-flows will be sorted according to their influence and balance sheet positions. This development of plan balance sheets represents on the passive side the interest rate and on the active side a correction in the cash positions [7-9]. Because of this every year fulfills this equilibrium:

Ct at the active side is the same as *Ct* of the passive side with:

$$C_t = C_{t-1} + i * C_{t-1} \tag{1}$$

$$C_t = [\sum_{t=0}^{T} CF_t(1+i)^{-t}](1+i)^t \tag{2}$$

$$CF_t = E_t - A_t \tag{3}$$

Et describes the cash inflow of the period *t* and *At* die cash outflow of the period *t*. *i* is the interest rate. *Ct* stands for the capital value in the period *t*. *T* describes in this case the end of the organization or the investment. When it comes to the cash in and outflows it can happen that they count for a different period because of a time lack. This will be taken into account in the concept by using positive or negative interest rates which lead to a cost reduction or cost increase [10].

As a result out of this, capital models for an investment project lead to the same results by using different calculation bases like Cash-Flow,

***Corresponding author:** Bjorn Preuss, BA, MSc, Department of International Management and Economics, Copenhagen Business School, Howitzvej 60, 2000 Frederiksberg, Denmark, E-mail: b.preuss@outlook.com

Profit-Loss, and Income-Cost. The theory shows furthermore that an investment calculation can be performed with all of these measures [10]. The Preinreich-Lucke-Theory shows that there is a connection between these measures and that they can be used inter exchangeable for one another [3,7].

A requirement for this theory is that after a specific time frame, the cahsflows and the profit loss accounts accumulate to the same amount. Another requirement is that all values are based on future prices for the sale and purchase of goods. It is furthermore not suitable to use in the calculation interest, repayment and dividend payouts [11].

The capital commitment in the period -1, *G-1*, and at the end of the timeframe in *T*, *GT*, should be both 0.

By using the theory of Hellauer to interest rates [12], it is possible to build the following equilibrium [13].

$$\sum_{t=0}^{T} \ddot{U}_t = \sum_{t=0}^{T} (Result_t) \quad (4)$$

$$\sum_{t=0}^{T} CF_t (1+i)^{-t} = \sum_{t=0}^{T} (\ddot{U}_t - i * G_{t-1})(1+i)^{-t} \quad (5)$$

$$\sum_{s=0}^{t-1} \ddot{U}_s - \sum_{s=0}^{t-1} CF_S = G_{t-1} fort = 0,1,...T+1 \quad (6)$$

$$\sum_{s=0}^{t} \ddot{U}_s - \sum_{s=0}^{t} CF_S = G_t fort = 0,1,...T+1 \quad (7)$$

Us is here the surplus out of the second control variable for example the cash flow (see for that formula 3) or profit/Losses, to the time *t*. *Gt* is the capital that is committed in the investment at the time *t*. This is based on the assumption that the sum of all cashflows *CFt* is the same as the sum of all profits *Üt*. In this case *G-1* = 0 and *Gt* = 0 applies. Formula (6) shows the definition for the capital commitment of the first period and formula (7) the definition for the capital commitment of the actual period. Formula (5) represents the equilibrium between the cash flow and the adjusted control variable *Ut*, as for example the residual income.

Residual income

The concept of the residual income is based on equal assumptions like the economic value added model which will be presented in the next part. The opportunity costs of the investor will be integrated into the model which leads to the fact that a decision for investment will be made only under the circumstances that the profit from the investment increases the costs of equity. This concept was developed by Edwards/Bell and Ohlson [14,15].

The concept adjusts the earnings by the interest for the equity which needs to be paid in each period on the invested capital. This can be summarized in the following:

$$RI = \sum_{t=0}^{T} (\ddot{U}_t - i * G_{t-1}) \quad (8)$$

Formula (8) describes the relation between the residual income concept and the Preinreich-Lucke-Theory. For this, look on the second part of the formula (5). *RI* describes in the formula the residual Income. The rest of the notions are the same as in the formulas above.

In the practical world will *Gt-1* be the equity of the company. *i* is here the interest rate that is used to discount the outcomes of the periods. This interest rate can be calculated by using the Capital-Asset-Pricing-Models (CAPM) or the Arbitrage-Pricing-Theory (ATP) [16,17]. The differences between these calculation methods for the discount factor will be not covered in this paper.

Economic value added

The Economic value Added (EVA) was developed in the 1990's by the consulting firm Stern & Steward. Mainly responsible for the concept are Stern J and Stewart G [18,19]. Like the residual Income so is also the EVA a member of the family of the residual income methods. This means that the earnings will be reduced by the capital cost which means that the opportunity costs for an investment will be a part of the calculation. According to certain scholars should it be possible to use the EVA concept in multiple areas of a business. One could be the resource allocation or the budgeting [18,19]. The calculation of the EVA is like followed:

$$EVA = NOPAT - WACC * NOA \quad (9)$$

NOPATt describes the earnings before interest. The tax effect will be not covered in this paper in order to reduce complexity in the equilibriums. Also the adjustments of the NOPAT that are suggested from Stern & Steward will be not applied in this paper [18,19]. The variable Weighted Average Cost of Capital *WACC* will be used instead of the interest rate *i*. Since the concept of the EVA is based on the whole capital of a business, it is crucial to cover all costs for resources in the *WACC* [5]. The Net Operating Assets (*NOA*) replacing here the position of the capital commitment G. See for this formula (7).

$$NOAt = \sum_{s=0}^{t} NOPAT_s - \sum_{s=0}^{t} FCF_s \quad (10)$$

The Free-Cash-Flow (*FCF*) needs to be used to make the equilibrium work since the whole capital is part of the calculation. Based on formula (9) and (10), the formula for the EVA can be generated.

$$EVA_t = NOPAT_t - WACC_t * NOA_{t-1} \quad (11)$$

With this the amount that is in addition to the capital costs produces will be described by the EVA measure.

Analysis of Concept Connection

Residual income

The Preinreich-Lucke-Theory shows that the residual value concept is able to be used as a calculation for short and long term focus. In a normal case the focus on cashflows would not lead to the same result as if the discounted profits of the periods would be analyzed. The reason for this is that the profits and the cashflows in each period differs and therefore lead to different results. In order to come with both values to the same result, the connection between the cashflows and the profits will be shown with the residual income (profit) and the free cash flow (Cashflow)

Based on formula (5) which shows the equilibrium of the Lucke-Theory and formula (8) which represents the residual income, it is possible to present the validity of the theory.

The formulas (6) and (7) can be set in relation to each other which results in formula (12) as shown here

$$G_t - G_{t-1} = \left(\sum_{s=0}^{t} \ddot{U}_s - \sum_{s=0}^{t} CF_S \right) - \left(\sum_{s=0}^{t-1} \ddot{U}_s - \sum_{s=0}^{t-1} CF_S \right) \quad (12)$$

Formula (12) describes the difference between the capital commitment in the current period and the period before. It is possible to change this formula to calculate the profit *Ut*.

$$\ddot{U}_t - CF_t = G_t - G_{t-1} \quad (13)$$

$$\ddot{U}_t = CF_t + G_t - G_{t-1} \quad (14)$$

Now it is possible to see that the profits in *t*, *Ut*, by using the cashflow and the difference in the capital commitment in *t* and *t-1*. In the next step it is possible to inset the formula (14) into formula (8) and simplify the formula.

$$\sum_{t=0}^{T}(Ü_t - i*G_{t-1})(1+i)^{-t} = \sum_{t=0}^{T}(CF_t + G_t - G_{t-1} - i*G_{t-1})(1+i)^{-t} \quad (15)$$

$$\sum_{t=0}^{T}(Ü_t - i*G_{t-1})(1+i)^{-t} = \sum_{t=0}^{T}(CF_t + G_t - (1+i)*G_{t-1})(1+i)^{-t} \quad (16)$$

It is possible to show the equilibrium (16) in a different way and split the last sum. Throughout this change it will be clear that the discounted cashflows and the discounted residual values are the same.

$$\sum_{t=0}^{T}\frac{Ü_t - i*G_{t-1}}{(1+i)^t} = \sum_{t=0}^{T}\frac{CF_t}{(1+i)^t} + \sum_{t=0}^{T}\frac{G_t}{(1+i)^t} - \sum_{t=0}^{T}\frac{G_{t-1}}{(1+i)^{t-1}} \quad (17)$$

$$\sum_{t=0}^{T}\frac{Ü_t - i*G_{t-1}}{(1+i)^t} = \sum_{t=0}^{T}\frac{CF_t}{(1+i)^t} + \sum_{t=0}^{T}\frac{G_t}{(1+i)^t} - \sum_{t=-1}^{T-1}\frac{G_t}{(1+i)^t} \quad (18)$$

$$\sum_{t=0}^{T}\frac{Ü_t - i*G_{t-1}}{(1+i)^t} = \sum_{t=0}^{T}\frac{CF_t}{(1+i)^t} + \frac{G_T}{(1+i)^T} - \frac{G_{-1}}{(1+i)^{-1}} \quad (19)$$

Since the capital commitment *G-1* is zero, so is the capital commitment at the end of the life of the investment/company *GT* zero. This leads to make the last two parts of the formula (19) zero.

$$\sum_{t=0}^{T}\frac{Ü_t - i*G_{t-1}}{(1+i)^t} = \sum_{t=0}^{T}\frac{CF_t}{(1+i)^t} \quad (20)$$

The equilibrium (20) is a version of formula (5). This shows the validity for the theory when it comes to the residual income. It needs to be mentioned that the equity value is already contained in the formula since the sum was calculated starting at *t=0*. See for that the following formula:

$$\sum_{t=0}^{T}\frac{Ü_t - i*G_{t-1}}{(1+i)^t} = \sum_{t=0}^{T}\frac{Ü_t - i*G_{t-1}}{(1+i)^t} + EQ_0 \quad (21)$$

EQ0 is the value of the equity in *t=0*.

Economic value added

According to Steward is the cumulated discounted EVA the same as the result of the discounted cash flow method (DCF) [19] Because of this it applies:

$$\sum_{t=0}^{T}\frac{EVA_t}{(1+WACC)^t} = \sum_{t=0}^{T}\frac{FCF_t}{(1+WACC)^t} \quad (22)$$

Already in this stage it can be seen a parallel to the relationship between the cash flow and the residual income. Steward wants to show with this statement that the company value can be calculated by using the EVA measure and therefore can be used inter exchangeable to the DCF [19]. It shows that the relationship needs to be equal to the one that Lucke described in his work [3]. In order to prove this, it should count the same assumptions as in the previous calculation. First the difference between the capital commitments of two following periods will be shown.

$$NOPAT_t - FCF_t = NOA_t - NOA_{t-1} \quad (23)$$

$$NOPAT_t = FCF_t + NOA_t - NOA_{t-1} \quad (24)$$

The formula is pretty equal to formula (13) and (14). The difference is here that it will be calculated with values of the total capital of the company. In the next step formula (11) will be placed in these which leads to the next formula (25).

$$\sum_{t=0}^{T}\frac{EVA_t}{(1+WACC)^t} = \sum_{t=0}^{T}\frac{NOPAT_t - WACC*FCF_t}{(1+WACC)^t} \quad (25)$$

$$\sum_{t=0}^{T}\frac{EVA_t}{(1+WACC)^t} = \sum_{t=0}^{T}\frac{FCF_t + (NOA_t - NOA_{t-1}) - WACC*NOA_{t-1}}{(1+WACC)^t} \quad (26)$$

$$\sum_{t=0}^{T}\frac{EVA_t}{(1+WACC)^t} = \sum_{t=0}^{T}\frac{FCF_t + NOA_t - (1+WACC)*NOA_{t-1}}{(1+WACC)^t} \quad (27)$$

It is possible to split the equilibrium (27) in sums.

$$= \sum_{t=0}^{T}\frac{FCF_t}{(1+WACC)^t} + \sum_{t=0}^{T}\frac{NOA_t}{(1+WACC)^t} - \sum_{t=0}^{T}\frac{NOA_{t-1}}{(1+WACC)^t} \quad (28)$$

$$= \sum_{t=0}^{T}\frac{FCF_t}{(1+WACC)^t} + \sum_{t=0}^{T}\frac{NOA_t}{(1+WACC)^t} - \sum_{t=-1}^{T-1}\frac{NOA_t}{(1+WACC)^t} \quad (29)$$

$$= \sum_{t=0}^{T}\frac{FCF_t}{(1+WACC)^t} + \frac{NOA_T}{(1+WACC)^T} - \frac{NOA_{-1}}{(1+WACC)^{-1}} \quad (30)$$

Like listed in the assumptions, *G-1* and *GT* are both zero. This leads to the effect that the last parts of the formula (30) are zero.

$$\sum_{t=0}^{T}\frac{EVA_t}{(1+WACC)^t} = \sum_{t=0}^{T}\frac{FCF_t}{(1+WACC)^t} \quad (31)$$

The formula (31) is the same as (22) and this shows that the Preinreich-Lucke-Theory counts also when it comes to the EVA and that the EVA can be used instead of the cashflow calculation.

Relationship RI and EVA

Now the paper has shown the connections between both the residual income and the cashflow and the EVA and the free cash flow. This part will focus on the relationship between the EVA and the residual income as well as the cashflow and the free cash flow. The previous parts of this paper have shown that both the EVA and the residual income lead under the assumptions of the Pre-inreich-Lucke-Theory to the same results as the linked measures cashflow and free cash flow.

In this part it should be present that also the EVA and the RI lead to the same result and with that give the decision maker the same base. The first situation in which both are the same is when the company is financed with 100% equity since then the interest is 0 and both formulas get the same result. It is then *WACC=i* und *NOPAT=U* and *NOA=G*. Since the input values are the same, the result will also not differ. However this holds only true when there are not changes when calculating the *NOPAT* [18,19].

Furthermore it will be shown that the discounted EVA has the same result like the discounted RI. This would lead to the same investment and divestment decisions. If the equilibrium (32) holds true, then also formula (33) needs to hold true.

$$\sum_{t=0}^{T}\frac{Ü_t - i*G_{t-1}}{(1+i)^t} \geq 0 \quad (32)$$

$$\sum_{t=0}^{T}\frac{EVA_t}{(1+WACC)^t} \geq 0 \quad (33)$$

For this calculation the NOA will be defined as the whole capital of the project and the capital commitment the same as the equity of a period. The author wants to raise the hypothesis that the graphs of both values over changing situations have a different increase but they meet at the point of zero. This means that both values give in all situations the same decision advice when they get discounted. In the following graphic the values of RI and EVA will be plotted by changing interest rates (Figure 1) and in the second graph over changing earnings or NOPAT (Figure 2).

In Figure 1 and 2 it is able to see that the increase of the function of the discounted EVA is higher as the one of the discounted RI. This leads to the interpretation that there is also a combination out of financing and interest rate where both values are the same. However it is much more important that both values cut the x-achses at the same point. This means that by changing variables both measures give the same decision support.

Now it needs to be examined whether EVA and RI can also have the same value. The WACC needs to be calculated on the base of market values to make this work.

$$WACC = \left(FK * i^{FK} + EK^m * i^{EK}\right) / GK^m \quad (34)$$

EK^m is the equity value based on market valuation and GK^m the market value of the total invested capital.

$$EK_t^m = EK_t + \sum_{t=1}^{T-1} \frac{RI_t}{\prod_{t=1}^{t}(1+i_t)} + \frac{RI_T}{i_T * \prod_{t=1}^{T-1}(1+i_t)} \quad (35)$$

The market equity value (EK^m) will be calculated based on the balanced equity EK at t and the cumulated residual income which will be calculated using the roll back method until the time t [20].

When the discounted residual income RI will be over the lifetime of the company with the perpetuity method be cumulated, then it generates the same result like the EVA if this measure will be calculated based on the market value of equity. Based on these assumptions it needs to hold true that the left sides of the equilibriums (17) and (22) needs to be the same. But to make this happen it is important to use the retrograde version while discounting [20,21].

$$\sum_{t=1}^{T-1} \frac{EVA_t}{\prod_{t=1}^{t}(1+WACC_t)} + \frac{EVA_T}{WACC_T * \prod_{t=1}^{T-1}(1+WACC_t)}$$

$$= \sum_{t=1}^{T-1} \frac{RI_t}{\prod_{t=1}^{t}(1+i_t)} + \frac{RI_T}{i_T * \prod_{t=1}^{T-1}(1+i_t)} \quad (36)$$

In this formula RIt is the residual income in t. $WACC$ is the based on market equity value calculated

$WACC$. The interest rate of the equity is i. Since a 3rd mathematical equilibrium would be too much for this paper, this relation will be shown in a practical example (Table 1). That the roll back method leads to an exact solution by doing business valuation, can be seen in the work of Casey [21]. The company value will be calculated starting with the entity value and to the time of the valuation [22].

Result

This work showed the assumptions connected to the Preinreich-Lucke-Theory. Furthermore it presented the relationship between the capital and profit accounting concepts. The core of the paper focused on the question in which cases the Preinreich-Lucke-Theory can be used also for the added value concepts. This showed the paper with the residual income and economic value added measure.

It came to the result that the residual income as well as the EVA can lead to the same result as their related cash flow measure (CF and FCF). Furthermore the paper elaborated more the relationship between the both concepts RI and EVA which are based on the one hand on the equity and on the other hand on the entity approach. The single discounted values of the RI and the EVA will give the user to all times the same decision direction (either invest or devest). The reason for this is that both measures change at the same time from negative to positive. The only difference it the increase of their curves. If the WACC in the EVA measure is calculated with market values and if

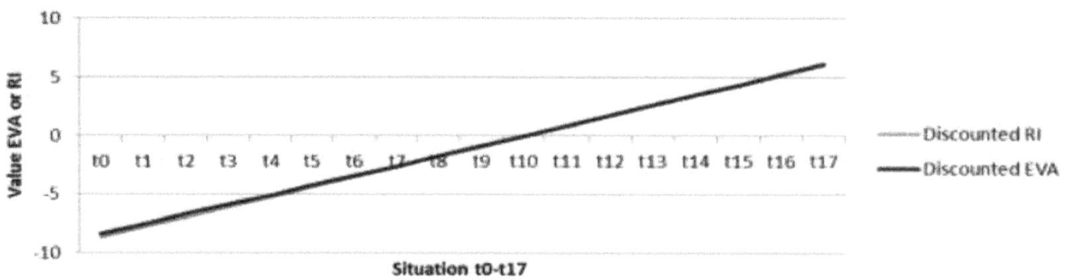

Figure 1: Comparison of RI and EVA in changing the borrowing interest rate.

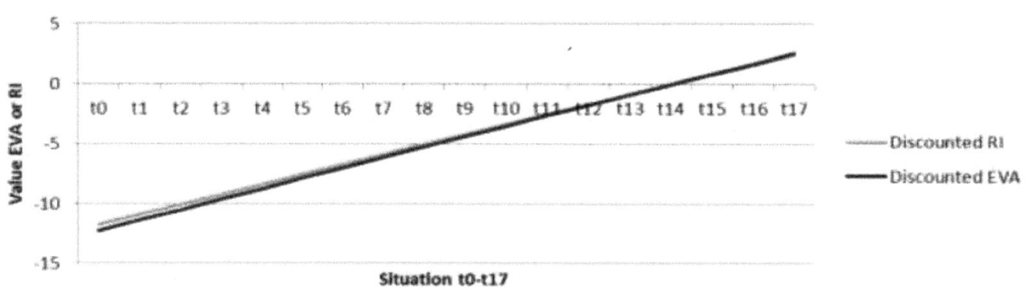

Figure 2: Comparison of RI and EVA at the change in earnings.

	C0	t0	t1	t2	t3
Equity	-	300	200	100	-
Market value equity	1.185	1.716	1.662	1.587	1.487
Debt	-	300	200	100	-
NOPAT		-	320	320	320
Interests		-	32	21	11
Profit	-	-	289	299	310
Interest rate equity	20%	20%	20%	20%	20%
Interest rate debt	11%	11%	11%	11%	11%
WACC		19,50%	18,16%	18,53%	18,97%
RI		-	230	260	290
Discounted RI	**1.185**	1.416	1.462	1.487	1.487
EVA		-	211	246	282
Discounted EVA	**1.185**	1.416	1.462	1.487	1.487

Comparison of KPIs

Table 1: Example calculation comparison EVA and RI.

both measures are calculated by using the perpetuity method, then the result of both concepts is identical.

Future Research

Since this paper answers the last question about the relationship between the EVA and the RI only with an example and not a mathematical equilibrium, future research could look on this and tries to solve this problem in a mathematical way.

References

1. Lucke W (1989) The concept of integration in the accounting of the company and the operation. In: Delftman W (ed.) The concept of integration in business administration. Assisted by Gap Wiesbaden pp: 219-253.
2. Mannel W (1985) Integration of cost accounting and capital budgeting. krp pp: 121-122.
3. Lucke W (1955) Investment calculation on the basis of expenditure or costs? ZfhF 7: 310-324.
4. Preinreich G (1937) Valuation and Amortization. The Accounting Review 12: 209-226.
5. Stewart BG, Chew D (1995) The EVA Financial Management System. Journal of Applied Corporate Finance 8: 32-40.
6. Eisner R (1978) Factors in business investment. Cambridge pp: 1-16.
7. Lucke W (1991) Investitionslexikon. Vahlen.
8. Lucke W (1977) Plan accounting and plan budgets. Applied planning 1: 47-56.
9. Lucke W, Hautz U (1973) Balances of future values. A theoretsicher contribution to the content and structure of plan balances. Wiesbaden.
10. Sierke B (1993) To take account of potential for success in the gap theorem. Management -oriented accounting pp: 85-102.
11. Lucke W (1960) Nature and significance of imputed interest. ZfhF 12: 353-375.
12. Hellauer J (1931) Costing in Trade and Industry. Accounting.
13. Lücke W (1965) The imputed interest in accounting. ZfhF 35: 3-28.
14. Edwards EO, Bell PW (1961) The theory and measurement of business income. Berkeley.
15. Ohlson JA (1995) Earning, Book Values and Dividents in Equity Valuation. Contemporary Accounting Research 11: 661-687.
16. French CW (2001) The Treynor Capital Asset Pricing Model. Journal of Investment Management 2: 60-72.
17. Burmeister E, Wall KD (1986) The Arbitrage Pricing Theory and Macroeconomic Factor Measures. Financial Review 1: 1-20.
18. Stern JM (2002) The EVA challenge. Implementing value-added change in an organization. Norwood, Mass.
19. Stewart GB (1991) The quest for value. A guide for senior managers. Business and economics, New York.
20. Crusselt N, Lohmann C (2012) Business valuation with the Residualgewinn modell: gross versus net approach. LexisNexis pp: 143-162.
21. Casey C (2004) New aspects of the rollback process in the Business valuation. Journal of Business economics 74: 139-163.
22. Baetge J, Niemeyer K, Kummel J, Schulz R (2009) Representation of the discounted cashflow method. Herne pp: 339-477.

2

Home-Bias Investment Measure: Evidence from a Repeated Experiment in Taiwan

Wei-Lung Huang[1*] and Yan-Kai Fu[2]

[1]Assistant Professor, Department of Finance, China University of Science andTechnology, Taiwan

[2]Assistant Professor, Department of BusinessAdministration, China University of Science andTechnology, Taiwan

Abstract

This study uses repeated experiment to explore the possible reasons of home-bias investment. The results indicated that the reasons for home-bias investment are information asymmetry or familiarity, resulting in over-investment in Taiwanese investment vehicles. The level of home-bias investment changed with the level of information asymmetry changes. A significant difference in home-bias investment was observed for different levels of education, investment experience, age, annual income and annual investment. Moreover, the difference in investment ratio did not change based on different levels of information asymmetry.

Keywords: Home-bias investment; Investment portfolio; Experimental questionnaire

Introduction

Today, cross-border investment barriers have been substantially reduced. To pursue the maximum rate of return of investment portfolios, investors actively invest in foreign financial markets. For example, as of the end of February 2010, Taiwanese investors held 1,004 accounts of offshore funds (the amount was NT $ 2.07 trillion). Various studies showed that the main reason for investors to hold foreign investment vehicles is the increase of the rate of return or risk reduction. For example, Karolyi and Stulz [1] reviewed the literature available on the international factors influencing the demand and prices of financial assets. They found that when cross-border investment barriers do not exist and the investor's investment decisions are affected by the mean and variance of the return of investment (ROI) in invest vehicles of various countries, an investor's portfolio should include investment vehicles in various countries.

At present, the investment portfolio of most investors is still primarily composed of Taiwanese assets (called home-bias investment in this study) and does not differ across countries, levels of knowledge and professional levels. Howell and Cozzini [2] observed that the proportion of domestic securities held by domestic investors in December 1986 was 92% in the United States, 95.7% in Japan, 92% in UK, 79% in Germany and 89.4% in France. Cooper and Kaplanis [3], Kang and Stulz [4] and Tesar and Werner [5] proved that investors in various countries all have home-bias investment. In addition, Karolyi and Stulz [1] observed that home-bias investment caused gradually reduced profit in cross-border investments, and Chan et al. [6] observed that home-bias investment also exists in mutual funds (investment professionals).

Based on the summary of various studies, home-bias investment occurred because of information asymmetries or familiarity; that is, over-investment into domestic investment vehicles occurred because information on domestic securities is easier to obtain and because domestic investors are more familiar with the information. French and Poterba [7] used the model of investor preferences to prove that the expected ROI of domestic assets is much higher than that of international ones and that the reason for home-bias investment is the investor's investment decision rather than institutional constraints. Using the framework of international expect at ions with background noise, Gehrig [8] and Brennan and Cao [9] observed that when investors have more accurate information on domestic investment vehicles, home-bias investment ma y occur. Shiller et al. [10], Kilka and Weber [11], Ackert et al. [12] and Strong and Xu [13] proved that familiarity will affect the investor's level of optimism and trust and then generate the expectation bias of risk and reward. Shiller et al. [10] noted that investors expect better performance for domestic securities than for foreign securities. Huberman [14] showed that investors are more prone to have a sense of trust with familiar things; thus, investors prefer to invest in more familiar companies. Ackert et al. [12] used an experimental questionnaire and determined that investors do not prefer domestic securities if the production is not home-based. For example, when the subjects were informed of the name of the securities, the y could associate the securities with the parent company. If the company's production base was not in the home country, the subject s would select other countries for investment.

Investors are unable to distinguish between the level of information asymmetry or familiarity for domestic and foreign investment vehicles; moreover, the existing studies have not yet clarified whether home-bias investment varies based on different degrees of information asymmetries or familiarity. Therefore, the first objective of this study was to use an experimental questionnaire to control for the level of information asymmetry and to explore the impact of the level of information asymmetry or familiarity with domestic and foreign investment vehicles on the investor's home-bias investment. The purpose of the experimental questionnaire used in this study was to investigate the investor's allocation status of funds to domestic and foreign assets when presented with different information. Moreover, in

***Corresponding author:** Wei-Lung Huang, Assistant Professor, Department of Finance, China University of Science and Technology, No.245, Sec.3 Academia Rd, Nangang Dist, Taipei City 11581, Taiwan
E-mail: hippoobee@yahoo.com.tw

the experimental questionnaire, in addition to controlling for the level of information asymmetry of the subjects, interfering variables such as the transaction costs and the risk level of the subjects' portfolio could also be controlled.

The experimental questionnaire used in this study controls for the level of information asymmetry; that is, the level of information received by various groups of subject s was different. Existing studies have not yet explored whether the domestic bias of investors changes depending on the amount of information at the starting point of investment (i.e., frame effect) or the amount of information (i.e., the level of information asymmetry). Therefore, the second objective of this stud y was to use the repetitive experimental questionnaire to change the level of information asymmetry and then to explore the framing effect and the impact of the changes in the level of information asymmetry on the home-bias investment. Earl and Morgan [15] divided information processing into three stages: acceptance, perception and action. In the perception stage, empirical experience is prone to cause subjective judgment bias (i.e., (the framing effect). Tversky and Kahneman [16] defined the framing effect refers as the phenomenon in which precisely the same decision-making situation will lead to different decision-making behaviors based on differences in the presentation of information. Levin et al. [17] explored three types of framing effects: risk selection framework, attribute framework and target framework. The risk selection framework explains how framing affects the willingness of consumers to take risks [16] the attribute framework explains how framing affects the consumer's assessment of the subject matter or event [18], and the target framework explains how framing affects the convincibility of communications [19].

Because the level of information asymmetry of domestic and foreign investment vehicles is subject to the investor's personal variables (such as gender, age, education level and occupation), home-bias investment may be affected by the investor's persona l variables and by familiarity with domestic and foreign investment vehicles. Therefore, the third objective of this study was to use an independent sample T test and correlation analysis to explore whether home-bias investment would change based on an investor's personal variables and familiarity with domestic and foreign investment vehicles and, moreover, whether the difference in home-bias investment changed with an adjustment in the level of information asymmetry. In addition, regression equations were used to explore the effect of the investor's personal variables and familiarity with domestic and foreign investment vehicles on the home-bias investment.

This paper is divided into four parts: an introduction, a description of the stud y design, an analysis of the results and conclusions and suggestions.

Study Design

To control for the subjects' level of information asymmetry and considering that the performance and basic information on the investment vehicles affects investment decisions, this study divided the information provided concerning the investment vehicles into four categories: no information, performance information, basic information and all information (i.e., both performance and basic information). The performance information included the ROI of investment vehicles, standard deviation, β Sharpe index and Treynor index. The basic information included the scale of the investment vehicles, management fees, custodial fees, service fees and investment targets[1].

To control for the framing effect and the type of subjects, this study divided the subjects into four groups, and four experiments were conducted in each group. The type of information received during the first experiment was different in each group, and the type of information received in each experiment was also different (Table 1). Each experiment lasted for 30 minutes. The subjects rested for one hour before the next experiment. The entire duration of the experiments was five hours[2].

The subjects answered six questionnaires. During the first experiment, the subjects answered three questionnaires related to personal data, the investment environment in various countries and their portfolio. During the second, third and fourth experiments, the subjects answered one questionnaire per experiment. The questionnaire on personal data was used to explore the personal factors that may influence home-bias investment. The questions included information on gender, age, educational level, occupation, annual income, the number of investment courses previously taken (number of investment courses), amount of annual investment and whether the investor had previously invested in more than two types of investment vehicles (investment experience). The purpose of surveying the number of investment courses previously taken was to understand whether the subjects understood the concepts of the pursuit of ROI and risk diversification. The purpose of surveying whether the subjects had previous experience investing in more than two types of investment vehicles was to understand whether the subjects understood the concept of an investment portfolio.

[1]The performance information of the investment vehicles provided in this study was the ROI (old Taiwanese currency) for 1, 3 and 6 months and 1, 2 and 3 years, 3-year standard deviation (NT), 3-β value (NT), 3-year Sharpe index (NT) and 3-year Treynor index (NT). The base point of the information was December 31, 2009. ROI provided the subjects with the profits and future trend of investment vehicles. The standard deviation, β, Sharpe index and Treynor index provided the subject with the risk of the investment vehicles. Basic information was provided so that the investors could understand the relevant fees for various investment vehicles and select investment vehicles believed to have potential for portfolio allocation, according to the scales and investment targets.

[2]To explore the effect of the framing effect and different levels of information on home-bias investment, this study used one hour as the interval between experiments because after one hour, the subjects may still have some memory of the information in the previous experiment. The forgetting curve in Ebbinghaus (1885) showed that the average memory retention rate was roughly 58% after 20 min, 44% after one hour and 35% after eight hours.

	1th group	2nd group	3rd group	4th group
1th	no information	performance information	basic informatio n	all information
2nd	performance information	basic information	all information	no informatio n
3rd	basic information	all information	no informatio n	performance informatio n
4th	all information	no information	performance informatio n	basic informatio n

Table 1: The order of various types of information received by the subjects in each group

The questionnaire on the investment environment in various countries was used to explore the subjects' familiarity with the investment environment in various countries. The questions included topics such as national financial markets, economic conditions, market risk, credit risk, liquidity risk, operational risk, regulator y risk and whether the subjects lived in the country before. In this study, the level of familiarity for each question was scored on a scale of 1-10. The average score of each question regarding Taiwan was defined as the level of familiarity with the Taiwanese investment vehicles, and the average score for each question related to other countries was defined as the level of familiarity with foreign investment vehicles. In this study, the countries included on this questionnaire were those that offered investment vehicles on the portfolio questionnaire, such as Taiwan, mainland China, the United States, India, Japan, South Korea, Thailand, Australia, Singapore, Hong Kong, UK and Switzerland. The questions on topics such as national financial markets, economic conditions and whether the subjects lived in the country before were designed to understand the subjects' level of understanding of the ROI of investment vehicles in various countries. Questions concerning market risk, credit risk, liquidity risk, operational risk and regulator y risk were designed to understand the subjects' level of understanding of the risk of the investment vehicles in various countries.

The portfolio questionnaire used in each experiment asked the subjects to full y allocate $ 1,000,000 into the portfolio tab le (the amount of investment could be zero, but it could not be negative), with reference to various types of information. Then, the answers were used to understand whether there was home-bias investment in the subject s' investment behavior and whether the extent of home-bias investment was affected by the level of information asymmetry and familiarity, the framing effect and the type of information change.

The fifteen domestic and foreign investment vehicles included in the portfolio questionnaire were three exchange-traded funds (ETFs), eleven publicly traded mutual funds and one time deposit. The Taiwanese investment vehicles included were one Taiwanese ETF (domestic ETF), one Taiwanese publicly traded mutual fund (domestic mutual fund) and the Taiwanese post office time deposit (domestic time deposit). The foreign investment vehicles included were two offshore ETFs (foreign ETFs) and ten offshore publicly traded mutual funds (foreign mutual funds). Because, among the foreign investment vehicles, investors were more likely to select ETFs and publicly traded mutual funds, the time deposit was the most common risk-free asset and home-bias investment was the focus of this study, the investment vehicles included on the portfolio questionnaire were divided into five types of investment vehicles: the Taiwanese ETF, Taiwanese mutual funds, foreign ETFs, foreign mutual funds and the Taiwanese time deposit[3].

To explore whether home-bias investment changed with different investment portfolios, this study divided the portfolio questionnaire into ETF and time deposit (Type A), publicly traded mutual funds and time deposit (Type B), and ETF, publicly traded mutual funds and time deposit (Type C). The different portfolio groups had a different number of investment vehicles that investors knew or could purchase, and the number of investment vehicles investors knew represented the level of information asymmetry. The number of investment vehicles investors could purchase represented the level of governmental control of the investment vehicles. For example, Taiwan's Financial Management Committee audited investment vehicles that were listed in the Taiwanese market, in accordance with political factors or the financial market and system.

Because the investment amount in the experimental questionnaire could require an alteration of our hypothesis, the reference value of the investment amount was small. Thus, this study focused on the investment ratio and used SPSS17.0 for the descriptive statistical analysis of the questionnaire data and hypothesis testing (such as correlation analysis, paired sample T tests, analysis of variance (ANOVA), regression analysis and single factor ANOVA analysis). For example, based on the overall data, the grouping of the type of information and the portfolio, the descriptive statistics of various investment ratios were calculated and compared. This study then explored whether there was home-bias investment in Taiwanese investors' investment behavior and whether Taiwanese investors' home-bias investment varied based on type of information or the grouping of the portfolio.

In addition, this study used Kolmogorov-Smirnova and Shapiro-Wilk normality tests to test the investment ratio of the subjects of different gender, educational level, occupation and investment experience and the experimental group. If the criterion of a normal distribution was met, then an independent sample T test was performed to compare the averages. Otherwise, the Kruskal-Wallis H test of K nonparametric independent samples and the Mann-Whitney U test of two independent samples were used to explore the following: (1) whether an investor's investment ratio would vary depending on gender, educational level, occupation and investment experience and whether the level of the investment ratio changed with the adjustment of the level of information asymmetry; (2) whether an investor's home-bias investment would vary based on differences in the type of information initially provided (framing effect).

Moreover, this stud y analyzed the correlation between the subjects' personal variables (age, annual income, the number of investment courses previously taken, annual investment amount, familiarity with Taiwanese investment vehicles and familiarity with foreign investment vehicles) and the investment ratio. This study then explored whether there was significant correlation between a Taiwanese investor's investment ratio and these personal variables and whether the correlation in the investment ratio varied significantly based on the level of information asymmetry.

Furthermore, this stud y used paired sample T tests to determine investment ratios when the same subject received different types of information (no information, performance, basic information, all information) or different portfolios (Type A, B, C) and then to explore whether a Taiwanese investor's home-bias investment changed with the adjustment in the type of information or portfolio (i.e., the level of information asymmetry).

Finally, this study used regression equations to verify the extent of the effect of investor's personal variables and familiarity

[3]As of the end of 2009, 14 ETFs (11 domestic component securities ETFs and 1 foreign component securities ETF) could be publicly traded in Taiwan. The ETFs selected by the portfolio questionnaire were the oldest and largest "Polaris Taiwan Top 50 securities investment trust funds" and the offshore ETFs, "Hang Seng H-Share ETF" and "Hang Seng ETF". The selection criteria for publicly traded mutual funds were: general equity funds invested in only one country, the funds from the top 11 countries with regard to the amount of holdings by Taiwanese investors and the funds with the highest 3-year ROI. Finally, the publicly traded mutual funds selected for the portfolio questionnaire were the Yongfeng SinoPac Securities Investment Trust Fund in Taiwan, Threadneedle (Lux) in the United States - American Equity Fund (USD), AIG Global Funds in India - AIG India Equity Fund Y, Fidelity Investment Fund in Japan - Japanese Potential Fund (Y share of cumulative shares - yen), JF South Korea Fund in South Korea, JF Thailand Fund in Thailand, Lion Capital Australia Fund in Australia (USD), Singapore UBS (Lux) Equity Fund in Singapore, UK Prudential Fund Company in Hong Kong - Prudential Hong Kong Fund, UK Prudential Group M & G New Opportunity Fund and Switzerland Falcon Swiss Equity Fund in Switzerland.

with domestic and foreign investment vehicles on the home-bias investment. The regression equation used was as follows

$$Y_i = \alpha_{0,i} + \beta_{1,i}X_{1,i} + \beta_{2,i}X_{2,i} + \beta_{3,i}X_{3,i} + \beta_{4,i}X_{4,i} + \beta_{5,i}X_{5,i} + \beta_{6,i}X_{6,i} + \beta_{7,i}X_{7,i} + \beta_{8,i}X_{8,i} + \beta_{9,i}X_{9,i} + \beta_{10,i}X_{10,i} + \varepsilon_i \quad (1)$$

where Yi is the investment ratio of the domestic investment vehicles, $X_{1,i}$ is gender, $X_{2,i}$ is age, $X_{3,i}$ is the education level, $X_{4,i}$ is occupation, $X_{5,i}$ is annual income, $X_{6,i}$ is the number of investment courses previously taken, $X_{7,i}$ is the annual investment amount, $X_{8,i}$ is the investment experience, $X_{9,i}$ is the familiarity with domestic investment vehicles and $X_{10,i}$ is the familiarity with foreign investment vehicles. i=1-4, i=1 is domestic ETF, portfolio A; i=2 is domestic mutual funds, portfolio B; i=3 is domestic ETF, portfolio C; and i=4 is domestic mutual funds, portfolio C[4].

Statistical Analysis

This study divided the subjects into four groups. 52, 36, 42 and 35 valid questionnaires were collected from Group 1, 2, 3 and 4, respectively. There were 53 male and 112 female subject s; 102 subjects were younger than 25 years of age, and 63 were older than 26 years of age; 139 had received a college education, and 26 had a graduate degree; 89 were students, and 76 were employed; 105 earned less than NT $ 300,000/year, and 60 earned more than NT $ 300,001/year; 87 had taken less than 10 investment courses, and 78 had taken more than 11 investment courses; 101 invested less than NT $ 25,000/year, and 64 invested more than NT $ 25,001/year; and 75 had previously invested into more than two types of investment vehicles, and 95 had never invested into more than two types of investment vehicles. The distribution of each group was similar to that of the overall d istribution[5].

Concerning the level of familiarity (mean of the sum) with the investment environment in various countries, the subjects were most familiar with Taiwan, followed by mainland China, the United States, Japan and Hong Kong. There was no significant difference for the remaining countries. The distribution of each question and each group was similar to that of the overall distribution.

Concerning the descriptive statistical results of the portfolio questionnaire, when the fifteen domestic and foreign investment vehicles were analyzed, there was home-bias investment in the investment behavior of Taiwanese investors. Regardless of the overall data, for grouping of the type of information or of the portfolio, the subjects' investment ratios (mean) were the highest for Taiwanese ETF, Taiwanese mutual funds and Taiwanese time deposit. The variance of the subjects' investment ratio demonstrated similar results.

According to the descriptive statistical results of the portfolio questionnaire, investor home-bias investment varied with the grouping of the type of information or of the portfolio. This study assumed that the number of investment vehicles could be viewed as the level of information asymmetry for investors; therefore, the level of information asymmetry was one of the reasons for home-bias investment, and the reduction of the level of information asymmetry (performance, basic information or the disclosure of investment vehicles) could reduce the investor's home-bias investment. For the groups that received different types of information, the investment ratio of Taiwanese ETF or Taiwanese mutual funds (mean) was decreased in the sequence of no information, basic information, performance and all the information. The effect of performance was far larger than basic information on home-bias investment. For the groups of different portfolios, the investment ratio of Taiwanese ETF or Taiwanese mutual funds (mean) was the highest for Type A, followed by Type B and Type C.

According to the descriptive statistical results of the portfolio questionnaire, the investment behavior of Taiwanese investors depended on their familiarity with the investment environment in various countries. Therefore, the level of familiarity was one of the reasons for home-bias investment. For example, the investment ratio (mean) of ETFs in mainland China, mutual funds in the United States, mutual funds in Japan, ETFs in Hong Kong and mutual funds in Hong Kong varied with the type of information or the grouping of portfolio; in the grouping method, the ratio was the second highest, and the investment ratios (means) of the aforementioned investment vehicles in the remaining countries were all small.

When the descriptive statistical results of the portfolio questionnaire were analyzed in terms of Taiwanese ETFs, Taiwanese mutual funds, foreign ETFs, foreign mutual funds and the Taiwanese time deposit, the level of Taiwanese investors' home-bias investment was smaller than in previous studies, which was caused by the high level of internationalization of Taiwanese financial market and the universality of financial knowledge among the Taiwanese population. Because the investment ratios of various foreign investment vehicles were quite small and the focus of this study was on home-bias investment, this study hypothesized that the investment ratio of foreign ETFs and foreign mutual funds was the sum of that of the two offshore ETFs and the ten offshore mutual funds. The subjects' investment ratios (mean) were mostly the highest in foreign ETFs or foreign mutual funds (except one group), and the order of the variance of the subjects' investment ratios indicated similar results.

The analysis of variance results of the subjects' investment ratio according to gender, educational level, occupation and investment experience is presented in Table 2. There was no significant difference in most of the investment ratios of Taiwanese investors regarding gender, educational level, occupation and investment experience. However, occupation had the largest effect, and the difference in the investment ratios did not vary with the level of information asymmetry. The results of the normality test verified that a normal distribution of the investment ratios was present when the subjects of different gender, educational level, occupation and investment experience were grouped according to investment portfolio, the type of information and investment vehicles. Moreover, this study used independent sample T tests to explore whether there was a difference in the investment ratios of Taiwanese investors based on gender, educational level, occupation and investment experience. Only 24 of the 176 T tests with an equal mean had significant results, of which 2 results indicated significance in gender, 7 in educational level, 10 in occupation and 5 in investment experience[6].

The results of Table 2 indicate that there was a significant difference in the investment ratio of Taiwanese investment vehicles based on the difference in educational level or investment experience. Moreover,

[4]The coding of each question on the questionnaire of personal data was: male = 0, female = 1; = age; college education = 0, graduate degree =1; student=0, employed =1; = annual income = the number of investment courses previously taken; = the annual investment amount; invested into more than two kinds of investment vehicles before = 0, never invested into more than two kinds of investment vehicles = 1; = familiarity with Taiwanese investment vehicles; = familiarity with foreign investment vehicles.

[5]Due to the complexity of the questionnaire results, this study only introduced the most important and significant results. If further details are needed, please contact the author.

[6]This study calculated the results of 176 T tests with an equal mean, based on the four questions concerning personal data (gender, educational level, occupation and investment experience), the four types of information and eleven investment vehicles (three types of portfolio).

	investment portfolio	Types of Information	investment vehicles	Levene Test(F)	T test	Average Difference
gender	Type A	basic information	foreign ETFs	0.420	-0.049*	-0.002
	Type C	basic information	foreign mutual funds	0.132	-0.033*	-0.001
education level	Type A	performance information	Taiwanese ETF	0.004	0.059*	0.002
	Type B	no information	Taiwanese mutual funds	0.802	-2.527*	-0.080
		all information	Taiwanese mutual funds	0.826	-0.041*	-0.001
	Type C	performance information	Taiwanese mutual funds	1.936	-2.899**	-0.083
			Taiwanese time deposit	2.308	-0.046*	-0.002
		basic information	Taiwanese mutual funds	4.590	-3.256***	-0.075
			Taiwanese time deposit	0.979	-0.039*	-0.002
occupation	Type A	no information	Taiwanese ETF	0.653	-0.035*	-0.001
		performance information	foreign ETFs	0.047	0.041*	0.002
	Type B	no information	foreign mutual funds	1.085	2.469*	0.094
		basic information	foreign mutual funds	0.622	2.011*	0.073
	Type C	no information	Taiwanese ETF	3.143	-2.467*	-0.050
			foreign mutual funds	2.534	3.095**	0.112
		performance information	foreign mutual funds	0.132	2.314*	0.081
		all information	Taiwanese ETF	0.044	-2.458*	-0.053
			foreign ETFs	7.081	-2.222*	-0.051
			foreign mutual funds	0.227	2.425*	0.088
investment experience	Type B	performance information	Taiwanese mutual funds	5.018	2.034*	0.050
		basic information	Taiwanese time deposit	0.006	-0.022*	-0.001
	Type C	performance information	Taiwanese ETF	0.373	2.677**	0.052
		basic information	Taiwanese time deposit	0.742	-0.029*	-0.001
		all information	Taiwanese time deposit	0.149	-0.002**	-4.500×10^{5}

Note * p < .05, ** p < .01, *** p < .000

Table 2: The analysis of variance of the subjects' investment ratio due to gender, educational level, occupation and investment experience.

the higher the educational level, the lower the investment ratio of the Taiwanese investment vehicles (roughly 8%). The investment ratio of the Taiwanese time deposit often decreased slightly with more investment experience. Furthermore, the investment ratio of the foreign mutual funds increased dramatically (roughly 8-11%) based on the occupation of Taiwanese investors.

The results of the correlation analysis of the subjects' personal variables (age, annual income, the number of investment courses previously taken and annual investment amount) and the investment ratios are provided in Table 3. There was no significant correlation between the majority of the investment ratios and age, annual income, the number of investment courses previously taken and annual investment amount, and the significance of a small number of investment ratios varied with the level of information asymmetry. Only 15 of the 176 correlation analyses had significant results, of which, 5 results were significant in age, 7 in annual income, 0 in the number of investment courses previously taken and 3 in the annual investment amount. Moreover, 14 of the 15 significant results were from the groups that received no information or basic information.

The results in Table 3 indicate that for Taiwanese investment vehicles, there was a significant positive correlation between the investment ratio of Taiwanese investors and age, annual income and annual investment amount. For the foreign funds, there was a significant negative correlation between the investment ratio of Taiwanese investors and age, annual income and annual investment amount. Therefore, the older the subject s, the higher the annual income, and the larger the amount of annual investment, it means that the higher the level of the Taiwanese investor's home-bias investment.

The results of the correlation analysis of the subjects' personal variables (familiarity with Taiwanese and foreign investment vehicles) and investment ratios are provided in Table 4. There was significant correlation between the investment ratio of Taiwanese investment vehicles and familiarity with Taiwanese and foreign investment vehicles, and there was no significant correlation between the investment ratio of foreign investment vehicles and familiarity with Taiwanese and foreign investment vehicles. In addition, the significance of the investment ratio did not vary with the level of information asymmetry. Twenty of the 56 correlation analyses of Taiwanese investment vehicles had significant results, and 3 of the 32 correlation analyses of foreign investment vehicles had significant results. Moreover, 10 results of the familiarity with Taiwanese investment vehicles were significant, and 13 results of the familiarity with foreign investment vehicles were significant. The results in Table 4 demonstrate that the investor's home-bias investment increased with higher familiarity with Taiwanese investment vehicles (which were consistent with those of Gehrig [8], Brennan and Cao [9]; however, the investor's home-bias investment did not decrease with higher familiarity with the foreign investment vehicles. Moreover, the amount of Taiwanese time deposit s decreased with increased

	investment portfolio	Types of Information	investment vehicles	Correlation coefficient
age	Type B	no information	foreign mutual funds	-0.156*
		basic information	Taiwanese mutual funds	0.175*
	Type C	no information	Taiwanese ETF	0.191*
		no information	foreign mutual funds	-0.207**
		basic information	foreign mutual funds	-0.184*
annual income	Type A	no information	Taiwanese ETF	0.156*
	Type B	basic information	Taiwanese mutual funds	0.216**
		all information	Taiwanese mutual funds	0.166*
	Type C	no information	Taiwanese ETF	0.245**
		performance information	Taiwanese ETF	0.208**
		basic information	Taiwanese ETF	0.197*
		basic information	foreign mutual funds	-0.153*
number of investment courses	N/A			
amount of annual investment	Type B	basic information	foreign mutual funds	-0.164*
	Type C	no information	Taiwanese ETF	0.165*
			foreign mutual funds	-0.160*

Note: * p < .05, ** p < .01

Table 3: Correlation analyses of the subjects' personal variables and investment ratio.

	Investment portfolio	Types of Information	Investment vehicles	Correlation coefficient
familiarity with Taiwanese investment vehicles	Type A	no information	Taiwanese time deposit	-0.184*
		basic information	Taiwanese time deposit	-0.169*
	Type B	no information	Taiwanese mutual funds	0.193*
		performance information	Taiwanese mutual funds	0.186*
		basic information	Taiwanese mutual funds	0.221**
		all information	Taiwanese mutual funds	0.158*
	Type C	no information	Taiwanese ETF	0.184*
		performance information	Taiwanese ETF	0.261**
		basic information	Taiwanese time deposit	-0.158*
		all information	Taiwanese ETF	0.174*
familiarity with foreign investment vehicles	Type A	no information	Taiwanese time deposit	-0.216**
		performance information	Taiwanese time deposit	-0.174*
		basic information	foreign ETFs	0.178*
			Taiwanese time deposit	-0.200*
		all information	Taiwanese time deposit	-0.154*
	Type B	no information	Taiwanese time deposit	-0.184*
		basic information	Taiwanese time deposit	-0.163*
	Type C	no information	Taiwanese time deposit	-0.179*
		performance information	Taiwanese time deposit	-0.184*
		basic information	foreign ETFs	0.190*
			Taiwanese time deposit	-0.189*
		all information	foreign ETFs	0.178*
			Taiwanese time deposit	-0.155*

Note: * p < .05, ** p < .01

Table 4 Correlation analyses of the subjects' familiarity with Taiwanese (Foreign) investment vehicles and each investment ratio.

familiarity with foreign investment vehicles. The purpose of including the Taiwanese time deposit (a risk-free investment vehicle) in this study was for investors to control the risk of the investment portfolio; the amount of the Taiwanese time deposit decreased with increased familiarity with foreign investment vehicles. The results were similar to those of previous studies in that the investor's risk tolerance level increased with familiarity with investment vehicles. For Taiwanese ETFs and Taiwanese mutual funds, there was a significant positive correlation between the Taiwanese investor's investment ratio and familiarity with the Taiwanese investment vehicles. For the Taiwanese time deposit, there was a significant negative correlation between the Taiwanese investor's investment ratio and familiarity with the Taiwanese investment vehicles. For foreign ETFs, there was a significant positive correlation between the Taiwanese investor's investment ratio and familiarity with the foreign investment vehicles. For the Taiwanese time deposit, there was a significant negative correlation between the Taiwanese investor's investment ratio and familiarity with the foreign investment vehicles.

The analysis of variance of the ratio of investment between the subject s in Group 1, 2, 3 and 4 and those in the other 3 groupings is provided in Table 5. The framing effect of home-bias investment may exist; however, it had insignificant effects. The results of the normality test (Kolmo gorov-Smirnova and Shapiro-Wilk) verified that there was a normal distribution in the groupings of the portfolio, the type of information and investment vehicles for the subjects from Groups 1, 2,

3 and 4. This study used independent sample T tests to explore whether there was a difference in the home-bias investment of Taiwanese investors based on the amount of information initially received. The results in Table 5 indicate that only 16 of the 176 T tests with an equal mean had significant results, of which 4 significant results were from Group 1, 0 from Group 2, 6 from Group 3 and 6 from Group 4.[7]

The results of the paired sample T test on the investment ratios when the same subject received different types of information or portfolios are presented in Tables 6 and 7. The home-bias investment of Taiwanese investors varied with the level of information asymmetry; therefore, the Taiwanese government could reduce the level of information asymmetry of investment vehicles or the level of control, thereby reducing investor's home-bias investment. The results in Tables 6 and 7 indicate that the paired sample T tests exhibited partly significant differences in the investment ratios when the Taiwanese investor received different types of information; moreover, the paired sample T test results were all significant when the same subject received different portfolios. In addition, the descriptive statistical results indicate that the investment ratio of Taiwanese investment vehicles decreased with an increase in the number of investment vehicles.

The results in Table 6 demonstrate that the reduction in the level of information asymmetry of investment vehicles could not improve the home-bias investment of Taiwanese investors in some investment vehicles (such as Taiwanese ETFs). Only the disclosure of a certain type of information (such as performance) could reduce the level of information asymmetry of investment vehicles. None of the results of the paired sample T tests were significant concerning the investment ratio of Taiwanese ETFs when the same Taiwanese investor received different types of information; moreover, the investment ratio of Taiwanese mutual funds when the same Taiwanese investor received the information of performance (or all of the information) was significantly different from that when the same Taiwanese investor received no information or basic information.

The result s of the regression equation that used the investment ratio of Taiwanese ETFs and Taiwanese mutual funds as the dependent variable and investor's personal variables and domestic and foreign investment vehicles as independent variables are provided in Table 8. The investment ratio of Taiwanese ETFs and Taiwanese mutual funds decreased with an increase in the number of investment vehicles (Table 8, constant value). When the controlled level of information asymmetry was excluded, the investor's familiarity with the Taiwanese investment vehicles significantly positively affected the investment ratio of Taiwanese ETFs and Taiwanese mutual funds, which is consistent with the hypothesis of this study. That is, one reason for the home-bias investment is the investor's over-investment in Taiwanese investment vehicles because of familiarity with the Taiwanese investment vehicles, while familiarity with foreign investment vehicles had no definitive effect[8].

The results in Table 8 indicate that when the controlled level of information asymmetry was excluded, the investor's educational level significantly positively affected the investment ratio of the Taiwanese mutual funds, and the investor's annual income significantly positively affected the investment ratio of the Taiwanese ETFs. When the results of Tables 2-4 and Table 8 are combined, it can be observed that the results are almost identical. Therefore, the effect of the subjects' personal variables on the investment ratios did not vary significantly based on the level of information asymmetry.

Conclusions

This study used experimental questionnaires to control the level of information asymmetry and explored the effect of an investor's level of information asymmetry and familiarity with domestic and foreign investment vehicles on home-bias investment. Based on the descriptive statistical results of the questionnaires and the analytical results of the regression equation, the reason for home-bias investment is the investor's over-investment into Taiwanese investment vehicles because of information asymmetry or familiarity. In addition, the level of home-bias investment of Taiwanese investors was lower than that in previous studies, which was due to the high level of internalization

[7]This study calculated the results of 176 T tests with an equal mean based on the four groups of subjects, the four types of information and eleven investment vehicles (three types of portfolio).

[8]This study compiled all the data (the level of information asymmetry was excluded) for the regression equation.

	investment portfolio	Types of Information	Investment vehicles	Levene Test(F)	T test
Group 1 VS. the other 3 groups	Type A	performance information	Taiwanese ETF	1.453	2.206*
			Taiwanese time deposit	0.545	2.082*
		basic information	Taiwanese time deposit	0.041	-2.164*
	Type C	no information	Foreign ETFs	0.519	-1.978*
Group 2 VS. the other 3 groups			None		
Group 3 VS. the other 3 groups	Type A	all information	Taiwanese ETF	1.690	2.729**
	Type B	no information	Foreign mutual funds	6.576*	2.511*
			Taiwanese time deposit	16.405***	-2.528*
		basic information	foreign mutual funds	1.954	2.033*
	Type C	no information	foreign mutual funds	1.359	2.258*
		basic information	Taiwanese time deposit	12.827***	-2.148*
Group 4 VS. the other 3 groups	Type A	no information	Taiwanese ETF	0.408	-1.973*
		performance information	Taiwanese ETF	2.303	-2.145*
		all information	Taiwanese ETF	1.034	-2.022*
			Taiwanese time deposit	3.185	2.066*
	Type B	no information	foreign mutual funds	2.716	-2.174*
	Type C	basic information	foreign ETFs	1.442	-1.977*

Note: * $p < .05$, ** $p < .01$

Table 5: The analysis of variance of the subjects' investment ratios between Groups 1, 2, 3 and 4 and the other 3 groups.

Investment portfolio	Types of Information	Investment vehicles	T tests
Type B	no information VS. performance information	Taiwanese mutual funds	-3.345*
	no information VS. all information		-2.402*
Type C	no information VS. performance information	Taiwanese mutual funds	-4.211**
		Foreign ETFs	3.587**
	no information VS. all information	Taiwanese mutual funds	-3.528*
		foreign mutual funds	-2.215*
	performance information VS. basic information	Taiwanese mutual funds	3.256*
		Foreign ETFs	-3.163*
	performance information VS. all information	Foreign ETFs	-2.167*
	basic information VS. all information	Taiwanese mutual funds	-2.455*

Note: * $p < .05$, ** $p < .01$

Table 6: Paired sample T test of the same subject's investment ratio when presented with different types of information.

investment portfolio	Types of Information	investment vehicles	T tests
Type A VS. Type C	no information	Taiwanese ETF	14.544**
		foreign ETFs	17.227**
	Performance information	Taiwanese ETF	13.613**
		foreign ETFs	16.739**
	basic information	Taiwanese ETF	14.682**
		foreign ETFs	14.922**
	all information	Taiwanese ETF	14.656**
		foreign ETFs	15.107**
Type B VS. Type C	no information	Taiwanese mutual funds	8.729**
		foreign mutual funds	12.661**
	Performance information	Taiwanese mutual funds	7.269**
		foreign mutual funds	13.108**
	basic information	Taiwanese mutual funds	9.621**
		foreign mutual funds	14.009**
	all information	Taiwanese mutual funds	7.773**
		foreign mutual funds	10.877**

Note: * $p < .05$, ** $p < .01$

Table 7: Paired sample T test of the same subject's investment ratio when presented with different portfolios.

	investment portfolio of type A's Taiwanese ETF	investment portfolio of type B's Taiwanese mutual funds	investment portfolio of type C's Taiwanese ETF	investment portfolio of type C's Taiwanese mutual funds
constant	0.290***	0.131***	0.083**	0.061*
gender	-0.009	-0.008	0.024*	-0.014
age	0.000	-7.923x10-5	0.000	9.737 x10-5
education level	-0.007	0.055**	0.018	0.054***
occupation	-0.053**	0.012	0.005	0.004
annual income	1.137x10-7*	6.885 x10-8	1.178 x10-7***	-2.743 x10-9
number of investment courses	0.000	0.000	-0.001	0.000
annual investment	-7	-8	-8	-7
investment experience	0.001*	-0.013	-0.014	0.029*
Domestic investment tool familiarity	0.010**	0.016***	0.014***	0.008**
Foreign investment tool familiarity	-0.006	-0.014**	-0.011*	-0.008

Note: * $p < .05$, ** $p < .01$

Table 8: The effect of the investor's personal variables and level of familiarity with domestic and foreign investment vehicles on their home-bias investment (regression coefficient).

of the Taiwanese financial market and the universality of financial knowledge among the Taiwanese population, as well as the fact that the subject s' behavior was simulated rather than actual. Therefore, this stud y suggests that future researchers can re-explore this topic using long-term real investigative data.

This stud y used repetitive experimental questionnaires, independent sample T tests and paired sample T tests to explore the effect of the framing effect and the level of information asymmetry on home-bias investment. The results demonstrate that the effect of the framing effect on home-bias investment may exist but is small. In addition, the home-bias investment of Taiwanese investors varied with the level of information asymmetry, and only the disclosure of certain types of information (such as performance) or an increase in the number of investment vehicles could change the level of information asymmetry. Therefore, the Taiwanese government could reduce the level of information asymmetry of investment vehicles (disclosure of the performance of investment vehicles) or the level of control (increase of number of investment vehicles), thereby reducing the level of investor home-bias investment.

This study used independent sample T tests, correlation analysis and regression equations to explore the effect of the investor's personal variables and familiarity with domestic and foreign investment vehicles on the home-bias investment. The majority of the investment ratios of Taiwanese investors did not vary significantly based on gender, educational level, occupation, annual income, the number of investment courses previously taken, annual investment amount or investment experience. However, the investment ratio of Taiwanese investment vehicles varied significantly based on educational level, investment experience, age, annual income and annual investment amount. Moreover, the difference in the investment ratios did not vary with the level of information asymmetry.

The level of the home-bias investment of Taiwanese investors increased with an increase in familiarity with Taiwanese investment vehicles but did not decrease with an increase in familiarity with foreign investment vehicles. In addition, the amount of Taiwanese time deposit decreased with an increase in familiarity with Taiwanese and foreign investment vehicles. The results were similar to previous studies in that the investor's risk tolerance level increased as the level of familiarity with investment vehicles increased.

The results of this study demonstrate that the framing effect existed; however, its effect was small, which may be due to the one-hour rest time between experiments. It is suggested that future researchers can adjust the rest time to explore the effect of different experimental rest times on the framing effect.

Reference

1. Karolyi GA, Stulz RM (2002) Are Financial Assets Priced Locally or Globally? Handbook of Economics and Finance 1: 975-1020.
2. Howell M and Cozzini A (1990) London: alomon Brothers European Equity Research. International Equity Flows.
3. Cooper I, Kaplanis E (1994) Home Bias in Equity Portfolios, Inflation Hedging, and International Capital Market Equilibrium. Review of Financial Studies 7: 45-60.
4. Kang JK, R. Stulz RM (1996) Why is There a Home Bias? An Analysis of Foreign Portfolio Equity Ownership on Japan. Journal of Financial Economics 46: 3-28.
5. Tesar LL, Werner IM (2001) Home Bias and High Turnover. J Int Money Financ 14: 467-492.
6. Chan k, Vicentiu MC, and Lilian KN (2006) What Determines the Domestic Bias and Foreign Bias? Evidence form Mutual Fund Equity Allocations Worldwide. Journal of Finance 60: 1495-1534.
7. French KR, Poterba JM (1991) Investor Diversification and International Equity Markets. American Economic Review 81: 222-226.
8. Gehrig TP (1993) An Information Based Explanation of the Domestic Bias in International Equity Investment. Scand. J. of Economics 95: 97-109.
9. Brennan MJ and Cao HH (1997) International Portfolio Investment Flows. Journal of Finance 52: 1851-1880.
10. Shiller RJ, Kon-Ya F, Tsutsui Y (1996) Why Did the NIKKEI Crash? Expanding the Scope of Expectations Data Collection. Review of Economics and Statistics 78: 156- 164.
11. Kilka M, Weber M (2000) Home Bias in International Stock Return Expectations. Journal of Psychology and Financial Markets 1: 176-192.
12. Ackert LF, Church BK, Tompkins J, Zhang P (2003) What's in a Name? An Experimental Examination of Investor Behavior. Review of Finance 9: 281-304.
13. Strong N, Xu X (2003) Understanding the Home Equity Bias: Evidence from Survey Data. Review of Economics and Statistics 85: 307-312.
14. Huberman G (2001) Familiarity Breeds Investment. Review of Financial Studies 14: 659-680.
15. Earl AA, Morgan B Jr (1976) Engineering Psychology and Human Performance. Annual Review of Psychology 27: 305-331.
16. Tversky A, Kahneman D (1981) The Framing of Decisions and the Psychology of Choice. Science 21: 453-458.
17. Levin IP, Schneider SL, Gaeth GJ (1998) All Frames Are Not Created Equal: A Typology and Critical Analysis of Framing Effects. Organizational Behavior and Human Decision Processes 76:149-188.
18. Levin IP, Gaeth GJ (1988) How Consumers are Affected by the Framing of Attribute Information Before and After Consuming the Product. Journal of Consumer Research 15: 374-378.
19. Meyerowitz BE, Chaiken S (1987) The Effect of Message Framing on Breast Self-Examination Attitudes. J Pers Soc Psychol 52: 500-510.

3

A Study of Business Students' Attitudes in Saudi Arabia: Generation C, Islamic Values, and Westernised Educational Video

G Martin Izzo[1] and Shaza W Ezzi[2*]

[1]Fulbright Scholar, Visiting Associate Professor, Department of Marketing, King Abdulaziz University, Saudi Arabia
[2]Assistant Professor, Department of Marketing, King Abdulaziz University, Saudi Arabia

Abstract

The present study investigated the relationships between Saudi Arabian college students and the "connected" Generation C, their use of small mobile devices to access video, video usage in the classroom, and behavioral variables like the willingness to seek and share video outside the classroom. Additionally, the study explored the relationship between Saudi Arabian students' attitudes about classroom learning through the use of Westernised videos where the content was presented in situations not in keeping with strict Islamic laws and traditions. Four research questions were generated and data was gathered using the Video Attitude Survey—a five point Likert scale instrument. The data was collected from college students (N=139) enrolled in business school classes at large public university. Descriptive statistics, Pearson correlations and selected Chi square analyses were conducted on the data. Frequency distributions were calculated to show the variables of interest for each research question, and then presented in concurrent tables.

The findings indicate that Saudi Arabian students living in a strict Islamic society still see themselves as part of the worldwide Generation C. That they use mobile devices to download and distribute video, more for social networking and trend-pacing than for news services. That their strong ties to Islamic tradition have a weak yet significant influence on learning from Westernised educational video. The study's most promising findings were the positive relationships between students' attitudes toward learning through educational video, improving their English speaking ability, and gaining a greater understanding of multi-cultural issues and differences.

Keywords: Saudi Arabia; Generation C; Islamic values; Educational video

Introduction

The present study investigated attitudes about the "connected" generation, video usage, and in particular Westernised educational video of business students at a large public university in Saudi Arabia. The social mores are different in Saudi Arabia, and the Islamic-influenced social structure is considered far more strict, even when compared to its Arab neighbors like Kuwait and Oman [1]. While Saudi Arabian college students based on age cohort are no less a part of the "connected" generation than their counterparts the world over their attitude toward membership in this group is relatively unknown [2,3].

Labeled by Nielsen, often shortened to Gen C by various media, Generation C (where C stands for connected) is a group so connected by mobile devices that it leads all other groups in the use of online videos, networking, blog sites and the ownership of tablets and smartphones [2,4,5]. As a rule, Generation C were born after 1990 and lived their adolescent years after 2000. In the developed world, Generation C encompasses everyone in this age group; in the BRIC countries (Brazil, Russia, India, and China), they are primarily urban and suburban [4]. The importance to marketers is that by 2020 Generation C will constitute the largest single cohort of consumers worldwide [6]. Additionally, when it comes to shopping and buying decisions, 85 percent of Generation C relies on peer input and approval [6]. Decision-making has become a team sport, where practically every product or service considered for purchase is reviewed, rated, and shared. "Marketing successfully becomes all about "talking to the community, not the individual" and creating a conversation for the swarm to run with" suggests Dan Pankraz, Youth Strategist, DDB Sydney [4].Thus, successful brand marketing with Generation C means getting into "tribal conversations" that are happening around and across different tribes, and connecting brand names, products and services with interesting ideas, cultural objects, causes and movements.

While their use of handheld technology and Internet prowess may be documented, little is known about the attitudes of Generation C toward video use in the classroom. The ways in which Saudi students embrace Westernised video in classrooms may provide insights to marketers as to how they will relate to similarly-styled advertising messages from commercial sources. Further, the present study is the first of its kind to actually go into the classrooms of Saudi Arabian students to find out how they associate with being part of Generation C, and what they think about Westernised educational video. Thus, understanding the attitudes of Saudi Arabian business students contributes to the overall research of Generation C, and adds information important to marketers everywhere.

Purpose of Study: the who, what, why and where for the study

Who

Following in the digital footprints of the millennials, Generation C — with the C standing for "connected" — is a term coined by Nielsen, a global leader in measurement and information, to describe young adults between the ages of 18 and 34 who lead a mainly digital

***Corresponding author:** Shaza W Ezzi, Assistant Professor, Department of Marketing, King Abdulaziz University, Jeddah, Saudi Arabia. PO Box 42623, 21551, E-mail: shazaezzi466@gmail.com

lifestyle. Although making up just 23 percent of the U.S. population, and an untold number worldwide, this group leads all other groups in their use of online videos, networking, blog sites and in owning tablets and smartphones [4]. As a rule, they were born after 1990 and lived their adolescent years after 2000. In the developed world, Generation C encompasses practically everyone in this age group [6]. By 2020, Generation C will make up 40 percent of the population in the U.S., Europe, and the BRIC countries [7].

With a median age of only 26 Saudi Arabia has a comparatively young population. According to [8] report, Saudi Arabia's population 15-24 years is 19.6% and 25-54 years is 44.8%. By contrast, population statistics in these ranges for two of Saudi Arabia's trading partners are: Turkey 17% and 42%, and United Kingdom 13% and 41%.For Saudi Arabia, these two age groups comprise about 64.4% of population, and slightly overlap the Generation C 18-34 range. However, this presents the statistic of a sizable, young demographic, and adds support for studying the "connected" behaviors of Generation C, as they represent a large portion of Saudi Arabia's population. Marketers and researchers call Generation C — connected, communicating, content-centric, computerized, community-oriented, and seemingly always clicking their personal digital devices [6]. Researchers needed to identify this group so that it could be accounted for in market research. Marketers, on the other hand, needed to update their thinking and revise their marketing plans and sales strategies to focus on this connected generations' buying power and affinity for group decision-making. Determining how pervasive this new Generation C is in light of other world cultures, and in particular in the strict social structure of Saudi Arabia, is a timely and relevant research endeavor [2, 3, 5].

What

While Generation C leads all other groups in its use of online videos and social networking, little is known about how this group feels about the use of educational video in the classroom. Much research has investigated the effects of television and video on children, from toddlers, to pre-school and as young adolescents, very little research has been published about young adults and college students [e.g. 9, 12]. Additionally, much of the research that involves evaluating the educational effects of video is proprietary in nature, and as a result, unpublished [13, 14]. However, researchers suggest that more research of educational aspects of television and video on different aged populations is needed [e.g. 10,12]. The present study helps to address this need by investigating college students. Since video, particularly viral video is a major part of the communications arsenal of Generation C, it is important to understand how this group feels about educational video used in the courses they study. Given the proclivity of this group toward social networking and participating in on-line group decision making, video in the classroom has the potential to become an attractive learning tool. Generation C already uses video as one of its main entertainment outlets information and fact-finding sources, so it may be reasonable to expect this group to embrace the use of education video.

However, the same may not hold true in Saudi Arabia. While educational videos are one of the most prolific modern educational methods being used in highly-developed countries, the same is not true in developing nations [15]. Prior research examined Saudi Arabian university students' cultural response to technological change by investigating acceptance of Internet banking [16]. Examining how firm contexts that are influenced by Islamic values such as in Saudi Arabia contrast with more Westernised business practices may shape business students' understanding of cross-cultural organizational mechanisms and processes. Using depth interviews with Saudi top-level managers and expatriate, customer-facing sales and marketing personnel [17] found harmony among firms using a formal Saudi top-down managerial structure, a slightly different model from the more interactive approach practiced at many Western firms. Culture does matter, and accordingly, the different aspects of Islamic values and Saudi tradition may influence student's acceptance as members of Generation C and the use of Westernised educational videos in the classroom.

Why

Beyond the challenges discussed above facing marketers and advertisers bootstrapping to understand Generation C, destined to be the largest consumer group on the planet by the year 2020, employers will have to deal with the "connectedness" of Generation C. "As the world becomes increasingly global and mobile, employers can benefit from workers who are in tune with the latest technology and are adept at communicating through the latest devices and collaborating with people all over the world" [2, p.1]. The connectedness of Generation C can empower and align workforces to levels never achieved before, creating on-line real-time collaboration through digitalized technology and with enhanced mobility [5,2]. Generation C members are experts with forming groups or tribes to share information, digesting large amounts of information quickly, and are resistant to processes and concepts that are not optimized for these proficiencies. For example, members of Generation C are much more comfortable seeking connections with other audiences and using their social networking skills to find solutions to well-defined problems [2]. This will be a key strength as they enter the workforces of today's interconnected business environments. However, in order to leverage the power of Generation C, businesses and other employers will be required to learn more about them in order to connect with them in their totally plugged-in lifestyles.

Where

While educational videos have been used in most education institutions of highly-developed countries, usage is still in its early stages in the developing countries [15]. This is especially true for conservative Islamic countries such as Saudi Arabia [e.g. 18,20]. Therefore, this research was conducted in Saudi Arabia because of its unique Islamic culture that influences practically every aspect of people's daily lives and behaviors. Gender separation, one of the most well-known and unique features or rules in Saudi culture, has influenced peoples' attitudes negatively toward the liberal lifestyles practiced in Westernised cultures [19,21,22]. For example, Saudi men and women are not permitted to attend public events together and are segregated in the work place. The separation concept, which originated from Islamic law has become a social tradition [19,21,22].Thus, further investigation is needed to determine if video use in Islamic cultures is appropriate in general. Saudi Arabia, the acknowledged heartland of Islam, presents a greater challenge as one of the most socially conservative Muslim countries in the Arab region [18,20]. Moreover, the city of Jeddah where the study took place is considered the center of Muslim religious thought, and gateway to Islam's two holy cities, Madinah (Medina) and Makkah (Mecca) [22].

The present study was conducted to investigate the attitudes of college students toward Generation C, and the use of on-line and Westernised educational videos. The social mores of Saudi Arabia are different, and Saudi Arabia's interpretation of Islam creates a social structure that is considered more strict, even when compared with other Arabic and Islamic countries. Would these factors have an impact on whether or not Saudi students see themselves as members of the "connected" Generation C? Do Islamic beliefs and Saudi Arabia's stricter social fabric affect Saudi Arabian college students' using on-line video? How do Saudi Arabian college students perceive the use of educational video? These inquiries led to the following research questions:

Research Question (RQ) 1. Do Saudi Arabian college students from a strict Islamic culture see themselves as part of the modern day Generation C?

Research Question (RQ) 2. Do Saudi Arabian college students use on-line video as a source of information used in their daily lives?

Research Question (RQ) 3. Are Saudi Arabian college students from a strict Islamic culture negativelyaffected by videos portraying Westernized beliefs and culture?

Research Question (RQ) 4. How do Saudi Arabian college students perceive the use of educational video in the classroom?

Materials and Methods

Sample

A judgment-type sampling procedure suitable for the present research objectives was used to collect data for the study [23]. Surveys were administered to 147 undergraduate male and female students. Due to unscorable responses 8 surveys were removed leaving 139 usable surveys. The respondents included in the study were from the student body of the business faculty at a large public university in Saudi Arabia. All students were enrolled in International business courses (classes where the subject language is taught in English). The rationale for using college students was that they fit well with the profile description of the study population. Specifically, the respondents in the study were age-appropriate, college students enrolled in International business courses where the classes are taught in English. In addition, the authors felt that students would be interested participants in the study by the nature of the subject of the research.

An important consideration was the issue of sufficiency in the number of observations to meet the purposes of the study, measuring attitudes. According to completed studies that investigated similar attitude phenomena, there should be at least 103 observations [24-26]. Thus, a sample size of 139 was considered sufficient for the purposes of the study.

Instrument

Video Attitudes Survey (VAS) [27] used the Computer Attitude Scale (CAS) in a study to measure students' computer attitudes and found improvement in respondents' feelings of comfort in using computers after completion of the activities. Video Attitude Survey (VAS) was adapted and modified from the attitudinal constructs of the CAS instrument to make it more applicable to the present investigation, measuring students' attitudes while reflecting the differences in technology between computers and video. The students were advised that the survey was assessing their beliefs, feelings, and behaviors in relation to using commercial video services, marketing subject educational video use in the classroom, and that there were no wrong or right answers. Survey respondents were assured of their anonymity with respect to filling out the surveys.

Data Analysis

The four research questions listed above are the basis for the analysis in the study. Some statistical procedures were used to accomplish the purposes of the study. First, descriptive statistics were calculated to present the characteristics of the sample and frequencies of certain categorical items. Second, Pearson correlations were computed to examine the relationships among the variables. Data was collected using the VAS, and scored on a five-point Likert scale where; 1 = 'Strongly Disagree'; 2 = 'Disagree'; 3 = 'Neither agree nor disagree'; 4 = 'Agree'; and 5 = 'Strongly Agree'. To aid in the discussion of each of the four research questions frequency tables were calculated and concurrently placed for the variables of interest (Table 1).

Finally, Chi-square analyses were conducted on selected variables to explore the potential relationships between Islamic values and video usage by gender to identify possible predictors of attitudes toward video usage by the connected generation (Table 2).

Results

Research Question RQ1

Table 1 presents the descriptive statistics of the basic characteristics of the sample and frequencies of several categorical variables. The first research question can be addressed with summary statistics contained in Table 1 Regarding RQ1 approximately 93% of student respondents see themselves members of Generation C. Table 2 shows Variable VC7-18 was strongly correlated with behavioral variable VU8-10 *downloading video to keep up with latest trends and information*(r=.37, P < .01). Providing additional support, in Table 3, frequency distributions for VC7-18 shows that,of those surveyed, approximately 88% agree with the statement, 62% 'Strongly Agree' and 26 % 'Agree. This belief has scored a high mean value, 4.45/5, representing a positive attitude of respondents toward the importance of Smartphones in their "connected" lives. These findings support that Saudi Arabian students surveyed do see themselves as part of Generation C (Table 3).

Research Question RQ2

RQ2 pertains to how Saudi Arabian college students use on-line video as a source of personal information and in their classes. Table 4 presents frequency distributions for usage variables. The overall results in Table 4 indicate that respondents have positive attitudes toward watching and using on-line videos as a source of information. Examination of responses to specific statements reveals that respondents believe that using on-line videos is a source of information for their education, and to keep up with the latest information and trends as a part of the Generation C's communications. In addition, VU1-1 watching videos from the Internet in general scored the highest mean, 4.13, indicating that Generation C depends on on-line videos as a source of information and a way to be connected with other members from their generation. Moreover, the correlation coefficient test found that there are moderate strength but significant relationships between some of the study variables. For example, the relationships between VU1-1 and VU8-10 (r=.-37, P< 0.01); VU3-7 and VU8-10 (r=.33, P< .01, and VU4-13 and VU8-10 (r=.41, P< .01 all were significant. VU2-2 has only significant relationship with VU4-13(r=.34, P< .01. These results highlight that respondents who like watching videos from the

Gender	Frequency	Percent	Major	Frequency	Percent	Course	Frequency	Percent
Female	72	51.8	Business Admin.	19	13.8	Accounting	5	3.6
Male	67	48.2	Marketing	51	36.7	Finance	18	13
Total	139	100.0	HR	11	7.9	HR	8	5.8
Age	Frequency	Percent	Finance	6	4.3	Management	9	6.5
19	5	3.6	MIS	14	10.0	Principles of Marketing	48	34.6
20	23	16.5	Accounting	22	15.8	Consumer Behavior	13	9.4
21	61	43.9	Other	16	11.5	Marketing Communication	11	7.9
22	34	24.5	Total	139	100.0	Sales	17	12.3
23	11	7.9	Connected Generation	Frequency	Percent	E-marketing	9	6.5
24	5	3.6	Yes	129	92.8			
Total	139	100.0	No	10	7.2			
			Total	139	100.0	Total	139	100.0

Table 1: Descriptive Statistics Analysis.

Variables	VU1-1	VU2-2	VU3-7	VU4-13	VC1-9	VC2-19	VC3-14	VL1-3	VL2-8	VL3-11	VL4-17	VC5-12	VU8-10	VC7-18	
VU1-1		-	.262**	.240**	.234**	.031	-.004	.033	.059	.176*	.026	.036	.231**	.372**	.171*
VU2-2			-	.051	.333**	.167*	.121	.102	.498**	.281**	.341**	.257**	.195*	.131	.166
VU3-7				-	.285**	-.048	.068	.026	.111	.092	.087	.070	.073	.331**	.240**
VU4-13					-	.137	.067	.061	.394**	.199*	.359**	.304**	.136	.408**	.321**
VC1-9						-	-.312**	.236**	.256**	.161	.257**	.211*	.075	.261**	.106
VC2-19							-	-.208*	.110	-.039	-.126	-.021	-.160	-.123	-.025
VC3-14								-	.094	.078	.043	-.043	.091	.022	.123
VL1-3									-	.195*	.386**	.243**	.118	.238**	.174*
VL2-8										-	.111	.321**	.573**	.300**	.331**
VL3-11											-	.619**	.206*	.164	.139
VL4-17												-	.430**	.164	.229**
VC5-12													-	.320**	.366**
VU8-10														-	.369**
VC7-18															-
N	N	139	139	139	139	139	139	139	139	139	139	139	139	139	139

**Correlation is significant at the 0.01 level (2-tailed)
*Correlation is significant at the 0.05 level (2-tailed)

Table 2: Pearson Correlations for Study Variables.

Variable – Description	1	2	3	4	5	Total	Mean	SD
VC7-18: I believe that small mobile device and Smart-phones have made accessing video easier for my generation.	1 0.7%	5 3.6%	11 7.9%	36 25.9%	86 61.9%	139 100%	4.4 5	0.84 4

Table 3: Mobile Devices and Video Usage.

Internet for their daily life needs are more likely to use video as source of information for educational purposes (Table 4).

Research Question RQ3

This question asks if Saudi Arabian college students' attitudes toward videos are negatively affected where the material may not be in keeping with strict Islamic values. From Table 2, the correlations between the 3 observed variables is if nothing else, interesting. VC2-19 negatively correlates(r=.-31, P < .01) (r=.21, P < .01), respectively, with variables VC1-9 and VC3-14 which correlate positively(r=.24, P < .01). While none of these relationships bordering between weak and moderate are particularly strong, the relationship may expose a bias. Chi-square analyses revealed that in terms of gender there was only a significant male difference on VC2-19 (13.84, *p* = .008, expected value 8.19, N = 139), suggesting that male students seem more offended than females by videos containing materials not in keeping with Islamic traditions. In Table 5, the frequency distributions show heavy midpoint or neutral response counts ranging from 25 to 30% which may mask the true meaning of the respondents, and contribute to the weak findings. However, if the neutral group's answers truly signal disinterest, then it might be quite reasonable to include them as unaffected, and thus increase positive responses. To summarize the data shows weak to moderate negatively affected correlation coefficients and a Chi-square of males over females on variable VC2-19. Given these findings it becomes difficult to suggest that students' attitudes toward videos with Westernized content are negatively affected by strict Islamic traditions. At the same time, it becomes difficult to say overall whether or not Saudi Arabian college students have a positive view of the educational benefits of Westernised videos. Clearly more research is needed with respect to these variables (Table 5).

Research Question RQ4

This question analyzed the relationships of Saudi Arabian college students' perceptions of and behavior to seek learning through educational video in the classroom. Four of the five variables in Table 6 clearly show that students perceived value of and a willingness to seek video in their classes. For classes in both Arabic and English, the summed percentages that indicated 'Strongly Agree' and 'Agree' ranges from 55% for VL1-3 up to 84% for VL2-8. Consequently the summations for those who 'Strongly Disagree' and 'Disagree' were particularly low ranging from just 4% for VC5-12 to a high of19%. VL3-11 was the only variable to break above trend, showing only 40% for those in agreement with 28% in disagreement. However, since this variable concerned behavior to seek access to video outside the classroom for classes taught in Arabic this result is somewhat understandable. From Table 3, the correlation between behavior seeking VL3-11 and VL4-17 (r=.-62, P < .01) was strong and significant. The interactions between VL4-17 and VC5-12 (r=.-43, P < .01) and VL4-17 and VL2-8 (r=.-57, P < .01) were both strong. These findings clearly point to a positive relationship between students taking classes taught in English and learning from educational videos. Overall students value educational video in the classroom, and are willing to seek them to increase their learning (Table 6).

Discussion and Conclusions

This study explored some of the possible relationships among the attitudes of Saudi Arabian college students toward Generation C and Westernised educational video. In doing so, four fundamental research questions were presented, analyzed, and discussed. The findings in RQ1 reveal that Saudi Arabian college students whose environment is characterized by strict Islamic traditions include themselves as members of the Generation C. In RQ2 these college students generally responded favorably toward the use of on-line video indicating a greater preference for social communication and popular content with less interest in major news information. These findings are completely consistent with the networking goals of Generation C members. With respect to RQ3 measuring the interaction between strict Islamic traditions and watching Westernized educational videos the results were not as clear. While most Saudi Arabian college students see moderate value in watching and learning from Westernized educational videos, correlations showed a weak but significant number (Males) were negatively influenced by their strong Islamic traditions. This indicates that while Saudi Arabian college students see themselves as being part of the Generation C, their beliefs are also influenced by Islamic culture. This particular finding may be important to advertisers and marketers trying to develop messages to reach out to this group of Saudi Arabians. RQ4 analyzed the interactions between Saudi Arabian college students' perceptions of and behavior toward seeking learning through educational video in the classroom. With exception of courses taught in Arabic, Saudi Arabian college students highly value educational video in the classroom, and are willing to seek videos outside to increase their in-class learning. The strongest and most promising findings of the study were the relationships between students' attitudes toward learning through educational video, improving their English speaking ability, and gaining greater understanding of multi-cultural issues and differences. Again, these findings on Saudi Arabian college students' attitudes toward educational video, and their use of small mobile devices for finding and sharing information and networking, are totally consistent with being both socially and technologically part of Generation C.

Variable	1	2	3	4	5	Total	Mean	SD
VU1-1: I like watching videos from the Internet	2 1.4%	9 6.5%	16 11.5%	54 38.9%	58 41.7%	139 100%	4.13	.954
VU2-2: I access videos as a source of information in my present courses	5 3.6%	21 15.1%	48 34.6%	53 38.1%	12 8.6%	139 100%	3.33	.958
VU3-7: Videos available through the Internet news services are a major source of my information	7 5%	37 26.6%	47 33.8%	36 26%	12 8.6%	139 100%	3.06	1.03
VU4-13: I send a lot of Internet videos to my friends	8 5.6%	31 22.3%	40 28.8%	45 32.8%	15 10.8	139 100%	3.20	1.01
VU8-10: I believe that downloading video to keep up with the latest information and trends is part of how my generation communicates	2 1.4%	11 7.9%	32 23%	57 41.1%	37 26.6%	139 100%	3.83	.960

Table 4: Saudi Arabian Student Usage of On-line Video

Variable – Description	1	2	3	4	5	Total	Mean	SD
VC1-9: I would not mind watching educational videos assuming the materials do not in-line with the Is lamic culture	13 9.3%	18 12.9%	40 28.8%	44 31.7%	24 17.3%	139 100%	3.35	1.184
VC2-19: I would be offended if some material is presented that is not in keeping with Islamic traditions	23 16.6%	24 17.3%	42 30.2%	33 23.7%	17 12.2%	139 100%	2.98	1.254
VC3-14: I believe watching videos that portray behaviors that are non-Islamic are/can be educational/helpful for learning	37 26.6%	24 17.3%	35 25.2%	32 23%	11 7.9%	139 100%	2.68	1.302

Table 5: Islamic Values and Westernized Videos

Variable	1	2	3	4	5	Total	Mean	SD
VL1-3: I feel that videos will enhance my learning for courses taught in Arabic	5 3.6%	21 15.1	36 25.9%	49 35.3%	28 20.1%	139 100%	3.53	1.09
VL2-8: I feel that videos will enhance my learning for courses taught in English	2 1.4%	10 7.2%	11 7.9%	56 40.3%	60 43.2%	139 100%	4.17	.952
VL3-11: I would access on my own time educational videos for my courses taught in Arabic	7 5%	32 23%	44 31.7%	40 28.8%	16 11.5%	139 100%	3.19	1.07
VL4-17: I would access on my own time educational videos for my courses taught in English	6 4.3%	10 7.2%	34 24.5%	55 39.6%	34 24.5%	139 100%	3.73	1.05
VC5-12: I believe that watching videos in English will help me to better understand multi-cultural issues or differences	1 0.7%	4 2.9%	18 13%	53 38.1%	63 45.3%	139 100%	4.24	.841

Table 6: Saudi Arabian Students' Perceptions of Educational Video

Implications

Tomorrows' college graduates, members of the Generation C, will contribute more than the skills and abilities learned through their college experiences. These constantly connected generation college graduates will also bring the value of their networking skills and technological expertise to the organizations that hire them. Their ability to network and stay connected has the potential to result in organizational productivity. Through their networking collaboration and technological mobility, these Generation C graduates will increasingly help organizations to achieve goals and objectives by creatively solving problems, taking on responsibility, working independently, and collaborating with peers. Accessing, using and sending videos to contacts are just some of the tools in Generation C's vast communications arsenal. Generation C members form their identities by belonging and expressing themselves within "tribes" reflecting the desire to "connect" around interesting ideas, cultural objects, causes and movements. Brands need to get into conversations that are happening within and across tribes. This will give their messages more credibility and attention compared to external sources– by expressing opinions, sharing ideas, observations and thoughts. Their influence depends on what they share and how often they share it.

Limitations and Future Research

Even though this study explored the relationships and interactions of several groups of variables that surround Generation C's attitudes toward video usage in the classroom, causal relationships were not explored. It is recommended that further studies examine the causal relationships through structural models and experimental designs. Further the study was geographically limited to one university, and only students of the college of business and administration. Future research would benefit from expanding the sample to include students of other college disciplines, and at different colleges. Finally, while this study focused on video usage in general, new research should attempt to focus and document specific educational video initiatives, and to evaluate them in terms of specific educational goals.

Acknowledgements

The authors wish to recognize Ms. Saga Shaabin, doctoral student, for her assistance in the current research particularly with survey item English-to-Arabic interpretation, some data collection and data entry, and help with preparing the exhibits and word processing.

References

1. Al-Khatib J, Vitell S, Rexeisen R and Rawwas M (2005) Inter-country differences of consumer ethics in Arab countries. International Business Review 14: 495–516
2. Harris I (2013) Connecting to Generation C. Human Resource Executive.
3. Brown G (2013) The Connected Generation.
4. Nielsen (2012) Introducing Generation C: Americans 18-34 Are the Most Connected.
5. Clear Focus (2013) How to Retain Talent in the Latest Generation C.
6. Friedrich R., Peterson M and Koster A (2011) The Rise of Generation C. Strategy +Business. Spring 62: 1-3.
7. Van Leeuven D (2011) How to prepare for the Connected Generation's transformation of the consumer and business landscape. Tomorrow-Today.
8. Central Intelligence Agency (CIA) (2013) The World Fact Book, People and Society Saudi Arabia.
9. Marshall JM (2002) Learning with Technology: Evidence that technology can and does support learning.
10. Shephard K (2003) Questioning, promoting, and evaluating the use of streaming video to support student learning. Brit J Educ Technol 34: 295-308.
11. Fisch SM (2004) Children's Learning from Educational Television: Sesame Street and beyond. Lawrence Erlbaum Associates. Mahwah. New Jersey.
12. Zhang D, Zhou L, Briggs RO and Nunamaker Jr JF (2006) Instructional video in e-learning: Assessing the impact of interactive video on learning effectiveness. Information & Management 43: 15–27.
13. Corporation for Public Broadcasting. (2004) Television goes to School: The Impact of Video on Student Learning in Formal Education.
14. Kirkorian HL, Wartella EA and Anderson DR (2008) Media and Young Children's Learning. Children and Electronic Media 18: 39-61.
15. Gulati S (2008) Technology-Enhanced Learning in Developing Nations: A review. The International Review of Research in Open and Distance Learning.
16. Alsajjan B and Dennis C (2010) Internet Banking Acceptance Model: Cross-Market Examination. J Bus Res 63: 1-19.
17. Malshe A, Al-Khatib J, Al-Habib M and Ezzi S (2012) Exploration of Sales-Marketing Interface Nuances in Saudi Arabia. J Bus Res 65: 1129-1125.
18. Rice G and Al-Mossawi M (2002) The implications of Islam for advertising messages: Middle Eastern context. Journal of Euromarketing 11: 71-96
19. Hamdan A (2005) Women and education in Saudi Arabia: Challenges and achievements. International Education Journal 6: 42-64.
20. Harden G and Al Beayeyz A (2013) A comparative analysis of social networking site use in two distinct cultures: evaluating the IT-culture conflict. Global Media Journal.
21. Nasr S (1980) The male and female in the Islamic perspective. Studies in Comparative Religion. 14: 1-2.
22. Islahi A (2009) Muslim economic thinking and institutions in the 10th AH/ 16th century. Scientific Publishing Centre King Abdulaziz University Jeddah, Saudi Arabia
23. Marshall NM (1996) Sampling for Qualitative Research. Family Practice. Oxford University Press 13: 522-525.
24. Aiken LS and West SG (1991) Multiple Regression: Testing and interpreting interactions. Sage Publication. Newbury Park, CA.
25. Bagozzi RP (1992) Self-regulation of Attitudes, Intentions, and Behavior. Social Psychology Quarterly 55: 178-205.
26. McClelland GH and Judd CM (1993) Statistical difficulties of detecting interactions and moderator effects. Psychological Bulletin 114: 376-390.
27. Escalda LT and Zollman DA (1997) An investigation on the effects of using interactive digital video in a physics classroom on student learning and attitudes. Journal of Research in Science Teaching. 34: 467-489.

4

Behavioral Intention of Taxpayers towards Online Tax Filing in India: An Empirical Investigation

Sharda Haryani[1]*, Bharti Motwani[2] and Sukhjeet Kaur Matharu[3]

[1]*M.Sc, (Ph.D pursuing), Prestige Institute of Management and Research, Indore, Madhya Pradesh, India*
[2]*MBA, PhD, Prestige Institute of Management and Research, Indore, Madhya Pradesh, India*
[3]*MBA, MPhil, PhD, Prestige Institute of Management and Research, Indore, Madhya Pradesh, India*

Abstract

Tax e-filing is one of the e-government services that have been adopted by many developed countries today, where the public has to discharge their responsibility to the government via online tax filing. In developing countries like India, due to high perceived risk by the public, a well establish integrated reliable system is required. It is very difficult to implant responsible behavior within a community, if an individual perception of risk of the e-government services is the concern. This paper attempts to develop an understanding of the factors that influence citizens' adoption of electronic tax filing services. This exploratory study elicited information using a structured questionnaire from 250 respondents from Indore city. The results revealed that the factors like perceived ease of use and perceived usefulness significantly affect the behavioral intention of the citizen towards the adoption of electronic tax filing. The study will serve as a useful guideline for strategic development in promoting e-government services, particularly the e-tax filing service.

Keywords: e-Tax Filing; Perceived ease of use; Perceived usefulness; e-Governance

Introduction

In this technology driven world, the use of internet has been widespread and diversified. The diversified use of internet will relatively be increased which also benefits the users [1,2]. In this digital era, governments of many countries are using the internet to provide public services to its citizens, known as e-Governance. Yildiz mentions that e-governance refers to the use of information and communication technologies by public administration to create a networked structure for; interconnectivity, service delivery, efficiency, effectiveness, transparency, and accountability [3]. Online tax filing commonly known as e-taxation is gaining more importance due to its wide applicability and usefulness. In India, income tax e-filing was introduced in September, 2004, initially on a voluntary usage basis for all categories of income tax assesses. But from July, 2006, it was made mandatory for all corporate firms to e-file their income tax returns. Taking this process further, from assessment year 2007 to 2008, e-filing of income tax return was made mandatory for all companies and for all other categories of income tax assesses, which also includes salaried individuals. About 81% of total revenue of the country is generated by direct taxes. Therefore the main aim of the department is to enable taxpayers to meet their normal tax obligations in a convenient manner without visiting Income Tax Office. To accomplish this objective, the department's high priorities are: e-delivery of taxpayer services, increase of departmental computer infrastructure and the setting up of Tax Information Network (TIN). The e-taxation system provides the key services like online registration, form download, returns filing, online payment, online tax accounting system, effective tax rates, key notifications and provisions and enactments. These services could be accessed through an internet connection without any geographical hindrance. The overall aim of e-taxation is to replace cumbersome manual, bureaucratic service systems with collaborative, efficient, process-driven and secure online delivery.

Despite the rapid adoption of tax e-filing in many countries, researchers have argued that it is yet to establish an integrated system that is reliable, especially in developing countries. The study is an attempt to understand the progress of e-taxation (Direct) in India in the recent past, the present and the future prospects. The present paper also attempt to investigate the impact of factors affecting users' perception about e-taxation on the citizens' behavioral intention of using e-taxation in future.

Literature Review

Electronic tax payment was first coined and implement in the US in 1986. Today, electronic taxation has been extended to many countries. Electronic taxation differs among countries hence the name of the system also differs from country to country. Electronic declaration is named electronic tax filing in International literature. e-tax payment is also called online taxation payment (UN, 2007) or e-tax lodgment [4].

Reima Soumi has discussed the meaning of e-taxation and also deals with the best practices in technology which would further help in the development of tax administration system [5]. Dr. Dimitris Gousco discussed about the concept of e-government, strategic objectives for electronic services, business planning for electronic services, technologies for delivering electronic services and evaluating the performance of electronic services [6]. Subhash Bhatnagar, has discussed about the different perceptions and delivery models of e-government and also about the cases resulting in multiple benefits: improved service delivery; reduced corruption; increased transparency; increased revenue; cost reduction; and empowerment [7]. Sanjiv K Chaudary in his article discussed about the advantages of E-Taxation and to provide clarity and certainty on various tax related issues to assess [8].

***Corresponding author:** Sharda Haryani, M.Sc., (Ph.D pursuing), Prestige Institute of Management and Research, Indore, Madhya Pradesh, India
E-mail: sharda_haryani@pimrindore.ac.in

Hussein Ramlah et al. investigated the factors influencing citizens' intention to use e-filing in the Malaysian context. He found that the perceived ease of use and perceived usefulness, trust of the government, image, compatibility and service quality were significant predictors of citizens' intention to use e-filing [9]. Carter Lemuria et al. investigated the influence of six determinants on taxpayers' intention to adopt e-file systems. Specifically, the results indicate that three factors from the Unified Theory of Acceptance and Use of Technology (UTAUT) model by Venkatesh, Morris and Davis, namely performance expectancy, effort expectancy, and social influence play a significant role in predicting taxpayers' e-filing intentions. More importantly, the research findings indicate that personal factors such as web-specific self-efficacy (WSSE) and perceived security control along with UTAUT factors, have a significant impact on taxpayers' e-file intentions [10,11].

Theoretical models such as Theory of Reasoned Action (TRA), the Theory of Planned Behavior (TPB), and the Technology Acceptance Model (TAM), attempt to explain the relationship between user beliefs, attitudes, intentions and actual system use [12-15]. Among these theories, TAM was widely used and accepted to explain the relationship between perceptions and technology use. In the e-government literature, various studies have also adopted TAM in their model to test or evaluate the citizen adoption of e-government services [16-19].

Rationale of Study

Since 2008, there is paradigm shift in the taxation system of India i.e. from manual to electronic. The data of number of e-filers from 2008 to 2014 (Table 1) signifies that e-filing experience reflects continued progress. The growth has occurred every year and has been driven particularly by the electronic filing of individual tax returns. The forward growth is seen in trend analysis of the data (Figure 1). The no. of ITRs filed increased from 2 million in 1998 to around 9 million for 2010. In 2012-13 the no. of e-filers were 13 million more than 2010. In 2016, 31 million people are estimated to file their tax through online system. This increase may be due to the benefits enjoyed by the people over manual Filing ITRs. The need of the study arises so as to know the strengths of this newly developed concept, the weakness or the hindrances in its progress, the opportunities and threats in its way to get a stronghold position in India. Considering the growth potential of e-fling which is beneficial for both the government and the taxpayers, Income tax department requires extra ordinary efforts to have a more user-friendly and error free software. Hence, the main aim of this study is to develop an understanding of the perception of taxpayers towards the e-taxation.

Objective

To propose a multivariate regression model where the factors affecting perception of taxpayers towards e-tax filing acts as predictors of the citizens' behavioral intention to adopt the e-taxation.

Financial year	No. of e-taxpayers'	Trend values
FY 2007-08	2169367	171117
FY 2008-09	4830122	4038950
FY 2009-10	5073977	7906783
FY 2010-11	9050242	11774616
FY 2011-12	16433684	15642449
FY 2012-13	21486807	19510282
FY 2013-14	29681794	23378114
FY 2014-15	--	27245947
FY 2015-16	--	31113780

Table 1: Number of ITR filers through online taxation.

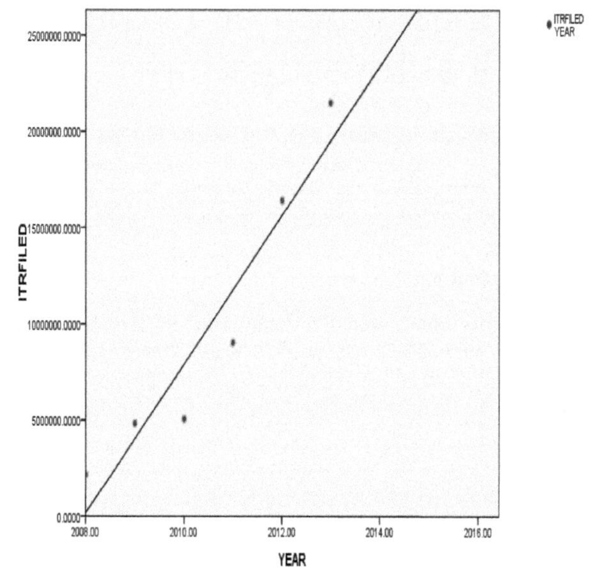

Figure 1: Trend Analysis.

Hypothesis

The heightened attention is being paid in the literature on e-taxation services offered by government of India. The e-filing system may offer potential benefits to improve administrative compliance efficiency, but the benefits gained may be obstructed by tax users' unwillingness to accept and use the available electronic services. José Carlos Pinho, Isabel Maria Macedo in a study analyzed the antecedents and consequences of online satisfaction towards the taxation services offered through the web-based electronic declaration system. It was found that convenience is an important antecedent of both satisfaction and online service quality. Also, findings suggest that both the degree of satisfaction and online service quality impacts on the intention of using the taxation website [20]. Fishbein and Ajzen defined usage intention as a measure of the strength of one's intention to perform a specific behavior [21]. Sheppard, Hartwick, and Warshaw found individuals' actual behavior could be predicted reasonably well from their intentions [22]. Therefore we hypothesized that:

H_0 There H_0 is insignificant impact of factors affecting the perception of taxpayers towards e-tax filing on the behavioral intention of e-taxpayers.

Methodology and Sampling Design

The study is exploratory in nature and intends to explore the impact of factors affecting the perception of e- taxpayers' towards the behavioral intention of using e-taxation.

A self structured questionnaire inspired by the scale developed by Venkatesh, Morris and Davis in their famous article on the Unified Theory of Acceptance and Use of Technology (UTAUT). The questionnaire comprises of three sections A, B and C. Section A contains general information of the respondents, section B consist of internet usage and behavior intention of using e-taxation. Section C comprises of 37 items base on five point likert scale anchored from strongly disagree to strongly agree. The cronbach alpha is found to be 0.81 indicating good consistency among the items and hence the questionnaire is considered to be reliable [11].

Sampling techniques and sample size description

A self structured questionnaire was used for primary data collection. Non probability judgmental sampling method was used for the collection of primary data. The data was collected from 250 respondents of which 237 have filed their returns personally, and out of those only 110 i.e 46.4 percent had attempted e-filing. The data of these 110 respondents was subjected to further analysis. The detailed profile of the sample is given below:

The respondents comprised 62 males and 48 females. 22% of the respondent was bachelor degree holders, 70.9% were master degree holders and 9.1% were Diploma/certificate/secondary school qualified. There are only 48 female respondents, which indicate that males appeared to be more technology adopters than females, females experienced greater difficulty with e-filing as compared to males. Also majority of the e-filers are professionals and aged between 25-40 years which indicates that older people tended to be less optimistic about e-filing and experienced more discomfort with e-filing as compared to younger people (Table 2).

Statistical tools for data analysis

Descriptive analysis including skewness and kurtosis, Kolmogorov and Smirnov test were used to check the normality of the data. To determine the important factors that affect the perception of e-tax payers principal component factor analysis was used. Multiple regression analysis was used to analyze the effect of independent variables on a single dependent variable. Durbin-Watson statistics was used to validate the independence of error term assumption. Breusch-Pagan and Koenker test was used to check the homoscedasticity.

Statistical Analysis and Results

Initially in a pilot study, the data was subjected to principle factor analysis. Factor analysis helps to reduce a vast number of variables to a significant, interpretable and convenient set of factors. The data of 40 respondents was subjected to principal component factor analysis which resulted in four factors namely perceived ease of use, perceived usefulness, perceived security and perceived attitude. Out of which perceived attitude was measured using 6 items, perceived usefulness was measured using 15 items, perceived ease of use was measured used 8 items and perceived security was measured using 8 items.

Feature	Description	Sample	Percentage
Age	18-25	38	34.5
	25-40	56	50.9
	40-60	16	14.5
Profession	Business	20	18.2
	Service	76	69.1
	Self employed	14	12.7
Education	Graduate	22	20.0
	Post graduate	78	70.9
	Others	10	9.1
Gender	Male	62	56.4
	Female	48	43.6
Marital status	Married	78	70.9
	Unmarried	32	29.1
Yearly income (in lakh Rs.)	2-4	50	45.5
	4-6	48	43.6
	Above 6	12	10.9

Table 2: Profile of samples.

The underlying assumptions of multiple regression analysis were also met before the analysis, the results are as follows.

Normality of variables

Regression assumes that variables should have normal distributions. Non-normally distributed variables (highly skewed or kurtotic variables, or variables with substantial outliers) can distort relationships and significance tests. The skewness and kurtosis value of all the variables in our study were found to belying between ±1 (Annexure 1). Thus this shows that the distribution of all the variables is normal. Also the Kolmogorov-Smirnov statistic of all the variables were found be significant which further confirms the normality of the data (Annexure 2).

Linearity

Standard multiple regression can only accurately estimate the relationship between dependent and independent variables if the relationships are linear in nature. A significant correlation between the variables confirms the linearity. In the present study the correlation between the variables were found to be lying between .485-.710 (Annexure 3). All the values are significant at the .01 level which indicates the existence of linear relationship between the dependent and independent variables.

Independence of errors

The Durbin-Watson value informs about whether the assumption independence of errors is defensible i.e there is no autocorrelation of error terms. The D-W value closer to 2 is better and in this study the statistic is 1.735 which is acceptable (Annexure 1).

Homoscedasticity

Homoscedasticity means that the variance of errors is the same across all levels of the independent variables. When the variance of errors differs at different values of the independent variables, heteroscedasticity is indicated. According to Berry and Feldman and Tabachnick and Fidell slight heteroscedasticity has little effect on significance tests; however, when heteroscedasticity is marked it can lead to serious distortion of findings and seriously weaken the analysis [23,24].

This assumption can be checked by visual examination of a plot of the standardized residuals (the errors) by the regression standardized predicted value. The Breusch-Pagan test fits a linear regression model to the residuals of a linear regression model (by default the same explanatory variables are taken as in the main regression model) and rejects if too much of the variance is explained by the additional explanatory variables.

In our analysis the scatter plot of the standardized residuals (the errors) by the regression standardized predicted value (Annexures 5 and 6) reveals that the data is Homoscedastic. This was further confirmed by the Breusch-Pagan and Koenker test. The Breusch-Pagan p-value=.316 (chi-square=2.319) which is greater than .05 andthus the null hypotheses is accepted i.e. the data is homoscedastic. Similarly the Keonker test p-value=.4665 (chi-square=1.525) is also greater than .05 and thus the null hypotheses i.e. the data is homoscedastic is accepted. The results of the test are shown in Annexure 7.

Multicollinearity

Multicollinearity occurs when you have two or more independent variables that are highly correlated with each other. This leads to problems with understanding which independent variable contributes to the variance explained in the dependent variable, as well as technical issues in calculating a multiple regression model. An inspection of correlation coefficients and Tolerance/VIF values help in detecting multicollinearity.

Here the the tolerance value of ease and usefulness was .566 and the Variance inflation factor (VIF) was 1.767 (Annexure 4-coefficients). The VIF recommendation of 10 or less corresponding to the tolerance recommendation of. 10 or more is acceptable. Thus no multicollinearity is seen in the data.

Model Summary

The stepwise multiple regression analysis was run using SPSS (Statistical Package for services and solutions) 16.0 version The behavioral intention of e-taxpayers which include satisfaction level and intention of using e-taxation in future was considered as dependent variable where as the factors extracted during the pilot study were taken as predictors (independent variables).

The model summary contains two models. $Model_a$ refers to the fisrt stage in the hierarchy when only perceived ease of use is used as a predictor. $Model_b$ refers to the final model. The final model produced R square of 0.466 which was statistically significant [F(2,107)=46.672, p<0.05]. Perceived attitude, perceived ease of use, perceived security, perceived usefulness can account for 46.6 percent of variance on behavioral intention of using e-taxation in future. The beta value (standardize coefficients) of perceived ease of use (β=.3 87, t=5.705 and p<0.05) and perceived usefulness (β=.095, t=2.106 and p<0.05) indicates that these independent variables are positively related to behavioral intention of using e-Filing. The independent variables perceived security (β=.071, t=.612 and p>.05) and perceived attitude (β= -0.10, t=-0.089 and p>.05) were found to be insignificant and could not enter the model. Similar results were found by Carter and Belanger, in their study. According to which Perceived usefulness and perceived ease of use were found to be significant constructs in the e-government adoption literature [25].

Past research was inconsistent on whether perceived usefulness (PU) or perceived ease of use (PEOU) was the stronger determinant. According to Davis, perceived usefulness (PU) is shown as a primary determinant and perceived ease of use (PEOU) as a secondary determinant of intentions to use a certain technology [15]. Fu et al. also found that behavioral intention was largely driven by perceived usefulness [26]. However, Wang (2002) found that perceived ease of use (PEOU) was a stronger predictor of people's intention to e-file than perceived usefulness (PU) [19]. According to the findings in Wixom and Todd (2005), perceived usefulness (PU) was influenced by perceived ease of use (PEOU) [27].

The results of regression analysis are shown in the Annexure 4. Since all the assumptions of multiple regression analysis are confirmed thus our model is acceptable and can be used for future predictions.

Conclusion

Indian economy is at a developing stage and there is still more to come in every stage of its development and e-taxation system is up-to-the-minute conception in India. Therefore it is necessary to know the progress done in this genre of direct tax system in India. Studies have shown that people tend to use on line tax filing as it is more convenient and quicker than traditional paper tax-filing. Every year there has been a substantial increase in the use of online tax filing. Technologies have made system more user-friendly in terms of ease-of-use, appealing user interface and smooth navigation.

The results of this study conclude that the behavioral intention of e-taxpayers towards the online tax-filing system is greatly influenced by perceived ease of use and perceived usefulness. Given the fact that the adoption of the electronic tax-filing system is voluntary in India, the findings suggest that a system that is easy to use ,customizable, user-friendly, provides range of services, convenient , provides easy mode of payment, secured and reliable has a positive impact on attitude of the tax payers to voluntarily e-file their tax returns.

Suggestions

The government of India should increase its efforts to promote the usefulness and user-friendliness of the e-filing system. Attempt should be made to emphasize the usefulness of e-filing by using a suitable advertising campaign that clearly denotes the usefulness of e-filing. Deliberately administering the campaign during tax filing months will give a better result. Apart from this the Indian Income tax department can also improve the user-friendliness of the system by creating web based tutorials or videos that guide the tax- payers regarding the use of the e-filing system.

Limitations

As with any research, this study has several limitations. Firstly, the survey concentrates on limited citizens of Indore city and does not represent the whole of India. The results may vary with different sample, geographical areas and demographics. Thus the results of the study cannot be generalized. Secondly, the research model is based on constructs namely perceived attitude (PR), perceived usefulness (PU), perceived security and perceived ease of use (PEOU)and this model only explains over half of the variance of the intention to use electronic tax-filing system [R2 = 0.466]. The unexplained 53% percent of variance suggests that other constructs could be included in this model. Also the responses of only online taxpayers were considered in the analysis. The responses of manual taxpayer may give different results. The comparison between the manual taxpayers and e-taxpayers can be considered for the future study.

References

1. Pavlou PA, Liang H, Xue Y (2007). Understanding and mitigating uncertainty in online exchange relationships: a principal-agent perspective. MIS Quarterly 31: 105-136.
2. Barako D, Rusmin R, Tower G (2008). Web communication: An Indonesian perspective. African Journal of Business Management 2: 53-58.
3. Yildiz M (2007) E-government research: reviewing the literature, limitations, and ways forward. Government Information Quarterly 24: 646-665.
4. Turner T, Apelt C (2004) Globalization, Innovation and Information Sharing in tax systems: The Australian experience of the diffusion and adoption of electronic lodgement. E Journal of Tax Research 2: 241-269.
5. Soumi R (2007) Governing Finnish taxation electronically, 5th Eastern European e|Gov Days, Prag, Czech Republik 11-13
6. Gousco D (2001) E-Government & E-Taxation Service: Rules of thumb, Benefits at hand, General Secretariat for Information System Greek Ministry of Finance.
7. Bhatnagar S (2006) E-Government: Opportunities and Challenges in India, IIM Ahmedabad.

8. Chaudary SK (2008) Time to make the country more tax-friendly for investor, Published in 'Daily News Analysis.

9. Hussein R, Mohamed N, Ahlan AR, Mahmud M (2011) E-government application: an integrated model on G2C adoption of online tax, Transforming Government: People, Process and Policy 5: 225- 248.

10. Carter L, Christian SL, Hobbs J, Campbell R (2011) The role of security and trust in the adoption of online tax filing, Transforming Government: People, Process and Policy 5: 303 -318.

11. Venkatesh V, Morris MG, Davis FD, Davis GB (2003) User Acceptance of Information Technology: Toward a Unified View, MIS Quarterly 27: 425-478.

12. Ajzen I, Fishbein M (1980). Understanding Attitudes and Predicting Social Behavior. Upper Saddle River: Prentice-Hall 1-278.

13. Ajzen I (1991) Theory of planned behaviour. Organizational Behavior and Human Decision Processes, 50: 179-211.

14. Davis FD (1989) Perceived Usefulness, Perceived Ease of Use, and User Acceptance of Information Technology, MIS Quarterly 13: 319-340.

15. Davis FD, Bagozzi RP, Warshaw PR (1989) User Acceptance of Computer Technology: A Comparison of Two Theoretical Models,Management Science 35: 982-1003.

16. Agarwal R, Prasad J (1999) Are Individual Differences Germane to the Acceptance of New Information Technologies? Decision Sciences 30: 361-391.

17. Morris M, Dillon A (1997) How User Perceptions Influence Software Use. IEEE Software 14: 58-65.

18. Carter L, Belanger F (2004) The Influence of Perceived Characteristics of Innovating on e-Government Adoption. Electronic Journal of E-government 2: 11-20.

19. Wang YS (2002). The adoption of electronic tax filing systems: An empirical study. Government Information Quarterly 20: 333-352.

20. Pinho JC, Macedo IM (2008) Examining the antecedents and consequences of online satisfaction within the public sector: The case of taxation services, Transforming Government: People, Process and Policy 2: 177-193.

21. Fishbein M, Ajzen I (1975) Belief, Attitude, Intention and Behaviour: An introduction to theory and research, Reading, MA: Addison Wesley.

22. Sheppard BH, Hartwick J, Warshaw PR (1988) The Theory of Reasoned Action: A Meta-Analysis of Past Research with Recommendations for Modifications and Future Research, Journal of Consumer Research 15: 325-343.

23. Berry WD, Feldman S (1985) Multiple Regression in Practice. Sage University Paper Series on Quantitative Applications in the Social Sciences, series no. 07-050. Newbury Park, CA: Sage.

24. Tabachnick BG, Fidell LS (2001) Using Multivariate Statistics (4th ed.). Needham Heights, MA: Allyn and Bacon

25. Carter L, Belanger F (2005) The utilization of e-government services: citizen trust, innovation and acceptance factors. Information Systems Journal 15: 5-25.

26. Fu JR, Farn CK, Chao W P (2006) Acceptance of electronic tax filing: A study of taxpayer intentions. Information and Management 43: 109-126.

27. Wixom BH, Todd PA (2005) A theoretical integration of user satisfaction and technology acceptance .information systems research. World Wide Web. International Journal of Electronic Commerce 1: 59-88.

5

Cultural Citizenship in the Constitution of the Islamic Republic of Iran

Tavana MA*

Assistant Professor of Political Science, University ofYazd, Iran

Abstract

Iran is a multicultural country including various groups of ethnic, lingual, religious and else. What is solution Constitution of Islamic Republic of Iran to organize this sociocultural diversity? To answer to this question we used the method of conforming theory with sample. The study uses cultural citizenship theories as a theoretical framework to analyze the solution of the Constitution of IRI. The most important finding of this study is: the Constitution of IRI has a two-layer solution for the issue of sociocultural diversity; in the beneath layer lays concentrated cultural policy which in turn is the result of domination of Islamic, Shiite, Persian, and patriarchal culture; in the layer above lays a combination of politics of wide recognition (especially in the area of language and ethnic); and politics of narrow recognition (especially in the areas of religion, women, and vulnerable social groups).

Keywords: Cultural citizenship; Constitution of Islamic republic of Iran; Cultural diversity; Cultural politics; Centralist; Wide recognition; Narrow recognition

Introduction

The victory of islamic revolution of Iran in 1979 significantly changed the political and sociocultural structure of iran. One of the areas highly influenced by the islamic revolution was the constitution of this country that is mashrouteh constitution (1906) was replaced by the constitution of islamic republic of Iran (1979). It seems that IRI constitution not only plays the role of institutionalizing IRI system, but also it reflects the historical, political, cultural, and social life of Iranian people. So it is expected that it present a fundamental solution for the basic issues of Iranian society. one of the most fundamental issues of iranian society is the diverse sociocultural structure consisted from various ethnicities (including fars, turk, lor, balouch, arab, sistani, mazani, gilak, gorji), languages (including persian, mazani, kurdish, pashto, balouchi, lori, laki, zazaki, gilaki, taleshi, tati, asi, semnani), schools (including imami, ismaili, hanafi, maleki, shafei, Hanbali), religions (including Islam, Judaism, Christianity (including Armenians, Ashourians, Kaldanis, Baha'i) [1]. Accordingly, main question is raised in the present study what is the specific solution of IRI constitution to organize the current sociocultural diversity? To answer to this question we used the method of conforming theory with sample (case). In this method, a case or a sample is measured with one or a set of theories [2].

Theoretical Framework

Cultural citizenship tries to organize the relationship between various sociocultural groups within a society based on the principle of equal respect [3]. In fact, cultural citizenship is one of the types of citizenship. In this sense cultural citizenship can be seen as involving membership, rights, duties and commitments, and participation of sociocultural groups (such as women, children, patients, the unemployed, the forsaken, the marginalized, ethnicities, races) within a political society [4,5].

Yet, cultural citizenship is a rebellion against centralist cultural policies of which ignore cultural differences [6]. The most important centralist cultural policies include assimilation and homogenization, benign neglect, and exclusion. Politics of assimilation and homogenization of try absorbing or merging minor groups into the culture of majority, so that the society becomes integrated [7]. Yet this process is accomplished significantly by knowledge builder and ideological organizations (such as training and education organization, media). Benign neglect is a liberal policy based on classifying the society into two sectors, public and private. According to this policy, in private sphere different sociocultural groups are free to follow their own cultural ideas and patterns, while they should forget their own culture in public sphere and get a common civic identity [8]. Exclusion policy is based on excluding distinct sociocultural groups, as abnormal, or at least tries to marginalize them. For example it is possible that dominant culture deprive them from having job, housing, and education opportunities equal to others. Suppression, genocide, contempt, and disdaining the minorities can also be regarded as parts of this policy [7]. In contrast, cultural citizenship tries to establish a plural sociocultural and political structure; provide the ground for membership of all sociocultural groups in this structure; and create a sense of cultural, social, and political solidarity among them. A significant theorist of cultural citizenship is Will Kymlicka. He presented the theory of multicultural citizenship, according to which not only all people benefit from public rights regardless what cultural groups they belong to, but also they should have special rights to maintain their identity. Kymlicka speaks of three types of group rights including Self-government Rights, Polyethnic Rights, and Special Representation Rights [9]. Bhikhu Parekh suggests that resolving the issue of diverse cultures requires the active participation of different sociocultural groups in the common political and cultural structure as well as protective policies of government in favor of minority groups, so that smaller groups have a strong sense of belonging to the larger society. He also demands for spreading justice, public rights, and multicultural education as other government plans for organizing a multicultural society [10].

According to the above, the macro solutions derived from recent cultural citizenship can be classified into two groups, narrow (weak) recognition policies, and wide (strong) recognition policies. Narrow recognition policy considers cultural differences as real issues which

***Corresponding author:** Mohammad Ali Tavana, Assistant Professor of Political Science, University of Yazd, Yazd, Safaeih, Iran
E-mail: tavana.mohammad@yahoo.com

can be controlled through tolerance, granting more freedoms, changing some general rules, granting financial exemption and even positive discrimination. In fact narrow recognition policy is based on non-discrimination [11]. By contrast, wide recognition policy considers no substantive difference between minority and majority groups and sees all sociocultural groups having equal inherent value and tries to contribute them in sociocultural and political structure through the principle of inclusion. Such a process requires not only granting autonomy, veto right, guaranteed representation, and equal access to public sphere, but also equality of values of minority to values of majority or dominant group [11]. Now we can deal with IRI Constitution with this background.

Cultural Citizenship in Constitution of Islamic Republic of Iran

IRI Constitution was passed in 1979 and in 1989 some amendments were applied to it. In the present study the latter (1989) will be explored. The Constitution has 1 Introduction, 14 Chapters and 177 Articles (principles).

The first issue in understanding the solution of IRI Constitution for sociocultural diversity is discovering the underlying structure or the general spirit governing it. It seems that the introduction of IRI Constitution has to some extent determined the underlying citizenship identity in Islamic Republic of Iran. According to the introduction, Iranian sociocultural, political, and economic institutions have been established based on Islamic principles [12]. In this sense Islam is the basic element of underlying structure of citizenship identity in Islamic Republic of Iran. This element (Islam) is more than anything representative of domination of Islamic (Shiite) culture on religious, historical, and political structure of Iranian society. In introduction we also read that Islamic revolution in 1979 was the result of anti-despotic and anti-colonialist struggles of Iranian Muslim people (Mansour 2012, 12) [12]. So, nation can be the second element of underlying structure of citizenship identity in Islamic Republic of Iran. At the same time these two elements are combined and integrated in Islamic identity in a unit sense. Yet, in introduction part of IRI Constitution, "Independence", "Freedom", and "Islamic Rule" were introduced as the other elements of underlying citizenship identity in Islamic Republic of Iran [12]. Above all, these elements represent contemporary evolutions in general and Islamic revolution (1979) in particular. However, in an overview we can consider region, history, political heritage, cultural heritage, rituals, national language, Islam religion, and nation as the underlying structure citizenship identity that are reflected for example in articles 17 and 18 [13].

The next issue is recognizing sociocultural groups approved in IRI Constitution. In this regard we can refer to articles 12, 13, 15, 19, 20, 21, 64, in which religious groups (Hanafi, Shafei, Maleki, Khanbali, and Zeidi), religions (Zoroastrian, Christianity, Judaism), all ethnic and lingual groups living in Iran, women and vulnerable groups like the elderly, widows, orphans, the disabled are recognized. While IRIs Marion Young considers people who have experienced exploitation, marginalization, cultural imperialism, violation, and powerlessness as sociocultural groups needing protection (eminenting differentiated citizenship) [14], it seems that the range of recognized groups in IRI Constitution is somehow more limited. According to this background, we can analyze the solution of IRI constitution based on the elements of cultural citizenship (membership, rights, duties, and participation).

Membership of sociocultural groups in IRI constitution

Membership is the basis of cultural citizenship. Although inclusive membership has not been realized yet, its scope is increasingly expanding [15]. In IRI Constitution, membership can be found under nationality title. Because nationality is a kind of political, legal, and spiritual relations which represents belongings of individuals to a society or State [16]. The articles 41 and 42 in IRI Constitution are assigned particularly to nationality. Article 41 states that: "Citizenship of Iran is the unquestioned right of all Iranians. The State may not deprive any Iranian of his citizenship, except at their own request, or if they take up citizenship of another country." According to this article then, we can recognize the citizenship of all Iranians regardless of their race, ethnicity, religion, language, gender, political trend. In this sense this article at least legally doesn't make any obstacle for citizenship of the members of different sociocultural groups. In any case this article considers Iranian identity as a cultural, historical, and political structure which is transfers generally by land and blood and entering to it or exiting from it requires individual will. So we can have a flexible attitude toward nationality. At the same time, in a strict interpretation, citizenship of sociocultural groups is subject to accepting dominant culture (Islamic-Iranian culture). Also, the article 42 states that "Foreign nationals may within the limits of the law take up Iranian citizenship. The citizenship of such persons may only be taken away if, possibly, another State accepts them into citizenship, or at their own request." This article confirms acquired citizenship. It seems this article is somehow similar to civic assimilation policies according to which the requirement for citizenship of foreign people in host culture is accepting the culture of majority or dominant culture. Generally these two articles indicate that in IRI Constitution citizenship is apparently inclusion-oriented. In this sense, privatively there is no obstacle for approving various people and sociocultural groups in society, but wide recognition policy in which cultural values of minority are inherently equal to cultural values of majority or the dominant group in society, is not necessarily extractable from these articles.

Rights of sociocultural groups in IRI constitution

The issue of Rights is the second base in cultural citizenship. As Kymlicka claims, cultural citizenship includes both public and private rights. So, cultural citizenship rights can be investigated in two dimensions.

Public rights of cultural citizenship: The article number 3 in IRI Constitution is one of the articles dealing with public rights of cultural citizenship. Clause 7 of this article states that "State is obliged to provide political and social freedoms within the framework of law"; this clause explicitly represents civil and political rights of cultural citizenship and has no constraining condition except for law. Clause 9 demands "the abolition of all forms of undesirable discrimination and the provision of equitable opportunities for all, in both the material and intellectual spheres". This article implies equal legal behavior with all citizens. Clause 12 emphasizes on just economic system and considers it aiming at "creating welfare, eliminating poverty, and abolishing all forms of deprivation with respect to food, housing, work, healthcare, and the provision of social insurance for all." This clause emphasizes particularly on public citizenship rights and as Riley believes, it can create the ground for active participation of citizens in political, social areas [17]. Clause 14 confirms "securing the multifarious rights of all citizens, both women and men, and providing legal protection for all, as well as the equality of-all before the law; this clause represents civil rights, especially judicial dimension of cultural citizenship, and at least because of the phrase men and women, it is considered as a sign of principle of non-discrimination about women which is a fundamental concept in narrow recognition policy. Generally, article 3 has a right-based view to citizenship; principally, there is no constrain indicating restriction, hence generalizing the range of citizenship rights to all members of sociocultural groups can be derived from it.

Article 20 states first that "all people, men and women, are equal before the law", and then considers "all human, economic, social, and cultural rights" as including "all people of the nation". It seems that this article implies civil rights and is particularly based on the principle of non-discrimination. Because it grants equal legal situation to all people of nation, regardless of race, religion, sex, and so on. Also stating the word all in this article makes the civil rights public. Yet, this article reminds that the only criteria violating legal equality and inclusive rights, is "opposition to Islamic criteria" which is one of the main infrastructures of Iranian citizenship identity. According to this article it can be followed that civil rights of sociocultural groups should not be opposed to the values of majority.

The articles 22 to 40 are generally about public civil political and social rights of citizenship. For example, article 22 declares that "The dignity, life, property, rights, residence, and occupation of the individual are inviolate, except in cases sanctioned by law". This article indicates personal, social, judicial, and economic civil rights. Article 23 is stating the forbiddance of inquisition and stipulates that "no one may be molested or taken to task simply for holding a certain belief". This article is corresponding to the principle of freedom of belief in citizenship civil rights [18]. Article 25 emphasizes forbiddance of "spy and investigating private and social relationships of citizens" except by the order of law. This article is corresponding to the principle of non-exposing civil rights of citizenship [19]. Article 26 implies "freedom of Political parties, societies, political and craft associations and Islamic or recognized minority religious associations", provided that "no violation is involved of the principles of independence, freedom, national unity, Islamic standards, and the foundations of the Islamic Republic". This article indicates part of political rights counted by Marshall [20]. Yet, its restrictive constraints especially the condition of keeping national unity and Islamic criteria reminds us of the underlying structure of citizenship (religious and national) in Iranian society. Article 27 states that "Unarmed assemblies and marches may be freely organized, provided that no violation of the foundations of Islam is involved". This article is about freedom of assemblies which is the intersection of pubic civil and political rights of citizenship [19]. Article 29 emphasizes "social security in retirement, unemployment, old age, being laid off (AZ KAR OFTADEGI), being without a guardian, casual misfortune, accidents, and occurrences giving rise to the need for health services and medical care and treatment, through insurance etc." and also declares that "health care and treatment insurance is the right of all people and State is obliged to provide these services and above mentioned financial supports for each individual in the country". This article is a complete reflection of public social rights in citizenship [20]. It is obvious that mentioning each individual in this article implies citizenship equality of citizens. At the same time this article particularly recognizes vulnerable groups. Article 32 states that "no one may be arrested without order of law". Article 33 "rejects ousting people from their residence or forbidding them to reside in the locality of their choice, or compelling them to reside in a particular locality, unless the law prescribes this". These two articles represent judicial and social aspect of civil rights [20]. Article 34 considers asking for justice as the unquestioned right of all people" and declares that "everyone may refer to the competent courts and no one may be prevented from recourse to any court to which the law entitles him to refer". This article as well is about judicial aspect of civil rights. Article 37 implies innocence of citizens and states that "No person is considered legally guilty, except in cases where his guilt is established in a competent court". This article is about the issue of immunity and not exposing in civil rights of citizens. Article 38 forbids "any kind of torture to extract an admission of guilt or to obtain information" and states that "compelling people to give evidence or confess or take an oath is null and void". This article emphasizes civil immunity of citizens and notes their human dignity. It seems that these articles are inclusive. In simple words, these articles are about superstructure of citizenship identity and no order indicating ejecting and not including members of sociocultural groups is observed in it, except that they violate infrastructure of citizenship identity in IRI Constitution including nationality, Islam, and law as the political convention. The article 43 also implies public social and economic rights of citizenship. For example first clause of this article states that "basic necessities for all citizens: housing, food, clothing, hygiene, medical treatment, education, and the necessary facilities for the establishment of a family must be provided". The second clause states: "conditions and opportunities for employment must be provided for all people"; in the third clause we read that "the plan for national economy must be structured in such a manner that each individual has sufficient leisure and energy for intellectual, political, and social activities leading to all-round development of his self, to take active part in leading the affairs of the country, improve his skills, and to make full use of his creativity"; clause 4 states that "people should be free in choosing their jobs and exploitation and compelled labor should be prevented". These clauses imply provision of social and economic facilities necessary for a better life for all citizens and refer implicitly to this fact that without fulfilling fundamental requirements, active participation in political, sociocultural, and economic structure is not possible. This clause can be compared with civil principles in European welfare state [21]. Article 47 emphasizes respecting "Private ownership, legitimately acquired". Although, this article is similar to liberal ownership right of Locke type [22]. But it seems that it has been derived from the principle of legitimate ownership in Islam. Generally it seems that these articles which imply particularly citizenship social rights are inclusive and there is no restrictive constraint in them to deprive an individual or a group for political, cultural, ethnic, ideological, gender, lingual reasons.

Also the articles 156 to 174 represent the judicial aspect of public civil rights. For example article 156 states: "judiciary power not only is the protector of rights of the individual and society, and responsible for the implementation of justice, but also investigates and passes judgment on grievances, violations of rights, and complaints; the resolving of litigation; the settling of disputes; and the taking of all necessary decisions and measures in probate matters as the law may determine. This article, while emphasizes the rule of law [23] considers no difference between people and groups and is inclusive in this sense. The article 165 emphasizes "open trials" or article 168 emphasizes not only "open political and press trials", but also claims that such trials should be held in courts of justice. It seems that these articles are written along with guarding judicial and civil rights of citizens.

Generally, it can be said that IRI Constitution has public civil, social, and political rights in it which is in turn part of cultural citizenship rights. Of course it should not be forgotten that these articles solely resolve legal obstacles of realizing cultural citizenship. In this sense they have a privative aspect, but we cannot necessarily derive wide recognition policy of the rights of minority sociocultural groups.

Specific rights of cultural citizenship: In cultural citizenship there is emphasis on specific cultural rights in addition to public rights. Because specific cultural rights not only compensate for structural injustice, but also make the equal access to public sphere and finally participation in cultural, social, and political structure possible [9,10,24]. Accordingly, the article 12 of IRI Constitution can be considered as one of the first articles about specific cultural rights, and introduces Islam and Twelver Ja'fari School as the formal religion of Iran, and at the same time recognizes the other Islamic schools including Hanafi, Shafei, Maleki, Hanbali, and Zeidi as well and represents the issue of freely holding rituals in these schools. This article also stipulates that in any region in which the followers of these schools constitute the majority, they can pass local regulations according to their own school provided that they don't violate the rights of other schools and religions. This means that in IRI Constitution religious self-ritual is recognized for some schools locally. The important point about this article is that it introduces Islam and Twelver Ja'fari School as the underlying citizenship structure and declares that this infrastructure is not changeable and tenable. Hence any kind of granting specific cultural rights should be formed based on that or at least not be in contrast with that. In article 13 the religions Zoroastrian, Jew, and Christianity are recognized but the right local rule according to these religions has not been granted to them, which represents the limitation of religious minorities. In any case these two articles determine the range of religious minorities and formal religion in Islamic Republic of Iran. Although in a restrict interpretation it seems that the other religious groups are excluded from this range [25]. But in a wide and more flexible interpretation it can be said that these articles are solely about religious rights and do not necessarily violate other citizenship rights of other religious minorities. In addition, the article 14 which documents verse 8 of Surah Al-Mumtahanah, obliges IRI State and Muslims to behave with good manner and Islamic justice toward non-Muslims and observe their human rights. Yet, such rights include people who do not act conspiracy against Islam and Islamic Republic of Iran. This article includes several fundamental points about specific cultural rights; first, the culture of Muslim majority in general, and yet Shiite culture in particular is considered as the base for granting cultural rights; second, it demands nice and just behavior with non-Muslims; third, recognizes fundamental human rights, aside from other religious rights which belong to human; fourth, it represents a condition in addition to not being opposed to Islam which is not acting conspiracy against Islamic Republic of Iran which is in turn another political infrastructure for citizenship identity in IRI Constitution. In this sense the article considers the superiority of Islam over the other religions as an unquestioned issue and recognizes other religious minorities solely out of benevolence and in the scope of human rights.

It may be said that these articles at first level (underlying layer) represents concentrated cultural policy and at the second level represents a kind of narrow recognition policy. Meaning that it tries to recognize religious freedom of minorities and promote a tolerant behavior with them by focusing on the culture and religion of majority. But deep and wide recognition of differences, equal opportunities of minorities with the majority or the equal participation of religious groups in political and sociocultural structure of Islamic Republic of Iran is not induced from it. Also it is not clear to what extent the religious groups have access to the public areas (sphere). Article 15 shows other aspects of specific cultural rights. It emphasizes maintaining the language of ethnic minorities and recognizes "the possibility of using local and ethnic languages in group press and media and teaching ethnic and local literature at schools beside Persian language". It makes it possible for minorities to keep their ethnic and local identity in public area. It should be remembered that language is the one of main elements of keeping ethnic identity [26]. According to this article ethnic minorities can establish bilingual schools and found press and TV networks with their local and ethnic language, as it is true in later cultural citizenship [27]. Hence, it not only recognizes the ethnic and language differences, but also based on wide recognition policy, provides access of ethnic and language groups to public area, but in a limited geography.

Article 19 emphasizes "Equal rights of Iranian people, regardless of their ethnicity, color, race, language, and so on". In fact it has public civil rights and specific cultural rights together, because it emphasizes the equality of rights of all Iranians and at the same time at least from a legal perspective puts minorities and various sociocultural groups in a similar position. Equal respect to sociocultural groups can be extracted from this article at least in social area which is in accordance with narrow recognition policy [28,29].

Article 21 of IRI Constitution represents women rights, as one of the sociocultural groups. It states that "State must: 1. create a favorable environment for the growth of woman's personality and the restoration of her rights, both the material and intellectual; 2. Protect mothers particularly during pregnancy and childbearing and protect children without guardians; 3. establishing competent courts to protect and preserve the family; 4. Provide special insurance for widows, and aged women adwomen without support; 5. Award guardianship of children to worthy mothers, in order to protect the interests of the children, in the absence of a legal guardian". This article represents the attention of Constitution of IRI to specific rights of women and implies enhancement of women abilities and their family and social situation. It seems that exemption of women from some public rules affecting them and even positive discrimination in favor of women can be derived from this article, as it is in narrow recognition policy [27].

Article 64 recognizes the representativeness assured for religious minorities (Zoroastrians, Jews, Ashourian, Kaldani, North and South Armenians). It is similar to special representatives presented by [27]. Although, it is perfectly obvious that generalizing special representatives to other sociocultural groups such as Sunnis, women, and disabled (other minorities) is not deduced from this article, it seems that at least it resolves the legal obstacles for such generalization. Generally, as Galeotti points out, granting assured representative to minorities and particular groups provide conditions so that they can not only determine their own destiny, but also belong to a larger society [28]. At the same time, it seems that the principle of special representative makes a bridge between narrow and wide recognition policy. It means that it provides a ground for resolving discriminations and at the same time makes it possible for them to access public arena.

In sum, it can be said that IRI Constitution has special cultural rights, although limited, for recognized sociocultural groups, including religious, ethnic, and language minorities, as well as women and vulnerable social groups. It should be said as well that the scope of such groups is limited, and does not for example include Dervishes or Baha'is. Also, the recognized groups enjoy narrow recognition including legal rights, holding their self-government, own rituals and so on somehow. At the same time some of such groups like religious and language groups enjoy wide recognition in some parts such as accessing public arena, but maybe deepening and expanding such recognition can make the belonging sense of sociocultural groups to the larger society stronger and as Parekh points out, help political and sociocultural enrichment in society [10].

Duties and commitments of sociocultural groups in IRI constitution

Citizenship right and duty are two sides of one coin. Meaning that my right determines the scope of other's duty and my duty determines the scope of other's right. Hence, cultural citizenship without commitments and duties is not only incomplete, but also fundamentally infeasible [30]. In this sense, the same principles including public and specific cultural rights, determine the scope of mutual duties and commitments. At the same time there are articles in IRI Constitution implying special duties and commitments. Yet, such articles are mostly regarding duties and commitments of State. For example we can refer to articles 3, 21, 28, 29, 30, 43, and 49. However, there are articles indicating duties and commitments of citizens and State together. For instance, article 8 considers al-'amr bilma'ruf wa al-nahy 'an al-munkar as a universal and reciprocal duty and sets the relationship between people together and between nation and State. It seems that it not only makes supervision of people by State possible, but also provides the ground for supervision of nation over State. This article has also been derived from original teachings of Quran of course it is not clear whether it involves all sociocultural groups. At least in a limited interpretation it can involve all Muslim sociocultural groups and provide the ground for their active participation in public arena. At the same time, not only it recognizes the possibility of public control over rulers, but also reminds them their responsiveness and responsibility [31]. Article 40 states that "No person may exercise his own rights as a means of constraining others or violating the public interest". Article 46 reminds that "Everyone is the owner of the fruits of his legitimate business and labor, and no one may deprive another of the opportunity of business and work under the pretext of his right to ownership." These two articles determine limitations of freedom of citizens in public arena which is somehow similar to negative liberty in the thoughts of Isaiah Berlin [32]. At the same time these articles represent a combination of public and individual duties. Article 50 represents the environmental commitments of citizens. It points out that environmental protection is a public duty and destroying and polluting environment is forbidden. Namely the article indicates the principle of sustainability in green citizenship [33]. Article 51 which is regarding paying tax, considers no difference among citizens. Also, as sociocultural minorities has the right to refer to competent courts, according to the articles 61 and 159 are obliged to follow their complaint through formal courts on the country. Interesting point is that the duties and commitments of sociocultural groups are general, and include all the cases of which all the other citizens are followers. In this sense, such duties and commitments are measured based on underlying citizenship structure in IRI Constitution (that is the principles of Islamic Republic of Iran, including Islam, Shiite school, independence and territorial integrity, national security, Faqih).

Participation of sociocultural groups in IRI constitution

According to wide recognition policy the possibility of participation of all sociocultural groups in political, social, and cultural structure is a part of cultural citizenship. Yet, it is not clear whether participation is in the category of citizens' rights or their duties. In any case, we can observe articles and clauses in IRI Constitution which are regarding public and particular participation of sociocultural groups. For example, in clause 8 of article 3 we read "State is obliged to provide the ground for the participation of the entire people in determining their political, economic, social, and cultural destiny". This clause involves all citizenship kinds for all people and groups and at least in the limited interpretation legal obstacles of participation of people and sociocultural groups in determining their own destiny is resolved by this article. Clause 15 of the same article demands for "the expansion and strengthening of Islamic brotherhood and public cooperation among all the people". This article which has an Islamic origin, reminds once again the most important citizenship infrastructure that is Islam. Also like new civic republic citizenship theories, it establishes a direct relationship between correlation and participation [34]. Article 56 emphasizes the right of human for determining his own destiny as a Devine and unquestioned right. It seems that in contrast to modern social convention which considers the right to determine destiny as natural, this article attitudes it to the status of God's Vicegerent of human. Yet, it is not clear if the principle of God's inheritor involves all people regardless their gender, religion, ethnicity and so on or only includes Muslims.

In article 59 "direct recourse to popular vote through a Referendum" has been represented as one way for political participation. Since in this article there is no restrictive limit, public participation can be derived from it. Article 62 is about "direct and secret ballot to elect representatives of people in The Islamic consultative Assembly". This article implies a maximum participation (at least with regard to electors), but it seems that the requirements set by the law for those who are going to be selected are derived from the citizenship infrastructure in Constitution, that are Islam and nation [35], hence it is a public participation to some extent.

Chapter 7 of IRI Constitution which is dedicated to councils can provide the ground for participation of citizens in controlling the issues of their own locality. For example article 100 states that: "Members of village, division, city, municipality, and province councils will be elected by the people of the locality in question". It seems that this article is a medium between narrow and wide recognition policy which in turn provides the ground for active participation of sociocultural groups in political and cultural structure of localities and regions. At the same time it can lead to a participation that is based on "equal respect policy" and is not ignorant to differences [36]. This article can implicitly provide the grounds for maintenance and flourishing local traditions and rituals and cultures. So, it can lead us to a multilayer citizenship according to which citizens establish connections in their underlying layers with their local culture and in higher layers with public culture of society [37].

Article 115 of Constitution which is regarding requirements of president represents one of the most controversial articles in IRI Constitution. This article states that the President must be elected from among religious and political personalities possessing the following qualifications: Iranian origin; Iranian nationality; administrative capacity and resourcefulness; a good past-record; trustworthiness and piety; convinced belief in the fundamental principles of the Islamic Republic of Iran and the official religion of the country. It is above anything derived from the underlying layer of citizenship in Islamic Republic of Iran (that is being Shiite and Iranian) and accordingly limits the scope of participation, with regard to being elected. It seems that religious minorities are excluded from this scope automatically. But there remain a question whether women can be elected as president? In this regard at least two interpretations can be presented both of which are resulted from etymology of the word "Rijal" (literally means men). In the first interpretation Rijal is perceived as meaning men [38]. It seems that this interpretation has been applied in ten presidential courses so far. Yet, the masculine structure of policy during Iranian history strengthens this kind of interpretation. In the second interpretation Rijal is known as being included in common words meaning people (Mardom) which involves both men and women. In any case in seems that this article is still limited. In this sense it prevents many people belonging to minority sociocultural groups from achieving high levels of political power. So this article is consistent with concentrating cultural policies which has been formed at least around men, the Shiite, and the limited circle of ruling powerful people. In general it seems that in IRI Constitution participation in public arena is more accessible for ethnic and local groups than other minority groups. At the same time, the issue of participation of such groups can be followed in subset of public participation.

Accordingly it may be said that participation of social groups such as women and disabled in political arena is not faced with fundamental legal barriers. But there seems to be two main barriers in this regard; first, the political interpretations made of their participation by power institutes, and second, treatment of public culture which because of historical belief, has not so much experienced political participation of these groups [39,40].

Conclusion

Now we return to our starting question: what is the particular solution of Constitution of Islamic Republic of Iran for the variety of sociocultural structure of Iranian society? Apparently, the solution of IRI Constitution is a combination of cultural policies concentrated in underlying layer and narrow and wide recognition policies on the top layer. Meaning that IRI Constitution is based on the culture of majority in the underlying layer which is raised to a high degree from Shiite school in particular, and Islam, being Iranian, Persian language, and patriarchal culture in general. At the same time we can see in this underlying layer the superiority of men over women and the ruling elite over other social classes. On the other hand narrow recognition of ethnic, language, and religious groups as well as women and other vulnerable groups (such as disables, elderly, children without guardian, and so on) can be observed on the upper layer. Yet, such recognition depends generally on the same underlying layer as was the result of historical, political, and cultural exploration in Iranian society. Hence, the sociocultural groups raised from new religions such as Baha'is are not recognized. At the same time women are protected generally and not necessarily as a particular sociocultural group. Yet, in regard with access to political power at high levels, women are faced with serious barriers both legally and culturally.

However, in Constitution of Islamic Republic of Iran both narrow and wide recognition of sociocultural groups can be traced. For example it has particular articles to resolve discrimination from sociocultural groups such as women, religious minorities and vulnerable ethnicities and classes. However, still there are restrictive articles. Accordingly not only should the barriers of formal equality resolved, but the sociocultural barriers of their access to public and private rights should also be eliminated. It can be said that attention to social and economic prerequisites of cultural citizenship is one of the strengths of IRI Constitution. However, its weakness is ambiguity in the scope of inclusion of cultural citizenship. The last point is that realizing perfect cultural citizenship in Iran requires fundamental arrangements and prerequisites, one of the most important of which is deepening citizenship in public culture. In simple words, inclusive and stable citizenship does not shape unless traditions, rituals, and social values get authenticity with rights and duties of cultural citizenship. Without changing culture, how much the rules are complete, cultural citizenship cannot be realized. Yet, it seems that the way to change culture is neither compelling from the upper powers nor leaving to invisible hand of history, but need have to Praxis in public arena. As Turner states, citizenship is a Praxis civil, legal, judicial, political, economic, and cultural in political society [20]. Hence, without forming citizenship rights movements and expanding them inside Iranian society, not only the legal barriers for cultural citizenship in IRI Constitution are not eliminated, but also the existing capacities cannot be used appropriately.

References

1. Maqsoudi M (2003) Ethnicity and its role in political evolutions in reign of Muhammad Reza Pahlavi. Document Center of Islamic Revolution, Tehran.
2. Matthew L (2012) Comparative-Historical Methods. Sage Publications, London.
3. Rosaldo R (1997) Cultural Citizenship. In: Flores WV, Benmayor R (eds.) Latino Cultural Citizenship: Claiming Identity, Space, and Politics. Beacon Press, Boston pp: 27-38.
4. O'Byrne D (2003) The Dimensions of Global Citizenship: Political Identity beyond the Nation-State. Frank Cass, London.
5. Stevenson N (2013) Cultural citizenship: cosmopolitan questions. Tehran, Tisa.
6. Fraser N (2000) Rethinking Recognition. New Left Review 3: 107-120.
7. Esman MJ (2004) An Introduction to Ethnic Conflict. Polity Press, Cambridge p: 4.4.
8. Gagnon A, Raffaele I (2005) Interculturalism: Expanding the Boundaries of Citizenship. Maiz R and Ferran R (eds.) In Democracy, Nationalism and Multiculturalism. Frank Cass, London and New York pp: 27-42.
9. Kymlicka W (1995) Multicultural Citizenship: A Liberal Theory of Minority Rights. University Press, Oxford, New York.
10. Parekh B (2000) Rethinking Multiculturalism: Cultural Diversity and Political Theory. Basingstoke, Macmillan.
11. Seglow J (2003) Theorizing Recognition. In: Haddock B, Sutch P (eds.) Molticulturalism, Identity and Rights. Routledge, London pp: 78-93.
12. Mansour J (2012) Constitution of Islamic Republic of Iran. (101thedn) Doran Publications, Tehran.
13. Ahmadi H (2011) Foundations of Iranian national identity. (2ndedn) Institute of Sociocultural Studies of Ministry of Science, Tehran.
14. Young IM (1990) Justice and the Politics of Difference. Princeton University Press, Princeton.
15. Bosniak L (2008) The Citizen and the Alien: Dilemmas of Contemporary Membership. Princeton University Press, Princeton.
16. Balazadeh Z (2004) Private international law and Iranian regulations regarding nationality, residence, and the status of foreigners. Mardomsalari Publications, Tehran.
17. Riley D (2009) Citizenship and welfare state. Translated to Persian by Jila Ebrahimi. Tehran, Agah.
18. Marshall TH (1992) Citizenship and Social Class. Battomore T (eds.) Pluto Press, London.
19. Castells S Allister D (2003) Citizenship and migration: globalization and politics of belonging. Translated to Persian by Faramarz Taghilou: Institute of Strategic Studies. Tehran.
20. Marshall TH (1994) Afterthought on Value of Problems of Walfare-Capitalism. In Citizenship: Critical Concepts. Turner BS and Hamiltion P (eds.) Routledge, London and New York 2:5-44.
21. Bussemaker J (1999) Citizenship and Walfare State Reform in Europe. Routledge London and New York.
22. Locke J (2009) Two treatise on government. Translated to Persian by Hamid Azdanlou, (2ndedn) Ney Publications, Tehran.
23. Qazi A (1994) Constitution and political institutes. (3rdedn) Publications of Tehran University, Tehran.
24. Young IM (2002) Inclusion and Democracy. Polity Press, Cambridge.
25. Aryamanesh B (2011) Rights of minorities from the perspective of constitution and international standards. Excellence of rights 4: 77-93.
26. Hermidas Bound D (2005) Language and national identity. In Discourses about language and identity. Goudarzi H (eds.) National studies, Tehran pp: 27-46.
27. Young IM (1989) Polity and Group Difference: A Critique of the Ideal of Universal Citizenship. In Citizenship: Critical Concepts. S. Turner and P. Hamiltion (eds.) Routledge, London and New York 2: 386-408.

28. Patten A (2000) Equality of Recognition and the Liberal Theory of Citizenship. In The Demands of Citizenship. C. McKinnon and I. Hampsher-Monk (eds.) Continuun, London and New York pp: 193-212.

29. Galeotti AE (1999) Neutrality and Recognition. In Pluralism and Liberal. R. Bellamy & M Hollis (eds.) Cambridge University Press, Cambridge pp: 37-54.

30. Delanty G (2000) Citizenship in a Global Age: Society, Culture, Politics. Open University Press Buckingham.

31. Haqiqat S (2008) Principles of political thoughts in Islam. Samt, Tehran.

32. Berlin I (1992) Two concepts of freedom. In Political philosophy. A. Quinten (eds.) translated to Persian by Morteza As'adi, Alhoda, Tehran pp: 281-303.

33. Dobson A (2000) Political theory and the environment: the grey and the green (and the in-between). In Political Theory in Transition. N. O'sullivan (eds.) Routledge, London and New York pp: 211-224.

34. Schwarzmantel J (2003) Citizenship and Identity: Toward a New Republic. Routledge, London.

35. Hashemi M (2004) The basic law in Islamic Republic of Iran. (8thedn) Mizban, Tehran.

36. Taylor C (1994) Multiculturalism and the Politics of Recognition. Princeton University Press, Princeton.

37. Lister R (1997) Citizenship: Feminist Perspective. Basingstoke, Macmillan.

38. Rostami V and Mousipour M (2011) An analysis of article 115 of Constitution of Islamic Republic of Iran regarding the requirements for president. Law magazine 40: 225-240.

39. Pateman C (1994) Feminism and Democracy. In Citizenship: Critical Concepts. S. Turner and P. Hamiltion (eds.) Routledge, London and New York 2: 372-385.

40. Turner BS (1993) Contemporary Problems in Theory of Citizenship. In Citizenship and Social Theory. B. S. Turner (eds.) Sage, London pp: 1-18.

6

Analysis of Marketing Function, Marketing Efficiency and Spatial Co-Integration of Rohu (Labeo Rohita) Fish in Some Selected Areas of Bangladesh

Umme Aymon Janifa[1*], Md. Imran Omar[2], Sabur SA[3], Moniruzzaman M[3] and Haque Md.S[4]

[1]*Department of Aquaculture, Faculty of Fisheries, Bangladesh Agricultural University, Mymensingh-2202, Bangladesh*

[2]*Agricultural Economics Division, Bangladesh Agricultural Research Institute, Joydevpur, Gazipur-1701, Bangladesh*

[3]*Department of Agribusiness and Marketing, Faculty of Agricultural Economics and Rural Sociology, Bangladesh Agricultural University, Mymensingh-2202, Bangladesh*

[4]*Department of Agricultural Economics, Faculty of Agricultural Economics and Rural Sociology, Bangladesh Agricultural University, Mymensingh-2202, Bangladesh*

Abstract

The study was undertaken to examine the value chain, value addition, marketing cost & margin, marketing efficiency and market integration of rohu fish in selected areas of Bangladesh during the month of July-August 2013. The objectives of the study were to estimate costs and margins, seasonal price variation and to test market integration of rohu fish. Primary and secondary data were used for this study. The higher marketing cost was incurred by paiker and the lowest by retailer. On the other hand, retailers earned the highest net marketing margins. Chain II was found the most efficient chain. Analysis of market integration shows that rohu fish market in Bangladesh was well integrated. The findings of the study revealed that the marketing of rohu fish was a profitable business and some recommendations were provided for the improvement of rohu fish marketing in the country.

Keywords: Value addition; Marketing cost & margin; Marketing efficiency; Spatial co-integration

Introduction

In the agro-based economy of Bangladesh, the fisheries sector contributes near about 58% of animal protein to the daily diets of the population, about 3.74% to GDP, 4.04% in export earnings and 20.87% to agriculture in 2010-11 [1]. This sector provide full-time employment of 1.4 million professional Fishers and Fish farmer, and 11 million part-time Fishers, fish farmer and women, which is about 10% of total population. The marketing system and structure is one of the main circumstances of socio economic condition of the local people and production system of any area. With intra-linkage and inter-linkage from production sector to consumer sector, it is a chain of various systems involved in marketing. As fish and fishery products are highly traded commodities, fish production is a necessary part of the marketing process to make a whole complete. The total fish production in Bangladesh was estimated to near about 2.56 million tons in 2009-2010, of which near about 2.07 (80.59%) and 0.5 (19.41%) million tons came from inland and marine waters respectively [1]. About 97% of the production is marketed internally for domestic consumption while the remaining 3% exported to the foreign [2]. Rohu fish is the most important among the three Indian major carp species used in carp poly culture systems. This graceful Indo-Gangetic reverie species is the natural inhabitant of the riverine system of northern and central India, and the rivers of Pakistan, Bangladesh and Myanmar. In India, it has been transplanted into almost all reverie systems including the freshwaters of Andaman, where its population has successfully established. The species has also been introduced in many other countries, including Sri Lanka, the former USSR, Japan, China, Philippines, Malaysia, Nepal and some countries of Africa. Bangladesh is considered one of the most suitable countries in the world for freshwater aquaculture, because of its favorable agro-climatic conditions. A sub-tropical climate and vast areas of shallow water provide ideal conditions for fish production. Rohu fish farming is widespread in many Asian countries including China, Indonesia, Philippines, Thailand and Vietnam due to its rapid growth rate, high market demand and increasing consumer acceptance [3]. The present study aimed to identify, particularly the marketing chains, to analyze the market integration. The study would make recommendation and suggestions to improve the organization and operation of rohu fish marketing with a view to enhancing efficiency by analyzing the present marketing problems. In view of these, the survey was conducted to examine marketing and price behavior of rohu fish in selected areas of Mymensingh district. Thus the study was conducted for understanding the present situation of marketing system of rohu fish in different regions of Bangladesh with following objectives.

The specific objectives of the study are to:

1. analysis of marketing function rohu fish and the marketing integration of rohu fish
2. identify different marketing chains of rohu fish
3. determine the extent of value addition in terms of costs in successive stages of rohu fish movement and
4. examine the marketing margins of the intermediaries of rohu fish.

Materials and Methods

The present study was conducted on the field survey method where the primary data were collected from the respondents. Secondary data was collected from journals, thesis and raw data from monthly bulletin of Directorate of Agricultural Marketing (DAM) and District Fisheries Office [4]. In Mymensingh district there were a number of successful rohu fish producers, trader's i.e.Aratdar, Bepari, Paiker and retailer etc. The study area is confined to two Upazilas namely Bhaluka Upazila and

***Corresponding author:** Umme Aymon Janifa, Professor of Fisheries, Bangladesh Agricultural University, Bangladesh
E-mail: janifa2011co@gmail.com

Phulpur Upazila in Mymensingh district, where the cultivation of rohu fish was concentrated. Purposive sampling techniques were used for selecting the sample. Total sample size of the study was 100. Selected samples consisted of 30 fish farmers and 70 traders. For this study, 30 stocking ponds were selected from Tarakanda and Baluka upazilas. The intermediaries dealing with rohu marketing were categorized into three groups, namely, Aratdar, Paiker and retailer. From different stages of fish marketing 25 Paikers, 10 Aratdars and 35 retailers were selected as respondents for the study. Among them two Aratdars, five Paiker and ten retailers from Tarakanda, three Aratdars, five Paiker and ten retailers from Trishal, and ten Paikers, five Aratdars and twenty retailers from Kawran Bazar of Dhaka city were selected. The data were collected intensively by using structured interview schedules. The weekly average wholesale prices of rohu of various markets like Dhaka, Chittagong, Khulna, Sherpur, Comilla, Bogra, Rangpur, Rajshahi, Mymensingh, Sylhet, Gazipur and Noakhali during 2000 to 2012 were collected from Department of Agricultural Marketing (DAM) [4]. Later it was converted into monthly figures.

Analytical techniques

Farmer's net prices, farmer's gross share, farmer's net share and Marketing efficiency were calculated by using following formulas:

5. Farmer's net price = Farmer's sale price - Farmer's marketing cost

6. Percentages of total value addition cost/net profit =

$$\frac{\text{Marketing cost / Net marketing margin}}{\text{Tota marekting cost / net marekting margin}} \times 100$$

7. Farmer's net share = $\frac{\text{Farmer's net price}}{\text{Retail price}} \times 100$

8. Gross margin = Sale Price – purchase Price.

9. Net margin = gross margin – marketing costs

Marketing efficiency was calculated using Acharaya's formula [5]:

$$ME = \frac{FP}{MC + MM}$$

Where,

ME = Marketing efficiency.

FP = Net price received by farmers

MC= Total marketing cost

MM= Total net marketing margin of intermediaries.

A higher value of ME denotes higher level of efficiency and vice versa.

Market integration

Market integration was measured by co-integration method.The bulk of econometric theories have been based on the assumption that the underlying data process is stationary. Stochastic process is said to be stationary if its mean and variance are constant over time and the value of co-variance between two time periods depends only on the distance or gap or lag between the two time periods and not the actual time at which the co-variance is [6]. In practice, most economic time series are non-stationary. An applying regression models to non-stationary data may arise the problem of "spurious or nonsense" correlation [6]. To overcome such problems, the concept of co-integration was used because it offers a means of identifying and hence avoiding the spurious. The underlying principle of co-integration analysis is that although trend of many economic series show upward or downwards over time in a non-stationary fashion, group of variables may drift together. **Unit root and Co-integration test:** The individual price series were tested for the order of integration to determine whether or not they are stationary which is known as the unit root test [6]. A number of tests for stationary are available in the literature; these include the Dickey-Fuller (DF) test, the Augmented Dickey-Fuller (ADF) test (Dickey and Fuller, 1981) and the Philips-Perron (PP) test.

For theoretical and practical reasons, the Dickey–Fuller test is applied to regressions run in the following forms:

Y_t is a random walk or without constant:

$$\Delta Y_t = \delta Y_{t-1} + e_t \text{ .... (1)}$$

Y_t is a random walk with drift or constant:

$$\Delta Y_t = \beta_1 + \delta Y_{t-1} + e_t \text{ .... (2)}$$

Y_t is a random walk with drift around a stochastic trend (constant plus trend):

$$\Delta Y_t = \beta_1 + \beta_2 t + \delta Y_{t-1} + e_t \text{ .... (3)}$$

Where t is the time or trend variable.

In each case the null hypothesis is $\delta = 0(\rho = 1)$; that is, there is a unit root in the time series i.e. the series is non-stationary. The alternative hypothesis is that δ is less than zero; that is, the time series is stationary. Under the null hypothesis, the conventionally computed t statistics is known as the τ (tau) statistic, whose critical values have been tabulated by Dickey and Fuller. If the null hypothesis is rejected, it means that Y_t is a stationary time series with zero mean in the case of (1), that Y_t is stationary with a non-zero mean $[= \beta_1/(1-\rho)]$ in the case of (2), and that Y_t is a stationary around a deterministic trend in equation (3).

It is extremely important to note that the critical values of the tau test to test the hypothesis that δ=0, are different for each of the preceding three specifications of the DF test. If the computed absolute value of the tau statistics (τ) exceeds the DF or MacKinnon critical tau values, we reject the hypothesis that δ = 0, in which case the time series is stationary. On the other hand, if the computed (τ) does not exceed the critical tau value, we do not reject the null hypothesis, were the time series is non-stationary.

In conducting the DF test as in (1), (2), or (3), it was assumed that the error term e_t was uncorrelated. But in case the e_t are correlated, Dickey and Fuller have developed a test known as the augmented Dickey-Fuller (ADF) test.

This test is conducted by "augmenting" the preceding equation by adding the lagged values of the dependent variable ΔY_t. The ADF test here consists of estimating if the error term e_t is auto correlated, one modifies (4) as follows:

$$\Delta Y_t = \beta_1 + \beta_2 + \delta Y_{t-1} + \alpha \sum_{i=1}^{m} \Delta Y_{t-i} + \varepsilon_t \text{ .... (4)}$$

where ε_t is a pure white noise error term and where, $\Delta Y_{t-1} = (Y_{t-1} - Y_{t-2}), \Delta Y_{t-2} = (Y_{t-2} - Y_{t-3})$ etc., that is, one uses lagged difference terms. The number of lagged difference terms to include is often determined empirically, the idea being to include enough terms so that the error term in (4) is serially uncorrelated. The null hypothesis is still that δ = 0 or ρ = 1, that is, a unit root exists in Y (i.e., Y is non-stationary).

To test the market integration, the following co-integration regression was run for each pair of price series:

$$Y_{it} = \alpha_0 + \alpha_1 Y_{jt} + \varepsilon_t \text{ .... } (5)$$

Where, Y_i and Y_j are price series of a specific commodity in two markets i and j, and ε_t is the residual term assumed to be distributed identically and independently. The test of market integration is straightforward if Y_i and Y_j are stationary variables but if the price series proved as non-stationary then we have to done another test (Engle-Granger test).

Testing whether the variables are co-integrated is merely another unit root test on the residual in equation (5).

However, since the Y_i and Y_j are individually non-stationary, there is the possibility that the regression is spurious. The DF and ADF tests in the present context are known as Engle-Granger (EG) test whose critical values was provided by Engle-Granger. The test involved regression the first-difference of the residual lagged level and lagged dependent variables (Engle-Granger test) is as follows:

For Engle-Granger (EG) test,

$$\Delta\varepsilon_t = \beta\varepsilon_{t-1} \text{ .... } (6)$$

If the computed value of 't' of regression coefficient β is higher (in absolute term) than tabulated value, our conclusion is that the residuals from the regression are I (0), that is they are stationary and the regression is not spurious even though individually two variables are non-stationary.

Results and Discussion

Buying and selling

An efficient marketing system is essential for earning fair profit for the fish farmers and traders. Marketing functions may be defined as major specialized activities performed in accomplishing the marketing process of concentration, equalization and dispersion [7]. The activities involved in the transfer of goods are completed through buying and selling functions. Aratdars do the functions of negotiation between buyers and sellers of fish and help them at their own business premises on receipt of commission. They do not take the ownership of the products. Rohu farmers sell 85% of their fish to paiker through aratdar, 15% to paiker directly and the final 4% to retailer. Paikers sell 74% of their fishes to retailers and 26% to retailers through aratdars. Retailers sell the entire fish to ultimate consumers. Paiker of Rohu purchases 88% from farmers through aratdar and 12% directly from farmers. Retailer purchases 87% from farmers through aratdar and 13% from farmers. Consumer purchases 100% of rohu from the retailers in the study area (Table 1).

Grading

Grading is the basic function of sales transactions and is defined as the classification of products according to some standards or measures [7]. Grading is the sorting of different market quality which facilitates exchange by simplifying buying and selling as it makes the sale by showing sample and description possible. It also simplifies the concentration process and makes easier and less costly the movement of goods through the marketing channel. Grading facilitates sale since different sizes of fish have different prices. In Bangladesh, all intermediaries grade fish on the basis of weight (Table 2).

Storage

The storage facilities help buyers and sellers to reduce the wide fluctuation of prices between peak and lean seasons. The storage function is primarily concerned with making goods available at the desired time and enables traders to receive better prices for their products. Because of high perishability, fish requires extremely specialized storage facilities matching the seasonal demand. Other intermediaries use only ice to transport fishes from one place to another. Surprisingly, no refrigerated vans are used in Bangladesh to transport fish. All intermediaries use ice during marketing, but their ice to fish ratio is not appropriate. So the quality of fish is deteriorated. In retail selling, some retailers use ice.

Transportation

Transportation is a basic function of making goods available at proper place and it creates place utility. Perishable goods must be moved as early as possible from the producing centre to the consumer centre. So transportation is essential for highly perishable commodities like fish. Adequate and efficient transportation is a cornerstone for the modern marketing system [7]. In the study areas, the fish farmers and intermediaries use various modes of transports such as van, rickshaw, truck, passenger bus, pickup, nasimon (locally made pick-up type van for transporting passengers and goods), head load etc, to transfer product from the producing areas to the consumption centre. Table 3, show different modes of transport used by the intermediaries to transport fish from one place to another.

Financing

The financing function is the advancing of money by someone to carry on the business. For effective operation, financing is of crucial importance in the whole marketing system of rohu. The source of finance for the value chain actors in the study areas are shown in Table 4 which show that most of the fish farmers, aratdars, paikers and retailers of rohu, are self-financed. Other sources of finance for farmers are banks, friends and relatives, and dadon. A minor portion of Aratdar's sources of finance are banks and friends and relatives. Paikers take loan from banks, NGO and friends and relatives. In addition to

Value chain actor	Purchase from (%)				Sold to (%)				
	Farmer	Farmer via *aratdar*	*Paiker*	Retailer	*Paiker*	*Paiker* via *aratdar*	Retailer	Retailer via *aratdar*	Consumer
Farmer	-	-	-	-	15	81	4	-	-
Aratdar	*Aratdars* negotiate between buyers and sellers of fish and help them at their own business premises on receipt of *Aratdari* commission.								
Paiker	12	88	-	-	-	-	74	26	-
Retailer	13	87	-	-	-	-	-	-	100
Consumer	-	-	-	100	-	-	-	-	-

Table 1. Percent of rohu fish transacted by value chain actors

Species	Size	Weight
Rohu fish	Large	2.5 kg above
	Medium	1.0 kg to 2.5 kg
	Small	Less than 1 kg

Table 2. Grading practices of *rohu* fish on the basis of size and weight

Farmers and Intermediaries	Mode of transport
Fish Farmer	• Rickshaw/Van: Three wheel non-mechanized man-driven carrier • Nasimon: Locally made mechanized small lorry/van • Pickup: Small lorry
Paiker	Bus: Passenger bus (Bottom cargo holder) • Truck: Cargo carrier (Non-refrigerated) • Pickup: Small lorry
Retailer	• Head load: Container carry on head • Rickshaw/Van: Three wheel non-mechanized carrier • Bus: Passenger bus (Bottom cargo holder/roof top) • Truck: Cargo carrier (Non-refrigerated) • Nasimon: Locally made mechanized small lorry/van • Pickup: Small lorry

Table 3. Mode of transport used by farmers and intermediaries for movement *of rohu* fish

Sources of finance	Market participants (%)			
	Farmer	*Aratdar*	*Paiker*	Retailer
Own fund	86	96	82	76
Bank	9	3	11	0
NGO	-	0	5	16
Friend and relatives	4	1	2	8
Dadon from *Aratdar*	1	0	0	0
Total	100	100	100	100

Table 4. Sources of finance of *rohu* fish farmers and intermediaries

the use of their own fund, retailers also borrow from NGOs and friends and relatives [8].

Packaging

Packaging may be defined as the general group of activities in product planning which involves designing and producing the container or wrapper for a product [9]. Packaging is essential for proper transportation of fish. 'Basket' made of bamboo, rope and polythene is used by farmers, paikers and retailers of major carps, pangas and tilapia fish. Plastic drums are usually used when fish is transported in live form. Currently, 'plastic crate' is commonly used by all types of intermediaries in Bangladesh (Table 5).

Pricing

In the study areas, all intermediaries are involved in buying and selling of fish. Farmer, aratdar, paiker, and processing plants practice open bargaining, auction and going market prices method for fixing price of their products in varying degree. Cent percent of the retailers follow open bargain for selling their fish to consumers (Table 6).

Characteristics of market participants

In the chain of fish marketing of the study areas, the product moves from farmers to consumers through market intermediaries such as Fish farmers, aratdar paiker, Faria and retailer.

Fish farmers and fishermen are the first link in the fish marketing channels. The fish Farmers (producers) of rohu fish usually sell their fish to the local aratdar.

The aratdars are at the centre of the entire marketing system and their role goes far beyond what one would normally expect of a commission agent, including financing of suppliers and buyers, and often dealing on their own account [10]. When fish arrives at the wholesale markets, aratdars take the responsibility and control of each sale. They sell the fish through an auctioning system and get a commission of 3% to 4% depending on fish species. Most of the time aratdars recruit koyal (person who organizes auction by uttering and offering different prices for buyers for sale). Koyals have a significant role on pricing the fish. Generally, the aratdars are self-financed. They hire necessary salaried persons or labourers depending upon their volume of business.

Paiker or bepari is conceptually same but used interchangeably in different fish marketing system in Bangladesh who transacts large volume of product. Another type of paiker is seen in hilsha marketing system called L/C paiker. They purchase fish from fishermen through aratdar and sell (export) their entire product to overseas market, especially the Indian markets. Some paikers/beparis receive money in advance from the aratdar on condition that they would sell their fish through them.

Faria is another type of intermediary in the marketing system. They purchase a small quantity of fish form distant fishermen far away from the market and carry it to the terminal point and sell it to aratdar or retailer in the study areas.

Retailer the last intermediaries of fish marketing channel, do not have any permanent establishment but they have fixed places in the market centre or are wandering with hari (aluminum pot) on head from door to door. Usually retailers buy fish from aratdar and sell directly to ultimate consumers. Mostly they purchase fish on cash. Sometimes they also purchase on credit for short term periods. If the size of fish is too large then buyers want the fish to cut into pieces as cutters have sufficient instruments to cut the large fish. Retailers may cut the whole fish for consumers or uses the services of cutters to remove scales and cut into pieces. Depending on the convenience, extra money is charged for removing scales or cut into pieces. In spite of being self-financed, the retailers often borrow money from non-institutional sources at the time of need.

Marketing chains

Marketing chains are the alternative routes of product flows from producers to consumers [7]. Value chain may be long or short for a particular commodity depending on the qualities of products, size and nature of consumers and producers and the prevailing social and physical environment (Figure 1). Dominant supply chains of rohu in the study areas are shown below:

Value chain - I Fish Farmer→*AratdarPaiker*→Retailer Consumer

→

Value chain – II Fish Farmer→*Paiker*→Retailer Consumer

Value chain – III Fish Farmer→ *Faria*→Consume

Value chain – IV Fish Farmer→Village market Consumer

Two major value chains are identified for *rohu* fish in Mymensingh district. These are:

Value chain – I Fish Farmer→*AratdarPaiker* →Retailer Consumer→

Value chain – II Fish Farmer→*Paiker*Retailer →Consumer

Value addition costs by different actors

The cost incurred to transport the product from producers to consumers is ordinarily known as marketing cost. In other words, the cost of marketing represents the cost of performing various marketing functions [7]. Marketing costs are incurred when commodities are shipped from the farm to the final market. Total marketing cost of fish includes all costs incurred by different intermediaries like inter district paikers, local paikers, aratdars, retailers and farmers who perform some marketing functions in the study areas. Products get value added during their movement across items. Share of transportation cost is the highest (40.54%) followed by aratdar's commission (26.92%), icing (8.23%), wages and salaries (4.81%) and tips & donations (4.32%) for rohu marketing (Table 7). Total value added cost per maund is Taka 953.13 from production point to consumption point. Amongst them, Paiker's value added cost is the highest while aratdar's value added cost is the lowest. Aratdars negotiate between buyers and sellers of fish and assist them in buying and selling at their own business premises on receipt of commission (Figure 2).

Marketing margin

A marketing margin is the percentage of the final weighted average selling Price taken by each stage of the marketing chain. The margin must cover the costs involved in transferring produce from one stage to the next and provide a reasonable return to those doing the marketing activities [11]. It is also termed as Price spread as it represents the difference between the buying and selling Price. Total marketing margin is the difference between the Price received by the fish Farmers and the Price paid by the final consumers. Marketing margins of fish are calculated separately for different intermediaries. Gross marketing margin of each type of intermediaries is calculated by deducting the purchase Price of fish from their sale Prices while net margin or profit component is calculated by deducting the marketing cost from gross marketing margins. Average net marketing margins of all intermediaries for rohu fish are presented in Table 3. Farmer average marketing cost is Taka 135.00 per maund for all fishes. Amongst all intermediaries, profit of retailers is the highest of Taka 624.29 per maund of fish. Profit of intermediaries varies due to variation in their costs; purchase Price and sales Price (Table 8).

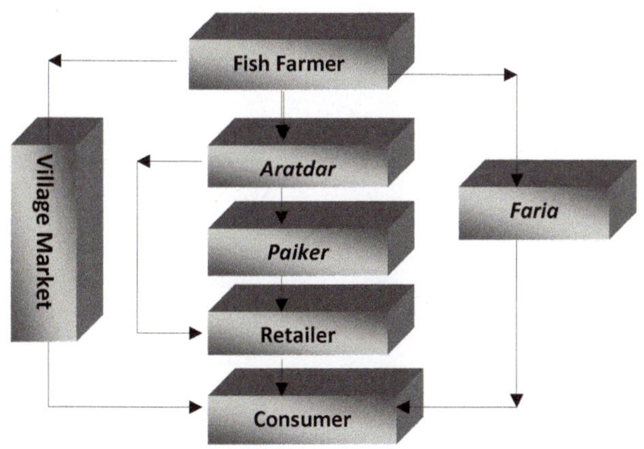

Figure 1. Value chains of *rohu fish* in Mymensingh district.

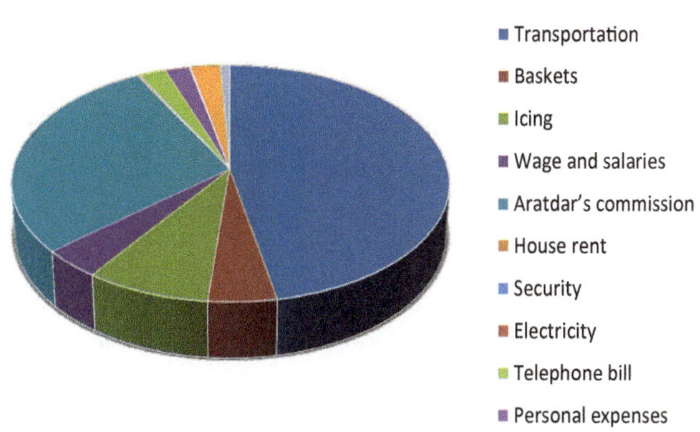

Figure 2. Total marketing cost involved in *rohu* fish marketing (Taka per maund)

Marketing efficiency

Marketing efficiency is essential for measuring the degree of marketing performance. On the basis of three methods for measuring marketing efficiency, chain 2 is more efficient (Table 9). In chain 2 the consumer paid lower price per maund rohu compared to chain 1.though in practice chain 1 is mainly used for selling rohu fish in the study area: Considering two value chain on the basis of product flow it was found that value chain-1 is more efficient than value chain-2. Consumer paid lower price in value chain-1 compared to value chain-2.

Distribution of value addition cost and net profit

Table 10 shows the percentages of total value addition cost and total net profit by different intermediaries for different fish marketing system in Bangladesh. For rohu fish, major cost is borne by paikers (32.03% of total cost) and major net profit is earned by retailers (51.98% of total net profit). Forrohu, major cost is borne by the inter district beparis, paikers and fishermen but major net profit is earned by retailers and processing plant owners. Farmers, in rohu marketing, bear the major marketing cost (23.70% of total cost) because they have to pay aratdar's commission which ultimately increases their marketing cost.

Market integration of rohu

To test the stationary of the data, the ADF (Augmented Dickey-Fuller) test with 13 lags of rohu Prices for Dhaka, Chittagong, Khulna, Sherpur, Comilla, Bogra, Rangpur, Rajshahi, Mymensingh, Sylhet, Gazipur and Noakhali were performed over 2000 to 2012 period and the estimated tau (τ)statistics and P values in their level and first difference are presented in Table 11. Real Price data were used and data were transformed into natural log. Real Price was calculated by multiplying nominal Price with the corresponding consumer price index (CPI) and dividing by the last CPI of the series. The tau (τ) statistics which were compared with p values indicate that all the rohu. Price series data were non-stationary at level. This set of regression was run once more after differencing all the markets. The tau (τ) statistics on the lagged first-difference terms are significantly negative indication that the series are stationary after first differencing. The study revealed that the rohu. Prices are stationary after differencing once that is they are all (11) processes.

Co-integration regression test results for rohu price in Bangladesh

To examine whether bivariate co-integration exists between

Packaging practices	Using materials	Capacity	Used by
Basket	Bamboo, Rope and Polythene	40 kg 20 kg	Farmer, Paiker and Retailer
Drum	Plastic	40 kg 20 kg	Farmer, Paiker and Retailer

Table 5. Packaging practices of *rohu* fish marketing in Bangladesh

Pricing methods	Farmer	Aratdar	Paiker	Retailer	Bepari
Auction	60	99	37	0	0
Based on going market prices	29	0	30	0	70
Prefixed prices	0	0	0	0	100
Cost-plus method	0	0	0	0	0

Table 6. Pricing methods followed in selling *of rohu* fishes in Bangladesh

Cost items	Farmer	*Aratdar*	*Paiker*	Retailer	Total
Transportation	39.6	-	276.49	70.35	386.44 (40.54)
Baskets	-	1.66	26.38	15.07	43.11 (4.52)
Icing	-	-	48.15	29.31	77.46 (8.13)
Wage and salaries	-	22.75	23.23	-	45.98 (4.82)
Aratdar's commission	88.08	-	168.55	-	256.63(26.92)
House rent	-	5.37	1.01	19.84	26.22 (2.75)
Security	-	0.10	0	1.89	1.99 (0.21)
Electricity	-	0.30	0.14	7.20	7.64 (0.80)
Telephone bill	3.85	3.26	13.07	16.10	36.28 (3.81)
Personal expenses	2.22	6.52	11.76	20.69	41.19 (4.32)
Tips and donation	4	0.70	0.52	1.02	6.24 (0.65)
Wastage	-	-	14.74	-	14.74 (1.55)
Others	-	0.26	4.71	4.25	9.22 (0.97)
Total	137.75	40.92	588.75	185.71	953.13 (100.00)

Table 7. Total marketing cost of different intermediaries involved in *rohu* fish marketing (Taka per maund)

different Prices of rohu market, Dhaka wholesale market was considered as reference market, Dhaka is a capital market and the largest city and it would appeared to be the dominant influences on inter districts rohu markets in Bangladesh. The reference market is a dominant market serving as a hub in a sort of "radial market structure" where different feeder (local) markets are at the rim. The reference market dominates the Price formation in the feeder markets. Every individual feeder market was affected by the reference market Price, though it alone cannot affect the reference markets Price.

Normally, the reference markets has a high turnover so that supply and demand shocks originating in the individual feeder markets are absorbed without creating much effect on the Price prevailing in the reference markets [12]. As there will be different combinations of the given 12 whole sale rohu Price markets, all combinations in a systems of bivariate relationships. The Engle-Granger (EG) and Augmented Engle-Granger (AEG) tests of residual equation confirm the stationary of the residual series [13]. Thus ADF results of unit root equation indicate that the real rohu Price series are I (1), while Engle-Granger (EG) and Augmented Engle-Granger (AEG) results of residual equation indicate that the residual series (which are linear combination of above rohu real Price series) are I(0). Thus above fact that the Price series being I (1) and their linear combination being I (0) point out that the series are co integrated without any exception. According to the Engle-Granger (EG) and Augmented Engle and Granger (AEG) test rohu markets of Bangladesh are statistically significance at 1% level (Table 12). An important finding of the study is that Dhaka market is significantly integrated to all regional markets of rohu markets in Bangladesh due to having the facility of information technology, which closely connected the markets to each other. This study strongly supports marketing efficiency in the selected rohu markets. Price move in the unison in all the markets together. Central Price policy making will be effective in these markets.

Strong forms of market integration

For testing strong form of rohu markets integration, the null hypotheses were applied to find rohu market integration against alternate hypotheses where rohu markets might not be integrated. The result of strong form of market integration in selected rohu markets is given in Table 13. It is seen from Table 13 that strong form of market integration was observed all the rohu markets in Bangladesh due to congenial atmosphere existed in these markets. This empirical finding strongly supports marketing efficiency in the markets. Price move in the unison in all the markets together. Central Price policy would be effective for these markets. For the estimation of strong form of market Integration we used the following restriction.

To calculate pair wise regression of the selected 12 domestic rohu markets prices, the time period was considered from January 2000 to December 2012 and the results are presented in Table 14. Monthly wholesale market price and Log linear model used for the study. The coefficient of Log linear model indicates the elasticity of prices. The entire coefficients are significant at 1% level. If price of Chittagong market increases 1 per cent then the price of Dhaka market increase 0.66 per cent and vice versa. And if the price of Comilla market increases 1 per cent then the price of Dhaka market increases 0.51 per cent and vice versa. Interpretations of all other coefficients are similar.

The coefficient of Log linear model indicates the elasticity of prices. The entire coefficients are significant at 1% level. If price of Chittagong market increases 1 per cent then the price of Dhaka market increase 0.66 per cent and vice versa. And if the price of Comilla market increases 1 per cent then the price of Dhaka market increases 0.51 per cent and vice versa. Interpretations of all other coefficients are similar.

Constraints of fish marketing

Main constraints of fish marketing are related to infrastructure, plant management and institutional management aspect. From the infrastructural constrains, lack of modern, hygienic fish landing centers; illiteracy, ignorance, lack of awareness and poor socio-economic condition of the fishers; shortage of adequate ice-plants with sufficient capacity, cold and freezer storage; lack of handling and preservation facilities etc are the most severe. Problems are particularly serious in certain inaccessible area where inadequate transportation and distribution facilities, lack of insulated and refrigerated fish vans, resulting in considerable wastage of ice; lack of electricity present and where open trucks are the main fish carriers. According to the traders, marketing and fish transporting also affected by political disturbances. As a result, fishes tend to damage and the traders sell these at lower price than that required obtaining these, sometimes they even unsuccessful to earn any revenue due to decomposition of this perishable commodity. The consumers have to pay higher price due to the participation of too many intermediaries in the marketing channel, but the actual fishers do not get the perfect price for their products and the lion shares go to the intermediary's pocket

Specific suggestions which are needed to improve marketing system are as follows:

- Establishment of more ice-plants, cold-storage and preservation facilities,
- Introduction of insulated and refrigerated fish vans and fish carriers to maintain cold-chain during transportation,
- Improvement of existing fish market structure,
- Improvement of fish transport, handling facilities,
- Establishment of modern wholesaling facilities,
- Improvement of sanitation, hygienic condition, drainage, washing facilities and sufficient auction places,
- Introduction of mechanical weighing equipment,

Intermediaries	Purchase Price	Sale Price	Gross marketing margin	Marketing cost	Net marketing margin
Farmer	-	3540	3540	135	3405.25
Aratdar	-	-	140	62.5	77.5
Paikar	3890	4650	760	305.31	454.69
Retailer	4650	5460	810	185.71	624.29

Table 8. Net marketing margin of different intermediaries for rohu fish marketing (Tk/maund)

Particulars	Unit	Amount	
		Value chain 1	Value Chain 2
1. Total marketing cost	Tk/Maund	689.69	370.38
2. Total net margins	Tk/Maund	990.50	689.09
3. Net price received by farmers	Tk/Maund	3405.25	3405.25
Marketing efficiency (ME) [3/1+2]	**Ratio**	**2.03**	**3.21**

Table 9. Marketing efficiency *of rohu* fish in Mymensingh market

Intermediaries	% of total cost	% of total profit
Farmer	15.45	-
Aratdar	4.29	4.40
Paikar	32.04	27.69
Retailer	19.45	51.98

Table 10. Percentage distribution of value addition cost and profit by intermediaries and marketing system

	Level				First difference			
Markets	Y_{t-1}	**ADF**	**P**	**Decision**	ΔY_{t-1}	**ADF**	**P values**	**Decision**
details	**In**	**(τ)**	**values**		**In**	**(τ)**		
	Coefficient				**Coefficient**			
Dhaka	-0.072	-1.89	0.12	Non-stationary	-0.142	-4.64	0.00	Stationary
Chittagong	-0.013	-1.32	0.18	Non-stationary	-0.032	-3.36	0.00	Stationary
Comilla	-.007	-0.79	0.42	Non-stationary	-0.44	-8.02	0.00	Stationary
Khulna	-0.08	-1.37	0.17	Non-stationary	-0.19	-5.20	0.00	Stationary
Sherpur	-0.04	-0.72	0.47	Non-stationary	-0.23	-5.89	0.00	Stationary
Bogra	-0.009	-0.94	0.34	Non-stationary	-0.29	-5.39	0.00	Stationary
Rangpur	-0.08	-1.62	0.13	Non-stationary	-0.20	-5.18	0.00	Stationary
Rajshahi	-0.06	-2.32	0.02	Non-stationary	-0.13	-4.06	0.00	Stationary
Mymensingh	-0.05	-1.56	0.11	Non-stationary	-0.24	-6.67	0.00	Stationary
Gazipur	-0.04	-1.42	0.15	Non-stationary	-0.17	-5.59	0.00	Stationary
Sylhet	-0.06	-2.40	0.01	Non-stationary	-0.13	-3.94	0.00	Stationary
Noakhali	-0.02	-0.13	0.02	Non-stationary	-0.04	-2.92	0.00	Stationary

Table 11. Unit root test for wholesale Price of *rohu* markets in Bangladesh

ADF= Augmented Dickey-Fuller,
Test critical values:
1% level -3.455096
5% level -2.872328
10% level -2.572592

Markets details	EG (lnU_{t-1})	P values	AEG ($dellnU_{t-1}$)	P values	Decision
Dhaka-Chittagong	-3.46	0.00	-3.41	0.00	Co-integrated
Dhaka-Comilla	-3.39	0.00	-3.29	0.00	Co-integrated
Dhaka-Khulna	-9.10	0.00	-7.24	0.00	Co-integrated
Dhaka-Sherpur	-3.88	0.00	-3.65	0.00	Co-integrated
Dhaka-Bogra	-3.31	0.00	-3.40	0.00	Co-integrated
Dhaka-Rangpur	-7.97	0.00	-6.02	0.00	Co-integrated
Dhaka-Rajshahi	-3.76	0.00	-3.62	0.00	Co-integrated
Dhaka- Mymensingh	-3.32	0.00	-3.39	0.00	Co-integrated
Dhaka- Sylhet	-4.35	0.00	-4.18	0.00	Co-integrated
Dhaka-Gazipur	-3.45	0.00	-3.35	0.00	Co-integrated
Dhaka-Noakhali	-3.32	0.00	-3.39	0.00	Co-integrated

Table 12. Co-integration regression test results for *rohu* fish price in Bangladesh (Price)

Dependent variable ln ΔY_t	Independent variable ln (ΔX_t)	When if β =1 Than: $\Delta Y_t - \Delta X_t = \alpha + \partial e_{t-1} + \mu_t$				t-value for α = 0
		Coefficient e_{t-1}	Standard Error	t-value β = 1 for	P values	
Dhaka	Chittagong	-0.90**	0.11	-8.03	0.00	-8.06**
Dhaka	Comilla	-0.09**	0.04	-2.09	0.03*	2.10*
Dhaka	Khulna	-1.31**	0.11	-11.00	0.00	-11.03**
Dhaka	Sherpur	0.20**	0.06	2.98	0.00	2.99**
Dhaka	Bogra	-0.85**	0.15	-5.67	0.00	-5.69**
Dhaka	Rangpur	-0.10	0.21	-0.47	0.63	-0.47
Dhaka	Rajshahi	-1.95**	0.12	-15.92	0.00	-15.98**
Dhaka	Mymensingh	-0.59**	0.16	-3.58	0.00	-3.59**
Dhaka	Gazipur	0.82	0.10	7.77	0.00	7.80**
Dhaka	Sylhet	-0.25	0.47	-0.54	0.58	-0.55
Dhaka	Noakhali	-0.07	0.04	1.67	0.09	1.68
Dhaka	Chittagong	-0.48**	0.10	-4.52	0.00	-4.53**

Table 13. Testing strong form of integration (β =1, α = 0) in selected *rohu* markets in Bangladesh .($\Delta Y_t = \alpha + \beta\Delta X_t + \partial e_{t-1} + \mu_t$)

- Proper electric supply,
- Increasing fish supply through improved culture practice,
- Proper attention should be paid to the personal hygiene,
- A study on socio-economic development, credit system,
- Financial and technical assistance,
- Training of manpower,
- An independent act or ordinance for fish landing and marketing.

Conclusion

The findings of this study indicated that the marketing of *rohu* is a profitable business. Thus, the selected *rohu* markets in Bangladesh are shown to be integrated. This is mainly attributed to close proxy, good communication facilities especially development of cell phone technology and good infrastructure availabilities among the market centers in Bangladesh. It also suggests that there is wide scope for the development of rohu farming and trading in this country. In this study the profit of retailer was higher than that of other intermediaries. Though fish marketing in Bangladesh is beset with a number of problems, there have been a number of positive changes that are expected to improve fish marketing environment in the country. These positive drivers includes, i) the shift from subsistence to commercial fish farming, ii) emergence of super-markets, and iii) a changing social attitude towards fish marketing, as it is less considered as a dishonorable

Dependent markets	Constant	P values	Independent markets (Coefficients)	P values	R^2
$\ln Y_t$ =	α		$+ \beta \ln X_t$		
In Dhaka	3.69**	0.001	+0 .65**InChittagong	0.00	0.39
	(0.79)		(0.10)		
In Dhaka	4.83**	0.00	+0.53**InComilla	0.00	0.35
	(.83)		(0.10)		
In Dhaka	1.83**	0.00	+0.87** InKhulna	0.00	0.92
	(0.21)		(0.02)		
In Dhaka	4.63**	0.00	+0.51** InSherpur	0.00	0.62
	(0.43)		(0.05)		
In Dhaka	5.26**	0.00	+0.48** InBogra	0.00	0.31
	(1.02)		(0.12)		
In Dhaka	2.44**	0.00	+0.82**In Rangpur	0.00	0.87
	(0.22)		(0.02)		
In Dhaka	4.27**	0.00	+0.59**In Rajshahi	0.00	0.59
	(0.50)		(0.06)		
In Dhaka	5.82**	0.00	+0.39**In Mymensingh	0.00	0.34
	(0.76)		(0.09)		
In Dhaka	5.03**	0.00	+0.51** In Gazipur	0.00	0.30
	(0.74)		(0.09)		
In Dhaka	2.12**	0.00	+0.81In Sylhet	0.00	0.64
	(0.42)		(0.05)		
In Dhaka	4.60**	0.00	+0.57 **In Noakhali	0.00	0.38
	(0.83)		(0.10)		

Table 14. Pair wise regression analysis in the selecting domestic *rohu* markets

job as it was in the past. But the government in Bangladesh needs to ensure that the proper infrastructure and necessary social capital are available for effective participation of all the market intermediaries of the seafood value chain. For better fish marketing, side by side with the private sector, government should also play active role in providing physical facilities like refrigerated storage, refrigerated vans, good market places with related facilities like water, ice, electricity, drainage facilities and sitting arrangements etc. The development of good road and transport networks can reduce superfluous involvement of intermediaries, which could be beneficial for both the fishers/farmers and consumers. Assembling centres with refrigerated storage facilities may be developed so that the perishability of fish is checked, which would enable the assembling centres to make bulk sell/transfer to the next destination. This could reduce post harvest loss and provide better price for the fishers/farmers.

References

1. Department of DOF (Department of Fisheries). 1999. Annual Report, Department of Fisheries, Dhaka, Bangladesh.
2. Ahmed M, Rab MA, Bimbao MAP (1993) Household socio-economic resource use and marketing in two thanas of Bangladesh. ICLARM Technical Report 04, p. 34.
3. ADB (2005) An evaluation of small-scale freshwater rural aquaculture development for poverty reduction. Operations Evaluation Department, Asian Development Bank, Manila, Philippines.
4. DAM (Department of Agricultural Marketing), (1998-2005). Wholesale price of Agricultural and Animal Products in Bangladesh.
5. Acharya SS, Agarwal NL (1999) "Agricultural Marketing in India", 3rd Edition, Oxford and IBH Publishing Co. Pvt. Ltd., New Delhi.
6. Gujarati DN (2003) Basic Econometrics, Fourth Edition, Tata McGraw-Hill Edition, India.
7. Kohls RL, Uhl JN (2005) Marketing of agricultural products. (9thedn). Macmillan publishing co., Inc., New York.
8. Bangladesh Bank, 2011. Annual Report of Central Bank of Bangladesh 2009-2013, Accessed date: 22.03.2011.
9. William J Stanton, Michael J Etzel (1991) Fundamentals of Marketing (Paperback).
10. Coulter R, Disney M (1987) A Handbook for Value Chain Research, International Development research Center (IDRC), Canada.
11. Crawford IM (1997) Agricultural and food marketing management. Food and Agricultural Organization of the United Nations, Rome, pp.261-262.
12. Ravallion (1986) Testing Market Integration. American Journal of agricultural Economics, February.
13. Engle RF, Granger CWJ (1987) "Co-integration and Error Correction: Representation, Estimation and Testing". Econometrica 55: 251-276.

Improving Service Quality in Hotels in Buea Subdivision before the African Nation's Cup (Afcon - 2016 and 2019): The Public Sector Role

Abam EN*

Department of Hospitality Management, Catholic University Institute of Buea, Cameroon

Abstract

The delivery of service quality within the tourism, hospitality and leisure industry is located firmly within marketing. Since services within the tourism, hospitality and leisure industry are intangible, the only option that can easily provide a competitive advantage to these restaurants and other sectors in this industry is the quality of service provided to clients. Human contact are necessary for the delivery of service, it is at this moment that front line staffs or employees need to show their best in order to sell the image or reputation of the firm, and there will be a repeat of purchase by the customers when they feel satisfied with the quality of services rendered to them. Quality enhancement is increasing and that service quality and customer satisfaction is central and vital to any business. The Ministry of Tourism and Leisure in collaboration with some proprietors have been carrying-out nationwide training to improve on guest satisfaction during the 2016 and 2019 African cup of Nations for female and male respectively.

Keywords: Service; Quality; African nation's cup; Public sector

Introduction

Consumers have many attributes such as personality traits, gender, number of consumptions, and the level of involvement on service recovery expectation. As consumers become increasing aware of their expectation, service industries too are faced with pressure to have new customers and maintain or keep existing ones. As far as customer retention is concern, most of the unsatisfied customers may not complain but they still however expect service recovery. When some of them do notice service failure, they automatically switch over. As long as there exist a gap between will-expectation and should - expectation shrinks or diminishes, consumers turn to feel positive about service quality.

Therefore employees have to develop stronger role in customer's loyalty and performance and need to have best skills and feel competent in their jobs, whereas managers have to use feedback to evaluate employee's performances and correct them when need do arise through short courses and training. It is critical for managers to understand their customer's perceptions of services. What distinguishes the features of its service styles are the power on which an organisation`s image and its brand are build, its services must be consistent.

Background of the study

Buea, according to social scientists was founded by a hunter in search of game; Eye Njie Tama Lifanje came from the Bomboko clan behind the Buea Mountain (Mount Cameroon or Mount Fako). On that fateful day he founded Buea, he had set out in search of animals but there were no game to be hunted only a vast peace of hospitable land that could harbor his family. Eyé Njie named it "Mwea", meaning, hospitable land for farming. The settlement soon grew into a clan but made tardy progress until the later part of the 19th century, when there was an influx of Europeans into Africa for exploration and colonialism purposes (www.bueacouncil.com).

Buea is presently the headquarters of the South West Region with an estimated population above 200.000 inhabitants. It is a highly complex community caught between a blend of urban, semi urban, rural and traditional settings and it covers 870 square kilometers surface area. Visitors to Buea are marveled by the town's picturesque landscape, iridescent vegetation, unique weather, and most especially its strategic position accentuated by the Majestic Mount Cameroon (4100m above sea level).

Buea has a booming economy with the agricultural, administrative, business, tourism and the financial sectors taking the central stage. Agriculture is the main occupation of the people; the rich volcanic soil, the equatorial climate and an almost all-year-round rainfall make Buea a fertile land for agriculture. The Muea Market, one of the biggest foodstuff markets in Cameroon, attracts traders from West and Central Africa. Two locally based Agro- Industrial Companies produce tea and banana for export. While tea is produced and marketed by the Cameroon Tea Estate (CTE), the Cameroon Development Corporation, (CDC), operates the Banana plantations. The tertiary sector is also witnessing an impressive growth with banks, corporative societies and other financial houses dotted around the town. There has been a rapid emergence of small and medium size enterprises especially in the Molyko neighbourhood (www.bueacouncil.com).

Literature Review

The importance of service quality in the Hospitality and Tourism industry is of paramount important to customers who expect or deserved to be treated well in relation to the money they pay.

Service quality, customer's satisfaction and price are important selection tools or criteria for a customer or guest and the key determinants of post-purchase or after purchase behaviour such as word- of –mouth and repurchase. Lots of research has been carried out all aimed at satisfying the customers expectation that is how the customer judge the services rendered to him or her.

***Corresponding author:** Evaristus Nyong Abam, MSc. in International Hospitality Management, Department of Hospitality Management, College of Business, Catholic University Institute of Buea, Cameroon
E-mail: enyongabam@yahoo.com

Hayes and Miller in their study on the revenue management for the hospitality industry concludes that service quality is perceived by most customers as more critical to value than is the product quality. Service industry is related to the importance of product quality and that service quality is the guests or customer`s perceptions of value and to the prices they are charged [1].

According to Tesone service consists of the interaction and transactions that occur between customers and members of staff from the time they enter the restaurants through the time of departure from the restaurants, this is called the customer relationship [2].

Bowie and Buttle revealed that some hotels and restaurants claim that their product is so unique that they don't have competitors; the reality is that all hospitality businesses compete against a variety of different types of competition which could be micro and macro-competition and what will make the difference is the quality of service they do offer [3].

Ahmed et al. thinks that the concept of service quality represents the social interaction between the service provider and the customer, and that the provider plays an important role in the delivery of product to the customer [4].

Helgadottir et al. believes that it is better to know whether the guest likes to be treated as a customer and knowing which methods adds more value to the experience of the guest [5].

Lee and Chen suggest that most service quality has both poor and versatile characteristics because service quality is based on the customer`s feeling [6]. When a customer feel that he or she was well cared for or served, this will surely encourage the customer to come for a another purchase, he or she may encourage his friends and relatives through word- of –mouth to come to this restaurant. In the case where the customer feels unsatisfied with the services offered to him or her, it will discourage them from coming and the customer can also to discourage friend and relatives from coming to patronised your business.

Barrows and Powers believed that service quality is often the best way to differentiate you from competitions [7]. Good services give an added advantage over new comers and it help to maintain your reputation. Customers perceptions of service quality is more directly linked to the morale, motivation, knowledge, skills and authority of front line staffs that are in direct contact with customers, than in the case of product selling organisation. Since the front line staffs are in constant or direct contact with customers, this researcher is suggesting that it would be good for managers to try to motivate these staffs and this will go a long way to providing best services hence increasing customer`s perception.

Kattara et al. believes that employees behaviours which could be negative or positive, are highly correlated to the customer overall satisfaction [8]. When the customer leave satisfied, the employee too will be happy as he or she knows that the customer will one day surely come back for another purchase or service.

Mohanty revealed that each customer regards various service attributes as more or less important and various service characteristics as more or less desirable while management ways of perception of quality of service frequently differs from that of customers [9]. This researcher is suggesting that Management should at times come and observe for some time what the front line staffs are doing in order to understand how customers feel about their services. This will in a long run help management to see the areas that need attention and therefore make necessary training [10].

Research Methodology

Veal indicated that an empirical approach is the collection and analysis of data; it could be quantitative or qualitative, primary or secondary. No research is purely empirical; it is usually informed by some sort of theory or conceptual frame work. Some researchers are of the opinion that a single research method may use both quantitative and qualitative techniques and procedures in combination as well as use primary and secondary data. The quantitative and qualitative data collection techniques and analysis procedure each have their own strength and weaknesses.

For this research work, the researchers used only secondary data that was information collected from documents and websites.

Analysis and Finding

The Government of Cameroon through its Ministry of Tourism and Leisure on November 25-26th 2015 in collaboration with some proprietors organised a five day workshop on the training of hotel managers, housekeeping managers, waiters/waitresses, bar tenders on the importance of good customer services, welcoming of guests, waste management in hotels and restaurants, good bar tending practices etc. This seminar or workshop was hosted in Mountain hotel - Buea and it is geared towards the hosting of the 2016 and 2019 African cup of Nations for female and male respectively.

On July 11th-15th 2016 another workshop for the training of hotel staff of the South West Region in view of the organization of the 2016 Female African Cup of Nations was organized by the Ministry of Tourism and Leisure at Buea - Mountain Hotel.

Also on September 15th-17th 2016 the same Ministry of Tourism and Leisure organized a seminar on the security of tourists, reception techniques, hygiene and quality of service for tourism actors in the South West Region at Buea Mountain Hotel.

Conclusion

Customers today expect a very high overall level of services, institutions that are able to better serve them; will have loyal customers and a better turnover. Every competitive organisation seeks some sort of advantages over its rivals; it seeks some way to distinguish itself in the eyes of its customers. This challenge is therefore to find an advantage that is long lasting and not easily copied. There is much competition in this field and this will be driven by the strategies or ways that focus on the quality of service to adding value as opposed to product.

The need of the customer is very important in the error reduction process in various areas and quality improvement leading to customer's satisfaction should be identified and implemented.

Service quality is largely based on reliability and responsiveness. This reliability and responsiveness in the hospitality industry (hotels and restaurants) have made significant and positive impacts on customer's satisfaction. The evaluation of service quality should not embrace only the service delivered, but also the manner in which this service is delivered.

References

1. Hayes DK, Miller A (2011) Revenue Management for the Hospitality Industry. John Wiley 7 Sons Inc. New Jersey.

2. Tesone D (2010) Principles of Management for the Hospitality Industry. Butterworth-Heinemann, UK p. 4.

3. Veal AJ (2006) Research methods for leisure and tourism - a practical guide. (3rdedn) Prentice Hall: Malaysia (CTP-VVP).

4. Bowie D, Buttle F (2004) Hospitality Marketing: An Introduction. Butterworth-Heinemann, UK p. 92.

5. Sadiq SM, Matthew HR, Mohammad S, Zafar UA (2007) Determinants of Service Quality in the Hospitality Industry: The case of Malaysian Hotels. Journal of Accounting- Business and Management 14: 64-74.

6. Helgadottir G, Sigurdardottir I (2008) Horse based Tourism, Community Quality and Disinterest in Economic Value- Scandinavian. Journal of Hospitality and Tourism 8: 105-121.

7. Lee Y, Chen T (2006) A Kano Two-Dimensional Quality Model in Taiwan`s Hot Spring Hotels Service Quality Evaluation. Journal of American Academy of Business, Cambridge.

8. Barrows CW, Powers T (2009) Study guide to Accompany: Introduction to Management in the Hospitality Industry (9thedn) John Wiley & Son, New Jersey.

9. Kattara SH, Weheba D, El-Said OA (2008) The Impact of Employee Behaviour on Customers` Service Quality Perception and Overall Satisfaction. Tourism & Hospitality Research 8: 309-328.

10. Mohanty P (2008) Hotel Industry and Tourism in India. APH Publishing Corporation. New Delhi, India.

Comprehensive Strategy Analysis for a Leading Firm in the UAE Precision Tooling Industry

Chaher Alzaman* **and Molham Chikhalsouk**

Business and Engineering Management Department, Higher Colleges ofTechnology, UAE

Abstract

This paper conducts an extensive analysis of the strategy of a leading UAE company in the precision tooling industry. The work starts by an introduction about the company and a comprehensive literature review about the strategy concept, how the scholars perceive strategy, and the tools that can be used to assess and analyze strategy. The paper analyzes the company's strategy in the light of Mintzberg's Ten Goals, Mckinzey's 7S model, Porter's Value Chain, Porter's Five Forces, SWOT analysis, and recommendation on *Balanced Scorecard* for supply chain analysis. Since the company is a leading one and has outreaching involvement in vital UAE businesses such as aerospace and oil and gas, the analysis serves as an insight into strategy for UAE companies.

Introduction

The paper aims at evaluating the depth and criticality UAE companies undertake in strategy building. Since the modeled company is a leading company in its *perspective* industry and has an encompassing reach over the oil and gas and the aerospace businesses, it can signify a fair understanding about strategy formulation in the UAE.

This paper sheds the light on strategic planning for a UAE leading company in precision tooling. The company core business is to deliver highly precise machining and manufacturing services in the following major business fields of Defense Equipment, Aerospace Equipment, and Oil & Gas Equipment. The company business is of high risk and competitiveness, which requires high potential and qualitative standards of achievement to *Position* the company in the right market *Position*. The vision of the company is to forge a world class precision manufacturing infrastructure serving as an industrial backbone to the UAE industries. The paper performs analysis for the UAE Company utilizing Mintzberg's strategy evolution process, McKinsey 7-S framework, and Porter's value chain. Further analysis is performed using Porter's Five Forces, SWOT analysis, and *Balanced Scorecard (BSC)*.

The business environment surrounding the company is quite competitive. Many suppliers are available in the market since the Gulf States are putting a lot of emphasis on defense. The suppliers originate from broad spectrum. The suppliers originate from many different countries such as the US, Russia, England, France, China, and other emerging nations. The market size is quite considerable since the Gulf States are putting top priority on defense. In regard to research and development, the company has several joint ventures with leading companies in the world. This makes their products very advanced.

Literature Review

In order to analyze an organization and its level of productivity, efficiency and success, it is important to define its operation strategy and analyze it. Advantageously, there are some approaches that help in understanding and analyzing its strategy such as Porter's five forces, McKenzie 7S framework and the Mintzberg's strategy evaluation process. Moreover, the Balanced Scoreboard is another tool that is used to evaluate the performance of the organization and how are their achievements close to their vision. To begin, researchers have made aggressive efforts in defining, studying, and evaluating strategy. Different perspectives and analysis of Operation Strategy (OS) are presented in the literature review.

Mintzberg [1] defined strategy as 'the *Pattern* in stream of significant decisions'. Porter highlighted a major question: What Is Strategy? In his paper he differentiated between the strategy and operational effectiveness. 'Operational effectiveness and strategy are both essential to superior performance, which, after all, is the primary goal of any enterprise. But they work in very different ways' [2]. Strategy is not that simple and hence, different scholars tried to study it more thoroughly. For example, Mintzberg [3] introduced a new approach in the comprehension of strategy. The approach is the 5 P's which are *Plan, Ploy, Pattern, Position*, and Perspective. These concepts broaden the angle that determines the role of the strategy in an organization. The *Plan* refers to the predetermined direction that the organization intends to lead to, while the *Ploy* assures that the strategy is going towards the realm of direct completion. *Pattern* focuses on actions. Mintzberg points out that 'the concept is an empty one if it does not take behavior into account'. If we want to see our organization's *Position* with respect to its competitors, the *Position* dimension helps us to look at organizations in context. Finally, *perspective* 'raises intriguing question about intention and behavior in a collective context' [4].

Drobis [5] believes that any strategy must be set and should be designed to achieve substantial competitive *advantages*. "In the long run, if you do not achieve a competitive advantage you would not have a profitable business. And in order to understand what the advantage would be, you must understand your customer needs and how you compare to your competitor in the ability to deliver value to your targeted customers; that is the core of effective decision-making in any company," [5].

Mintzberg [1] stressed that the fundamental issues that determine the level of the strategy success is creativity and keen understanding of the organization's objectives. 'Managers take one narrow *perspective* or

***Corresponding author:** Dr. Chaher Alzaman, Business and Engineering Management Department Higher Colleges of Technology, UAE, E-mail: calzaman@hct.ac.ae

another- the glories of planning or the wonder of learning, the demands of external competitive analyses or the imperatives of an internal "resource-based" view' [1].

Strategy has witnessed several stages of evolution. This is because of the change in the economic activities and learning and exploring the optimal ways to improve our organizations performance and revenues. Mintzberg [4] studied the strategy evolution and classified it into ten schools (streams). The *Design School* is the oldest school based on a simple concept which is we format our strategy according to the organization internal strengths and weaknesses and fit it perfectly with external opportunities and threats. The *Planning School* is prevalent in machine- type organization. In this school, the planning staffs play the most important role in the strategy formation and replace senior managers. The *Positioning School* is a kind of "Strategy Reduction", where reduced to general *Positions* chosen for formalized analyses of industry situations [4]; and the planners are replaced with analysts. The need for the analysts is fundamental, where they can sink too deeply in data and prompt their scientific truths to their clients. The *Entrepreneurial School* shifts the process for precise designs, plans to vague visions (wide perspectives). The process is centered about the Chief Executive (CE). It can be seen in dynamic organizations. The *Cognitive School* is the school of creative strategy. It is does not rely on the reality mapping but it goes beyond that and proposes a creative strategy that leads the organization to higher levels of success. The *Learning School* is the practical school (Emergent Process). This school assumes that the strategy is emergent; and we can develop our strategy from our own organizations. The intertwining between the formulation and implementation is used in this school. The *Power School* is the power of negotiation school as an orientation in strategy making. There are two orientations can be recognized by this school, which are *Micro Power* and *Confrontation Power*. The *Micro Power* suggests that the strategy progress inside the organization is a result of political- a process involving- argument. And the *Confrontation Power* is among parties who divide the power. It is focused on self-interest and fragmentation. The *Cultural School* has started in Japan and became popular in the USA in the 1980s. This school is reverse of the *Power School*. It is focused on common interest and integration. Hence, the strategy formation is seen as a social process bounded with cultures and we cannot sometimes modify our strategy because of the culture influence. *Environmental School* is connected to the "*Contingency* theory" which predicts what response under environmental conditions and population ecology can limit our strategy choices. It is a hybrid between the cognitive and *power schools*. It is also influenced by the "Institutional Pressures" which is concerned with the institutional pressure faced by organizations. *Configuration School* happens when an organization is moving from a level to another; this will be as transformation (configuration) process. In practice, more than one school can be seen for one organization strategy.

In 1988, Mintzberg proposed criteria for strategy evaluation due to the different and broad meaning for strategy. He guaranteed that any strategy should fit within one or more of the criteria he proposed. The criteria are *contingency* that must not present mutually inconsistent goals and policies, *consonance* in which the strategy must represent an adaptive response to the external environment, *advantages* that must provide for creation and/or maintenance of competitive *advantages*, and *feasibility* that will neither overtax available resources nor create unsolvable sub problems. Hence any strategy that will not meet one or more of the previous criteria is a suspect [6].

Alternatively in 1996, Porter [2], a Harvard business professor, proposed a model that is now commonly used to analyze industries and competitive structures. Porter's Five Forces model is a powerful tool that combines five competitive forces which limit any industry's profit according to external factors. These forces are the threat of new entrants, the customer bargaining power, the supplier bargaining power, the substitution to an alternative product or service, and the intensity of competition among current rivals inside the industry.

Alternatively, Boyer et al. [7] comment that operation strategy refers to the decisions and plans involving developing, *Position*ing, and aligning managerial policies and needed resources for consistency with the overall business strategy [7]. While Cousins [8] highlights that there are some situations when the outcomes do not come as they have been planned. This is because of the 'mismatch between the way resources are de*Ploy*ed and the competitive priorities established by the firm' [8].

Furthermore, Peters and Waterman [9] published a book about the most successful companies in 1980's. They proposed the McKinsey 7-S model. The book came as an extensive study for 'leading 1980s companies with records of long-term profitability and continuing innovation' [9]. According to the 7-S model, there are seven factors that shape a strategy and make it effective; these factors are: *strategy, structure, systems, staff, skills, style* (Culture), and *shared* value. The McKinsey 7-S model factors can be divided into hard elements and soft element. Hard element, which includes *strategy, structure*, and *system*, can be easily discovered and controlled by the management:

- *Strategy*: The *Plan* implemented to keep the company ahead of its competitors.
- *Structure*: The *Position* of each em*Ploy*ee in the company, and to whom he reports.
- *System*: The operations and activities done by each em*Ploy*ee to complete the job.

Soft elements are more complicated to identify and are usually influenced by the culture of the company and its environment.

- *Shared* values: These are the values that the company was founded on.
- *Style*: Adopting a leadership style.
- *Staff*: The em*Ploy*ees and their qualifications and the ability to accomplish their jobs.
- *Skills*: The proficiency and expertise of the em*Ploy*ees.

Ka*Plan* [10] mentions that the diagram for the 7-S model looks like a spider web, where each of the 'S's' connecting to the other six. Carlos and Morris [11] citing other studies classify strategy, according to the stage of implementation, into three models of static, dynamic, and mixed models. The 7-S lies in the static model and every S emphasizes specific dimensions of the organization [11]. The strategy should be flexible and modifiable to absorb any external changes and maintain the organization at a maximum profit level. Ka*Plan* and Norton [12] stated that 'It's more effective to choose a design that works reasonably well, and then develop a strategic *system* to tune the structure to the strategy.'

Analysis

Mintzberg's ten goals

To begin, based on the company mission, vision, and Functional Organizational Chart (FOC), the following observations have noted that he organization has social role in the development of the country by preparing national manpower that helps in enabling a sustainable industry. With accordance to Mintzberg's ten strategy schools, we found that the organization implements a strategy that is a blend of different schools. The strategy is a blend of design, planning, entrepreneurial, and *cultural schools*. While, it appears that there is no significant influence for the other schools. From the *Design School* perspective, the company starts from its internal strengths and weaknesses and aims to take *advantages* of its strengths to gain new customers, enter new markets, and manufacture new products. From the *Planning School*, the company is a high tech company and its state of the art machines are the core of this industry. Here, its strategy is machine-centric; the organization seems to place technology and state of the art machine procurement at the center of its strategy. The decisions and the strategy are developed from the B.O.D. and C.E.O. levels and hence there is a hint of *Entrepreneurial School*. The company also resembles the strategy of *Cultural School* as the company adopts social goals and aims to contribute to the community and develops the national manpower to enable sustainability. Concerning the other schools, the company shows no significant influence in them as illustrated in the following:

- *Positioning School*: The Company has a strategy and there is no strategy reduction, and the important decisions are taken from the highest level.
- *Cognitive School*: The organization is new (started in 2007), and they are still in learning and establishing stages and they have not reached to the cognitive level and creative strategy.
- *Learning School*: In order to avoid any additional losses, the organization is stick to its strategy and they do not modify the strategy. Also, the three years can be considered as a building stage for experience and data collecting that enables the organization to learn from.
- *Power School*: The Company is a young company and they are trying to build their name and reputation. The company does not have the bargaining power over the customers. This is because of the high completion in this industry and reputation of the other competitors.
- *Environmental School*: This industry does not expose a real impact on the environment. Hence, the company can expand without any serious impact on the environment.
- *Configuration School*: As mentioned before, the company with its recent start did not reach to this transformation stage.

The McKinsey7S model

The McKinsey 7-S framework is a technique to evaluate a company's performance in order to identify its *Position* in a certain industry. This technique helps in improving the performance of a company by looking at the effect of changes on it, aligning the departments, and deciding the best way for implementing a strategy.

Strategy

The company is continuously searching for the latest technologies and implementing them to improve the operations performance and customer satisfaction. The company aims at providing high quality products to regional and international customers. Accordingly, the company has adopted rigorous standards and rules to maintain high internationally recognized quality qualifications. Hence quality is important in the company's strategy as after being established to provide products for the defense industry, the company grew in a short period to serve the aerospace and oil & gas industries due to its outstanding quality records. The company is continuously acquiring quality certifications from well reputed bodies and establishing good relations with suppliers to ensure good quality and the sustainability of their resources. The company is also gearing its strategy towards the environment as it is more and more involved in projects that have an impact on the UAE and regional environment.

Shared values

Through our review of the company's mission and the overall work environment, the company's *shared* values have cohesiveness around the importance of a friendly and safe work environment: a foundation stone for the company. The company applies the regulations of health, safety, and environmental set by international recognized certification bodies.

Structure

As shown in Figure 1, the structure of the company resembles a common hierarchal tree found in most companies with functional departments. Em*Ploy*ees report to their direct supervisors and tasks coming from other departments or higher management *Position* has to go through the supervisor before being carried out by the em*Ploy*ee. This could be an impediment to collegiality.

As in many of the manufacturing organizations, the operations department plays a pinnacle part. The sub-departments under operations are concerned with planning the production of new items and improving the production of existing items, purchasing raw material to produce the item, production, logistics and inventory, and quality and control. The operational processes are set by the operations manager and approved by the strategy development manager and the C.E.O. based on financial analysis, cultural constraints, and standards and rules required by the government and the certification bodies.

Style

The company assigns each year a significant budget for training purposes. All em*Ploy*ees including all level management are required to attend at least one seminar or workshop relating to their duties in a year. The board of directors usually doesn't address operations issues. It is the C.E.O. and the Strategy Development Manager who deal with operations issues.

Staff

The company has a priority to recruit UAE Nationals whenever possible. It is making immense efforts in preparing UAE Nationals for the precision industries by partnering with educational institution.

Skills

The company aims to hire well qualified workers with international experience to ensure worldwide competency. The company holds multiple skill management seminars for managers aiming to assist them in achieving the goals and strategy of the company.

Porter's Value Chain

Operations strategy for a manufacturing company is more than transforming raw material into valuable goods. Companies should be able to create the greatest possible value for their customers. A useful tool for analyzing value in a company would be Porter's Value Chain [13].The work chooses the following three steps to perform value chain Analysis:

- **Activity analysis**

  The evaluated the activities carried from production till delivery at two levels. The company should map all the activities at the organization and personal level

  - Organizational level: Going in depth into all the business processes: marketing, sales, operations, delivery, support, etc.
  - Personal level: Recruiting skilled em*Ploy*ees, motivation, keeping updated with the latest techniques, seeking feedback from customers.

- **Value analysis**

  Trying to figure out how more value can be added in the eyes of the end customers (Table 1). Most important is to identify the *value factor* of each activity and what should be done in order to obtain a better value. Table 1 identifies *value factors* of great importance to the company.

- **Evaluation and planning**

  Decisions should be taken whether the changes should be implemented by the company. A smart move would be to start by easy, quick, and cheap tasks, guaranteed to succeed. Prioritization of the tasks is important in this step.

Porter's five forces

Many organizations use Porter's five forces analysis to evaluate their potential in making profits within a given industry. Figure 2 explains well Porter's Five Forces.

The first force to analyze is the *Bargaining Power of Buyers*. Buyers in all the different market, which the company functions in, have a good bargaining power due to the criticality of quality in precision tooling. This is more pronounced in the aerospace industry where customers perceive products more in terms of value: the buyer is looking for high quality, low cost goods. They are looking for quality and cost. In this market international suppliers are a real threat. Hence, the company keeps the buyer interest in mind.

Second is the *Bargaining Power of Suppliers*. Due to the nature of precision tooling, parts can be procured from a variety of vendors. There a large pool of vendors and hence the company can assert its imperatives in controlling cost and improving quality.

Third is the *Relative Power of Stakeholders*. Shareholders of the company have a visionary and strategic view of the company. The company is UAE based which entrusts the shareholders and also impacts on the social benefits. Furthermore, the company has been successful in entering new market, which in all has satisfied the shareholders. The company should invest more in hiring UAE nationals and winning important contracts in the UAE to sustain the support of the shareholders.

Next is the force of ***New Entrants.*** We choose important factors that influence the threat of new entrants which are *economies of scale*, *product differentiation*, capital requirement, *switching cost*, and *access to distribution channels*. In terms of *economies of scale*, the company is making good strands towards economy of scale but it is still lacking and hence affection the company's performance. This is an opportunity

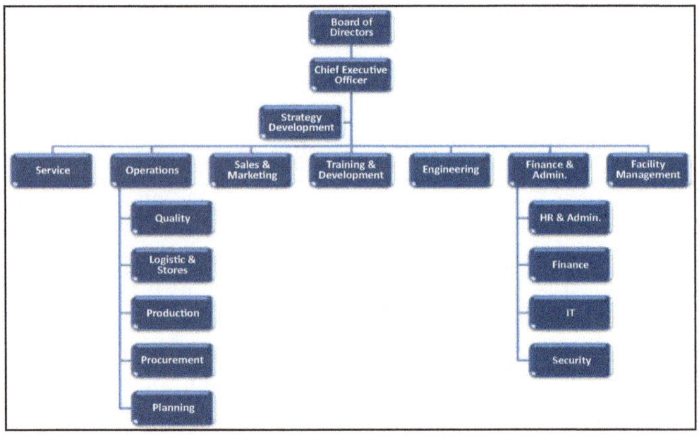

Figure 1: Company's Organizational Structure (EPI HR Department 2009) System.

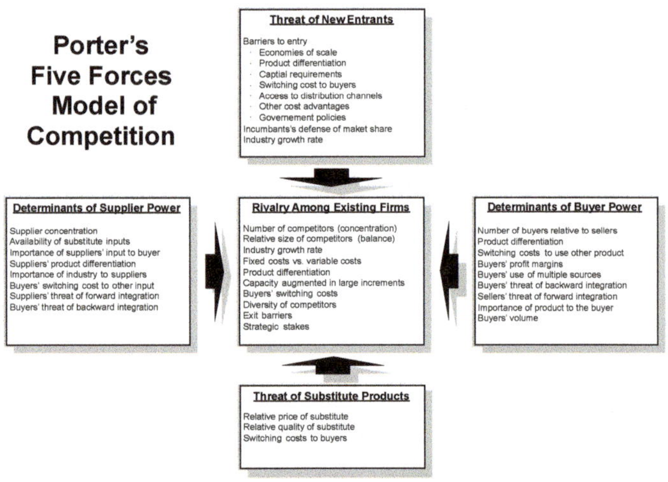

Figure 2: porter's five forces structure (strategic advantage 2005).

which the company can focus on. In terms of *product differentiation*, the company has a strong competitive advantage in *product differentiation*. It answers to customers' specification very well. In terms of *capital requirements*, as many of the precision industry, the capital requirement is quite intensive especially in the start-up phase. The technology needed in this industry is quite expensive. It is a major factor that could be a threat for the company. The company has been aggressively investing in technology but unless it can translate that into higher production and higher value, this would impede the company's bottom line of profit. In terms of *Switching Cost*, this is an area of strength for the company as it has not faced problem in switching from market to another. This is due to the nature of the industry, as precision tooling is quite extendable and could entertain the criteria of different industries. It has been not difficult for the company to switch from one market to another as the machines are not customized for certain products. The machine can be used for different product which gives an opportunity for the company but certainly affect the company's ability to mass produce. The company needs to find the right balance between customization and mass production. Finally concerning *Access to Distribution channels*, for new entrants, *access to distribution channels* could be a hinder while given the company's ongoing projects and extensive experience with the UAE. It has built for itself a good base for access into distribution

Value Chain	Value Factors	Changes Needed
Purchasing Raw Material	• Building the best relations with suppliers • Getting the maximum value for purchased products • Getting the best quality of raw material	• Making deals with the maximum number of suppliers to create competition between them • Purchasing higher number of products to control the price • Forcing standards of the suppliers to get the best quality products
Manufacturing/ Production	• Minimizing manufacturing throughput time • Reducing operational costs • Increase utilization of the company's operational capacity	• Creating an operation strategy to minimize the time and cost for manufacturing • Using all available resources in the manufacturing process in an effective way
Sales & Marketing	• Having a complete database containing all the potential clients • Making the product popular • Selling all the manufactured products	• Making a long term marketing plan • Searching for high potential clients • Proposing the best pricing scenarios to maximize sales.
Delivery	• Delivery all the required products with the exact specifications • Always delivering on time	• Taking care of every purchase order to make sure that the packed products match the requirements • Finding more efficient and reliable ways for delivery • Should consider JIT
Support	• Replacing defected products	• When costing the product, the selling price should reflect the cost of replacing a certain number of defective products • Statistical Process Control can be used to minimize defectives

Table 1: Porter's Value Chain Analysis

channels. However, the company might need to invest more to compete regionally.

Next in our discussion is ***Rivalry among Existing Firms***. Here we analyze the *number of competitors*, the *product or service characteristics*, the *overhead costs*, *capacity*, and exit high barrier cost. In terms of the *Number of Competitors*, given the quality level at which the company functions, competition is quite scarce. Also, given the high capital requirement in the precision tooling industry, it is quite difficult for companies to compete on high quality products and services; with the exception of the aerospace industry where competitors are global. In terms of *Product or Service Characteristics*, the main factor for success for our model company is its excellent quality standings. The company retains important customers in this manner. Correspondingly, this makes it very difficult of new entrants to attract the company's important customers. This is a key to the company's competitive advantage. In terms of *overhead costs*, fixed costs maybe the main threat on the existence of the company as it is in its start-up phase as there are a high amount of fixed costs associated with the operations runs regardless the amount or production. CAPIX is a critical issue as all machines are depreciated. In terms of *capacity*, the *capacity* non-flexibility is affecting the company's productivity. The ability of the company to increase its *capacity* to accept more orders from customers is limited. This is an area which the company should concentrate on. Finally for *exit barriers*, as mentioned before the company has a strong record in switching between industries. The company can exit markets effectively and soundly as it has done in the past.

Overall, we can conclude that the modeled company has a great opportunity to succeed in its respective market given it invests more in the opportunities discussed and improve in the areas where improvement is needed such as *capacity*, *overhead costs*, and *economies of scale*. In the aerospace market, the company should invest heavily in those elements to reduce cost

SWOT Analysis

A SWOT analysis, Table 2, was carried. From the SWOT analyses, it is clear that the organization faces serious difficulties on the supply chain level. Hence, using *Balanced Scorecard (BSC)* in the supply chain process, the supply chain can be analyzed further: This is done in the next section. In general, strategies are executed through short-term goals, functional tactics, and staff motivations.

Strengths	Weaknesses
• Well established direct contact with global aerospace OEMs. • Secured Contracts locally and regionally through Offset program due to customer base in defense and civil aerospace. • Raw material available for oil & gas components. • The company is one of the shops for the manufacturing of oil & gas components due to high manufacturing capabilities. • Close proximity with customers in the oil & gas industry. • Outsourcing of repair and maintenance services of oil industry. • High level of experience and knowledge of local defense market. • Outsourcing of repair services.	• Basic requirement which needed to handle large aerospace structure in not available. • Lack of knowledge/competency in aerospace industry. • Certification required in aerospace industry and oil & gas industry (e.g. AS 9100, ISO 14001). • Just-in-time supply chain needs to be developed • Lack of knowledge and experience in oil field components • Difficult to get engineering grade raw materials in Middle East • Lack of required production technology to develop sufficient production.
Opportunities	**Threats**
• Aviation and airline fleets market growth domestically and regionally. • Government efforts to diversify the UAE economic by moving to aerospace industry. • Advantage of cost position in Middle East aerospace industry. • Government support in getting the supply contracts of approved components to oil & gas industry. • High demand for low cost components in the oil & gas industry (e.g. Flanges, bolts, gaskets...etc). • Low competition on local level for the high technology oil industry components (like drill heads, valves...etc). • Growing PMA (Parts Manufacturer Approvals) which required production capacity and securing contacts with defense.	• The difficulties to get the complete aviation authority certification. • Economic crisis lead to cancellation of orders for many OEM (Original Equipment Manufacturer). • High competition located in low-cost region. • Difficulties in preserving the needed skilled talents. • Difficulties in acquiring the complete aviation authority certification. • High international competition from China & Korea. • Growing competition locally. • Lack of modules and system assemblers of oil's equipment. • Required Industry's certification. • Difficulties to retain the talented skilled workforces. • Cross-Country entry barriers affecting competition. • Cost Optimization due to Economic Crisis. • High requirements to attract the required talented workforce beside the difficulties to preserve talented workforce.

Table 2: SWOT Analysis.

Short Term vs. Long Term

The company with the assistance of external partners on the short term is trying to gain some local market and enter new foreign market mainly in the Middle East and Africa. The main objective in the short run for the company is to win the confidence of defense contractors and render good reputation. Immediately, the company should capitalize on the market growth. At the start, the company had considerable investment and was able to allocate it effectively. And from the very start, the company had significant amount of funds that enabled it to hire talented personnel who have clear understanding of the products and markets of which to penetrate. In the long term, the company should dominate the local and surrounding markets. Given that the company is UAE-based, this should give it a strong future presence in the UAE and also accessibility to Middle East markets.

Conclusion

Initially, it is important to state that the modeled company has far reaching arms into different businesses in the UAE and faces competition locally, regionally, and internationally as many other companies in the region. The modeled company is much aware of the importance of strategy. As many other companies in the gulf region, strategy is critical for the company to have a sound business strategy. From this work, the company seems to focus on its strengths, weaknesses, opportunities, and threats in the formulation of its strategy. The company also puts a lot of stress on planning as it continuously seeks new technologies that would render competitive advantage. The company also places emphasis on recruiting UAE nationals to gain support of society- an important stakeholder for any company. Alternatively, the company does not put emphasis on *Positioning*. The company doesn't prioritize studying the market and analyzing what other world class companies are doing.

A very important component of the company's strategic thinking is quality. In the precision industry quality is all important. Here small minor errors are not allowed. For this, the company is committed to fishing out the latest technologies. The *shared* values of the company also show dedication to providing good work environment. While the company's hierarchal structural is quite traditional. This quite important in the region where hierarchal structure requires progression.

Some of the potential problems inherited in the company might be due to the classical hierarchal structure which lacks the flexibility required to respond to market changes or cost avoidance opportunities. The company needs to have a more flexible structure in order to be more responsive. The company should alternatively focus on niche products and excellence in quality keeping in mind that the necessity of the market is excellent quality.

Performance Measure	Primary measures	Secondary measures
Customer satisfaction/ quality	Perfect order fulfillment Customer satisfaction Product quality	Delivery- to- commit date Warranty costs, returns, allowances
Time	Order fulfillment lead time	Supply chain response time Product plan achievement
Cost	Total supply chain costs	Value-added productivity Forecast accuracy Inventory obsolescence Capacity utilization
Assets	Cash-to cash cycle time Inventory days of supply Asset performance	

Table 3: Measures to improve supply chain measurements in PI (Handfield and Ernest, 1999).

Advantageously, the company evaluates its *value factors* very well and is quite aware of what is important to the customer. Quality is over and over again identified as important. In line to Porter's Five Forces, identified *rivalry among existing firms* as important. The company incurs a high fixed cost due to high *product differentiation*. This is tradeoff between customer customization and mass production. Also, *capacity* is another problem the company is facing and limited *capacity* could threaten customers' loyalty.

Since the company focuses on its strengths, weaknesses, opportunities, and threats in the formulation of its strategy, then a SWOT analysis becomes important. The paper performed a SWOT analysis and the findings shine the light on the challenges arising from the aerospace business where competition is ripe. One of the weaknesses identified is in the supply chain. The company requires JIT supply chain capabilities. It is advisable that the company reassesses its supply chain partners and further analyzes its supply chain *capacity* requirements. As form of recommendation the company should perform *Balanced Scorecard (BSC)*. In the BSC, there are four strategy processes that are addressed [12], which are:

- Financial perspective
- Customer perspective
- Process (internal) perspective
- Innovation and learning (training) perspective

This work recommends applying BSC to supply chain performance measurements. In BSC, we the supply chain goals and strategy are aligned with the entire performance measures. We need to apply the BSC on the different (four) levels of the supply chain and these levels are:

- Supply chain
- Organization
- Function
- Team/individual

The improvements on the supply chain level will definitely lead into improvements on the organization level. The chain supply goals, strategies, and performance measures at its level will be led to the organization level, which will improve the function level. As a last step, the team level will improve depending upon the functional level. For every level of the four forgoing levels, the BSC address the four keys (customer, financial, internal, and innovation), and within each area, the fundamental objectives are characterized and the entire performance measures, performance targets, and new ideas and plans are developed. Handfield and Ernest [14,15] proposed a measure of supply chain performance. We strongly recommend the organization to apply it in order to improve the process by improving the supply chain measurements.

References

1. Mintzberg H (1972) Research on Strategy Making. Proceedings of the Academy Of Management Conference. First Notions of Strategy as Pattern 29-34.
2. Porter ME (1996) What is strategy? Harvard Business Review 74: 61-79.
3. Mintzberg H (1987) The Strategy Concept I: Five Ps for Strategy. California Management Review 30: 11-25.
4. Mintzberg H, Lampel J (1999) Reflecting On Strategy Process. Sloan Management Review 40: 21-30.
5. Drobis, David R (1991) Competitive Thinking for Competitive Advantage. Public Relations Quarterly 36: 9-13.

6. Rumelt R (1999) Note on Strategy Evaluation. The Anderson School at UCLA 1: 1-12.

7. Boyer K, Swink M, Rosenzweig ED (2005) Operations Strategy Research in the POMS Journal. Production and Operations Management 14: 442-449.

8. Cousins PD (2005) The alignment of appropriate firm and supply strategies for competitive advantage. International Journal of Operations & Production Management 25: 403-428.

9. Peters T, Waterman R (1982) In Search of Excellence: Lessons from Americas Best Run Companies. Harper & Row, USA 51-85.

10. Kaplan RS (2005) How The Balanced Scorecard Complements The Mckinsey 7-S Model. Strategy & Leadership 33: 41-46.

11. Carlos JF, Morris DS (2001) The implications of service quality gaps for strategy implementation. Total Quality Management & Business Excellence 12: 825-833.

12. Kaplan RS, Norton DP (1996) Using the Balanced Scorecard as a Strategic Management System. Harvard Business Review 74: 75-86.

13. Krishnan R, Szmerekovsky J, Cowing M (2009) An Examination of Inter-Firm Cooperative Arrangements of U.S. Manufacturing Firms. Journal of Transnational Management 14: 16-26.

14. Handfield RB, Ernest NL Jr (2002) Supply Chain Redesign: Transforming Supply Chains into Integrated Value Systems. Prentice Hall, New Jersey 101-180.

15. Handfield RB, Ernest NL Jr (1999) Introduction to Supply Chain Management. Prentice Hall, New Jersey 27-84.

9

Islamic Microfinance in Sudanese Perspective

Elsadig Musa Ahmed[1] and Anwar Ammar[2]

[1]*Faculty of Business, Multimedia University, Cyberjaya, Malaysia*

[2]*Faculty of Management, Multimedia University, Cyberjaya, Malaysia*

Abstract

Microfinance-providing affordable financial services to the poor- has been identified as an important tool in increasing the productivity of the poor and in enhancing economic development. Although conventional microfinance products have been very successful in Muslim countries the traditional microfinance contract which involves the payment of interest (riba) is strictly prohibited with the principles set forth in the Sharia of Islam. Sharia-compliant microfinance is one among many interventions designed to bring poor people into the formal financial mainstream. Islamic microfinance leaders have taken the initiatives to meet the increasing needs of the poor Muslim customers with the aim of alleviating poverty among poor Muslim people. While conventional microfinance institutions (MFIs) have expanded their operations in the last two decades, Islamic microfinance products are still quite small relative to the conventional microfinance sector. Sudan emerges as the most prominent market for Islamic banking in terms of number of Islamic banking providers. This is driven by the fact that the country requires full compliance with Sharia principles for the entire financial system. In this respect, the aim of this paper is to shed light on Islamic microfinance in Sudan.

Keywords: Islamic microfinance; Sharia-compliant; Sudan

Introduction

Sudan a country with a population of approximately 36.2 million, of which two-thirds is rural, holds abundant land and livestock, rich mineral resources and, solid manufacturing base. Despite these large endowments of natural resources, and its agricultural potential; Sudan is ranked the fifth hungriest nation in the world by the Global Hunger Index. "Much of this potential has not been realized due to long-running conflict and governance challenges; and the gains of the last growth decade have not advanced productive public investment that contributes to poverty reduction, or been widely shared [1].

The Sudanese economy is witnessing a crucial downturn since the separation of the south in 2011; Sudan loosed 75% of its oil revenue due to this secession. Growth rate of the country's GDP show declines from 3.5% in 2010 to -3.3% and -10.1% in 2011 and 2012, respectively (WDI) [2]. This is reflected on the livelihoods of many Sudanese in forms of increasing poverty statistics. Average rural poverty rates in Sudan are estimated at 58%, much higher than the national average and the urban poverty rate (47% and 27%, respectively) (National Baseline Household Survey [NBHS]. The main constraints on rural livelihoods are poor access to markets, lack of access to financial services. Unemployment is also high (19.8%) in rural than in urban (12.1%) areas (FAO 2015) Other factor contributed to the unemployment and poverty is longest civil wars and the internal conflicts across the regions.

Promotion of economic growth, reduction of poverty, achieving MDGs (Millennium Development Goals) and employment creation are among the first important policy priorities and strategy pillars of the Government of Sudan to address the challenges of high poverty, unemployment, an increase of inflation due to the secession of the South in 2011.Within this context and as articulated in theInterim Poverty Reduction Strategy Paper IPRSP for Sudan, microfinance is one of the major tools which is given due priority by the government to alleviate poverty particularly in marginalized and conflict areas [3].

Islamic Microfinance

Earlier studies of the application of Islamic finance in microfinance was carried by Rahul and Sapcanin cited by Khan [4] they demonstrate that Islamic banking, with its emphasis on risk sharing for certain products and collateral-free loans, is compatible with the needs of some micro-entrepreneurs. Islamic Microfinance is very effective and essential for creating hope for the poor and those above the poverty line as shown by the traditional microfinance, but also for the extremely poor in the community the Islamic microfinance, based on a partnership mode, is fair and does not require poor clients' payment, or lead to a loss of the livelihood of the poor in the case of project failure beyond the client's control. It also does not require strong guarantees [5]. Viable projects that are rejected by conventional lending institutions because of insufficient collateral might prove to be acceptable to Islamic banks on a profit-sharing basis. Poor Muslims remained excluded from traditional microfinance for several reasons, voluntarily due to the practices of the interest rate by conventional lending institutions which considered riba, can be excluded non-voluntarily due to inability to repay back the loan plus the interest rate accrued to it. Hence, Islamic microfinance can easily overcome these challenges due to its wide scope to cover various diversity of customer whether based on their expertise or sectorial dimension.

On the funding side, Islamic microfinance services providers can mobilize additional resources through zakat (Zakah is instruments of charity occupy a central position in the Islamic scheme of poverty alleviation) and waqf (Waqf is a trust or pious foundation), and on the lending side they mainly use financial instruments that are based on Profit and Loss Sharing (PLS) schemes such as mudarabah and musharaka (Musharaka and mudaraba are contracts which share risks and benefits) rather than loans. Qard-al-Hassan (Qard-al-Hassan is an interest-free loan that the Qur'an encourages Muslims to make to the needy) resources should be made available to Islamic microfinance

***Corresponding author:** Elsadig Musa Ahmed, Faculty of Management Multimedia University, Cyberjaya, Malaysia, E-mail: elsadig1965@gmail.com

institutions to reduce the burden of high interest charges on their borrowers Zakat funds could be used to cover the default risk of microenterprises and to build capacity and skills. Takaful (Takaful is a mutual insurance) - micro-insurance – can be used for protection against unpredicted risks by borrowers. Murabaha (Murabaha is a "cost plus markup" sale contract) sale is used to finance goods. Salam is an advance payment in exchange of a future delivery, and istisna the exchange contract between a seller and a buyer.

Many studies show that poor Muslims refrain from taking interest-based microfinance products due to religious beliefs [4,6-8]. Salwana et al. [9] study revealed that traditional microfinance has failed to satisfy the Muslims communities because of its shift from poverty to focus on profit oriented business. Riwajanti [10] suggests that Islamic Microfinance should be considered contributing to poverty alleviation, financial development, and also financial inclusion because it offers unique characteristics with rich of values and human oriented. Shabrawy [11] favours the Islamic Microfinance because risk is shared between financial institutions and beneficiaries, allowing the entrepreneurs to concentrate on what they do best. A survey conducted in Azad Kashmir Pakistan by Al Huda Centre of Islamic Banking and Economics in 2011, exhibited that 99% of respondents showed strong demand for Islamic microfinance services [12].

Islamic microfinance in Sudan

Islamic microfinance is one of the essential unconventional outlets of lending that use by Islamic financial institutions to relieve the negative impact of the extreme poverty and unemployment among the people in Muslim countries. Being the majority are Muslims and more than 35 Islamic banks in addition to others non- banks Islamic financing providers, the country has become a suitable host for Islamic microfinance.

Microfinance existed in Sudan for decades as an informal economic activity. Traditionally villagers borrowed from local merchants in cash or in-kind consumption or emergency loans and paid back the loan when their anticipated funds become available. Microfinance was officially formalized by Bank of Sudan when it recognized Micro entrepreneurs and micro-enterprises in 1990 and included Artisan and skilled workers among the priority sectors to receive finance from commercial banks, especially for projects in rural areas. In 1994, micro-enterprises and low-income productive families were added together with agriculture, manufacturing, exports, mining, power generation, low cost housing, transport, and warehousing as priority sectors to receive finance from commercial banks. Social funds and donor supported programs have also been in operation for quite a while and many communities have benefited from their contributions. Islamic financial infrastructure has witnessed tremendous growth and improvement since 1989. The government transformed the existing dual economic system into Islamic financial system. This initiative has improved Islamic financial infrastructures and made enabling environment for Islamic microfinance.

Central Bank of Sudan (CBOS) in 2006, took the initiative of formulating a vision for developing and expanding microfinance sector in Sudan [13]. The vision detailed the creation of a conducive legal environment by: reviewing current law and policies of the CBOS to encourage banks to provide micro financing through i) monetary and flexible pricing policy, ii) restructuring and of some specialized bank like the Savings and Social Development Bank, and the Agriculture Bank of Sudan, iii) improving outreach of financial institutions though more bank branches and downscaling, iv) licensing of MFIs. The vision specified the requirements for a regulatory framework such as minimum capital requirements, capital adequacy, loan provisioning etc. in order to expand the financial resources. The vision also called for wholesale lending by banks to MFIs. Diversification of products and services including making use of traditional modes of finance and setting conducive modes of investments was emphasized in the vision. Institutionally; the vision called for the establishment of a MF Unit at the CBOS for regulating, supervising and promoting the development of micro finance and establishing an Apex institution outside CBOS to help in coordination among all stakeholders.

Since 2007, the policies issued annually by the CBOS incorporated specific section on microfinance. The CBOS started gradually to develop an enabling policy environment for microfinance adding elements that addresses constraints facing the sector from year to year. The major CBOS polices encompassed establishing a special MFU in CBOS to regulate, develop and supervise microfinance, encouraging banks to allocate specific resources to microfinance, resolving guarantees issues, allowing diversified Islamic modes of finance that are suitable for microfinance, developing wholesale financing and encouraging intermediaries and support services [14].

Microfinance providers

Total windows serving microfinance, both provisions of financial and non-financial services all over the country amount to 501 windows of which 466 are financial services windows and 35 windows are non-financial services. For financial services, it was found that micro are being provided by 21 banks (representing 54% of the operating banks) through 286 service windows, (i.e. 47% of the total branches providing banking services); a total number of 27 MFIs operating and under establishment through 37 windows; 18 mediators delivering their services through 87 windows (double number of the specialized MFIs windows); 33 windows of social security institutions and 23 supervision institutions. Non-financial micro financing services are provided by about 35 institutions of which: 4 are training and capacity building centres, 19 are technical support and development of small scale projects, 6 are consultancy firms and 6 are specialized collages. This is beside the informal sector spreading all over the country [3].

Outreach

Outreach is an important aspect of microfinance in view of the fact that the fundamental aim of microfinance is to reach the largest number of unnerved poor people who do not have access to financial services. Limited outreach can impact on the sustainability in terms of benefits linked to economies of scale.

The capacity of providers is very far from meeting the demand for this service. Potential microfinance customers in the country may exceed 8 million individuals, while coverage as shown by the number of clients of the microfinance services providers by this study hardly exceeds 350,000. Even discrepancies exist in the distribution between the state and between urban and rural. Most of the service providers are concentrated in the states with the lower poverty rates and are less in poverty stricken states, contrary to the policy and rationale that was behind the support for micro financing. Most windows are not in rural areas. There is only one rural micro finance service provider in all states out of 48 representing only 2% [14].

The number of clients (Banks and MFIs) increased from 244,000 in 2011 to 494,000 in 2012 and to 700,000 in 2013further to 970,000 in mid-2014, the banking MF portfolio increased from 1% in 2007 to 5% in 2013, MFIs increased from 3 in 2007 to 23 in 2013, The

MFIs' Non-Performing Loan NPL down from 6% in 2012 to 1.9% in 2013. According to IMF (2013) the number of MF borrowers went from 49,000 at end-2007 to 494,000 by 2012. The growth has occurred in both bank portfolios (49,000 to 300,000) and at the dedicated MF institutions (zero to 194,000) [15].

Penetration

UNICONS [16] study indicates that microloans are concentrated in urban areas; Microfinance Providers MFPs are far from achieving the CBOS directive for channelling 70% of their MF loans to rural areas. The Mapping (2012) shows that total windows serving microfinance, both provision of financial and non-financial services all over the country amount to 501 windows of which 466 are financial services windows and 35 windows are non-financial services. For financial services, it was found that microfinance are being provided by 21 banks (representing 54% of the operating banks) through 286 service windows, (i.e., 47% of the total branches providing banking services); a total number of 33 MFIs operating and under establishment through 37 windows; 18 mediators delivering their services through 87 windows (double number of the specialized MFIs windows); 33 windows of social security institutions and 23 supervision institutions. Non-financial microfinance services (Training and capacity building; Technical support, and consultation) are provided by about 35 institutions of which: 4 are training and capacity building centres, 19 are technical support and development of small scale projects, 6 are consultancy firms and 6 are specialized collages.

Sudan microfinance experience

The Sudanese experience showed that Islamic microfinance has a positive impact on income generating activities. Agricultural Bank of Sudan Microfinance Initiative (ABSUMI) Offer sharia-compliant credit, savings and micro insurance, particularly to women, ABSUMI was supported by three key stakeholders: the IFAD-funded Western Sudan Resources management Programme, ABS and the Microfinance Unit of the Central Bank of Sudan. As of May 2012, ABSUMI had reached 36,000 members of 6,000 households through 350 women's groups. It had mobilized savings worth US$72,000 with a client base of 4,500 borrowers and a loan portfolio of US$700,000. Its loans based on murabaha and musharaka are supporting small agricultural activities, livestock fattening and rearing, and a range of microenterprises such as petty trading, tea stalls and brick-making (IFAD [17]. Impact Evaluation (2013) study show that microfinance clients respondents reported an improvement in nutrition for their families (46.7% of clients), followed by better access to education (36.3%), better access to health services (33.8%), and purchase of property (30%). When compared to non-clients, less impact is reported by non-clients in all areas. Amira [18] study main findings revealed that participation of women in micro-credit program helps in promoting women's empowerment, in particular the economic and socio cultural dimensions of empowerment. The targeted women became economically empowered by (1) having their own income, (2) contributing to household purchases and (3) financing the education of their children; however, they did not manage to make savings to promote their micro-small operations. Fadul et al. [19] study impact of microfinance in North Kordofan, Sudan, results of the descriptive statistics show that there is a positive effect of microfinance on poverty reduction by 16%. Microfinance institutions enable poor low-income households to develop their microenterprises, which enhance their income earning capacity, and improve their living standard [20]. Maruod study was conducted to investigate the role of North Kordofan Rural Development Project (NKRDP) as a microfinance institution in women development, in Bara Locality. The results showed that 80%, 96.3%, 60%, 63.8% and 65% of the respondents mentioned that the project helped in providing education services, health services, water services, fuel services and handcrafts respectively. Results also showed that about 91.25% of the respondents had got profits from their investments.

Within the internal context, a survey for the collection of data on Islamic microfinance in the Arab region was conducted by Sanabel show that Sudan holds 70% of Islamic microfinance within the Arab region. CGAP [21], described Sudan Islamic microfinance model as: A laboratory for Islamic microfinance delivery where developments could shed light on effective Islamic microfinance practices. The IMF Sudan Article of Consultation, Sep. 2013, stated that "The microfinance sector is small but growing rapidly. The results of this push have been impressive to date. In terms of active clients, Sudan & Bangladesh are easily the global leaders in Islamic finance microfinance, with Sudan likely to take top spot given current growth rates". Issa et al. mapping exercise of Islamic banking/institutions in Africa, reveals that over 40% of these institutions are located in Sudan which imposes compliance with Shariah on the entire financial sector [22,23]. Within the three top countries with the highest Islamic microfinance outreach, two institutions dominate: (i) in Sudan the Agriculture Bank serves 75 percent of clients using Sharia-compliant products and (ii) in Bangladesh, the Islamic Bank of Bangladesh serves 67%. Task Team Leader Andres, Economist and Country Sector Coordinator with the World Bank say that "I have never seen a country so committed to microfinance as Sudan. The microfinance sector is growing in Sudan and it seems to be a healthy sector compared to other countries where the sector grows and then begins to drop."

Challenges of Islamic microfinance in Sudan

However, in spite of its successes, microfinance in Sudan has barely scratched the surface of need .Nonetheless late statistics show that the total number of clients in 2014 is 970,000 i.e. 8% coverage of total polemical clients (estimated at 7.2 mill.). Leaving more than 6 million individuals in Sudan have a need of microfinance services. This was also supported by the World Bank recent survey conducted in urban areas (state of Khartoum), showing that 1.5 million people-21% of the total population—expressed interest for such loans. Yet at the same time, 72% of the micro entrepreneurs surveyed said they had no access to formal or informal credit services [1]. In the same vein according to Asli Demirguc [24] 92% of the Sudanese adults who report having used mobile money in 2011do not have a formal account, 7% of adults have an account with formal financial institutions, 3% have saving with formal financial institutions, 2% get loans during 2011 from formal financial institutions, and only 1% have a credit card. This might be due to several reasons briefed below.

1. Sudan microfinance market maintains a high operating expense ratio at 56% (Situational Analysis 2006). Equally, for MFPs, the cost of reaching people is high. The lack of physical infrastructure increases the transaction costs for micro- and small enterprises. In addition, limited market information flows discourage market entry and formalization, particularly for subsistence farmers and rural micro entrepreneurs. Equally, for MFPs, the cost of reaching people is high. Distance of microfinance institutions [25]: is a variable that is always associated with high transaction costs. Time gaps to receive loans are 53, 59 and 86 days in Um Rwaba, Shiekan and Enuhud localities, respectively. These long time gaps have encouraged many borrowers to

drop out after one cycle of credit or not to ask for credit in the future [25].

2. There is no sustainable, i.e. profitable, microfinance model for the rural areas, which constitute about 90% of the geographical area of Sudan, mainly due to the lack of road and transportation infrastructure, lack of market access, lack of business skills and recurring conflicts [26]. Banks do not specifically target the rural poor [27]. The weakness on basic infrastructure represents big challenge, which hinders Islamic microfinance institutions to reach the poor in the very remote areas. the poor communication, and the weakness of the Sudanese basic infrastructures, microfinance providers deliberately ignoring the rural areas clients' because of the high risk/cost, only 20% of the available microfinance resources appear to be reaching the rural areas which have 80% of the microfinance market. Moreover, putting in mind the nature of Islamic finance such as Al-salam and Istisna'a in to consideration, the availability of warehouses and cheap in-land transportation are even more essential [28].

3. Limited range of microfinance products being focusing on micro loans for productive purposes only [29].

4. The diversity of Islamic microfinance beneficiaries in Sudan in terms of the geographical rural areas, climates, tribalism system, farms and non-farms based activities, livestock, trading, religious and the political climate need well trained microfinance providers staff to deal with different issues at the same times [28] most of Islamic microfinance providers currently active in Sudan are by international standards small and display serious weaknesses in operational, financial, managerial and strategic management capabilities [13].

5. Although there are many Islamic modes of finance, Murabaha seems to be the favoured mode for many providers, even though it might not be the most suitable for some clients and their projects. UNICONS (Situational analysis 2006) study show that the lending methods used by all organizations and institutions engaged in micro-credit are Murabaha (40%), Quardhasan (17.6%), hire-purchase (14.5%), Salam (10%) and Mudaraba (3.7%). Although CBOS directive places a ceiling of 30 per cent of the loan portfolio to be dedicated to murabaha and at the same time restricts the profit margin on murabaha contracts to a maximum of 9% [30]. Darfur [31] study revealed that the vast majority of microfinance loan products are traditional murabaha, Impact Evaluation [32] show that majority of clients (87.1%) have Murabaha as their Islamic mode of finance for their microfinance loan, while other modes of finance account for less than 5% each. As noted by Ibrahim in Crossfire [33] current practice of Islamic banking worldwide is heavy dependent on murabaha which is similar in practise, but not in principle to interest rate, might not be a suitable formula to combat poverty and profiting from the poor.

Conclusion and Implications

This study demonstrated Sudan's experience in implementing Islamic principles in developing Islamic microfinance. It has shown the financial models practiced in Sudan compared with the conventional microfinance models in general and those practice in the Muslim world in particular. The paper also, highlighted the Islamic microfinance implemented in Sudan and showed the shortcomings in these projects to be solved by taking the experiences of other countries into consideration.

Based on the aforementioned studies, this study concludes that there are a lot of opportunities for Islamic microfinance in Sudan and other Muslim countries if governments and regulators paid attention to the business model and profit and loss share products.

References

1. Banker Africa Issue (2014) 010.CPI Financial.
2. WDI (2013) World Development Indicators of the World Bank, Washington DC, USA.
3. (2012) Mapping, Capacity Assessment and Capacity Development of Microfinance Providers in Sudan.
4. Khan AA (2011) What role for Islamic finance in promoting development? Paper presented at the Institute of Social Studies, Netherlands.
5. Badr EDAI (2013) Islamic Microfinance-Why is it worth considering? Posted by Microfinance Nigeria, J Islam Banking Finance 30: 98.
6. IFC (2007) Syria Microfinance Market Assessment, Draft Report. Washington DC:IFC/The World Bank.
7. IFC/FINCA (2006) Business Plan for a Microfinance Institution in Jordan, Commissioned by IFC and FINCA.
8. (2006) Frankfurt School of Finance and Management (Bank akademia International), Access to Finance in Algeria, Final Report. Frankfurt: Frankfurt School of Finance and Management, Algeria.
9. Salwana H, Abdul Rahman R, Abu Bakar N, Mohd R, Muhammad AD, et al. (2013) Designing Microfinance Products for Islamic Banks in Malaysia, Middle-East Journal of Scientific Research 17: 359-366.
10. Riwajanti NI (2013) Islamic Microfinance as an Alternative for Poverty Alleviation: A Survey Afro Eurasian Studies 2: 254-271.
11. Shabrawy EA (2011) Innovation in Micro Entrepreneurship and Islamic Microfinance the model of Family bank in Bahrain, 10th International Entrepreneurship forum, Bahrain 1-18.
12. Mohsin S (2011) Overview of Microfinance. Education, Economy and Finance, Technology, International Conference on Islamic Microfinance, US.
13. Abukasawi MG, Hasssan AI (2006) Situational Analysis of the Microfinance Sector in Sudan Unicons.
14. (2013) Impact Evaluation Assessment MFI Sector in Sudan 2007-2012 Sudanese Microfinance Development Facility (SMDF) Draft Report, PACT, Sudan.
15. Badr EDAI (2014) Microfinance Sectors in two African countries-Sudan and Ethiopia, AEMFI 8th biennial conference, Hawassa, Ethiopia.
16. (2008) Unicons Evaluation of Implementation of the Strategy For Expansion and Development of The Micro Finance Sector In Sudan.
17. IFAD (2012) Islamic microfinance: Unlocking new potential to fight rural poverty From a market niche to a growing industry, Italy.
18. Amira YB (2013) The Role of Micro-credit System for Empowering Poor Women, Developing Country Studies 3: 71-84.
19. Elmola SF, Belal I (2013) The Impact of Microfinance on Rural Poor Households, Income and Vulnerability to Poverty: Case Study of North Kordofan State Tropentag 17-19.
20. Habeeb EEH, Maruod EM, Mohammed SE (2014) The Role of North Kordofan Rural Development Project (NKRDP) in Women Development in Bara locality, North Kordofan State. Int J Edu Res 2: 39-52.
21. CGAP (2008) Islamic Microfinance: An Emerging Market Niche, Focus Note No. 49.
22. Badr IEDA (2014) President, Microfinance Unit, Successful Models in Agricultural Microfinance Sponsored by the Central Bank of Sudan, (CBoSCTA-AFRACA) Revolutionizing finance for agri-chain 14-18.
23. Faye I, Triki T, Kangoye T (2013) The Islamic finance promises: Evidence from Africa. Review of Development Finance 3: 136-151.
24. Demirguc KA, Klapper L (2012) Measuring Financial Inclusion, The Global Findex Database. The World Bank Development Research Group Finance and Private Sector Development Team.
25. Ibrahim AH, Bauer S (2013) Access to Micro credit and its Impact on Farm Profit among Rural Farmers in Dryland of Sudan, Global Advanced Research Journal of Agricultural Science 2: 088-102.

26. (2006) Unicons: A Vision for the Development and Expansion of the Microfinance Sector in Sudan.

27. Sinha S (2007) Microfinance Consultant, IFAD-First National Consultative Forum on Microfinance in Sudan.

28. Ali ASE (2013) The Challenges of Islamic Trade Finance in Promoting SMEs In IDB Member Countries, Central banks of Sudan reports, J Eur Sci.

29. (2010) Evaluation report, The Savings and Social Development Bank SSDB-UNICONS, Sudan.

30. Laura A (2009) Government of Sudan Issues Directives Requiring Banks to Allocate 12 Percent of Portfolio to Microfinance, Sudan.

31. Badr IEDA (2014) Sudan-Enabling Policies, Supervisory and Regulatory Framework for Microfinance Sector, Roundtable Discussion on Regulatory and Supervisory Framework in Islamic Microfinance, Idb, Sudan University Of Science and Technology, Khartoum.

32. (2013) Country Programming Framework for Sudan "Plan of Action (2015-2019)" Resilient Livelihoods for Sustainable Agriculture, Food Security and Nutrition, FAO Representation in Sudan Khartoum.

33. (2013) Trends in Sharia-Compliant Financial Inclusion", Consultative Group to Help the Poor, CGAP, The World Bank, Focus Note.

Attitude of the Tourists towards the Availability of Facilities in and around Madurai Region

Selvaraj N*

Saraswathi Narayanan College, Madurai,Tamilnadu, India

Abstract

The early history of tourism is the story of the development of mobility of man. Both in the pre-historic era and later, man searched for things he wanted and he travelled for food, shelter or just for curiosity. 'Attitude' is an abstract concept; it cannot be directly measured in quantitative terms. There is no fixed value or score which will help measure the attitude. But the attitude can be measured indirectly with the help of scaling technique. The level of attitude may vary from one tourist to another and from time to time. A comprehensive study has been made to highlight the level of attitude, the variation in the levels of attitude and their relative importance to each component identified for measuring the level of attitude. This paper presents the attitude of tourists towards tourist facilities available in and around Madurai region. An airstrip with facilities for landing and takeoff, of mini planes and helicopters of private travel agencies at least should be established at Cape Comorin. It will put the entire district on the international and national tourist map.

Keywords: Tourism; Attitude; Facilities; Chi-square

Introduction

The early history of tourism is the story of the development of mobility of man. Both in the pre-historic era and later, man searched for things he wanted and he travelled for food, shelter or just for curiosity. He was awed and wonder-struck by the vividness of nature and the environment. In due course, other urges, other motivations made man travel from one place to another. Large-scale movements were also caused by natural elements or human pressure, which forced man to move to other locations. The absence of roads or other transport facilities, made travel hard and this led slowly to the development of land routes, as also of river and sea navigation. Man exploited the facilities and with the passage of time, this resulted in increased travel for a variety of reasons including wander-lust, conquest and gain, propagation of religion or pilgrimage. The hazards of travel were many and these often meant death caused by wild animals, marauders, inclement weather, sickness and lack of food and water [1].

This paper presents the attitude of tourists towards tourist facilities available in and around Madurai region. 'Attitude' means 'settled behaviour'. Since more tourist facilities are available to tourists, the level of attitude will indicate the extent of satisfaction on tourist facilities available in and around Madurai region.

Since 'attitude' is an abstract concept, it cannot be directly measured in quantitative terms. There is no fixed value or score which will help measure the attitude. But the attitude can be measured indirectly with the help of scaling technique. The researcher has identified 17 components for measuring the attitude. A five-point scale has been devised for measuring the attitude of tourists towards tourist facilities available in and around Madurai region by following the scale developed by Likert.

The level of attitude may vary from one tourist to another and from time to time. A comprehensive study has been made to highlight the level of attitude, the variation in the levels of attitude and their relative importance to each component identified for measuring the level of attitude [2].

Period of Study

The field survey was conducted from September 2014 to June, 2015 for the collection primary data. The reference period of survey was 2014-2015.

The attitude scale

For analysing the attitude of tourists towards tourist facilities available in and around Madurai region, some statements were given to the respondents. With a view to measuring the opinion of the respondents, they were requested to indicate whether they strongly agree (or) agree (or) neither agree nor disagree (or) disagree (or) strongly disagree about each given statement. For eliciting the responses the following 17 statements were given to them [3].

i. ATM card facility is easily available
ii. RBI approved agents render better foreign exchange services
iii. Car hiring facility is not plenty
iv. Auto drivers/Taxi drives/Cycle rickshaw are not reliable
v. Auto charges are discriminating
vi. Madurai city is not clean
vii. Madurai is well connected by railways
viii. Madurai does not have more flights
ix. Guide facility is very good
x. Catering facility is satisfactory
xi. Lodging facility is adequate

***Corresponding author:** Selvaraj N, Assistant Professor of Commerce, Saraswathi Narayanan College, Madurai, Tamilnadu, India
E-mail: selvaraj_narayanan@yahoo.com

xii. Entertainment facilities in Madurai are plenty

xiii. Availability of adequate medical facility

xiv. Shopping facility is limited

xv. Communication facility is more advanced one

xvi. The services of Tourist Information Centre are prompt and reliable

xvii. Sri Meenakshi Amman Temple is the main attraction for tourists

The responses were anlaysed with the help of Likert's five-point scale technique. The answers supporting the given statement fully receive the maximum score of five, while the answers on the other end get a score of one. Then the total scores will be divided by the total number of respondent. The resultant value, namely, the mean score will be provided for each statement [4].

In this study, the maximum score is 100 and the minimum is 20. If a tourist gets a total score which is below 36, he belongs to low level attitude group. If a tourist gets a total score between 36 and 77, he belongs to medium level attitude group. If a tourist gets a total score which is above 77, he belongs to high level attitude group.

The level of attitude

On the basis of scores allotted, the respondents have been categorised into three groups namely, Low, Medium and High. When the scale has been applied to the sample tourists, it has been found out that none of the respondents belong to 'Low' level attitude group, 197 respondents to 'Medium' level attitude group and 303 respondents to 'High' level attitude group. Table 1 shows the level of attitude of 500 tourists under the study.

Table 1 reveals that 197 tourists belong to medium level attitude group and 303 tourists belong to high level attitude group. So, it is a fact that all tourists get satisfaction in visiting Madurai region and this may influence other potential people to make a visit to Madurai region [5].

Age of tourists and level of attitude

Whenever a tourist moves from one place to another place in his/her nation, age factor need not be considered. But if a tourist moves from one country to another, there is the possibility of hesitation, when a tourist is not a major. So, age group of tourists and their attitude have been considered. Age is also a factor which may influence tourists to enjoy themselves the beautiful temples, historical places and the like in Madurai region. Table 2 presents the age-wise classification of sample tourists.

The above Table 2 shows that out of 199 respondents in high level of attitude in the case of domestic tourists majority of 126 (63.32%) of the respondents belonging to the age group upto 34 years and rest of 73 (36.68%) of the respondents belonging to the age group of above 35 years. In the case of medium level attitude out of 139 respondents majority of 90 (64.75%) of the respondents belonging to the age group of upto 34 years and remaining 49 (35.35%) of the respondents belonging to the age group of above 35 years [6].

Sl. No.	Category	Number of Tourists	
		Domestic	Foreign
1.	Medium	139 (41.12)	58 (35.80)
2.	High	199 (58.88)	104 (64.20)
	Total	338 (100)	162 (100)

Note: Figures in brackets indicate percentages

Table 1: Level of attitude of sample tourists.

Age	Attitude Level					
	Domestic		Total	Foreign		Total
	High	Medium		High	Medium	
Upto 34 Years	126 (63.32)	90 (64.75)	216 (63.91)	51 (49.04)	33 (56.90)	84 (51.85)
Above 35 Years	73 (36.68)	49 (35.25)	122 (36.09)	53 (50.96)	25 (43.10)	78 (48.15)
Total	199 (100.00)	139 (100.00)	338 (100.00)	104 (100.00)	58 (100.00)	162 (100.00)

Source: Primary data.

Note: Figures in brackets represent percentages to total.

Table 2: Age of tourists and the level of attitude.

In order to see whether there is any relationship between age and attitude in domestic tourists, Chi-Square test has been applied and results are given below:

- Degrees of freedom: 1
- Calculated Value: 8.0432
- Table value at 5% level: 3.841

The results of Chi-Square test shows that the calculated value is greater than the table value and hence the Chi-square test reveals that the relationship is significant. Thus there is a relationship between the age of domestic tourists and the attitude level.

The above table observed that out of 104 respondents in high level of attitude in foreign tourists majority of 51 (49.04%) of the tourist belonging to the age group upto 34 years and remaining 53 (50.96%) of the respondents belonging to the age group of above 35 years. In the case of medium level of attitude, out of 58 respondents majority of 33 (56.90%) of the respondents belonging to the age group of upto 34 years and rest of 25 (43.10%) of the respondents belonging to the age group of above 35 years [7].

In order to see whether there is any relationship between age and attitude in foreign tourists, Chi-Square test has been applied and results are given below:

- Degrees of freedom: 1
- Calculated Value: 0.9680
- Table value at 5% level: 3.841

The above Chi-Square test shows that the calculated value is less than the table value and hence there is insignificant. Thus there is no relationship between the age of foreign tourists and the attitude level.

Sex of tourists and level of attitude

India is a land of contracts from tropic to snow. It is vast, varied and strikingly beautiful. It does not restrict any man or woman coming to India. Therefore, sex of tourists has been identified as one the factors influencing the attitude. Table 3 shows the sex-wise classification of sample tourists.

As could been seen from Table 3, out of 199 respondents in high level attitude, majority of 128 (64.32%) of the domestic tourists are male and remaining 71 (35.68%) of the respondents are female. In the case of medium level attitude out of 139 respondents, majority of 94 (67.63%) of domestic tourists are male and rest of 45 (32.37%) of the respondents are female [8].

In order to find out whether there is any relationship between sex of domestic tourists and the attitude level, Chi-Square test has been applied and the results are given below:

- Degrees of freedom: 1
- Calculated Value: 0.4874
- Table value at 5% level: 3.841

Since the calculated value is less than the table value, hence there is no significant relationship between the sex of domestic tourists and their level of attitude.

Table 3 also shows that out of 104 respondents in high level attitude, majority of 85 (81.72%) of foreign tourists are male and rest of 19 (18.27%) of the respondents are female. In the case of medium level of attitude out of 58 respondents, majority of 44 (75.86%) of foreign tourists are male and remaining 14 (24.24%) of the respondents are female [9].

In order to find out whether there is any relationship between sex of foreign tourists and the attitude level, Chi-Square test has been applied and the results are given below:

- Degrees of freedom: 1
- Calculated Value: 2.0313
- Table value at 5% level: 3.841

Since the calculated value is less than the table value, there is no significant relationship between the sex of foreign tourists and their level of attitude.

Marital status of tourists and level of attitude

Tour operators approach both married and unmarried persons to have a visit to India. Generally unmarried persons are free from family commitments and hence their responsibility is lesser than that of married persons. Financially unmarried persons are well-off. When they are persuaded by the tour operator, they visit India.

In the case of married persons, they take their dependents to selected countries like India, for their interest and development.

Thus married as well as unmarried persons feel that it is necessary to visit India. Therefore, marital status has been identified as a factor which may influence the attitude of tourists. Table 4 shows the classification of tourists on the basis of marital status.

Table 4 observed that out of 199 respondents in high level attitude of domestic tourists majority of 124 (62.31%) of the respondents are married and remaining 75 (37.69%) of the respondents are unmarried. In the case of medium level attitude out of 139 respondents majority of 92 (66.19%) of the respondents are married and rest of 47 (33.81%) of the respondents are unmarried [10].

In order to find out whether there is any relationship between the marital status and the attitude level, Chi-Square test has been applied and the results are given below:

- Degrees of freedom: 1
- Calculated Value: 0.4769
- Table value at 5% level: 3.841

Since the calculated value is less than the table value, hence there is no significant relationship between the marital status of domestic tourists and the level of attitude.

The above Table 4 also shows that out of 104 respondents in high level attitude of foreign tourists, majority of 66 (63.46%) of the respondents are married and remaining 38 (36.54%) of the respondents are unmarried. In the case of medium level attitude out of 58 respondents majority of 32 (55.17%) of the respondents are married and rest 26 (44.83%) of the respondents are unmarried.

In order to test any relationship between the marital status and the

Sex	Attitude Level					
	Domestic		Total	Foreign		Total
	High	Medium		High	Medium	
Male	128 (64.32)	94 (67.63)	222 (65.68)	85 (81.73)	44 (75.86)	129 (79.63)
Female	71 (35.68)	45 (32.37)	116 (34.32)	19 (18.27)	14 (24.14)	33 (20.37)
Total	199 (100.00)	139 (100.00)	338 (100.00)	104 (100.00)	58 (100.00)	162 (100.00)

Source: Primary data.

Note: Figures in brackets represent percentages to total.

Table 3: Sex-wise classification of tourists and the level of attitude.

Marital Status	Attitude Level					
	Domestic		Total	Foreign		Total
	High	Medium		High	Medium	
Married	124 (62.31)	92 (66.19)	216 (63.91)	66 (63.46)	32 (55.17)	98 (60.49)
Unmarried	75 (37.69)	47 (33.81)	122 (36.09)	38 (36.54)	26 (44.83)	64 (39.51)
Total	199 (100.00)	139 (100.00)	338 (100.00)	104 (100.00)	58 (100.00)	162 (100.00)

Source: Primary data.

Note: Figures in brackets represent percentages to total.

Table 4: Marital status of tourists and the level of attitude.

attitude level, Chi-Square test has been applied and the results are given below:

- Degrees of freedom: 1
- Calculated Value: 1.0167
- Table value at 5% level: 3.841

Since the calculated value is less than the table value, there is no relationship. Hence, the null hypothesis, the marital status does not influence the level of attitude holds good [11].

Educational qualification of tourists and level of attitude

Tourism is an essential aspects of any human being whether a tourists is educated or uneducated. The educated tourists are able to understand the significance of the various parts of the world when compared to the uneducated.

Education widens the knowledge and understanding of all including the tourists. Therefore qualification is identified as one of the factors which may influence the attitude of tourists. Table 5 exhibits the educational qualification of the sample tourists.

It is understood from Table 5 that out of 199 respondents in high level attitude of domestic tourists majority of 53 (26.63%) of the respondents are undergraduates followed by 49 (24.62%), 27 (13.57%), 25 (12.56%), 24 (12.06%) and 21 (10.56%) of the tourists are post-graduates, high school, diploma, professional degree and research degree respectively. In the case of medium level attitude out of 139 respondents majority of 43 (30.94%) of the respondents are under-graduates, post-graduates, high school, diploma, professional degree and research degree respectively [12].

In order to find out whether there is any relationship between the educational qualification of the domestic tourists and the attitude level, Chi-Square test has been applied and the results are given below:

- Degrees of freedom: 5
- Calculated Value: 2.5710
- Table value at 5% level: 11.070

Since the calculated value is less than the table value, hence there is no significant relationship between the educational qualification of domestic tourists and the level of attitude.

Table 5 also indicates that out of 104 respondents in high level attitude of foreign tourists, majority of 26 (25.00%) of the respondents are undergraduates followed by 24 (23.08%), 15 (14.42%), 14 (13.46%), 13 (12.50%) and 12 (11.54%) of the foreign tourists are post-graduates, high school, diploma, professional degree and research degree respectively. In the case of medium level attitude of foreign tourists, out of 58 respondents majority of 26 (25.00%) of the respondents are undergraduates followed by 24 (23.08%), 15 (14.42%), 14 (13.46%), 13 (12.50%) and 12 (11.54%) of the respondents are post-graduates, high school, diploma, professional degree and research degree respectively.

In order to find out whether there is any relationship between the educational qualification of the foreign tourists and the level of attitude, Chi-Square test has been applied and the results are given below:

- Degrees of freedom: 5
- Calculated Value: 7.5790
- Table value at 5% level: 11.070

Since the calculated value is less than the table value at 5% level of significance. Hence there is no significant relationship between the educational qualification of foreign tourists and the level of attitude.

Occupation of tourists and level of attitude

Nature of occupation varies from one person to another. Whatever may be the source of occupation, every human-being wants to enjoy their leisure hours. Many of the travellers explore new places and seek a charge of environment and experiences. But most of the foreign tourists want to enjoy their leisure in India irrespective of their occupation. Getting away from the routine work of everyday life is perhaps the most important desire of all. If the tourists is in employment, then there is the possibility of regular income as compared to other categories. So, the researcher has identified this occupation category as a factor influencing the attitude of tourists. Table 6 shows the classification of respondents on the basis of their occupation [13].

Table 6 shows that out of 199 domestic tourists in high level attitude, majority of 130 (65.33%) of the respondents are belonging to the category of other than employment and rest of 69 (34.67%) of the respondents are belonging to the employment. In the case of medium

Qualification	Attitude Level					
	Domestic		Total	Foreign		Total
	High	Medium		High	Medium	
High School	27 (13.57)	17 (12.23)	44 (13.02)	15 (14.42)	4 (6.90)	19 (11.73)
Diploma	25 (12.56)	15 (10.79)	40 (11.83)	14 (13.46)	6 (10.34)	20 (12.35)
Under-Graduates	53 (26.63)	43 (30.94)	96 (28.40)	26 (25.00)	22 (37.93)	48 (29.63)
Post-Graduates	49 (24.62)	38 (27.34)	87 (25.74)	24 (23.08)	14 (24.14)	38 (23.46)
Professional Degree	24 (12.06)	14 (10.07)	38 (11.24)	13 (12.50)	9 (15.52)	22 (13.58)
Research Degree	21 (10.56)	12 (8.64)	33 (9.77)	12 (11.54)	3 (5.17)	15 (9.25)
Total	199 (100.00)	139 (100.00)	338 (100.00)	104 (100.00)	58 (100.00)	162 (100.00)

Source: Primary data.

Note: Figures in brackets represent percentages to total.

Table 5: Educational qualification of tourists and the level of attitude.

level attitude, out of 139 respondents, majority of 93 (66.91%) of the respondents are belonging to the category of other than employment and remaining 46 (33.09%) of the respondents are belonging to the category of employment.

In order to find out whether there is any relationship between occupation of the domestic tourists and the level of attitude, Chi-Square test has been applied and the results are given below:

- Degrees of freedom: 1
- Calculated Value: 7.6802
- Table value at 5% level: 3.841

Since the calculated value is greater than the table value at 5% level of significance. Hence, there is a relationship between the occupation of the domestic tourists and the level of attitude.

Table 6 also indicates that out of 104 foreign tourists in high level attitude, majority of 69 (66.35%) of the respondents are belonging to the category of other than employment and rest of 35 (33.65%) of the respondents are belonging to the category of employment. In the case of medium level attitude, out of 58 respondents, majority of 41 (70.69%) of the respondents are belonging to the category of other than employment and remaining 17 (29.31%) of the respondents are belonging to the category of employment respectively.

In order to find out whether there is any relationship between occupation of foreign tourists and the attitude level, Chi-Square test has been applied and the results are given below:

- Degrees of freedom: 1
- Calculated Value: 0.4850
- Table value at 5% level: 3.841

Since the calculated value is less than the table value. Hence, there is no significant relationship between the occupation of the foreign tourists and their level of attitude.

Tendency of tourists and level of attitude

Whenever a person moves from one place to another, he may move either individually or collectively as a group. The researcher has made an attempt towards the movement of tourists. For this purpose, the tendency of tourists has been identified as a factor influencing the attitude of tourists. Table 7 shows the classification of respondents on the basis of their tendency [10].

Table 7 reveals that out of 199 domestic tourists in high level attitude, majority of 90 (45.23%) of the respondents arrived as group followed by 64 (32.16%) and rest of 48 (22.61%) of the respondents arrived as individual and family respectively. In the case of medium level attitude, out of 139 respondents, majority of 52 (37.41%) of the domestic tourists arrived as group followed by 48 (34.53%) and remaining 39 (28.06%) of the respondents arrived as individual and family respectively.

In order to find out whether there is any relationship between tendency of the domestic tourists and the level of attitude, Chi-Square test has been applied and the results are given below:

- Degrees of freedom: 2
- Calculated Value: 1.9802
- Table value at 5% level: 5.991

Since the calculated value is less than the table value at 5% level of significance. Hence, there is no relationship between the tendency of the domestic tourists and the level of attitude.

Table 7 also indicates that out of 104 foreign tourists in the case of high level of attitude, majority of 44 (42.31%) of the respondents are arrived as group followed by 35 (33.65%) and 25 (24.04%) of the

Occupation	Attitude Level					
	Domestic		Total	Foreign		Total
	High	Medium		High	Medium	
Employment	69 (34.67)	46 (33.09)	115 (34.02)	35 (33.65)	17 (29.31)	52 (32.10)
Other than Employment	130 (65.33)	93 (66.91)	223 (65.98)	69 (66.35)	41 (70.69)	110 (67.90)
Total	199 (100.00)	139 (100.00)	338 (100.00)	104 (100.00)	58 (100.00)	162 (100.00)

Source: Primary data.
Note: Figures in brackets represent percentages to total.

Table 6: Occupation of tourists and the level of attitude.

Category	Attitude Level					
	Domestic		Total	Foreign		Total
	High	Medium		High	Medium	
Individual	64 (32.16)	48 (34.53)	112 (33.14)	35 (33.65)	13 (22.41)	48 (29.63)
Family	45 (22.61)	39 (28.06)	84 (24.85)	25 (24.04)	12 (20.69)	37 (22.84)
Group	90 (45.23)	52 (37.41)	142 (42.01)	44 (42.31)	33 (56.90)	77 (47.53)
Total	199 (100.00)	139 (100.00)	338 (100.00)	104 (100.00)	58 (100.00)	162 (100.00)

Source: Primary data.
Note: Figures in brackets represent percentages to total.

Table 7: Tendency of tourists and the level of attitude.

Category	Attitude Level					
	Domestic		Total	Foreign		Total
	High	Medium		High	Medium	
Self	71 (35.68)	43 (30.94)	114 (33.73)	46 (44.23)	19 (32.76)	65 (40.12)
By Travel agent	47 (23.62)	39 (28.06)	86 (25.44)	23 (22.12)	17 (29.31)	40 (24.69)
By Tour Operator	49 (24.62)	41 (29.50)	90 (26.63)	25 (24.04)	15 (25.86)	40 (24.69)
By Department of Tourism	32 (16.08)	16 (11.50)	48 (14.20)	10 (9.611)	7 (12.07)	17 (10.50)
Total	199 (100.00)	139 (100.00)	338 (100.00)	104 (100.00)	58 (100.00)	162 (100.00)

Source: Primary data.

Note: Figures in brackets represent percentages to total.

Table 8: Planning of tour and the level of attitude.

respondents are arrived as individual and family respectively. In the case of foreign tourists of medium level attitude, out of 58 respondents, majority of 33 (56.90%) of the respondents arrived as group followed by 13 (22.41%) and 12 (20.69%) of the respondents arrived individual and family respectively.

In order to find out whether there is any relationship between tendency of the foreign tourists and the level of attitude, Chi-square test has been applied and the results are given below:

- Degrees of freedom: 2
- Calculated Value: 2.9787
- Table value at 5% level: 5.991

Since the calculated value is less than the table value at 5% level of significance. Hence, there is no relationship between the tendency of the foreign tourists and the level of attitude.

Planning of tour and level of attitude

Planning is an essential function of management. Likewise, tour planning is an essential aspect of tour programme. The planning task is carried out either by tourists themselves or others. Therefore, planning of tour has been identified as a factor influencing the attitude of tourists. Table 8 shows the planning of tour of respondents.

Table 8 shows that out of 199 domestic tourists in the case of high level of attitude, majority of 71(35.68%) of the respondents planned themselves followed by 49 (24.62%), 47 (23.62%) and 32 (16.08%) of the respondents planned by travel operator, by travel agents and by Department of Tourism respectively. In the case of medium level attitude, out of 139 respondents, majority of 43 (30.99%) of the respondents planned themselves followed by 41 (29.50%), 39 (28.06%) and 16 (11.50%) of the respondents planned by tour operator, by travel agent and by Department of Tourism respectively.

In order to find out whether there is any relationship between planning of domestic tourists and the level of attitude, Chi-Square test has been applied and the results are given below:

- Degrees of freedom: 3
- Calculated Value: 3.4556
- Table value at 5% level: 7.815

Since the calculated value is less than the table value at 5% level of significance. Hence, there is no relationship between the planning of the domestic tourists and the level of attitude.

Table 8 also revealed that out of 104 foreign tourists in the case of high level attitude, majority of 46 (44.23%) of the respondents planned as themselves followed by 25 (24.04%), 23 (22.12%) and 10 (9.61%) of the respondents planned as by tour operator, by travel agents and by Department of Tourism respectively. In the case of medium level attitude, out of 58 respondents, majority of 19 (32.76%), of the respondents planned as themselves followed by 17 (29.31%), 15 (25.86%) and 7 (12.07%) of the respondents planned as by travel agents, by tour operators and by Department of Tourism respectively [7].

In order to find out whether there is any relationship between planning of foreign tourists and the level of attitude, Chi-Square test has been applied and the results are given below:

- Degrees of freedom: 3
- Calculated value : 2.4327
- Table value at 5% level: 7.815

Since the calculated value is less than the table value at 5% level of significance. Hence, there is no relationship between the planning of the foreign tourists and the level of attitude.

Summary of Findings

Regarding the analysis of the attitude of tourists towards tourist facilities available in and around Madurai region, Chi-square test was applied. In case of domestic tourists, it was found that there was significant relationship between the factors such as age and occupation of the tourists with level of attitude. The other personal variables such as sex, marital status, education, tendency of tourists and planning of tour were not influencing the level of attitude. In case of foreign tourists, it was found that no variables have significant relationship with level of attitude towards tourists facilities available in and around Madurai region.

Recommendations

A special website should be started for the centres of tourist attraction in the internet regarding Kanyakumari.

The government should come forward to facilitate the growth of travel convenience in the district to assist the foreign and domestic tourists thus enabling them to gain easy access to the tourist spots here.

An airstrip with facilities for landing and takeoff, of mini planes and helicopters of private travel agencies at least should be established at Cape Comorin. It will put the entire district on the international and national tourist map.

References

1. Rivera MA (2015) A Destination Performance Analysis through the Comparison of Tourists and Stakeholders' Perceptions: The Case of Curaçao. J Tourism Hospit 4: 171.
2. Singh V (2015) Eco-Tourism as a Sutainable Alternative to Conventional Tourism. J Tourism Hospit 4: 168.
3. Kidane-Mariam T (2015) Ethiopia: Opportunities and Challenges of Tourism Development in the Addis Ababa-upper Rift Valley Corridor. J Tourism Hospit 4: 167.
4. Aynalem S, Akele B, Alemayehu H, Molla G (2015) Assessment and Identification of the Tourism Resources of Bale Zone, Ethiopia. J Tourism Hospit 4: 176.
5. Horotwitz MD, Posensnerg JA (2007) Medical tourism-health Care in the Global Economy. Physician Executive 33: 24-30.
6. Lindvall O, Hyun I (2009) Medical innovation versus stem Cell tourism. Science 324: 1664-1665.
7. Lunt N, Smith R, Exworthy M, Green ST, Harstall R, et al. (2013) Medical Tourism: Treatments, Markets and Health System Implications: A Scoping review. OECD Report.
8. Merrell C, Boxcher D, Carabello L, Herrick M, Lozzano V, et al. (2008) Roundtable discussion Medical Tourism. Telemedicine and Health 14: 14-20.
9. Sarwar A (2013) Medical tourism in Malaysia: Prospect and challenges. Iranian Journal of Public Health 42: 795-805.
10. Unti JA (2009) Medical and Surgical Tourism: The new World. Healthcare globalization and what it means for the practicing surgeon. Bulletin of American College of Surgeons 94: 18-25.
11. Inoue S, Lee (2011) Effects of Different Dimensions of Corporate Social Responsibility on Corporate financial Performance in Tourism - Related Industries. Journal of Tourism Management 32: 790-804.
12. Baltruschat A (2011) Exploring the Scope and Relevance of Corporate Social Responsibility for Small and Medium Size Tourism Enterprises: A Situation Analysis and Future Outlook for Inbound Tour Operators in Thailand.
13. Argandona A (2010) Corporate Social Responsibility in the Tourism Industry: Some Lesson from the Spanish Experiences. IESE Business School, University of Navarra, Spain.

A Fair Value and Hedge Activities

Doan Van Dinh[1]* and Guangming Gong[2]

[1]College of Economics and Trade Management of Hunan University, China and Faculty of Finance and Banking of the Industrial University of Ho Chi Minh City, Vietnam
[2]Business school Hunan University in China

Abstract

This article, author consider the fair value of financial instruments whether it is appropriate for economic development and the volatility of the stock market or not through investors' financial statement analysis and to help the Managers, Investors and someone else understand about reasonable economic information in financial statements. Because, Use of fair Value method plays an important role in measurement of financial instruments and help entity can decrease risk financing. However, Vietnam entities have not applied fair value method yet to revalue financial assets. So value financial assets in financial statements are not exact. This problem impacts on Vietnam financial market for long time. This article shall consider the fair value and historical cost methods measure financial instruments on the stock market through economic transactions to find out the difference of value financial assets, when using two these method to revalue them. The usage of fair value measurement accounting is a necessary factor for the development of Vietnamese stock market. Currently, Vietnamese accounting is using a book method for financial instruments; besides that the fair value accounting has not been thoroughly applied by entities under the standards of international financial instruments accounting.

Keywords: Fair value; Historical cost; Financial statements; Financial instruments; Financial statements

Introduction

When financial assets are transacted by firms, the value of financial assets will be varied from the market price. Therefore, the companies need to apply fair value method to measure them, and ensure that the value of financial assets appropriate real value of assets [1]. Because, information on financial reports play an important role in managers and investors to analyze the accounting data give reliable results, and this information Results as a basis for making management decisions or investing in the stock market. As we see, historical cost is determined the initial value of investment securities and recognition in accounting books, after that value of the securities will be varied according to the market price. Therefore, the historical cost of the securities will be unreasonable in the future. So the firms need to apply fair value method for their value revaluation [2]. In addition, using the fair value method to measure financial assets will help managers, investors avoid financial risks. The IASB'S researches show that the economic crisis is affected by financial risks. Specifically, in 2008 the economic crisis started from the economy of the U.S. and then it spread out the global economy. This economic crisis was due to bad debt credits and frozen properties investment. Besides, the accounting method is also an important factor and impact on the relevance and reliability of Financial Statements. If the accountants apply inexact accounting method, it will lead to inexact financial information in Financial Statements.

So the International Accounting Standard Board (IASB) has issued international accounting standards (IAS), such as IAS 32 (Financial Instruments: Presentation); IAS 39 (Financial Instruments: Recognition and Measurement); international financial reporting standard (IFRS 7 - Financial Instruments: Disclosures) [3] and international financial reporting standard (IFRS 9 - Financial Instruments) for firms' application.

From the above reasons, the author considers the relevance and reliability of Vietnam's current Financial Statements and finds out that when the firms apply the inexact accounting method to evaluate the financial assets, their financial statements will be irrelevant and unreliable. In fact, almost foreign investors and domestic investors don't dare to make more investment on Vietnam stock market. They doubt about the relevance and reliability of Financial Statements. Because, they cannot understand accounting method that the firms have applied to make financial statements. So, they cannot identify that the accounting data in financial statements are exact or inexact. Although the financial statements were audited by auditors, auditor's audit statements are the only reference for the Investors. So they can get risk financial information. Why? This problem needs to discuss, and find out unreasonable financial information or reasonable financial information on Financial Statements. In 2000 the stock market of Vietnam officially went into operation with the operation of the Stock Exchanges in Ho Chi Minh City on July 20, 2000 and in Hanoi on March 8, 2005. But, the Vietnam Stock Exchanges have not been developed for 11 years yet [1](Vietnam stock market loses over $10b of capitalization in 2011). The author assesses the irrelevance and unreliability of financial statements whether it impacts on the Decline of Vietnamese stock market or not and why? Besides, the Vietnam accounting policy is also a factor to make an impact on the Vietnamese stock market. Because, from 2001 to now, the Vietnamese Ministry of Finance issued 26 Vietnamese Accounting Standard (VAS) include: VAS 1- General provisions, VAS 2- Inventories , VAS 3- Property, VAS 4- Intangible Assets, VAS 5- Investment Property, VAS 6- Leases, VAS 7- Investments in Associates, VAS 8- Interests in Joint Ventures, VAS 10- The Effects of Changes in Foreign Exchange Rates, VAS 11- Business Combinations, VAS 14- Revenue, VAS 15- Construction contracts, VAS 16-Borrowing Costs, VAS 17- income tax, VAS 18- Provisions, Contingent Liabilities and

http://en.stockbiz.vn/News/2012/1/3/262166/vietnam-stock-market-loses-over-10b-of-capitalization-in-2011.aspx

***Corresponding author:** Doan Van Dinh, College of Economics and Trade Management of Hunan University, China and Faculty of Finance and Banking of the Industrial University of Ho Chi Minh City, Vietnam
E-mail: citydinhninh@yahoo.com

Contingent Assets, VAS 19- Insurance Contracts, VAS 21- Presentation of Financial Statements, VAS 22- Financial Instruments: Disclosures, VAS 23- Events after the Reporting Period, VAS 24- Statement of Cash Flows, VAS 25- Consolidated and Separate Financial Statements, VAS 26- Related Party Disclosures, VAS 27- Interim Financial Reporting, VAS 28- Operating Segments, VAS 29- Accounting Policies, Changes in Accounting Estimates and Errors, Plant and Equipment, VAS 30- Earnings per Share.

The financial instrument accounting standards play an important role in the measurement and classification of financial instruments. However, the Ministry of Finance has not issued them yet. So the Vietnamese firms are applying the historical cost method to recognize value of financial assets, leading to affect the relevance and reliability of Financial Statements [4].

The Rationale for Fair Value

Currently, it is very difficult to measure fair value of the assets because there have not been any measurement standard to evaluate them. Because of the fair value measurement based on the market, that is not an entity specific measurement. Therefore, measurement of fair value should be determined based on the assumptions that the market would use in pricing the asset or liability. According to the definition of the fair value (paragraph 5) in Statement of Financial Accounting Standards 157 (SFAS 157) as "the price that would be received if an asset is sold or paid to transfer a liability in an orderly transaction between market participants at the measurement date". In case of fair value measurement, the firms should base on the market price or the other methods to evaluate their assets. Generally accepted accounting principles (GAAP) U.S give three methods of determining the assets that are the market approach, income approach, and/or cost approach. The market approach is "The market approach uses prices and other relevant information generated by market transactions involving identical or comparable assets or liabilities (including a business)". The income approach is "The income approach uses valuation techniques to convert future amounts (for example, cash flows or earnings) to a single present amount (discounted). The measurement is based on the value indicated by current market expectations about those future amounts" and the cost approach is "The cost approach is based on the amount that currently would be required to replace the service capacity of an asset (often referred to as current replacement cost). From the perspective of a market participant (seller), the price that would be received for the asset is determined based on the cost to a market participant (buyer) to acquire or construct a substitute asset of comparable utility, adjusted for obsolescence".

The Fair Value Accounting is based on International Accounting Standard (IAS 39 - financial instruments: recognition and measurement), Fair value is defined as "the amount for which an asset could be exchanged, or a liability settled, between knowledgeable, willing parties in an arm's length transaction" (paragraph 9) [5]. Underlying the definition of fair value in IAS 39, International Accounting Standards Board (IASB) gives also three approaches: Market approach, Income approach and Cost approach. Besides, the market approach is observable market prices and information on actual market transactions will be used to estimate the fair value of an asset, a liability; the income approach is the technical approach and will be applied to convert the funds in the future on the present value. (The money from the exploitation and use of assets or cash flow to pay liabilities) and the cost approach is the fair value of an asset and is determined on the basis of considering the cost incurred to obtain an equivalent replacement asset to manufacturing capacity (cash flow to spend to buy production assets). However, within the scope of this article, the author shall deal with a market approach (quoted prices) to evaluate securities and to find out their effects.

The fair value is only an evaluation method, thus the firms can base on IAS 39 or SFAS 157 to choose a suitable measurement method to evaluate the financial assets for financial hedging activities. Before the firms choose the measurement method, the financial assets need to be classified. From the classification of financial assets, the firms can use the method of asset valuation simply and exactly. According to Measurement of Financial Instruments and Recognition of Gains and Losses in International Financial Reporting Standard (IFRS 9 – Financial Instruments) as Assets under [6]:

-Loans and receivables and Held-to-maturity investments are measured by amortized cost method, and then they are recognized in net income when the asset is derecognized or impaired (foreign exchange and impairment are recognized in net income immediately).

-Available-for-sale financial assets and Held for trading are measured by Fair value method. But Available-for-sale financial assets are recognized in other comprehensive income (impairment is recognized in net income immediately) and Held for trading are recognized in Net income immediately.

The Rationale for Historical Cost

Assets are recognized at cost. Cost of assets is recognized by cash or cash equivalents paid payable or evaluated under the fair value of the asset on that date. The original cost of the assets cannot be changed (except) the other regulations in the specific accounting standards. The cost of inventories includes purchase costs, processing costs and other direct costs associated with inventory. Historical cost of assets is used for the initial recognition in the financial statements and to compare its value variable on the market, and is the base for calculating the Gains and losses in income statements. Recognition principle of the historical cost is as follows: all assets need recognizing their historical cost of the assets.

Underlying the definition in IAS 32, cost is defined as follows [7]:

Inventories are assets

a. Held for sale in the ordinary course of business;
b. In the process of production for such sale; or
c. In the form of materials or supplies to be consumed in the production process or in the rendering of services. And Net realizable value is the estimated selling price in the ordinary course of business less the estimated costs of completion and the estimated costs necessary to make the sale. Fair value is the amount for which an asset could be exchanged, or a liability settled, between Knowledgeable, willing parties in an arm's length transaction. This case, the firm needs to determine the inventory value according to two measurement methods that are net realizable value and fair value of the inventory. Underlying also the definition in IAS 2, the inventory's value needs to be evaluated in the process of business, when their values are variable in the market. The assumptions that: firm purchased 2,000 shares, at $ 10 per shares in 31/3/N, and the firm paid cash. The next month hypothesis, the firm sell 2,000 shares with selling price $ 12 per share. On 31/12/N, in case, the firm has not sold securities and then the market price can increase or reduced. Meanwhile, the inventory stock value of the firm will be variable; assuming that the stock price drops $ 8 per share, the firm loses $ 2 per share. Now, the firm needs

to adjust the value of securities at fair value. In case, the firm doesn't adjust the historical cost of the securities they will be irrelevant on the balance sheet. So, historical cost is irrelevant longer. Therefore, assets on the balance sheet are recorded at historical costs until sold (Table 1).

Cost-based IFRS measures

According to international accounting standards IFRS the historical-cost method is stated in different standards for different accounting objects such as [8-14]:

- Few things measured at historical cost:
  - Unimpaired land (IAS 16 + IAS 40 cost model)
  - Unimpaired indefinite life intangibles (IAS 38)
  - Unimpaired inventories (IAS 2)
- Cost-based measures are more common
  - Unimpaired depreciated historic cost (IAS 16)
  - Unimpaired amortized historical cost (IAS 38)
  - Amortized cost (IFRS 9)

Through the guidelines of international accounting standards given above, show that recording assets at historical cost right after being purchased is essential in ensuring accuracy of the property after formation. However, the asset value will change over time and be influenced by factors of market value, if assets are still recorded at the historical cost, then the asset value is unsuitable to be recorded and mentioned in the financial statements to be presented by the enterprise. Hence it is inevitable that the original value of assets needs to be replaced by the fair value. The international accounting standards have well adopted the measurement and recognition of assets at the fair value to match the current assets (Table 2) [15].

The System of Vietnamese Accounting Standards

The Vietnamese accounting standards are not much different from international accounting standards, particularly for accounting standards of inventory. However, the standards IAS 16, IAS 38 and VAS 3, VAS 4 have basic differences; these differences lead to differences between information on Vietnam's financial statements and international financial statements. Additionally, the Accounting Standards System of Vietnam lacks some basic standards for the financial instruments of accounting, which is the reason why fair value methods are not being applied for calculating assets on the financial statements of Vietnam [16].

Presently, the financial statements of Vietnam still apply the historical cost method, in the case of decreased inventory price; it is adjusted by the provisional method. The inventory is defined by Standard No. 2 VAS 02: "The inventory is calculated at original cost. Where the net realizable value that is lower than the original cost must be calculated according to the net realizable value". For financial instruments, the Vietnamese accounting system has no financial instruments standard

Date	Account and Explanation	Debits	Credits
31/3/N	Common securities	$ 20,000	
Initial recognition	Cash		$20,000
Revenue - Financial activities recognition	Cash	$24,000	
	Common securities		$ 20,000
	Revenue - Financial activities		$4,000

Table 1: Sale of Equipment at Historical Cost.

that can be implemented. Therefore, Vietnamese firms still apply the historical cost method by the following rules [17-23]:

1. Short-term investment securities must be recorded in the accounting books according to the actual purchase of securities (at original cost) including: purchase price (+) purchase cost (if any), such as costs of brokering, transactions, information supply, tax, fee and banking fee.
2. Short-term investment securities, including long-term securities are purchased for sale in the stock market which can recover capital for a period of not more than one year.
3. At the end of the accounting year, if the market value of short-term investment securities is lower than the original price, accounting for the value impairment of short-term investment securities.
4. The accountant must open detailed books to track each type of short-term investment securities (In each class of shares, bonds, securities with different values; under each investment partner; each type of face value and the actual purchase price).

In the case of declining stock prices, the enterprises must make provision for a reduced price at the end of the accounting year under the following principles [24-26]:

1. The appropriation and reversal of provision for value impairment of short-term investments are made at the time of closing the accounting books for presentation of the yearly financial statements. For the businesses that make the interim financial statements, if there are any big changes in provision, the appropriation or reversal of provision will be adjusted.
2. Making provision for value impairment of short-term investments is determined by the difference between the net realizable value (market value) and the historical cost recorded in the accounting books. If the amount of the provision being made in this period is higher than the provisional balance being made at the end of the previous accounting period, the difference is recognized in financial costs in the period. If the amount of the provision made this year is lower than the provisional balance been recognized in the accounting books, the difference shall be recorded at reduced price from the financial cost.
3. Conditions of appropriation of provision for value impairment of short term investments are as follows:

- The enterprises can make legal investment in securities;

- Freely being purchased and sold on the market at the time of inventory and presentation of the financial statements with the market price down as compared with the original price recorded in the accounting books (for securities that are not freely traded, cannot make provision).

4. The enterprises must make provisions for each type of short-term investment security when fluctuations of decreased prices happen at the end of the accounting period by the following formula 1:

Provision for decreased value of short-term investment securities = Number of securities with decreased price at the end of yearly accounting period X [The original price of securities recorded in the accounting books - Market price of short-term investment securities]

The enterprises must determine the amount of provision to set up for each type of short-term investment security whose price are

Asset Type	Measurement at Initial Recognition	Cost Model	Basis of Impairment Test
IAS 2 *Inventory*	Cost of purchase and/or conversion costs, transportation costs and costs to get the item in condition for sale	Cost unless impaired	Lower of initial recognition cost and net realizable value
IAS 16 Property, Plant and Equipment	Purchase costs + construction costs + transportation costs and costs to get the item in working condition as intended by management	Accounting policy choice: cost less accumulated depreciation and impairment, if any	Compare carrying amount to recoverable amount. The recoverable amount is greater of value in use and fair value less disposal costs (IAS 36)
IAS 38 Intangibles Assets	Purchase costs + development costs + transportation costs and costs to get the item in working condition as intended by management	Accounting policy choice: cost less accumulated amortization (unless indefinite life asset) and amortization, if any	
IAS 40 Investment Property	Cost including transaction costs	Accounting policy choice: cost less accumulated depreciation (unless land) and impairment(if any)	
IFRS 9 Financial Instruments	Fair value	For particular business models amortized cost	IAS 39 specifies impairment rules

Table 2: Process of Asset Measurement.

decreased and they are synthesized into a detailed provision list for the decline in security price and comparing with data made at the end of the previous accounting period to determine more provision or reversal of the reduced financial costs.

Provisions for long-term investments are made in principle as follows [27-29]:

1. The appropriation and reversal of provision for value impairment of long-term investments are made at the time of the yearly accounting period. For the enterprises who are approved by the Ministry of Finance to apply fiscal year other than the calendar year (fiscal year does not begin on January 1 and not end on December 31 every year), the time for provision is the last day of the fiscal year. For the businesses that make the interim financial statements, if there are any big changes in provision, the appropriation or reversal of provision will be adjusted at the end of the interim accounting period (quarterly accounting period).
2. The provision for value impairment of long term investments must be made in accordance with the rules of each type of long-term investment. The provision level is determined by the difference between the net realizable values (market price) or withdrawn investments and the original price recorded in the accounting books. If the amount of the provision for this year is higher than the provisional balance recorded in the accounting books, the difference shall be recognized in business & production expenses in the period. If the amount of the provision which is made in this year is lower than the provisional balance which was made in last year but not used up, the difference shall be recorded reduction in the business & production expenses.
3. The preparation and treatment of provision for value impairment of long-term investment securities are made at the end of the fiscal year if the market price of the long-term investment securities is often lower than the original price recorded in the accounting books.

Conditions of appropriation of provisions for value impairment of long-term securities are as follows:

- The enterprises make legal investment in securities;

- Freely being purchased and sold on the market at the time of inventory and presentation of the financial statements with the market price down as compared with the original price recorded in the accounting books.

4. The enterprises must make provisions for each type of short-term investment security when fluctuations of decreased prices happen at the end of the accounting period by the following formula 2:

Provision for decreased value of short-term investment securities for next year	=	Number of securities with [decreased price at presentation time of yearly financial statements	X	The original price of securities recorded in] the accounting books Market price of short -term investment securities

The enterprises must determine the amount of provisions to set up for each type of long-term investment security whose prices are decreased and then they are synthesized into a detailed provision list of declining security prices and compared with data which was formulated at the end of last year but not used up to determine more provision or reversal of the reduced financial costs.

Data Analysis and the impact it has on the Relevance and Reliability of Financial Statements

The stock market's development depends on the relevance and reliability of financial statements through investors. Therefore, the use of the historical cost method by Vietnamese firms is inappropriate because it makes a provision for impairment in asset value according to the principles mentioned above, the information in the financial statements did not reflect the nature of the assets at the time when the financial statements are presented. Below are some accounting assumptions that prove the relevance and reliability of financial statements (Tables 3-5):

Using Historical cost.

Accounting assumption:

On date 19/02/2012, the firm A bought $ 1,555 of common stocks that are, face value of a share is $10, brokerage fees of share are $2. This time, current price of a share is $20.

On date 12/8/2012, the firm sold $555 of common stocks, current price of a share is $25, Brokerage fees of share are $1.

- The first case: on the 31/12/2012, Firm A with a debit balance of securities is 1,000,000 shares. This time, Current price of security is$30.

- The second case: On 31/12/2012, Firm A has a debit balance of securities are 1,000,000 shares. Current price of Security is $15.

Determinant of double entry is as follows:

* The amounts of 1,555,000 shares are purchased.

* The amounts of 555,000 shares are sold.

Using fair value method

The same Accounting assumption as above:

On date 19/02/2012, the firm A bought 1,555,000 of common stocks with a face value of a share of $10, brokerage fees of the share is $2.

This time, current price of a share is $20.

On date 12/8/2012, the firm sold 555,000 of common stocks, current price of a share is $25, Brokerage fees of share are $1.

- ***The first case:*** on the 31/12/2012, Firm A with a debit balance of securities is 1,000,000 shares. This time, quoted price of securities in an active market is $30 per share.

- ***The second case:*** On 31/12/2012, Firm A with a debit balance of securities is 1,000,000 shares; quoted price of securities in an active market is $15 per share.

Solution 3

The part of the determinant of double entry is same as a determinant of double entry of solution 1. However, there is a different result of financial reporting as follows.

- ***The first case:*** on date 31/12/2012, the firm revalues fair value of the security base on securities debit balance when the firm forms financial reporting of accounting period.

- When a quoted price of security in an active stock market is $30, it means that the firm needs to adjust the security's value by quoting prices in an active stock market. Now the quoted price is higher than historical cost: ($30 – $22) = $8; (1,000,000 shares x $8) = $8,000,000.

* ***Write – up.***

- The second case: When a quoted price of security in an active market is $15 per share, that means, the firm needs to adjust the security's value by quoting prices in an active market. Now the quoted price is less than historical cost: ($15 – $22) = ($7); (1,000,000 shares x $7) = $7,000,000. ****Write – down.***

Discussion and Conclusion of How Financial Statements have an Impact on the Vietnamese Stock Market

Discussion about the impact of the relevance and reliability of financial statements

Problem 1: Unmatched accounting of the historical cost method: Assets which are available-for-sale and financial assets cannot use the historical cost method for recognizing and presenting the accounting year-end financial statements. Because, the security value is a type of financial asset held for trading, their value is usually a variable on the stock market. Therefore, the firms' application of this method will affect the suitability of the assets held for trading. The results of the above analysis show that when the firms use the historical cost method, the results in the income statement are inappropriate for the fair value of the assets.

- In a scenario whereby security prices increased at the time when the year-end financial statement is presented, then the security value on the market is $30, while the security value on the balance sheet still presents the original value that is $22. A different ratio compared with the original price is 36%, the greater the difference rate is then the greater the error degree of current security's price will be, leading to the information on financial statements to have a greater difference than the actual security value at the time when financial statements are presented. This difference has clearly affected the income statement and balance sheet. For the income statement of solution 1, the business results only reflect securities trading that have already occurred, but do not reflect the actual value of inventory securities that have brought profits for the business. The security prices rise on the stock market meaning that the profits that were not achieved are also increasing but the income statement has not presented this item. The balance sheets also do not show the increased value of securities at the market price but only show retained achieved from financial activities.

- In the case of a security's price falling at the time when financial statements are presented as the above analysis depicts the security's price will drop to $15. If the securities are sold with this price at this time, the securities shall be lost, because the market price is lower than the original price of securities. To preserve capital, according to the Vietnamese accounting system, the entities are required to make financial provision at accounting period. This financial provision level is made on the basis of the hedge accounting for financial activities, the first formula is for the provision for short-term investments and the second formula of accounting estimates is for provision for long-term investments. The above assumptions applied the first formula and got decreased and different results in the stock market compared to the original price, the decreasing rate is 32%. This ratio reflects the correct fluctuation level of security prices on the stock market at the time when financial statements are presented. However, according to this method, the company made a provision appropriate for short-term investments without revaluation of fair value of securities on the stock market price. This made the stock inventory value of financial statements not change as a result of solution 2 (stock inventory value of solution 1 and the stock inventory value of solution 2 is equal to $22,000,000).

The table of the income statement did not reflect the actual results from financial activities. Because at the time of securities sale, the security's price did not reduce, the business got profits. But the security's price unexpectedly fell last year, forcing the business to make a stock provision. The security provision made financial costs increase, leading to a drop in financial profits that exceed a safe level. In this case, the financial profits fell below the breakeven point; the business could not get the profits that were lost. Actually, the business still got profits of $1,110,000 to replace the lost profits ($5,890,000) as expressed in the results of the income statement in solution 2. For the balance sheet, the short-term investment provision increases because the business makes provision for a decreased security's price, but the securities investment item does not change, it still remains original. Thus, the securities investment item did not reflect the true market price of the securities at the time when financial statements are presented. Specifically, the security's price at this time has dropped to $15,000,000, instead of $22,000,000 as an analysis result above. Although, the ultimate results of the two methods are the same and is $28,320,000, but the items for analysis will have different results. When the retained earnings item on the balance sheet is also down, leading to a decrease of total capital source. Otherwise, the retained earnings item on the balance sheet has not been shown correctly. Because the reduced capital source is affected by the reduced value of inventory security, but profits from trading

Date	Account and Explanation	Debits	Credits
19/02/2012, shares are purchased.	Securities.	$34,210,000	
	Cash.		$34,210,000
12/8/2012, shares are sold.	Cash.	$13,875,000	
	Securities.	-	$12,210,000
	Revenue – Financial activities.		$1,665,000
Arising of financial expenses of brokerage.	Financial expenses	$555,000	
	Cash.		$555,000

Note: (1,555,000 shares x $22) = $34,210,000; (555,000 shares x $25) = $13,875,000; (555,000 shares x $22) = $12,210,000; (555,000 shares x $3) = $1,665,000; (555,000 shares x $1) = $555,000.

The first case: on the 31/12/2012, Firm A has a debit balance of securities of 1,000,000 shares; price of security is $30. This case, the Vietnamese accounting system states that the prices of securities are not adjusted at "market prices" when shares' prices increasing arise in the stock market.

- Debit balance of cash: $13,875,000 - $555,000 $ equal to $13,320,000.
- Debit balance of Securities investments: 1,000,000 shares x $22 equal to $22,000,000.
1. The result of income statement on 31/12/2012:

- Revenue – Financial activities: (1)	**$1,665,000**
- Financial expenses: (2)	**$ 555,000**
- Profit after Income Tax (3) = (1) – (2)	**$1,110,000**

2. The result of Balance sheet on 31/12/2012:
A. Assets:

1) Cash:	**$13,320,000**
2) Investment securities:	**$22,000,000**
3) Provision for short - term investments *:$	**$0,000**
4) Total Assets:	**$35,320,000**

B. Equity:

1) Investment securities:	**$12,210,000**
2) Common stock:	**$22,000,000**
3) Retained Earnings:	**$1,110,000**
4) Total Equity:	**$35,320,000**

In the above case, A profits of company A is: $1,110,000, when the market price of securities increases. Company A didn't revalue value securities. So profits of sale securities were presented in Income statements. The profit estimate of value securities increasing weren't presented in income statements and balance sheet.

For assumption above:

The second case: On 31/12/2012, (the securities are dropping in price in the stock market at the end of the accounting period). Firm A has a debit balance of securities of 1,000,000 shares. Security price is $15 per share. This case, the Vietnamese accounting system states that the prices of securities are adjusted at "market price" when shares are dropped in, this time, the current price of a share is $15 per share (the historical cost of a share is $22). This means that historical cost > current price leads to the firm A making provision for impairment of securities.
Solution 2

The principle of the Vietnamese accounting system follows.

Provision for short term securities investment rate = Total of provision for short term security investments x [Historical cost of short term security investments – Fair value of short term security investments]: 1,000,000 shares x ($15– $22) equal to $7,000,000.

Table 3: Purchase and Sale of securities at Historical Cost Method.

activities of securities have still increased, simultaneously increasing the retained earnings of $1,110,000, instead of $5,890,000 as on the balance sheet.

In the Vietnamese accounting system businesses usually apply the historical cost method for inventory securities when they have to present financial statements but this is irrelevant to the fact that the financial statements represent the variability of the security's price which affects the rationality and reliability of the financial statements. The historical cost method does not reflect the volatility of the security value on the financial statements and does not provide the necessary information to investors. Under international accounting standards, the historical cost method is not applied and not presented in financial statements for financial assets.

Problem 2: The match accounting principle of the fair value method: The historical cost principles still have an initial recognition about the asset value so to ensure that the quality of accounting information presented in financial statements is reliable. However, the asset value will be changed under fluctuation in the market on the different phases.

Additionally, the asset value is also worn invisible, because the assets are no longer appropriate in design, decreased quality leading to decline in the asset value. For this reason, the fair value method is applied for asset revaluation when making financial statements. So, if the firms have still applied the historical cost method, the assets would have been longer irrelevant to the market value, especially for the financial assets of Available-for-sale and Held for trading, the firms should apply the

Date	Account and Explanation	Debits	Credits
31/12/2012, Provision for short – term securities investment.	Financial expenses.	$7,000,000	
	Provision for Securities impairment		$7,000,000

And now,	
- Debit balance of Financial expenses:	**$7,000,000 + $555,000 = $7, 555, 0000.**
- Debit balance of cash:	**$13,875,000 - $555,000 $ equal to $13,320,000.**
- Debit balance of Securities investments:	**1,000,000 shares x $22 equal to $22,000,000.**
1. **The result of income statement on 31/12/2012:**	
- Revenue – Financial activities: (1)	**$1,665,000**
- Financial expenses: (2)	**$ 7, 555, 0000**
- Profit after Income Tax (3) = (1) – (2)	**($ 5,890,000)**
2. **The result of Balance sheet on 31/12/2012:**	
A. Assets:	
1). Cash:	**$13,320,000**
2). Investment securities:	**$22,000,000**
3). Provision for short – term investments *:	**($ 7,000,000)**
4) Total Assets:	**$28,320,000**
B. Equity:	
1). Investment securities:	**$12,210,000**
2). Common stock:	**$22,000,000**
3). Retained Earnings:	**($5,890,000)**
4). Total Equity:	**$28,320,000**

In the second case: company A applies Vietnam provision accounting methods, the profits in income statements is loss , and value financial assets on the balance sheet is reduced. Financial statements results did not reflect the true nature of financial asset's value. Actually, the company A still has gained profit from a securities sale. The part of losses is only being a valuation of financial assets in the future. We can see the difference profits in the financial statements when using the fair value method and historical cost to revalue financial assets. The author uses the second method. That is the fair value method below:

Table 4: Purchase and Sale of securities at Historical Cost Method.

fair value method to evaluate the assets at the time of financial statement presentation. The benefit of this method is to get high reliability of the information on the financial statements, and measure the market value of the securities. Besides, the enterprises apply the fair value method for financial risk prevention and effective measurement of the financial assets. For assets on hold for trading, according to the international accounting standards, no provisions for it but use the fair value method for revaluation through loss/profit. Thus, the assets always guarantee their real value and the high relevance and reliability in the financial statements are better. We may consider the results in the financial statements through the above assumptions as follows:

In regards to the results presented on income statements, there are two items to be recorded concerning the two different profit parts; these profits are from financial activities and other comprehensive incomes. These two items are important for analyzing financial statements and are helpful to investors because they can easily see where the profits come from: Stock trading activities or from the gains or losses that come from different levels of the asset prices. Specifically, when a business sells its securities it gets a profit of $1,110,000, because the stock prices increase at this time and an unrealized profit becomes $8,000,000 due to increase in security price in the market at the time of financial statement presentation. This information is very important for the stock investors, because they can immediately see the future profits given by their stock inventory. So, they can make decisions in the investment or not.

For the balance sheet, the inventory item clearly presents the security value when the security prices increase in the market. Specifically, when the security prices in the market were increased to $30 in 31/12/2012, on the short-term stock investment item the value also changes to $30,000,000. These results indicate that security prices in the market are favorable for investors and if the securities are sold at this time, they will get profits of $8,000,000. For the equity item, it also shows two separate items that are retained earnings and other comprehensive income. These items help the investors to clearly see the capital source that increased from security activities that have been executed and the capital source that increased from security activities but that have not been executed yet. From this information investors may evaluate the potential value and profitability of the securities in the future such as: the profit brought from security activities is $1,110,000, the unrealized profit is $8,000,000.

When the security prices fall, the results in the financial statements also show the security trading effectiveness and future damages. The income statements show the increased profits and lost profits, from this information, the investors can avoid the financial risks. Because two items are separate, the investors see the damage of the inventory security and can use the accounting hedge method or hedge derivative instruments (usage of the hedge derivative instruments will be studied in the next topic). Based on the above hypothesis, the profits from financial activities are $1,110,000 and the unrealized loss is $7,000,000. The realized profits from financial activities show that the company still gets profits and is very productive in the financial year. The unrealized loss is in the information that the investors are interested in for making reasonable and timely decisions. For the capital source, the inventory security value is reduced to $15,000,000 as the market prices are in the item of short-term investment securities. This value indicates that security prices in the market pose a disadvantage for the investors and the investors know the real value of financial assets. This is useful information for financial analyses as a means of assessing the results of business assets. For the capital source, two separate items also help the investors to see the realized profits and unrealized losses.

Problem 3: The results of difference between the use of historical cost method and fair value method: The results in Table 6 show the

Date	Account and Explanation	Debits	Credits
- ***The first case:*** 31/12/2012, the quoted price is higher than historical Common securities:. cost. * ***Write – up.***	Common securities:	$8,000,000	
	Other comprehensive income		$8,000,000
- ***The second case***: 31/12/2012, the quoted price is less than historical cost. ****Write – down.***	Other comprehensive income.	$7,000,000	
	Common securities		$7,000,000

Debit balance of securities is $30,000,000: ($22,000,000 + $8,000,000).

- The result of first case:

1. The result of income statement on 31/12/2012:

- Revenue – Financial activities: (1)	**$1,665,000**
- Financial expenses: (2)	**$ 555. 0000**
- Profit after Income Tax (3) = (1) – (2)	**$1.110.000**
- Other Comprehensive Income (gain/loss): (4)	**$8.000.000**
- Total Profit: (5) = (3) + (4):	**$9.110.000**

2. The result of Balance sheet on 31/12/2012:

A. Assets:	
1). Cash:	**$13,320,000**
2). Investment securities:	**$30,000,000**
3). Provision for short – term investments *:	**000.000**
4) Total Assets:	**$43.320.000**
B. Equity:	
1). Investment securities:	**$12,210,000**
2). Common stock:	**$22,000,000**
3). Retained Earnings:	**$1.110.000**
4). Net Other Comprehensive Income. (Gain/loss):	**$8.000.000**
4). Total Equity:	**$43.320.000**

- The result of second case:

*** Debit balance of securities is $15,000,000: ($22,000,000 - $7,000,000).**

1. The result of income statement on 31/12/2012:

- Revenue – Financial activities: (1)	**$1,665,000**
- Financial expenses: (2)	**$555, 0000**
- Profit after Income Tax (3) = (1) – (2)	**$1.110.000**
- Other Comprehensive Income (gain/loss): (4)	**($7.000.000)**
- Total Profit: (5) = (3) + (4):	**($5.890.000)**

2. The result of Balance sheet of 31/12/2012:

A. Assets:	
1). Cash:	**$13,320,000**
2). Investment securities:	**$15,000,000**
3). Provision for short – term investments *:	**000.000**
4) Total Assets:	**$28.320.000**
B. Equity:	
1). Investment securities:	**$12,210,000**
2). Common stock:	**$22,000,000**
3). Retained Earnings:	**$1.110.000**
4). Net Other Comprehensive Income. (Gain/loss):	**($7.000.000)**
4). Total Equity:	**$28.320.000**

The analysis of data and results of the financial statements shown above demonstrates the interactive impacts to the financial markets through investors. The financial information on the financial statements plays an important role in financial analysis and the provision of economic targets for the investors to evaluate the profitability or the financial health of a quoted company on the stock market. To analyze and clarify how these factors affect the stock market, as well as investors' comments on Vietnam's financial statements and the solutions for Vietnam's stock market development will be presented in the discussion part.

Table 5: Purchase and Sale of securities at Fair value method.

difference in percentage rate in a scenario whereby there is an increased security's price. Using the historical cost method, the difference in profit is 88%, when security prices reduce the total income there is no difference (0%). However, the income after tax has a big difference (631%) and some items also have differences [30].

The results of the Table 7 above, show that a scenario whereby there is a decreased security's price, the total assets and total capital have no difference when using two methods (0%). However, there is a big difference in other items such as: Investment securities with a difference of 47%, Retained Earnings with a big difference of 631 % and Net Other Comprehensive Income (gain/loss) with a difference of 100 %. In a scenario whereby there is an increased security's price, there are differences in total assets and total capital (18%), these differences are due to that the historical cost method does not recognize the increased securities. Some items in the balance sheet also have differences such as: Investment securities with a difference of 47%, Retained Earnings with a difference of 631 % but these basic differences have a large effect on the quality and reliability of financial statements. The items presented in financial statements are impact factors of the financial analysis results that was done by investors, this part will be elaborated further in problem 4 [31].

Problem 4: The items presented in the financial statements are analysis of security targets: The accounting information presented in financial statements provides some basic elements to be used by investors, these elements assist in assessing the profitability of investing in securities and assist in analyzing indicators related to investments in the stock market, investors base their decisions upon these indicators. The basic criterion used to analyze security investment is as follows:

* Assuming usage of profitability indicators and usage of the company A's assets, the financial statement is as follows:

$$\text{Return on Assets } (\text{ROA})\text{H} = \frac{\$1{,}110{,}000}{\$35{,}320{,}000} \text{ x } 100\% = 3\%$$

$$\text{Return on Assets } (\text{ROA})\text{F} = \frac{\$1{,}110{,}000}{\$43{,}320{,}000} \text{ x } 100\% = 2.6\%$$

✓ **In the case of a decreased security's price:**

$$\text{Return on Assets } (\text{ROA})_{\text{H}} = \frac{\$5{,}890{,}000}{\$28{,}320{,}000} \text{ x } 100\% = 21\%$$

$$\text{Return on Assets } (\text{ROA})_{\text{F}} = \frac{\$1{,}110{,}000}{\$28{,}320{,}000} \text{ x } 100\% = 4\%$$

Through the above analyzed data it shows that there is a difference from the result of return on assets. In the case of increased security prices, the return on assets ROA (H) is equal to 3% that means:

ROA provides the investors with information about the profits generated from the investment capital (or assets). The ROA for joint-stock firms has a big difference and depends on business fields. That is why when using ROA to compare firms, it is better to compare each company's ROA over years and compare it among similar firms. Assets of a company are formed from loan capital and equity both funds are used to finance the company's activities. The effect of the transfer of investment capital into the profit is shown by ROA. The higher ROA is better because the company is earning more money on less investment. The analyzed data above shows that there is a difference from the result of return on assets. In the case of security price increases, the profitability ratio of ROA (H) is equal to 3% > ROA (F) is equal to 2, 6% that means: if the Company uses this method, the ROA is higher than ROA of the fair value method. Nevertheless, this ROA (H) is unreal because the company ignored the increased security's value when making financial statements. In the case of a decreased security's price, ROA (H) and ROA (F) have a big difference such as: ROA (F) is equal to -21 % much less than ROA (H) is equal to 4 %. If the investors use the result of ROA (H) to make decisions in security investment, they will get many risks. This result reflects unrealistic and not highly reliable information as the above analysis. For ROA(H) is equal to 4 %, showing that the company still gets profits but only has unrealized losses due to decreased price of inventory security.

Conclusions

From the problems mentioned above, it shows that the fair value method is always appropriate and contains high reliability of financial information. The information provided by financial statements brings great benefits to investors; for businesses have reliable information for financial analysis. Therefore investors have a basis for making investment strategies that bring high effectiveness to the economy. The international standard system emphasizes that the fair value method should be applied for the hedge financial activities or revaluation of financial assets.

The results also show that the accounting system is very important for the application of collecting data and incidental business data processing. In this phase, it is necessary for firms to apply appropriate accounting methods for economic transactions to ensure that the accounting information correctly reflects the economic nature. The accounting system affects the chain, the chain starts from recognizing, processing and presenting the financial statement and eventually released to the public. When the financial statements are released to the public, it is a period of great influence for the stock market through decisions taken by those who use financial statements. Thus, the use of the fair value accounting method should be comprehensively and fully applied. The Vietnamese accounting system needs to be reviewed, it lacks fair value accounting instruments that can be applied by firms; this has a big impact on the stock market. Presently, Vietnam's stock market has developed in two areas of Hanoi and Ho Chi Minh City and has about 500 quoted local firms; the number of participating firms is large enough to impact the Vietnam's stock market [32]. Therefore, the Vietnamese accounting system needs a comprehensive reform and to quickly complete accounting standards of financial instruments; these are a set of standards that are very important for firms to apply on the financial hedge and very important to apply to the category of financial assets and liability assets. The Vietnamese stock market has developed since the year 2000 up to now, more than a decade, but there are still no financial instruments of accounting standards applicable for this field. In today's environment, the Vietnamese Accounting System should apply the fair value method for financial asset evaluation instead of using the historical cost method to evaluate financial assets as currently [33]. This helps investors to get full and correct information to make

Items	Results		Different ratio ((H-F)/F)x100%
	Historical cost method (H)	Fair value method (F)	
In the case of an increased price.			
- Revenue – Financial activities.	1,665,000	1,665,000	0%
- Financial expenses.	555,000	555,000	0%
Profit After Income Tax	**1,110,000**	**1,110,000**	**0%**
Other comprehensive income.		**8,000,000**	**-100%**
Total profits	**1,110,000**	**9,110,000**	**-88%**
In the case of a decreased price.			
- Revenue – Financial activities.	1,665,000	1,665,000	0%
- Financial expenses.	7,555,000	555,000	1261%
Profit After Income Tax	**(5,890,000)**	**1,110,000**	**-631%**
Other comprehensive income.		**(7,000,000)**	**-100%**
Total profits	**(5,890,000)**	**(5,890,000)**	**0%**

Unit: $

Table 6: Comparison of income.

http://www.thesaigontimes.vn/Home/taichinh/chungkhoan/83489/Bao-cao-tai-chinh-nen-huong-toi-nha-dau-tu.html

Items	Results		Different ratio
	Historical cost method (H)	Fair value method (F)	((H-F)/F)x100%
In the case of an increased price.			
Assets.			
- Current assets.	13,320,000	13,320,000	0%
- Investment securities.	22,000,000	30,000,000	-27%
- Provision for short – term investments *			
Total assets.	**35,320,000**	**43,320,000**	**-18%**
Equity.			
- Investment capital.	12,210,000	12,210,000	0%
- Common stock	22,000,000	22,000,000	0%
Retained Earnings	**1,110,000**	**1,110,000**	**0%**
Net Other Comprehensive Income. (Gain/loss)		**8,000,000**	**-100%**
Total Equity.	**35,320,000**	**43,320,000**	**-18%**
In the case of a decreased price.			
Assets.			
- Current assets.	13,320,000	13,320,000	0%
- Investment securities.	22,000,000	15,000,000	47%
- Provision for short – term investments *	(7,000,000)		
Total assets.	**28,320,000**	**28,320,000**	0%
Equity.			
- Investment capital.	12,210,000	12,210,000	0%
- Common stock	22,000,000	22,000,000	0%
Retained Earnings	**(5,890,000)**	**1,110,000**	**-631%**
Net Other Comprehensive Income. (Gain/loss)		**(7,000,000)**	**-100%**
Total Equity.	**28,320,000**	**28,320,000**	**0%**

Unit: $

Table 7: Comparison of balance sheets.

effective investments. According to the plan of the Ministry of Finance, from now to the year 2015 the standard system will be completed. In particular, for the financial instruments standard system, Vietnam will study the basic principles of international standards, and then re-evaluate to set up standards specific to Vietnam. This is a good sign for the Vietnamese stock market; there will be major changes in the completeness of accounting standards this change will ensure that appropriate accounting principles are used towards the economy and international rules [34,35].

[2]In fact, the implementation of Vietnamese accounting standards meets great difficulties, because in the accounting standard system, there are many guidance circulars which the accounting industry often follows without consulting accounting standards consequently this leads the accounting industry to become passive and compliant. In the opinion of Mr. Bui Hoang Hai, Deputy Director under the Release Management Department of the State Securities Committee, Vietnam now has 26 Vietnamese accounting standards, but in reality, the supervision of full implementation of 26 standards is difficult. So according to Mr. Hai's opinion, the implementation of standards is not more important than actually keeping the enterprises under discipline in the implementation of standards, so that investors are not misled into believing in the information presented on the enterprises financial statements. He also gives examples of administrative decisions for governance. Mr. Dang Thai Hung, Director of the Accounting Regime Department of the Ministry of Finance said that: for treatment of the exchange rate difference, the accounting standards allow allocation into the financial activity costs but in accordance with Circular No. 201/2009/C-MOF the allocation is made in 5 years. Hence, the enterprises will not be lost if following this circular. Currently, the Ministry of Finance has changed the above circular and issued the same as in the accounting standards to avoid the aforesaid phenomenon. But the accounting policies issued by micro- managers have an impact on the stock market through investors. In particular, the biggest impacts are that the financial analysis targets are based on the items on financial statements of quoted firms. Therefore, the financial statements of the enterprises with high reliability and reasonability will bring benefits to the economy or stock market. If financial statements are inappropriate and lack reliability subsequently they will constrain the economy and the stock market. It will impact any economy or nation but not only one country, such as Vietnam's economy.

References

1. Laux C, Leuz C (2009) Did Fair-Value Accounting Contribute to the Financial Crisis? National Bureau of Economic Research, NBER Working Paper 15515.
2. Ryan SG (2008) Fair Value Accounting: Understanding The Issues Raised by the Credit Crunch. Council of Institutional Investors, New York University, NY, USA.
3. Historical Cost and Fair Value Accounting: Relevance and Reliability Revisited.
4. International Accounting Standard (2011), IAS 39 (Financial Instruments: Recognition and Measurement).
5. International Accounting Standard Board "IASB" (2012) IFRS 9: Financial Instruments.
6. International Accounting Standard (2003) IAS 32 (Financial Instruments: Presentation).
7. International Accounting Standard (2005) IFRS 7 (Financial Instruments: Disclosures).
8. International Accounting Standard (2008) IAS 40 (Investment Property).
9. International Accounting Standard (1991) IAS 30 (Disclosures in the Financial Statements of Banks and Similar Financial Institutions).
10. International Accounting Standard (2008) IAS 38 (Intangible Assets).
11. International Accounting Standard (2008) IAS 16 (Property, Plant and Equipment).
12. International Accounting Standard (2008) IAS 2 (Inventories).
13. International Accounting Standard Board "IASB" (2008) IAS 39: Financial Instruments: Recognition And Measurement.
14. Bischof J, Elbert M (2007) IAS 39 and basis in rick perception of financial instruments. Universitat Mannheim, Deutsche, Germany.
15. Horton J, Macve R (2000) 'Fair value' For Financial Instruments: How Erasing Theory is leading To Unworkable Global Accounting Standard Performance Reporting. The Australian Accounting Reviews 11: 26-39.
16. Ow Yong KK, Fair Value Accounting: SFAS 157 and IAS 39 2of 6.
17. Ministry of Finance (2009) Circular No. 210/2009/C -MOF, 06/11/2007.
18. Minister of Finance (2001) Vietnam accounting standard 2 (Inventories), 31/12/2001.
19. Minister of Finance, (2001), Vietnam accounting standard 3, Tangible fixed assets, 31/12/2001.
20. Minister of Finance (2005) Vietnam accounting standard 22, Disclosures in the Financial Statements of Banks and Similar Financial Institutions, 15/02/2005.
21. Minister of Finance (2003) Vietnam accounting standard 5, Investment property, 30/12/2003.
22. Minister of Finance (2001) Vietnam accounting standard 4, Intangible fixed assets, 30/12/2003.
23. Ministry of Finance (2006) Decision No. 15/2006/QD-MOF, 15/7/2006.
24. Ministry of Finance (1995) Decision No. 1141-TC/Q Đ/C ĐKT, 1/ 11/1995.
25. Ministry of Finance (2001) Decision No. 149/2001/Q Đ-BTC, 31/12/2001.
26. Ministry of Finance (2002) Decision No. 165/2002/ Q Đ-BTC, 31/12/2002.
27. Ministry of Finance (2003) Decision No. 234/2003/ Q Đ-BTC, 31/12/2003.

28. Ministry of Finance (2005) Decision No. 12/2005/ Q Đ-BTC, 15/2/2005.

29. Ministry of Finance (2005) Decision No. 100/2005/ Q Đ-BTC, 18/12/2005.

30. PricewaterhouseCoopers (2008) Similarities and Differences: A Comparison of IFRS and Thai GAAP, Vietnamese GAAP, Cambodian GAAP and Laos GAA, Vietnam.

31. www.acsbcanada.org

32. http://www.thesaigontimes.vn/Home/taichinh/chungkhoan/83489/Bao-cao-tai-chinh-nen-huong-toi-nha-dau-tu.html

33. http://www.investopedia.com/terms/h/historical-cost.asp#ixzz2FGfBbQQo

34. http://business-accounting-guides.com/historical-cost/

35. http://en.stockbiz.vn/News/2012/1/3/262166/vietnam-stock-market-loses-over-10b-of-capitalization-in-2011.aspx

Measuring Corporate R&D

Natesa Prasad*

Economics & Finance, College of Business, University of Bahrain, Bahrain

Abstract

The essay critically examines measurement of R&D. R&D capital and cited patents are used in the literature to measure R&D intensity and investigate market returns for R&D. The results are ambiguous. Previous literature suggests that patents are distinct from R&D expenditure, and R&D is influenced by competition. We suggest eight new measures based on the interplay between R&D and competition. We empirically test these measures on pharmaceutical and computer software industries which have the highest R&D intensities of all industries. The new measures are more significant than R&D capital and offer further insights on R&D in these industries. These measures help in capital allocation for R&D at firm level which maximizes stock returns.

Keywords: R&D; Stock Valuation; R&D capital; Capital allocation; Measuring corporate R&D

Introduction

We focus on the long-term stock market return to R&D expenditure, arguably the riskiest of investment decisions made by a firm. The extensive literature in this area is discussed in the next section. In these studies R&D efforts by the firms are measured in two ways. R&D capital focuses on the long term nature of R&D projects and aggregates R&D expenditure over the past five/ seven years depreciated at an appropriate rate. Another measure is to calculate the number of patents registered by the firm each patent being weighted by its subsequent citations. The cited patent measure follows the logic that stock markets would value the output of R&D efforts proxied by patents rather than R&D expenditure which represents inputs. We suggest that both these measures fail to capture key elements of firm level R&D efforts. To better understand the stock market rewards for R&D, we suggest new measures which involve R&D expenditure and competitive position of the firms. Empirical tests show that these measures are superior to R&D capital and offer greater insights on R&D in the industries studied.

The growing interest in R&D by policy makers, practitioners, and academics alike is driven by the increasing importance of the high-tech sectors and firms that compete on superior research know-how. Investing in R&D is risky because of its typically long gestation period. Unlike investments in physical assets, R&D dollars are expensed thereby reducing current earnings. Despite these short-term disadvantages, the investment in R&D continues unabated. Empirical studies that investigate the returns to R&D include Megna and Klock [1], Klette and Griliches [2], Lev and Sougiannis [3], Chan et al. [4], Al-Horani et al. [5], and Eberhart et al. [6]. The results are ambiguous, with many studies finding a positive correlation while some find no significant correlation. These studies use R&D capital and/or cited patents to measure R&D [4,5].

Megna and Klock [1] find that R&D and patents are distinct and measure separate aspects of intangible capital. Hall [7], Hall et al. [8] find that in several industries, firms do not value patents for protecting their know-how but for other reasons such as financing and patent portfolio race. Hall and Ziedonis [9] report that as R&D capital includes many lags, the sum of the coefficients is roughly the same as the estimated coefficient of current R&D expenditure without lags. They therefore recommend using current R&D expenditure especially in industries with short history or technological cycles. Megna and Klock [1], Hall and Ziedonis [9], Hall [8] also emphasize the importance of competition in understanding firm level R&D an aspect both R&D capital and cited patent measures ignore.

We develop eight measures which incorporate R&D and the competitive position of the firm. We test the measures formulated on a data set of all firms in computer software and pharmaceutical firms ranked by Chan et al. [4] as the highest in R&D intensity amongst all industries. The empirical results show that the new measures are highly significant, compare favorably with R&D capital and offer useful insights in our understanding of R&D in these industries.

The rest of the paper proceeds as follows. Section 2 surveys the previous literature in this area. Section 3 formulates the hypothesis. Section 4 describes the data and methodology. Section 5 discusses the findings and their implications. Section 6 provides the conclusions.

Literature Review

Several studies have examined the impact of R&D spending by firms on the long term stock market returns and firm value. Megna and Klock [1] find a significant relationship between firm values and R&D efforts. Lev and Sougiannis [3] study the value relevance of R&D expenditure and find a significant association between R&D capital and subsequent stock returns. Eberhart et al. [6,10] examine long term stock returns following unexpected R&D increases. They observe significantly positive long-term abnormal stock returns and conclude that R&D investments are beneficial. Booth et al. [11] observe that R&D expenditure increases long-term market returns, but the effect varies across countries and samples. On the other hand Hall [7] finds that during 1980s, stock markets significantly undervalued R&D. Chan et al. [4] find that the average historical stock returns of firms engaged in R&D matches the returns of firms not so engaged. They suggest that the stock market is apparently too pessimistic about the prospects of beaten-down R&D-intensive technology stocks. Al-Horani et al. [5]

***Corresponding author:** Natesa Prasad, Economics & Finance, College of Business, University of Bahrain, Bahrain
E-mail: prasadrespaper@gmail.com

study the long-term returns to R&D on a cross section of UK stocks and their findings confirm those of Chan et al. [4]. These studies use R&D capital or cited patents. Subsequent studies have modified the patent measure to incorporate additional information on patents. Pakes [12] suggests that the number of renewals of a patent and the number of countries covered should also be included. Megna and Klock [1] suggest that along with their own patents the patent stocks of competitors should also be considered. They observe that if the technology advance is cumulative and patents are not able to fully protect the know-how, then patents by rival firms should impact the share price of the firm positively. It would be negative otherwise. McGahan and Silverman [13] study the patent filings by 4168 firms over 25 years from 1975 to 1999 and find that firms gain both when they file for a patent as well as when their competitors file for a patent. Asthana and Zhang [14] find that a high R&D intensity in the industry as a whole leads to competition mitigation via entry barriers. In such a scenario, a high R&D intensity of the firm coupled with a high R&D intensity by its competitors may turn out to be beneficial. Overall, R&D efforts by competitors play a significant role that could be positive or negative depending on the industry characteristics. Researchers have also questioned whether patents really measure R&D efforts. Megna and Klock [1] note that "Patents are commonly thought of as the output of a process in which R&D is the input." "We argue that patents and R&D are distinct measures of intangible assets since patents are marketable commodities, whereas R&D is inchoate." "R&D stocks and patents stocks appear to measure different elements of intangible capital". Cohen et al. [15] find that firms protect their R&D in a number of ways including patents, secrecy, lead time advantages etc and patents tend to be the least emphasized in a majority of industries and secrecy and lead time are the favored options to protect R&D. They also find that patents are registered for other purposes such as blocking a rival or to force rivals into negotiations. Hall and Ziedonis [9] observe that the reasons for the recent surge in patenting have to do with a patent portfolio race rather than a surge in R&D activity. They point out that patents per million dollars of R&D had gone up from 0.3 to 0.6 between 1982 and 1992. They find that "pro patent shift in many industries seems to be an increase in patenting rather than an increase in R&D activity per se"[6]. Based on their extensive study of one million patents issued over a 30 year period, Hall et al. [8] conclude that "patent related measures cannot win a "horse race" with R&D as a determinant of market value, but this is hardly surprising: even if citations are a reasonably informative signal of success, this does not mean that they will be more correlated with value than R&D, because optimizing firms will increase their R&D in response to success." It is fair to infer from the above literature that previous measures for R&D have not found wide acceptance in the literature and there is a need for new measures of R&D which incorporate competition. In the next section, we examine such measures for R&D closely following previous literature.

Hypotheses

We develop various measures for R&D and assess their impact on firm value and stock returns following the cited literature. Not all measures may be significant across all industries and industry-specific empirical testing may be needed. This follows previous literature that each industry is different depending on its technology cycle. Measures derived from R&D expenditure have several advantages over the measures for patents. First, annual R&D expenditure is based on audited financial information and is universally available. Second, they are useful in industries where every successful R&D is not patented. Third, patents measure past R&D. Fourth, some literature suggests that patents and R&D measure different intangible capital Megna and Klock [1] and R&D expenditure is superior to patents in measuring market value Hall et al. [8].

R&D capital is the most researched measure of R&D Hausman et al. [16], Megna and Klock [1], Lev and Sougiannis [3], Chan et al. [4], and Blundell et al. [17]. However, Hall and Ziedonis [9] report that when many lags are included in the model, the sum of the coefficients is roughly the same as the estimated coefficient of current R&D expenditure without lags. They therefore recommend using current R&D expenditure especially in industries with short history or technological cycles. We examine as a robustness check whether R&D capital provides more information as compared to current R&D expenditure as a measure for evaluating stock market returns.

Researchers have held that the impact of R&D efforts have to be studied in the context of competition forces in the industry. Megna and Klock [1], Sundaram et al. [18], Garlappi [19], and Asthana and Zhang [14]. The impact of competitors' R&D could be either positive or negative. Megna and Klock [1] suggest that if the intangible capital cannot be appropriated perfectly and the technological advance is cumulative, then the innovation stock of rivals should positively impact the R&D efforts of the firm and be negative otherwise. Overall literature suggests that to ascertain the impact on firm value, R&D expenditure has to be analyzed with the competition. Our measures evaluate R&D interacted with firm level competition. Based on previous literature, firm-level competition can be calculated in four different ways, based on sales, total assets, physical plant and equipment, and operating profit margin. These methods are discussed in the next section.

The impact of competition on innovation can be positive or negative depending on the industry as noted by Megna and Klock [1]. Even within an industry at a given time, competition can either hinder or enhance R&D for different firms. The intuition for this is supplied by Gilbert [20]. He suggests that "There is an intuitive argument that moderate levels of competition should be most effective in promoting innovation." "To the extent that market concentration is a reasonable proxy for the degree of competition, this suggests that intermediate levels of market concentration are the most fertile environments for innovative activity". Aghion et al. [21] postulate that competition and R&D have an inverted-U shaped relationship by assuming a sequential structure of innovation. That is to say, if the competition increases, R&D should increase, but beyond a point increased competition reduces R&D. They suggest an exponential quadratic function of competition to model R&D. Following this, we suggest that, in every case, the squared term of the competition measure is also correlated with R&D and hence the return. The correlation of the squared term is expected to have a sign opposite to that of the competition term. Klock and Megna [22], and Hall and Ziedonis [9] also suggest that R&D and its valuation depend the number of employees and the per capita R&D effort. Following this, we also calculate R&D expenditure per employee. Lanjouw and Schankerman [23] examine the value of patents with respect to the size of the firm. They find that smaller firms are less capable of tackling the litigations arising out of patents and protecting the intellectual know-how generated by R&D. They conclude that patents are more valuable to larger firms rather than smaller firms. Following this analogy, we suggest that a measure of R&D to impact shareholder returns is the number of employees of the firm. Thomas [24] suggests that, in industries where R&D itself is regulated, such as in pharmaceutical industry, complying with regulatory environment calls for establishing an infrastructure of qualified personnel that the smaller firms with few R&D projects are ill equipped to do. This further emphasizes the employee factor in measuring R&D.

We hypothesize that firm value and stock returns are positively impacted by R&D capital and significantly affected by the interaction of R&D with competition based on sales, total assets, physical plant and equipment, and operating profit margin. The impact may be positive or negative depending on the industry characteristics. We further suggest that the impact of R&D interaction with the squared R&D capital and competition are significant and bear an opposite sign. R&D value is also affected by the number of employees. We also suggest that these measures will have to be individually tested and identified for each industry.

In the following section, we operationalize the measures for R&D interaction with competition and squared competition so that they can be empirically tested.

Data and Methodology

Our data set includes all pharmaceutical (SIC code 2834) and computer software (SIC code 7372) firms for which accounting and share prices data are available from Compustat data base. We collect data for the 21 years period from 1985 to 2005. After discarding observations with missing data, we have 492 firm-years of data for the pharmaceutical firms and 957 firm-years of data for the computer software firms. We also need additional information to calculate Tobin's q and Lerner index. For the extra variables needed for these computations, we are left with 466 firm-years of data for pharmaceutical firms and 918 firm-years of data for computer software firms. Real Tobin's q is unobserved and there are several methods to calculate its proxies. Erickson and Whited [25] find that the average q explains less than two-thirds of the variation in its best proxy. They suggest using instrumental variables but also concede that finding such instruments is not easy. They also find that when Tobin's q is used as a dependant variable as in our case the measurement error does not bias any slope coefficient but renders the R^2 smaller. They recommend adopting the "book" method of computing Tobin's q. Our calculations are based on the book method, while noting its limitation. Summary statistics for all firms in the pharmaceutical industry are provided in Table 1. Panel A provides the summary statistics for pharmaceutical industry and Panel B the summary statistics for the computer software industry. Sales of pharmaceutical firms displayed in Panel A range all the way from no sales to $52 billion. Similarly we have firms with negligible ($630) to nearly $17 billion of annual R&D. There are both profitable firms and loss-generating firms. The sample includes firms with losses ($5 million), all the way to a net income of $11 billion. The total assets vary from $3 million to $123 billion and the plant and equipment from negligible to $18 billion. The number of employees ranges from 100 to 122,000. Thus, the sample of pharmaceutical firms has a wide cross section of firms to study the stock returns for R&D. We observe a similar situation with regard to the computer software firms displayed in Panel B. We have 957 firm-years of data for most variables and 918 firm-years of data for tests involving Tobin's q and cost competition measures. The sales vary from $10 million to $39 billion and the research and development expenditure varies from nil to $7.8 billion. The firms include both highly profitable and loss-generating firms. The net income varies from a loss of $1 billion to profits of $12 billion. The sample includes firms whose total assets range from $4 million to $ 92 billion and possess plant and equipment from negligible to $23 billion. Thus for both industries, we have a wide range of firms to test our measures.

We develop measures for R&D that have an impact on firm value and stock returns based on the existing literature and in particular, measures developed in the patent literature on R&D. The summary statistics of the measures are provided in Table 2 and the details of various measures are provided in Appendix. Capitalized value of R&D, known as R&D capital is widely used in the literature. The commonly accepted measure uses R&D expenditure for the past five years with an annual depreciation rate of 20% as suggested by Chan et al. [4]. We adopt that measure. To our knowledge, no other calculated measure of R&D at the firm level is available in the literature. The other measures proposed by us as are discussed below.

R&D and Competition

Megna and Klock [1], Sundaram et al. [18], and Asthana and Zhang [14] find that value of R&D is moderated by a firm's competitive position in the industry. We develop measures for the firms' competitive position in the industry and interact them with R&D. There are two widely used measures for industry concentration or competition. One set of measures is derived from industry concentration namely, the Herfindahl-Hirschman Index (HHI) [14,26,27]. We use a firm level scaled version of HHI to capture the competitive position of the firm. Another measure is the cost-competitive position of the firm based on Lerner index(LI), calculated as (1- Lerner index) [21,28-31]. We evaluate measures for R&D both with respect to HHI and LI. Further, concentration with respect to HHI can be measured in three ways. Computing HHI for sales is more common and is employed among others by Tingvall and Poldahl [26] and Asthana and Zhang [14]. Danzon et al. [32] note the significant presence and growth of contract research organizations (CROs) which carry out R&D for other firms on contract and sometimes on their own. These firms have assets in place and carry on research but have very little sales. Asset based HHI better incorporates the role of such firms. Hall and Ziedonis [9] advocate using physical plant and machinery (PPE) and the interaction of R&D with PPE to evaluate patents. Following this, we also calculate a measure of competition based on a scaled HHI of PPE. We thus have four measures of R&D interacted with competition namely, R&D Capital, R&D Asset Dominance, R&D Sales Dominance, R&D Plant Dominance, R&D operating Margin Dominance. Appendix provides the definitions of measures.

R&D and competition, second-order interaction

Aghion et al. [21] and Gilbert [20] suggest an optimum level of R&D for a given level of competition. We argue that if firms decide an optimum level of R&D based on competition in the industry, then market should also reward or penalize R&D efforts that are above or below these levels. Following Aghion et al., we use squared measures of interaction term with competition Aghion et al. [21] use squared measure of the competition]. We investigate if the impact of the R&D interaction with the squared measures of competition has the opposite sign from those of the interaction terms with competition measures.

We thus generate four measures of R&D based on the second-order interaction of competition with R&D. These measures are Sq. R&D Asset Dominance, Sq. R&D Sales Dominance, Sq. R&D Plant Dominance, and Sq. R&D operating Margin Dominance. Following the same reasoning, we define Sq. R&D capital. The definitions are provided in Appendix. These measures will have an opposite sign to the competition measures and will be significant [21].

R&D Measure	Expected Impact on Stock Return	Expected Impact on Tobin's q
R&D Capital	+	+
R&D Asset Dominance	- In some industries	- In some industries
R&D Sales Dominance	+/-	+/-
R&D Plant Dominance	+/-	+/-
R&D operating Margin Dominance	+/-	+/-
R&D per Employee	-	-
Squared. R&D Capital	opposite sign as the first order measure in some industries	opposite sign as the first order measure in some industries
Sq. R&D Asset Dominance		
Sq. R&D Sales Dominance		
Sq. R&D Plant Dominance		
Sq. R&D operating Margin Dominance		

Variable	**Mean**	**Standard Deviation**	**Minimum**	**Maximum**
Panel A: Pharamaceutical firms under SIC code 2834. Number of firms 492				
Sales	4596.42	9242.89	0	52516
R&D	668.08	1550.89	0.06	16923.85
Net Income(NI)	703.67	1745.36	-4887.22	11332
Total Assets	7034.9	15944.98	3.48	123684
Physical Plant & Equipment (PPE)	1618.07	3155.13	0.02	18385
Book Equity	1911.01	4207.8	16131.17	28178
Employees	16.01	27.72	0.01	122
Share Price Fiscal Year	31.9	24.51	5.06	122.03
Operating Profit	1411.26	3085	-220.23	22181
Depreciation	251.16	627.23	0.01	5661.66
Current Liability	500.2	1389.95	0	11589
Inventory	583.33	1082.01	0	6660
Panel B: Computer Software Firms under SIC Code 2834. Number of Firms 957				
Sales	659.66	2641.77	10.01	39788
R&D	104.04	446.47	0	7779
Net Income(NI)	114.83	790.56	-1102	12254
Total Assets	1078.2	5479	4.7	92389
Physical Plant & Equipment (PPE)	78.39	241.83	0.03	2346
Book Equity	566.37	3941.85	-7168	71141
Employees	2.31	5.98	0.03	61
Share Price Fiscal Year	19.58	22.33	1	198.75
Operating Profit	181.17	1027.04	-490	13584
Depreciation	31.07	99.73	0.02	1536
Current Liability	12.55	107.66	0	2693
Inventory	7.06	32.1	0	673

Note: 1.The number of observations for Operating Profit, Depreciation, Cost Competition, Current Liability, and Inventory is 466 in case of pharmaceutical firms and 918 for the Computer Software firms.
2. Share Price is in $, and Employees are in thousands. All other figures are in $ million

Table 1: Profile and Summary Information of Firms used in the Study.

Variable	Mean	Standard Deviation	Min	Maximum
Panel A: Summary statistics of R&D Measures for Pharma industry. Number of observations 492				
R&D Capital	39.32	43.65	1.65	383.25
R&D Asset Dominance	73.13	394.96	0.00	5858.20
R&D Sales Dominance	59.72	228.57	0.00	2764.32
R&D Plant Dominance	60.08	234.40	0.00	3360.44
R&D operating Margin Dominance	18.25	187.49	0.05	3983.71
R&D per Employee	106.26	256.39	0.75	4748.20
Sq. R&D Capital	3446.91	10295.14	2.72	146880.70
Sq. R&D Asset Dominance	17.15	152.07	0.00	2820.00
Sq. R&D Sales Dominance	55.70	456.00	0.00	7640.00
Sq. R&D Plant Dominance	58.40	581.00	0.00	11300.00
Sq. R&D operating Margin Dominance	5.67	10.40	0.05	222.00
Variable	**Mean**	**Standard Deviation**	**Min**	**Maximum**
Panel A: Summary statistics of R&D Measures for Pharma industry. Number of observations 492				
R&D Capital	261.54	1089.44	0.14	17801.20
R&D Asset Dominance	33.17	358.77	0.00	6759.36
R&D Sales Dominance	31.06	334.65	0.00	6194.21
R&D Plant Dominance	23.521	216.46	0.00	3451.61
R&D operating Margin Dominance	91.38	356.43	0.00	7484.14
R&D per Employee	36.71	23.00	0.00	181.78
Sq. R&D Capital	1254.04	15100.00	0.02	317000.00
Sq. R&D Asset Dominance	130.00	1900.00	0.00	45700.00
Sq. R&D Sales Dominance	113.00	1690.00	0.00	38400.00
Sq. R&D Plant Dominance	47.40	611.00	0.00	11900.00
Sq. R&D operating Margin Dominance	93.32	331.50	0.00	7200.46

Note: 1.The number of observations for R&D operating Margin Dominance and Sq. R&D operating Margin Dominance is 466 in case of pharmaceutical firms and 918 for the Computer Software firms.
2. Share Price is in $, and Employees are in thousands. All other figures are in $ million. Squared R&D dominance measures are in $ billion.

Table 2: Summary Information of R&D Measures used in the Study

Size factor

Following Thomas [24], Hall and Ziedonis [9] and Lanjouw and Schankerman [23], we suggest that R&D expenditure interacted with a size factor (R&D per employee) have a significant negative impact on market value and stock returns.

The R&D measures, the signs of the coefficients and the expected significance are summarized in Table 1.

Table 3 Panel A presents the summary statistics for the eleven measures proposed by us calculated for all firms in the pharmaceutical industry and Table 2 Panel B presents the same data for the computer software industry. For the firms in the pharmaceutical industry, R&D capital varies from 1.65% to 383.25%. The R&D asset dominance varies from near zero $5.85 million, the R&D sales dominance varies from zero $276 million, and R&D plant dominance varies from near zero to $336 million. The R&D per employee varies from near zero to $4.75 million. The squared R&D dominance measures are expressed in $ billions and have a corresponding range. Thus the measures have a wide range for measuring the impact of R&D on stock returns. Similarly for the firms in the computer software industry, R&D capital varies from near zero to $17.81 million, R&D dominance for assets varies from zero $675.93 million, R&D dominance for Sales varies from zero to $619.42 million, and R&D dominance for Plant and equipment varies from zero $345 million. The R&D intensity for employee varies from near zero to $0.18 million. The values for the second order interaction terms expressed in $ billions show a similar variation. Thus for both industries, our measures cover a wide range to test for the impact of stock value and stock returns on R&D.

Table 4 presents the correlation matrix of R&D measures for both pharmaceutical and computer software industries. As expected, R&D

measures for assets, sales, and plant dominance (HHI based) show close correlation in both the industries. Their correlation with operating margin dominance (LI based) is strong in the computer software industry but weak in the pharmaceutical industry. This emphasizes the industry specific nature of these dominance measures. Further, Tingvall and Poldahl [26] observed an inverted-U relationship for R&D based on HHI measure but not for the LI measure. Our findings also suggest that HHI and LI competition measures are distinct and their correlation depends on the industry. R&D capital is not significantly correlated with other measures. Appropriate measures should be identified for each industry from our wide range of measures. Choosing appropriate measures for specific industries is in line with patent literature.

Findings and implications

We evaluate the impact of each of our measures individually on stock values and annual share returns by univariate regressions for each industry. Our data is a panel data set for firms in the industry over several years. We anticipate that time series correlation of error terms across the years will affect the consistency of the results and therefore avoid regressions on the pooled data set. To ensure consistent results across the years and to avoid time series correlation of error terms, we use separate regressions for each year and calculate Fama-Macbeth coefficients and t statistics across the years [Fama and Macbeth [33]. Our analysis and presentation of the results closely follows Fama and French [34] and Asthana and Zhang [14]. R&D capital uses four lag variables and therefore we have seventeen years of data from 1989 to 2005. We carry out, for each industry for each year, separate univariate regressions for each of the eleven measures

With Tobin's q and annual return as the dependant variables. Thus, we carry out in all a series of 748 regressions (eleven regressions over seventeen years for two dependant variables over two industries). For regressions involving annual return as the dependant variable, the return for the previous year is included as a control variable. In addition, we also wish to assess the combined effect of each pair of the dominance and squared dominance measures on annual returns and Tobin's q. This requires an additional 340 regressions, making it, in all, and 1088 OLS regressions [9]. Due to the bulkiness of these results, we report only the results for the 64 Fama–Macbeth combined coefficients and t statistics. Table 5 Panel A presents the univariate regression results for the pharmaceutical industry. Column 1 presents the results for annual returns and column 2 presents the corresponding results for Tobin's q. None of the coefficients for the univariate regressions against annual returns are significant. This agrees with the finding by Chan et al. that the historical returns for firms that carry out R&D are not different form firms which do not. Chan et al. [4] suggest that this finding is in conformity with the efficient market hypothesis that when a firm engages in high R&D activity on a regular basis, the market does not re evaluate the return every year. On the other hand such firms may have a higher stock valuation as compared to other firms that carry out minimal R&D. This is indeed borne out by the significance of the coefficients in the regressions against the Tobin's q shown under column 2. For the firms in the pharmaceutical industry this indicates well defined classes of firms which regularly carry out substantial R&D or minimal R&D over the years. In other words, these firms follow a consistent R&D policy over the years. Empirical literature in pharmaceutical industry suggests a three way classification of firms [35], namely, pioneers that carry out high risk research on a new family of products, imitators that research on a known family of products aiming at new products with marginal improvements, and generic firms that aim to produce existing drugs at lower prices through minimal research. Grabowski and Vernon [35] further suggest that R&D strategies of the pharmaceutical firms are based on this role and a pioneering firm will not change into a generic firm for a few products. This characterization of industry by Grabowski and Vernon [35] is in conformity with our findings of low significance for our computed R&D measures in relation to annual returns but a high correlation with firm value, as represented by Tobin's q. Overall we

Variable	R&D Capital	R&D Asset Dominance	R&D Sales Dominance	R&D Plant Dominance	R&D operating margin dominance	R&D per Employee
Correlation Matrix for R&D measures–Pharmaceutical Industry						
R&D Capital 1	1					
R&D Asset Dominance	-0.07 1	1				
R&D Sales Dominance	-0.09	0.82 1	1			
R&D Plant Dominance	-0.09	0.89	0.93	1		
R&D operating Margin Dominance	0.06	0.06	0.05	0.05	1	
R&D per Employee	0.24	-0.02	-0.05	-0.04	0.08	1
Correlation Matrix for R&D measures–Computer Software Industry						
R&D Capital 1	1					
R&D Asset Dominance	-0.06 1	1				
R&D Sales Dominance	-0.06	0.99 1	1			
R&D Plant Dominance	-0.07	0.98	0.98 1	1		
R&D operating Margin Dominance	-0.09	0.91	0.92	0.91	1	
R&D per Employee	0.33	0.24	0.23	0.24	0.33	1

Table 3. Correlation Matrix.

Dependant Variable/ Independent Variables	Return		Tobin Q	
	Slope	Statistics	Slope	Statistics
Fama Macbeth Univariate Regressions				
R&D Capital	2.48	0.78	24.10	0.89
R&D Asset Dominance	-0.01	-0.14	-0.19	-5.82****
R&D Sales Dominance	0.01	0.69	-0.24	-4.0****
R&D Plant Dominance	0.01	0.12	-0.21	-5.94****
R&D operating Margin Dominance	-0.05	-0.27	-2.64	3.68****
R&D per Employee	2.43	0.66	35.31	2.15**
Squared. R&D Capital	0.03	0.51	0.32	1.52
Sq. R&D Asset Dominance	-0.01	-0.65	-0.01	-4.48****
Sq. R&D Sales Dominance	0.01	0.63	-0.01	-2.31**
Sq. R&D Plant Dominance	-0.01	-0.10	-0.01	-4.13****
Sq. R&D operating Margin Dominance	-0.06	-1.29	-0.16	-0.32
Fama Macbeth Bivariate Regressions				
R&D Capital	15.10 1.18	168.84	1.10	15.10 1.18
Squared. R&D Capital	0.03	-0.20	1.16	1.57
Squared. R&D Capital	0.06	0.73	0.88	-3.32****
Sq. R&D Asset Dominance	-0.01	-1.02	0.04	3.74***
R&D Sales Dominance	0.07	0.94	-0.83	3.99****
Sq. R&D Sales Dominance	0.01	-1.05	0.01	3.52****
R&D Plant Dominance	-0.15	-0.67	-0.88	-4.10***
Sq. R&D Plant Dominance	0.01	0.81	0.01	3.89****
R&D operating Margin Dominance	-0.32	-0.46	-2.84	-3.30****
Sq. R&D operating Margin Dominance	0.60	0.94	0.07	0.11

Note: *, **, ***, and **** represent 10%, 5%, 1%and 0.1% and more of significance

Table 4: Fama-Macbeth Regressions - Pharmaceutical Industry

find significant support for the use of our computed R&D measure in the pharmaceutical industry.

It is also interesting to note that all the five measures suggested by us [R&D asset dominance, R&D sales dominance, R&D plant dominance, R&D operating margin dominance, and R&D per employee] have high significance and R&D capital, the widely used measure for R&D in the [3,4] is not significant for pharmaceutical industry. Anecdotally, we also observe that the significance for the coefficient of R&D sales dominance is lower than that for asset and plant dominance. This is in conformity with the observation by Danzon et al. [32] on the significance of CROs, although this is not a rigorous empirical finding. Megna and Klock suggest that R&D measures related to competition can have a positive or negative impact but should be significant. For the pharmaceutical industry, three of our measures (all based on HHI) show a negative impact and the measure based on LI shows a positive impact, while all of them are highly significant. The divergence of the results can be compared to that of Tingvall and Poldahl who report that, in their investigation of R&D with respect to competition, that they obtain very different results when they use HHI and LI to measure competition. The difference between these two sets of measures is an interesting area for further study.

Table 4, Panel B presents the regression results for Fama-Macbeth combined coefficients and t statistics for the bivariate regressions for dominance and the corresponding squared dominance measures. Literature [20,21] suggests that there could be an inverted-U shape relationship between R&D and competition resulting in an optimum R&D for a given level of competition. If so, firms whose R&D is higher or lower than this optimum would be penalized by the market. This would suggest opposite signs for the coefficients of the two measures. The regressions for Tobin's q fully bear this out for HHI competition measures while the relationship is insignificant for LI competition measure. Again this finding can be compared with similar findings by Tingvall and Poldahl who find divergent results for HHI and LI measures.

Table 6 Panel A presents Fama-Macbeth combined coefficients and t statistics for the univariate regressions of R&D measures for the computer software industry. Column 1 presents the results for annual return and column 2 presents the results for Tobin's q.

Annual returns are significantly correlated with all the four measures of R&D dominance namely, asset, sales, plant, and operating margin dominance as well as R&D per employee. R&D capital is not significant. For the computer software industry stock returns are significantly correlated with R&D measures, unlike, pharmaceutical industry. Guy [36] points out that R&D in computer software is highly portable in the global market along with availability of free software. Patent protection is not very significant and hence R&D expenditure is volatile. This contrasts with the empirical findings for the pharmaceutical industry. Thus our findings are in broad conformity with the industry characteristics and empirical literature. R&D capital, the commonly used measure is not very significant for stock return but it is significant for Tobin' q. This could imply that in view of the unpredictability of R&D expenditure, annual returns depend on the current R&D, while firms that have a track record of high R&D and have survived the competition have a high firm value. The signs of the coefficient are all negative, the same as in the case of pharmaceutical industry. Table 5, Panel B provides the results for Fama-Macbeth bivariate regressions. As in the pharmaceutical industry, there is a divergence between HHI-based measures and LI-based measures. The impact on Tobin's q shows a high significance for LI measure and marginal significance for HHI measures. The findings in the two industries indicate that all the four R&D competition based measures are important and need to

Dependant Variable/ Independent Variables	Return	Tobin Q		
	Slope	Statistics	Slope	Statistics
R&D Capital	-12.11	-0.29	-75.04	-3.21***
R&D Asset Dominance	-2.60	-2.72***	-1.50	-1.85*
R&D Sales Dominance	-1.64	-2.70***	-0.91	-1.80*
R&D Plant Dominance	-1.20	-2.35**	-0.87	-1.75*
R&D operating Margin Dominance	-22.34	-3.13***	-5.77	-1.74*
R&D per Employee	-10.47	-4.30****	-8.88	-0.57
Squared. R&D Capital	-0.04	-0.09	-0.52	-2.57***
Sq. R&D Asset Dominance	-0.01	-1.27	-0.01	-1.26
Sq. R&D Sales Dominance	-0.01	-1.36	-0.01	-1.33
Sq. R&D Plant Dominance	-0.01	-1.57	-0.01	-1.54
Sq. R&D operating Margin Dominance	-24.69	-3.18***	-6.35	-1.81*
R&D Capital	-437.92	-1.56	-30.77	-2.61***
Squared. R&D	6.12	1.40	2.65	1.81*
R&D Asset Dominance	-13.81	-1.17	-7.50	-1.17
Sq. R&D Asset Dominance	-0.01	-0.65	-0.01	-0.07
R&D Sales Dominance	-10.82	-1.23	-6.28	-1.29
Sq. R&D Sales Dominance	-0.01	-0.20	-0.01	-0.34
R&D Plant Dominance	-10.65	-0.78	-10.68	-1.69*
Sq. R&D Plant Dominance	-0.01	-0.21	-0.01	-1.63*
R&D operating Margin Dominance	-4.70	-0.15	-40.70	-2.73***
Sq. R&D operating Margin Dominance	-25.29	-0.82	-55.52	-3.46****

Table 5: Fama-Macbeth Regressions - Computer Software Industry

be judiciously applied to specific industries. We also wish to ensure that the results of Fama-Macbeth regressions reported in Tables 4 and 5 are robust across individual years and do not show significant variations within the sample. Following the presentation of results in Fama and French [34], we sub-sample the data into three sets for the years 1989 to1994, 1995 to1999, and 2000 to 2005. We compute Fama-Macbeth combined coefficients and t statistics separately for each of the sub-sample for the six R&D measures namely, R&D Capital, R&D asset dominance, R&D sales dominance, R&D plant dominance, R&D operating margin dominance, and R&D per employee. Regressions are carried out against Tobin's q for the pharmaceutical industry and annual return for the computer software industry. The results are shown in Table 6 for the pharmaceutical industry and Table 8 for the computer software industry. We find that the main results shown in Tables 4 and 5 hold true for each of the sub samples. The results are robust across years. We further note that in our analysis, the competition measures suggested by us, namely, R&D asset dominance, R&D sales dominance, R&D plant dominance, R&D operating margin dominance, and R&D per employee are more significant for the two samples and sub-samples than R&D capital, the measure most commonly used in the literature. R&D capital is significant for the computer software industry in predicting Tobin's q as shown in Table 6, Panel A. Hall and Ziedonis [9] observe that including the lag variables of R&D does not capture more significance than current R&D because R&D dollars over the years are highly correlated. They advocate using current R&D. We investigate this possibility for the computer software industry. Table 8 presents the analysis. We regress separately Tobin's q against R&D capital, Squared R&D capital and current R&D and also all three measures together. We find that R&D capital does convey significant information over and above the current R&D. The coefficient for R&D is not significant and R^2 improves marginally from 0.15 to 0.18. We suggest that this may because firm R&D dollars over the years may not be highly correlated in computer software industry. This would also explain why R&D dominance measures based on current R&D are able to significantly predict annual stock return for computer software industry unlike in pharmaceutical industry. The findings by Hall and Ziedonis [9] across their sample of industries on R&D capital and current R&D could be extended to imply that current R&D would score over R&D Capital in industries where firm R&D is predictable and highly correlated over the years. An example could be pharmaceutical industry as characterized by Grabowski and Vernon [35]. In other industries R&D capital may be a useful measure of R&D. Obviously, this requires further research and it may turn out that R&D capital is not a universal measure across industries as currently used , but only appropriate for certain industries. We also wish to explore for the two industries the impact on the regressions by combining multiple measures. We investigate the combination of R&D per employee with the most significant amongst the R&D dominance measures. Table 10 presents the analysis for the pharmaceutical industry. The most significant R&D dominance measure (R&D plant dominance) is combined with R&D per employee. We find that the inclusion of R&D per employee, by itself a significant measure considerably adds to the overall predictability and significance in Fama-Macbeth regression over the entire sample. The coefficients are all significant and the R^2 improves from 0.08 to 0.27. Table 10 shows a similar analysis for computer software industry. We combine R&D operating margin dominance with R&D per employee. Both coefficients are significant and the R^2 improves from 0.08 to 0.11. This again conforms to the patent literature that appropriate measures need to be developed separately for each industry to better understand the impact of R&D and a single measure such as R&D capital may not be appropriate across all industries.

Conclusions

To better explain the stock market valuation of R&D expenditure, patent literature suggests that stock market looks at the R&D output such as patents rather than R&D expenditure. While considerable work has been done in investigating patents and patent related measures, measures based on R&D expenditure have not been investigated. This is

Year	1989/1994		1995/1999		2000/20005	
	Slope	Statistics t	Slope	Statistics t	Slope	Statistics t
Fama Macbeth Univariate Regressions – Dependant Variable Tobin's q						
R&D Capital	74.64	1.46	63.42 1.42	45.54	0.92	R&D Capital 74.64 1.46 63.42 1.42
R&D Asset Dominance	-0.21	4.32****	-0.11	-1.96**	-0.26	-4.81****
R&D Sales Dominance	-0.23	-3.16***	-0.11	-2.41**	-0.41	-2.58***
R&D Plant Dominance	-0.23	-3.78****	-0.1	-2.54**	-0.3	-5.78****
R&D operating Margin Dominance	-0.28	-2.41**	-0.15	-1.60	-0.38	-2.21**
R&D per Employee	41.48	1.43	25.76	2.52**	39.39	0.84

`**Table 6:** Fama-Macbeth Regressions Pharmaceutical Industry – Sub samples

Year/ Dependant Variable	1989/1994		1995/1999		2000/20005	
	Slope	Statistics t	Slope	Statistics t	Slope	Statistics t
Fama Macbeth Univariate Regressions – Dependant Variable Annual stock return						
R&D Capital	-65.48	-0.59	-41.82	-1.51	65.99	65.99 1.74*
R&D Asset Dominance	-5.56	-3.05***	-0.06	-2.02**	-1.77	-1.24
R&D Sales Dominance	-4.07	-3.46****	-0.09	-1.61	-0.51	-1.47
R&D Plant Dominance	-3.19	-2.68***	-0.16	-1.34	-0.24	-1.54
R&D operating Margin Dominance	-49.52	-3.57****	-4.44	-3.1***	-10.08	-1.67*
R&D per Employee	-11.56	-2.08**	-69.01	-2.71***	-121.48	-3.16***

We regress stock returns against various R&D measures. Our data comprise all computer software firms (SIC code 7372) from Compustat data base. We gather data from 1985 to 2005.We have 957 firm years of data in seventeen groups. For regressions involving R&D operating profit dominance we have 918 firm years of data in seventeen groups. We analyze the data separately for the three periods 1989/1994, 1995/1999, and 2000/2005. Appendix provides the definitions of variables and measures.

Table 7: Fama-Macbeth Regressions Computer Software Industry – Sub samples

all the more necessary since all R&D is not patented and some literature suggests that patents are distinct from R&D. Literature also discounts the universal use of R&D capital the only R&D measure investigated so far. We suggest ten new measures for R&D closely following the patent literature, along with R&D capital. We investigate these eleven measures on pharmaceutical and computer software firms, industries which are ranked first and second in R&D intensity. We find that our suggested measures are significant and score over R&D capital. The measures also reveal significant insights on R&D expenditure in the two industries. The findings and the significant differences we observe between the industries are in conformity with other empirical literature for the two industries. We also suggest that R&D capital may not be an appropriate measure for all industries and appropriate R&D measures have to be chosen from the eleven measures for specific industries. We readily acknowledge the limitations in this study, namely that we study only two industries and better insights are possible by including other industries as well as further classification of industries. The appropriateness of these measures across other industries may provide useful area for further research in this area (Table 2).

We investigate all pharmaceutical firms (SIC code 2834) and computer software firms (SIC code7372) for which accounting and share prices data is available from Compustat data base. We gather data from 1985 to 2005. After discarding observations with missing data, we have 492 firm years of data for the pharmaceutical firms and 957 firm-years of data for the computer software firms. For calculations involving Tobin's q and Lerner index, we have 466 and 918 firm years of data respectively. Appendix provides the definitions of variables and measures (Table 3).

We investigate all pharmaceutical firms (SIC code 2834) and computer software firms (SIC code 7372) for which accounting and share prices data is available from Compustat data base. We gather data from 1985 to 2005. After discarding observations with missing data, we have 492 firm years of data for the pharmaceutical firms and 957 firm-years of data for the computer software firms. For calculations involving Tobin's q and Lerner index, we have 466 and 918 firm years of data respectively. Appendix provides the definitions of variables and measures (Table 4).

We investigate all pharmaceutical firms (SIC code 2834) and computer software firms (SIC code 7372) for which account is available from Compustat data base. We gather data from 1985 to 2005. After discarding observations with missing years of data for the pharmaceutical firms and 918 firm-years of data for the computer software firms. Appendix pro variables and measures (Table 5).

We regress stock returns and Tobin's q against various R&D measures. Our data comprise all pharmaceutical firms (SIC code 2834) for which accounting and share prices data is available from Compustat data base. We gather data from 1985 to 2005. After discarding observations with missing data, we have 492 firm years of data in seventeen groups. For regressions involving Tobin's q and R&D operating profit dominance, we have 466 firm years often in seventeen groups. Appendix provides the definitions of variables and measures (Table 6).

Independent variables			
R&D Capital	75.04 (-3.21)**	-30.77 (-2.61)**	-30.8 -(2.67)**
Squared R&D Capital		2.65 (1.81)*	2.67 (1.75)*
R&D			(0.66)
R^2	0.06	0.15	0.18

We regress Tobin's q stepwise against R&D Capital, Sq. R&D Capital and R&D.. We gather data from 1985 to 2005. After discarding observations with missing data, we have 957 firm years of data. Appendix provides the definitions of variables and measures.

Table 8: Fama-Macbeth Regressions Computer Software Industry

Independent variables			
R&D Plant Dominance	-0.21 (-5.94)****	-0.88 (-4.1)****	-0.66 (-2.45)**
Sq. R&D Plant Dominance		-0.01 (3.89)****	-0.01 (3.31)****
R&D per Employee			29.92
R	0.04	0.08	0.27

We regress Tobin's q against R&D Plant Dominance, Sq. R&D Plant Dominance, and R&D per Employee. We gather data from 1985 to 2005. After discarding observations with missing data, we have 492 firm years of data. Appendix provides the definitions of variables and measures.

Table 9: Fama-Macbeth Regressions Pharmaceutical Industry

Independent variables			
Previous Return	-21.57 (-2.11)**	-18.41 (-2.14)**	-19.51 (-2.00)**
R&D operating Margin Dominance	-22.34 (-3.13)***		-20.15 (-2.92)***
R&D per Employee		-103.99 (-4.3)****	-86.42 (-3.56)****
R^2	0.08	0.08	0.11

We regress annual stock return against Previous Return, R&D operating Margin Dominance, and R&D per Employee. The observations comprise of all computer software firms (SIC code 7372) for which accounting and share prices data is available from Compustat data base. We gather data from 1985 to 2005. After discarding observations with missing data, we have 918 firm years of data. Appendix provides the definitions of variables and measures.

Table 10: Fama-Macbeth Regressions Computer Software Industry

We regress stock returns and Tobin's q against various R&D measures. Our data comprise all computer software firms (SIC code 7372) for which accounting and share prices data is available from Compustat data base. We gather data from 1985 to 2005. After discarding observations with missing data, we have 957 firm years of data in seventeen groups. For regressions involving Tobin's q and R&D operating profit (Table 7).

We regress Tobin's q against various R&D measures. Our data comprise all pharmaceutical firms (SIC code data base. from 1985 to 2005. We have 466 firm years of data in seventeen groups. We analyze the data s periods 1989/1994, 1995/1999, and 2000/2005. Appendix provides the definitions of variables and measures (Table 8).

We regress stock returns against various R&D measures. Our data comprise all computer software firms (SIC code 737 base. We gather data from 1985 to 2005.We have 957 firm years of data in seventeen groups. For regressions involving dominance we have 918 firm years of data in seventeen groups. We analyze the data separately for the three periods 198 2000/2005. Appendix provides the definitions of variables and measures (Table 9).

We regress Tobin's q stepwise against R&D Capital, Sq. R&D Capital and R&D. We gather data from 1985 to 2005. After discarding observations with missing data, we have 957 firm years of data. Appendix provides the definitions of variables and measures (Table 10).

We regress Tobin's q against R&D Plant Dominance, Sq. R&D Plant Dominance, and R&D per Employee. We gather data from 1985 to 2005. After discarding observations with missing data, we have 492 firm years of data. Appendix provides the definitions of variables and measures.

We regress annual stock return against Previous Return, R&D operating Margin Dominance, and R&D per Employee. The observations comprise of all computer software firms (SIC code 7372) for which accounting and share prices data is available from Compustat data base. We gather data from 1985 to 2005. After discarding observations with missing data, we have 918 firm years of data. Appendix provides the definitions of variables and measures.

References

1. Megna P, Klock M (1993) The impact of intangible capital on Tobin's q in the semiconductor industry. The American Economic Review 83: 265.
2. Klette TJ, Griliches Z (2000) Empirical patterns of firm growth and R&D investment: A quality ladder mdoel interpretation. The Economic Journal 110: 363.
3. LevB, Sougiannis T (1996) The capitalization, amortization, and value-relevance of R&D. J Account Eco 21: 107.
4. Chan LK.C, Lakonishok J, Sougiannis T (2001) The stock market valuation of research and development expenditures. J Financ 56: 2431.
5. Al-Horani A, Pope PF, AW Stark (2003) Research and Development Activity and Expected Returns in the United Kingdom. European Finance Review 7: 27.
6. Eberhart AC, Maxwell WF, Siddique AR (2006) Does the Stock Market Under react to R&D Increases? J Investment Manag : JOIM, 1.
7. Hall BH (1993) The stock market's valuation of R&D investment during the 1980's. The American Economic Review 83: 259.
8. Hall BH (2005) Exploring the Patent Explosion. J Technol Transfer 30: 35.
9. Hall BH, Ziedonis RH (2001) The patent paradox revisited: An empirical study of patenting in the U.S. semiconductor industry, 1979-1995. Rand J Eco 32: 101.
10. Eberhart AC, Maxwell WF, Siddique AR (2004) An Examination of Long-Term Abnormal Stock Returns and Operating Performance Following R&D Increases. J Financ 59: 623.
11. Booth GG, Junttila J, Kallunki, JP, Rahiala M, Sahlstrom P (2006) How does the financial environment affect the stock market valuation of R&D spending? J Finance Intermed 15: 197-214.
12. Pakes A (1986) Patents as Options: Some Estimates of the Value of Holding European Patent Stocks. Econometrica 54: 755.
13. McGahan A, Silverman B (2006) Benefiting from Rivals`Breakthroughs. MIT Sloan Management Review 48: 6.
14. Asthana SC, Zhang Y (2006) Effect of R&D investments on persistence of abnormal earnings. Review of Accounting & Finance 5: 124.
15. Cohen W, Nelson R, Walsh J (2000) Protecting Their Intellectual Assets: Appropriability Conditions and Why US Manufacturing Firms Patent (Or Not). National Bureau of Economic Research w7552.
16. Hausman J, Hall BH, Griliches Z (1984) Econometric Models for Count Data with an Application to the Patents-R&D Relationship. Econometrica (pre-1986) 52: 909.
17. Blundell R, Griffith R, Windmeijer F (2002) Individual effects and dynamics in count data models. J Econometrics 108: 113.
18. Sundaram AK, John TA, John K (1996) An empirical analysis of strategic competition and firm values: The case of R&D competition. Journal of Financial Economics 40: 459.
19. Garlappi L (2004) Risk Premia and Preemption in R&D Ventures. J Financ Quant Anal 39: 843.
20. Gilbert R (2006) Competition and Innovation. J Indus Organization Edu.
21. Aghion P, Bloom N, Blundell R, Griffith R, Howitt P (2005) Competition and Innovation: An Inverted-U Relationship. Quarten J Eco 120: 701.

22. Klock M, Megna P (2000) Measuring and valuing intangible capital in the wireless communications industry. Quarterly Review of Economics and Finance 40: 519.

23. Lanjouw JO, Schankerman M (2004) Protecting intellectual property rights: Are small firms handicapped? J Law Econ 47: 45-74.

24. Thomas LG (1990) Regulation and Firm Size: FDA Impacts on Innovation. Rand J Eco 21: 497.

25. Erickson T, Whited TM (2006) On the Accuracy of Different Measures of q. Financial Management 35: 5.

26. Tingvall PG, Poldahl A (2006) Is there really an inverted U-shaped relation between competition and R&D? Economics of Innovation and New Technology 15: 101.

27. Al-Muharrami S, Matthews K, Khabari Y (2006) Market structure and competitive conditions in the Arab GCC banking system. J Bank Financ 30: 3487.

28. Fischer T, Kamerschen DR (2003) Price-cost margins in the US airline industry using a conjectural variation approach. J Transp Econ Policy 37: 227.

29. Maudos J, Guevara JFD (2004) Factors explaining the interest margin in the banking sectors of the European Union. J Bank Financ 28: 2259.

30. Toolsema LA (2004) Monetary Policy and Market Power in Banking. J Econ 83: 71.

31. Matthews K, Murinde V, Zhao T (2007) Competitive conditions among the major British banks. J Bank Financ 31: 2025.

32. Danzon P, Nicholson S, Nuno S (2003) Productivity In Pharmaceutical - Biotechnology R&D: The Role of Experiance and Alliances. National Beaureau of Economic Research.

33. Fama EF, Macbeth JD (1973) risk, return and equilibrium - empirical tests. J Politic Econ 81: 607.

34. Fama EF, French KR (2006) Profitability, investment and average returns. J Financ Econ 82: 491.

35. Grabowski HG, Vernon JM (1987) Pioneers, Imitators, and Generics - A Simulation Model of Schumpeterian Competition. Quartern J Econ 102: 491.

36. Guy F (2000) Strategic bundling: Information products, market power, and the future of globalization. Review of International Political Economy: RIPE 14: 26

Audit Tenure, Rotation and Accounting Conservatism: Empirical Evidences from Nigeria

Babatolu Ayorinde[1] **and Oyewo Babajide**[2]*

[1]*Department of Accounting, Federal University of Agriculture, Abeokuta, Ogun State, Nigeria*

[2]*Department of Accounting, University of Lagos, Nigeria*

Abstract

Accounting regulators have, for many years, had concerns about the possible lack of Independence between auditors and their clients, which arises from a long-standing professional relationship between the two parties. The reservation stems from a widely-held belief that the risk of audit failure increases when an auditor and a client remain together for a long period of time. The possibility exists that auditors might get too familiar with their clients and in consequence loses professional scepticism and objectivity when the relationship goes on for too long. Stakeholders are therefore interested in if long-term relationship between companies and their auditors gives rise to closeness that impairs auditors' independence and reduces quality of audit work. With these in view, an attempt was made by the research to examine the link between audit tenure, rotation, and accounting conservatism using empirical data from Nigeria. Secondary data were randomly gathered by drawing 100 observations from the published financial statements of sample companies operating in the financial and non-financial sectors. Quantitative methods such as descriptive statistics, correlation, and multiple- regression analysis were used for data analyses. Findings were that; the tenure of auditor has a significant positive influence on firms accounting conservatism; the rotation of audit firms also significantly influences accounting conservatism. The study recommends the mandatory rotation of audit firms' lead engagement partner and the review partner on an engagement for publicly listed companies, and the strict prohibition of providing non-audit services by auditors to their clients to enhance auditors' independence and the quality of audit services.

Keywords: Audit failure; Audit tenure; Auditor rotation; Conservatism; Nigeria

Introduction

History is replete with recurring instances of prominent corporate failures and collapses that have ensued in recent times, raising serious concern about the authenticity and reliability of companies' financial statements. While the preparation of an accurate financial statement is a statutory duty vested on the company directors by S.334 (1) of the companies and allied matters Act [1], questions are further been put forward in respect of the quality and independence of external auditors who render assurance services. Accounting regulators have, for many years, had reservations about the independence gap that exist between auditors and their clients; this arises from a long-standing professional relationship between the two parties. Auditors working with clients for a long time would likely have increased specific knowledge about the activities of their clients, thereby increasing conservatism and result in a positive association between auditor tenure and accounting conservatism [2].

Attempts have been made by regulators to boost audit quality through formulation of rules impacting on auditors' independence. Concerns about auditors' independence were accountable in part for the development and passage of the Sarbanes Oxley Act of 2002 and the formation of the Public Company Accounting Oversight Board (PCAOB). The concern stems from a widely publicized belief that when an auditor gets too familiar with his client for a long period of time, it increases the risk of audit failure. There is every possibility that once auditors get too acquainted with their clients, they can lose professional scepticism and objectivity when such a relationship goes on for too long. It is of great interest to relevant stakeholders whether long-term relationships that exist between auditors and their client can bring about some level of closeness which can impair auditors' independence and reduces audit quality. To check this tendency, mandatory audit firm rotation has been suggested as a possible way out of it. The concept of mandatory auditors' rotation was introduced as a result of widely publicized corporate collapses that led to litigation. The topical issue of mandatory rotation of external auditor was perceived to be a way out of threat posed to the independence of an auditor as a result of the long relationship that may exist between the client and the auditor [3-5].

To ensure audit quality and investor confidence in the financial statements, a case could be made for mandatory rotation as an avenue to foster a more independent auditor-client relationship. In the mist of the scandals rocking Enron, the Comptroller General was directed by the Sarbanes-Oxley Act to study the merit and demerit of mandatory rotation. On the other hand, short term auditor-client relationships may also be associated with a high risk of audit failure due to an auditor's lack of familiarity with a client and its operations. The AICPA is of the view that new auditor-client relationships has more inherent risk, with reference to a study carried out by the SEC Practice Section, which came up with the findings that audit failures are three times more likely to occur in the case where the auditor is new to the client. Nonetheless, the Sarbanes Oxley Act requires audit partner rotation the question remains: what is the relation between audit firm tenure and audit quality?

There are two views on the issue of mandatory rotation of external auditors: one derives from the audit profession which is of the view

***Corresponding author:** Oyewo Babajide, Department of Accounting, University of Lagos, Nigeria, E-mail: meetjidemichael@ymail.com

that rotation is unnecessary because it would be costly to client and may reduce the quality of audits. The second perspective is from the regulators, which is in support of the rotation of the external auditors requiring audit firm to periodically let go of their client because of the notion that it could solve the problem of independence. It is against this background that the research attempts to empirically examine audit tenure, rotation and accounting conservatism using empirical data from Nigeria.

Review of Related Literatures

Conservatism has been seen as an integral part of accounting practice, which is usually expressed as the anticipation of losses and the non-recognition of profit [6]. Anticipating profits could be seen as recording profits before there is legal claim to their associated future cash flows and before the revenues are verifiable [7]. Financial Accounting Standards Boards (FASB) Statement of Concepts No. 2 justifies this behaviour by defining conservatism as "a prudent reaction to uncertainty to try to ensure that uncertainties and risks inherent in business situations are satisfactorily considered" [8]. Many construe this as traditional guidance for choosing between various methods of accounting for similar transactions. Conservatism suggests that when accountants are to make professional judgements and there is insufficient evidence as to information taking a position, the position to be taken should be the one which will less likely lead to overstatement of assets and income. Basu [9] viewed conservatism as representing the accountant's predisposition to involve a high sense of authentication to see good news as gains than to see bad news as losses. In other words, conservatism can be defined as accountants' asymmetric acknowledgment of unrealized gains and losses in reported earnings. Building on this interpretation, Basu [9] posits that accountants spot bad news in earnings more promptly than good news. Thus, if we are of the opinion that current equity returns efficiently put together good and bad news regarding firms' expected future cash flows, we expect that the slope coefficient and *R2* in a regression of earnings on unexpected returns should be higher for firms with negative unexpected returns (proxy for "bad news") and lower for those with positive unexpected returns (proxy for "good news"). The empirical results from Basu [9] are consistent with this prediction. Basu's measures have been used in so many studies to assess the degree of accounting conservatism [10-14].

The importance of accounting conservatism principle in accounting practice cannot be over emphasized, as it is essential to understand the variance, and the inherent link between the traditional concept of accounting conservatism and the unevenness of recognition presented by Basu [9]. Going by how recent the literature is, the concept of conservatism was inconsistent across studies. The traditional conservatism is called ex ante conservatism [15-17], news independent conservatism [18] or unconditional conservatism [19-21]. Basu's concept of conservatism was referred to as ex-post conservatism, news-dependent conservatism [18], or conditional conservatism [17-19]. For the purpose of discussion, we will use the concept of unconditional and conditional conservatism throughout this study. Unconditional conservatism arose from policies that reduce earnings free of current economic news or from the application of generally accepted accounting principles (GAAP), denoting that aspects of the accounting process determined at the time of acquisition of assets and liabilities yield expected undervalued assets. Prompt expensing of the costs of most internally developed intangibles, accelerated depreciation of property, plant, and equipment, and historical cost accounting for positive net present value projects are examples of unconditional conservatism. As noted in Basu [9], since unconditional conservatism is independent of current-period news, it will lower the intercept in a regression of earnings on returns but will not affect the slope coefficient. That is, the implementation of unconditional conservatism will not have an impact on the relation between earnings and returns in the current period.

On the other hand, conditional conservatism implies that bad news is recognised asymmetrically compared to good news: which means that, book values are written down under unfavourable circumstances but not written up under favourable circumstances. Examples of conditional conservatism include, the market accounting rule for inventory, impairment accounting for long-lived tangible and intangible assets, and the asymmetric recognition of contingent losses and contingent gains. Thus, in an efficient market situation if good news and bad news are arrested promptly and totally in equity prices, the use of conditional conservatism will snowball to the slope coefficient in the regression of earnings on current returns being higher for firms with negative unexpected returns (proxy for bad news) than for those with positive unexpected returns (proxy for good news).

Only recently have researchers begun to study the interaction between the two types of conservatism. For example, Basu [22] notes that less conservative news-unrelated accounting allocation methods are more likely to result in asset write downs, and hence, greater asymmetric news-driven conservatism. DeAngelo [23] argued that audit firm size could be a surrogate of audit quality. Thus, big audit firms are expected to provide high quality earnings in financial statements. Consistent with this argument, Basu [22] demonstrated that the earnings reported by big auditees are more conservative than the earnings of non-big auditees. Earnings conservatism can be used by audit firms as a risk management strategy. Audit firms can maintain higher reported audit quality by demanding more conservative earnings for their clients even under the 'threat' of auditor independence.

To critically examine the relationship between audit firm tenure, audit firm rotation and conservatism as an intrinsic attribute of earnings quality, an in-depth understanding of earnings quality is essential. Most of the studies opined that, the quality of financial reporting depends on the company's management and the audit firm since financial statements are perceived as a joint product of the duo [24,25]. Supposing that auditor independence has a directly effect on the quality of an audit, this will imply that any such change in auditor independence will translate to a change in the quality of the financial statements, hence affects the quality of reported earnings. Proponents of auditor rotation are of this argument that auditors would provide more support for aggressive accounting by the client's management when their independence is compromised, which in due course result in failures to spot material errors [4]. Further, when the auditor-client relationship lengthens, management is likely to gain more reporting flexibility which could result in earnings management quality [26,27] opined that utmost criticism with respect to reduced auditor independence and its effect on earnings quality "seems to be premised on instances of overly aggressive reporting, whereby the underlying deterioration in the profitability of collapsing firms has been concealed". Aggressive reporting has been defined as using reporting methods that portray "the client's financial situation favourably when that method is not clearly indicated by the facts and relevant professional literature". The methods in totality are likely to result in an increase of earnings and/or liquidity in the sense that managers have incentives to partially estimate the future values in favour of current earnings [9].

The relationship between a long audit-client relationship and audit quality is not farfetched because economic, financial and social factors could drive the final result. Most empirical studies define audit quality relative to risk which is the risk that an auditor will fail to modify the opinion on audited financial statement that are materially misstated. If auditors are more independent, there is the likelihood that they will not compromise their integrity by attempting to manipulate earnings management, which would be shown in more income decreasing items being recorded [28]. Given that audit firm rotation impacts the independence of the auditor and also impact aggressive reporting, a variation in earnings depicting losses on a timely basis than gains would exist after audit firm rotation. Francis et al. [14] argued that conservative accounting results in higher accounting quality. This research takes the position that the level of earnings conservatism in reported earnings can be used to identify changes in the quality of those earnings after audit firm rotation.

Research Method

Population and sample of study

The population of the study consists of all quoted firms in Nigerian Stock Exchange. Samples were drawn from these sectors using the NSE classification of publicly quoted companies: Agriculture, Automobile and Tyre, Breweries, Building Materials, Chemical and Paints, Conglomerates companies, Food/Beverages and Tobacco, Construction, Healthcare, Industrial/Domestic Products, Packaging, Printing and Publishing, Textiles, Petroleum marketing companies, Banking, Insurance and others. 30 companies covering these sectors were randomly selected using the published financial statements for two years - 2009 and 2010. On the whole, 100 observations comprising of 50 from the financial sector and 50 from the non-financial sector were used.

Research hypotheses and model specification

The purpose of the present study was to investigate association between accounting conservatism (financial report quality) and audit tenure and rotation in Nigeria.

The following hypotheses have been formulated and expressed in the alternative form for the study:

H_1^1: The tenure of auditor exerts a positive influence on the firm's accounting conservatism.

H_1^2: The rotation of a firm's auditor exerts positive influence on its accounting conservatism.

H_1^3: Firm's accounting conservatism is positively associated with the rotation of audit partner.

The model adopted for the study started with a focus on measuring accounting conservatism (financial report quality) using total accruals, which were then partitioned into discretionary and non-discretionary accruals. Chen et al. [28] opined that the absolute discretionary accruals (ADA) which is a more popular and widely use indicator for measuring mangers accounting estimates and accounting choices. Thus, discretionary accrual was used to proxy accounting conservatism. In establishing discretionary accruals, we used the modified Jones model. Beaver and Ryan [20] identified the Jones model as a strong tool for measuring accounting conservatism (discretionary accruals). Dabor and Adeyemi [29] identified that the model uses components of annual financial statements such as turnover (Sales revenue), account receivables, profit and assets to establish discretionary accruals. Added to the above, the model establishes total accruals by subtracting cash flow from operations from net income before extraordinary items. Thus,

$$TACC = EBEI - CFO \quad (1)$$

Where TACC represents total accruals, EBEI is the net income before extraordinary items, and CFO is cash flow from operations. Total accruals are then partitioned into two components i.e non-discretionary accruals, which relate to normal activities of the company and discretionary accruals, which are determined according to the subjective reasoning of management. That is, discretionary accrual is a function of accounting conservatism (management choice of accounting policies) [30-32].

$$TACC = \alpha_0 + \alpha_1 (\Delta REV - \Delta REC) + \alpha_2 PPE + \alpha_3 ROA_{t-1} + e \quad (2)$$

Where ΔREV is change in revenue; ΔREC is change in accounts receivable; PPE means plants, property and equipment (Fixed Assets) and ROA is return on assets managed in the previous accounting period. All the variables that enter the equation are scaled by total assets (TA) of the previous year- $TA_{t-1.}$

The non-discretionary accruals portion (NDA) is also modelled as a function of the change in revenue, change in accounts receivable, plants, property and equipment and return on assets in the previous accounting period as follows;

$$NDA = \alpha_0 + \alpha_1 (\Delta REV - \Delta REC) + \alpha_2 PPE + \alpha_3 ROA_{t-1} \quad (3)$$

The difference between (2) and (3) above is the residual e, and this is the discretionary accruals (DA). Thus,

$$DA = TACC - [\alpha_0 + \alpha_1 (\Delta REV - \Delta REC) + \alpha_2 PPE + \alpha_3 ROA_{(t-1)}] \quad (4)$$

All the variables, except $ROA_{t-1,}$ are scaled by total assets in previous year.

In the light of the above and the research hypotheses we specified a multiple regression econometric model (4). By definition, multiple regression econometric models is one that seeks to explain change or variation in the values of one variable called the dependent variable(accounting conservatism) on the basis of changes in other variables known as the independent or explanatory variables (audit firm rotation and audit partner rotation). The assumption is that the dependent variable is a linear function of the independent variables. The function form of the model is express as follows;

$$ACC = f(AUTEN, AUDROT, AUDPAT) \quad (5)$$

The multiple regression with an error term (ε_t) is express in equation (6)

$$ACC = \alpha_0 + \beta_1 AUTEN + \beta_2 AUDROT + \beta_3 AUDPAT + \varepsilon_t \quad (6)$$

Table 1 provides a summary of variable definitions and expected signs for relations.

The study used Descriptive Statistics, Correlation Analysis, and multiple Ordinary Least Square (OLS) Regression Analysis. The model was estimated using the ordinary least square (OLS) estimation technique with the aid of computer software (Eviews 7). The hypotheses stated was tested using the t-ratios obtained from the regression result. To ensure that our model is statistical and econometrically valid we conducted diagnostic test such as goodness fit and heteroscedaticity test.

Variables	Apriori Sign	Explanation
ACC		Accounting conservatism is measured as discretionary accruals(DA); DA = TACC – $[\alpha_0 + \alpha_1 (\Delta REV-\Delta REC) + \alpha_2 PPE + \alpha_3 ROA_{t-1})$
AUTEN	+/-	Auditor Tenure (number of years the current auditor has been firms). The following code was used to measure firms auditor tenure; we assign the values of "1" for Less than one year, "2" for more than one years but less than 3yeras and "3" for more three years.
AUDROT		Firms Auditor rotation. We use three dummy to proxy firms type of auditor rotation. These three dummy are express as follows; (i) AUDROTD1 = is assign the value of "1" when there is a change of auditor from non-big 4 to Big 4 (CROSS UP) otherwise "0" (ii) AUDROTD2 = is assign the value of "1" when there is a change of auditor from big 4 to non-Big 4 (CROSS DOWN) otherwise "0" (iii) AUDROTD3 = is assign the value of "1" when there is a change of auditor from big 4 to another Big 4 (LATERAL) otherwise "0"
AUDPAT		Firms Auditor partner rotation. The value of "1" is assign when there is a change of firms auditor partner, otherwise "0"

Table 1: Definition of Variables and Expected Signs.

	TENURE	AUDROTD1	AUDROTD2	AUDROTD3	ACC
Mean	4.5	0.02	0.02	0.55	97381941
Median	5	0	0	1	3925558
Maximum	5	1	1	1	3.36E+09
Minimum	1	0	0	0	-9072908
Std. Dev.	1.267304	0.140705	0.140705	0.5	4.04E+08
Skewness	-2.319302	6.857143	6.857143	-0.201008	6.737039
Kurtosis	6.57114	48.02041	48.02041	1.040404	50.39974
Jarque-Bera	142.7904	9228.828	9228.828	16.67347	10117.86
Probability	0	0	0	0.00024	0
Observations	100	100	100	100	100

Table 2: Descriptive statistics of study variables.

	TENURE	AUDROTD1	AUDROTD2	AUDROTD3	ACC
TENURE	1	-0.056647	-0.113293	-0.231144	0.051144
AUDROTD1	-0.05665	1	0.489796	-0.014358	-0.345209
AUDROTD2	-0.11329	0.489796	1	-0.014358	-0.345009
AUDROTD3	-0.23114	-0.014358	-0.014358	1	-0.043303
ACC	0.051144	-0.345209	-0.345009	-0.043303	1

Table 3: Correlation analysis between Audit Tenure, Rotation, and Accounting conservatism.

Data Presentation and Analysis

Descriptive statistical analysis

The descriptive statistical analysis result of variables is captured in Table 2. Result shows that the minimum audit tenure of firms quoted on the Stock Exchange is about a year while the maximum audit tenure is about 5 years. On average the audit tenure is about 4.5 years. 63 firms have had the same auditor from 2006 to 2010 which indicates No audit rotation. Hence majority of firms quoted on the Stock exchange do not rotate their auditors.

The minimum auditor rotation from non-big4 to big4 (AUDROTD1) is 0 while the maximum auditor rotation from non-big4 to big4 (AUDROTD1). It was observed that only one firm had changed from non-big4 to big4 audit firm. The minimum auditor rotation from big4 to non-big4 (AUDROTD2) is 0 while the maximum auditor rotation from big4 to non-big4 (AUDROTD2). It was observed that only three firms had changed from big4 to non-big4 audit firm. The minimum auditor rotation from big4 to big4 (AUDROTD3) is 0 while the maximum auditor rotation from big4 to big4 (AUDROTD3). It was observed that only six firms had changed from big4 to non-big4 audit firm. The jarque-Bera statistics revealed that all the variables are normally distributed.

Variable	Coefficient	Std. Error	t-Statistic	Prob.
C	-1.20E+08	1.59E+08	-0.755601	0.4518
TENURE	-34855898	30746418	-2.133657	0.0348
AUDROTD1	-6.67E+08	3.07E+08	-2.175414	0.0321
AUDROTD2	-7.01E+08	3.08E+08	-2.273202	0.0253
AUDROTD3	60897974	77439048	0.786399	0.4336
R-squared	0.373564	Mean dependent var		97381941
Adjusted R-squared	0.338767	S.D. dependent var		4.04E+08
S.E. of regression	3.74E+08	Akaike info criterion		42.36866
Sum squared resid	1.33E+19	Schwarz criterion		42.49892
Log likelihood	-2113.433	F-statistic		4.987863
Durbin-Watson stat	1.995234	Prob(F-statistic)		0.001080

Table 4: Ordinary Least Square regression result for 2009.

Inferential statistical analysis

Correlation analysis: In exploring the relationship between accounting conservatism and the variables used in the study, we carried out correlation analysis using Pearson product moment correlation method. The results are presented in the Table 3. There is a weak positive relationship of about 5% between accounting conservatism and audit tenure. An increase in audit tenure would lead to an increase in accounting conservatism. There is fairly weak negative relationship between accounting conservatism and auditor rotation from non-big4 to big4 (AUDROTD1) with correlation co-efficient of -0.35). With a correlation co-efficient of -0.35, the relationship between accounting conservatism and auditor rotation from big4 to non-big4 (AUDROTD2) is fairly weak and negative. There exists a weak negative relationship between accounting conservatism and auditor rotation from big4 to big4 (AUDROTD3) with a correlation value of 0.04.

An increase in auditor rotation from non-big4 to big4 audit firm, rotation from big4 to non-big4, or rotation from big4 to big4 should lead to a decrease in accounting conservatism.

Regression analysis: Regression Analysis for 2009- The result from the ordinary least square regression result is presented in Table 4. The coefficient of determination (R-Square) with a value of 0.37 means that about 37% of the total systematic variations in accounting conservatism(ACC), have been explained by the explanatory variables taken together. The Adjusted R-square shows that even after adjusting for the degree of freedom the model could still explain only about 33% of the total systematic variations in accounting conservatism (ACC) while about 67% of the systematic variation in accounting conservatism (ACC) was left unaccounted for by the model which has been captured by the stochastic disturbance term in the model. This implies that other factors apart from audit tenure and audit rotation affect accounting conservatism in Nigeria.

It was observed that the overall model was statistically significant since the calculated F- value of 4.92 was greater than the critical F-value at 5% level of significance. On the basis of the individual statistical significance, as shown by the t-ratios in the table above, it was observed that TENURE, AUDROTD1, and AUDROTD2 was statistically significant since their calculated t-values of 2.13, 2.17 and 2.27 respectively was greater than the critical t-value of 2.0 at 5% level of significance under the two tailed test. This means that TENURE, AUDROTD1, and AUDROTD2 had a significant impact on accounting conservatism while AUDROTD3 was not statistically significant since the calculated t-value of 0.78 was less than the critical t-value of 2.0 at 5% level of significance under the two tailed test (Table 5). The Durbin Watson statistics of 1.99 indicates the absence of first order autocorrelation of the stochastic variables inside the error term in the model.

Regression Analysis for 2010-The coefficient of determination (R-Square) with a value of 0.24 means that about 24% of the total systematic variations in accounting conservatism(ACC), have been explained by the explanatory variables taken together. The Adjusted R-square shows that even after adjusting for the degree of freedom the model could still explain only about 20% of the total systematic variations in accounting conservatism (ACC) while about 80% of the systematic variation in accounting conservatism (ACC) was left unaccounted for by the model. Overall, the model was statistically significant since the calculated F-value of 6.03 was greater than the critical F-value at 5% level of significance.

On the basis of the individual statistical significance, as shown by the t-ratios in the table above, it was observed that TENURE, AUDROTD1, and AUDROTD2 was statistically significant since their calculated t-values of 3.2, 1.85 and 2.02 respectively was greater than the critical t-value at 5% and 10% level of significance under the two tailed test. This means that TENURE, AUDROTD1, and AUDROTD2 had a significant impact on accounting conservatism while AUDROTD3 was not statistically significant since the calculated t-value of 0.97 was less than the critical t-value at 5% and 10% level of significance under the two tailed test. Thus, audit rotation from big4 to big4 audit firm has no significant impact on accounting conservatism. Furthermore, it was observed that TENURE, AUDROTD1, and AUDROTD2 had a negative relationship with accounting conservatism while AUDROTD1 had a positive relationship with accounting conservatism. The Durbin Watson statistics of 2.16 indicates the absence of first order autocorrelation of the stochastic variables inside the error term in the model.

Variable	Coefficient	Std. Error	t-Statistic	Prob.
C	1.90E+08	95851995	1.984407	0.0487
TENURE	-33668373	19164255	-1.756832	0.0806
AUDROTD1	-3.17E+08	98391253	-3.224391	0.0015
AUDROTD2	-55068027	83607088	-2.658653	0.0309
AUDROTD3	-22252045	62997046	-0.353224	0.7243
AR(1)	0.062273	0.073264	0.849981	0.3964
R-squared	0.119767	Mean dependent var		35373807
Adjusted R-squared	0.096105	S.D. dependent var		1.80E+08
S.E. of regression	1.71E+08	Akaike info criterion		40.78292
Sum squared resid	5.44E+18	Schwarz criterion		40.88471
Log likelihood	-3909.160	F-statistic		5.061543
Durbin-Watson stat	2.037436	Prob(F-statistic)		0.000225

Table 5: Pooled Ordinary Least Square regression result.

Pooled regression analysis: The coefficient of determination (R-Square) with a value of 0.119 means that about 12% of the total systematic variations in accounting conservatism(ACC), have been explained by the explanatory variables taken together. The Adjusted R-square shows that even after adjusting for the degree of freedom the model could still explain only about 10% of the total systematic variations in accounting conservatism (ACC) while about 90% of the systematic variation in accounting conservatism (ACC) was left unaccounted for by the model which has been captured by the stochastic disturbance term in the model. This implies that other factors apart from audit tenure and audit rotation affect accounting conservatism in Nigeria.

The F-statistics shows that the overall model was statistically significant since the calculated F- value of 5.06 was greater than the critical F-value at 5% level of significance. it was observed that TENURE, AUDROTD1, and AUDROTD2 was statistically significant since their calculated t-values of 1.75, 3.22 and 2.65 respectively was greater than the critical t-value at 5% and 10% level of significance under the two tailed test. Thus, audit rotation from big4 to big4 audit firm has no significant impact on accounting conservatism. Furthermore, it was observed that TENURE, AUDROTD1, AUDROTD2 and AUDROTD1 had a negative relationship with accounting conservatism. Durbin Watson statistics of 2.0 indicates the absence of first order autocorrelation of the stochastic variables inside the error term in the model.

Hypotheses testing

Hypothesis 1

H_1^1: The tenure of auditor exerts a positive influence on the firm's accounting conservatism.

The empirical result reveals that TENURE with a calculated t-value of 1.75 is greater than the critical t-values of 1.64 at 10% level of significance under the two-tailed test. Hence, we reject the null hypothesis and accept the alternative hypothesis that the tenure of auditor exerts a significant influence on firms accounting conservatism.

Hypothesis 2

H_1^2: The rotation of a firm's auditor exerts positive influence on its accounting conservatism.

The empirical result reveals that AUDROTD1 with a calculated t-value of 3.22 is greater than the critical t-values of 1.64 at 10% level of significance under the two-tailed test. Hence, we reject the null hypothesis and accept the alternative hypothesis that the rotation of audit firms from Big 4 to Non-Big4 audit firms exerts a significant influence on firms accounting conservatism.

Hypothesis 3

H_1^3: Firm's accounting conservatism is positively associated with the rotation of audit partner.

The empirical result reveals that AUDROTD2 with a calculated t-value of 2.65 is greater than the critical t-values of 1.64 at 10% level of significance under the two-tailed test. Hence, we reject the null hypothesis and accept the alternative hypothesis that the rotation of audit firms from Non-Big 4 to Big4 audit firms exerts a significant influence on firms accounting conservatism.

Discussion of Findings

The study revealed that the tenure of auditor has a significant positive influence on firms accounting conservatism; conservatism increases as auditor tenure lengthens. This is consistent with the findings of Jenkins and Velur that conservatism increases as auditor tenure lengthens. The study also showed that the rotation of audit firms from Non-Big 4 to Big4 audit firms and from Big 4 to Non- Big4 audit firms has a significant influence on accounting conservatism which is in tandem with the findings of Sinnett that mandatory auditor rotation will adversely affect not only the auditors' accumulation of specific knowledge about their clients, but also auditors' independence because it undermines the incentives to build up a reputation for auditors' honesty, especially in the last period before rotation. Meanwhile, a newly appointed auditor might fail because of lack of a thorough understanding of the client. Incumbent auditors can profit from their learning curve effect in the detection of material errors or breach.

The study establishes the necessity to have properly defined maximum legal audit tenure, in order to minimize audit tenure elongation in Nigeria. There has been recent expression of concern by the Institute of Chartered Accountants of Nigeria, ICAN, that a long involvement of an individual or audit team with a client could lead to circumstances that could threaten objectivity and independence. It therefore suggested an orderly rotation of senior personnel serving on an audit engagement (section 4:76 of Rules of Professional Conduct for Members).

The study found out that long audit tenure impacts negatively on the quality of the auditor's report when the audit tenure is prolonged. This indicates that the longer the audit tenure, the lower the quality of audit. This disagrees with the findings of Ghosh and Moon, Carcello and Nagy [31] that prolongation of audit tenure increases audit quality because an auditor is able to gain firm-specific expertise and a better understanding of the client's business as the auditor's tenure. The study revealed that audit rotation can minimize the negative impact of long tenure, but the audit firms rather than audit partners should be rotated.

Conclusion and Recommendations

The study has attempted to empirically examine audit tenure, rotation and accounting conservatism in Nigeria. We therefore conclude that: the tenure of auditor has a significant influence on firms accounting conservatism; the rotation of audit firms from non-big4 to big4, rotation from big4 to non-big4, or rotation from big4 to big4 has a significant influence on accounting conservatism. In Nigeria, there exists a negative relationship between audit tenure and audit quality. This indicates that the longer the audit tenure, it may create familiarity threat by virtue of a close relationship with the client, its directors, officers or employees. The audit opinion of the auditor will favour the client, thus, impairing the independence of the auditor. Low-quality audits can mislead investors and result in misallocated resources. To ensure quality of audit and enhance auditor's independence, a period of five years has been suggested and adopted in some countries as the maximum audit tenure in an audite company for a principal partner of a firm.

The research contributes to knowledge in that it scientifically examines the connection between audit tenure, rotation and accounting conservatism. It also empirically established that the tenure.

The study recommends the mandatory rotation of audit firm lead engagement partner and the review partner on an engagement for publicly listed companies. A partner rotated after a pre-defined period should not resume the lead engagement role until a further period of time, say minimum of two years. The tenure of the Appointed Auditor should be one year in the first instance, renewable annually subject to satisfactory performance for 3 years and on no account should annual renewal extend the total tenure of the appointed firm or firms beyond 5 years. This is to ensure that the independence of the auditor is not placed in jeopardy. Professional bodies such as the Institute of Chartered Accountants of Nigeria (ICAN) should strictly ensure that their members who audit for their clients do not audit for more than three years at a stretch to preserve the independence of the auditor and his objectivity. There should be strict prohibition as to the provision of non-audit services by auditors to their audit clients. This could impair an auditor's independence. The auditor would lack independence if he represents an audit client before a law court on matters outside their main audit job such as maintaining or preparing the audit client's accounting records, preparing financial statements and originating source data underlying the audit client's financial statements.

References

1. (2004) Companies and Allied Matters Act (CAMA).
2. Jenkins D, Velury U (2008) Does auditor tenure influence the reporting of conservative earnings? Journal of Accounting and Public Policy 27: 115-132.
3. Jackson AB, Moldrich M, Roebuck P (2008) Mandatory audit firm rotation and audit quality, Managerial Auditing Journal 23: 420-437.
4. Myers J, Myers L, Omer T (2003) Exploring the term of the auditor-client relationship and the quality of earnings: A case for mandatory auditor rotation? The Accounting Review 78: 779-799.
5. Coopers P (2002) Mandatory rotation of audit firms: will it improve audit quality? New York.
6. Bliss J (1924) Management through accounts. New York: Ronald Press.
7. Watts R (2003) Conservatism in accounting Part1: Explanations and implications, Accounting Horizons 17: 207-221.
8. FASB (1980) Statement of Concepts No.2: Qualitative characteristics of accounting information, Financial Accounting Standard Board, Norwalk.
9. Basu S (1997) The conservatism principle and the asymmetric timeliness of earnings. J Account Eco 24: 3-37.
10. Givoly D, Hayn C (2000) The changing time series properties of earnings, cash flows and accruals: has financial reporting become more conservative?, J Account Eco 29: 287-320.
11. Ball R, Kothari S, Robin A (2000) The Effect of International Institutional Factors on Properties of Accounting Earnings. J Account Res 29: 1-51.
12. Chaney P, Philipich K (2003) The price-earnings relation in troubled times: the case of Arthur Andersen. Working paper, Vanderbilt University and The Ohio State University.
13. Krishnan G (2003) Audit quality and the pricing of discretionary accruals, Auditing: A Journal of Practice and Theory 22: 109-126.
14. Francis J, Olsson R, Schipper K (2004) Costs of capital and earnings attributes. The Accounting Review 79: 967-1010.
15. Giner B, Rees W (2001) On the asymmetric recognition of good and bad news in France, Germany and the United Kingdom, J Bus Financ Account 28: 1333-1349.
16. Pope P, Walker M (2002) Ex-ante and ex-post accounting conservatism, asset recognition, and asymmetric earnings timelines. Working Paper, Lancaster University.
17. Richardson G, Tinaikar S (2004) Accounting based valuation models: what have we learned? Accounting and Finance 44: 223-255.
18. Chandra U, Wasley C, Waymire G (2004) Income conservatism in the U.S. technology sector. Working paper, University of Rochester.
19. Ball R, Shivakumar L (2006) The Role of Accruals in Asymmetrically Timely Gain and Loss Recognition, J Account Res 44: 207-242.

20. Beaver W, Ryan S (2005) Conditional and unconditional conservatism: concepts and modelling, Review of Accounting Studies 10: 269-309.

21. Ryan S, Zarowin P (2003) Why has the contemporaneous linear returns earnings relation declined? The Accounting Review 78: 523-553.

22. Basu S (2001) Discussion of 'on the asymmetric recognition of good and bad news in France, Germany and the United Kingdom. J Bus Financ Account 28: 1333-1349.

23. DeAngelo L (1981) Auditor size and audit quality. J Account Eco 3: 113-127.

24. Antle R, Nalebuff B (1991) Conservatism and auditor-client negotiations. J Account Res 29: 31-54.

25. Hamilton J, Ruddock C, Stokes D, Taylor S (2005) Audit partner rotation, earnings quality and earnings conservatism, Working paper, and University of New South Wales, Sydney.

26. Davis LR, Soo B, Trompeter G (2000) Auditor tenure, auditor independence and earnings management. Working paper, Michigan Tech University and Boston College.

27. Kaplan S, Mauldin E (2008) Auditor rotation and the appearance of independence: Evidence from non-professional investors, J Account Public Policy 27: 177-192.

28. Chen K, Elder R, Hsieh Y (2007) Corporate Governance and Earnings management: The Implication of Corporate Governance Best Practice Principles for Taiwanese listed companies. J Contemp Acc Eco 3: 73-105.

29. Dabor E, Adeyemi S (2009) Corporate Governance and the Credibility of Financial Statements in Nigeria, J Bus Sys Governance and Ethics 4.

30. Ghosh A, Moon D (2005) Does auditor tenure impair audit quality? The Accounting Review 80: 585-612.

31. Carcello J, Nagy A (2004) Audit firm tenure and fraudulent financial reporting Auditing: A Journal of Practice and Theory 23: 55-69.

An Empirical Analysis to Assess the Impact of Inconsistency of Exchange Rate on Share Market: A Case Study of London Stock Exchange

Hossain SA*

Teaching Assistant, London college of business management and Information technology, UK

Abstract

This study evaluated the impacts of inconstancy of exchange rate on the London Stock Exchange (LSE). An assessment of writing on inconstancy of exchange rate and stock exchanges was led coming about into detail of an observational model. The Regression model was utilized as a part of making the relationship between conversion standard instability and securities exchange execution. The study utilized month to month United Kingdom information for the period August, 2004 - July, 2014. The information recurrence chose guaranteed a sufficient number of perceptions. An extremely feeble relationship between money instability and the share trading system was affirmed. The exploration finding is upheld by past studies. US premium rates were found to have a positive effect on Market capitalisation. Also GBP volatility makes greater impact on the money supply.

This study prescribed that, since the United Kingdom securities exchange is not by any means presented to the negative impacts of inconstancy of exchange rate, government can utilize conversion scale as an arrangement device to pull in outside portfolio speculation. The feeble relationship between inconstancy of exchange rate and money markets proposes that the LSE could be advertised as a safe business for remote speculators. Nonetheless, financial specialists, investors and portfolio directors still need to be vigilant concerning the overflows from the remote swapping scale into money markets. Despite the fact that there is a powerless relationship between GBP inconstancy and stocks in United Kingdom, this does not so much imply that financial specialists and portfolio administrators require not screen the improvements between these two variables.

Introduction

Rationale

The trend of volatility has been regarded as one of most prominent difficulties or the UK economy in recent years. Despite the fact that exchange markets, various firms and various industries are working together for diminishing the GBP volatility, in the same way as, vitality worth producers mentioned lowering the costs with diverse arrangements, steadiness inside conversion scale also been regarded as a long shot. For UK, Instability additionally has made an economy dilemma and it is introducing the as lower weight currency against EURO. Volatility of currency is mainly functioning as an important reactor for the UK economy growth. Exchange rate unpredictability caused basically by the tsunami of structural movements in the worldwide economy. In most of the cases, it is influencing stocks too. It is exceptionally critical for strategy creators to comprehend the relationship between fluctuations of exchange rate and stock market. Likewise there are such a large number of debates around nature's domain also. Analyzing fluctuations of exchange rate will provide such important knowledge which will determine the factual impacts exchange rate on London Stock Exchange (LSE).

Relevance to the management study

The Exchange rate ideal has changed fundamentally inside most recent 100 years. Since the starting till now guidelines have changed namelessly. Just extravagant nations had fluctuating exchange rates and level cash a while ago. Anyway, by the end of the century the parameter has been changed. It is not any more similar to the recent past. It has now ended up more evident to try for a coasting conversion standard. To extra, these drifting trade rates have affected the stock exchanges not at all like different apparatuses of economy. In purpose of certainty, decision is significantly more confounded than some time recently. In the Bretton Wood framework, one of the significant concerns of approach producers is the vitality of unpredictability of exchange rates. This evident to be, a projecting adaptability of exchange rates framework. Instability of exchange rates has significant derivations inside financial commercial center, especially stock markets. Above analysis settled the point of exchange rate and share market importance for any kind of management. It is very much relevant to the management studies and therefore, the study significance is higher for study of management.

Purpose of the project and achieving aim

Various researches have proved that exchange rate fluctuation has impacted on the stock market. It has been regarded as one of the top priority of business and finance area. This has prejudiced researcher to involve a research on such subject. Researcher aims to define the impact of exchange rate fluctuation on LSE. Below objective and question certainly will provide a greater idea about the impacts.

Research Objective

Research objective is "to measure the impact of inconstancy of exchange rate on the London Stock Exchange (LSE)".

***Corresponding author:** Hossain SA, Teaching Assistant, London college of business management and Information technology, United Kingdom
E-mail: ssahossain@gmail.com

Research question

- Research question is "what the impact of inconstancy of exchange rate on the London Stock Exchange (LSE)?

Structure

The paper report is separated into 6 tiers. Introduction, is the essential portion is the that demonstrated the foundation besides assorted establishments for the work report including research background, research objective, research question and targets and the essentialness of the study. Literature Review is second portion which kept an eye out for the aide perspectives of research. Overview of LSE and exchange rate is the third portion that outlines LSE (London Stock Exchange) and exchange rate summary. Research methodology, is the fourth portion that explains the procedure of the research, research plan where the research method and technique moreover the parts of vital and optional research and information get-together have been tended to. Data presentation and analysis, is the fifth portion where data assortment is done and then analyzed accordingly. Discussion is the sixth portion where all the results are discussed and evaluated whether it matches the objectives or not. Conclusion is the section of the where researcher addresses the proposal and further proposal on the research to conclude the work (Figure 1).

Literature Review

Introduction

A few scholastics, for example, Ross [1,2] furnished speculations with evidences on exchange rate fluctuation and stock market. Not, one or the other has provided such important models that actually can identify the actual relationships of exchange and stock market. This chapter is divided into two parts. First researcher will present the theoretical base and provide the gathered empirical evidences of exchange rate fluctuations.

Flow oriented model

Relying on the grounds of microeconomics Flow oriented model was established. is focused around the grounds of microeconomics. Flow oriented model shows associating connection presence which runs from exchange rate to stock prices. As such, stock costs are influenced through fluctuations of exchange rate. Saleh [3] mentioned that flow oriented model involves that worldwide intensity along with offset of exchange points that are influenced through exchange rate. Thusly it makes influences the future and present expected association's money stream and qualities of the stock. Local currencies positive reception captures a floating framework can regulate organization's increase and aggressive execution of trading stocks [4]. In this manner they maintain their cost of stock. Joseph accepts it that it can affect the data and yield costs, intensity of associations which are influenced through progressions within return rate.

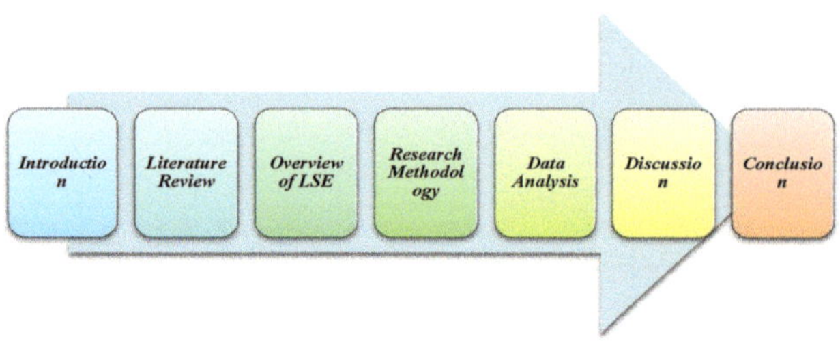

Figure 1: Structure of study.

Adverse consequences of exporters are conspicuous whether rate of trade. Subsequently, worldwide aggressiveness would be decreasing. Thusly, lessening benefit would influence the residential aggressiveness of the association. Resultantly, a discouraging correspondence between household money and stock cost might be perceived. In any case importing firms are profited if the trade rates acknowledge through encouraging the lessening in info costs. Low costs for the last items and administrations would be made by the decrease in expenses. Therefore benefits will be supported by the expanded deals. The appeal of the association in the residential securities exchange will build and the normal level of stock costs will be helped. Subsequently, the pattern of the effect relies on upon whether the organizations work essentially in an import or trading industry [3].

Legitimacy of flow orient model's

Aggarwal [5] mentioned about the flow orient model that it is backed through procurement of proof. Author also inspected the relationship of exchange rate and stock price. This concentrated the relationship of US exchange weighted conversion standard and US securities exchange files of every month within the period of 1974 and 1978. The optimistic correspondence within US securities exchange records and the exchange rate volatility is found in the study that presumes two variables are interrelated with a consistent style along with the flow orient model. In between the period of 1980 to 1986, US dollar and US stock price maintained a link that is downbeat. This figure was achieved through the monthly figures [6]. This also represented the flow model. Casualty and cointegration research was used by Bahmani and Sohrabian [7] for investigating the exchange rate and stock price correlation. To add on it, Fang and Miller investigated same kind of research on Korea of a period 1997 to 2002. Bhattacharya and Mukherje, Chow, et al., Solnik, Young and Frank all established a verification that flow oriented model is not consistent [8-11].

Stock oriented model

In spite of the fact that the remote cash business is overwhelmed by the worldwide capital developments, a clear issue with the stream arranged model was brought up by Pilbeam [12] as being that they don't identify with the global monetary developments. This model's fundamental nature provides the capital record parity of installments. Money related record for determining the exchange rates were pushed by this stock oriented model. While exploring this stock oriented model, Adjasi and Biekpe confirmed the supply and request for possessions are likened through swapping scale. In this way, value developments of fiscally held holdings are affected altogether by the possibilities of relative money developments. In this manner swapping scale developments may affect or be affected by the stock value developments. Harmony of stock within currency business sector decides the supply and interest for coinage; the money related model suggests. Financial model distinguishes the swapping scale as a relative stake cost.

Legitimacy of stock oriented model

To a large extent, present value of asset is influenced by expected rate of return. Three variables that determine the exchange rate are relative national yield, relative cash supply and the relative premium rates. These variables also focuses on the on the stock trade rates. Friedman [13] established such financial model that incorporates the costs of stock. Friedman [13] has also outlined the interest determination for elevating the trading system of share. For accompanying capacity the model is demonstrated below $E(R_i) = R_f + [E(R_m) - R_f]xB_i$

$$m_t = p_t + \alpha y_t - \beta i_t + \chi s_t$$

Portfolio balance model

Portfolio balance model hypnotizes a negative relationship in between the exchange rate and costs of stock. It mainly expresses the effect of exchange rate on costs of stock. For building the interest strength and the stake of national and international, the part of trade rates and all-inclusive spread portfolios are assumed by the model Stavárek [14]. Using immediate and roundabout channel, the energy about residential coin is headed by an expand in local stocks costs. A conversion standard with a negative relationship is relied upon to be headed by stock cost since the local riches is lessened by decline in the stock cost, which thus prompts lower cash request and premium rates as far as the household prospect [15]. Along these lines one currency gratefulness and inflows of capital will be headed to the circumstance.

The accompanying mathematical statement exhibits the business sectors which the model comprises of; where the aggregate of outside securities if, residential securities B and cash M would characterize the aggregate riches W. The model is

$$W = M + B + e^F$$

Welfens [16] mentioned that rather than the residential security markets, securities exchange is incorporated through a modified approach of portfolio offset.

Practical validity of portfolio balance model

Richard, et al. [17] examined the interface of exchange rate and costs of stock in Australia. While determining the exchange rate and costs of stock author involved the granger causality test and which clashed with the portfolio theory approach. Ajayi, et. al depicted the connection in between these two variables. Bahmani and Sohrabian [7] utilized the causality research for realising the connection in between the exchange rate and stock exchange. Many other authors like, frank and Young, Aggarwal [5,11] used this model for realising the same relationship. However, Sonen and Hennigar [6] determined a negative association of this relationship.

Hypothesis of efficient market

The data that is accessible for securities and reflects on the costs of securities is known as efficient market hypothesis. This mainly works on the productivity of the capital market where handling data is initiated by theories. Security cost increases the value of characteristics. Kasper [18] commented that it creates effective business speculation.

Practical validity of efficient market hypothesis

Business like proof supportive EMH gets to be noticeable when return to of alterably overseen common stores is surpassed by the reappearance of business sector midpoints. The current stock costs after the report of a takeover in the UK has been considered by Firth (; cases Mandal [19]. Semi-solid structure effectiveness of (United Kingdom) securities exchange and the completely quick alteration for offering costs to their right levels were noticeable in the conclusion from study of Firth.

Capital Asset Pricing Model (CAPM)

Capital Asset Pricing Model (CAPM) is a model that actually works with a facilitating set for forecasting yield of the asset for the year. It was developed in the 60's. Yield of the asset [σ2] is displayed by the icon. This model explicates doubt about estimation where yield's standard deviation is charecterized [20]. Grosman and Livingstone mentioned that the mathematical statement CAPM is anticipated by the yield of stock. The model is

$$E(R_i) = R_f + [E(R_m) - R_f]xB_i$$

As per the solution, the yield got for initiating interest in danger free securities, Rf must equivalent the anticipated yield of any dubious stock i-E (Ri). The yield adjusted stands on an unsafe possession which is biased through precise factors.

Validity of CAPM

Roll evolved an empirical test with stock indicator and other features of markets and identified it as hard for empirical test. Taylor [21] also supported the critique of roll. Fama and McBeth (1973) found the correlation of risk and return which is positive. Taylor [21] suggested that their firm and market ratio was very much reliable and CAPM actually calculates the evident.

The arbitrage pricing theory and its practical validity

Drake and Fabozzi proposed the model APT (Arbitrage Pricing Theory) for Differentiating CAPM's market danger, one set of risky factors make impact on an advantage's normal yield. Model APT (Arbitrage Pricing Theory) creates a direct relationship of the yield on a basis of benefit with the H component. Vernimmen [22] mentioned that APT counts the Yield stock.

Discussion

From, above theories researcher found that Richard [17] examined the interface of exchange rate and costs of stock in Australia. While determining the exchange rate and costs of stock author involved the granger causality test and which clashed with the portfolio theory approach. Ajayi depicted the connection in between these two variables. Therefore, researcher followed portfolio model for this research paper.

Empirical Analysis

The conduct of unpredictability of stock exchange has been broadly contemplated utilizing the Regression structure spearheaded by Engel and further created by Bollerslev, and others. These studies endeavored to explore the relation of exchange rates and stock costs association within the rising monetary markets and industrialized nations. Notwithstanding, the aftereffects of some of these studies are uncertain. The present study might take a gander at studies that have been carried out in creating nations, developing markets and in created nations.

Developing Countries

Adjasi and Biekpe [12] researched the relationship between stock costs and swapping scale development in Ghana, South Africa, Egypt, Kenya, Mauritius and Nigeria. Vector Auto Regressive cointegration (VAR) was utilized by them and drive reaction investigation for focusing the short run linkage and long run linkage within stock costs and exchange rates. Long run relationship standard between stock costs and the conversion are discovered from their study in Tunisia, where swapping scale devaluation drove down stock costs. A short-run mistake adjustment display likewise demonstrated comparative results.

Adjasi, Harvey and Agyapong [12] utilized the Exponential Generalized Autoregressive Conditional Heteroskedascity (EGARCH) display in making the relationship between conversion standard unpredictability and securities exchange instability in Ghana. In their study, it was discovered that there was negative relationship between swapping scale unpredictability and securities exchange returns, deterioration in the nearby cash prompts a build in stock exchange returns over the long haul. Moreover, there was instability determination in the vast majority of the macroeconomic variables; current period's rate had an impact on conjecture change of future rate. It was likewise uncovered that an expand (diminish) in exchange shortfall and desire in future climb in exchange shortage will diminishing (build) stock exchange unpredictability. Furthermore, the buyer value file demonstrated a solid association with stock exchange instability. This implied that a build in buyer value prompted an ascent in securities exchange unpredictability. At long last, there was the vicinity of influence impact and instability stuns in stock profits for the Ghana Stock Exchange.

Pilinkus and Boguslauskas examined the short-run relationship between stock exchange costs and macroeconomic variables in Lithuania. One of their macroeconomic variables was swapping scale. The Augmented Dickey Fuller test was utilized to check the stationary of the chose time arrangement since a spurious relapse may happen if a period arrangement is not stationary. The study utilized the Impulse reaction capacity to test the presence of the short-run relationship between securities exchange costs and macroeconomic variables. As the consequences of the Impulse reaction capacity are dependable just with a stationary time arrangement the information was transformed into stationary after the second distinction. The consequences of the study unmistakably showed that macroeconomic variables are critical determinants at stock exchange costs in Lithuania. Their study presumed that unemployment rate, swapping scale, and transient premium rates adversely impact securities exchange costs. Through the Error Correction model, Subair and Salihu explored the impacts of exchange rateinstability on the Nigeria securities exchanges. It was observed that the swapping scale instability produced by means of GARCH procedure pushes a stronger negative effect on the Nigeria securities exchanges. Notwithstanding, the rate of swelling and premium rate did not have long run association with securities exchange promotion since the significant member in the business sector was the administration. In light of this, it was proposed that a facilitated money related and monetary strategy ought to be placed set up to check mate the vacillation of swapping scale so as to extend the profundity of the Stock Market.

Olugbenga analyzed the long-run and short-run impacts of exchange rate on stock exchange advancement in Nigeria in excess of 1985:1–2009:4 utilizing the Johansen cointegration tests. A bi-variate model was pointed out and observational results demonstrated a huge positive stock exchange execution to swapping scale in the short-run and a noteworthy negative stock exchange execution to conversion standard over the long haul. The Granger causality test indicated solid proof that the causation runs from swapping scale to securities exchange execution. This suggested that varieties in the Nigerian securities exchange are clarified by exchange rate instability. The study reasoned that the negative impact of exchange rate on Nigerian stock exchange execution could have been an aftereffect of overwhelming degrading of the coin since the presentation of the structural alteration program in 1986.

General evaluation

An investigation of studies from creating nations was directed and it was watched that there is no general accord concerning the connection between swapping scale and the stock exchange. Whilst a few studies found that swapping scale unpredictability pushes a stronger negative effect on the securities exchanges, others found that there is no relationship between these two variables. It was additionally watched that diverse studies connected distinctive methodologies to attain their targets. Confirmation of remarkable connections between trade rates and the stock exchange has been seen in various African nations. Notwithstanding, because of the distinctive approachs that were utilized by diverse studies furthermore the way that studies were directed in distinctive nations, diverse results could be acquired.

Developing markets

Murinde and Abdalla explored associations within stock cost and exchange rate among the rising monetary markets like, Philippine, Pakistan, Korea, India. The inspiration was to make the causal linkages between heading costs in the outside trade business sector and money markets; the linkages had suggestions for the on-going endeavors to create stock exchanges in rising economies all the while with an approach shift towards freely skimming trade rates. A bivariate vector autoregressive model was connected as an estimation strategy and the study utilized month to month perceptions on the IFC stock value list and the genuine viable swapping scale in excess of 1985:01 - 1994:07. Their finding has strategy suggestions; it recommended that separate governments ought to be mindful in their execution of swapping scale strategies, given that such approaches have repercussions on their securities exchanges.

The essential instinct behind Karoui's examination was that the instability of the stock returns could be incompletely clarified by the unpredictability of the money rates. The study concentrated on the accompanying 18 rising nations which are- Turkey, Thailand, Taiwan, South korea, South Africa, Russia, Philippines, Poland, Peru, Mexico, Malaysia, Indonesia, India, Hungary, Colombia, Chile, Brazil, Argentina. The study discovered a huge relationship between cash rate instability and stocks returns unpredictability for an expansive piece of the records mulled over. Additionally, a positive relationship between the outside conversion standard instability and the stock return unpredictability in an expansive piece of the division records concentrated on was found.

Spirits explored the degree of instability overflows between stock returns and exchange rate changes for six Latin American budgetary markets to be specific: Venezuela, Colombia, Chile, Brazil, Argentina and Mexico one European monetary market, and Spain in the 1998-2006 periods. The study partitioned the example into sub periods, before and after the presentation of the Euro and it connected the EGARCH technique to model unpredictability. The results demonstrated that the instability of stock returns influences the unpredictability of trade rates; nonetheless, no proof of instability transmission in the inverse course was found. The after effects of the study are predictable with those of Kanas and Yang and Doong who both discovered proof of instability overflows from stock comes back to trade rates. However the results vary on the proof of overflows in the inverse course from trade rates to securities exchanges. Spirits' study found that in spite of the fact that unpredictability overflows are substantially less pervasive from the different two-sided trade rates to the stock exchanges in the nations inspected, and also less steady crosswise over nations and about whether than the overflows from stock exchanges to trade rates.

Agrawal and Srivastav observationally inspected the motion between the unpredictability of stock returns and development of Rupee-Dollar trade rates, as far as the degree of interdependency and causality. Supreme estimations of information were changed over to log ordinary structures and checked for typicality. Application of Jarque-Bera test yielded facts that confirmed non-typical conveyance of both the variables. These postured inquiries on the stationary of the two arrangements. Stationary of the two arrangements was checked with ADF test and the results demonstrated stationary at level structures for both the arrangement. The coefficient of relationship between the two variables was registered, which showed slight negative connection between them. This cleared a path for deciding the course of impact between the two variables. Granger Causality test was connected to the two variables and it demonstrated unidirectional causality running from stock comes back to trade rates, that is, a build in the reappearances of Nifty brought on a decrease in the trade rates yet the opposite was not discovered to be genuine.

Eissa, Chortareas and Cipollini inspected the vicinity of unpredictability overflows between ostensible trade rates and stock returns in three nations: Egypt, Morocco and Turkey. The study considered day by day division files in Egypt, Morocco and Turkey. The multivariate GARCH show that was utilized did not deliver proof of cross-business sector impacts for the general stock lists returns. Anyway it was seen that a bidirectional stun and unpredictability overflows between trade rates and stock returns existed at the business division level. These discoveries were considerably more declared in Egypt and Turkey. The diverse results were because of the distinctive swapping scale administrations/approaches received by the three nations. While trade rates in Egypt and Turkey were permitted to buoy, Morocco took after an all the more firmly oversaw exchange rate administration.

In an alternate study in Turkey, Yıldiz and Ulusoy inspected the impact of conversion standard unpredictability on Turkish stock returns utilizing month to month information for the period 1987-2010. The squared residuals from the Autoregressive Moving Average (ARMA) models were utilized to create a measure of exchange rate unpredictability and after that tried against Turkish stock returns. The month to month shutting file estimations of the Istanbul Stock Exchange 100 Index (ISE) were utilized as a part of request to acquire Turkish stock returns. The consequences of the study underlined that Turkish exporters did not consider exchange rate instability as a vital issue.

General Evaluation

Above observational investigation writing in developing markets demonstrated that there is no exact congruity among the studies directed to analyze the effect trade rates on securities exchange in developing markets. A few systems have been utilized with distinctive methodologies to test the connection between trade rates and the share trading system. Procedures, for example, the Engel-Granger Causality, Johansen Cointergration, GARCH, and ARMA were utilized by different studies. On the other hand, results from these studies are uncertain; there are blended results as to the connection between the two variables. There are differentiating results and a conclusion can't be attracted as to the relationship between conversion standard and stocks. This legitimizes the need of more research around there to help existing writing.

Developed countries

Aggarwal [5] inspected the relationship between trade rates and stock costs by taking a gander at the association between progressions in the US exchange weighted exchange rate and changes in US securities exchange records every month for the period 1974 to 1978. The study found that the exchange weighted exchange rate and the US securities exchange records were emphatically connected amid this period. The study reasoned that developments in the swapping scale could specifically influence the stock costs of multinational firms by impacting the estimation of its abroad operations, and in roundabout way impact household firms through affecting the costs of its fares and/or its foreign made inputs.

Results demonstrated that nations like France, Germany, and Hong Kong don't display solid proof of positive commitment to swapping scale vacillations. This suggested that deteriorating neighborhood coinage are connected with climbing US stock exchanges, recommending a negative effect of exchange rate vacillations on the US/nearby value market association. Factual confirmation exhibited in Mun's study showed that higher exchange rate variability, generally, helped higher nearby value market instability however to a lower US value market unpredictability.

As far as their causality examination, Morales' results demonstrated an unidirectional causal relationship structure the trade rates to the stock costs on account of Hungary, Poland and Czech Republic. There was likewise proof of causality from the Hungarian exchange rateto the United Kingdom stock costs, from the Polish trade rates to the United Kingdom stock costs, from the Czech Republic exchange rateto the United Kingdom stock costs and from the Slovakian trade rates to the United Kingdom stock costs. At long last, the study likewise discovered proof of causality from the stock costs to the stock costs on account of Hungary to United Kingdom, United Kingdom to Poland, and the United States to Poland.

In an alternate study, Korsgaard analyzed the relationship between firm esteem and exchange return predictability in the accompanying European nations; Denmark, Spain and German. An alternate numerous relapse models was created and resultantly, the typical Ordinary Least Squared (OLS) technique was supplanted by the Newey-West standard slips test. The information on Danish, Spanish and German organizations was synchronized such that the time compass went from May 2001 to October 2008. Conversion standard instability was tried against stock returns. The discoveries proposed that stock returns are to a certain degree delicate to swapping scale instability.

Sekmen inspected the impacts of exchange rate instability, utilizing the squared residuals from the autoregressive moving normal (ARMA) models, on stock returns for the U.S for the period 1980 to 2008. The study tried the impact of exchange rate unpredictability on the benefits of firms in the US utilizing the squared residuals from the ARMA model to create appraisals of unpredictability. In general, the study found that conversion standard instability adversely influenced US stock returns.

Evaluation

Table 1 explicates that a few studies, for example, those by Aggarwal [5] help the view that there is a relationship between exchange rate and stock exchanges. Others by Morales, Nieh and Lee [23] and Alagidede, Panagiotidis and Zhang demonstrate that there is no relationship between trade rates and the share trading system. The table also demonstrates that distinctive methods were utilized by diverse studies to acquire results. Studies utilized the EGARCH, Johansen system, Granger Causality Tests and the Autoregressive moving normal (ARMA), Regression models for estimation purposes. Diverse results were gotten in created nations. This may have been created by distinctive elements and diverse monetary circumstances that every nation was laid open to. Studies led in created nations are uncertain; the results are blended. From the table, it can be seen that Chi, Fang and Yang FU emphasises on the relationship of exchange rate and stock exchange can be followed up by either EGARCH or

Regression analysis. This advocates this study in looking at the effect of swapping scale and securities exchange London.

Overview of Exchange Rate Policy and LSE

Exchange rate history of UK

Exchange rate administration ideal has changed fundamentally inside most recent 100 years. Since the starting till now principles have changed secretly. Just extreme nations had drifting trade rates and level cash awhile ago. However, the parameter changed by end of the century. It is no more like some time recently. It has now gotten to be clearer to try for a gliding exchange rate. To extra, these gliding trade rates have affected the securities exchanges dissimilar to different instruments of economy.

A history of LSE (London Stock Exchange)

One of the most seasoned stock trade businesses of the world is London Stock. It began exchanging more than 300 years back. London Stock Exchange quickly raised to wind up most vital monetary establishment of the City since Starting its life in the cafés of London in the seventeenth century, Years after years, London Stock Exchange has been reliably heading the method for developing a solid, generally directed securities exchange. By today it exists in the heart of the world monetary group. In 1995, it touched one of the breakthroughs including AIM (Alternative Money Investment) into their administrations. In 2007, it developed with Borsa Italiana and shaped London Stock Exchange Group.

Exchange rate policy and maintenance

Exchange rate approach is a basic part of arrangement contentions identifying with worldwide intensity and macroeconomics concerns. Farrell and Todani, contend that developments in return rates can have a huge effect on financial development, vocation, expansion and the equalization of instalments and on the prosperity of people. Exchange rate progressions influence macroeconomic components, for example, expansion, monetary development, vocation creation and salary appropriation. Financial arrangement creators subsequently need to nearly screen exchange rate improvements to settle on the right choice. Exchange rate improvements are a critical part of the economy which the legislature should dependably stand watch on. The consequence of having unseemly conversion standard arrangements would be a misaligned Exchange rate. This misalignment has been rebuked for an arrangement of monetary fiascos endured by economies around the globe. Expand in globalization has likewise made the exchange rate approach to be one of the key determinants of both inner and outer strength. Exchange rate administration strategy of United Kingdom.

In UK, exchange rate administrations have developed from being altered, to oversee skimming lastly to free drifting in the year 2000. The appropriation of the expansion focusing on administration in the year 2000 had suggestions on the way with which the swapping scale strategy is led. The Bank of England decided to direct expansion focusing on and having an adaptable exchange rate. The expansion focusing on skeleton, as in any state where it is connected has permitted the conversion scale to buoy and there are no exchange rate targets. Under an unadulterated expansion focusing on administration that the Bank of England decided to direct, the national bank has constrained control in the outside trade market. When the GBP devalued forcefully against the primary monetary forms, the Bank of England consistently abstained from interceding in the remote trade business sector to backing the GBP. The estimation of the GBP swapping scale was regardless is controlled by the strengths of interest and supply in the remote trade market. Despite the fact that the swapping scale is seen as an essential transmission system for fiscal approach that could influence swelling and financial development, the Bank of England is of the view that a lot of worry about conversion standard security can affect the wrong arrangement reaction.

The globalization process has permitted budgetary transactions and cash to moderately move crosswise over national limits and this has made the conversion scale to be a standout amongst the most critical instruments for dealing with the nation's economy. UK is no special case to this. Hentz (2005:18) prominent that exchange rate now be a standout amongst the most vital costs in the economy. As a consequence of this, general conversion standard arrangements are currently being coordinated to some proximate goals, including outside parity, interior offset, and micro financial productivity (Boker, Boraine, and Krafchik, 1993:138). The inquiry, nonetheless, of attaining proximate goals (for instance inside and outside offsets) are truly chosen by the decision of exchange rate administration.

The decision of Exchange rate administrations has been a focal choice confronting policymakers in very nearly all economies around the globe. The conversion standard has essential ramifications for exchange, inflation, Gross Domestic Products (GDP), budgetary markets and numerous different parts of the economy. Diverse exchange rate administrations could be worked to attain the picked targets these incorporate settled trade rates, free skimming and a mixed bag of halfway administrations, for example, movable peg or creeping peg.

Economic Indicators of LSE

Structural, administrative and mechanical changes over the previous decade have made the LSE to have numerous positive progressions. Numerous positive improvements have been recognized and as an aftereffect of this "the LSE is on the radar screen of numerous universal financial specialists today". Positive improvements have been portrayed by noteworthy changes in the financial pointers predominantly made out of, in addition to everything else, complete volume what's more estimation of shares exchanged on the LSE, All Share Index, Liquidity and business capitalisation. This area might inspect the patterns that have been going on the LSE in manifestation of graphical and numerical dissection. Graphical and numerical dissection serves to break down the patterns in the monetary markers on the LSE. This will give a measuring stick of assessing the general execution of the LSE. The aggregate volume and estimation of shares exchanged on the LSE, market capitalization, liquidity on the LSE, All Share Index are the monetary pointers broke down by this study.

Research Methodology

Introduction

This exploration expects to assess the effect of swapping scale instability on London Stock Market. Section 2 concentrated on writing audit of speculations and clarifications identified with the point. This part explains the philosophy to perform the examination. This predominantly incorporates the models and related variables picked for exploration, foreseen priori, research standard, information gathering and exact examination procedure of information.

Style of Research

Research philosophy

The term that portrays a change of learning and the way of

information is known as exploration theory [24]. It impacts real perspective of the association in the middle of learning and the procedure through it is created. Saunders [24] specified around three examination methods of insight epistemology, philosophy and axiology.

Epistemology

Scientist should work from a position of common researcher when assets give information. At times, specialist might picked reality where information are considered as true. In this viewpoint scientist can contend that gathered information less open and therefore more target. All things considered, specialist would view question through sentiments and demeanour.

Positivism

One positivism system acknowledges the truth may be explored prevented from securing annoying the made case. This technique may be performed really if the reality of the situation is reliable (Levin, 1988). It has a couple of mixtures. Alavi and Carlson, communicated all trial investigates are positivist in nature.

Interpretivism

Saunders [24], said in regards to the examination rationale where expert commonly go about as a social performing craftsman to perceive change of human. It is known as Interpretivism. It generally focuses on human contrasts as opposed to considering matters like, machines. Remenyi, communicated that interpretivism has subjective point of view.

Realism

Saunders [24], raise legitimacy as an epistemological locus. Genuineness is focused on the inclination of truth. It truly infers that dissents subsist autonomously on individual's mind. Free identity of people is the center motivation behind legitimacy theory.

Pragmatism

The rationale that stands amidst a position of interpretivism and positivism is known as calm mindedness. It practices focused solicitation for the examination. Solicitation may be seen as an on-going strategy. Segregating deduction picks waverings and request and over the long haul attested in topple. Saunders [24], said there is no true position to get.

Chosen philosophy

Fundamental objective of the momentum exploration is to discovering effect of swapping scale instability. This money based paper will be examining optional information which are true and accessible. Enough measure of learning is accessible is around also. Consequently scientist likes to work with epistemological reasoning.

This exploration objective affirms that examination conducts both subject and item. Therefore the flow examination affirms that it remains in an in the middle of positivism and interpretivism and practices center request and discriminating thinking. Along these lines the analyst plans to practical methodology of epistemological reasoning.

Research approach

Ghauri and Gronhaug, expressed that while channeling an exploration scientist needs to spare the apparent information without any preference. Result may match supremely with speculations and laws perceived around. Exploration methodology is required so as to discover reality and false and finishing the examination.

Inductive

An inductive technique of investigation is performed with down to business annotations by re-searcher. Contingent upon it, researcher improvises distinctive hypotheses, begins new theories and adds them to routine speculations. Grazino communicated that this procedure remains closer to the recouped data and high-lights on incitation. As needs be new made hypotheses could be all the more compelling.

Deductive

Bryman and Bell said that examiners fortifies theory from the open theories in deductive approach of investigation. Later on master performs the investigation and find precise results. Cooper and Schindler tagged that conclusions give the vital in deductive technique. Grazino et al. refered to that deductive approach principally focuses on the actuations recouped from theories. From speculations it starts and later on it is observationally investigated later on.

Chosen approach

Fundamental objective of the flow examination is to discovering effect of conversion standard instability. This money based paper will be inquiring about optional information which are genuine and accessible. Enough measures of information and speculations are accessible around too. Scientist does not expect to manufacture theory namelessly and build new hypothesis. As opposed to that, scientist likes to fabricate speculations on the premise of made hypothesis, inspect information and give genuine result. In this manner analyst will pick inductive methodology of exploration.

Quantitative technique

Quantitative technique for exploration predominantly depends on the strategy of information accumulation, dissect them and produce numeric information resultant. Results are clarified by diagrams or detail in this system for exploration [24].

Qualitative strategy

Qualitative strategy for examination mostly depends on the hypotheses and clarifications investigate them and create non-numeric information resultant. Results are clarified by hypotheses and clarifications in this strategy for examination [24].

The picked system

Principle objective of the momentum examination is to discovering effect of conversion standard instability. This account based paper will be looking into auxiliary information which are genuine and accessible. Numeric examination will give conclusions. These will be clarified too. Accordingly scientist will pick both qualitative and quantitative technique for the exploration.

Saunders [24] referred to that there are 2 sorts of exploration techniques Specified routines change in the standings numeric and non-numeric information.

Data Analysis

Analyse model

So as to measure the effect of money unpredictability on the stock exchange in United Kingdom, this study emulated Subair's model.

Subair utilized the regression model to explore the effect of swapping scale instability on money markets execution in London. His study utilized the accompanying model:

This present study might change Subair's model. The informative variables that are incorporated in this current study's model are: money supply (M3)fares, GBP volatility, Market capitalization and US premium rates. The model should, in this way, take the structure:

Lsmc=f(GBPVOL,MC,M3,USINT (4.1)

Meaning of Variables

LSMC is the characteristic logarithm of the stock exchange capitalisation (LSE). Market promotion is the piece of the pie value for every offer increased by the quantity of shares exceptional. Market underwriting will change in accordance with progressions in offer cost and the quantity of shares issued. Financial specialists focus an organization's offer esteem by taking a gander at its market promotion. Olalere held that, in United Kingdom, the conversion scale has a more noteworthy effect available promotion than stock costs. This is the motivation behind why market underwriting instead of stock costs is picked in this study.

Gbpvol is the US/GBP Exchange rate - The US dollar has been utilized as a part of perspective of the predominance of the dollar in universal transaction and also close connections between the United Kingdomn and US economies. Since 2001 the LSE execution takes after the GBP swapping scale.

M3 is utilized to catch cash supply. M3 is utilized to be a sign of the aggregate sum of cash supply accessible in the economy. M is the broadest measure of cash thus it is utilized to gauge the whole supply of cash inside an economy. Bhattacharya and Mukherjee [8] likewise utilized this variable when they were leading a study on the way of the causal relationship between stock exchange and macroeconomic totals in India.

US investment rates - The expanded openness of the United Kingdomn economy permits the USA financial advancements to assume a urgent part in value costs in United Kingdom. The US premium rates have been assuming an immense part in deciding interest in developing markets. The LSE pulls in an extensive measure of remote investment from institutional financial specialists in the created world, including the US (Ocran, 2010). Subsequently changes (particularly diminishes in premium rates) in the US premium rates will make speculators to move far from the US and look for appealing venture ends of the line, for example, United Kingdom. Thus the United States investment rates are essential in clarifying the offer cost on the LSE.

Expected priori

Cash Supply - The indication of M3 is relied upon to be sure. Higher M3 additionally bestows additional liquidity to the securities exchanges since the overabundance cash is channelized into the stock exchanges, along these lines pushing up the business capitalisation. Thus, stock valuations climb as a quick response to an expand in M3. The productive business sector theory (EMH), as formalized by Fama [2], proposes that changes in macroeconomic variables, for example, cash supply can impact the conduct of securities exchange exercises. In an effective business, present and additionally past data on the development of these essential macro-variables are completely reflected in possession.

US investment rates: The US premium rates sign is required to be negative. A lessening in the US investment rate is relied upon to cause the stock costs to climb. When US premium rates fall, financial specialists move their speculation from the US to United Kingdom since it is a developing business sector. This build in speculation will result in the stock costs to climb because of the accessibility of numerous purchasers on the stock trade. In this way a negative relationship is relied upon to exist between the US premium rates and the stock exchange costs.

GBP Volatility: The indication of the GBP unpredictability is required to be negative. At the point when there is expanded unpredictability, speculators won't contribute much on stocks. It would be unsafe to contribute and they will take their venture somewhere else. This will result in stock costs to decline. Hence a negative relationship is perceived on the stock costs. Adjasi [12] (additionally discovered a negative relationship between conversion standard vacillations and the London securities exchange returns.

Information for the study should be acquired from optional sources, for example, the Johannesburg Stock Exchange and the United Kingdom Revenue Services, Statistics United Kingdom, United Kingdom Reserve Bank, and Department of Trade and Industry. Ostensible figures should be utilized for the study. The study utilizes month to month United Kingdom information for the period 2000 – 2010. The information recurrence chose should be month to month to guarantee a satisfactory number of perceptions. A perception lower than this (yearly or quarterly) won't give enough perception of which a solid conclusion might be drawn as the information won't be a sufficient representation of unpredictability while a higher recurrence will be influenced by impacts of settlements and clearing deferrals which influence returns over a shorter inspecting interims. The results from month to month data are more exact and are better equipped to catch the elements between trade rates and the LSE. The information should first test for stationary or the request of incorporation of the information arrangement keeping in mind the end goal to dispose of spurious relapse results. This should be carried out utilizing the Augmented Dickey Fuller system and the Phillip Peron test. This is the center of the following are

The ADF Test

Mernard held that the Dickey Fuller tests figure an autoregressive model and test whether the coefficient is measurably unique in relation to one. On the off chance that it is not, it will be important to distinction the arrangement to accomplish stationary. The Dickey Fuller test is of the model:

A significant issue with normal D.f test is that their discriminating qualities are pre dispositioned if there is autocorrelation in the residuals of the D-F relapse. To redress this, Dickey and Fuller (1981) concocted the increased rendition of the Dickey Fuller Test. They included the same number of slacked variables as important to evacuate any autocorrelation in the residuals. The ADF methodology controls for higher-request connection by including slacked contrasts terms of the ward variables to the right hand side of the relapse held that the Augmented Dickey Fuller will, then, take the structure: For the reasons of this study the Augmented Dickey Fuller is utilized.

Phillips peron test

In spite of the fact that the ADF is a standout amongst the most generally utilized tests5, it some of the time carries on inadequately, particularly in the vicinity of serial connection. As a consequence of this, Phillips and Peron created a more far reaching hypothesis of unit root non stationarity. The tests are like the ADF tests, however they fused programmed adjustment to the DF methodology to take into consideration auto correlated residuals. The Phillips Peron test performs better than (or at any rate and additionally) the ADF test regarding near force and yields tighter certainty interims. Notwithstanding this, the Phillips and Peron tests are non-parametic tests of the invalid of the unit root and are viewed as all the more influential, as they utilize reliable estimators of the change. The Phillips Perron unit root test contrasts from the ADF tests for the most part by the way they manage serial association and hetero scedasticity in the slips.

Conclusion

This part set out the model which decides the effect of money instability on stocks. Included in this model are variables that are liable to influence the operation of money markets. These variables are the local investment rates, US premium rates, GBP unpredictability, aggregate mining creation and fares. For stationarity/unit roots purposes, the model utilized the Dickey-Fuller and the Phillips Perron tests. Indicative tests, for example, the Normality test, Ramsey RESET test and the LM test were talked about. The regression system has been picked as the estimation method for the effect of coin unpredictability on money markets in United Kingdom. The succeeding section will run the talked about preparatory examination of the information and the last regression model utilizing the econometric bundle EVIEWS 7. At long last, demonstrative tests should be performed on the residuals.

Data Analysis

Introduction

The past section set the systematic structure and assessed the model and estimation methods to be utilized as a part of this study. This section introduces the primary aftereffects of relapse on month to month information for the period from August 2004 to July 2014. The effect of exchange rate inconstancy on stock exchange is evaluated utilizing three macroeconomic variables. It is through this part that the destination of this study might be accomplished. The fundamental target of this study has been to research the exchange rate inconstancy on the stock exchange in United kingdom.

This part is separated into 4 sub-segments. The primary exhibits the consequences of enlightening detail. This is done by descriptive statistics. This part has mainly followed the market capitalisation exchange rate fluctuation. The second part, Collinearity test, took after by stationarity tests for finding mean and variance change in the third area. Final test, regression is performed on the last part for finding the result of research question.

Descriptive statistics of market capitalisation and exchange rate fluctuation in last 10 years

Xuezheng, Rusell and Tiao held that numerous monetary arrangements, for example, returns on stocks and remote trade rates, show leptokurtosis and time-shifting unpredictability. These two gimmicks have been the subject of broad studies following the time when Mandelbrot (1963) and Fama (1965) initially reported them. In this respect it is important to perform some engaging facts to look at if the GBPvol and MC display time differing instability and leptokurtosis qualities. The two primary variables of the study are inspected in light of the fact that these variables focus the estimation system for the study. The facts of the GBPvol and MC arrangement are shown in Table 2 below.

Descriptive Statistics

Table 2 demonstrates the spellbinding detail of the GBPvol variable. Correspondingly, skewness and kurtosis speak to the way of flight from typicality. Emenike contends that in an ordinarily disseminated arrangement, skewness is 0 and kurtosis is 3. The coefficient of skewness measures asymmetry. The GBPvol esteem for skewness is .462 and it reflects positive skewness. A positive skew demonstrates that the tail on the right side is longer than the left side and the majority of the qualities lie to the left of the mean. Additionally, if skewness is sure, the normal extent of positive deviations is bigger than the normal size of negative deviations. The coefficient of the GBPvol variable is showing that there is asymmetry within GBPvol. Thus, a variable that takes after a typical dissemination ought to be symmetric. The coefficient of kurtosis measures the peakedness of dissemination. The quality for kurtosis is -1.083 and this recommends that there is peakedness in the GBPvol. Kurtosis coefficients have values short of what 0. From this it could be watched that the GBPvol variable displays noteworthy deviations from ordinariness. The coefficient of kurtosis is -1.083 and it is more modest than zero. This shows noteworthy lerptokurtosis. A dissemination with a coefficient bigger than 3 is said to be leptokurtic and unified with a coefficient more modest than 3 is platykurtic. The MC variable reflects positive skewness with an estimation of 4.6 and this demonstrates that there is asymmetry in the MC variable. Defusco, Mcleavey, Pinto, Runkle (2006) held that a few specialists accept that speculators favour positive skewness, all else measure up to that is, they ought to lean toward portfolios with appropriations offering a moderately vast recurrence of uncommonly huge settlements. The

Study	Methodology	Findings
Choi, Fang and Yong Fu (2009) (New Zealand)	EGARCH	The exchange rate affected the stock market
Moracles (2007) (Czech republic, Hungary, Poland and Slovakia)	Regression Analysis, Johansen technique, Cointegration, Vector Error, Correction Modelling and the standard Granger Casuality test	No evidence of stock prices and exchange rates moving together either in the long-run or in the short-run was found.
Alagidede, Panagiotidis and Zhang (2010)	Cointegration tests and Granger casuality test	There is no long-run relationship between two variables.
Sekmen (2011)	ARMA	Exchange negatively stock returns rate volatility affected U.S

Table 1: Evaluation Studies.

	N	Minimum	Minimum	Mean	Std. Deviation	Variance	Skewness		Kurtosis	
	Statistic	Statistic	Statistic	Statistic	Statistic	Statistic	Statistic	Std. Error	Statistic	Std. error
GBP/USD	119	1.42	2.07	1.7117	.17257	.030	.462	.222	-1.083	.440
Market Capitalization	119	414193.00	793432.00	5689427.899	1.12448E5	1.264.E10	.143	.222	27.981	.440
Valid N	119									

Table 2: Descriptive Statistics.

estimation of kurtosis demonstrates that the MC variable has high circulation than a typical conveyance. The kurtosis worth is 27.981 and this demonstrates leptokurtosis.

From the month to month standard deviation, it might be seen that the MC is substantially more unpredictable than the Gbpvol henceforth there is requirement for it to be caught under the relapse model. Overall, both the Gbpvol and MC variables don't adjust to typical dissemination however show negative skewness and leptokurtic appropriations. Deviations from typicality of time arrangement information have been seen by past studies. Emenike watched that the Stock return arrangement don't fit in with typical appropriation yet show negative skewness and leptokurtic dispersion. Agrawal and Srivastava, likewise recognized that these variables are non-ordinarily dispersed.

Finding the linear correlation between variables

Collinearity Test: Collinearity was performed to see in there is no direct correspondence between illustrative variables. Rationale behind suspicion of no multicollinearity is if two variables are collinear it gets to be hard to divided the individual impact of every variable on the ward variable. So as to check multi collinearity among autonomous variables, a correspondence examination was performed. The closer the r coefficient approaches ± 1, paying little mind to the course, the stronger is the current affiliation demonstrating a more straight relationship between the two variables. Notwithstanding, a recommended dependable guideline is that if the pair insightful relationship between two repressors is high, in abundance of 0.8, multicollinearity may posture genuine issue. The association examination results are accounted for in Table 3 underneath.

Table 3 demonstrates that the most elevated relationship coefficient worth is 0.984which is low. It is well beneath 0.8. Since the most noteworthy correspondence numbers are higher than 0.8, the results plainly demonstrate that none of the autonomous variables are exceptionally corresponded and multi collinearity amongst free variables exist.

Finding the mean and changes in variance

Stationarity test : On the off chance that the mean and fluctuation are consistent about whether, then the arrangement is stationary. Stationarity is vital for standard econometric hypothesis. Without it we can't get predictable estimators. One method for telling if a procedure is stationary is to plot the arrangement against time. Graphical representations taking the manifestation of time arrangement plots provide for us especially valuable methods for imagining data and leading similar dissects about whether. In the event that the chart crosses the mean of the specimen commonly, risks are that the variable is stationary; overall that is an evidence of diligent patterns far from the mean of the arrangement. On the off chance that the mean and difference change, then the arrangement is non-stationary. To identify if an arrangement is stationary graphical plots were carried out on watched estimations of the information. It demonstrates the GBPVOL and MC plots.

Model		Colinearity Statistics	
		Tolerance	VIF
1	Market Capitalization	.826	1.210
	US interest rate	.984	1.016
	Money supply	.821	1.218

Table 3: Elevated relationship coefficient.

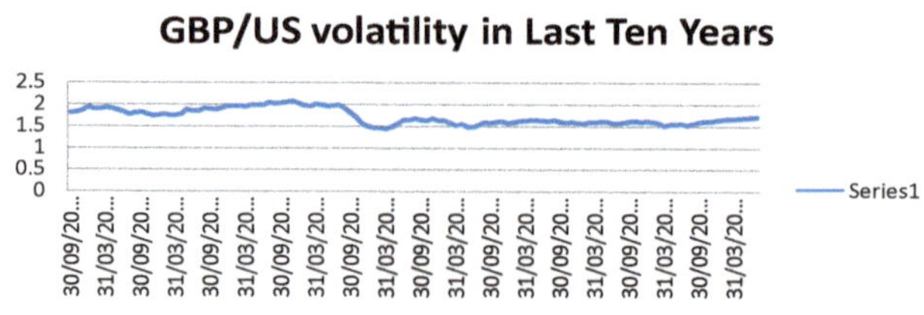

Figure 2: GBP/US Volatility in last ten years.

Figure 3: Market Capitalisation in last ten years.

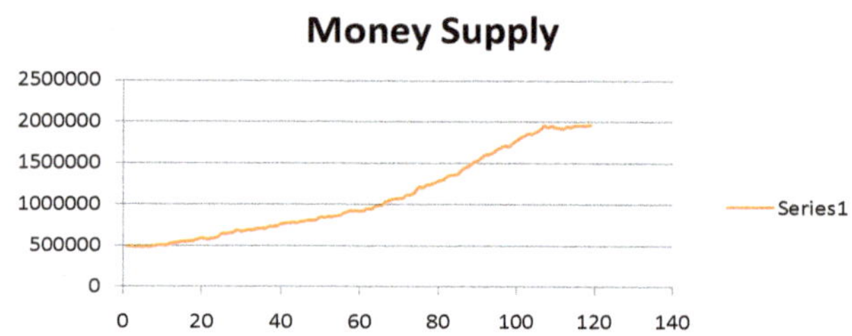

Figure 4: Money supply rate.

It proposes that the GBPVOL variable shows changes about whether. The level information demonstrates no propensity to come back to its mean demonstrating the requirement for differencing. The arrangement plot of the MC information shows that the arrangement is fluctuating about whether. This demonstrates that it is not stationary. The two variables have a period variation mean and change proposing that they are not stationary in their levels. The MC arrangement has a fluctuating conduct and with such a fluctuating example, a period arrangement is non-stationary, it doesn't demonstrate a propensity of mean inversion (Figure 2).

Graphical representations taking the manifestation of time arrangement plots was additionally done on the other informative variables; US premium rate, Money supply (M3). Their diagrams are shown in Figure 3 underneath.

Figure 4 demonstrates that the M3 information arrangement is emphatically straightly drifted and subsequently it is in this way non-stationary. The arrangement likewise demonstrates no inclination of coming back to its mean.

Figure 5 demonstrates that the Interest rate information arrangement is emitted and non- straightly drifted and subsequently it is stationary. The arrangement additionally demonstrates inclination of coming back to its mean.

Notwithstanding visual assessment, formal econometric tests were connected to unambiguously choose the genuine nature of time arrangement. Essential examination of graphical presentation of the information demonstrated conceivable non-stationary of the variables

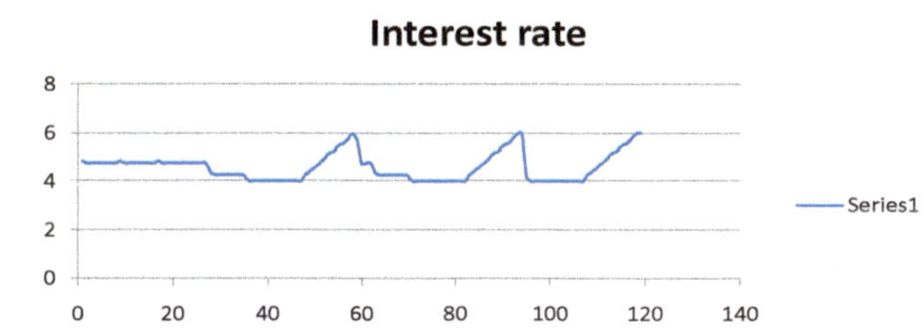

Figure 5: Interest rate.

which encourages for unit root testing. This study emulated the standard methodology of unit root testing by utilizing the Augmented Dickey Fuller (ADF) test. Since the ADF test is regularly reprimanded for low power, the study supplements this test with the Phillips Perron (PP) test. Results from these tests are indicated in the tables underneath.

ADF test: In the event that the mean and change are consistent about whether, then the arrangement is stationary. Stationary is key for standard econometric hypothesis. Without it we can't get steady estimators. One method for telling if a methodology is stationary is to plot the arrangement against time. Graphical representations taking the type of time arrangement plots provide for us especially valuable methods for imagining data and leading similar examines about whether. On the off chance that the chart crosses the mean of the example ordinarily, risks are that the variable is stationary; overall that is an evidence of constant patterns far from the mean of the arrangement. In the event that the mean and fluctuation change, then the arrangement is non-stationary. To discover if an arrangement is stationary graphical plots were carried out on watched estimations of the information. Figure 2 demonstrates the GBPVOL and MC plots.

Figure 2 proposes that the GBPVOL variable shows vacillations about whether. The level information demonstrates no inclination to come back to its mean showing the requirement for differencing. The grouping plot of the MC information shows that the arrangement is fluctuating about whether. This demonstrates that it is not stationary. The two variables have a period variation mean and fluctuation recommending that they are not stationary in their levels. The MC arrangement has a fluctuating conduct and with such a fluctuating example, a period arrangement is non-stationary, it doesn't demonstrate a propensity of mean inversion.

Graphical representations taking the manifestation of time arrangement plots was additionally done on the other illustrative variables; POR, Export Money (M3).

It demonstrates that the M3 information arrangement is emphatically straightly slanted and henceforth it is along these lines non-stationary. The arrangement additionally demonstrates no propensity of coming back to its mean.

Notwithstanding visual review, formal econometric tests were connected to unambiguously choose the real nature of time arrangement. Essential investigation of graphical presentation of the information showed conceivable non-stationary of the variables which encourages for unit root testing. This study took after the standard strategy of unit root testing by utilizing the Augmented Dickey Fuller (ADF) test. Since the ADF test is regularly condemned for low power, the study supplements this test with the Phillips Perron (PP) test. Results from these tests are demonstrated in the tables underneath (Table 4).

The results from the ADF tests are given in tables. The results are organized as per level information arrangement and for first contrasts in the information arrangement.

Table 4 demonstrates that all variables were not stationary in levels. The p- estimations of the variables all being more noteworthy than 0.05 show that we couldn't dismiss the invalid theory of the presence of unit establish in levels for all variables. Be that as it may, the variables are stationary will be stationary after first differencing them. The greatness of the p –values (short of what 0.05) are huge, demonstrating that the variables are stationary from the start contras

PP Test: The results from the Phillip Perron test are given in Table 5 beneath.

In applying the Phillips Peron test to the variables, MC and TMP were discovered to be stationary at levels. On the other hand, the test detail of M3, POR, USINT and GBPVL were short of what the discriminating worth at 1% and 5% individually and subsequently not stationary. In any case, these variables achieved stationary after the first differencing. The discriminating qualities at 1% and 5% were 3.480818 and 2.883579 individually.

After the stationary tests, graphical plots were carried out to watch the way of the mean and difference of the stationary information. The graphical plots of the differenced variables are appeared.

It demonstrates that the initially differenced variables hint at coming back to its mean recommending that the arrangement is pitifully stationary. In the wake of differencing, the run arrangement plot shows that the information has a steady area and fluctuation, in spite of the fact that the example of the residuals demonstrates that the information leave from the model in a methodical way. The same is seen in the other four illustrative variables.

		ADF test (intercept)		ADF (Trend and intercept)	
Variables		**Levels**	**1ST Difference**	**Levels**	**1ST Difference**
M3 (P value)		1.931176 0.9998	9.723775** 0.0000	-2.274915 0.4442	-10.03535 0.0000
GBPVOL (P value)		2.224457 0.1987	8.076612** 0.0000	-2.340393 0.4090	-8.085405 0.0000
USINT (P value)		-1.769695 0.3941	-4.679856** 0.0002	-1.764772 0.7162	-4.670071 0.0002
MC (P value)		-0.786105 0.8191	-6.921686** 0.0000	-2.561822 0.2985	-7.155631 0.0000
Critical values	1%	3.480818	3.480818	4.036310	4.036310
	5%	-2.885654	-2.885654	3.447699	3.447699
** and * denotes rejection of the null hypothesis at 1% and 5% respectively					

Table 4: Unit root/stationary test: ADF test.

		Phillips perron (intercept)		Phillips perron (Trend and intercept)	
Variables		**Levels**	**1ST Difference**	**Levels**	**1ST Difference**
M3 (P value)		1.194002 0.9980	-10.49386 0.0000	-2.122939 0.5279	-10.59217 0.0000
MC (P value)		10.51483 0.0000		-11.11609 0.0000	
GBPVOL (P value)		-2.143811 0.2281	-8.037357 0.0000	-2.245581 0.4602	-8.046197 0.0000
USINT (P value)		1.357667 0.6011	-4.581038 0.0002	-1.467586 0.8358	4.527591 0.0020
Critical values	1%	3.480818	3.480818	4.036310	4.036310
	5%	-2.883579	-2.883553	-3.444487	2.883753
** and * denotes rejection of the null hypothesis at 1% and 5% respectively					

Table 5: Unit root/Stationary tests: Phillips person tests.

Exchange rate vs Market capitalization

Researcher performed regression analysis here. Researcher aimed to find the inconstancy of exchange rate impact on market capitalization. Picked invalid theory here is that there is no such association in the middle of enhancement of monetary position and availability to Market Capitalization. Reverse theory is that there is association in the middle of them. Utilizing SPSS programming figuring is carried out. Bivariate relapse examination results are demonstrated in above tables. Model rundown table gives R2 = to the relapse model. R2 delineates level of variety between two variables. If there should arise an occurrence of loaner's originations of change of their monetary circumstance for 88.6% of the aggregate variety in Market Capitalization. The ANNOVA table outlines the F degree planned for the relapse model. This detail assesses centrality of the facts for the general relapse. More prominent F proportion gives more noteworthy change inside the ward variable which is illuminated by the free variable. F degree here assigns the relapse show that is profoundly noteworthy at the 0.000 level. The relapse coefficient table demonstrates the dock named "Unstandardized Coefficients" uncovers the unstandardized relapse coefficient for better budgetary positions, 0.168. T-test demonstrates the centrality level of relapse coefficient which is (0.000) here. Investigation above rejects the invalid speculations that demonstrate existing associations in the middle of 2 variables which could be seen specifically above sober minded bend of total likelihood. Hence, it demonstrates that conversion standard instability has more noteworthy effect on Market Capitalization.

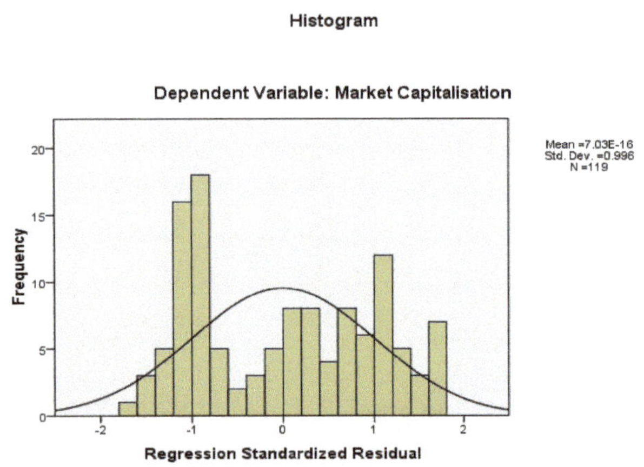

Figure 6: Exchange rate vs Market Capitalisation.

Exchange rate vs Interest rate

Researcher performed regression analysis here. Researcher aimed to find the inconstancy of exchange rate impact on Interest Rate. Picked invalid theory here is that there is no such association in the middle of enhancement of monetary position and availability to Interest Rate. Reverse theory is that there is association in the middle of them. Utilizing SPSS programming figuring is carried out. Bivariate relapse examination results are demonstrated in above tables. Model rundown table gives R2 = to the relapse model. R2 delineates level of variety between two variables. If there should arise an occurrence of loaner's originations of change of their monetary circumstance for 88.6% of the aggregate variety in Interest Rate. The ANNOVA table outlines the F degree planned for the relapse model. This detail assesses centrality of the facts for the general relapse. More prominent F proportion gives more noteworthy change inside the ward variable which is illuminated by the free variable. F degree here assigns the relapse show that is profoundly noteworthy at the 0.000 level. The relapse coefficient table demonstrates the dock named "Unstandardized Coefficients" uncovers the unstandardized relapse coefficient for better budgetary positions, 0.168. T-test demonstrates the centrality level of relapse coefficient which is (0.000) here. Investigation above rejects the invalid speculations that demonstrate existing associations in the middle of 2 variables which could be seen specifically above sober minded bend of total likelihood. Hence, it demonstrates that conversion standard instability has more noteworthy effect on Market Capitalization (Figure 6, Tables 6 and 7).

Exchange rate vs Money Supply

Researcher performed regression analysis here. Researcher aimed to find the inconstancy of exchange rate impact on market capitalization. Picked invalid theory here is that there is no such association in the middle of enhancement of monetary position and availability to Money Supply. Reverse theory is that there is association in the middle of them. Utilizing SPSS programming figuring is carried out. Bivariate relapse examination results are demonstrated in above tables. Model rundown table gives R2 = to the relapse model. R2 delineates level of variety between two variables. If there should arise an occurrence of loaner's originations of change of their monetary circumstance for the aggregate variety in Money Supply The ANNOVA table outlines the F degree planned for the relapse model (Figures 6 and 7). This detail assesses centrality of the facts for the general relapse. More prominent F proportion gives more noteworthy change inside the ward variable which is illuminated by the free variable. F degree here 3.740 assigns the relapse show that is profoundly noteworthy at the 0.000 level. The

Model	R	R Square	Adjusted R Square	Std. Error of the Estimate	Change Statistics				
					R Square Change	F Change	df1	df2	Sig. F Change
1	.208[a]	.043	.035	.56438	.043	5.309	1	117	.023

a. Predictors: (Constant), GBP/USD

b. Dependent Variable: US Interest Rate

Table 6: Model Summary[b] of Exchange rate vs interest rate.

Model		Sum of Squares	Df	Mean Square	F	Sig.
1	Regression	1.691	1	1.691	5.309	.023[a]
	Residual	37.268	117	.319		
	Total	38.959	118			

a. Predictors: (Constant), GBP/USD

b. Dependent Variable: US Interest Rate

Table 7: Anova.[b]

relapse coefficient table demonstrates the dock named "Unstandardized Coefficients" uncovers the unstandardized relapse coefficient for better budgetary positions, 0.168. T-test demonstrates the centrality level of relapse coefficient which is (0.000) here. Investigation above rejects the invalid speculations that demonstrate existing associations in the middle of 2 variables which could be seen specifically above sober minded bend of total likelihood. Hence, it demonstrates that conversion standard instability has more noteworthy effect on Money Supply (Tables 8 and 9).

Discussion and Conclusion

The principle goal driving this study has been to analyze the effect of currency fluctuations on stocks market in United Kingdom. To accomplish this destination, a few appraisals were performed. Firstly, an outline of the advancements of the GBP and the stock exchange was carried out. An outline of the advancements of the GBP swapping scale and the share trading system was important as this gives a premise to our understanding of the reason for its fluctuation. The exchange rate in United Kingdom has been described by respectable fluctuation and these were seen to spill into money markets. Changes in the GBP have extensive impacts on the route with which the stock exchange works.

An evaluation of writing on exchange rate fluctuation and securities exchanges was led and from it an exact model was tagged. It was seen that there is a blended supposition as to the relationship that exist between conversion scale and the share trading system. The study utilized month to month United Kingdom's information for the period August, 2004- July, 2014. The information recurrence chose guaranteed a satisfactory number of perceptions. The variables utilized within the study were GBP conversion standard, market capitalisation; supply of money (M3), and United States premium rate. Spellbinding facts were utilized to explore the factual properties of the two principle variables; exchange rate standard and business capitalisation. Results demonstrated that these two variables were absolutely skewed and notwithstanding this they had fat tails. The study utilized the regression model to measure the effect of exchange rate fluctuation on the share trading system of LSE.

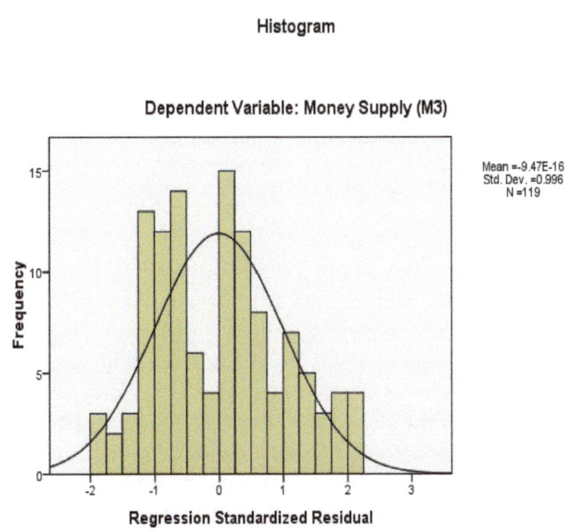

Figure 7: Exchange rate vs Money Supply.

The imperative experiences of the results could be abridged as takes after

To begin with, the examination reported powerless relationship between exchange rate fluctuation and the stock exchange. This result is not steady of the assumption that the instability encompassing conversion scale business sector misshapes proficient speculation distribution. Showcases that are presented to cash instability generally confront extensive vulnerability about the reappearances of venture ventures. This can prompt interruption of these organizations on stocks. Unpredictability influences the stream of data about the nature of undertakings to speculators and subsequently twists asset distribution.

Results from this study did not discover any confirmation that backing the above declaration. Actually, unpredictability was seen to bring positive effects on the stock exchange in United Kingdom. This may be a consequence of the accompanying;

1. The organizations on the LSE now understand the negative effects of coin unpredictability and thus have created measures that pad against the impacts of cash instability.

2. Cavallo held that "working together in an economy that is occasionally presented to turmoil in relative costs implies that business visionaries must face generous vulnerability about the benefit of option tasks. Under this situation, a key peculiarity is the capacity to adjust to a nature's domain". Organizations and firms working on the LSE have taken different instruments to fence against swapping scale hazard. Results from this study propose that the LSE has approached towards educational productivity in any event as for swapping scale and cash supply unpredictability. The frail relationship between money unpredictability and stocks appear to give prove that the LSE

Model	R	R Square	Adjusted R Square	Std. Error of the Estimate	Change Statistics				
					R Square Change	F Change	df1	df2	Sig. F Change
1	.608[a]	.369	.364	3.95317E5	.369	68.474	1	117	.000

a. Predictors: (Constant), GBP/USD
b. Dependent Variable: Money Supply (M3)

Table 8: Model Summary[b] of Exchange rate vs Money Supply.

Model		Sum of Squares	Df	Mean Square	F	Sig.
1	Regression	1.070E13	1	1.070E13	68.474	.000[a]
	Residual	1.828E13	117	1.563E11		
	Total	2.898E13	118			

a. Predictors: (Constant), GBP/USD
b. Dependent Variable: Money Supply (M3)

Table 9: Anova.[b]

is not a proficient business sector. Results propose that organizations on the LSE can utilize swapping scale data to anticipate the future conduct of stocks. This results in the organizations' capability to gauge the developments that the GBP would take later on consequently empowering them to pad against the future variances of the GBP. As a consequence of this, money unpredictability won't influence the stock operations on the LSE.

3. The frail relationship between conversion scale unpredictability and the stock exchange may have been brought on by the diverse variables that influence each of these businesses. The variables/news that causes changes in return rates may be unique in relation to the components that cause changes in stock costs. Under such situation, there ought to be no connection between the said variables (Muhammad and Rasheed, 2011). On the off chance that there were normal elements that impact both swapping scale unpredictability and securities exchange, then a solid relationship between these two money related variables would have been found.

Second, stocks was seen to be influenced by other macroeconomic variables to be specific: premium rates, aggregate mining generation, cash supply and the United States premium rates. Premium rates were seen to have a negative effect on stocks. This is upheld both by monetary hypothesis and various studies including that of Alam and Uddin. Expands in premium rates builds the opportunity expense of holding cash and consequently substitution in the middle of stocks and enthusiasm bearing securities and thus falling stock costs. In different words, climbs in premium rates propel speculators to put less in stocks and this, subsequently, prompt a fall in business sector capitalisation.

Aggregate mining creation was likewise seen to have a negative effect on securities exchange capitalisation; a build altogether mining generation prompted a decrease in securities exchange capitalisation. A build in the supply of cash was seen to have a positive effect on the stock exchange. Expand in cash supply prompts build in liquidity that eventually brings about upward development of ostensible value costs. Li discovered a comparative bring about a study which evolved an examination of cash supply and stock exchange relation in Europe.

In conclusion, the results demonstrated a optimistic relationship within US premium rate and market capitalisation. The estimation of the US premium rates was sure; implying that an expand in US premium rates will prompt an ascent in business sector capitalisation. The US investment rates sign was required to be negative yet comes about have demonstrated the positive. This may be the way that developing markets like United Kingdom are still seen as alluring by speculators paying little mind to other macroeconomic elements, for example, world premium rates.

Indicative tests on the model demonstrated a steady and strong model. The Q-detail test demonstrated that there was no serial association in the residuals. Issues of ARCH were additionally killed by the GARCH model. In any case, the typicality test demonstrated that the residuals were not typically disseminated and this situation is confronted by a few studies.

Policy implications and recommendations

The discoveries from this study have various strategy suggestions. Firstly, the frail unpredictability transmission from the GBP to stock exchange may be characteristic of expanded utilization of supporting instruments by firms on the LSE. Additional supporting instruments needs to be placed set up to guarantee the disposal of negative impacts of GBP unpredictability. These supporting instruments ought to be proficient and they ought not contort the ordinary working of the LSE. There has been sizeable proof in backing of hypotheses recommending that relative value instability gives motivations to ambitious people to embrace more "flexible" however less beneficial generation advances, empowering them to oblige money volatility8. Supporting operations are, on occasion, expensive and can diminish the execution of the organizations.

Besides, Since the United Kingdom n stock exchange is not by any stretch of the imagination presented to the negative impacts of money unpredictability. Important arrangement creators in government can utilize swapping scale as an approach instrument to pull in remote portfolio speculation. In addition, the capacity of the LSE to support against the negative impacts of cash instability could be utilized as a device to pull in outside financial specialists to stocks. The capacity of securities exchanges to pad against macroeconomic vulnerabilities has been connected with created nations' stock exchanges, for example, the United States and United Kingdom. Be that as it may, this has additionally been seen, in this study, and this demonstrates that the LSE could be showcased as a safe business for remote financial specialists. The feeble unpredictability transmission from the conversion scale business to money markets shows that there is prospect for remote speculators to differentiate their interests in these two businesses.

Thirdly, The LSE needs to keep up its co-operation with world class stock exchanges, for example, the LSE. This may be one of the reasons the LSE can pad negative impacts of coin unpredictability. Macroeconomic overflows from created nations are normally difficult to manage however in the event that there is some joining between the LSE and created nations, news about any conceivable improvements in these business sectors will achieve the LSE quick and measures to manage any conceivable impacts of these macroeconomic advancements will be placed set up route before the businesses are influenced.

In conclusion, Investors, brokers and portfolio chiefs still need to be vigilant on the overflows from the remote conversion standard into stocks. In spite of the fact that there is a feeble relationship between GBP instability and the share trading system in United Kingdom , this does not so much imply that speculators and portfolio chiefs require not screen the improvements between these two variables. Different methodologies to ensure money markets from the hurtful impacts of cash instability need to be brought into stocks. These instruments would then be utilized to further fence against trade hazard. Conversion standard incited instability is a pressing issue in United Kingdom and numerous different nations that have adaptable swapping scale administrations.

Possible regions for further research

Swapping scale unpredictability is at the center of the boiling over verbal confrontation on the execution of conversion standard administrations. This worry was fortified by the huge developments in ostensible trade rates that portrayed world budgetary markets since the move to an oversaw skimming conversion scale framework in 1973. A significant concern of approach producers at the downfall of the Bretton Wood framework is the outcome of swapping scale instability saw to be a noticeable peculiarity of an adaptable conversion standard framework. Money unpredictability has respectable ramifications in the monetary markets, particularly the stock exchange.

The GBP has been the most unstable among rising monetary standards over the recent years. United Kingdom 's late measures to diminish the GBP's unpredictability haven't had a craved effect as the cash's vacillation is powered by worldwide financial shakiness and capital inflows from created nations (Davies, 2010). United Kingdom has encountered significant and proceeded with money unpredictability amid the recent years notwithstanding of solid monetary basics. Pretorius and de Beer (2002) note that the stressing instability of the GBP brought about the erGBP of the Myburgh Commission of investigation into the devaluation of the GBP. Policymakers and scholastics have progressively pondered about the way of the money instability emergencies, the variables in charge of their spread and especially whether a nation with apparently suitable residential and outer essentials can experience the ill effects of cash emergency.

"The joining of the LSE into the world business has been supported by the proceeded with development and improvements it has been making. Mboweni contends that amid 2001, the LSE entered into two concurrences with the London Stock Exchange (LSE) to accommodate co-operation in admiration of information dispersal and the likelihood of remote participation and double essential postings on both trades. The relations with the London Stock Exchange (LSE) have been solid and have to a great extent enhanced the operations on the LSE. The LSE Tradelect, which is the LSE's completely robotized exchanging framework, is worked under the permit from the LSE. These and different improvements have helped the LSE's worldwide standing and this has enhanced LSE's effectiveness and its risks of pulling in financial specialists both generally and abroad. This has made it to be one of the best performing stock trades on the planet.

It is recognized that United Kingdom 's ostensible conversion scale unpredictability is among the most astounding of all merchandise exporters and developing markets and that, in time of "unnecessary instability", money developments don't go about as a stun absorber reflecting changes in relative costs, however as a "wellspring of powerlessness". Notwithstanding real upgrades in the organization of financial and fiscal approach, money instability discourages speculators in tradable products and administrations outside of the merchandise segment. "The GBP remains to some degree unstable; however the level of instability has been decreased. At present, the relative instability is joined by a coin that is over-esteemed as in monetary assets are redirected into limited territories of venture, establishing a shaky framework for what's to come"

Knedlik kept up that expanded unpredictability of trade rates in developing markets is additionally ascribed to the more modest size of their economies and therefore the littler size of the business for their money. Higher swapping scale instability in developing business sector nations is in this way a reasonable desire and reflects principal contrasts in the structure of economies. Regardless, it is evident that a real snag for effective arranging in the business area, and the powers would have wanted to have more prominent conversion scale soundness. Yet, under the current circumstances, conversion scale variances are most likely unavoidable. Unstable money related streams now and then created by advancements in different monetary forms make the accomplishment of swapping scale steadiness almost unimaginable (Van de Merwe and Mollentze, 2009).

Benita and Lauterbach (2004) demonstrated that conversion standard unpredictability have genuine financial expenses that influence value steadiness, firm benefit and a nation's solidness. Swapping scale unpredictability has suggestions for the monetary arrangement of a nation particularly money markets. Conversion standard instability produces quality of vulnerability as the fluctuation of expected benefits climbs and its net present worth falls. Stock exchange assumes an extremely essential part in evaluating financial states of any nation through enhanced stock returns normally meant by higher benefit to firms. This thusly causes financial development and the other way around. Essentially stock trade business serves as a channel through which surplus trusts are moved from Lender-Savers to Borrower-Spenders who have deficiencies of stores. In view of this reason, instability in stock costs can essentially influence the execution of the budgetary area and the whole economy.

Also, cash instability prompts the issues of conversion scale hazard. Swapping scale danger, or money danger, is the hazard that a business' operations or a venture's worth will be influenced by progressions in return rates. Case in point, if cash must be changed over into alternate money to make certain venture, changes in the estimation of the coin with respect to the US dollar will influence the aggregate misfortune or increase on the speculation when the cash is changed over back. This danger typically influences organizations yet it can likewise influence singular financial specialists who make global speculations. Subsequently trade danger is higher under states of conversion scale unpredictability.

The majority of the studies that looked to analyze the relationship between conversion scale unpredictability and the share trading system, including this one, focused on utilizing month to month information to inspect the relationship that exists between the two variables. Then again, it must be noted that day by day information or week by week information give more helpful comes about that month to month information. It is along these lines, recommended that the centrality of this present study's results could be enhanced by applying day by day or week by week information.

Utilizing more incessant perceptions better catches flow of conversion scale and stock exchange interrelationships.

References

1. Branson W, Halttunen H, Masson P (1977) Exchange rate in the short run: The dollar Deutsche mark rate, European Economic Review 10: 303-324.
2. Fama EF, French RK (2004) The Capital Asset Pricing Model: Theory and Evidence.
3. Saleh G (2009) The Dynamic Relation Between Stock Prices and Exchange Rates in Egypt, Saudi Arabia and UAE. United States, UMI.
4. Choi JJ, Papaioannou MG (2009) Credit, Currency, or Derivatives: Instruments of Global Financial Stability. U.K, Emerald Group Publishing.
5. Aggarwal R (1981) Exchange Rates and Stock Prices: A Study of the US Capital Markets under Floating Exchange Rates, Akron Business and Economic Review.
6. Soenen LA, Hennigar ES (1988) An Analysis of Exchange Rates and Stock Prices: The U.S Experience between 1980 and 1986.
7. Bahmani OM, Sohrabian A (1992) Stock Prices and the effective exchange rate of the dollar, Applied Economics 24: 459-464.
8. Bhattacharya B, Mukherjee J (2003) Causal Relationship Between Stock Market and Exchange Rate. Foreign Exchange Reserves and Value of Trade Balance: A Case Study for India.
9. Chow EH, Lee WY, Solt MS (1997) The exchange rate risk exposure of asset returns.
10. Solnik B (1987) Using financial prices to test exchange rate models: A note. J Financ, 42: 141-149.
11. Franck P, Young A (1972) Stock Price Reaction of Multinational Firms to Exchange Realignments.
12. Pilbeam K (1998) International Finance. 2nd ed. UK, Basingstoke: Mac Adjasi C, Harvey SK, Agyapong D (2008) Effect of Exchange rate volatalitity on the Ghana stock exchange. African Journal of Accounting, Economics and Banking research.

13. Friedman M (1988) Money and the Stock Market, Journal of Political Economy 96: 221-245.

14. Stavárek D (2004) Linkages between Stock Prices and Exchange Rates in the EU and the United States, Cech Republic, Silesian University in Opava School of Business Administration in Karviná Department of Finance.

15. Aydemir O, Demirhan E (2009) The Relationship between Stock Prices and Exchange Rates Evidence from Turkey, Int Res J Financ Eco, 23: 207-215.

16. Welfens PJ, Ryan C (2007) Financial Market Integration and Growth: Structural Change and Economic Dynamics in the European Union. London, Springer.

17. Richards ND, Simpson J, Evans J (2009) The Interaction Between Exchange Rates and Stock Prices: An Australian Context, Int J Eco Financ 1: 3-23.

18. Kasper LJ (1997) Business Valuations: Advanced Topics. USA, Green wood Publishing.

19. Mandal BN (2009) Global Encyclopaedia of Welfare Economics: The Principle of Population. India, Singh Global Vision for Publishing

20. Herekar H (2006) Capital Asset Pricing Model (CAPM) for Dummies.

21. Taylor (2005) An Empirical Evaluation of the Capital Asset Pricing Model.

22. Vernimmen P, Quiry P, Fur Y, Dallochio M, Salvi A (2005) Corporate Finance: Theory & Practice. England, John Wiley and Sons.

23. Nieh CC, Lee CF (2001) Dynamic relationship between stock prices and exchange rates for G-7 countries, The Quarterly Review of Economics and Finance 41: 477-490.

24. Saunders M, Lewis P, Thornhill A (2007) Research Methods for Business Students, Harlow: Pearson Education Ltd.

Female Students get More Marks as Compared to Male Students: A Statistical Study

Hassan N[1]* and Hassan T[2]

[1]Department of Statistics, University of Peshawar, KPK, Pakistan
[2]Department of Economics, University of Malakand, KPK, Pakistan

Abstract

The main purpose of the study is to find various causes which leads towards the success of the female students rather than male students. Nowadays in educational institutions most of the position holders are females. For these investigations sample of 200 students of University of Peshawar selected from different departments and investigated through a questionnaire. There were 55.5% male respondents and 44.5% are females respondents. 75% respondents were agreed that female students get more marks rather than male students, 25% were disagreed. The investigation of marks percentage showed that 8.11% male students and 1.12% female students were in the range of 51-60 percentage marks, low range of marks have less number of female students. As the range increased from 50-60 percentage to interval of 71-80 percentage of marks so there were found 44.14% male students and 46.06% female students. And in the range of 81% and above there were 18.01% males and 40.45% females students. These results showed that more female students have high range of marks as compared to male students. And at low range of marks only 1.12% females compared to 8.11% males. Over all comparison showed that more female students have high marks rather than male students or female students perform better than male students. 60.5% of the respondents believe that female students are more studios as compare to male students. And 21% responses were thinking that female students are not more studios than male students and 18.5% respondents had no opinion that who are more studios. 76% of the respondents said that female students are more serious toward their studies comparatively to male students. Technique of odds ratio analysis was performed to check at the association of female students get more marks as compare to male students with females attend classes (lectures) more regularly, females know the art of attempting paper in a better way, females ask more questions in the class from teachers. The odds ratio analysis suggests that the female students get more marks as compare to male students were significantly associated with females attend classes (lectures) more regularly, females know the art of attempting paper in a better way, and females ask more questions in the class from teachers.

Keywords: Female students; Marks; Male students; Statistical study

Introduction

Education is the crucial need of human being. Education plays a vital role in the development of human capital in any society and also linked with an individual's well-being and opportunities for better living. It enables individual to improve the quality of life. This increase in productivity also leads towards new sources of earning which enhances the economic growth of a country. There are some factors that affect students' performance these factors may be family problems, social and economic problems etc.

In 1951 the literacy rate of Pakistan was 17.90% (Male literacy rate 86.1%, Female literacy rate 13.9%) and now based on 1998 census the literacy rate is 43.9%. Male literacy rate is 67.98%, female literacy rate is 32.02%. In 2012 the literacy rate of Pakistan is increased to 57% and urban literacy rate is 75% and rural is 49% [1]. Female literacy rate in 2012 is 45% and male literacy is 69.7%. The literacy rate of Pakistan is increasing time to time. Female literacy rate of rural areas is low as compare to urban females, rural areas female literacy rate is 35% (2012) and urban female literacy rate is 68% (2012). Rural areas literacy rate is low because they have not enough facilities for education there are lack of educational institutions. In rural areas people do not want to send her females to other villages or urban areas for education, rural areas people not encouraged females for education. Most of rural areas people involve in labour field, small business and forming etc. They not like to get education as compare to urban areas because of some factors like financial resources, educational institutions, transport resources, employments/jobs etc.

In Pakistan total educational institutions are approximately 162,939, there universities number are 139 in which 7 are women universities. In Pakistan total numbers of female educational institutions from primary to degree collages are approximately 61269. In past females are not encouraged for education but now female getting education equally to males. Males and females have equal rights to get education. And now females have competition with males in any field of study [2]. Generally in school and college results in recent years, is that female students in many cases are better performing than males. And females also behave better in class so there for teachers are cooperative with females.

Nowadays Pakistan has two different education systems, one is annual (BSC/M.Sc) examination system and 2nd one is Semester (Hons/Bachelors) system. In annual system the exams are conducted on annual base but in semester system exams are conducted after every 3 or 2.5 months in this system students are more involve in study activities like assignment, Presentations and monthly tests. Semester system is adopted in Pakistan in most of educational institutions so large numbers of students are studying in semester system. Comparison between annual and semester systems is very often done. Both the

***Corresponding author:** Noor Hassan, Department of Statistics, University of Peshawar, KPK, Pakistan, E-mail: nhassan230@yahoo.com

semester and annual systems have its own merits and demerits. Annual system covers the entire syllabus and then students remember all this till the end of the study year. In this system teacher and students both have enough time for study and easily cover all topics of syllabus. In annual system University/Collage have enough time to prepare questions paper. In semester system examinations are held within five months so what the students studied will remain afresh in their mind. In semester system the syllabus load also will be less on students. In this system different topics have no need to be combined in the same paper. In semester system students have more chances to improve also.

Literature Review

A study of University of Agriculture, Faisalabad showed that performance of female students is better than males. In a study of university level the female students performance compared to male students. There were 265 respondents in which female students were only 36.2% [3].

Comparison between the performance of male and female students with reference to their GPA "up to 2.00" in first semester, this comparison showed that there were 4.7% males and 1% females placed in this GPA range but the range of GPA increased to "above 3.00" so in this range 49.1% males and 59.4% females were counted.

When the performance of males and females was studied till the end of sixth semester, the situation further trended in favor of female students. In CGPA category of "up to 2.01 to 3.00", only 16.7% females were placed, whereas in contrast more than 44% male students fell in this category. Mean of these results was that majority of males probably did not effort to get better grades. The situation became further interested when their performance was considered with reference to the CGPA in "above 3.00", wherein compared to males, about 28% more females secured higher than 3.00 CGPA, the difference being highly significant [4].

The above study concludes that the overall performance of female students was better than male students. This study showed that females work hard and females are more studies as compare to males. Males involve themselves more in social activities and also in physical activities. University of Punjab also showed (December, 2011) that there is a significant difference between male and females marks. There were studied 300 samples of student's marks. And hypothesis were tested that there is no difference between male and females in performance. But there *t*-values (t=-5.405, -2.745, -2.034) indicate that there is a significant difference in the marks of male and female students [5]. Null hypothesis was rejected. And conclude from the result of this study that female students perform better than the male (mean values=295.03; 38.71; 38.47) in the subjects of English and Mathematics as well as in the overall scores/performance.

Study limitation

Due to the limitation of time and resources the study is delimited to;

- University of Peshawar Students
- Survey/Data Collection from 200 respondents

Need of the study

In most of the educational institutions females are position holders. Females perform better than males there should be some main causes which lead towards the success of female students rather than male students. There are some factors which affects the performance of students. Therefore need to investigate these factors and causes.

Main objectives of research are:

- To examine the study trend of male and female students
- To study the activities of students
- To study the seriousness of students about her/his study
- To point out the weaknesses of male students in study
- To find different factors affecting on students' performance
- To study the teachers cooperation

Methodology

Data was collected through a questionnaire for this study, from 200 students of university of Peshawar. One of the sampling method known as simple random sampling (SRS) was used.

According to this method 200 students were taken randomly and then information has been collected. The response of the questionnaires was coded, tabulated and analyzed under Statistical Packages for Social Sciences (SPSS 20) [6]. University of Peshawar is one of the largest educational institution of Khyber Pakhtunkhwa (KPK) Pakistan have different Faculties like faculty of Medical sciences, faculty of Numerical and Social sciences, faculty of Islamic and Oriental studies, faculty of Management and Information Sciences and faculty of Life and Environmental Sciences.

Statistical techniques were used to analyze the collected information and to investigate the records/data. For illustration of joint distribution of the responses the descriptive statistics (bar chart, frequency distribution and pie chart) were used. Odds ratio were used for measuring associations of different categorical variables with one main variable. Odds of an event is the probability of event occurring divided by the probability of the event does not occurring. And the odds ratio is the odds of the event for one group divide by the odds of the event for second group or odds ratio is a measure of association of two binary variables. The odds ratio shows the association between a predictor and the response of interest. And as logistics regression is used to fit a best model and to investigate that which variables have impact on main/dependent variable and how much explaining the response variable. The forward stepwise (Wald) technique is used to get best model. Binary Logistic regression is a type of regression which can be used a situation where the dependent variable is categorical and has only two categories [7].

Result/Analyses

Table 1 showed the result of this question. 8.11% male students and 1.12% female students were in the range of 51-60 percentage marks, low range of marks have less number of female students.

As the range increased from 50-60 percentage to interval of 71-80% of marks so there were found 44.14% male students and 46.06% female students. And in the range of 81% and above there were 18.01% males and 40.45% female students. Over all comparison showed that more female students have high marks rather than male students or female students perform better than male students (Table 1).

It is clear from Table 2 "Female students get more marks as compare to male students". There 75% of the respondents were agreed that female students get more marks rather than male students, 25% of the respondents were disagreed (Table 2).

Marks (%)	No. of male students	%	No. of male students	%	Total	Percent
51-60	9	8.11	1	1.12	10	5
61-70	33	29.72	11	12.36	44	22
71-80	49	44.14	41	46.06	90	45
81-90	20	18.01	36	40.45	56	28
Total	111		89		200	100

Table 1: Your last semester (previous year) GPA/CGPA or (Marks %).

	Frequency	Percent
No	50	25
Yes	150	75
Total	200	100

Table 2: Female students get more marks as compare to male students.

	Frequency	Percent
No	42	21
Yes	121	60.5
Don't Know	37	18.5
Total	200	100

Table 3: Do you think that female students are more studios as compare to male students?

	Frequency	Percent
No	48	24
Yes	152	76
Total	200	100

Table 4: Do you think that girls are more serious towards their studies comparatively to male?

	Frequency	Percent
No	20	10
Yes	180	90
Total	200	100

Table 5: Females attend classes (lectures) more regularly?

	Frequency	Percent
No	25	12.5
Yes	175	87.5
Total	200	100

Table 6: Females complete assignments on time?

	Frequency	Percent
Male	181	90.5
Female	19	9.5
Total	200	100

Table 7: Who's more involved in extra curriculum activities?

Table 3 results clearly showed that female students are more studios than male students. 60.5% of the respondents said that female students are more studios as compare to male students (Table 3).

According to the Table 4 findings 76% of the respondents said that female students are more serious toward their studies comparatively to male students (Table 4).

It is clear from Table 5 that female students attend classes (lectures) more regularly. 90% of the respondents said that female students attend classes (lectures) more regularly (Table 5).

According to the Table 6 that female students complete assignment on time. 87.5% of the respondents were agreed that females complete assignments on time (Table 6).

It is clear from Table 7 that male students are more involved in extra curriculum activities. 90.5% of the respondents said that males are more involved in extra curriculum activities and 9.5% of the respondents answered that females are more involved in extracurricular activities (Table 7).

Odds ratio analyses (Tables 8-14)

Table 9 showed that the odd ratio of female students get more marks as compare to male students is 2.19. Female students have 2.19 times more chance to get more marks if they are attend classes (lectures) regularly as compared to non-regular female students. The 95% Confidence interval (0.840, 5.715) shows a significant relationship between getting more marks and attending classes (lectures) regularly. Female students are more regular then male students because the male students are mostly involve in extra curriculum activities.

It is clear from Table 11 that female students have 1.408 more chance to get more marks if they are know the art of attempting paper

		Females attend classes (lectures) more regularly?		Total
		No	Yes	
Female students get more marks as compare to male students	No	8	42	50
	Yes	12	138	150
Total		20	180	200

Table 8: Female students get more marks as compare to male students. Females attend classes (lectures) more regularly?

	Value	95% Confidence Interval	
		Lower	Upper
Odds Ratio	2.19	0.84	5.715

Table 9: Risk Estimate.

		Females know the art of attempting paper in a better way?		Total
		No	Yes	
Female students get more marks as compare to male students	No	15	35	50
	Yes	35	115	150
Total		30	150	200

Table 10: Female students get more marks as compare to male students. Females know the art of attempting paper in a better way? Cross tabulation.

	Value	95% Confidence Interval	
		Lower	Upper
Odds Ratio	1.408	0.69	2.874

Table 11: Risk estimate.

		Females ask more questions in the class from teachers?		Total
		No	Yes	
Female students get more marks as compare to male students	No	33	17	50
	Yes	97	53	150
Total		130	70	200

Table 12: Female students get more marks as compare to male students. Females ask more questions in the class from teachers? Cross tabulation.

	Value	95% Confidence Interval	
		Lower	Upper
Odds Ratio	1.061	0.541	2.081

Table 13: Risk estimate.

		B	S.E.	Wald	Df	Sig.	Exp(B)
Step 1a	Gender	1.493	0.39	14.691	1	0	4.451
	Constant	0.574	0.198	8.424	1	0.004	1.775
Step 2b	Gender	1.949	0.459	18.069	1	0	7.023
	Responsibilities	-0.797	0.404	3.894	1	0.048	0.451
	Constant	0.819	0.24	11.689	1	0.001	2.268
Step 3c	Gender	1.972	0.463	18.101	1	0	7.182
	Study Time	-0.717	0.354	4.093	1	0.043	0.488
	Responsibilities	-0.842	0.41	4.21	1	0.04	0.431
	Constant	1.218	0.321	14.438	1	0	3.381

Binary logistic regression, Forward Stepwise (Wald).

Table 14: Logistic regression model (Variables in the Equation).

in a better way as compared to those who are have no art of attempting paper. The 95% Confidence interval (0.690, 2.874) shows a significant relationship between female students get more marks as compared to male students and female student know the art of attempting paper in a better way [8].

It is obvious from Table 13 that the odd ratio of female students is 1.06. There female students have 1.06 times more chance to get more marks if they are asking more questions in the class room from teachers [9]. The 95% Confidence interval (0.541, 2.081) shows a significant relationship between female students get more marks as compared to male students and female students ask more questions in the class from teachers.

After applying forward stepwise logistic regression the required best model has only three variables are

X_1=Gender

X_2=Study Time (Are you studying at start of semester/session?)

X_3=Responsibilities (Who has more responsibilities at home?)

The simplest model which represents the data is given by

$$\ln\left(\frac{p}{1-p}\right) = 1.218 + 1.972X_1 - .717X_2 - .842X_3$$

From the fitted logistic regression model, the β_1=1.972 means that being a male the odds of female students get more marks as compare to male students increased by 1.972 times or 97%.

There β_2=-0.717 indicates if the respondents does not study at start of semester/session than the odds of female students get more marks decreased by -0.717 (1-0.717=0.283) times. β_3=-0.842 means if male student is responsible at home than the odds of female get more marks as compare to male decreased by -0.842 times.

Conclusion

To find various causes of that female students get more marks as compare to male students, in most of the educational institutions the positions holders are females therefore this study is important. For this study a survey in University of Peshawar was conducted. According to the survey 75% respondents were agreed that female students get more marks rather than male students, 25% disagreed (Table 2). Generally the performance of the students mostly depend on study, these students will get more marks when they should be more studious as compare to others. So according to the Table 3 60.5% of the respondents believe that female students are more studios as compare to male students. And 21% responses were thinking that female students are not more studios than male students. These results clearly showed that female students are more studios than male students so there for female students get more marks than male students. And female students also more regular in attending classes, according to the survey 90% of the respondents said that female students attend classes (lectures) more regularly.

From Table 7 majority male students are involved in extra curriculum activities therefore male students not giving full concentration on study. Therefore female students get more marks as compared to male students.

Recommendation

On the basis of above findings the following recommendations are made. The trend of female students getting more marks as compared to male is very challenging in educational institutions. To improve male performance, concentration and hard work of male students is required and male students need to avoid those weaknesses that affect the performance of male students like extra curriculum activities. Male students need to improve class attendance, study seriousness, art of attempting paper, completion of assignments on time, study hours, and responsibility.

References

1. Peng CJ, Lee KL (2002) An introduction to logistic regression analysis and reporting. The Journal of Educational Research 96: 3-14.
2. Khan BB, Nawaz R, Chaudhry KM, Hyder AU, Butt TM (2012) Evaluation of comparative academic performance of undergraduate students at university level. The Journal of Animal & Plant Sciences 22: 798-801.
3. Farooq MS, Chaudhry AH, Shafiq M, Berhanu G (2011) Factors affecting students' quality of academic performance: A case of secondary school level. Journal of Quality and Technology Management 7: 1-14.
4. Azhar M, Nadeem S, Naz F, Perveen F, Sameen A (2013) Impact of parental education and socio-economic status on academic achievement of university students. International Journal of Academic Research and Reflection 1: 25-33.
5. Pakistan Economy Survey (2012-13). Government of Pakistan, ministry of finance.
6. Pedhazur E (1997) Multiple Regression in behavioral research. (3rdedn) New York, Harcourt Brace College.
7. Chaudhry SM, Kamal S (1996) Introduction to Statistical Theory. Pakistan.
8. Stephen FE (2007) The analysis of cross-Classified Categorical Data. Statistical Theory and Methods pp: 120-121.
9. Fuller WA (2016) Sampling Statistics. Iowa State University pp: 1-10.

Are Negative P/E and P/B ratio Firms Different?

George Athanassakos*

Ben Graham Chair in Value Investing, Richard Ivey School of Business, The University of Western Ontario, London, Ontario, N6A3K7 Canada

Abstract

Using separately AMEX, NASDAQ and NYSE stock market data for the period 1968-2011, the purpose of this paper is to examine whether negative multiple firms are different from positive ones by examining the performance of negative P/E or P/B firms and how this performance compared with the most widely examined positive multiples firms. We find that firms with negative multiples are indeed different than firms with positive in that (a) a relatively small number of firms with negative multiples experience high forward stock returns even though the majority of them does not resulting in a large difference between mean and median returns and (b) the small firm-low liquidity effect observed in positive multiple firms is not as clearly observed in the case of negative multiple firms. This indicates that prior academic research was right in excluding negative multiple firms from their analysis as inclusion would have affected the homogeneity of their sample and would have diluted their findings and tests of significance.

Keywords: Financial statement analysis; Positive and negative price-to-earnings; Positive and negative price-to-book

JEL Classification: G12, G14, M41

Introduction

A large body of academic research has examined the performance of firms with different levels of positive price-to-earnings (P/E) or price-to-book (P/B) stocks, but there is not much research with regards to the performance of negative P/E or P/B firms and how this performance compares with the most widely examined positive multiples firms [1-10]. Academic papers, such as the ones referred to above, exclude from their analysis negative P/E or P/B firms. Negative P/E or P/B firms were considered to be different from the positive multiple firms and had to be segregated in order to keep the homogeneity of the sample intact. But are they really different?

Using separately AMEX, NASDAQ and NYSE stock market data for the period 1968-2011, the purpose of this paper is to answer this question by examining the performance of negative P/E or P/B firms and how this performance compares with the most widely examined positive multiples firms.

While previous studies [3-8] derive trailing price to earnings (P/E) and price to book value (P/B) ratios using price as at the end of June of year (t) and earnings per share and book value per share as of December of year (t-1), this study will derive trailing ratios where price is as at the end of April of year (t), given that our sample only include firms that already have reported financials by the end of April of year (t). We see no reason to wait until June given that a stock selection strategy can be implemented at an earlier time.

First, we will examine the performance of positive multiple firms and then that of the negative multiples firms and draw conclusions. Given the implicit assumption made by academic papers to date regarding positive and negative multiple firms, our null hypothesis is that negative and positive multiple firms exhibit similar return and fundamental financial characteristics.

This paper shows that firms with negative multiples are indeed different than firms with positive in that (a) a relatively small number of firms with negative multiples experience high forward stock returns even though the majority of them does not resulting in a large difference between mean and median returns and (b) the small firm-low liquidity effect observed in positive multiple firms is not as clearly observed in the case of negative multiple firms. This indicates that prior academic research was right in excluding negative multiple firms from their analysis as inclusion would have affected the homogeneity of their sample and would have diluted their findings and test of significance.

The rest of the paper is structured as follows. Section 2 discusses the data sources and sample selection. Section 3 reports the empirical results and compares the performance of positive and negative multiples stocks and Section 4 concludes the paper and discusses the implications of findings.

Data and Methodology

Our sample includes all AMEX, NASDAQ, NYSE companies that traded on US Stock Exchanges for the period 1969-2011, as well as their financials for the period 1968-2009.

As in Athanassakos [11], this paper uses data from COMPUSTAT from which earnings per share (E), book value per share (B), shares outstanding, trading volume, stock prices and dividends paid, as well as company financials are obtained, and from which trailing price to earnings (P/E), trailing price to book (P/B), total returns, stock liquidity, market cap and firm fundamentals are derived.[1] For the trailing P/E (P/B) ratios, the price (P) is as of the end of April of year (t) and E (B) is the fully diluted annual earnings per share (book value per share) for companies with fiscal year end in year (t-1), as reported in COMPUSTAT. Annual total stock returns are calculated as the price change plus the dividend from May 1 of year (t) to April 30 of year (t+1) over the price in May 1 of year (t).

[1]There is no survivorship bias in the COMPUSTAT data employed in this paper as dead/merged companies are included in our sample.

***Corresponding author:** George Athanassakos, Ben Graham Chair in Value Investing, Richard Ivey School of Business, The University of Western Ontario, London, Ontario, N6A 3K7 Canada, E-mail: gathanassakos@ivey.uwo.ca

Firm fundamentals, derived from company financials, are defined as follows: CASH is cash over assets. EBIT MARGIN is EBIT over Revenues (i.e., operating margin). TURNOVER is assets over revenues (times). CURRENT RATIO is the ratio of cash plus short term investments, inventories and accounts receivable to current liabilities (times). DEBT is short and long term debt to equity. EPS GROWTH, EBIT GROWTH and REV GROWTH are the annual growth rates of EPS, EBIT and revenues, respectively for fiscal year (t-1). Market metrics are defined as follows: MARKET CAP is derived by multiplying price per share time's shares outstanding at the end of April of year (t). LIQUIDITY is the annual stock trading volume of the year prior to May of year (t) over shares outstanding as at April of year (t) [11].

To eliminate likely data errors [12,13], we have excluded firms with P/E values over 500 and P/B values over 30. Finally, to be included in our sample a stock had to have a price over $1 and to have reported financials in COMPUSTAT.

After all aforementioned screenings, the sample with the positive multiples ends up with 90,423 cross sectional-time series (firm-year) observations belonging to a cumulative number of 8,570 unique companies. Of those companies 1,217 are AMEX, 3,244 are NYSE and 4,109 are NASDAQ companies.

The negative multiples sample includes 6,232 firms or 22,133 observations with negative P/E ratios and 927 firms or 2,246 observations with negative P/B ratios over the sample period. For the negative P/E group, 3,564 unique companies (14,332 observations) are NASDAQ companies, 838 are AMEX (2,616 observations) and 1,830 are NYSE (5,185 observations). For the negative P/B group, 294 unique firms (834 observations) are NYSE, 134 are AMEX (339 observations) and 499 are NASDAQ (1,083 observations).

Non-overlapping forward annual stock returns (adjusted for stock splits and stock dividends) are obtained from May 1, 1969 to April 30, 2011. Trailing company fundamentals, as defined earlier, are for the period 1968 to 2009.

Empirical Results

Table 1 and 2 report the summary statistics for key variables of firms with positive multiples (Table 1) and those with negative multiples (Table 2). The tables include the mean, median, minimum and maximum of each variable.

In Table 1, we see that the EBIT margin and turnover for the median positive multiple firm are 9.88% and 0.857, respectively. The median annual growth rates of revenues, EPS and EBIT have all been positive over the sample period. The median firm is not overleveraged as indicated by the debt to equity ratio of .28 and has a market cap is US$182.5 million. Median values for cash to assets and current ratio are 3.7% and 2.1, respectively. Moreover, the median firm trades about 48% of the shares outstanding over the previous year. Finally, the median stock return of firms with positive multiples is 8%.

Comparing Table 1 and 2, we see that firms with negative P/E or P/B have very low or negative median EBIT margin, and EPS, EBIT and revenue growth rates as opposed to a very positive one for firms with positive multiples. Negative P/E or P/B firms also have very low market cap and higher debt, turnover and liquidity (annual trading volume to shares outstanding) than firms with positive multiples. Median tests, reported in Table 2 (Panel C) and based on CHI-SQUARE tests for testing the null hypothesis that median values for the variables of Tables 1 vs. Table 2 (i.e., of positive vs. negative multiple firms) are equal, show the following. Median values of Table 1 variables are statistically different from the median values of same variables in Table 2 (Panel A), with the exception of current ratio and debt, at conventional levels of significance. Moreover, all median values of Table 1 variables are statistically different from the median values of the same variables in Table 2 (Panel B), at conventional levels of significance. Finally, we see that firms with negative P/B also have negative P/E, but not the other way around.

More importantly, there is a very large difference between mean and median returns when firms have negative P/E (21.1% and 0%, respectively) or P/B ratios (30.6% and 6.8%, respectively) vis-à-vis corresponding numbers when firms have positive multiples (16.8% vs. 8%, respectively). Although, on average, returns are much higher for negative P/E (P/B) firms than positive ones, 50% of the negative P/E (P/B) firms experience a return of less than zero (6.81%) as opposed to positive P/E firms whereby 50% of the returns are less than 8%. Not shown here, this is also true when we look at individual exchanges. AMEX firms with negative P/E have a mean return of 9.14% and a median return of -6.98%, NASDAQ firms 21.54% and -3.31% and NYSE firms 25.87% and 9.37%. For negative P/B firms, the mean return for AMEX is 17.5%, for NASDAQ 34.44% and for NYSE 30.54%; the corresponding medians are -3.71%, 5.28% and 11.52%, respectively. Again, not shown here, the mean and median return figures by exchange for the positive multiples firms in the sample are: 12.7% vs. 2.42% for AMEX, 18.5% vs. 5.4% for NASDAQ and 16.7% vs. 10.4% for NYSE stocks.[2]

Variable	Median	Mean	Maximum	Minimum
EBIT margin	0.0988	0.1207	1.334	-22.82
Current Ratio	2.10355	2.676	113.37	0
Cash	0.037	0.0824	0.9968	-0.09928
Debt	0.28	0.2921	1.17	-0.06
Turnover	0.8569	1.2787	864.222	0.0582
EPS growth	0.05	0.1557	823	-3212.43
EBIT growth	0.14	0.1668	3372	-1993
REV growth	0.13	0.3512	6500.8	-199.29
Liquidity	0.479	0.9473	272.905	0
Market Cap	182.477	2430.306	596475.75	0.02724
Return	0.0799	0.16899	22.8745	-0.9907
P/E	15.8655	25.679	500	0.00636
P/B	1.8252	2.6067	29.824	0.0000921

Table 1: Positive P/E or P/B ratios

The table reports summary information for 90,423 firm-year observations of 8,570 unique firms that are listed in AMEX, NASDAQ and NYSE exchanges. Of those companies 1,217 companies are AMEX, 3,244 are NYSE and 4,109 are NASDAQ. All data are from COMPUSTAT and are available from 1968-2011. P/E is price as at April of year (t) over earnings per share as fiscal year end (t-1). P/B is price as at April of year (t) over book value per share as fiscal year end (t-1). Return is the annual return for the year following the sorting into portfolios. Cash is cash over assets. EBIT Margin is EBIT over Revenues. Turnover is assets over revenues (times). Liquidity is trading volume for the year prior to May of year (t) as a percentage of shares outstanding. Current Ratio is the ratio of cash plus short term investments and accounts receivable to current liabilities (times). Market Cap is market cap in millions of US dollars determined by multiplying shares outstanding by price per share as at April of year (t). Debt is short and long term debt to equity. REV, EBIT and EPS growth are the annual growth rates of revenues, EBIT and EPS, respectively for the fiscal year (t-1).

[2]We also repeated the analysis by excluding the upper 10% and bottom 10% of the ranked data and found that the results were not materially different for all variables examined both in terms of mean and median values.

Panel A: Negative P/E ratios

Variable	Median	Mean	Maximum	Minimum
EBIT Margin	-0.0553	-0.0161	3.083	-69.99
Current Ratio	2.117	3.5846	100.192	0
Cash	0.0829	0.159	0.9988	-0.0357
Debt	0.27	0.3611	113.24	-62.4
Turnover	1.3557	4.5587	1206.73	-0.4524
EPS growth	-0.66	-1.4631	1341	-1021
EBIT growth	-0.33	1.1615	28985	-2364.5
REV growth	0.04	2.319	11651	-20.24
Liquidity	0.8454	1.484	139.37	0
Market Cap	96.66	819.38	232826	0.0157
Return	0	0.2109	36.1316	-0.9942
P/E	-10.9375	-42.3236	-0.0015	-4120.83
P/B	1.7	4.6973	8100	-2345.68

Panel B: Negative P/B ratios

Variable	Median	Mean	Maximum	Minimum
EBIT Margin	0.0299	-0.6924	0.9338	-63.8813
Current Ratio	1.1709	1.5236	45.4358	0
Cash	0.0586	0.1221	0.8961	-0.0139
Debt	1.14	1.3611	470	-73.17
Turnover	0.9519	2.4956	409.024	0.0055
EPS growth	-0.215	-0.733	391	-796
EBIT growth	-0.01	0.5733	810.32	-291.06
REV growth	0.06	7.3656	11651	-0.98
Liquidity	0.7262	1.2613	23.37	0
Market Cap	109.12	837.3	40181.5	0.0157
Return	0.0681	0.3056	17	-0.9942
P/E	-1.461	5.3509	3975	-2082
P/B	-4.8407	-35.8924	-0.0003	-2345.68

Panel C: Median Tests (p-values)

Variable	Table 1 ≠ Table 2 (Panel A) Metrics	Table 1 ≠ Table 2 (Panel B) Metrics
EBIT Margin	0.0001	0.0232
Current Ratio	0.431	0.0001
Cash	0.0221	0.043
Debt	0.576	0.0001
Turnover	0.0001	0.017
EPS growth	0.0001	0.0001
EBIT growth	0.0001	0.0001
REV growth	0.014	0.0366
Liquidity	0.0001	0.0001
Market Cap	0.0001	0.0001
Return	0.0001	0.049

Table 2: Negative P/E or P/B ratios

The table reports summary information for 22,133 firm-year observations belonging to 6,232 unique firms that have negative P/E ratios and 2,246 firm-year observations belonging to 927 unique firms that have a negative P/B ratios for the total sample. For the negative P/E group, 3,564 unique companies (14,332 observations) are NASDAQ companies, 838 AMEX (2,616 observations) and 1,830 NYSE (5,185 observations). For the negative P/B group, 294 unique firms (834 observations) are NYSE, 134 AMEX (339 observations) and 499 NASDAQ (1,083 observations). All data are from COMPUSTAT and are available from 1968-2011. P/E is price as at April of year (t) over earnings per share as fiscal year end (t-1). P/B is price as at April of year (t) over book value per share as fiscal year end (t-1). Return is the annual return for the year following the sorting into portfolios. Cash is cash over assets. EBIT Margin is EBIT over Revenues. Turnover is assets over revenues (times). Liquidity is trading volume for the year prior to May of year (t) as a percentage of shares outstanding. Current Ratio is the ratio of cash plus short term investments and accounts receivable to current liabilities (times). Market Cap is market cap in millions of US dollars determined by multiplying shares outstanding by price per share as at April of year (t). Debt is short and long term debt to equity. REV, EBIT and EPS growth are the annual growth rates of revenues, EBIT and EPS, respectively for the fiscal year (t-1). Median tests are based on CHI-SQUARE tests for testing the null hypothesis that median values for the variables of Tables 1 vs. Table 2 (i.e., of positive vs. negative multiple firms) are equal.

Firms with negative multiples are thus different than firms with positive multiples and hence our null hypothesis is rejected. As we see in Table 2, negative P/E or P/B firms experience, on average, high stock returns even though their medians are relatively low. This indicates that while some low P/E or P/B value firms have high returns the majority of such firms do not, resulting in much larger differences between mean and median returns than firms with positive multiples, both for the total sample and by exchange. The implication of this is that one can find real gems within negative P/E or P/B firms but he/she needs to be extremely cautious as the majority of such firms are anything but. In other words, prior academic research was right in excluding negative multiple firms from their analysis as inclusion would have affected the homogeneity of their sample.

Further analysis also shows that negative P/E (P/B) firms are different than positive P/E (P/B) firms in another dimension as is shown in Table 3 (Panels A and B). While smaller and less liquid positive P/E (P/B) firms tend to perform unequivocally economically and statistically better than larger/more liquid firms [14-16], for negative P/E (P/B) firms the evidence is not as clear cut as the bigger and more liquid firms seem to earn median annual returns comparable to the smaller and less liquid firms. The markets seem to reward liquidity and size more when it comes to negative P/E (P/B) firms than when it comes to positive multiple firms. Market participants may view negative P/E or P/B firms as riskier thus preferring to focus on the safer larger/more liquid firms among them, which enable them to exit quickly if the need arises, resulting in higher than normal returns for these vs. equivalent positive multiple firms. This further exemplifies the importance of segregating negative from positive multiple firms in related research as inclusion would undermine the clarity and generality of findings and dilute the significance of empirical evidence.

Conclusions

Using separately AMEX, NASDAQ and NYSE stock market data for the period 1968-2011, the purpose of this paper was to examine whether negative multiple firms were different from positive ones by examining the performance of negative P/E or P/B firms and how this performance compared with the most widely examined positive

Panel A: Negative P/E ratios

No of OBS	Small cap/low liquidity		Large cap/high liquidity	
	Median	Mean	Median	Mean
2706	0.069	0.3001	0.0498	0.131

Panel B: Negative P/B ratios

No of OBS	Small cap/low liquidity		Large cap/high liquidity	
	Median	Mean	Median	Mean
266	0.0817	0.435	0.096	0.232

Table 3: Returns of Small - Low liquidity Firms vs. Returns of Large - High Liquidity Firms: Negative P/E or P/B firms

The table reports the mean and median returns of firms with small cap/low liquidity vs. large cap/high liquidity firms within the negative P/E or P/B sample for the period 1968-2011. For the negative P/E sample, low market cap are firms with market value of less than US$28.5 million, while large cap firms are those with a market value of over US$342.2 million. At the same time, low liquidity (annual trading volume to shares outstanding) firms are those with liquidity of less than 0.37 and high liquidity firms are those with liquidity of over 1.80. For the negative P/B sample, low market cap are firms with market value of less than US$27 million, while large cap firms are those with a market value of over US$533.8 million. At the same time, low liquidity firms are those with liquidity of less than 0.34 and high liquidity firms are those with liquidity of over 1.51.

multiples firms. We found that firms with negative multiples are indeed different than firms with positive in that (a) a relatively small number of firms with negative multiples experience high forward stock returns even though the majority of them does not resulting in a large difference between mean and median returns and (b) the small firm-low liquidity effect observed in positive multiple firms is not as clearly observed in the case of negative multiple firms. This indicates that prior academic research was right in excluding negative multiple firms from their analysis as inclusion would have affected the homogeneity of their sample and would have diluted their findings and tests of significance.

References

1. Basu S (1977) Investment Performance of Common Stocks in Relation to their Price to earnings Ratios: A Test of the Efficient Market Hypothesis. Journal of Finance 32: 663-682.
2. Chan LKC, Hamao Y, Lakonishok J (1991) Fundamentals and Stock Returns in Japan. Journal of Finance 46: 1739-1764.
3. Fama EF, French KR (1992) The Cross Section of Expected Stock Returns. Journal of Finance 47: 427-465.
4. Fama EF, French KR (1993) Common Risk Factors in the Returns on Stocks and Bonds. Journal of Financial Economics 33: 3-56.
5. Fama EF, French KR (1995) Size and Book-to-Market Factors in Earnings and Returns. Journal of Finance 50: 131-155.
6. Fama EF, French KR (1996) Multifactor Explanations of Asset Pricing Anomalies. Journal of Finance 51: 55-84.
7. Lakonishok J, Shleifer A, Vishny RW (1994) Contrarian Investment, Extrapolation, and Risk. The Journal of Finance 49: 1541-1578.
8. Chan LKC, Lakonishok J (2004) Value and Growth Investing: Review and Update. Financial Analysts' Journal 71-84.
9. Athanassakos G (2009) Value versus Growth Stock Returns and the Value Premium: The Canadian Experience 1985-2005. Canadian Journal of Administrative Studies 2: 109-129.
10. Athanassakos G (2011) The Performance, Pervasiveness and Determinants of Value Premium in Different US Exchanges: 1986-2006. Journal Of Investment Management 9: 33-73.
11. Athanassakos G (2013) Separating winners from losers among value and growth stocks in different US exchanges: 1969-2011, Working Paper, Western University, USA.
12. Griffin JM, Lemmon ML (2002) Book to Market Equity, Distress Risk, and Stock Returns. Journal of Finance 57: 2317-2336.
13. Cohen RB, Polk C, Vuolteenaho T (2003) The Value Spread. Journal of Finance 58: 609-641.
14. Baker M, Stein JC (2004) Market Liquidity as a Sentiment Indicator. Journal of Financial Markets 7: 271-299.
15. Fang VW, Noe TH, Tice S (2008) Stock Market Liquidity and Firm Value. Journal of Financial Economics 94: 150-169.
16. Kothari SP, Shaken J, Sloan RG (1995) Another Look at the Cross Section of Expected Stock Returns. Journal of Finance 50: 185-224.

17

Operational Risk, Fund Performance and Investors Protection: Evidence from China

Robin H Luo*

School of Economics and Finance, Wuhan University, China

Abstract

This paper investigates the operational risk, fund performance and investor protection in the seven years subsequent to the 2001 liberalisation of the Chinese open-end funds market. The empirical results indicate that the fund type and fund manager's qualification are positively associated with selecting the Big 4 auditing firms, while the size and profitability of open-end funds are not. The results also indicate that the open-end funds audited by the Big 4 firms do not outperform the funds audited by non-Big 4 firms.

Keywords: Big 4 Firms; Investor protection; Open-end funds; Operational risk; China

Introduction

As the investment fund industry has grown explosively, so too has the list of fund failure. One of the famous examples of hedge fund failure is the Long Term Capital Fund managed by the Long-Term Capital Management (LTCM)[1] . In September 2006, another large hedge fund, Amaranth, reported losses of more than $6 billion apparently incurred in only one month, representing a negative return over that month of roughly 66 percent [1]. A recent example is the Madoff scandal. On December 11, 2008, the Securities and Exchange Commission (SEC) charged Bernie Madoff and his firm, Bernard L. Madoff Investment Securities LLC, with securities fraud for a $65 billion dollar Ponzi scheme[2].

To better understand why investment funds, including both the hedge funds and mutual funds, fail and how these failures could be avoided, researchers attempt to predict the fraud and other operational risks in financial firms. Brown, Goetzmann, Liang, and Schwarz [2,3] use a contemporaneous cross-section of hedge funds' Form ADV filings with a summary of historical violations to create a measure of operational risk based on the correlations between historically available hedge fund data and Form ADV variables. They then test if this measure is associated with hedge fund death, flows, and returns.

Hedges IV [4] concludes that the primary cause of fund's failure attributed to one of three categories of risk, investment risk, business risk, and operational risk. Operational risks are associated with supporting the operating environment of the fund. The operating environment includes trade processing, accounting, administration, valuation, and reporting. These are the types of risks that investors do not intend to take as part of their investment strategy. For example, it could be the risk that an investment might be fraudulent, or that managers might misrepresent performance. The most common operational issues related to investment fund losses have been misrepresentation of fund investments, misappropriation of investor funds, unauthorized trading, and inadequate resources. The most significant operational issue is the misrepresentation of investments, which is defined as the act of creating or causing the generation of reports and valuations with false and misleading information. This may be due to deliberate deception or to operational errors.

It is widely believed that the internal fraud and operational risk are alleviated by selecting a good external auditor and larger and more prestigious auditors have greater incentives to monitor the firms closely. The auditor selection can be viewed as an indication of firm's willingness to control the operational risk [5,6].

Nevertheless, most of the existing auditor selection literature ignores the financial companies or investment companies because there is no comparability between them and normal companies. In the present study, I investigate the choice of auditor and investor protection in China's open-end fund market over the period 2001-2007. The present study contributes to the literature in a number of ways. First, the 2001 liberalisation of open-end funds market in China provides an environment for the study of auditor selection in the fast-growing investment industry. It is thus possible to investigate which slices of the fund audit market the international firms gained in the booming Chinese funds market. Second, previous studies suggest that high-quality auditors provide a source of protection for equity investors in the US and other developed countries[3]. This study sheds light on this issue in an emerging market. In particular it explores the question whether the Big 4 auditors are associated with the open-end funds which have abnormal returns.

In the present paper, I first investigate the determinants of choice of auditor by developing several hypotheses based on characteristics of China's open-end funds, such as fund type, fund manager's qualification, fund size and profitability. In the second step, I study whether the Big

[1]LTCM was founded by a number of star traders and Nobel laureate economists in 1994. The fund was spectacularly successful until the middle of 1998 with an average annually return of 33.4% during the period of 1995-1997. It had capital of $4.8 billion and assets of $120 billion at the beginning of 1998. In the aftermath of the Russian crisis in August 1998, the fund lost almost all its capital in one month.

[2]SEC Charges Bernard L. Madoff for Multi-Billion Dollar Ponzi Scheme. US Securities and Exchange commission.

[3]See, Khurana and Raman [33], Leuz et al. [31], and Newman et al. [35].

***Corresponding authors:** Robin H Luo, School of Economics, Wuhan University, Luojia Hill, Wuhan, 430072, China, E-mail: robin.h.luo@gmail.com

4 auditors protect the open-end funds investors by extending Krishnan [7] and Francis and Wang [8] method.

The rest of this paper is organised as follows. Section "Literature Review" reviews the related literature. Section "Hypotheses Development and Models" develops the hypotheses and models. Section 4 presents the data and empirical results. Conclusion is in the last section.

Literature Review

Early researches on the investment funds have centred on the performance persistence of investment funds[4] and the investor behaviour and cash flows to funds[5]. Operational risk and illegal behaviour by fund managers were ignored in these studies.

Several recent papers examine the returns manipulation of hedge fund manager and illegal behaviour conducted by mutual fund managers. Agarwal, et al. [9,10], Bollen and Pool [10,11] present strong evidence that hedge funds' manipulate their reported returns. Zitzewitz [12] shows that late trading in mutual funds was widespread. Goetzmann, et al. [13] develop pricing rules that prevent investors from late trading. Choi and Kahan [14], Houge and Wellman [15] show that fund families that allowed late trading suffered significant outflows.

A number of other studies investigate the operational risk in lending institutions. The overall conclusion of these papers is that operational risk is a major source of risk for lending institutions and internal fraud is the largest component of operational risk. Chernobai, et al. [16] find financial institutions with weak corporate governance are more likely to have operational events. Perry and de Fontnouvelle [17] test stock price reactions to operational risk events at lending institutions. For internal fraud, the firms' market capitalization drops by double the value of the loss. For other operational losses, the market capitalization only drops by the value of the loss.

It is widely believed that the internal fraud and operational risk can be alleviated by using a good external auditor and larger and more prestigious auditors have greater incentives to monitor the firms. The auditor selection is motivated from three possible sources - client characteristics, audit firm characteristics or the audit environment [5,6]. The existing literature has concentrated on exploring how either auditor or client characteristics determine auditor choice. Auditor section research has been conducted in the U.S. and other developed countries[6]. DeFond [18] summarises the previous literature and concludes that larger companies and those making securities issues are more likely to select larger or higher reputation (as proxied by Big Six)[7] audit firms. DeFond [18] also finds support for the propositions that companies with lower management ownership and those with higher gearing tend to select larger audit firms. Firth and Smith [19] find similar variables significant for the New Zealand companies in the new issue market.

In addition to the choice of auditor, the association between earnings quality and large international accounting firms has also been investigated extensively. DeAngelo [5] documents that higher audit quality is associated with Big six auditors, where audit quality is defined as the joint probability of detecting and reporting material financial statement errors. Francis and Krishnan [20] argue that investor may perceive Big 4 auditors as having higher quality because these auditors have more of the observable characteristics associated with quality, such as specialised training and peer reviews, than non-Big 4 auditors.

There is evidence that earnings of U.S. companies with Big 4 auditors are of higher quality and that the stock market values earnings surprises of Big 4 clients more highly than earnings surprises of firms with non-Big 4 auditors [21,22]. Kinney and Martin [23] analyse nine data sets of audit-related adjustments from more than 1,500 audits across 15 years, and conclude that audit-related adjustments are overwhelmingly negative on pre-audit net earnings and net assets. Another reason investors have greater confidence in the reported earnings of Big 4 clients is that Big 4 auditors are more likely to issue going concern warnings than non-Big 4 auditors for the same set of client circumstances [24].

Hypotheses Development and Models

Auditor selection

The first set of hypotheses (H1a to H1d) test what are the determinants of choice of auditor in China's open-end funds market.

Theoretical studies have shown that larger or more prestigious accounting firms have greater incentives not to perform a low-quality service at a high-quality price because they have more wealth [25] and more valuable reputations [5]. The fund managers who have obtained the relevant degrees from developed countries or the professional certifications, such as Chartered Financial Analyst (CFA), are deemed to have stronger links with the Big 4 firms. I therefore expect the open-end fund with its manager is a Chartered Financial Analyst (CFA) or has an overseas qualification to be more likely to select a Big 4 auditor. This leads to the following hypothesis:

H1a: There is a positive relationship between an open-end fund manager is a Chartered Financial Analyst (CFA) charter holder or has relevant qualification from overseas and the likelihood of selecting a Big 4 auditor.

There are four types of open-end funds in China. Stock funds are investing heavily on common stocks and the objective of this type of funds is long-term growth through capital appreciation. The other three categories include bond funds, money market funds and hybrid funds. These funds have a more diversified portfolio containing bonds, money market instruments and other assets. Kelley [26] and Granzin [27] compare the value and growth indices based on the behaviour of value and growth funds and report higher volatility of the funds investing heavily on the growth stocks. In the present study, I divide the open-end funds into two groups, stock funds and non-stock funds, which include bond funds, money market funds and hybrid funds. Non-stock funds have lower risk given the nature of the instruments they invested. In the light of the above discussion, I expect that the stock funds tend to

[4]See Hendricks et al. [36] and Brown and Goetzman [37].

[5]See Gruber [38] and Zheng [39].

[6]Craswell [40] studies the auditor selection in Australia. Firth and Smith [19] and Beattie and Fearnley [41] investigate the similar issue in New Zealand and UK, respectively.

[7]The Big Six accounting firms were Arthur Andersen, Coopers and Lybrand, Deloitte, Ernst and Young, KPMG, and Price Waterhouse prior to the merger of Price Waterhouse and Coopers and Lybrand in 1997. Arthur Andersen collapsed in 2002. The remaining Big 4 accounting firms are Deloitte, Ernst and Young, KPMG, and PricewaterhouseCoopers. We use the term Big 4 throughout the paper to refer to the above set of large international accounting firms.

select a local auditor because of the embedded risk in their investment portfolio. This hypothesis is formulated in the alternative form as:

H1b: There is a positive relationship between an open-end fund being a non-stock type fund and the likelihood of selecting a Big 4 auditor.

Previous auditor selection studies have generally included a client size measure as a control variable [18,19]. There are some good reasons that the large open-end funds to be targeted by the Big 4 firms. First, targeting large open-end funds would have been an effective way of gaining market share quickly. Second, such open-end funds may have been considered less risky and may be able to afford high-quality auditing fees. For similar reasons they may be expected to have sought funds with relatively better performance as clients. These hypotheses are formulated in the alternative form as:

H1c: There is a positive relationship between the size of an open-end fund and the likelihood of selecting a Big 4 auditor.

H1d: There is a positive relationship between the profitability of an open-end fund and the likelihood of selecting a Big 4 auditor.

These hypotheses are tested by running a binomial logistic regression. It takes the following form:

$$FIRM_{it} = \log it(\lambda_0 + \lambda_1 FUNDTP_{it} + \lambda_2 COE_{it} + \lambda_3 \Delta NAV_{it} + \lambda_4 ASSET_{it}) \quad (1)$$

Where, from H1a to H1d,

$FIRM$ =1 if auditor is Big 4

=0 otherwise

$FUNDTP$ =1 if the fund is a stock fund

=0 otherwise

COE =1 if the fund manager is a Chartered Financial Analyst (CFA) or educated overseas

=0 otherwise

$\Delta NAV = (NAV_{t+1} - NAV_t)/[(NAV_{t+1} + NAV_t)/2]$

$ASSET$ =total assets

Investor protection

Subsequent set of hypothesis tests whether the Big 4 firms protect the open-end funds investors in China. It is widely accepted that Big 4 firms in the US impose a high level of earnings quality in order to protect their brand name reputation form legal exposure and reputations risk which can arise from misleading financial reports by clients [5]. However, cross-country comparative accounting studies show that the Big 4 firms' behaviour with respect to client earnings and investor protection varies systematically with the incentives in different institutional environments [28-34]. A more recent study by Francis and Wang [8] investigates the joint effect of investor protection and Big 4 audits on earnings quality for a large sample of firms from 42 countries. They find that earnings quality increases for firms with Big 4 auditors when a country's investor protection regime gives stronger protection to investors. In the light of the above discussion, I expect that the open-end funds audited by Big 4 firm offer higher return to the investors because of investor protection associated with the high-quality audits. This hypothesis is formulated in the alternative form as:

H1e: An open-end fund being a Big 4 firm's client tend to provide higher return to the investors.

Following Krishnan [7] and Francis and Wang [8], I pool the clients of Big 4 auditors and other auditors, and add an additional dummy variable DR^{it} in the regression. This model directly examines whether the contemporaneous association between earnings and negative returns is statistically different for clients of Big 4 firms and clients of other auditors.

$$\begin{aligned}\Delta NAV_{it} &= \alpha_0 + \alpha_1 DR_{it} + \alpha_2 FIRM_{it} + \alpha_3 DR_{it} \times FIRM + \beta_0 R_{it} \\ &+ \beta_1 R_{it} \times DR_{it} + \beta_2 R_{it} \times FIRM_{it} + \beta_3 R_{it} \times DR_{it} \times FIRM_{it} + \varepsilon_t\end{aligned} \quad (2)$$

Where ΔNAV_{it} is the change of net asset value per share for fund ^{i} in year ^{t}; R_{it} is annual market return calculated over a 12-month period; and DR_{it} is a dummy variable that equals 1 if $R_{it}<0$ and 0 otherwise. $FIRM_{it}$ equals 1 for clients of Big 4 firms and 0 for other auditors' clients.

Data and Results

My sample consists of 902 fund-year observations between 2001 and 2007 obtained from CSMAR Open-end Fund database. Investment funds were not available to Chinese investors until the late 1990s. A number of closed-end funds emerged after the government passed the *Provisional Measures of the Administration of Securities Investment Funds* in November 1997. This guideline for institutional stock trading was replaced by the *Securities Investment Funds Law* promulgated on 28 October 2003 and effective as of 1 June 2004. A detailed *Administration of Securities Investment Fund Operations Procedures* was then passed by the China Securities Regulatory Commission (CSRC) on 16 September 2004 and implemented on 1 October 2004.

The first two closed-funds emerged with 20 per cent of their capital in bonds and 80 per cent in stocks in April 1998. As of June 2000, there were 22 closed-end funds with total assets of 50.5 billion Renminbi (RMB). China's first open-end fund, Hua-An Innovation open-end

	Number of open-end funds	Deloitte	Ernst and Young	KPMG	PWC	Big 4 Total	Big 4 Market Share	Number of Non-Big 4 Auditors	Non-Big 4 Market share
2001	2	-	-	-	2	2	100%	-	-
2002	13	-	3	-	10	13	100%	-	-
2003	50	3	9	1	33	46	92%	4	8%
2004	99	6	21	3	56	86	87%	13	13%
2005	157	14	35	5	81	135	86%	22	14%
2006	249	20	58	10	124	212	85%	37	15%
2007	332	26	73	14	169	282	85%	50	15%

Note: Data are obtained from CSMAR Open-end Fund database for the years 2001-2007. The Big 4 firms include Deloitte, Ernst and Young, KPMG and PricewaterhouseCoopers (PWC). Da-Hua CPAs was one of the oldest CPA firms in Shanghai, China. It reached an agreement with Ernst and Young to form a join firm at the end of 2001. The newly established firm was registered under the name Ernst and Young Da-Hua with the Chinese government in February 2002. The number of open-end funds audited by Ernst and Young Da-Hua is included into that of Ernst and Young.

Table 1: Descriptive information on the number of open-end funds and their auditors.

	Number of open-end funds	Fund Type				CFA and Overseas Education (COE)			
		Stock Fund	%	Non-Stock Fund	%	Yes	%	No	%
2001	2	1	50.00%	1	50.00%	2	100.00%	-	-
2002	13	6	46.15%	7	53.85%	6	46.15%	7	53.85%
2003	50	23	46.00%	27	54.00%	22	44.00%	28	56.00%
2004	99	40	40.40%	59	59.60%	40	40.40%	59	59.60%
2005	157	56	35.67%	101	64.33%	60	38.22%	97	61.78%
2006	249	96	38.55%	153	61.45%	86	34.54%	163	65.46%
2007	332	151	45.48%	181	54.52%	109	32.83%	223	67.17%
Total	902	373	41.35%	529	58.65%	325	36.03%	577	63.97%

Note: Non-stock fund includes bond fund, money market fund and hybrid fund.

Table 2: Descriptive information on the characteristics of open-end funds.

	Variables		
	ΔNAV	*ASSET*	*R*
Mean	0.1167	4.7947	0.6872
Median	0.0219	1.8373	0.9666
Maximum	1.3122	48.1740	1.3043
Minimum	-1.1673	0.0197	-0.2062
Std.Dev	0.3081	7.1722	0.5888
Skewness	0.4289	2.5745	-0.4607
Kurtosis	4.4907	10.3577	1.4545
Observations	902	902	7

Note: *ΔNAV* is the percentage change of funds' net asset value. *ASSET* is the market value of open-end funds in billion RMB. *R* is the market return computed based on Shanghai Composite Index

Table 3: Descriptive information on the characteristics of open-end funds.

Independent Variables	*Variables*		
	Coefficient	Std. Error	Prob.
Intercept (λ_0)	1.3395	0.2924	0
FUNDTP (λ_1)	0.4860	0.2911	0.095*
COE (λ_2)	0.6564	0.3111	0.0348**
ΔNAV (λ_3)	-0.0725	0.0793	0.3607
Ln(ASSET) (λ_4)	0.1258	0.0919	0.1711
LR statistic: 9.9079 Prob (LR stat): 0.042			

Notes: The standard errors are estimated using quasi-maximum likelihood (Huber/White) method. Parameter estimates are obtained using quadratic hill-climbing algorithm. ***, **, * stand for 1%, 5%, and 10% significance level, respectively. The unit of ASSET is 1 billion RMB.
FIRM =1 if auditor is Big 4; =0 otherwise
FUNDTP =1 if the fund is a stock fund; =0 otherwise
COE=1 if the fund manager is a Chartered Financial Analyst (CFA) or educated overseas;=0 otherwise

$\Delta NAV = (NAV_{t+1} - NAV_t)/[(NAV_{t+1} + NAV_t)/2]$

ASSET =total assets

Table 4: Regression analysis of auditor selection.

fund (fund code: 040001), was established in September 2001. The open-end funds thrived in the period of 2001 to 2007. The number surged from 2 to 332 and the total assets managed soared from 8.56 billion RMB to 3,063.09 billion RMB.

Table 1 presents the number of open-end funds and the number of funds audited by the Big 4 on an annual basis. It demonstrates that the Big 4 firms dominate the auditing market of open-end funds in China in the sample period. However, the percentage of funds audited by the Big 4 exhibits a decline over time from 100 per cent in 2001 to 85 per cent in 2007. PricewaterhouseCoopers has always been the major player in this market. The other three Big 4 accounting firms, Deloitte, Ernst and Young, and KPMG, have similar market shares with a number of local accounting firms. One of the oldest CPA firms in China, Da-Hua CPAs, reached an agreement with Ernst and Young to form a join firm at the end of 2001. The newly established firm was registered under the name Ernst and Young Da-Hua with the Chinese government in February 2002. The number of open-end funds audited by Ernst and Young Da-Hua is included into that of Ernst and Young.

Table 2 presents the summary statistics of two binomial variables of 902 fund-year observations on an annual basis. For the full sample, 41 per cent of the open-end funds are stock funds, which are mainly investing on stocks, and the rest of 59 per cent are non-stock funds, including bond funds, money market funds, and hybrid funds. The other binomial variable is the *CFA and Overseas Education* (COE). The fund managers who are a CFA charter holder or obtain undergraduate or postgraduate degree from an oversea university manage one third of the open-end funds in China.

Table 3 reports the summary statistics of other key variables. During the period of 2001-2007, the open-end funds in China have obtained an annual return of 11.67% measured by the percentage change of funds net asset value. The average total assets value is 4.79 billion RMB. *R* is the market return computed based on Shanghai Composite Index in the sample period. Chinese stock market has been booming since 2001. The index was 1645.97 at the end of 2001 and surged to 5261.56 at the end of 2007. Therefore it is not a surprise that the mean of market return is nearly 69%.

In order to test the significance of the above four determinants in the presence of the others, I run the logistic regression for the pooled data from 2001-2007. The result is shown in Table 4. The regression is statistically significant at 5% level on an overall basis, with one individual variable significant at 5% level and one individual variable significant at 10% level. As expected, there is a positive relationship between the fund manager's qualification and the likelihood of selecting a Big 4 auditor. The fund type is marginally significant at 10% level. However, the empirical result is not able to provide support for the positive relationship between the size and profitability of open-end funds and the likelihood of selecting a Big 4 auditor.

The investor protection analysis is reported in Table 5. The model (2) is insignificant with adjusted R-squared of around 12%, and the significance levels of individual coefficients are reported as two-tail p-values. The terms R and $R \times DR$ are positive and significant at 1% level. This illustrates the co-movement of open-end funds' return and market return. The three-way interaction term $R \times DR \times FIRM$ tests the investor protection of Big 4 clients relative to non-Big 4 clients. The coefficient is negative and insignificant. Overall the evidence indicates that the open-end funds audited by the Big 4 firms do not outperform

Independent Variables	Variables		
	Coefficient	Std. Error	Prob.
Intercept (α_0)	-0.1856	0.1131	0.1012
$DR(\alpha_1)$	0.2768	0.1160	0.0173**
$FIRM\ (\alpha_2)$	0.1120	0.1093	0.3060
$DR\ X\ FIRM\ (\alpha_3)$	-0.1117	0.1127	0.3216
$R\ (\beta_0)$	0.2943	0.1015	0.0038***
$R\ X\ DR\ (\beta_1)$	0.6640	0.2510	0.0083***
$R\ X\ FIRM\ (\beta_2)$	-0.0491	0.0979	0.6164
$R\ X\ DR\ X\ FIRM\ (\beta_3)$	-0.0434	0.2682	0.8713
Adj. R-squared: 0.1165 Durbin-Watson: 1.8147			

Note: The heteroskedasticity consistent covariances are estimated using Newey-West method. ***, **, * stand for 1%, 5%, and 10% significance level, respectively

Table 5: Regression analysis of investor protection.

the funds audited by non-Big 4 firms. Therefore Big 4 firms do not provide any investor protection apart from their high-quality auditing service.

Concluding Remarks

In recent years, the Chinese investment funds market has emerged as one of the fastest growing emerging markets in the world. The investment funds, especially the open-end funds, are becoming the major institutional investors in China's stock and bond markets. There are a few systematic studies, however, on the operational risk, fund performance and investor protection on the investment funds in China.

In this paper, I investigate the determinants of auditor selection using a sample of China's open-end funds from 2001-2007. The results indicate that the fund type and fund manager's qualification are positively associated with the Big 4 firms, while the size and profitability of open-end funds do not have any positive relationship with the likelihood of selecting Big 4 auditor.

Unlike the previous studies, I am not able to identify the investor protection effect in China's open-end funds market. The empirical results also indicate that the open-end funds audited by the Big 4 firms do not outperform the funds audited by non-Big 4 firms. It indicates that the operational risk is not effectively alleviated in the Chinese investment fund industry by selecting the auditors.

References

1. Stulz RM (2007) Hedge Funds: Past, Present, and Future. J Econ Perspect 21: 175-194.
2. Brown Stephen J, William N Goetzmann, Bing Liang, Christopher Schwarz (2008) Mandatory Disclosure and Operational Risk: Evidence from Hedge Fund Registration. J Finance 63: 2785-2815.
3. Brown Stephen J, William N Goetzmann, Bing Liang, Christopher Schwarz (2009) Estimating Operational Risk for Hedge Funds: The ω-Score. Financial Analysts Journal 65: 43-53.
4. Hedges IV JR (2005) Hedges on Hedge Funds: How to Successfully Analyze and Select an Investment. Hoboken NJ, John Wiley.
5. DeAngelo L (1981) Auditor size and auditor quality. J Account Econ 3: 183-199.
6. Shapiro C (1983) Premiums for high quality products as returns to reputations. Q J Econ 98: 659-680.
7. Krishnan GV (2005) Did Houston clients of Arthur Andersen recognize publicly available bad news in a timely fashion? Contemp Account Res 22: 165-193.
8. Francis J, Wang D (2008) The joint effect of investor protection and Big 4 audits on earnings quality around the world. Contemp Account Research 25: 1-39.
9. Agarwal Vikas, Naveen D Daniel, Narayan Y Naik (2008) Why is Santa so Kind to Hedge Funds? The December Return Puzzle! Working Paper, London School of Business.
10. Bollen Nicolas PB, Veronika K Pool (2008) Conditional Return Smoothing in the Hedge Fund Industry. J Financ Quant Anal 43: 267-298.
11. Bollen Nicolas PB, Veronika K Pool (2009) Do Hedge Fund Managers Misreport Returns? Evidence from the Pooled Distribution. J Finance 64: 2257-2288.
12. Zitzewitz Eric (2006) How Widespread Was Late Trading in Mutual Funds? American Economic Review 96: 284-289.
13. Goetzmann William, Zoran Ivković, K Geert Rouwenhorst (2001) Day Trading International Mutual Funds: Evidence and Policy Solutions. J Financ Quant Anal 36: 287-309.
14. Choi Stephen J, Marcel Kahan (2007) The Market Penalty for Mutual Fund Scandals, Boston University Law Review 87: 1021-1057.
15. Houge Todd and Jay W Wellman (2005) Fallout from the Mutual Fund Trading Scandal. J Bus Ethics 62: 129-139.
16. Chernobai Anna, Philippe Jorion, Fan Yu (2009) The Determinants of Operational Risk in U.S. Financial Institutions, J Financ Quant Anal 46: 1683-1725.
17. Perry Jason, Patrick de Fontnouvelle (2006) Measuring Reputational Risk: The Market Reaction to Operational Loss Announcements, Working Paper, Federal Reserve Bank of Boston.
18. DeFond ML (1992) The association between qualified opinions and auditor switches, Auditing: A Journal of Practice and Theory 11: 16-31.
19. Firth M, Smith A (1992) Selection of auditor firms by companies in the new issue market. Applied Economics 24: 247-255.
20. Francis J, Krishnan J (1999) Accounting accruals and auditor reporting conservatism. Contemp Account Res 16: 135-165.
21. Teoh S, Wong TJ (1993) Perceived auditor quality and the earnings response coefficient. The Accounting Review 68: 346-366.
22. Krishnan G (2003) Audit quality and the pricing of discretionary accruals, Auditing: A Journal of Practice and Theory 22: 109-126.
23. Kinney W and Martin R (1994) Does auditing reduces bias in financial reporting? A review of audit-related adjustment studies. Auditing: A Journal of Practice and Theory 13: 149-156.
24. Francis J and Krishnan J (2002) Evidence on auditor risk management strategies before and after the Private Securities Litigation Reform Act of 1995. Asia-Pacific Journal of Accounting and Economics 9: 135-157.
25. Dye RA (1993) Auditing standards, legal liability and auditor wealth. J Polit Econ 101: 887-914.
26. Kelley J (1996) Style matters – but so does substance, Morningstar Investor, Apr, 8-9.
27. Granzin A (1999) Vanguard Growth Index, Morningstar Fund Investor, Sep, 14-15.
28. Hung M (2000) Accounting standards and value relevance of financial statement: An international analysis. J Account Econ 30: 401-420.
29. Ball R, Robin A, Wu J (2003) Incentives vs. standards: Properties of accounting numbers in four East Asian Countries, and implications for acceptance of IAS. J Account Econ 36: 235-270.
30. Francis J, Khurana I, Pereira R (2003) The role of accounting and auditing in corporate governance and the development of financial markets around the world, Asia-Pacific. J Account Econ 10: 1-30.
31. Leuz C, Nanda D, Wyscocki PD (2003) Earnings management and investor protection: An international comparison. J Financ Econ 69: 505-527.
32. Hope OK (2003) Disclosure practices, enforcement of accounting standards, and analysts' forecast accuracy: An international study. J Account Res 41: 235-272.
33. Khurana I, K Raman (2004) Litigation risk and the financial reporting credibility of Big 4 versus Non-Big 4 audits: Evidence from Anglo-American Countries. The Accounting Review 79: 473-495.
34. Barniv R, Myring M, Thomas W (2005) The association between the legal and financial reporting environments and forecast performance of individual analysts. Contemp Account Res 22: 727-758.
35. Newman DP, Paterson E, Smith JR (2005) The role of auditing in investor protection. The Accounting Review 80: 289-313.

36. Hendricks D, Jayendu P, Zeckhauser R (1993) Hot hands in mutual funds: short-run persistence of relative performance 1974-1988. Journal of Finance 48: 93-130.

37. Brown S, Goetzman W (1995) Performance persistence. Journal of Finance 50: 679-698.

38. Gruber M (1996) Another puzzle: the growth in actively managed mutual funds. Journal of Finance 51: 783-810.

39. Zheng L (1999) Is money smart? A study of mutual fund investors' fund selection ability. Journal of Finance 54: 901-933.

40. Craswell AT (1988) The association between qualified opinions and auditor switches, Accounting and Business Research 19: 23-31.

41. Beattie V, Fearnley S (1995) The importance of audit firm characteristics and the drivers of auditor change in UK listed companies. Accounting and Business Research 25: 227-39.

Wining the Talent War via Effective Employee Engagement

Maniam Kaliannan* and Samuel Narh Adjovu
School of Business, University of Nottingham Malaysia

Abstract

As the corporate sector entrenches itself among the players of the global economy, more sophisticated strategies and novel business trends are required so as to enhance profitability and lower business costs. It is against this backdrop that the researchers undertook this study to explore possible alternatives of addressing the talent war rather than the orthodox methods. A multinational telecommunication company located in Ghana (Mobile Telecommunication Network, MTN Ghana) was selected as a case, due to its competitiveness and world presence, especially for its dominance in Africa.

With substantive review of the literature, five thematic effective engagement variables were discovered: the work environment, supervisor-employee relationship, job satisfaction, HRM Practices, and organization culture. A quantitative approach was adopted as the main tool to gather 137 valid responses from employees of MTN Ghana. Some comprehensive interviews were also conducted to saturate the robustness of the findings. Therefore, the methodological approach to this research outcome could be best described as triangulation. Interestingly, the findings were insightful, intriguing and competitively viable.

The role of human capital in the success of every giant firm certainly could not be overemphasized. Obviously, our findings shed amazing light on why the company is beating its industry competitors like Tigo and Vodafone hands down. The company is committed to her employees and the inverse is also true-commitment begets engagement. Though, few gaps were identified, on a whole the talent war is a done deal when the engagement strategies are sound.

Keywords: Effective employee engagement; Talent management; Talent war; Paper type: case study

Introduction

"In the war for talent, even firms that are not interested would have no choice but to partake and it's only those firms that are prepared beforehand that would prevail"-Gladwell

The on-going war for talent seems to be building momentum progressively and creating the need for concern among top firms as the obvious realities of employee attrition stare senior management officers in the face. Thus, most employees rather feel robbed of physical, emotional, mental and even spiritual energy by their respective companies [1].

A survey conducted by Srinivasan Pillay, an assistant clinical professor and a psychiatrist at Harvard Medical School via random sampling of 72 senior executives discovered almost all of them admitted some level of burnout signals. In broader terms, just about 30 percent of employees in America are highly engaged to their work as reported by Gallup 2013. In global terms, among 142 countries the engaged proportion of employees is 13 percent. To most employees, the dispiriting and depleting nature of work is obviously taking an endless toll on their health. Not only are employees getting choked by the disequilibrium created in modern work setting and quality of family life but also the peaking need for organizations to remain competitive in order to survive [2]. When Gallup interviewed most of the CEO's they acknowledged that the constant demand for time, puts them in a position where they are compelled to pay more of their mental and emotional resilience than they ever bargained.

Interestingly, a survey conducted by Harvard Business Review which involved 12,000 dominantly white collar employees across varied firms and industries which also include employees of two energy projects- one manufacturing company of 6000 employees and the other, a financial services firm of 2,500 employees. A homogeneous outcome was found to exist among the three populations [3]. Employee satisfaction and productivity level proved to be significantly linked with their mental, emotional, physical and spiritual equilibrium. Obviously, the pattern of engagement gets stronger as these core needs are being supported and inversely, it reduces the perceived stress level among employees. In a meta-analysis of 263 research studies among 192 companies to correlate engagement components such as enthusiasm, passion, commitment, involvement and focused effort with corporate performance, it was discovered organizations that fall within the top quartile for engaged employees, compared with the bottom quartile, achieved 22 percent higher profitability, 10 percent higher customer satisfaction, 28 percent less theft and 48 percent fewer safety issues. It comes as no surprise that in the surveys mentioned above, a happy, engaged workforce translates into high productivity, low turnover and strong internal branding. The emotional attachment of employees in relation to their work environment influences speed and the overall job clarity. However, more profound evidence lies in the findings of [4] where it was discovered that high employee engagement had led to a reduction of 25 percent lower turnover in high attrition firms and that of 65 percent lower turnover in low attrition firms. Additionally, it revealed the capacity of employee engagement leading to "job recreation" where employees have the natural flow to do what they do best, thereby invoking a sense of satisfaction in their job role. Besides, it reduces the relentless pressure on HR to make itself relevant via defensive and

***Corresponding author:** Maniam Kaliannan, School of Business, University of Nottingham, Malaysia Jalan Broga, 43500 Semenyih, Malaysia
E-mail: maniam.kaliannan@nottingham.edu.my

retaliatory strategies. Defensively, they are compelled to alter internal human resource practices such as increasing salaries and benefits as well as employee training. On the retaliatory side, actions might be taken directly or indirectly to threaten the departing employees or the firm to which they are hired. For instance, an aggressive enforcement of non-compete clauses by managers. An epitome of such case was when Microsoft Corporation filed a lawsuit that prohibit its vice president from carrying out a specific project offered by Google Incorporated in the year 2005 [3]. Finally, effective employee engagement could be a strategic tool in creating organizational good will [5] argues that strong internal relationship among employees and their supervisors tend to build mutual cohesiveness that project the external brand of the firm.

Nonetheless, the influx of researches carried on the topic was tilted towards the western context with rare examples within the jurisdiction of Africa, especially relating to Ghana. To saturate the robustness of our fact findings, the framework had been underpinned by a rigorous selection of the variables endorsed by the literature [6]. Our optimism resides in the resourcefulness of the findings in enriching academic literature as well as building the knowledge pool of professionals. All in all, this paper presents an explicit outlook of the relevant literature that backs our study, the methodological approach, and finally, the outcomes clearly dissected. A comprehensive elucidation of the findings proceeds then after in the manner that draws the reader into the flow of the presentation. The discussion of the findings and the possible implications were critically assessed whilst the research limitations were also evaluated on their overall impact.

Literature Review

"As the corporate ship takes on water, sinking deep into the financial maelstrom, the fate of the deckhands, cooks and cabin boys we cannot guarantee...but surprisingly, there came an order from the captain for preparation of life rafts for the group whose lives we dare not sacrifice-the performance drivers"- [7].

The official launching of the concept, "talent war", occurred in 1998 when the largest America's most prestigious and management consulting-organization, McKinsey and Company's now famous publication reported hat "a battle over better talent is worth it". Their data emerged from a rigorous study of 77 firms across varied industries and almost 6000 executives as well as managers for a period of one year. This data however, was saturated with additional 20 case studies of firms perceived to be talent endowed [8,9]. The conclusion of McKinsey's research highlighted that the most crucial corporate resource for the span of 20 years ahead would be those with technological literacy, global astuteness and acute operational agility. In short, they are the embodiment of smartness and sophistication. To McKinsey, talent represents the summation of one's capabilities, skills, learning, attitude, judgment and drive [10]. In other words, talent connotes the best the brightest [11]. Also viewed talent as high-impact group of elite, yet individuals with high maintenance capable of dealing with complex situations but are more complex themselves. In contrast, some organizations use the concept synonymously to represent the entire workforce whilst others refer to the entire workforce when used [12]. David Ulrich, a professor and HR guru approached the concept holistically, when he defined it as "the possession of the required knowledge, skills, and cherished norms presently and beyond as employee puts in time and effort towards the success of the organization and at the same time enthused by what they do." Ulrich further dissect the talent war as the aggressive search for individuals with the needed competencies and commitment towards their job because it gives them a sense of purpose and fulfillment and more also, the relentless willingness to develop and keep them when found. In spite of these definitions, McKinsey's became more pervasive after their study found 89% of respondents agreeing that talent attraction is even more difficult than it was in three years ago with 90% admitting that their retention leaves the HR in a state of endless brainstorming. In their publication entitled "The old reality replaced by new reality" explained as the era of moving from "people needing companies" to "companies needing people", it is highlighted that the future demand for talent would hike leading to a costly battle [8]. The study also found that the firms that are up to the task on talent management are delivering greater value to their shareholders with an improvement in operational productivity as well as sales revenue and profit compared to average performers.

Nonetheless, the critical reasons that make the issue of talent war more alarming and bewildering challenge that all competitive organizations need to address reside in: improved longevity with dramatic decline in birth rate; gradual exist of the baby boomers; spurt of globalization; shift from product-based to knowledge-based economies and finally, rising employee consumerism.

To begin with, in countries like Italy, Germany, China, Singapore and Japan the average number of children per woman are below the replacement rate of 2.1 offspring per woman in order to maintain population levels [13]. Eventually, this would lead to gradual reduction in the human capital in these countries over a period of time. And truly, they cannot flee its stunt impact making the talent battle even tougher for firms in these nations.

Besides, as the baby boomer advance in age with Europe and Japan already coming under the weight of the dramatic shifts in population profiles, it is simply impossible for businesses to stay aloof and just watch on. The die is cast and organizations that respond aptly might be above the ship-wrenching tides of the talent battle yet to roll. With 7%, 9% and 14% decline in ages 15-64 within Germany, Italy and Japan respectively, a bigger picture unfolds and the changes could be fast and abrupt [13].

In addition, spurt in globalization as well as tremendous economic integration across the globe, inevitably impact the supply of labor and consequently the talent war. The economic barriers at varied geographical locations are losing their threat potency and grip as nations are getting more flexible with their international interaction laws than before. This however, is driven by labour market integration which in turn derives resilience from foreign direct investment with value of $1833 billion as of 2007 despite the financial down-turn [13]. Interestingly, in countries like Malaysia and Mexico FDI is linked with the import of best managerial and technological practices which heightens the labour power of employees. Typically, China multinational firms had to deal with 20-30% year turnover and poaching of executive staff [14-16].

Furthermore, Johnson et al in a study found that the services sector globally provides 42.7% jobs compared to 34.9% produced by agriculture and 22.4% generated by industry with even larger value as 71.5% relative to developed economies. This radical shift from product-based to knowledge-based economies in transformation of business trends is inimical to the global war for talent. And it gets more frightening as service economies pursue investment in areas of human and intangible assets [12].

Finally, the growing speed of technology and increase in data accessibility is creating a breed of employees who are largely informed about employment markets, options and opportunities, thereby complicating the hurdle to find and hire top talents [17]. For instance, the rather linear trend of work life cycle- education, job, retirement, it now gets interwoven where the period of education, job and recreation intertwined progressively along lifespan [18].

How does effective employee engagement meet this mind boggling business challenge that robs firms of their best profitability- battle over the brightest and the best? The researchers' line of argument is substantively supported by the literature in critical analysis from the firm's as much as the employee's perspective. To start with, the concept employee engagement is relatively green and still finding its footings in both business and academic literature. But its linkage to various organizational outcomes such as turnover, customer loyalty as well as performance error [19] safety, profitability and customer focused-behavior is on-going [20]. The current popularity of engagement is schematically represented in Table 1. In spite of the impressive outlook of the figures available, it is in sharp contrast to engagement publication available in *PsychINFO*, the leading database of scholarly publications in Psychology with the low values indicated [21].

Kahn [22] as the first to predict a co relational link between employee engagement and firm outcome levels, did so on the premise that employees work for other reasons aside their remuneration. He defined employee engagement as the manner of coordinating members' self to the roles of their works and essentially expressing themselves cognitively, emotionally and physically relative to their role performance. Effective employee engagement saves proactive firms from the war for talent in various matrixes.

First and foremost, based on the research findings of the Corporate Leadership Council it had been discovered that the highly engaged employees are 87% more likely to stay and work for their organization. Similarly, it had been found that more than half of the disengaged employees would be willing to abandon their current employer for another firm. Meanwhile, only 25% of highly engaged employees have an intention to leave their current job [23] and the impact of retention on firm's bottom line is significant intriguing [24]. Also, [25] found a positive correlation between employee engagement and the brand value of a firm. For instance, in the year 2005 when it was reported of Walmart's unfair treatment of employees, the news went viral because most employees and customers persistently discussed the issue. This affected the brand reputation and eventually its equity. And most employees if not all would like to work for a company with great brand value [26]. More also, it has been highlighted that one of the main factors of consideration when employees look out for a firm to work for is the serenity, conduciveness and safety of the work environment. Consistently, research findings have indicated a relationship between employee engagement and safety results. In meta-analysis by [27], it was brought to the fore that the top 25% of highly engaged employees experienced 49% less issues of safety. In the same vein, the findings revealed 41% less client safety incidents among most engaged employees within the health sector. Furthermore, [28] contends based on the findings of a study among 500 Junior High Schools. The results touched on inferiority complex as an answer to the lingering question why most youngsters prefer to stay out of school. And this explains why top companies such as Intel, Apple and Walmart promote a culture that encourages transparency, free flow of information and team-spirit. They also enforce the pattern of bridging the traditional gap that long existed between employees and their superiors [29]. Finally, [30] describes the HRM unit of every competitive organization as the engine house since the implemented policies determine the direction of the entire firm. No wonder firms without employee-centered policies though welcome gifted talents via the front door, those talents escape through the back door even long before it is noticed. Meanwhile, one of the tools that fix employee engagement swift and smart is the HR policies enacted by the firm. It is against this backdrop that the researchers believe there is no better time for this study relative to its relevance and competitive strategy.

	The Internet		Psych INFO	
	Google	Google scholar	Anywhere	In Title
Employee Engagement	626000.	1120	12	35
Work Engagement	21400	785	20	66
Total	645130	1898	32	1000

Source: Bakker and Leiter (2010)

Table 1: The Popularity of Engagement.

Summary

In sum, the field of employee engagement is steadily gaining the attention of researchers and human resource practitioners as available evidences from findings turn to highlight its niche potentialities. But more essentially, as the battle for talents intensifies, it arouses a natural awakening among firms to explore more novel zones for competitive advantage and core competences. On this premise, the potential winners of the "war" are not the mightiest but the meekest; not the most powerful but the most passionate firms driven in the spirit of employee centeredness. Thus, the main research question is: how explorative could effective employee engagement be in addressing the war for talent?

Methodology

Procedure and sample

In collection of the primary data, the researchers employed simple random sampling which is defined by [31] as a random selection from the sampling frame which could be online based, computer generated, or random number table usually generated manually. It was crucial however that the survey was carried out based on three main criteria as guiding rule: In the first place, all participants were employees who have worked with the company for at least a year. Secondly, they all have a permanent working appointment with MTN Ghana. Finally, they experience direct or indirect supervision from their superiors to whom they are accountable. Having carried out a rigorous data cleaning (e.g. looks out for repeated records, ambiguous values, and limited time of survey completion), a sample of 137 employees was reached.

The gender classification in the research instrument after analysis produced a summation of 82 (60%) male and 55 (40%) female of the workforce of MTN Ghana. Chunk of the employees engaged by MTN Ghana are young adults, within the age range of 26-30 years which constitute 75 (55%) of the employee aggregate whilst those above 30 years and those between 20-25 years were 39 (28%) and 23 (17%) respectively. Most of the employees are executive position holders 58 (42%), 30 (22%) are heads of departments, 17 (12%) are junior executives, 17 (12%) are experts in management training, 9 (7%) as assistant managers and 6 (5%) with professional qualification of managers.

Data collection

The design of the research instrument took into account the exposition from the literature with 35 items specifically fashioned to examine the extent to which effective employee engagement is linked to powerful talent management. For instance, the questionnaire intends to address employee direct needs such as work resources as well as indirect ones like relationship with supervisors and conduciveness of the work environment. Moreover, the culture of the organization; human resource management practices and the satisfaction level of employees were closely assessed. The 5-Point Likert scale measurement was used in the development of the research instrument. Likert scale is one of the most commonly used scaled-response in survey design in recent times. The three main reasons why the researchers adopted the 5-point Scale as explained by includes: the argument that respondents in a survey might genuinely feel neutral about a given statement, and the research instrument might be predisposed to respondent bias as a result of the absence of a neutral midpoint, also, neutrality is a legitimate opinion that cannot be overruled among respondents. It is inevitable except that a researcher is not interested in neutral opinion. Finally, a nice midpoint is usually offered by 5-Point Scale. The 3 rating is exactly in the middle and it is an indication of mixed satisfaction or neutrality. The two most emphasized ethical behaviors in research conduction which include: confidentiality and informed consent underpinned the data collection process [32].

Analysis

The researchers hugely engaged the quantitative approach [33] with adept focus on capturing both participants' data and also protecting its accuracy and then, to integrate the results with theoretical findings. For the purposes of validity and reliability, the instrument was put through a meticulous scrutiny based on the underpinning logic. Establishing validity through logic implies the justification of each question in relation to the objectives of the study with sufficient priority on brevity, simplicity, and disambiguated sentences [34]. The analysis involved the usage of version 20 of IBM's SPSS as well as Microsoft Windows Excel.

This was preceded by data cleaning which is one of the most crucial and initial steps among the routines of processing a given data. The process was void of any missing data from the source file therefore heightened the credibility and confidence in the data. The prime goal of reliability test was to assess the internal consistency of the instrument using the Cronbach's Alpha as evaluative tool. The reliability results of Cronbach's Alpha vary between 0 and 1 and esteemed if the results of the Cronbach's Alpha transcend the minimum requirement of 0.7 [35]. Refer to Table 2 for details on reliability results.

To ensure effective interpretation of the data, the items were appropriately coded (1=Strongly Agree; 2=Agree; 3=Neutral; 4=Strongly Disagree and 5=Disagree). The overall mean for each of the variables (both independent and dependent) provides a summative disposition of respondents' views towards that particular variable [36]. This implies that the responses or views of respondents towards a particular variable can either be positive or negative depending on the magnitude of the response towards that variable. In lieu of this, a mean below 2.5 in this study signals positivity in the overall tendency of respondents relative to that particular variable. On the contrary, a mean above 2.5 is an indication of negative perception of respondents towards that variable.

To further ensure that no possible gaps exist in the findings, skype interviews were also conducted with some of the employees to enrich the integration of the results. The interviews were carefully transcribed and analysed where specific themes were identified in support of the quantitative data. In sum, triangulation was the approach adopted by the researchers.

Results

The outcome of our investigation produced an explicit overview of employee engagement trend at MTN Ghana. The results captured the health of the work environment as sane and sound. With HRM practices in their most attractive package presented, the employee-supervisor relationship could not go haywire but to yield a cohesive bonding and compassionate reciprocity. Serving as an umbrella, the consistent culture of quality, safety and value for both employee and customer provides an irresistible shade under which most employees found their satisfaction. These were the evidences uncovered with respect to each engagement strategy purported for scrutiny. The facts found include: resilience of the engagement strategies, correlational values and finally, variation of demographic information on effective employee engagement.

The strategic employee engagement variables included in the research questionnaire had their findings summarized as depicted in Table 2 below. Each of these variables is explained in the light of the findings with acute focus on the aggregate mean and overall percentage agreement.

Apparently, the work environment was strategically included in the survey instrument to assemble views, opinions and responses of participants with reference to the serenity of the physical and social environment prevailing at the workplace of MTN Ghana. With reference to the HRM practices, it targets the views, opinions and responses of participants with reference to employee-centred policies, reward systems and other motivational packages available in the company and the extent to which they stir up engagement drives of the employees. The focus of this variable was mainly towards the solicitation of views, opinions and responses of participants with reference to cordiality, peace and tranquility that ensue among the workforce of MTN Ghana, especially employees and their superiors. The premise of this reinforcement was based on the literature that strong and buoyant relationship between the two parties impacts engagement effectiveness. The main aim of including this variable was to assemble views, opinions and responses of participants with reference to their enthusiasm and degree to which they feel excited about what they do. A culture of an organization, though, seemingly intangible is like the rudder of a ship. It steers the direction of the firm and creates a sense of belongingness for both employees and customers alike. Just like the other variables the opinions, views and responses regarding nurturing and cherishing

Engagement variables		Cronbach's alpha/No. of items		Mean	Variable viability (%)	Pearson Correlation N
1	Work Environment	5	.890	1.590	86.9	.461**
2	HRM Practices	6	.814	1.600	91.4	.528**
3	Employee-Supervisor Relationship	7	.885	1.720	86.3	.530**
4	Job Satisfaction	5	.903	1.710	87.4	.468**
5	Organizational Culture	7	.892	1.810		.979**
6	Overall means of engagement			1.686	88.0	
7	Engagement (MTN Ghana)	5	.778	1.710		
	Total	35	.962			

Table 2: Description of findings.

the values and norms that create the corporate identity are irresistibly embraced and accepted by most employees.

A critical look at Table 3 suggests that participants responses were almost the same irrespective of their gender, with means=2.35 and 2.32 respectively.

The t-value (.451) has a significance (p) value (.633) which is greater than the alpha (0.05) confirming that the variation between the means is not significant. Therefore there is no significant difference in effective employee engagement with regards to the employee's gender at 5% level of significance. Table 4 contains the outcome of the ANOVA results. This is to examine possible variation in engagement levels with reference to age of employees.

Critical look at Table 4 suggests that the level of effective employee engagement does not differ with respect to age. However, the participants in the age group of 26-30 obtained the highest mean (2.5), with those in the age group of 20-25 obtaining the lowest mean (2.3). The obtained F-value (2.535) has a significant p-value of 0.43 which is greater than the alpha (0.05). This affirms that effective employee engagement does not vary with regards to employee's age at 5% level of significance.

The mean of 2.3 as indicated in Table 4 suggests that there is no significant difference in the level of effective employee engagement with respect to the marital status of employees at MTN Ghana. The obtained F-value (1.405) has a significant p-value of 0.373 which is greater than the alpha (0.05). This affirms that effective employee engagement does not vary with regards to employee's marital status at 5% level of significance.

The means of years of working experiences have not differed significantly from one another. However, having F-value of 6.323 with p-value of .000 which is less than the alpha (0.05), confirm the conclusion that effective employee engagement varies with years of working experience at 5% significant level. And this could explain the fact that as employees advance on their job, their level of confidence thrives, build stronger emotional ties with colleagues and job setting and are more willing to make sacrifices in their firm's interest.

The mean of 2.4 as indicated in Table 4 suggests that there is no significant difference in the level of effective employee engagement with respect to educational background of employees at MTN Ghana. The obtained F-value (5.551) has a significant p-value of 0.05 which is equal to the alpha (0.05). This affirms that effective employee engagement does not vary with regards to employee's educational background at 5% level of significance.

Gender	Mean	T	Sig. (2-tailed)
Male	2.32	.451	.633
Female	2.35		
Total	2.33		

Table 3: The T-test results.

It could therefore be concluded that among all the key demographic data examined by the researchers, it is insightful to find that employees get more engaged as they gain sufficient experience.

Discussion

This study evaluates effective employee as an antidote in dealing with the mind boggling challenge of the unending war over talent using a telecommunication firm, Mobile Telecommunication Network (MTN) Ghana. The epic awareness of increasingly complex and hyper competitiveness in global economy creates the acute sensitivity to re-evaluate the criticality of managing talent as a resource to firms' longevity. Picking on a thought provoking statement by the CEO of Siemens, Joe Kaeser which says: the rate of continuous rise in talent scarcity is beating up its predictable estimates and requires the fullest management to avert the trends. According to Teng, one of the most strategic tools in combating the talent is talent engagement [36]. It is in this light, that the confidence of the researchers is anchored that the insightful findings could trigger a shift that gives firms vigour to nurture their own core competences, thus competitive advantage that would be firm-specific.

Given the primary data above, the obtained mean for work environment (1.590) indicates employee positivism towards the variable. An agreement level of 86.9% yielded by same variable confirms its viability and the confidence employees have in the work environment of the "Mobile telecomm giant". Alongside, the Pearson's correlation coefficient (r=0.461) yielded a positive a correlation though it's the smallest correlational value obtained.

Imperatively, the HRM practices of every firm have the propensity to invoke passion or bitterness among employees towards the firm and its very vision. For instance, when the transformational leadership style was adopted by Lee Kun-hee during his era as CEO of Samsung Company, it became imperative that strong employee-supervisor relationship received a boost and was inevitably infused into the culture of the organization [37].

The HRM Practices obtained a mean of mean equivalent to 1.600. This signifies participants' general attitude concerning the HRM Practices at MTN Ghana is potent, proactive and highly embraced. Similarly, the rate of viability indicates homogeneous signal with the overall engagement trend (91.4% and 88.0). The Pearson's Correlation Coefficient for this variable in relation to the dependent variable is positive (r=0.528), moderately correlated and third highest value produced.

Surprisingly, the impact of networking between employees and

	Age		Marital Status		Years of experience		Educational Background	
		Mean				Mean		Mean
	20-25	2.3	Single	2.3	Less than 3 years	2.3	PhD	
	26-30	2.3	Married	2.3	4-6 years	2.5	Master	
	Above 30	2.4	Divorced	2.4	7-9 years	2.1	Degree	2.4
					10 years and above	2.4	Diploma	2.5
	Total	2.4	Total	2.3	Total	2.3	Total	**2.4**
F	2.535		1.404		6.323		5.551	
Sig	.43		.373		.000		.05	

Table 4: The ANOVA results.

their superiors is contingent on the level of cordiality existing between the two parties. A flat pattern of organizational structure encourages coherence and cooperation which promotes an insightful learning atmosphere. Evidence shows an interview results where employees pointed that though they had an opportunity to move to better paying firms, the amicable interaction with their supervisors denied them the confidence to quit [38].

The findings of this study produced a primary data of 1.720 indicative of the resilience demonstrated by employee-supervisor relationship. In a critical comparison of the viability values of 'employee-supervisor relationship' and 'engagement at MTN Ghana' brings to light the coherency in workers opinions (86.3% and 88.0%) as uncovered.

In support of this assertion, the Pearson correlation coefficient (r=0.530) though this variable is moderate, it is the second highest correlated value. Due to the evidential support from literature regarding the fit between job satisfaction and employee engagement informed the decision for its inclusion as a controlling variable [39]. The survey has a mean of mean of 1.710 obtained in favour of employees' job satisfaction. Close analysis of 'Job satisfaction' and 'Engagement at MNT Ghana' in terms of their viability values shows 87.9% and 88.0% respectively. The Pearson correlation coefficient shows a positive and moderate value (r=0.468), however Organizational Culture has been come an intricate element of business strategies as a result of the complexities, sophistications, and the global call. For instance, Egypt Airline has been competitive in the airline industry over the years, especially in most destinations in Africa for its culture of affordability. This culture singles out the company among its cohort with its target customers as middle and lower class customers [40]. Several studies have indicated that the prevailing culture in a particular organization determines the breed of employees attracted to that company and how long they stay [41].

Obtaining a mean of mean of 1.810 signifies a positive attitude of most employees towards 'Organizational culture' in the company whilst the figures for variables viability equate 84.4% and 88.0% respectively. To buttress this assertion, the Pearson correlation coefficient shows a positive and very strong value (r=0.979). This is the highest correlated variable among the five independent variables included in this research. It turns to announce that as much as employees cite positive views towards the culture of the organization, they also believe it has a very strong relationship with the dependent variable. In order to formulate a robust argument saturated in empirical evidence, the talent scarcity index of the selected Asian (presumed to form the chunk of the global population) nations: China, India, Singapore, Indonesia and Malaysia are shown in Table 5.

Assessing the intensity and progression of the talent need in the countries of selection, it is quite obvious that though Singapore has good talent retention rate, the impressions of outside talents dangle. As India seem to be doing slightly better, the struggle of Indonesia and Malaysia speaks louder than could be concealed. Even, China the supposed "hub of talent" still feels the impact of the war. The evidence had been further highlighted in Weiss and MacKay's insightful book, "The talent advantage".

Surprisingly, the survey has a mean of mean (1.710) obtained as the summative performance of the overall employee engagement at MTN Ghana given the data analysis.

The analysis has also revealed the top most exhibited engagement characteristics among employees in the company as 'Achiever Tendencies' and 'Energetic Disposition'. It was followed by 'Employee Proactivity' then, 'Active Involvement' and then 'Organizational pride'.

Radical implications

As proven from the literature, the underlying forces that underpin talent attrition and mobility are inherent within the physical, social and psychological environment. Other factors include degree of satisfaction derive from the job and the smoothness of the top-bottom relationship. Contrary to these is the brand image which is contingent on the culture of the firm as well as the HRM practices.

Yet, the impact of stress and discomfort caused by the physical working environment could be eliminated to large extent by investing sufficiently mental, social and work-related resources into the design of the work setting. Essentially, there is the need for moderation and emphasis on both organizational and individual interests which usually underpins the motivation and drive to achieve. In order to give weight and substance to this view [42], deepens the urgency and criticality to prioritize employee safety and welfare policies. Aside, the power of employee recognition is paramount. It is believed that employees with high positive esteem usually abound in confidence which enhances efficiency and accuracy. And mostly the confident employees have echoes firm's most dependable human asset.

Conclusion

This study carefully examined and evaluated in detail the core employee engagement strategies in mitigating the war over talent recently. The researchers adopted a quantitative analysis in assembling the views of employees and drawing meaningful conclusions via descriptive and inferential statistics. In order to authenticate and enrich the findings of the survey, interviews were conducted to conceal possible gaps. The researchers through rigorous literature review found the core engagement strategies as: work environment, HRM Practices, employee-supervisor relationship, job satisfaction, and organizational culture.

The analysis of the data gathered indicated that all the engagement strategies of the company are in good shape and more vibrant. This turns to explain the unparalleled performance of the company in its industry of operation. However, the greatest enemy of the company's current achievement is the tendency to be complacent.

In order to avert becoming a victim in the talent war, MTN Ghana must make every effort to stay abreast with the commitment pattern of her employees. This can be achieved through periodic assessment of employees' opinions and picking their thoughts on probable dissatisfied matters relative to the organizational management. As employees are radically engaged via strategic human resource management, the trend of attrition would ultimately fall to the lowest limit possible, thereby strengthening the corporate brand and its preference among clients. In practice, the talent war is immune to prevention yet, the

	Talent identification	Talent attraction	Talent retention	Overall scarcity
China	53%	80%	83%	60%
India	55%	72%	72%	62%
Indonesia	63%	80%	83%	70%
Malaysia	68%	87%	84%	77%
Singapore	66%	75%	88%	90%

Source: Wellins et al, 2012

Table 5: Distribution of the talent war in Asia.

smart companies have the option to escape even its fiercest impact via effective employee engagement.

References

1. Nohria N (1999) The war for global talent. Chief Executive Magazine 16.
2. Mendenhall ME, Osland JS, Bird A, Oddou GR, Maznevski ML (2008) Global Leadership: research, practice, and development. Routledge, London.
3. Yanadori Y, Kato T (2007) Average employee tenure, voluntary turnover ratio, and labour productivity: evidence from Japanese Firms". Int J of Hum Resour Mange 18: 1841-1857.
4. Somaya D, Williamson IO, Lorinkova N (2008) Gone but Not Lost: The Different Performance Impacts of Employee Mobility Between Cooperators Versus Competitors. Acad M J 12: 13-27.
5. Nahapiet, Ghoshal S (1998) Social Capital, Intellectual Capital and the Organizational Advantage. Acad Manage Rev 23: 242-266.
6. Heidrick G, Struggles J (2007) Mapping global talent: Essays and insights. Economist Intelligence Unit Ltd, Switzerland.
7. Smith F (2008) Workspace: companies will keep top staff. Australian Financial Review 50: 33-45.
8. Chambers E, Foulon M, Handfield-Jones H, Hankin S, Michaels E (1998) The war for talent. The McKinsey Quarterly 3: 44-57.
9. Axelrod B, Handfield-Jones H, Welsh T (2001) War for talent, part two. McKinsey.Quarterly 2.
10. Michaels E, Handfield-Jones H, Axelrod B (2001) The war for talent. Harvard Business School Press, Boston, MA.
11. Robertson A, Abbey G (2003) Managing talented people. Momentum/Pearson Education, Essex.
12. The Economist (2006) Survey: talent. The Economist.
13. United Nations Conference on Trade and Development (UNCTAD) (2008) World investment report: transnational corporations and the infrastructure challenge. United Nations, New York and Geneva.
14. The Economist (2007) Briefing: manpower: the world of work.
15. Farrell D, Grant A (2007) China's looming talent shortage. Sage Publications, Newbury Park.
16. Prieur M (2007) In the same boat: China and India bogged in shallow talent pools. New York: McGraw-Hill
17. Potter E (2005) Part 1: changing workforce demographics and management challenges.
18. Pfeffer J, Sutton R (2006) Hard facts, dangerous half-truths, and total nonsense: profiting from evidence-based management. Harvard Business School Press, Boston, MA.
19. Gonring MP (2008) Customer loyalty and employee engagement: an alignment for value. J Bus Strategy 29: 29–40.
20. Harter JK, Schmidt FL, Hayes TL (2002). Business-unit-level relationship between employee satisfaction, employee engagement, and business outcomes: A meta-analysis. J Appl Psychol 87: 268-279.
21. Bakker AB, Leiter MP (2010) Work engagement: A handbook of Essential Theory and Research, New York Press.
22. Kahn WA (1990) Psychological condition of personal engagement and disengagement at Work. Acad Manage J 23: 692-723
23. Towers Perrin (2003) Working Today: Understanding What Drives Employee.
24. Haid M, Sims J (2009) Employee Engagement: Maximizing Organizational Performance via Right Management.
25. Taleo Research (2009) Alignment Drives Employee Engagement and Productivity.
26. Eisenhardt K, Schoonhoven CB (1990) Organizational growth: linking founding team, strategy, environment, and growth among U.S. semiconductor ventures. Administrative Science 35: 504-529.
27. Harter JK, Schmidt FL, Killham EA, Agrawal STL (2009) Meta-Analysis: The Relationship Between Engagement at Work and Organizational Outcomes.
28. Nink M (2009) Employee disengagement plagues Germany, Good workers and bad management crimp the country's productivity and GDP, Gallup Management Journal.
29. Hobfoll (2002) A program for Africa's computer people. Science and Technology 19: 79-89.
30. Brockner J, Grover S, Reed T, De Witt R (1996) Layoffs, Job Insecurity and Survivors' Work Effort: Evidence of an Inverted-U Relationship. Acad Manage J 33: 413-435.
31. Thomas RM, Brubaker DL (2007) Theses and Dissertations: A guide to Planning, Research and Writing London: Corwin.
32. Tait M, Padgett MY, Baldwin TT (1989) Job and life satisfaction: A re-evaluation of the Strength of the relationship and gender effects as a function of the date of the study. J Appl Psychol 74: 503-507.
33. Crewell JW (2009) Research Design: Qualitative, Quantitative, and Mixed Methods Approaches, London: Sage.
34. Barney JB, Hesterly WS (2008) Strategic Management and Competitive Advantage: Concepts and cases, USA: Pearson Education Incorporated.
35. Haslam SA, McGarty C (2003) Research Methods and Statistics in Psychology, London: Sage.
36. Morgan D (1998) Practical strategies for combining qualitative and quantitative methods: Applications to health research. Qualitative Health Research 8: 362-376.
37. Teng A (May 2007) Making the business case for HR: Talent management aids business earnings. HRO Today magazine.
38. Baruch Y, Budhwar P, Khatri N (2006) Brain drain: inclination to stay abroad after studies. J World Bus 42: 99-112.
39. Spector PE (1997) Job Satisfaction: Application, Assessments causes, and consequences, California, Sage Publications.
40. Barney JB, Hesterly WS (2008) Strategic Management and Competitive Advantage: Concepts and cases. USA: Pearson Education Incorporated.
41. Lane AM, March JG, Sutton RI (2001) attitudinal organizational commitment and job performance: a meta-analysis. Journal of Organizational Behavior 23: 257-266.
42. Myer (1989) Driving performance and retention through employee engagement, Corporate Leadership Council.

The Impact of Credit Risk on Profitability of the Commercial Banks

Saeed MS* and Zahid N
Glasgow Caledonian University, Glasgow Business School, Glasgow, UK

Abstract

This paper aimed to analyse the impact of credit risk on profitability of five big UK commercial banks. For measuring profitability, two dependent variables ROA and ROE were considered whereas two variables for credit risks were: net charge off (or impairments), and nonperforming loans. Multiple statistical analyses were conducted on bank data from 2007 to 2015 to cover the period of financial crisis. It was found that credit risk indicators had a positive association with profitability of the banks. This means that even after the deep effects of credit crisis in 2008, the banks in the UK are taking credit risks, and getting benefits from interest rates, fee, and commissions etc. The results also reveal that the bank size, leverage, and growth were also positively interlinked with each other, and the banks achieved profitability after the financial crisis and learned how to tackle the credit risk over the years.

Keywords: Credit risk; UK commercial banks; Bank profitability; Net charge off; Nonperforming loans; ROA; ROE

Introduction

The banking industry worldwide has been more complex over the years because of rapid development and growth of financial security market [1]. Consequently, the banks started to practice multiple compound operations without even perceiving the risks associated with these transactions. As a result, the risk attitude and risk exposure of banks became more composite and subject to system failure and thus they caused to break down to economic system of the country where they operate. The governments of various countries tried to control the situations by practicing regulatory reforms in order to stabilise the economy. However, it is worth to declare that these reforms did not work well and ended up with the similar outcomes such as financial volatility and economic downturn around the globe including UK, USA and other economies on which worlds' institutions are based to great extent. During all the circumstances the most exposed risk, which was difficult to discover, was the credit risk [2]. The significance of credit risk is enlarged by the reality that it is associated with the collateral problem. Hence, it becomes the most controversial topic to be discussed and explored. For dealing with credit risk, Basel II also practiced and adopted different credit risk management techniques [3]. The primary objective of these practices was to improve the quality of credit risk management without limiting the competitiveness of the banks worldwide.

Over the last 10 years, the quality of the loan and its portfolios across many economies worldwide stayed comparatively stable until the emergence of 2007-08 financial crises. Since then the quality of the bank assets declined quickly because of the world economic downturn. The reality is that the loan performance is closely associated with the economy of any country and decline in the loan performance was not yet standardised across the world economies [4]. For instance, some cross-country analyses and evaluations in terms of GDP performance during the time of crises reveal extensive enlargements in non-performance loans. In 2009, the economy of Latvia squeezed by 18 percent decline in GDP. Simultaneously, the economy of Germany also shrank by nearly 5% in terms of GDP and when it appears to non-performing loan ratio, it also contracted by great extent [5].

Banks face too many serious problems due to unsuccessful credit risk management but the credit lending remains the chief activity of the banking sector throughout the world. The core cause behind it that banks can no longer survive without this activity. This is the reason that credit worth is considered as a key sign of financial health and soundness of financial institutions particularly the banks. The interests charged by the banks on advances and loans shape large part of the bank's assets and delays and defaults of credits and advances create solemn circumstances for both the lenders and borrowers and even the whole economy can be disturbed as evident in the 2008 financial crisis. Different studies in the context of banking crises across the world uncover the fact that poor credits (asset quality) are the primary cause of failure of the banks [6]. Stuart indicates that the ratio of non-performing loans (bad loans) all around the world was extremely high between 1999 and 2009 in commercial banking sector [7]. And this was due to a number of reasons such as absence or inadequate loan collaterals, poor loan processing, ineffective credit risks management, excessive intervention during loan lending procedure, and several negative impacts on bank profitability.

Therefore, by considering the importance of credits in the banking sector and their severe economic impact, it is extremely important to find the relation and impact of credit with/on profitability of the bank. The banking theory points out 6 major risks associated with the credit policy of banks. These risks are: credit risk (or repayment risk), credit deficiency risk, operating risk, portfolio risk, interest risk, and trade union risk [8]. However, credit risk is the most vital risk among them and thus, it requires special awareness and concentration. Hence, a sincere attempt is made in this dissertation to make the modest contribution to the credit risk literature by analysing the impact on UK banking sector with particular focus on five big UK commercial banks including HSBC, Barclays, Royal Bank of Scotland, Lloyds Banking Group, and Standards Chartered Bank.

Literature Review

Figure 1 illustrates the proposed theoretical model of this study. The model consists of two profitability indicators (ROA and ROE)

***Corresponding author:** Muhammad Sajid Saeed, Glasgow Caledonian University, Glasgow Business School, Glasgow, Cowcaddens Rd, Lanarkshire G4 0BA, Scotland, UK, E-mail: msaeed14@caledonian.ac.uk

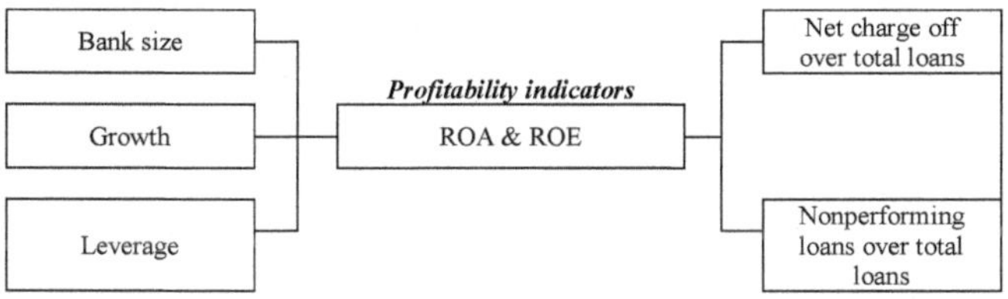

Figure 1: Theoretical model.

which are considered as dependent variables; and five independent variables (bank size, growth, leverage, and credit risks (ratio of net charge off and non-performing loans to total loan) (Figure 1).

There are several risks linked with the banking sector namely credit risk, earning risk, interest rate risk, market risk and liquidity risks are key risks. There are three dominant categories of these risks like, credit risk, operations risk and market risks. Among all types of risks the vigorous part is played by the credit risk without any suspicion that bank's biggest asset is loan which is normally consists of 50 to 70 per cent of banks value. Credit risk is well-defined by the Basel committee on Banking supervision as "potential that a bank borrower or counterparty will fail to meet its obligations in accordance with agreed terms" [9].

The credit risk based upon the obtainable internal data which is measured by investigating the adjustments in quality loans (medium or low) over total asset ratio. The credit risk can be controlled and dropped down by the chance provided by this ratio. However several scholars have stated the conventional ratios which can be employed to recognise the credit risk if no data about medium loan quality is available, for example;

- Total loans to total deposits
- Total loans to total assets
- Nonperforming loans to the total loans
- Nonperforming assets to total loans and advances
- Loan loss reserves to the total loans
- Net charge-offs of loans to total loans and advances [5,10-12].

Literature on non-performing loans has extended along with the attention towards investigating the major reasons behind the financial vulnerability over the last few years. Financial weakness is primarily because of critical role impaired assets have, proven by the evidence which shows the firm link between banking/financial crises and NPLs in Sub-Saharan African countries and East Asian countries during the 1990s. The prevailing literature to scrutinise the determinants of non-performing loans in Guyana is studied in the current section to formulate a theoretical framework.

Keeton and Morris made an examination on the causes of loan losses in their earliest study [13]. Latterly they estimated the 2470 losses insured by commercial banks in the US during the time period of 1975 to 1985. NPLs are used by them as the prime method of calculating loan gains and losses. The findings of their study indicate the variation in loan losses documented by banks is mainly described by the local economic situations and inadequate performance of particular industries.

The publication of Keeton and Morris is followed by several other studies which anticipated interrelated reasons for problems regarding credits in the United States. Another study was conducted by Sinkey and Greenwalt on the loan gain/loss experience of major banks in the United States [14]. The results of their study postulate that Loan – loss rate is affected by both internal and external factors of these banks. The term loan loss rate refers to an addition of NPLs and net loan charge offs and dividing this sum by net charge offs plus total loans. The main findings of their study showing that internal factors namely High rate of interest, Excessive lending and volatile funds significantly and positively influence the loan-loss rate. Sinkey and Greenwalt also discovered that loss rate of banks is also based on the economic conditions. They used the data of giant banks in the US during the Time period of 1984 to 1987 by employing simple log-linear regression.

Another study on the effect of loan expansion in the United States is conducted by Keeton [13]. The author took the data from 1982 to 1996 by employing the regression model for empirical analysis. Evidence show that credit growth is strongly associated by impaired assets stated by the author. The major credit loss in particular US States is affected by the rapid credit growth that has a relationship with lower credit standards.

Many studies also provided similar results conducted other than US financial system. Kodan and Chhikara examined the Indian banking industry through statistical tools and techniques by analysing the trends and composition of NPAs [15]. The analysis of data showed the significant reduction in NPAs in Indian industry over the time.

Salas and Saurina conducted a study on the Spanish commercial and savings banks by using a comprehensive dataset and framework for 1985 to 1997 [16]. The key aim of this research was to explore the determinants of problem credits in Spanish banks. Their findings indicate that major variation in NPLs is mainly explained by market power, capital ratio, bank size, rapid credit expansion, and true GDP growth. Similarly in another study Spanish banking sector was investigated for the period of 1984 to 2003. The empirical evidence shows that loan terms, higher interest rates, and GDP growth are key determinants of NPLs. This study points out that managers in commercial banks provide more loans when economic conditions are excellent and trigger several issues such as agency problems, herd behaviour and disaster myopia.

Rajan and Dhal conducted a study on the commercial banks of India by utilising panel regression analysis [17]. They reported that encouraging economic situations and other financial indicators such as credit direction, bank size, credit terms, and maturity have significant influence on the NPLs of Indian commercial banks.

Fofack made an attempt to examine the determinants of NPLs in several countries of Sub-Saharan Africa by using a pseudo panel-based model [18]. The researcher found that NPLs are determined by many factors such as interest margins, interest rate, economic growth, interbank loans, and exchange rates etc. The NPLs and these economic factors have important role to play in the undiversified African countries.

The study of Hu et al. indicates the association between commercial bank's ownership structure and NPLs in Taiwan for the period of 1996 to 1999 using panel dataset [19]. The results indicate that Non-performing loans are negatively associated with higher government ownership and bank size while diversification seems indifferent and may not be a determinant.

Ratio analysis is used to measure and analyse the bank's profitability. Financial statements of banks demonstrate some ratios and some can be calculated based on requirements if needed. Koch and MacDonald stated that relatively appropriate measures for measuring the bank's profitability level are Return on Assets (ROA) and Return on Equity (ROE) [20]. These measures are described in the light of the existing literature in this section.

ROA is calculated as a percentage of net income and total assets. ROA is used as main profitability measure in most of the organisations including banks and financial institutions. The ROA demonstrates the level of net income produced by the bank and also determines how the assets utilised by banks to generate profit over the years [6]. The competence and proficiency of banks in transforming their assets into profits is also indicated by it. Hence, to improve the performance of banks, they always attempt to achieve higher ROA. The ranking of banks is usually based upon the higher ROA ratio and total assets. As a general view, particularly in banking sector, ROA is known as good profitability multiplier for the reason that equity multiplier does not influence it [21].

A percentage of net income over shareholder's equity is termed as ROE. The net income comprised of all types of earnings like preferred stock income, surpluses, undivided profits and capital reserves. The difference between net assets and liabilities is termed as shareholder's equity on the other hand. The most common measure to determine the effectiveness of banks of generating revenue based on every element of shareholder's equity.

To attain sufficient level of profitability, Both ROE and ROA refer to bank's managerial ability. According to Golin and Delhaise, the ROE between 15 to 20 per cent is considered to be good for a banking institution [6].

The significant difference between ROA and ROE measures is debt. The total assets and shareholder's equity will become equal in the absence of debt; consequently the results drawn from each measure would be equivalent. According to the Koch and MacDonald, a greater value of ROE is not always considered as inspirational indicator of good performance of the bank, consequently ROA is known as suitable measure of profitability and efficiency of the banks [20].

An extensive stock of earlier literature has discussed the ROE as a significant indicator to quantify the profitability of the banks. Foong revealed that ROE is used to measure the efficiency of banks which explains to make upcoming profits; the reinvested income is used to what extent [22].

According to Riks bank's Financial Report to define the profitability in the banks, the technique which is normally used is to associate profit with shareholder's equity [23]. Moreover, in the paper "Why Return on Equity is a Useful Criterion for Equity Selection", the author has found a very useful instrument for profit generating efficiency provided by ROE for its ability to measure the extent of company's earnings on the equity capital.

Company's after tax annual net income divided by shareholder's equity is termed as ROE. NI is the deduction of all expenditures and taxes from total earnings. Retained earnings added to capital invested in the company are called equity. Basically, the amount of earnings made from equity is termed as ROE. The higher value of ROE indicates that, without injecting new capital into the company profit is rising.

Each year shareholders are provided with more of their investment referred by a progressively growing ROE. Conclusively, the greater ROE is fruitful for them as well as for the growth of the company. Additionally, ROE guides the investors how efficiently the capital is reinvested by taking the retained earnings.

According to the study of Waymond, the indicators widely used with greater esteem for credit analysis in banks is profitability ratios, as results of management performance is associated with the profitability [24]. Most widely used ratios are ROE and ROA, and the ROE level of quality ranges from 15-30 percent and at least 1 per cent for ROA.

Joetta suggested that the aim of ROE as the investigation of total profit produced by the firm's equity. It is also mentioned that to engender profit from equity the ROE is used as a gauge of the efficiency [25]. This ability is associated with how accurately the collaterals are utilised to yield the earnings. The assets' quantity produced by the company against each equity dollar, considerably determined through the effectiveness of assets utilisation. Thus, after bringing the evidence of ROE used as the profitability indicator, the discussion can be moved towards credit risk management indicators.

Research Methodology

Research design

The research design embraces the methods on which the research work is founded on Saunders et al. [26]. In other words, it can be said that it is composed of the type of the study which is employed by the researchers to accomplish the objectives. The type of study covers various aspects such as hypotheses, variables, methods, and analyse framework. Descriptive and exploratory research designs are the two fundamental categories of research design. The use and adoption of both research designs is primarily based on the nature and requirements of the study [27].

The descriptive research design is inappropriate for this research because of scientific necessity such as laboratory experiment. The exploratory research design can better fit in this research because of highlighting the links (significant or insignificant) between credit risk and bank profitability. It is supposed that finding these links will help the UK banks to avoid credit risks in the future. In addition, the study's nature is elastic and distinct in answering the research questions. Therefore, the research objectives can be accomplished more explicitly while adopting exploratory research design [28]. Moreover, the results of this study are largely rooted in the quantitative data and thus careful and thorough investigation is needed which can be achieved by adopting exploratory research.

Population

The key aim of this research is to determine the links between bank profitability and credit risks associated with banks. The numerical data for analyses is acquired from five big UK banks for the period of eight years starting from 2007 to 2015. The big five UK banks refer top five UK commercial banks which include:

1. HSBC
2. Barclays
3. Royal Bank of Scotland (RBS)
4. Lloyds Banking Group (consists of Lloyds TSB, Halifax, and Bank of Scotland)
5. Standard Chartered Bank (SCB)

The updated list of top UK banks is acquired from the MarketCensus.com. The data required for selected variables is acquired from Bank Scope database which extracts information from the financial statements of the banks. The financial statements of some banks were also considered to find double check the information/data extracted.

Data collection

The empirical data about study variables for the period of eight years (2007 to 2015) is collected from Bank Scope database which contains the data of all commercial UK banks. This period is important because it covers the financial crises of 2008 as well. Two types of empirical data (dependent variables and independent variables) are collected based on the theoretical model of the study (Figure 1). The dependents variables are ROE (Return on Equity) and ROE (Return on Assets) and conversely the independent variables are the factors that affect bank profitability including the credit risk. So the independent variables include credit risk variables, bank size, growth, and leverage as shown in Table 1.

Model

This study investigates the impact of credit risk on profitability of big five UK commercial banks. For this purpose, it is essentially required to find the relationship between credit risk and profitability indicators and that is why the regression model is used to declare dependent and independent factors. A general linear model of regression is outlined in equation 1 where 'Y' indicates the dependent variables and 'X' are the independent factors. 'C' shows the coefficient.

$$Y=c+f(X) \tag{1}$$

By putting the study variables in above equation, two equations 2 and 3 can be formed where $ROE_{i,t}$ and $ROA_{i,t}$ represent the profitability factors (i=1,...N, and t=1,...,T) which depend upon the independent factors such as credit risk factors including CRIMP (Credit risk calculated as impairments divided by total loans), CRNPL (Credit risk calculated as non-performing loans divided by total assets), BS (bank size), GR (growth in bank interest income), and LV (leverage ratio).

$$ROA_{i,t=}c_0+\alpha CRIMP_{i,t}+\beta CRNPL_{i,t}+\chi BS_{i,t}+\delta GR_{i,t}+\gamma LV_{i,t}+_{i,t} \tag{2}$$

$$ROE_{i,t=}c_0+\alpha CRIMP_{i,t}+\beta CRNPL_{i,t}+\chi BS_{i,t}+GR_{i,t}+\gamma LV_{i,t}+\varepsilon_{i,t} \tag{3}$$

Apart from the regression analysis, the descriptive and correlation analyses are also performed. The descriptive analyses indicate the calculation of fundamental statistical formulas such as central tendencies like mean, median, mode; and deviations like standard deviation. The central tendencies show the averages of the particular variables while standard deviation indicates the variability of data or the standard error.

The links or associations between credit risk variables and profitability indicators can be found through correlation analysis. The correlation analysis in this study is used to find the association of each profitability indicator (i.e. ROA and ROE) with all credit risk variables. The formula of correlation is as follows which is given by Karl Pearson.

$$r=\frac{\sum(x-\bar{x})(y-\bar{y})}{\sqrt{\sum(x-\bar{x})^2-\sum(y-\bar{y})^2}} \tag{4}$$

The Karl Pearson's formula of coefficient of correlation (r) is popular for finding correlations and according to its assumption the results should remain within the range of -1 to +1. The results near to +1 show stronger correlation or links between variables, and results close to -1 point out weaker relationships. Moreover, if the result of 'r' is perfectly zero then it shows that both variables have no relationships at all (Peck *et al.* 2011).

Results and Discussion

Regression results

The regression model considered two profitability measures ROA and ROE which depend upon 5 independent credit risk indicators including: CRIMP - Credit Risk due to net off-charge or impairments, CRNPL - Credit risk due to non-performing loans, BS - bank size, GR - growth and LV - leverage. Table 2 indicates independent variables as credit risk indicators which are entered into both regression equations (i) and (ii) (Table 2).

$$ROA_{i,t=}c_0+\alpha CRIMP_{i,t}+\beta CRNPL_{i,t}+\chi BS_{i,t}+\delta GR_{i,t}+LV_{i,t}+\varepsilon_{i,t} \tag{i}$$

$$ROE_{i,t=}c_0+\alpha CRIMP_{i,t}+\beta CRNPL_{i,t}+\chi BS_{i,t}+GR_{i,t}+\gamma LV_{i,t}+\varepsilon_{i,t} \tag{ii}$$

Two regression models are indicated in Table 3 showing the variability percentage of independent variables. The "R square" demonstrates the relationship between dependent and independent variables whereas "R" represents the square root of R. The value of R points out how independent variables are associated to ROA and ROE. Moreover, the "adjusted R square" mentions the statistical shrinkage of credit risk variables. Simply, adjusted R square refers the compatibility of independent variables with dependent ones in order to validate the decisions based on regression model [29].

In model 1, the value of R square is 0.281 which demonstrates a suitable level of association between all the variables. The shrinkage level for model 1 is 0.089 (8.9%) which is calculated by taking difference of R square and adjusted R square values. In fact, there is no hard and fast rule for assessing the shrinkage level; however, it is acceptable if lies between 10 and 15% [30]. The shrinkage level of model 1 is between this specific range and therefore accepted because it represents the significance of variables involved as predictors (Table 3).

The value of R square in model 2 is 0.154 and the shrinkage level is 0.106 (10.6%) which is relatively higher then model 1 but lies between 10 and 15% and thus accepted. Both models are similar in terms of R, R square and adjusted R square but standard error of the estimate of model 2 demonstrates high value as compared to model 1. This shows the significance of the effect of random changes [31].

The ANOVA analysis in Table 4 shows the statistical significance of predictors (or independent factors) and their unpredictability over ROA and ROE. This significance is showed in Table 4 using 'F' and "Sig." values. The "Sig." value is also known as P-Value. In model 1, the p-value 0.007 is below 0.01 and 0.05 standards which shows that the

	Measure	Formula	Impact	Source
Dependent variables	ROA	=Net income/Total assets		Bank scope
	ROE	=Net income/Shareholder equity		Bank scope
Independent variables	Credit risk	=Net Charge Off (impairments)/Total loans and advances (to customers and banks)	+/-	Bank scope
	Credit risk	=Non-performing loans/Total loans and advances (to customers and banks)	+/-	Bank scope
	Bank size	=Total assets	+	Bank scope
	Growth	=Growth in net interest income of bank	+	Bank scope
	Leverage	=Total debt/Total assets	+	Bank scope

Table 1: Study variables.

Model	Variables Entered	Variables Removed	Method
(i) and (ii)	CRIMP, CRNPL, BS, GR, LV[a]		Enter

Table 2: Variables entered/removed.

Model	R	R Square	Adjusted R Square	Std. Error of the Estimate
1	0.530[a]	0.281	0.192	4.01
2	0.391[a]	0.154	0.048	16.801

a. Predictors: (Constant), CRIMP, CRNPL, BS, GR, LV.

Table 3: Summary of the models.

Model		Sum of Squares	Mean Square	F	Sig.
1	Regression	388.62	50.822	3.202	0.007[a]
	Residual	1014.054	16.578		
	Total	1398.674			
2	Regression	3115.714	392.937	1.419	0.222[a]
	Residual	17880.561	281.423		
	Total	20984.734			

[a]Predictors: (Constant), CRIMP, CRNPL, BS, GR, LV.
[b]Dependent Variable: ROA.
[c]Dependent Variable: ROE.

Table 4: ANOVA[b,c].

Variables	ROA			ROE		
	Coefficients	t-value	Sig.	Coefficients	t-value	Sig.
Constant	76.514	1.690	0.095	109.811	0.572	0.573
CRIMP	0.069	1.27	0.894	0.715	1.202	0.247
CRNPL	0.210	0.370	0.722	0.713	-1.170	0.248
BS	0.059	0.521	0.610	0.138	1.050	0.300
GR	0.178	1.362	0.175	0.289	2.110	0.039
LV	0.340	1.491	0.134	0.134	0.570	0.633

Table 5: Coefficients.

relationship between predictor variables and dependent factors. The F-value 3.202 in Table 4 denotes an appropriate link between dependent and independent factors in model 1. However, model 2 demonstrates 0.222 p-value which is higher than 0.01 and 0.05 standards. This means that the association between dependent and independent variables is non-linear. In contrast, the F-value 1.419 indicates apt level of association between variables (Table 4).

Table 5 provides detail of beta coefficients of model 1 and model 2 of regression. Based on Table 5 coefficients, the following regression models of ROA and ROE are formed.

ROA=76.514+0.069 (CRIMP)+0.210 (CRNPL)+0.059 (BS)+0.178 (GR)+0.340 (LV) (Model 1)

ROE=109.811+0.715 (CRIMP)+0.713 (CRNPL)+0.138 (BS)+0.289 (GR)+0.134 (LV) (Model 2)

In both models, all credit risk variables have positive impact on ROA and ROE. These results are similar to various researchers including Sinkey and Greenwalt, Ahmed et al, Berríos and Ueda and Mauro (Table 5) [14,32-34].

Validity of regression results

Multicollinearity statistics is the reliable measure to calculate the validity of regression analysis and this is usually done through SPSS. Using multicollinearity statistics, the Variance Inflation Factor (VIF) and tolerance level are calculated (Table 6). The outcomes in Table 6 can be evaluated on the particular criteria. For instance, it is suggested by Gujarati that the VIF value should be under 5 and the 1/VIF (or multicollinearity) value should be nearer to zero [35]. If these conditions are met then the regression analysis is considered to be validated. As shown in Table 6 that VIFs of variables is under 5 and 1/VIF values are also nearer to zero. This shows the absence of multicollinearity in regression analysis (Table 6).

Correlation analysis

The correlation analysis is done to correlate ROE and ROA profitability indicators with credit risk factors that are considered independent in this research. Therefore, this section is divided into two subsections:

- Correlating ROA with credit risk factors
- Correlating ROE with credit risk factors

The correlation matrix in Table 7 carries the correlation between ROA and credit risk variables having influence on bank profitability. Table 7 shows that all factors including Net off-charge impairments, non-performing loans, bank size, growth and leverage are positively correlated with ROA. However, bank size and leverage have weak association as compared to other factors. It is evident in Table 7 that all other factors are also positively correlated with each other apart from leverage and net-off charge impairments. These two have slightly negative relationship which is not a big issue. These correlation results are similar to various studies conducted in the past where Sinkey and Greenwalt and Berríos are prominent (Table 7) [14,33].

Like ROA, ROE is another measure to quantify profitability. The correlation matrix in Table 8 demonstrates the correlation between ROE and credit risk variables. It is shown in the Table 8 that all credit risk factors (apart from Net off-charge impairments - CRIMP) are positively correlated with ROE. However, they have no strong

Variables	Variance Inflation Factor (VIF)	1/VIF
CRIMP	4.848	0.206271
CRNPL	3.752	0.266525
BS	1.822	0.248847
GR	1.349	0.34129
LV	4.640	0.215517

Table 6: Multicollinearity Statistics.

	ROA	CRIMP	CRNPL	BS	GR	LV
ROA	1					
CRIMP	0.223	1				
CRNPL	0.211	0.98	1			
BS	0.015	0.036	0.054	1		
GR	0.429	0.095	0.116	0.171	1	
LV	0.082	-0.028	-0.044	0.77	0.558	1

Banks=5, Variables=6

Table 7: ROA relationships.

	ROA	CRIMP	CRNPL	BS	GR	LV
ROA	1					
CRIMP	-0.006	1				
CRNPL	0.041	0.704	1			
BS	0.155	0.043	0.126	1		
GR	0.176	0.048	0.137	0.271	1	
LV	0.087	-0.085	-0.019	0.782	0.45	1

Banks=5, Variables=6

Table 8: ROE relationships.

association with ROE in contrast to ROA. The key reason of positive correlation between ROE and bank size and gearing is when bank increases its activities, than it received greater opportunities of success in achieving profitability which consequently reflects increase in shareholder's equity [36]. It is interesting to see that leverage and credit risk of non-performing loans have weak association with ROE. This does not mean that they have lower impact on ROE; rather it shows weak relationships with the selected banks and their profitability. It is also indicated in Table 8 that credit risk of impairments (CRIMP) has negative correlation with ROE which is not a surprise because of its slightly negative association (Table 8).

As compared to ROA, Golin and Delhaise found ROE only 15 to 20 per cent relevant to banking institutions [6]. Similarly, ROA is also preferred by Koch and MacDonald and Waymond when evaluating the performance and profitability of a bank [20,24]. Joetta suggested that the aim of ROE as the investigation of total profit produced by the firm's equity [25]. Based on these observations and authentic references, it can be said that the results produced by ROA is preferable in both regression and correlation models.

Conclusion

Banks like other financial institutions face a number of risks and hazards including credit risks, liquidity risks, operational risks, exchange rate risks, interest rate risks, political risks, and all other internal and external risks. However, credit risk is considered as the most common and dangerous risk especially for the banks that can put them into deep trouble and even they may face bankruptcy. During the financial crisis of 2008, several banks passed through a deep recession due to mismanagement of credit risks and therefore, in this study 5 top UK banks are critical analysed to measure the level of relationship between credit risk and profitability of these banks and to find out what degree/extent credit risk obstructs the growth of the banks. The profitability in the banking sector is often measured through ROE and ROA indicators whereas the credit risk is measured in various ways. But in the light of literature, two variables (net off charge over total loans, and non-performing loans over total loans) are used for measuring credit risks of 5 topmost UK banks.

Although many banks learned a lesson after financial crisis of 2008, but still there is a need to improve the credit risk management system of banks to avoid credit risks. In this way, banks can effectively deal with credit and other risks that have severe impact on bank's profitability. Credit risk management is a crucial part of measuring the optimising profitability of financial institutions. A bank can improve the overall credit system by tackling asymmetrical information flow, and giving guarantee of loan repayment. Policies and strategies involved in appropriate credit management system (consisting of identification, quantification, analysing, and monitoring and controlling stages) clearly indicate the allotment of credit facilities in banks and the methods used for managing credit portfolio. This method is usually used to originate, appraise, supervise and collect loans. The most significant factors during the improvement of credit risk management are the development of a transparent procedure of approving new credit and extending the existing credit by observing credit rating of the borrowers. Banks in the UK and other developed countries use tools like credit rationing, collateral, covenants, and loan syndication and securitisation for monitoring credit losses. In this way, they ensure a successful management of credit risks in banks. However, this process is weak and needs a rapid improvement.

Interestingly, the credit risks calculated on the basis of impairments (or net credit charge off) reveals risky positions of top UK banks particularly RBS and Lloyds. Similarly, RBS fell into crisis because of non-performing loans and the ratio of these loans which was comparatively higher than other banks. Besides RBS, Barclay and Lloyds also faced difficulties in managing non-performing loans during the period of financial crisis.

Based on regression models, it is interesting and quite surprising to find out that credit risk indicators have a positive association with profitability of the banks. This means that even after the deep effects of credit crisis in 2008, the banks in the UK are taking credit risks and earning benefits from interest rates, fee, and commissions etc. The results also reveal that the bank size, leverage, and growth are also positively interlinked with each other. It is also unveil that the banks achieved profitability and growth after the financial crisis and learned how to tackle the credit risk over the years. Thus, the results do not disclose any major negative association between bank profitability and credit risk variables. However, few minor negative relationships indicate that credit risk improves bank profitability. Hence, UK banks should be confident in minimising the lending rates, and also decreasing commission and fee charges. It is also important for the borrowers to repay their full loans on time settled in the beginning of the agreement.

References

1. Thiel M (2011) Finance and economic growth – a review of theory and the available evidence. European Communities.
2. Nijskens R, Wagner W (2011) Credit Risk Transfer Activities and Systemic Risk: How Banks Became Less Risky Individually but Posed Greater Risks to the Financial System at the Same Time. Journal of Banking and Finance 35: 1391-1398.
3. Hassan H, Maher A, Khalil L (2009) Credit Risk under Basel II. KPMG.
4. Gestel TV, Baesens B (2008) Credit Risk Management: Basic Concepts: Financial Risk Components, Rating Analysis, Models, Economic and Regulatory Capital: Basic Concepts: Financial Risk Components, Rating Analysis, Models, Economic and Regulatory Capital. OUP Oxford Publishing.
5. Beck R, Jakubik P, Piloiu A (2013) Non-performing loans: what matters in addition to the economic cycle? European Central Bank, Working Paper Series 1515, Germany.
6. Golin J, Delhaise P (2013) The Bank Credit Analysis Handbook: A Guide for Analysts, Bankers and Investors. (2ndedn), John Wiley & Sons, p: 1056.
7. Stuart T (2005) New Players, New landscape: The Banker, special supplement. Financial Times.
8. Muraleedharan D (2009) Modern Banking: Theory and Practice. PHI Learning Pvt Ltd p: 428.
9. Glantz M (2003) Managing Bank Risk: An Introduction to Broad-base Credit Engineering. Academic Press, Business and Ecnomics p: 667.
10. Casu B, Girardone C, Molyneux P (2006) Introduction to Banking. (2ndedn), Pearson Education Ltd, England.
11. Rose P (2002) Commercial Bank Management. (5thedn) Mc Graw-Hill/Irwin, USA.
12. Bratanovic SB, Greuning VH (2000) Analyzing Banking Risk: A Framework for Assessing Corporate Governance and Risk Management. (3rdedn) The World Bank, Washington D.C.
13. Keeton WR (1999) Does Faster Loan Growth Lead to Higher Loan Losses? Economic Review pp: 57-75.
14. Sinkey JF, Greenwalt MB (1991) Loan-Loss Experience and Risk-Taking Behaviour at Large Commercial Banks. Journal of Financial Services Research 5: 43-59.
15. Kodan A, Chhikara KS (2013) Analysis of Non-performing Assets in Indian Banking Industry. Indian Journal of Finance and Economic Management 1: 113-136.
16. Salas V, Saurina J (2002) Credit Risk in Two Institutional Regimes: Spanish

Commercial and Savings Banks. Journal of Financial Services Research 22: 203-224.

17. Rajan R, Dhal S (2003) Non-performing Loans and Terms of Credit of Public Sector Banks in India: An Empirical Assessment. Occasional Papers 24: 81-121.

18. Fofack H (2005) Non-performing loans in sub-Saharan Africa: Causal Analysis and Macroeconomic Implications. World Bank Policy Research.

19. Hu J, Li Y, Chiu YH (2004) Ownership and Non-performing Loans: Evidence from Taiwan's Banks. The developing Economics 42: 405-420.

20. Koch TW, MacDonald SS (2009) Bank management. (7thedn) Cengage Learning pp: 1-888.

21. Grier WA (2007) Credit Analysis of Financial Institutions. Euromoney Books p: 333.

22. Foong KK (2008) Return-on-equity ratio can show how efficient banks are. Malaysian Institute of Economic Research.

23. Riks bank Financial Stability Report (2002) The major Swedish banks in an international comparison.

24. Waymond AG (2007) Credit analysis of financial institutions. (2ndedn) Euromoney Books.

25. Joetta C (2007) Credit risk management: how to avoid lending disasters and maximize earnings. (3rdedn) McGraw-Hill Professional, Business and Economics p: 372.

26. Saunders M, Lewis P, Thornhill A (2009) Research methods for business students. (3rdedn) Prentice Hall.

27. Creswell JW (2003) Research Design: Qualitative, Quantitative, and Mixed Methods Approaches. SAGE pp: 1-26.

28. Blanche MJT, Durrheim K, Painter D (2006) Research in Practice: Applied Methods for the Social Sciences. Juta and Company Ltd pp: 1-565.

29. Cameron AC, Trivedi PK (1998) Regression Analysis of Count Data. Cambridge University Press p: 566.

30. Slavkin ML (2000) Juvenile Firesetting: An Exploratory Analysis. Universal-Publishers p: 216.

31. Hosmer DW, Lemeshow S, Sturdivant RX (2013) Applied Logistic Regression. John Wiley & Sons p: 528.

32. Ahmed AS, Takeda C, Thomas SE (1998) Bank Loan Loss Provisions: A Reexamination of Capital Management, Earnings Management and Signaling Effects. SSRN pp: 1-39.

33. Berríos MR (2013) The relationship between bank credit risk and profitability and liquidity. The International Journal of Business and Finance Research 7: 105-118.

34. Ueda K, Mauro BW (2013) Quantifying Structural Subsidy Values for Systemically Important Financial Institutions. International Monetary Fund, Washington DC.

35. Gujarati (2007) Basic Econometrics. Econometrics, Tata McGraw-Hill Education.

36. Saeed MS (2014) Bank-related, Industry-related and Macroeconomic factors affecting bank profitability: A Case of the United Kingdom. Research Journal of Finance and Accounting 5: 42-50.

Reciprocity Based Concept of Nonprofit Marketing

Novatorov EV*
Department of Management, Higher School of Economics, National Research University, Russia

Abstract

The author deconstructs the prevailing conceptualization of nonprofit marketing and concludes it rests on three principles: voluntary exchange, an open system organization, and self-interest motivation. A review of the genesis of these principles revealed that alternative principles were ignored in the social science literature. Based on a qualitative analysis and critical hermeneutic approach a revised conceptualization of nonprofit marketing was suggested which incorporated the principles of reciprocity, the features of a contingency-choice system model of formal organizations, and collectivistic interest motivation. A revised definition of nonprofit marketing is offered based on these principles.

Keywords: Nonprofit marketing; Reciprocity; Substantivist economic anthropology; Public interest; Nonprofit sector; Collectivist sociology

Introduction

Interest among nonprofit administrators in the application of marketing tools to nonprofit sector services emerged from the tax revolt of the late 1970s and early 1980s in the US. With theshrinkage and withdrawal of grants from federal and state governments, municipalities and nonprofit organizations were confronted with the issue of how to satisfy the growing expectations of taxpayers in a milieu of reduced financial resourses. During this period of financial scarcity, the public administrationabd nonprofit literature witnessed an attempt to rethink the nature of public and nonprofit sectors management through theactive importation and borrowing of private sector techniques. Several commentators labeled thisprocess of importation as integration of public and private sector management or in briefer terms "managerialism" [1-3]. Marketing in the public sector was part of the managerialism movement [4,5]. From the beginning, the concept of marketing in the nonprofit and public sectors was criticized in the marketing literature as confusing [6,7]. Nevertheless eventually, it became widely embraced by marketing scholars and consultants [8]. In 1978, Lovelock and Weinberg noted that by the end of the 1970s there was no longer any serious controversy among marketing scholars about the appropriateness of the concept for the public and nonprofit sectors [9]. However, despite this apparent agreement among marketing academics, public administrators and academics in public administration and nonprofit areas have not unanimously embraced the utility of the concept of non-profit and public sector marketing [4,5,10-12]. During the subsequent three decades the "marketing to nonmarketers" problem in thecontext of the public sector, has split public administrators into two camps comprised of its supporters and opponents. Roberto [12], an active proponent of marketing, observed: "Marketing's recent and growing participation in public sector management has received a bipolar love-hate evaluation." Supportive commentators refer to public sector marketing as "a comprehensive strategy for effecting social change" with "unique concepts and techniques" which are "coming of age" and are merely "misunderstood" [9,11-13]. Critical commentators do partially recognize the need of public administrators to adopt new management techniques to deal with the prevailing environment of «less-government-more- user-fees». However, they refer to the application of marketing principles within the nonprofit and public administration fields as "confusion compounded", "an inappropriate model", "intellectualization", "absurd", "the megalomaniac marketing supremacy syndrome", and "a dramatic imitation" of social relationships [14-17]. Ironically, the ultimate goal of proponents and opponents was essentially the same—to increase the effectiveness and responsiveness of public organizations in a changed financial environment. The essence of the difference in opinions appears to relate to the means by which this commonly recognized goal should be achieved. The "marketing to nonmarketers" issue has wide geographic and disciplinary scope. It can be found in such diverse disciplines as political science, arts and culture, health promotion, fundraising, and nutrition education. The geography of the debates ranges from the Republics of the former Soviet Union, across Europe and Scandinavia, through North America, to New Zealand and Australia. The problem was perhaps best articulated by Walsh [3] who suggested the need to redefine public marketing "...if it is to be specifically public service marketing rather a pale imitation of a private sector approach within the public sector." The intent of this paper is to deconstruct the prevailing conceptualization of public sector marketing into a set of underlying principles, contrast these principles with alternative principles, and use the alternative principles as a basis for developing a superior conceptualization of public sector marketing.

Method

To pursue the objectives the study employed a critical hermeneutic approach that focused on deconstruction, understanding, and interpretation [18]. The major tool employed to attack the problem was negative case analysis. Kidder [19] compares procedures of negative case analysis with statistical tests of significance. A goal of both methods is "to handle error variance." During negative case analysis all existing propositions, null hypotheses, or assumptions underlying theories or concepts, are tested and refined against alternative explanations until no or a minimum possible number of alternative explanations are left. Kidder [19] notes: "negative case analysis requires that the researcher look for disconfirming data in both past and future observations. A single negative case is enough to require the investigator to revise a hypothesis." This method is consistent with the Hegelian method of dialectic, which suggests that any proposed thesis should be countered

***Corresponding author:** Novatorov EV, Professor, Department of Management, Higher School of Economics, National Research University, Russia
E-mail: enova@mail.ru

by an antithetical proposition in order to achieve synthesis. Application of negative case analysis in this study included two major elements. The first element dealt with results of the investigative research and included a search for alternative concepts or disconfirming data. For example, if investigative research found that some concepts from the social science disciplines were borrowed to develop the public sector marketing concept (e. g. the concept of formal organizations from organizational theory, or the concept of social exchange from sociology), then these concepts (the concepts of formal organization and social exchange in our example) were analyzed and the existence of alternative conceptualizations was investigated in the organizational theory or sociological literatures. If alternative conceptualizations were found then they were studied and analyzed in the context of their usefulness for the public sector marketing discussion. The second step in negative case analyses was to investigate the potential for conceptual consistency among and between the existing and the revealed alternative concepts. For example, if alternative conceptualizations of both social exchange theory and formal organizations were found, they could be compared with each other looking for possible consistency, connections, or links among them. The negative case analysis attempts to find out if researchers who developed the concept of public sector marketing suppressed evidence. Kahane [20] contends that such actions can occur when a researcher "conceals evidence unfavorable to his own position." It does not necessarily means that a researcher on purpose hid or omitted evidence or al ternative concepts. As suggested by Douglas [21] a researcher may have a diversity of reasons for suppressing evidence. Negative case analysis assists in avoiding the suppression of evidence by checking if alternative conceptualizations were considered and consequentially incorporated. Maxwell [22] noted that: "the most serious threat to the theoretical validity of an account is not collecting or paying attention to discrepant data, or not considering alternative explanations or understandings of the phenomena you are studying." The conceptualization of public sector marketing cannot be generic and universal if its originators purposefully or mistakenly ignored alternative explanations. The issue is analogous to public hearings and legal proceedings, where both offensive and defensive parties are given the right to be heard. In order to be fair, the negative case analysis focused on the evidence available and reported prior to, and not after, development of the concept of public sector marketing.

Prevailing Conceptualization of Public Sector Marketing

Kotler and Murray [23] suggested one of the earliest and most influential conceptualizations of public sector marketing. It was elaborated upon in a text published in the same year [24]. Kotler adopted [25,26] definition, and Blau and Scott's [27] classification, of formal organizations. In Kotler's [24] interpretation, a formal organization is "a purposeful coalescence of people, materials, and facilities seeking to accomplish some purpose in the outside world." Different purposes determine different types of formal organizations: business concerns seek to benefit their owners: service organizations seek to benefit their clients; mutual benefit organizations seek to benefit their members; and commonweal organizations seek to benefit the public at large. In spite of differences in goals, Kotler contended that all formal organizations were involved in exchange relationships with various categories of publics. However, the concept of voluntary exchange is only one of several possible philosophical alternatives for explaining the relationships between formal organizations and their publics. Other options include: the love system, characterized by the underlying motive of benevolence on one side without any necessary reciprocation by the other; and the threat system characterized by an underlying motive of malevolence on one side. Thus, in Kotler's interpretation, a church and its members, a police department and citizens, a charity and its donors, and so on: are all engaged in exchange transactions that involve taxes, services, money, contributions, feelings of well-being, or other tangible and intangible benefits. If an organization is willing to exchange resources with an identified public, then this category of public becomes the organization's market or "distinct group of people and/or organizations that have resources which they want to exchange, or might conceivable exchange, for distinct benefits" . Having introduced the notions of organization, public, market and exchange, Kotler explained the differences between marketing and a sales orientation. The marketing concept involves continuously adjusting the firm's offerings to the targeted customers' needs. In contrast, a sales orientation involves continuous adjustment of buyers' needs to the firm's offerings. He asserts that a sales orientation is likely to be characteristic of an unresponsive organization, while a marketing orientation is likely to result in a highly responsive organization. Kotler [24] favors the latter and defines marketing as being applicable for all types of formal organizations: The analysis, planning, implementation, and control of carefully formulated programs designed to bring about voluntary exchanges of values with target markets for achieving organizational objectives. It relies heavily on designing the organization's offering in terms of the target market's needs and desires, and on using effective pricing, communication, and distribution to inform, motivate, and service the markets.

Assumptions of the prevailing conceptualization of public sector marketing

Advocates of the prevailing conceptualization of public sector marketing believe that public administrators should be interested in "understanding what the organization exchanges with each public; i.e., what each party gives and gets... [and what are]...the motivations underlying their transactions and satisfactions received" [28]. Three major principles underling this conceptualization of public sector marketing are: (1) An open-system model of formal organizations, borrowed from organizational theory [29]; (2) the concept of social exchange, adapted from individualistic sociology [30]; and (3) Self-interest motivation, advocated by formalist's economic anthropologists [31]. These principles and their origins are discussed in the follow sub-sections.

An open-system model of public agencies

This principle assumes that an organization is "a purposeful coalescence of people, materials, and facilities seeking to accomplish some purpose in the outside world" [28]. The primary functions of such an organization are: (1) Input—attraction of sufficient resources; (2) Throughput—conversion of these resources into various products; and (3) Output—distribution of these throughputs to the public. This conceptualization of a formal organization as a resource conversion machine is consistent with the precepts of an open-system model of organizations, designed to respond to external and internal pressures.

Self-interest motivation

The doctrine contends that pursuit of personal self-interest is the essential motivation for exchange between any organization and their publics. Although Kotler [28] avoided the term "self-interest," Bagozzi [32], who acknowledged Kotler's influence and advice, openly recognized the central role of self-interest motivation in the context of public sector marketing: " many individuals, groups, and firms pursue their own self-interest. This is what Adam Smith meant by his reference to an "invisible hand, the pursuit of self-interest can be the foundation for the web of kinship, economic, and social institutions". Adam Smith [33] described the quid pro quo principle that underlies his philosophy of the invisible hand in the following terms: "whoever offers to another a bargain of any kind, proposes to do this: give me that what I want and you shall have this which you want". Shapiro [34] similarly believed that this central role of self-interest in the context of public and nonprofit marketing was sufficiently self-evident that there was no need to discuss it: "I shall not bother discussing theconcept of self-interest; it can be taken for granted."

Voluntary exchange and public agencies

A central assumption underlying this principle is that all organizations seek to attain their goals through the voluntary exchange mechanism. They perceive voluntary exchange to be the only viable mechanism through which formal organizations can attract, convert, and distribute resources [28]. Kotler argues that voluntary exchanges are not limited to such conventional resources as: goods, services, and money [but] include other resources such as time, energy, and feelings" [26]. He believes that voluntary exchange in all of its resource forms should be conceptualized as a transaction, and that it is the central tenet underpinning the notion that marketing is generic. Such exchanges require the existence of at least two conditions: (1) The availability of two parties, and (2) That each party possesses some resource that is valued by another party [28].

Limitations of the prevailing conceptualization of public sector marketing

Some negative comments towards applying the marketing philosophy and techniques in the public sector have emerged in the public administration literature. Opponents of marketing in the public administration field felt uncomfortable with Kotler's generic transactional conceptualization of public marketing, which suggests no differences between public and private management; public, private and the nonprofit sectors; and the role and application of marketing in these different sectors. Rainey, Backoff, and Levine [35] contested Kotler and Murray's and Murray's [2,23] positions that there were only limited differences between formal organizations and between managing public and private entities; that their trends converged; and that as a result, marketing was appropriate in the public sector. In contrast, Rainey et al. [35] postulated that there are crucial differences between the two sectors and, thus, in the role of marketing in public agencies. Drawing from the literature existing at that time and organizing their data into three major categories (environmental factors, organization-environment transactions, and internal structure and processes), Rainey et al. [35] contended that a public organization: works in an environment with less market exposure; has more legal and formal constraints on its procedures and spheres of operation; relies more on the "coercive" and "monopolistic" nature of many government activities; and has less decision-making autonomy. Allison and Walsh [3,36] reached similar conclusions. These analyses challenged the notions of the appropriateness of both the marketing philosophy and voluntary exchange in the delivery of public services services. Differences between the public and private sectors were at least partially recognized in subsequent literature on public sector marketing. Crompton and Lamb [37] argued that government organizations are committed to allocate resources equitably, while private sector organizations direct resources only at the most responsive target markets. Equity principles require public organizations to deliver services to all citizens on a fair basis. In contrast, commercial organizations selectively serve only responsive customers. Although differences were recognized and incorporated into some conceptualizations of public sector marketing, the controversy remained salient. Crompton and Lamb, Mokwa and Permut, and Coffman, who all accepted the distinctive positions of commentators on both sides of the debate, demonstrated the centrality of controversy [37-39]. They recognized Rainey et al.'s [35] crucial differences between public and private organizations, but they accepted the Kotlerian conceptualization of marketing based on the voluntary exchange paradigm as the basis of their conceptual frameworks. Doubts were raised that the conceptualization of public sector marketing authentically reflected the public realm [3]. Walsh and Loveday argued that public sector marketing as it is operationalized has little in common with the public realm. According to Walsh, marketing has not developed in a fashion that is specific to the context of government. He believes that the current conceptualization of marketing reflects a simple semantic adjustment of commercial marketing definitions, for example, by dropping the notion of profit without substantive adaptations to the political context of the public realm. Loveday questions whether public sector marketing is in any way innovative. He argues that "what the marketers claim as their own has been developed by a lot of other people as well; marketers have made a distinctive contribution in thinking it through in the context of selling products, first tangibles and more recently intangibles, to a mass market" (p. 174). Both authors support Walsh's conclusion that there needs to be a rethinking and re-examination of public sector marketing in order to develop its new politically informed form. Empirical studies seem to support these critical voices. Contrary to Lamb and Crompton's [37] findings about the growing acceptance of marketing philosophy in public agencies, Graham [1] found that after 10 years of attempting to implement it in public sector organizations, most agencies still were not customer-oriented as defined by the generic marketing concept. Smith's [40] study found that marketing was viewed only as a promotion technique concerned with specific problems such as an AIDS campaign. Marketing continued to be perceived by many public administrators as unethical, goal distorting, and as an inappropriate model and framework for public service delivery [17,41-43]. It appears that public sector marketing should undergo further modifications to address the concerns of those public administrators who remain skeptical towards it.

Results of negative case analysis

Negative case analysis found that alternative assumptions (negative cases) were available to those who introduced the public sector marketing concept. A search for negative cases and rival hypothesis revealed that those available were : (1) open-system and closed-system perspectives on formal organizations that could be operationalized using microeconomic or political system paradigms; (2) individualistic and collectivistic versions of social exchange theory; and (3) "formalist" and "substantivist" perspectives in economic anthropology with distinct views on the history of marketing exchange and types of economic analysis. The following subsections discuss the overlooked concepts in more detail.

A Closed-system Model of Formal Organizations

A search for rival hypotheses in the organizational theory literature suggests that formal organizations can be conceptualized not only from an open-system model perspective but also from a closed-system model perspective. Hall [44] summarized major differences between these two approaches: The closed-system model views organizations as instruments designed for the pursuit of clearly specified goals, and thus directing organizational arrangements and decisions toward goal achievement and toward making the organization more and more rational in the pursuit of its goal. The open-system model views organizations as not only concerned with goals, but also responding to external and internal pressures. In some cases, the open perspective virtually ignores the issue of goals. The closed-system conceptualization of organizations is an older perspective that stems from Weber's classical analysis of bureaucracy. Weber [45] defined an organization as "a system of continuous purposive activity of a specified kind." This perspective suggests that an organization has a clear and explicit goal that determines its internal structure and the tasks undertaken to achieve this goal. Tasks are divided among members of the organization so that each member has responsibility for an area of activity that matches his/herc ompetence. Decision-making in a closed-system organization is based on an established normative order and is manifested by clearly specified rules and a chain of command. Selection of members is based on an individual's skills and technical competence. The person's membership with the organization is documented in the form of a written contract that delineates the individual's duties and level of remuneration [45]. The open-ended or "natural-system" perspective on organizations emanates from a critique of the closed-ended system [29] and is based on the conventional microeconomic paradigm. This perspective puts lesser emphasis on an organization's concern with goals and greater emphasis on its responsiveness to external pressures: The major misconception [of the closed-system model] is the failure to recognize fully that the organization is continually dependent upon inputs from the environment and that the inflow of materials and human energy is not constant. This perspective is based on assumption of scarce energy and resources. The main goal of the organization is perceived to be survival in a competitive surrounding environment that consists of other organizations that compete for the same resources. A need to survive, forces the organization to adapt to both controllable internal and non-controllable external forces. Therefore, it is conceptualized as a "natural system" which imports energy in the form of people and materials (input) from its external environment, alters it in some way (the throughput), and distributes it back to the environment (output). Survival dictates a "broadening of organizational goals" because the organization is dependent on what is imported to it, how it transforms inputs, and how the environment accepts the organization's output. Finally, there has been an attempt in the organizational literature to develop a balanced model of formal organizations that encompasses elements of the both the open-system and closed-system perspectives. The major assumption of this perspective is that organizations have multiple conflicting goals and thus have to make strategic choices in response to internal and external threats. This perspective tries to control three major factors: individuals within an organization; the environment of the organization; and form of the organization. Individuals within the organization are seen as the mechanism through which environmental and organizational characteristics are shaped. The environment is considered as being unstable and varying from predictable to non-predictable. By choosing the best strategic choice-response to a changed environment, the organization attempts to fit itself to the changed environment and accordingly changes its form. That is why contingency and choice are major elements of this perspective [44]. The negative case analysis suggests that the open-system definition of an organization, in contrast to the closed-system definition, invites an organization-environment approach, which implies that an organization is engaged in xchange relationships with the competitive environment [46]. In such an approach, differences between the goals of formal organizations become less apparent since all types of organizations are concerned with the issue of survival through efficiently attracting and distributing scarce and valued resources, and ensuring there is a difference between accrued revenues and expenditures. An open-system model interpretation of the four types of formal organizations classified by Blau and Scott [27] suggests the generic nature of operational goals [29], management functions [23], and marketing applications [47] for both public and private types of organizations. The alternative Weberian closed-system definition of organizations emphasizes the critical role of clearly specified organizational goals that will result in different, not generic, operational tasks; management functions; and internal and external arrangements of organizations. From the Weberian perspective it is important to distinguish between profit organizations concerning with goal of survival and budget organizations concerning with bureaucratic goals. For example, a goal to maximize profit institutionalizes the existence of business organizations that are concerned with profit management. In the internal arrangements, subparts or units are accountable for the success or failure to attain this goal as well the whole organization. Therefore, management and accountability are decentralized, and responsibility is divided among the organization's parts without jeopardizing the unity of the total operation's achievement of the profit goal. Subordinates are empowered and have discretion to amend rules or regulations in order to keep their operations profitable [48]. In the external arrangements, the profit goal directs decision-making relating to selection of the most profitable market segments for an organization. However, similar to the Weberian separation of profit and bureaucratic organizations Von Mises notes that: "There are areas of man's activities in which there cannot be any questions of profit management and where bureaucratic management must prevail." Bureaucratic management is bound by law and budget and concerned with those areas where profit management cannot operate. Bureaucratic management means management in strict accordance with the law and budget, so bureaucratic organizations do what the law and the budget order them to do. Accordingly, as Von Mises notes [48]: "bureaucratic management is bound to comply with detailed rules and regulations fixed by the authority of a superior body. The task of a bureaucrat is to perform what these rules and regulations order him to do. His discretion to act according to his own best conviction is seriously restricted by them." Bureaucratic management requires very rigid internal and external arrangements. Internally, it implies detailed discretion based on bureaucratic procedures and codes of ethics such as, for example, the American Society for Public Administration (ASPA) Code of Ethics [49]. Externally, the law and budget requires bureaucratic managers to serve members of the community equally, and without showing preference to one client over another. The open-system model assumption about formal organizations fits well with the activities of business agencies and profit management. Business concerns are encouraged to compete for scarce financial resources with other business concerns in a competitive environment that is boosted by this economic development. However, the social exchange school by ignoring the closed-system model of formal organizations fails to acknowledge the difference between profit oriented and bureaucratic oriented management. Profit and bureaucratic organizations are situated in different economic and political environments. Public agencies often enjoy the status of monopolists with no need to compete and with relatively stable funding in the form of tax-support from the public-at-large who own these organizations. Von Mises [48] noted: "In public administration there is no connection between revenue and expenditure. The public services are spending money only; the insignificant income derived from special sources is more or less accidental." The main general goal common to most public agencies is effective implementation of the tasks established by the public at large, based on rigid compliance with detailed rules and regulations established by the authority or superior body that politically represents the public at large. However, the open-system interpretation of public agencies distorts the pursuit of such a goal and inevitably arouses conflict between the requirement to comply with detailed regulations and the need to generate revenue. Negative case analysis suggests that the term "bureaucracy" does not necessarily have negative connotations, and the term "overbureaucratized" when used to characterize an organization does not necessarily imply an unresponsive organization as was suggested by the social exchange school [24]. Blau and Scott [27] in an introduction to their classification of formal organizations cautioned about this fallacy: Note also that the criticism that an organization is "overbureaucratized" means quite different things in the four types of organizations. In the case of mutual-benefit associations, such as unions, overbureaucratization implies centralization of power in the hands of officials. Here it does not refer to inefficiency; indeed, bureaucratized unions are often ruthlessly efficient. But in the case of business concerns overbureaucratizion implies an elaboration of rules and procedures that impairs operation efficiency, and here the term is not used in reference to the power of management officials to decide on policies, since such managerial direction is expected and legitimate. In other words, if business concerns are bureaucratized it means that they are unresponsive and there is an authentic need to move towards a de-bureaucratization process and higher responsiveness through application of the marketing concept, as the social exchange school suggests. However, if commonweal organizations are bureaucratized it does not necessarily mean that they are unresponsive and that there is an urgent need to implement the marketing concept. On the contrary, Blau and Scott [27] argue that "the maintenance of efficient bureaucratic mechanisms that effectively implement the objectives of the community" is the major task of commonweal organizations. According to Blau and Scott [27], the de-bureaucratization of commonweal organizations (or Kotler's suggestion to apply the marketing concept to make them more responsive) may lead to commonweal organizations jeopardizing their ability to effectively implement community objectives. Public Interest and "Coercion Mutually Agreed Upon Negative case analysis revealed the existence of alternative conceptualizations of motivation. Hardin [50] formulated the limitation of self-interest motivation in the context of commonly held resources (commons) in his essay "The Tragedy of Commons." Hardin [50] illustrated the tragedy of the commons by using the example with of a pasture fixed in size that is accessible to all the residents of a village. Motivated by self-interest all the villagers sought to maximize their own use of the pasture by grazing as many cattle as possible and expanding the size of their own herds. Since each villager followed the same logic, the tragedy occurs. Receiving personal benefits, villagers fail to recognize that all villagers will share the costs of the increased grazing. In other words, they fail to recognize that in the end the cumulative effect of their short run independent pursuit of self-interest will harm their collective interest. Without adequate and timely collective measures, the pasture will be destroyed. The example demonstrated that increasing demand on limited resources and a philosophy of unlimited access to commonly held resources eventually might lead to mutual destruction and harm. Hardin argued that education efforts to prevent the tragedy of commons are not enough since there can be free riders who will take advantage of others' voluntary self-restrained actions. The solution suggested by Hardin to this type of problem is "mutually agreed upon coercion," a coercion agreed upon by a majority of the people affected through democratic voting procedures. Mutually agreed upon coercion may take the form of a law, rule, regulation, fine, or a graduated tax. Such an approach, however, requires people and agencies that will be responsible for enforcement of these procedures: that is, bureaus and bureaucrats. The limits of self-interest motivation in different non-economic contexts have been articulated conceptually and supported empirically in the social science literature. For example, the sociological literature introduced game The Prisoners Dilemma when two captured suspects are confronted with several alternatives for confession/non-confession and different types of punishments. A usual result of this game suggests that both suspects could receive minimum punishment if they co-operate with each other. However, each of them by following personal self-interest to minimize personal punishment inevitably harms each other's' personal self-interest. Nevertheless, Hardin's position was debated by libertarians who associate the word "coercion" with the word "anathema" and by representatives of the public choice solution in the public administration literature. Representatives of this school questioned if "the mutually agreed upon coercion" is democratic and voluntarily agreed upon by a majority of citizens. Representatives of the public choice solution coined the term "free rider," arguing that there would be members of a community who would prefer to use common resources while others ere paying for them. Public choice school advocates of the "user pays system" and "vouchers" seek to increase the discretion of individuals by compelling them to "vote with their feet" for levels of taxation and a need government services. The social science literature seems to give a balanced consideration of the self-interest and the coercion perspectives. The self-interest motivation was recognized in sociology, anthropology, and social psychology [30,51,52]. The "coercion mutually agreed upon" perspective was also recognized by many as a legitimate principle for doing things appropriate for a democratic country. Writers, whose studies were cited by the social exchange school, characterized it either as a "visible hand," "quid pro without quo," "pure gift," "one-way transfer," "grant economy," "bureaucratic management" or simply "government" and "public administration." For example, the philosopher Berdyaev [53] distinguished two motivational principles in regard to economic life: "One of them says: In economic life follow up your own personal interest and this will promote the economic development of the whole, it will be good for the community, for the nation, for the state. The other principle says: In economic life serve others, serve the whole community and then you will receive everything which you need for your life." Similarly, the economist Von Mises referred to the same distinction as "two contrary methods of doing things" in a democratic society: "the private citizens' way and the way in which the offices of the government and the municipalities are operated." Von Mises termed them, "profit management" and "bureaucratic management." Another economist Boulding [54], adapting from the philosopher Sorokin [55] the distinction between compulsory and familistic types of social relationships, discussed the malevolence and benevolence types of motivation that underlie the threat and love integrative forces. The anthropologist Sahlins [56] distinguished between altruistically motivated transaction and subordination to central authority, as did Polanyi and Dalton [57,58] who differentiated between politically or socially defined obligations and self-interest motivation. Finally, one of the definitions of government articulated by Abraham Lincoln recognized the limits of invisible hand and a need for bureaucratic management: "a legitimate object of government, to do for a community of people, whatever they need to have done, but cannot do, at all, or cannot, so well do, for themselves-in their separate, and individual capacities" [59]. Negative case analysis suggests that self-interest motivation fits well with the activities of business organizations or profit management. However, negative case analysis also suggests that there is a contradiction in the social exchange school's conceptualization of public sector marketing between self-interest motivation and the code of ethic practiced by public administrators. Contrary to the social exchange school interpretations, Blau and Scott [27] argued that self-interest plays a limited role in the governance of nonbusiness formal organizations such as mutual-benefit associations, service organizations, and commonweal organizations. They contended that in the case, for example, of a mutual benefit association such as a labor union, self-interest condemns the organization: "If union leaders usurp the role of prime beneficiary and run the union as if they owned it for their personal benefit, the oganization is condemned for no longer serving the proper functions of a labor union". Service organizations are in a similar case. In service organizations, such as social work agencies, hospitals, schools and universities, the welfare of clients, participants, patients, and students is presumed to be the chief concern. This concern usually is cemented in codes of ethics adopted by professions as, for example, oaths, rules, or codes of ethic in the medical, military, law enforcement, and jurisprudence professions. These regulations are based on an assumption that while customers are able to look after their own self-interest in a store, the same customers often do not know what will best serve their own interest in relationships with professional service organizations.

For example, patients in a hospital may or may not want surgery intervention in their bodies. However, it is a doctor or medical professional who determines and decides for patients what is in their best interest and what is the best treatment for a particular health problem based on professional and ethical considerations. Similarly, clients who pay lawyers for legal advice may guess what is good in their case, but it is the lawyers who decide what is in the client's best legal interest on the basis of professional and ethical standards, and not considerations of personal gain at the expense of the client. Lawyers who personally gain at the expense of client interests are usually condemned by the bar association and deprived of their practice. Finally, in the example of a university used by Kotler [24], Blau and Scott argue: "students are best served when professional educators determine what and how they are to be taught and not when students themselves decide what and how they need to study". Blau and Scott [27] identified clear differences between the motivations of business and public decision-makers: while the businessman's decisions are expected to be governed by his self-interest--as epitomized in the phrase "caveat emptor"--the professional's decisions are expected to be governed not by his own self-interest but by his judgment of what will serve the client's interest best. The professions are institutionalized to assure, in the ideal case that the practitioner's self-interest suffers if he seeks to promote it at the expense of optimum service to clients.

In the Code of Ethics developed by the American Society for Public Administration (ASPA) employees of public sector organizations are seen to "serve the public interest beyond serving oneself [49]. The ASPA's guidelines are consistent with contention that public servants must "abstain from exchange relationships" with clients and serve the public interest in "detached manner" with personal "disinterest." The presence of self-interest in the relation of clients with commonweal organizations inevitably leads to ethical and even legal conflicts. For example, Locke and Woicenshyn [60] argue that the cynical egoism code that is commonly taught in business schools as the subjective expected utility (SEU) model is inappropriate for the character of social service because it advocates dishonesty ", if one feels like it, if it helps gratify one's immediate desires, and if the cost (likelihood of getting caught) is low" (p. 406). In the like vein, Blau and Scott [27] note: Commonweal organizations, in sharp contrast, are not expected to be oriented to the interests of their "clients," that is, those persons with whom they are in direct contact. A police department, for example, that enters into collusion with racketeers fails to discharge its responsibility to the public-at-large and is no longer the protective organization it is assumed to be. Likewise, if policemen solicit bribes instead of enforcing the law, or the police commissioner runs the department to further his political ambitions, the public's position as prime beneficiary of the organization suffers.

Redistribution and Reciprocity Arrangements

Negative case analysis suggests that arrangement of formal organizations with environments can be explained from not only an exchange perspective, as suggested by the social exchange school, but also from the redistribution or reciprocity perspectives. The concept of redistribution, as well as the concept of reciprocity, was developed by those adapting a substantivist perspective in economic anthropology [56-58,61]. This perspective attempts to analyze economic life in primitive and modern societies from three different approaches: reciprocal arrangements based on the symmetry principle; redistributive arrangements based on the centricity principle; and marketing exchange arrangements based on price-making markets.

Reciprocity implies a symmetrical sequence (AB/ BA) between just two partners or (AB/BC/CA/AC) between more than two fixed partners. Redistribution is centripetal movement of resources among many actors within a group upon one central figure followed by the action of that central figure upon the actors within the group in unison and repartition (BA/CA/DA/ and then A/BCD). Finally, marketing exchange is chaotic movements (A/BCD, B/ACD, and C/ABD) [61]. This "sunbstantivist" perspective is different from the "formalist" perspective that recognizes only marketing exchange arrangements [31]. Substantivists theorize that redistribution is payment to, and disbursement by, a central political authority. It implies a hierarchically structured group and that there is a center of the group. The primary mechanism of redistribution is sharing. Members of a group pool their resources at a center, and this pooled or common resource is then shared among the group members according to commonly accepted distributive rule. The tax systems of industrial countries or payments to the chief in primitive societies are typical examples of redistributive arrangements. Sahlins [56] referred to redistribution as "pooling." Pooling is "centralized movements: collection from members of a group, often under one hand, and redivision within this group. This is "pooling" or "redistribution" ... pooling is socially a within relation, the collective action of a group." The most important principles that characterize redistribution arrangements are centricity and the group membership rules. While Sahlins believed that it was wise to separate the array of economic transactions in the ethnographic record into two types (reciprocity and redistribution) because their social organizations are very different, Ekeh [62], whose study was adopted by the social exchange marketing school to develop public sector marketing concept, used a different approach. Referring to Levi-Strauss's [63] studies of kinship, Ekeh [62] distinguished between direct reciprocity and generalized reciprocity. Direct reciprocity characterizes relationships where actor A expects to be benefited directly by actor B, whenever A benefits B. Ekeh refers to this type of reciprocity as restricted exchange and notes that restricted exchange can take two major forms. Given only two parties, A and B, restricted exchange has the form A→B, and this is referred to as exclusive restricted exchange. Given several parties, for example, three individuals A, B, and C, restricted exchange has the form A→B→C and this is referred to as inclusive restricted exchange.

Both types of restricted exchange based on direct reciprocity are characterized by the notion of quid-pro-quo, emotional load, attempts to maintain equality, tensions, distrust, frequent conflicts over fairness, instability, mechanical solidarity, and brittle relationships [62,64-66]. Restricted or dyadic exchange is traditional economical exchange motivated by self-interest motivation and profit considerations. This exchange is characterized by Adam Smith's quid-pro-quo notion: "whoever offers to another a bargain of any kind, proposes to do this: give me that what I want, and you shall have this which you want" [33]. Univocal reciprocity characterizes relationships that involve at least three actors and where actors do not benefit each other directly, but only indirectly. Ekeh refers to this type of relationship as generalized exchange that also has two forms. Chain generalized exchange has the form A→B→C→A, where, "→" signifies "gives to." It is operated by chain univocal reciprocity when actors in the system are so positioned that they operate a chain of univocal reciprocations to each other as individual units. Net generalized exchange operated by net univocal reciprocity. Net univocal reciprocity denotes empirically observed situations where relationships can be individual-focused or group-focused. In individual-focused exchange relationships, the group as a whole benefits each member consecutively until all members have each received the same amount of benefits and attention (ABC→D; ABD→C; ACD→B; BDC→A). In a group-focused exchange, individuals give to the group as a unit and then gain back as part of the group from each of the unit members (A→BCD; B→ACD; C→ABD; D→ABC). Generalized exchange produces a high degree of social solidarity among parties, and establishes trust and commitment. Ekeh believed that generalized exchange and univocal reciprocity generate collective rights and lead to concepts such as "payment of taxes" and "citizenship".

This negative case analysis suggests that interpreting of a formal organization's interaction with its environment as a voluntary exchange of values, fits well with business organizations and the profit management philosophy. Business and marketing scholars have commonly accepted this law of exchange. However, negative case analysis and a review of original sources used by the social exchange school [23,24] suggests some contradictions in the interpreting public agencies' interaction with their environment in terms of voluntary exchange. For example, contrary to the assertions of the social exchange marketing school that adopted the Blau and Scott taxonomy of organizations, Blau denied that voluntary exchange was applicable to public organizations. The reason for his denial was the inherent conflict between bureaucratic rules of conduct and exchange relationships in these types of organizations. For example, when discussing service organizations, Blau noted: Professionals are expected to be governed in their work exclusively by professional standards of performance and conduct and not by considerations of exchange with clients. Although free professionals depend on fees from clients for their livelihood, the professional code of ethics demands that they do not let this fact influence their decisions and that these economic transactions do not affect the social interaction in which professional services are rendered to clients. The professional must refrain from engaging in reciprocal social exchange with clients lest his decisions be influenced by the exchange instead of being based only on his best judgment in terms of professional standards.

Discussing commonweal organizations, Blau noted the existence of the same conflict between bureaucratic rules and exchange transactions citing the empirical studies that he and Scott used in their work on classification of formal organizations in 1962: The situation of bureaucratic officials who provide services to clients is similar to that of professionals. Officials in a bureaucracy are expected to treat clients in a detached manner in accordance with official rules, and this requires that officials abstain from exchange relationships with clients, because exchange transactions would make them obligated to and dependent for rewards on clients. Even if it is only the gratitude and approval of clients an official wants to earn, his concern with doing so can hardly fail to influence his decisions and lead him to depart from official procedures. If officials become dependent on clients either for rewards they personally seek or for services of clients the oganization needs, they must enter into exchange transactions with clients, which means that they cannot strictly follow bureaucratic procedures in their relations with client.

The absence of direct exchange relationships between nonbusiness organizations and their clients based on the quid pro quo notion was a principal argument used by Luck [6,7] against acceptance of the broadened marketing proposition and the social marketing concept. Luck noted the existence of exchange relations of public organizations with their clients as a process of "corruptly committing illegal acts," which is consistent with Blau's position of a "departure from official procedures." In response to its critics, the social exchange marketing school attempted to use the notion of an indirect quid pro quo and to introduce concepts of indirect, restricted, generalized, and complex exchanges [32,47]. However, a closer analysis of these concepts revealed that this school still relies heavily on an exchange paradigm that ignores the "absence of exchange relations with clients" requirement as a fundamental condition in the functioning of public agencies. The results of negative case analysis suggest that consciously or unconsciously the social exchange school of marketing overlooked the main condition for governing the functioning of public organizations suggested by Blau: An essential element of professional and bureaucratic detachment is the absence of exchange relations with clients. Exchange transactions create obligations that make it impossible to conform undeviatingly to professional or bureaucratic standards.

Thus, the complex exchange concept has limited adequacy for conceptualization and explanation of public agencies' interaction with their environment. It appears that the concept of redistribution might be superior conceptual constructs for operationalizing and accounting for such interactions, because it recognizes the "absence of exchange relations with clients" requirement to be crucial for bureaucratic management. Development of the redistribution conceptualization of public sector marketing . The redistribution conceptualization of public sector marketing is based on a closed-system model of formal organizations; "coercion mutually agreed upon" motivation; and a redistribution arrangement mode. This perspective attempts to view a public agency as a bureaucratic organization. The agency is viewed as a substantively constrained subsystem of a larger political system having relatively little freedom for responsive action without approval from a dominant political center that governs the system. A public agency is subject to tight central control enforced by the city manager's office and/or by a city council. Almost all decisions have to "go through channels" and be authorized by the central authorities before actions can be taken. This perspective stresses pursuit of clearly specified goals and procedures, and a pyramidal hierarchy of positions and regulations. They are designed in accordance with the philosophy that says, "If this is the goal, then these are the most rational procedures for achieving it." The tasks, sphere of activities, and authority to make deci sions are clearly delineated, tightly defined and proscribed. They are assigned to members of the agency based on their position in the hierarchical pyramid. All decisions are centralized and employees in the middle and lower echelons of the pyramid have very limited discrete decision-making authority. This perspective implies that a public agency achieves its goals through the notion of redistribution. Redistribution entails obligatory payments of money objects (taxes) by community members to a democratically elected government. The government uses the receipts for its own maintenance, as emergency stock in case of individual or community disaster, and for the provision of needed different community services. Redistribution payments (taxes) to a government (socially recognized center) are an expression of politically and democratically defined obligations, and redistribution disbursements (public services) by government are determined democratically by political, legislative decisions, and voting procedures. This perspective postulates that the collective needs are best met when the managers and it employees of a public agency serve the public interest rather than their own self-interest. From this perspective, a public agency's interaction with its interest groups diagrammatically can be represented as: C ← AB, then C → BA, where: "←" signifies "redistributive payments"; "→" signifies "redistribution disbursements;" and "C" is a city council or the city manager's office with a subservient agency, and "B" and "A" are groups of citizens.

Redistribution Marketing

The data and results of the study suggest that the marketing-like activities of public organizations could be descriptively termed as "redistribution marketing." The historical root of redistribution marketing is administered trade. Under administered trade "prices, as well as all other terms, had been negotiated with the king before any transactions could take place" [67]. Historical records document that under the system of administered trade the king "fixes the price of every sort." After "the terms were agreed upon and the king's customs paid" the merchant had "full liberty to trade, which is proclaimed throughout the country by the king's cryer" [67]. Although records of administered trade stem from the eighteenth century, they seem to aptly describe the modern regulation policies of local government regarding collection of taxes and the approval of fee structures for some government services. Redistribution is the central concept underlying redistribution marketing. A city council, as an elected and commonly recognized political authority collects property and sale taxes from citizens and deposit them into the general fund. After taxes have been collected, they are distributed among the different services delivered to the community. Government establishes the agency, finances it, determines its goals, mission, and rules, and authorizes it to provide services for the community including some that require fees. An agency is a bureaucratic closed-system organization with a clearly defined mission, moral principles, hierarchical structure, and internal arrangements designed to effectively implement the mission. A professional administrative marketer is someone who seeks to understand, plan, and manage redistributive arrangements. She or he would not be expected to focus upon selling the agency's services and generating revenue, but to look at the agency, its mission, and its problems in a rational manner: identifying objectives; discovering the recreational needs of citizens through research; weighing the opportunities and constraints; determining the resources available to the agency and exploring alternative sources of resources; examining the various ways, in which client requirements can be met and the amount of human resources and type work that needs to be done. Additionally, an administrative marketer would be concerned with the resources, efforts, and time that citizens, donors, and partners are willing to contribute; location of the agency's facilities and scheduling of times when these services are offered; behavior of employees in accordance with established moral standards and, finally, control mechanisms which help to determine if the agency is functioning as planned, or whether changes and adjustments are required in response to new citizen demands. All of this is embraced in the following definition of administered marketing:

Redistribution marketing is the analysis, planning, implementation, and control of programs designed to facilitate redistributive arrangements within a community for achieving established objectives.

Conclusion

The concept of redistribution marketing developed in this study differs from existing conceptualizations in several important ways. Conceptualizations of nonprofit marketing can be characterized as a continuum. On one side would be located perspectives that consider marketing as a set of tools for managing exchanges [9,24,38,39,68,69]. Marketing is perceived as being concerned with satisfying clientele needs and, hence, the marketing is defined as identifying and fulfilling people' needs through the integrated use of marketing tools with the goal of creating consumer satisfaction, which is the organization's primary goal [24]. At the other end of the continuum are perspectives that do not consider marketing to be defined by with exchange processes. These perspectives discard both the voluntary exchange of values and marketing concept as means for meeting visitors' needs. According to these conceptualizations, marketing is a set of tools designed to induce behavior change. From this premise, the marketing concept is defined as inducing changes in existing patterns of behavior. Persuasive communications and adapting to existing patterns of behavior are seen as marketing's two primary characteristics. This perspective distinguishes between a core area of mission and an augmented mission and argues that tools of persuasion are central to achieving the core area of mission, while marketing and sales orientations are appropriate for the augmented mission activities [15,70,71]. Between the continuum extremes, there are conceptualizations that incorporate elements of both extremes. For example, Dixon does not accept the conceptualization of marketing as a management technology, arguing that marketing is a social activity and a social science concerned with study of such market activities as buying and selling. A similar conceptualization but with different nuances is offered by Pandya and Dholakia [72] who positioned their approach in the political economy paradigm developed in the marketing literature by Arndt [73]. Their perspective advocates conceptualization of social marketing based on both exchange, redistribution and reciprocity arrangements, although the authors mistakenly perceive the later two arrangements as other forms of exchange.

Redistribution marketing is a synergetic concept. It accepts the premise of supporters of exchange conceptualizations that marketing is a management technology [74-78]. However, it rejects the concept of voluntary exchange as being universal and as underlying all of marketing activities. Instead, it recognizes the concept of redistribution, but does not accept that it is merely another form of exchange. Economic anthropologists and historians derive it from the classic notion of redistribution with all the rules and premises that comprise this system that have been developed and documented.

References

1. Graham P (1995) Are public sector organizations becoming customer centered? Marketing Intelligence and Planning, 13: 35-47.
2. Murray MA (1975) Comparing public and private management: An exploratory essay, Public Administration Review 35: 364-371.
3. Walsh K (1994) Marketing and public sector management, Euro J Market 28: 63-71.

4. Mansfield H (2011) Social Media for Social Good: A How-to Guide for Nonprofits, McGraw-Hill.

5. Miller KL (2013) Content Marketing for Nonprofits: A Communications Map for Engaging Your Community, Becoming a Favorite Cause, and Raising More Money. The Jossey-Bass Nonprofit Guidebook Series. San Francisco, CA: Jossey-Bass. Mokwa MP, Dawson WM, EA Prieve (1980), Marketing the arts. New York: Praeger Publishers.

6. Luck D (1969) Broadening the concept of marketing-Too Far. Journal of Marketing 33: 53-55.

7. Luck D (1974) Social marketing: Confusion compounded, J Market 38: 70-72.

8. Nickels WG (1974) Conceptual conflicts in marketing, J Eco Busines 27: 140-3.

9. Lovelock CH, Weinberg CB (1978) Public and nonprofit marketing comes of age. In G. Zaltman and T. Bonoma (Eds.), Review of Marketing, 413-452. Chicago, IL: American Marketing Association.

10. Adreasen AR (1995) Marketing social change: Changing behaviour to promote health, social development, and the environment, San Francisco, CA: Jossey-Bass Publishers.

11. Hastings G, Haywood A (1991) Social marketing and communication in health promotion, Health Promotion International 6: 135-145.

12. Roberto E (1991) Applying a marketing model in the public sector, In O'Fairchellaigh C, Graham P, Warburton J (1991) Service delivery and public sector marketing (112-134), Sydney: Macmillan & Co.

13. Leathar DS, Hastings GB (1987) Social marketing and health education, J Service Market 1: 49-52.

14. Arndt J (1978) How broad should the marketing concept be? J Market 42: 101-103.

15. Capon N, Mauser G (1982) A review of nonprofit marketing texts. J Market 46: 125-128.

16. Monieson DD (1988) Intellectualization in macromarketing: A world disenchanted, J Macromarketing 8: 24-36.

17. Vanden Heede A, Pelican S (1995) Reflections on marketing as an appropriate model for nutrition education, J Nutrition Education 27: 141-150.

18. Bleicher J (1980) Contemporary hermeneutics, London: Routlege and Kegan Paul.

19. Kidder LH (1981) Qualitative research and quasi-experimental frameworks. In MB Brewer, BE Collins (Eds.), Scientific inquiry and the social sciences (123-145). San Francisco, CA: Jossey-Bass.

20. Kahane H (1973) Logic and philosophy, (2d ed.) Wadsworth, CA: Belmont.

21. Douglas JD (1976) Investigative social research, Beverly Hills, CA: Sage Publications.

22. Maxwell P (1996) Qualitative research design: An interactive approach. London: Sage Publications 27.

23. Kotler P, Murray M (1975) Third sector management: The role of marketing. Public Administration Review, 35: 467-72.

24. Kotler P (1975a) Marketing for nonprofit organizations, Englewood Cliffs, NJ: Prentice Hall.

25. Kotler P, Levy SJ (1969a) Broadening the concept of marketing, J Market 33: 10-15.

26. Kotler P (1972) A generic concept of marketing. Journal of Marketing 36: 46-54.

27. Blau P, Scott D (1962) Formal organizations. San Francisco, CA: Chandler Publishing Co.

28. Kotler P (1975b) Overview of political candidate marketing, Advances in Consumer Research 2: 761-769.

29. Katz D, Kahn RL (1966) The social psychology of organizations. New York: John Wiley & Sons.

30. Homans GC (1969) Social behavior: Its elementary forms, New York: Harcourt, Brace, and World.

31. Belshaw CS (1965) Traditional exchange and modern markets. Englewood Cliffs, NJ: Prentice-Hall.

32. Bagozzi RP (1975) Marketing as exchange, J Market 39: 32-39.

33. Smith A (1850) An Inquiry into the Nature and Causes of the Wealth of Nations, Edinburgh: Black.

34. Shapiro B (1973) Marketing for nonprofit organizations, Harvard Business Review 51: 123-132.

35. Rainey HG, Backoff RW, CH Levine (1976) Comparing Public and private Organizations, Public Administration Review 36: 233-244.

36. Allison GT (1992) Public and private management: Are they fundamentally alike in all unimportant respects? In JM Shafritz, Hyde AC (Eds.) Classics of public administration. Pacific Grove, CA: Brooks/Cole Publishing Company.

37. Lamb C, Crompton JL (1981) The status of the concept in public recreation and park agencies, Journal of the Academy of Marketing Science 9: 1-14.

38. Mokwa MP, Permut SE (1981) Government marketing: Theory and practice. New York: Praeger Publishers.

39. Coffman LI (1986) Public sector marketing: A guide for practitioners, New York: John Wiley and Sons. 25

40. Smith G (1988) Applying marketing to the public sector: The case of local authority leisure centers, Int J Public Sector Management 1: 36-45.

41. Buchanan DR, Reddy S, Hossain Z (1994) Social marketing: a critical appraisal, Health Promotion International 9: 49-57.

42. Ehling WP, White J, Grunig JE (1992) Public relations and marketing practices, In J.E. Grunig (Ed.), Excellence in public relations and communication management, Hillsdale, N J:Lawrence Erlbaum Associates.

43. O'Fairchellaigh C, Graham P, Warburton J (1991) Service delivery and public sector marketing, Sydney: Macmillan & Co.

44. Hall RH (1972) Organizations: Structure and process. Englewood Cliffs, NJ: Prentice-Hall.

45. Weber M (1946) Bureaucracy. In M. Weber. Essays in Sociology 23-34, Edited and translated by Gerth HH, Wright Mills C, Oxford University Press 8: 63-71.

46. Yuchtman E, Seashore SE (1967) A resource approach to organizational effectiveness, American Sociological Review 32: 891-903.

47. Kotler P, Levy SJ (1969b) A new form of marketing myopia: Rejoinder to professor Luck, J Market 33: 55-57.

48. Von Mises (1944) Bureaucracy. New Haven: Yale University Press.

49. Van Wart M (1996) The sources of ethical decision making for individuals in public sector, Public Administration Review 56: 525-533.

50. Hardin G (1968) The tragedy of commons, Science 1245-1248.

51. Belshaw CS (1976) jkhkh, NewYork: Pergamon Press Inc.

52. Thibaut JW, Kelley HH (1959) The social psychology of groups, New York: Wiley.

53. Berdyaev NA (1948) The origin of Russian communism. Glasgow: Geoffrey Bles, The University Press.

54. Boulding K (1970) A primer on social dynamic, NewYork: Free Press.

55. Sorokin PA (1964) Basic trends of our times. New Heaven, CT: College & University Press Publishing 28.

56. Sahlins MD (1965) On the sociology of primitive exchange, In M Banton (Ed.) The relevance of models for social anthropology (139-236) London: Tavistock Publications.

57. Polanyi K (1944) The great transformation, Boston: Beacon Press.

58. Dalton G (1971) Primitive, archaic, and modern economies, In G. Dalton (Ed.) Economic anthropology and development New York: Basic Books.

59. Shafritz JM, Russell EW (1997) Introducing public administration, New York: Longman.

60. Locke EA, Woiceshyn J (1995) Why businessman should be honest: The argument from rational egoism, J Organizational Behavior 16: 405-414.

61. Polanyi K, Arensberg CM, Pearson HW (1957) Trade and market in early empires. New York: The Free Press.

62. Ekeh PP (1974) Social exchange theory: The two traditions. Cambridge, Mass:

Harvard University Press. Frazer J (1919) Folklore in the Old Testament Vol. II. London: Macmillan & Co.

63. Levi-Strauss C (1969) The elementary structures of kinship, Boston: Beacon Press. English translation of Claude Levi-Strauss, Les Structuresa Elementares de la Parenete. 1967, Revised Edition.
64. Gillmore MR (1987) Implications of general versus restricted exchange, In K. Cook, (Ed.) Social exchange theory, 27-34, Beverly Hills, CA: Sage Publications.
65. Uehara E (1990) Dual exchange theory, social networks, and informal social support, American Journal of Sociology 96: 521-57.
66. Yamagishi T, Cook KS (1993) Generalized exchange and social dilemmas, Social Psychology Quarterly 56: 235-248.
67. Arnold R (1957) A port of trade: Whydah on the guinea coast. In Polanyi, Arensberg KCM, Pearson HW (Eds) Trade and market in early empires, 145-174 New York: The Free Press.
68. Manoff RK (1985) Social marketing: New imperative for public health, New York: Praeger Publishers.
69. McCort DJ (1994) A framework for evaluating the relational extent of a relationship marketing strategy: The case of nonprofit organizations, J Direct Marketing 8: 53-59.
70. Lauffer A (1984) Strategic marketing for not-for-profit organizations, New York: The Free Press.
71. Rados DL (1981) Marketing for nonprofit organizations, Boston, MA: Auburn House.
72. Pandya A, Dholakia N (1992) An institutional theory of exchange in marketing, Euro J Market 26: 19-41.
73. Arndt J (1981) The political economy of marketing systems: Reviving the institutional approach, J Macro market 1: 36-47.
74. Arndt J (1985) On making marketing science more scientific: The role of orientations, paradigms, metaphors, and puzzle solving, J Market 49: 11-23.
75. Arnold MJ, Fischer JE (1996) Counterculture, criticism, and crisis: Assessing the effect of the sixties on marketing thought, J Macro market 16: 118-133.
76. Crompton JL, Lamb CH (1986) Marketing government and social services. NewYork: John Wiley and Sons.
77. Kotler P (1979) Strategies for introducing marketing into nonprofit organizations, Journal of Marketing 43: 37-44.
78. Kotler P, Roberto E (1989) Social marketing: Strategies for changing public behaviour, New York: The Free Press.

The Influence of the Greek Economic Crisis on FYROM Exports

Ljupco Davcev[1] and Nikolas Hourvouliades[2*]
[1]*Faculty of Economics, Goce Delcev University, Stip, FYROM*
[2]*American College of Thessaloniki, Greece*

Abstract

According to the contemporary political and economic conditions, there is still an existing possibility for Greece to exit the Euro zone. If this scenario comes true, it will further decrease FYROM imports from Greece, as this will most probably result in the return of the Drachma with an assumed 50% devaluation to the Euro. On the other hand, FYROM exports Greece will become equally more expensive. The economic crisis which currently trembles our neighbour Greece has emerged as a new variable in the prediction and planning of economic activity along with main economic variables in the Macedonian economy. Analysis of the economic and trade relations between Greece and FYROM shows a steady decline during the last five years. FYROM exports to Greece in the first quarter of 2012 are at the lowest level in the history of trade relations between the two countries, at €39m. Even worse is that the coverage of imports from Greece with exports from FYROM is only 25.2 basis points, which is also at the lowest historical level. This is a clear indication that FYROM is losing Greece, neighbouring country and EU member, as a significant business partner. This paper is trying to determine the potential effects on Macedonia economy due to the contemporary Greek crisis, taking into consideration that our neighbour is one of the largest investors and trading partners of FYROM.

Keywords: Foreign effective demand; GDP growth;Income elasticity coefficient; FYROM exports growth rate

Introduction

This has been the fifth consecutive year (2013) that the Greek GDP is still falling, keeping the country in the deepest recession period of its modern history. The government has recently announced, in the last quarter of 2013, that a primary surplus has been achieved for the first time, after almost a decade that the country has had four times higher budget deficit than that allowed for Eurozone member countries. But the current situation in Greece after more than three years later is alarming. During the economic crisis Greece received an unprecedented financial aid from the European Union and the International Monetary Fund. Government also made huge cash savings in the budget, severing public wages and pensions and minimizing public expenditure. In the same fashion, the private sector has also taken the blown, since it is called upon to support the ailing public sector of the economy. Nevertheless, results have not yet met expectations and the country has cumulatively lost more than a quarter of its wealth during the past five years.

The Greek economy was not in an ideal situation even before the crisis. GDP in 2008 fell by 0.2%; a year later it fell by another 3.1%. In 2011, GDP fell by 7.1%. The draft state budget for 2013 foresaw another year of crisis, specifically reducing GDP by an additional 3.8%, but economic analysts believe that GDP will finally fall by 4.2% as a result of reduced economic activity. On February 2013 the Chairman of the Bank of Greece projected a 4.5% recession and 26% unemployment for the current year. The impact of unemployment is phenomenal: four years ago, the unemployment rate stood at 7.7% and has since been in continuous growth. In August 2013 it stood at 27% or more than quarter of the total active working population and latest announcements report a stable 27% in the end of 2013. Government debt three years ago stood at 129.4% of GDP, and the end of 2013 it is expected at about 170%.

FYROM exporters and Greek companies operating in the country during the last few years have strongly felt the effects of the Greek debt crisis. What is more important, the crisis is not appeased, but is gaining impetus. Direct result of the poor financial situation of Greece is the reduction in Macedonian exported goods and services. As the difficult economic situation escalates in Greece, FYROM exports are the most endangered in the aggregate economic cooperation between the two countries. The point here is on the most exported products, i.e. iron, steel, textiles, tobacco and marble. These five products count for about 55% of the total exports to Greece.

Likewise, Greek debt crisis has a negative impact on Greek investments in the country. Greek companies are expected to begin intensive efforts to extract profits from abroad, rather than reinvest in the business in the country, in order to distribute dividends to their shareholders in Greece. State statistics already show a declining trend in both export and direct investment in Greece in recent years. According to official records, in particular the office of financial and business affairs in Skopje, Greece in 2013 still stood as the largest investor in the country, followed by Germany, Serbia, Bulgaria and Italy.The report noted that the country's exports to Greece totaled around 188 million US dollars, while imports totaled 804 million dollars. According to Hellenic Statistical Authority, Greek exports to FYROM -excluding oil- totaled 255.7 million euros in the January-November 2012 period, up 1.14% from 2011, while imports totaled 156.4 million euros, up 1.88% over the same period, respectively. The value of bilateral trade transactions in the 11-month period totaled 412 million euros, up 1.42% from 2011.

The economic crisis which presently shakes our neighbour has emerged as a new variable in the prediction and planning of economic activity along with main economic variables in the FYROM economy. This paper is trying to determine the potential effects on our economy from the economic crisis in Greece, considering that our neighbour is one of the largest investors and trading partners of our economy. The

***Corresponding authors:** Nikolas Hourvouliades, American College of Thessaloniki, Greece, E-mail: hourvoul@act.edu

dominant part of the analysis will focus on determination of the future effects of the economic crisis in Greece, including FYROM's foreign effective demand.

Literature Review

The significance of exports on national economy and their relationship to GDP levels has been analysed by many empirical studies. The categorization of these studies varies depending on either the methods applied or the scope of geographical regions. As far as the methods are regarded, some articles try to distinguish causality links between exports and GDP as well as existence of co-integration, whereas other look into short term relationships that could help policy makers adjust their decisions. As far as geographical regions are concerned, there are studies that examine one country-domestic characteristics, whereas other cover multiple countries or economic zones that share common economic and political characteristics.

Another important issue that influences all variables is the country's monetary policy. The local currency, the Denar, is at a semi-pegged rate to the Euro and has been kept stable for the last decade or so. Until recently, the annual capital inflows were sufficient for the country to pay its debt and maintain the rate to the Euro. Current conditions however have raised the question of the future monetary policy of the country and the extend up to which the Euro peg can have more benefits than disadvantages.

According to a research by Nenovski et al. [1]the domestic economy of FYROM has been found to have some basic parameters, namely: a) the economy is heavily dependent on the only a few sectors (metals, textiles and agriculture), b) the movement of international prices has a great effect upon import and export goods, and c) the domestic demand on goods and services is relatively limited, discouraging the development of the economy.

In an earlier study by Kostoska and Petreski [2]on the state of competitiveness of the economy they claim that the country had an unsuccessful attempt to transition characterized by low growthrates and high unemployment. They also underline the dependence of the economy and its growth potential upon export competitiveness.

In a cointegration based analysis, Sharma and Panagiotidis [3] examine the case of India over a thirty year period 1971-2001 and fail to find convincing evidence of a Granger causality between exports and GDP or exports and investments. Interestingly enough Ramos [4] examines data from the Portuguese economy and also cannot prove causality between exports-imports and growth.

On the contrary, Konya [5]analyses a vast set of OECD countries and finds one-way and two-way causality in most countries between real exports and real GDP over a forty year period, with the exception six countries that do not have any causality in any direction. Likewise, Awokuse [6]examines transition European economies and suggests that trade stimulates economic growth; the same applies in another article of the same author [7]that refers on the Japanese economy.

In another cross-border analysis, Silaghi and Ioana [8]examine data from Central and Eastern European countries and find various forms of one-way causality between GDP existing in most cases. Hsiao and Hsiao [9]examine eight rapidly developing Asian economies, i.e. China, Korea, Taiwan, Hong Kong, Singapore, Malaysia, Philippines and Thailand, applying panel data analysis on the relationship between GDP, exports and FDI. They find mixed evidence of unidirectional causality varying from country to country depending also on economic and policy implications.

Finally, in their recent study Sadiku et al. [10]investigate the impacts of the Greek crisis on Western Balkan countries including FYROM by applying a binary logit model than includes variables such as real GDP growth, ratio of domestic bank loans, current account deficit, inflation and budget deficits. The authors conclude that the probability of a systemic crisis and contagion appears higher in countries like FYROM (Albania and Serbia as well) where Greek banks have a strong presence and suggest that policy makers take pre-emptive measures to prevent financial spill-over effects.

Effects on Foreign Effective Demand

This part of the paper analyses the effects of the Greek crisis on the FYROM foreign effective demand, i.e. FYROM exports to Greece and FYROM total exports. Initially, foreign effective demand is modelled and estimated (in accordance with the methodology of the Central Bank), as a weighted sum of the indices of the gross domestic product of the most important trade partners of FYROM. The weights are calculated based on the participation of these countries in exports. The calculation of the index includes Germany, Greece, Italy, Netherlands, Belgium, Spain and Serbia. In order to determine future foreign effective demand (2012 - 2015) this paper uses estimates of the IMF for GDP in constant prices[11,12].

For the sake of the calculations to evaluate the effects of the Greek crisis on the total FYROM exports and exports to Greece we use the income elasticity coefficient of 1.51, which is found as a result in the research of the Macedonian Central Bank (Kadievska-Vojnovic and Unesca) as the income elasticity coefficient of FYROM exports in terms of total world GDP. The results of the research from Kadievska-Vojnovic and Unesca show that income and price elasticity of exports are statistically significant at the 1%-5% level, have the expected signs, and amounted to 1.51 and -0.73, respectively This means that in the long run, in terms of growth of world income by 1%, the demand for FYROM exports will increase by 1.51%, while relative export prices growth at 1% will have a decline in exports by 0.73% (higher domestic prices from foreign prices determine decline in exports). Thus, FYROM exports are more sensitive to changes in world income than price changes. This indicates that the price characteristics of FYROM exports are not the main significant determinant of foreign demand, which is more directed towards non-price (qualitative) aspects of exporting. Thus, if exporters wish to increase their turnover in world markets, they need to increase export non-price aspects (quality, distribution, marketing, etc.)

Given the high concentration of FYROM exports in a few products, mostly for reproduction (iron-steel and their derivatives, petroleum derivatives, as well as clothing and textiles based on a CMT-production), it becomes obvious that it is necessary to invest in qualitative aspects of products in order to attract foreign consumers whose standards grow in accordance with the growth of their income.

In regard to the above (FYROM exports sensitivity to changes in world income rather than price changes) this paper takes into account only the income elasticity of the FYROM exports. The approximation of the income elasticity of FYROM exports to Greece is taken the coefficient -1.511, which means in case of decline of Greece's income for 1%, the demand for FYROM exports will decrease by 1.5% and vice versa. Table 1 summarizes the calculations for foreign effective demand, effective demand by Greece and foreign effective demand without Greece.

Proven from global experience, a small and open economy like that of FYROM cannot reach solid growth rates and operate successfully isolated from its surrounding countries (trading partners and foreign investors). Therefore, the various shocks in the economic and business environment, which is important for our economy, can very easily be transmitted as a spiral to our economy. Exports and FDI (in our economy a significant part comes from private transfers) are the main pillars on which in terms of de facto fixed exchange rate, the stability of the FYROM economy is based. To get a clearer picture of the importance of foreign effective demand (exports) for the FYROM economy Figure 1 shows the movement of real GDP and foreign effective demand in the period from 1999 to 2015 (historical and forecast).

The Figure 1clearly shows the dependence relationship between GDP growth rates and foreign effective demand (before the economic crisis, during the crisis and expected recovery period). From the Figure 1 it can be concluded that by mid-2013 the economy starts recovering, simultaneously with are our major trading partners. This comes as a direct result of the increased exports and positive growth rates of our GDP (specific rates Table 1). During 2012 we witnessed a modest GDP growth, a decline in industrial production and a modest export growth, which was expectable due to the lowest foreign effective demand. But the expectations for 2013 and the following two years are more optimistic, mainly due to the expected positive foreign effective demand in the middle of 2013 and expected higher percentage growth in real GDP (1.9% in 2013; 3.5% in 2014 and 4.2% in 2015).

In addition Figure 2 isolates the effective demand by Greece and shows its movement along with the movement of real GDP of FYROM. Figure 2 also presents a close connection of the movement of the effective demand by Greece and the movement of GDP, but here we can highlight the fact that the Greek effective demand is recovering slower than the Macedonian economy (seen from the GDP perspective). This leads us to the conclusion that the expected economy growth in other major trading partners, will affect our growth rates despite the prolonged economic crisis in Greece. Here we should mention that in decline of Greek effective demand, the strong effect of the economic crisis which presently affects Greek economy is calculated[13].

At a first glance there seems to be little relationship between real change in GDP and the effective demand that comes from Greece. The volatility in our GDP does not seem to closely follow the Greek demand during this period. In order to offer an improved way to view the movement of the total foreign effective demand and effective demand by Greece we report in Graph the following variables: foreign effective demand, foreign effective demand without Greece and effective demand by Greece.

From Figure 3 it becomes obvious that the effective demand that originates from Greece is far below the total foreign effective demand of FYROM. In the period from 2010 – 2011, as well as in the second half of 2013, a clear distinction can be seen between the foreign effective demand and foreign effective demand without Greece, which leads us to the conclusion that the reduced effective demand by Greece would lead to reduction of total foreign effective demand. Especially interesting are the situation in 2012 and the first half of 2013, where foreign effective demand is reduced and has a negative sign, as a result of the enormous cuts of effective demand by Greece. From the overall analysis of this graph it is obvious how much is the negative impact of the Greek contemporary crisis on Macedonia's exports[13].

Two Possible Scenarios

In order to calculate the effects of the economic crisis from our neighbor country Greece, two scenarios are designed for the period 2012 – 2015 that are most likely to take place in the Greek economy and have strong effects on FYROM's foreign effective demand. The assumptions used to design these two scenarios are Greek GDP growth estimates from the IMF (World Economic Outlook Database), and an income elasticity coefficient of FYROM exports with a value of 1.5.

GDP on constant prices (real GDP % changes)								Foreign effective demand	Foreign effective demand from Greece	Foreign effective demand without Greece	GDP in MKD on constant prices (real GDP% change)
Year	Belgium	Germany	Greece	Italy	Netherlands	Spain	Serbia				
1999	3.547	1.932	3.42	1.464	4.684	4.745	-11.173	-1.296108872	0.511576023	-1.8076849	4.348
2000	3.677	3.224	4.477	3.693	3.941	5.053	5.254	3.085824181	0.669685923	2.416138258	4.539
2001	0.807	1.151	4.197	1.818	1.926	3.645	5.579	2.430780704	0.627802506	1.802978199	-4.525
2002	1.352	0.006	3.439	0.454	0.76	2.704	3.882	1.564833335	0.514418112	1.050415222	0.853
2003	0.786	-0.231	5.943	-0.017	0.336	3.098	2.448	1.517857338	0.888975528	0.628881809	2.82
2004	3.091	1.176	4.623	1.532	2.237	3.267	8.295	3.178218713	0.691525133	2.48669358	4.08
2005	1.997	0.732	2.241	0.656	2.047	3.615	5.614	2.008962967	0.335216921	1.673746047	4.104
2006	2.78	3.167	4.522	2.036	3.394	4.017	5.213	2.846305763	0.676417186	2.169888576	3.903
2007	2.843	2.517	4.472	1.482	3.613	3.563	6.905	3.069998168	0.668938005	2.401060163	5.9
2008	0.832	1.248	2.015	-1.319	1.996	0.858	5.536	1.744321367	0.30141102	1.442910347	4.801
2009	-3.006	-4.973	-1.963	-5.038	-3.983	-3.639	-2.873	-2.515293758	-0.293632671	-2.22146109	-0.9
2010	1.153	1.21	-2	0.843	1.302	-0.41	1.968	0.492960075	-0.029916727	0.79212734	2.89
2011	1.605	1.999	0.16	1.543	1.726	1.463	5	1.77693343	0.023933381	1.753000049	3.1
2012	0.037	0.936	-6	-2.292	-0.457	-1.538	-0.477	-3.171684049	-1.276595745	-1.895	0.956
2013	0.34	0.852	-4	-0.73	0.394	-13.16	2.049	-1.161406114	-0.85106383	-0.31	1.951
2014	0.952	1.372	0	501	1.353	1.004	2.545	3.097485948	0	3.097	3.543
2015	1.322	1.381	2.7	1.203	1.821	1.552	2.2	4.846544331	0.574468085	4.272	4.226

Table 1: Foreign effective demand of FYROM (1999-2015)

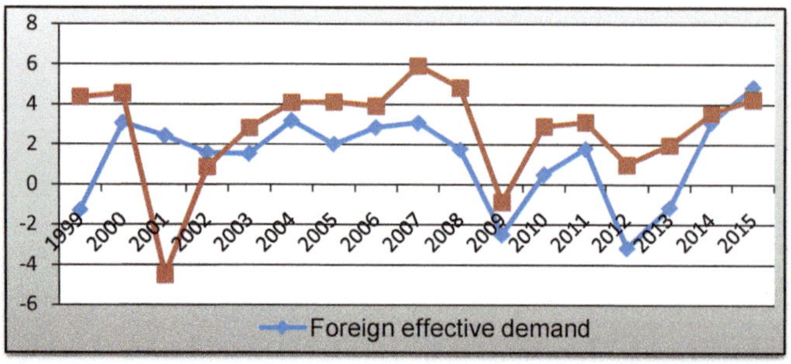

Source: Authors, based on data from IMF - World Economic Outlook Database

Figure 1: The interdependence between the real GDP of FYROM and foreign effective demand (1999-2015)

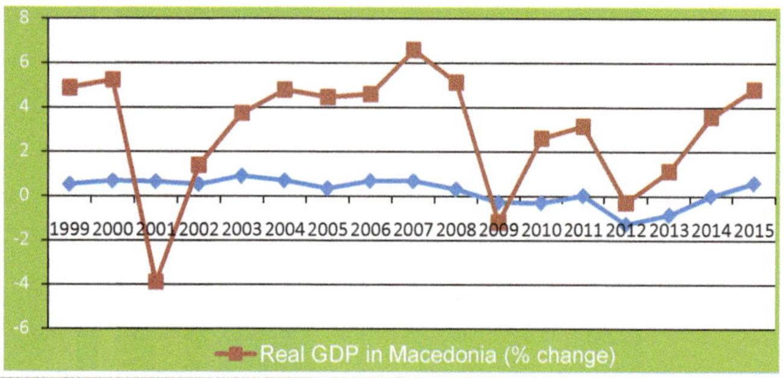

Source: Authors, based on data from IMF - World Economic Outlook Database

Figure 2: The interdependence between the real GDP of FYROM and foreign effective demand from Greece (1999-2015)

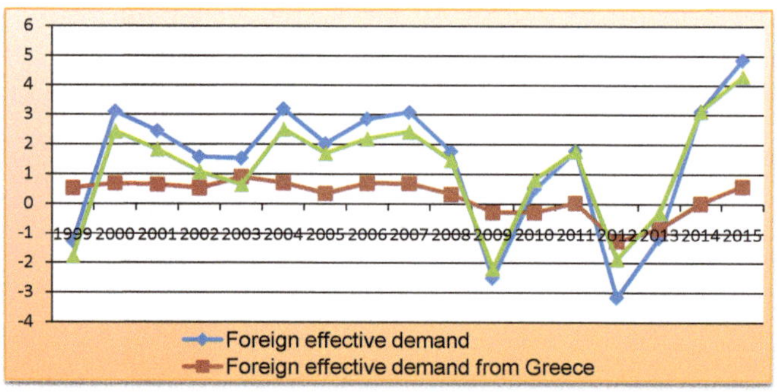

Source: Authors, based on data from IMF - World Economic Outlook Database

Figure 3: Foreign effective demand, foreign effective demand without Greece and effective demand by Greece

The first scenario is the reduction of the projected rate of GDP of Greece by 1 percentage point and the ratio of income elasticity of FYROM exports of 1.5.

Table 2 presents the effects of this scenario on the value of FYROM exports in thousands of U.S. dollars (2012 - 2015), as well as FYROM export growth rates (2012 - 2015). The last column shows the amount of FYROM exports in thousands of U.S. dollars that will be lost if Greece's GDP fell by 1 percentage point below the projected rate, and income elasticity coefficient of FYROM exports stays at 1.5. The first scenario shows that in 2013 the effects of the reduction of the projected rate of Greek GDP by 1% are not so alarming, but in the following two years, even though the Greek economy starts to recover in 2014 and 2015 at a slower rate in comparison to the decline in 2012 and 2013, the effects will be more noticeable, leading to a loss of 214.69 million USD in 2015 (a figure that is by no way negligible for FYROM economy).

The second scenario is the growth of the projected rate of GDP of Greece by 1 percentage point and the ratio of income elasticity of FYROM exports of 1.5.

Table 3 reports the second scenario with the growth of the projected rate of GDP of Greece at 1 percentage point and the ratio of income elasticity of FYROM exports of 1.5. Table 3is presenting the effects of this scenario of 1 percentage point of Greek GDP growth on the value of FYROM exports in thousands of U.S. dollars (2012 - 2015), as well as Macedonian export growth rates (2012 - 2015). The last column shows the amount of Macedonian exports in thousands of USD that will be gained if Greece's GDP increase by 1 percentage point above the projected rate of IMF, and income elasticity coefficient of FYROM exports is the same 1.5. This can be better seen at the growth of FYROM exports in 2015, which is 214.69 million USD[14].

Nevertheless, it should be noted that based on the last two tables, the most significant issue is that the growth rate of Macedonian exports presented in USD, when there is 1% increase in projected Greece GDP growth, is bigger compared to the losses that FYROM exports will have if the Greek GDP fell by 1 %. In particular, Figure 4 summarizes this case:

The above shows FYROM exports, in absolute values, in two case scenarios, and in the first scenario there is a decline in the Macedonian exports, and in the second there is a growth in FYROM exports. Analyzing year by year, there is no difference in the numbers considering 2013, but in 2014 there is difference of 1.8 million USD more in growth compared to the decline, taking the absolute numbers. In 2015 there is even bigger difference of about 6 million USD in absolute numbers.

Conclusion

Although there are signs of recovery and exit from the crisis for some major economies (Germany, France etc.), pace of recovery is with lower intensity than expected, and on the other hand there are economies that are still struggling with the effects of the crisis, such as Portugal, Spain, Italy and many other EU economies.

The effects of the Greek crisis on the total Macedonian exports, according to our analysis are expected to be significant, but not devastating for our economy, taking in consideration the fact that when calculating the effective demand in this paper it was provided only a drop in GDP of Greece. According to the IMF GDP projections for other economies - which are part of our effective demand growth – there will be a smaller, almost insignificant decrease in GDP just in 2012. The IMF projections that were used, assume that growth in other economies will entail greater import demand and thus absorb some of the negative effects of the Greek crisis on the FYROM export. But here comes the question: what will happen and what will be the effect on the FYROM economy be if the effects of the Greek economic crisis spill over into other economies that are major trading partners and investors in FYROM? The answer to this question would go in the direction - if there is such a scenario as the Macedonian economy whose GDP growth is highly determined - dependent on foreign effective demand will face a decline in exports, FDI, private transfers, which could lead to pressure on the foreign exchange market, a decline in production, increase in unemployment (which is currently at the highest level in Europe) and devastating meltdown of our economy[15].

The significance of the Greek GDP growth is confirmed with the

				Scenario for Greek GDP decline by 1 %			
Year	GDP growth rates of the Greek economy	Macedonian export value (thousand USD)	Macedonian export growth rate	GDP growth rates of the Greek economy	Macedonian export value (thousand USD)	Macedonian export growth rate	Decline in Macedonian exports
2012	-6,00%	4 001 857	5,00%	-7,00%	4 001 857	/	/
2013	-4,00%	4,322,005,777	8,00%	-5,00%	4,261,977,919	6,50%	-6,002,785,801
2014	0,00%	4,746,858,945	9,83%	-1,00%	4,617,000,679	8,33%	-1,298,582,652
2015	2,70%	5,316,482,018	12,00%	1,70%	5,101,785,751	10,50%	-2,146,962,673

Source: Authors, IMF Country Report 2012

Table 2: Reducing the projected rate of GDP of Greece by 1 percentage points and the ratio of income elasticity of FYROM exports of 1.5

				Scenario for Greek GDP growth by 1 %			
Year	GDP growth rates of the Greek economy	Macedonian export value (thousand USD)	Macedonian export growth rate	GDP growth rates of the Greek economy	Macedonian export value (thousand USD)	Macedonian export growth rate	Growth of Macedonian exports
2012	-6,00%	4 001 857	5,00%	-5,00%	4 001 857	/	/
2013	-4,00%	4322005,78	8,00%	-3,00%	4382033,63	9,50%	6,002,785,801
2014	0,00%	4746858,94	9,83%	1,00%	4878518,05	11,33%	131,659,101
2015	2,70%	5316482,02	12,00%	3,70%	5537117,98	13,50%	2,206,359,638

Source: Authors, IMF Country Report 2012

Table 3: Growth of the projected rate of GDP of Greece by 1 percentage points and the ratio of income elasticity of FYROM exports of 1.5

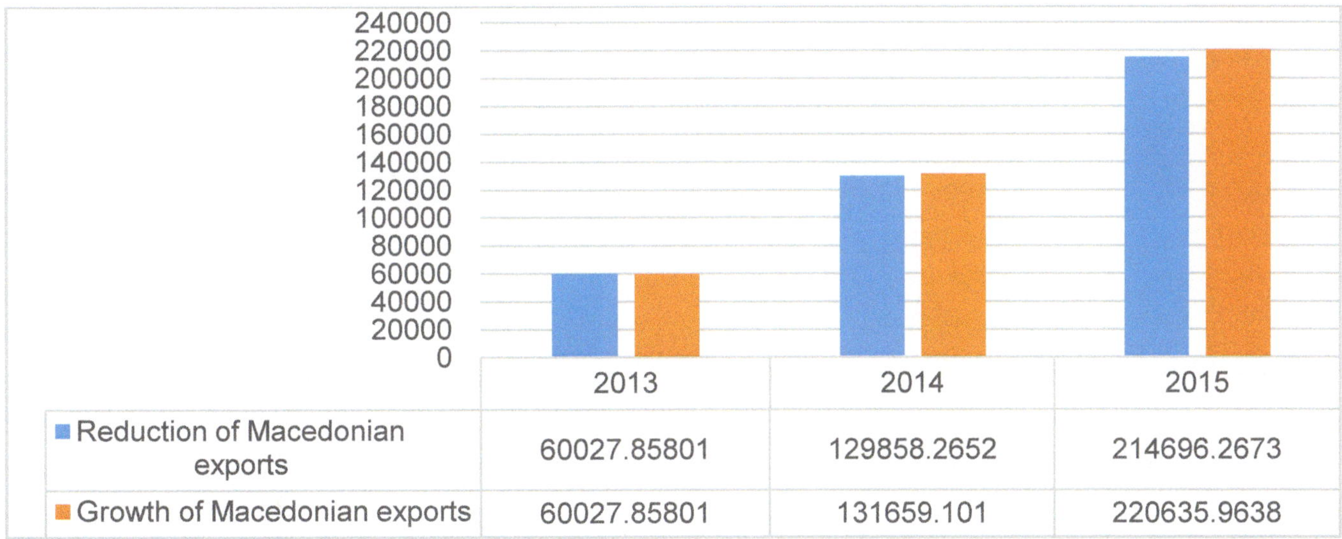

Source: Authors, IMF Country Report 2012

Figure 4: FYROM exports (in absolute values) according to two scenarios (reduction and growth of the projected rate of GDP of Greece by 1 percentage points)

two case scenarios where the increase of Greece GDP growth by 1% is provoking bigger increase in the FYROM exports, than in the opposite case, where there is 1% decrease in Greek GDP and smaller decrease in FYROM exports, taking the absolute values of the FYROM exports. Further investigation into the matter should include the inter-related partner economies of FYROM and the potential integrated result that could stem from the different recovery rates of the economies of our partners.

References

1. Nenovski T, Smilkovski I, Poposki K (2001) Remodeling of the Macedonian Economy. Chinese Business Review 20: 1156-1166
2. Kostoska, O,Petreski, G (2009) Modelling the determinants of Exports and Imports: Assessment of the Macedonian Competitive Performances, Management & Marketing.
3. Sharma A, Panagiotidis T (2005) An Analysis of Exports and Growth in India: Cointegration and Causality Evidence, Loughborough University working papers.
4. Ramos F (2001) Exports, Imports and Economic Growth in Portugal: evidence from causality and cointegration analysis. Economic Modelling, 18: 613-623.
5. Konya L (2006) Exports and growth: Granger causality analysis on OECD countries with a panel data approach, Economic Modelling 23: 978-992.
6. Awokuse T (2007) Causality between exports, imports and economic growth: Evidence from transition economies. Economic Letters, 94: 389-395.
7. Awokuse, T. (2006) Export-led growth and the Japanese economy: evidence from VAR and directed acyclic graphs, Applied Economics, 38(5): 593-602.
8. Silaghi, P. and Ioana, M. (2009) Exports-Economic Growth Causality: Evidence from CEE Countries, Romanian Journal for Economic Forecasting, 6: 105-117.
9. Hsiao F, Hsiao M (2006) FDI, exports and GDP in East and Southeast Asia - Panel Data versus time-series causality analyses. Journal of Asian Economics, 17(6): 1082-1106.

10. Sadiku, M., Sadiku, L. and Berisha, N. (2014) The financial crisis in Greece and its impacts on Western Balkan Countries. Economic Crisis in Europe and the Balkans, Problems and Prospects (eds.) Karasavvoglou and Polychronidou, XII.

11. International Monetary Fund (2012) Retrieved from IMF Country.

12. International Monetary Fund (2012) World Economic Outlook Database. Retrieved from International Monetary Fund.

13. Basic Economic Data (2012) Retrieved from National Bank of the Republic of Macedonia.

14. Volume of foreign trade (2013) Retrieved from State Statistical Office.

15. EUROSTAT Database (2012) Retrieved from Eurostat.

The Impact of Firm-Level Shareholder Protections on Abnormal Returns on Insider Trading

Christopher von Koch*, Ola Nilsson[1], Micael Jönsson, Jeff Andersson and Erik Matthiesen

School of Business and Economics, Linnaeus University, Sweden

Abstract

This study is the first to investigate the relationship between firm-level shareholder protections and abnormal returns on insider trading. We thereby extend the few studies that have analysed insider trading from a shareholder protection perspective. The novelty of this study is its concentration on firm-level shareholder protection. Our results show that firm-level shareholder protections have a significantly positive impact on abnormal returns on insider purchases, indicating that firm-level shareholder protection is more influential than country-level shareholder protection. We found support that the information content hypothesis is valid for explanation of abnormal return on insider trading, which is in line with earlier studies. This result is an indication that insider purchases in firms that have adopt strict corporate governance rules are viewed by the market as trustworthy leading to positive market reactions on insider trading.

Keywords: Shareholder protection; Insider trading;Firm-level

Introduction

This study investigates the relationship between firm-level shareholder protections and abnormal returns on insider trading. Insider trading has been a central topic within both practice and research. A main question in this discussion asks whether insider trading should be seen as a problem or if it actually contributes to a more effective market [1].

The most general view is that insider trading is a symptom of imperfection within the market because it presents the opportunity for insiders to take advantage of superior information [2-4]. Insiders exploit outsiders because they can receive abnormal returns. The way to handle this problem is to implement regulations with the purpose of reducing the opportunity for insider trading [5-14].

A contrasting view is that insider trading must be accepted as a part of the game and that it is an effective and fast way to transfer expectations to the market. Outsiders can respond quickly to the signs of insider trading and therefore also gain profits or reduce losses. According to this view, regulation with the purpose of reducing insider trading makes the market more inefficient in the long run. Instead, regulations should support fast responses to insider trading trading [1,15-17]. These contrasting views have initiated empirical studies that examine how regulative settings and regulations affect insider trading and its consequences [18-21]. Two recently published studies by Fidrmuc et al. [22] and Dardas [23] extend existing research by highlighting howshareholder protections affect insider trading and the possibility of abnormal returns. These authors also compare countries with different legal origins based on the assumption grounded in the legal origin hypothesis, i.e. that legal origin affects how effective a regulation will be. However, the results of these studies are contradictory. Fidrmuc et al. [22], who use data from 16 countries, find that abnormal returns on insider transactions are positively correlated with country-level shareholder protections. The authors suggest that shareholder protection laws are highly relevant in shaping the information environment between the insiders and outsiders of a firm. According to the authors, this conclusion supports the information-content hypothesis that stipulates that market reactions to insider purchases increase with greater shareholder protection because shareholder protection enhances both the trustworthiness and the transparency of their actions. However, Dardas [23] usedata from 17 countries and categorises countries based on their belonging to different legal origins, resulting in three groups representing different levels of shareholder protection. English law countries represent high levels of shareholder protection, German and Scandinavian law countries represent medium levels shareholder protection and French law countries represent low levels of shareholder protection. The results show that abnormal returns on insider trading are highest in German and Scandinavian law countries, i.e. the countries representing medium levels of shareholder protection, compared to the other countries. French law countries show the lowest abnormal returns on insider trading, while English law countries exhibit mid-level abnormal returns. Dardas [23] explains that the results for English law countries stem from their longer history of using directors to address investment strategies, which results in smaller opportunities for abnormal returns.

We find the contradicting results interesting and a basis upon which to analyse the relationship between shareholder protections (beyond shareholder protections at the country level) and abnormal returns on insider trading. We build upon the implicit assumption of earlier studies that shareholder protections do not differ between firms within a country [22,23]. This assumption is supported by several studies that examine both country- and firm-level shareholder protections and show that it is not necessary for firms in strong shareholder countries to have strong shareholder protections in reality; instead, shareholder protections on the firm level vary greatly within a given country [24-27]. Markets throughout the world are becoming increasingly integrated, and several companies are currently cross-listed in exchanges in two or more countries. As previously explained, this conclusion implies that firm-level shareholder protections would have a more profound impact on the transparency and trustworthiness of insider actions and therefore may have a more direct impact on the

***Corresponding authors:** Christopher von Koch, School of Business and Economics, Linnaeus University, Sweden
E-mail: christopher.von.koch@lnu.se

effects of insider trading. Fully compiling the effects of insider trading in a specific company with country-level shareholder protections may therefore be quite misleading and would explain the contradictory results. The primary objective of this study is to deepen the results obtained by Fidrmuc et al. [22] and Dardas [23] by taking shareholder protections on the firm level into account to analyse their effects on abnormal returns for corporate insiders. Additionally, by taking the country dimension into account and choosing firms in three countries representing different levels of shareholder protections on the country level, we will be able to include a complementary analysis of the impact of shareholder protections on this level.

We used a comprehensive dataset to establish each firm's shareholder protections, and we analysed firms from three different countries and collected over 5,700 insider transactions from insiders within these firms. Our results confirm our expectations that firm-level shareholder protection affects abnormal returns on insider trading and appears to be moreimportant than shareholder protection levels on the country level. Insider trading in firms with strong shareholder protection results in significantly higher abnormal returns than does insider trading in firms with low shareholder protection. This result indicates that a firm's corporate governance is very important in shaping the information environment between insiders and outsiders of the firm. Our results support the information-content hypothesis, i.e. that insiders in firms with strong corporate governance are perceived to be more trustworthy in their actions in the market because they respond faster than outsiders. This hypothesis is in line with the findings of Fidrmuc et al. [22].

This study contributes to the extensive research on insider trading by proposing an important explanation of abnormal returns on insider trading. The novel contribution of our study is particularly an examination of the relationship between firm-level shareholder protections and abnormal returns. Our results also shed light on the agency cost problem in which insiders exploit superior information to gain profits from insider trades, indicating that stricter corporate governance on the firm level may not mitigate these agency costs.

Research Question

Fidrmuc et al.[22] and Dardas [23] build upon the notion that shareholder protection contributes to returns on legal insider trading. We agree with this notion because earlier studies have shown that shareholder protection or corporate governance is influential in shaping the information environment in the capital market. The present research question involves whether shareholder protection on the country level or firm level is the most important factor in determining returns on insider trading. The literature on corporate governance is extensive, and there are many studies from both the country-level perspective [27,28] and the firm-level perspective [29,30]. Within the line of research from a country-level perspective, there has been a stream of comparative governance literature [31,32] focused on how economies, capital markets and firms perform under different legal regimes. In general, these studies demonstrate that country-level corporate governance influences firm performance. Additionally, within the line of research from a firm-level perspective, there are many studies that examine the value and relevance of firm-level corporate governance. These studies typically find that higher standards of firm-level governance are associated with increased firm value, decreased costs of capital, greater access to external financing, and other beneficial aspects of firm value [20,33-41]. There are also several examples that analyse whether and how corporate governance affects the information environment as well as the impact of dealing with problems with asymmetric information, which could be directly translated to the problems between insiders and outsiders. Particularly relevant is the empirical research on financial analysts in which comparative studies of analyst performance and country-level shareholder protection have shown that analysts perform better (by producing more accurate earnings forecasts, for example) in countries with strong shareholder protection than in countries with weak shareholder protection [42-46]. These studies suggest an association between legal and financial reporting environments and analysts' forecast behaviour. The main argument of these studies is that strengthening country-level shareholder protection improves firms' public information, which can lead to a decreased need for analysts to gain private information. If more information is known by an outsider (as is the case in strong shareholder protection countries),an insider would have less private information with which to earn abnormal returns on insider purchases or sales.

However, although firm-level corporate governance has been studied extensively, there are not many studies on this issue as it relates to firm-level corporate governance. One of the few studies combining an analysis of firm-level corporate governance and analyst performance is by Beekes and Brown[47]. They find that Australian firms with better corporate governance have a greater analyst following and that there is less bias and greater accuracy but greater disagreement in their forecasts. Their results are therefore in line with those of Heflin et al. [48] and Irani and Karamanou[49], who argue that if analysts seek to gain an advantage by gathering private information in response to an increase in public information, this improvement of public information may improve accuracy while simultaneously increasing dispersion.

To conclude this section, research on both the firm level and the country level indicates that strengthening shareholder protection (on both levels) improves the availability of public information relative to the availability of private information. If so, insiders would have relatively less private information with which to trade when shareholder protection strengthens. However, this notion does not address the ability of insiders to use this private information to earn abnormal returns. We present a result similar to that reported by Acharya et al. [50], which indicates that firm-level governance systems effectively mitigate potential agency conflicts between managers and shareholders even without any country-level governance mechanisms. We therefore determine that within the context of insider trading, it is much more important to use firm-level shareholder protection than country-level shareholder protection to analyse insider trading. The firm-level shareholder protectionsexamined in this study were constructed using firm-level shareholder protection attributes such as board effectiveness and audit quality. Because abnormal returns from insider trading mainly tend to be viewed as agency problems between shareholders and managers, it can be argued that these agency problems may be handled more effectively with firm-level, rather than country-level, shareholder protection mechanisms.

However, as mentioned in the introduction, strengthening firm-level shareholder protection may result in two divergent outcomes; the literature identifies these outcomes as rent extraction and information content. For example, Leland [51] argues that insider trading transfers wealth from uninformed shareholders to informed insiders.

Additionally, Bebchuk and Fried [52] report abnormal trading profits made by corporate insiders as agency costs. By contrast, Carlton and Fischel[15] argue that insider trading facilitates the flow of information and the rapid reflection of private information in stock prices. In support of the informational role of insider trades, Piotroski and Roulstone [53] show that insider trading increases the relative amount of firm-specific information incorporated into stock prices. The results presented by Fidrmuc et al. [22] support the information content outcome by showing that abnormal returns on insider purchases are higher in countries with high shareholder protection. The authors conclude that these results favour the information-content perspective based on the notion that insider trades reveal private information to the market and contribute to prices that better reflect fundamental firm values.

Method and Data

A firm-level measure of corporate governance

To measure firm-level corporate governance, we use the Corporate Governance Quotient CGQ dataset in accordance with Aggarwal et al. [24], Bruno and Claessens [25], and Chhaochharia and Laeven [26]. The provider, ISS, began collecting data from U.S. firms in 2002 and from non-U.S. firms in 2003; in total, ISS collects firm-level data from samples of firms from 30 countries. Several of the variables within the dataset were created from data gathered through other included variables, which could explain why researchers have previously chosen to use only part of the dataset. However, the parts of the dataset that these authors used differ. Chhaochharia and Laeven[26] use 17 of the dataset's attributes to create their governance index, Bruno and Claessens [25] use 18 attributes to create six different indices, and Aggarwal et al [24] use 44 attributes. For our analysis, we choose the same 44 attributes selected by Aggarwal et al [24] . This dataset gives us the opportunity to perform the most comprehensive firm-level analysis possible. Aggarwal et al.'s [24] methodology includes four subcategories of firm-level governance metrics: (1) Board (25 attributes), (2) Audit (3 attributes), (3) Anti-takeover (6 attributes), and (4) Compensation and Ownership (10 attributes). Table 1 lists the 44 specific attributes that are used in this study, classified according to the four aforementioned subgroups. If a firm possesses all of the attributes, its index is recorded as 100 per cent.

Research design

Because this study focuses on information asymmetry between insiders and outsiders, we develop a design with which to handle this issue. The literature has shown that information asymmetry between insiders and outsiders vary between firms, especially between smaller firms and larger firms or between specific industries. For example, smaller firms and somespecific industries receive lower analyst coverage and less public information, which could also be less reliable. Therefore, it is assumed that these firms have higher information asymmetry between insiders and outsiders than other firms do. We therefore develop a research design to mitigate this problem of different information asymmetry. We aim to include as many similar firms as possible in our sample despite analysing firms from three different countries. The countries are chosen because they represent different shareholder protection regimes. The U.S., Germany and Sweden are representative of the three legal traditions described by La Porta et al. [32] Anglo-Saxon, German and Scandinavian - and therefore have different shareholder protection laws on the country level. Because the size of firms varies within countries, we choose a method for obtaining a sample of similar firms from each country. We therefore select Swedish

BOARD
1. All of the directors attended 75% of the board meetings or had a valid excuse.
2. The CEO serves on the boards of two or fewer public companies.
3. The board is controlled by more than 50% independent outside directors.
4. The board size is greater than 5 but less than 16.
5. The CEO is not listed as having a related-party transaction.
6. No former CEO is on the board.
7. The compensation committee is composed solely of independent outsiders.
8. The chairman and CEO are separate, or there is a lead director.
9. The nominating committee is composed solely of independent outsiders.
10. A governance committee exists and has met in the past year.
11. Shareholders vote on directors that are selected to fill vacancies.
12. The governance guidelines are publicly disclosed.
13. The board is annually elected (no staggered board).
14. A policy exists regarding outside directorships (with a limit of four or fewer boards).
15. Shareholders have cumulative voting rights.
16. Shareholder approval is required to increase/decrease board size.
17. There is a majority vote requirement to amend the charter/bylaws (not necessarily a supermajority).
18. The board has the expressed authority to hire its own advisors.
19. The performance of the board is reviewed regularly.
20. A board-approved succession plan is in place for the CEO.
21. The outside directors meet without the CEO and disclose the number of times that they meet.
22. The directors are required to submit their resignation upon a change in position.
23. The board cannot amend the bylaws without shareholder approval or can do so only under limited circumstances.
24. The board does not ignore shareholder proposals.
25. The board qualifies for combination points in proxy contest defences.
AUDIT
26. The consulting fees paid to auditors are less than the audit fees paid to auditors.
27. The audit committee is composed solely of independent outsiders.
28. Auditors are ratified at the most recent annual meeting.
ANTI-TAKEOVER
29. Single class, common.
30. There is a majority vote requirement to approve mergers (not necessarily a supermajority).
31. Shareholders may call special meetings.
32. Shareholders may act by written consent.
33. The company either has no poison pill or has a pill that was shareholder-approved.
34. The company is not authorised to issue blank check preferred stock.
COMPENSATION & OWNERSHIP
35. The directors are subject to stock ownership requirements.
36. The executives are subject to stock ownership guidelines.
37. There are no interlocks among compensation committee members.
38. The directors receive all or a portion of their fees in stock.
39. All stock incentive plans are adopted with shareholder approval.
40. Options grants align with company performance and demonstrate a reasonable burn rate.
41. The company expenses stock options.
42. All of the directors with more than one year of service own stock.
43. Officers' and directors' stock ownership is at least 1% but not over 30% of the total shares outstanding.
44. Repricing is prohibited.

Table 1: Forty-four firm-level corporate governance attributes
The above approach used by Aggarwal et al. (2008), we construct four subcategories of firm-level governance attributes: (1) Board (twenty-five attributes), (2) Audit (three attributes), (3) Anti-takeover (six attributes), and (4) Compensation and Ownership (ten attributes). The table presents the forty-four attributes that are considered in this study, divided into these four subgroups.

companies because Sweden is a small economy, and companies that are publicly traded in the Nasdaq OMX Stockholm Exchange are generally much smaller in size compared to companies in Germany and the U.S. To obtain a sample of companies with a reasonable number of insider trades, we choose the 26 companies in Sweden with the greatest rates of turnover. We then select the same number of firms from the U.S. and Germany, which have characteristics most similar to the firms from Sweden based on industry and sales. After checking for these characteristics, the chosen firms were included in the CGQ dataset; the final sample consists of 78 firms in total, i.e. 26 from each country.

Firm-level sample

The sample for the study is based on company data retrieved from the Orbis database and has been designed based on companies listed in the Nasdaq OMX Stockholm Exchange, the New York Stock Exchange and the Frankfurt Boerse.

Table 2 presents a summary of the CGQ statistics for the 78 firms in our sample. As expected, the levels of firms' shareholder protections are the highest for U.S. firms and the lowest forGerman firms. The median U.S. firm has a shareholder protection of 0.68 or 68 per cent, meaning that the median firm in our U.S. sample complies with 68 per cent of the 44 CGQ attributes. On the other hand, the median German firm complies with only 51 per cent of the CGQ attributes. Notably, there is a wide variation in firm-level shareholder protection among firms in each country. For example, the minimum value of shareholder protection for a firm from a strong shareholder protection country such as the U.S. is lower than the median values for firms in Sweden and Germany. Table 2 therefore supports the aim of this study to not only look at country-level shareholder protection but also analyse firm-level shareholder protection because country-level and firm-level shareholder protection might not correlate in a substantial way. Next, we use the median of the full sample from Table 2 to divide the firms into to two groups: firms with high shareholder protection (median values higher than 0.59) and firms with low shareholder protection (median values lower than 0.59). Each group includes firms from each country. The first group is hereafter named High CGQ, whereas the other group is hereafter named Low CGQ. We also determine each firm's ownership structure, and ownership concentration is defined according to the general information on ownership reporting in 2011 from the Orbis database. To reclassify whether a company was concentrated or dispersed, we use the definition by La Portas et al. [32]. Companies with a single owner and voting shares of 20 per cent or more are considered to be companies with concentrated ownership, whereas those with voting shares below 20 per cent are considered to be companies with dispersed ownership.

Data on insider trading were collected from January 2006 until the end of December 2012, a period equivalent to seven years. The German companies in the sample were registered in 999 insider transactions, the Swedish companies were registered in 1,974 insider transactions, and the American companies were registered in 2,809 insider transactions. In total, data on 5,782 transactions were collected. A difference exists between the numbers of insider transactions analysed between countries because the German and American data were retrieved by hand. The collection of Swedish data was extracted from the Financial Supervisory Authority (FI) website. The German data were retrieved from Insider Daten, which compiles the publications under the Federal Financial Supervisory Authority (BaFin), while the U.S. data were taken from a similar page, SecForm4, which compiles trade data from the U.S. Securities and Exchange Commission (SEC). For all transactions, we collected the following information: the names and identifiers of the company, transaction dates, announcement dates, transaction types (e.g., buy, sell, grant), the number of shares traded, transaction prices, and the insider's name and position in the firm (CEO, board Member, major Owner, other).

Table 3 summarises the trade statistics. In total, we collected data on 2,312 purchases (785 were trades in High CGQ firms while 1,527 were trades in Low CGQ firms) and 3,470 sales (2,487 were trades in High CGQ firms while 983 were trades in Low CGQ firms) for the 78 sample firms over the seven-year time period. Additionally, Table 3 shows the origin country of the High CGQ transactions. The majority of these transactions come from Sweden (purchases) and the U.S. (sales).

In Table 4, the transactions are divided by the position of insiders within the firm. A large portion of the trades were made by insiders other than CEOs, board members and major owners. In addition, we show the median ownership concentrations for the firms with dispersed ownership in Table 4. Of the 26 firms, 94 per cent have dispersed ownership, while only 35 per cent of Swedish firms in this sample have dispersed ownership. Compared to earlier studies (Fidrmuc et al.), we therefore measure ownership concentration on the firm level and not on the country level.

Comparative statistics

Table 5 shows the results for CARs over 6-, 11- and 101-day windows from the transaction day. For purchases recorded in Panel A, the overall average market is positively significant over the three windows, with the market adjusting on average by 0.7%, 0.6% and 7.0%, respectively. For the three windows, the markets react positively for all countries as well as for the full sample, except for the 6-day and 11-day windows in Germany. The long-term abnormal returns are larger on average and are significant at the 1% level. For all windows, we find that the markets react more significantly for firms with high shareholder protection relative to firms with low shareholder protection.

CARs for sale trades are presented in Panel B of Table 5. The results

	CGQ for firms			
	Min	Max	Median	Mean
Sweden	0.43	0.64	0.54	0.55
Germany	0.41	0.59	0.51	0.51
USA	0.41	0.77	0.68	0.67
Full Sample	0.41	0.77	0.59	0.60

Table 2:CGQ for firms
Firm-level shareholder protection measured with 44 attributes from the Institutional Shareholder Service. The numbers in the table are percentages of how many of the attributes are compiled by the firms. Note that the median for the sample is 59%, which is used to divide the sample into firms with strong shareholder protection (above 59%) and firms with weak shareholder protection (below 59%).

	Purchase transaction		Sale transaction	
	Total	High CGQ	Total	High CGQ
Sweden	1,396	462	578	179
Germany	638	58	361	11
USA	278	278	2,531	2,297
Full sample	2,312		3,470	
High CGQ	785		2,487	
Low CGQ	1,527		983	

Table 3: Summary of statistics from insider trades shown for the three countries as well as for the full sample. The transactions are broken down by the type of transaction and High CGQ firms and Low CGQ firms.

	Position				Ownership concentration
	CEO	Board Member	Major owner	Other	
Panel A: Purchase					
Sweden	82	446	86	786	0.35
Germany	80	161	440	393	0.44
USA	27	156	10	85	0.94
Sum	189	763	536	1,267	
Panel B: Sale					
Sweden	5	84	49	440	
Germany	32	62	0	267	
USA	161	1,089	114	1,157	
Sum	198	235	163	1,864	

Table 4: Descriptive statistics for different insider positions, transactions and ownership concentrations, broken down by different countries.

	CAR (0.5)		CAR (0.10)		CAR (0.100)	
	Mean	Median	Mean	Median	Mean	Median
Panel A: Purchase						
Sweden	0.89%**	0.37%**	0.32%	-0.03%	4.00%***	1.00%**
Germany	-0.47%	-0.59%	-0.26%	-0.49%	7.27%***	6.07%***
USA	2.80%***	1.96%***	3.71%***	1.75%***	21.50%***	10.87%***
Full sample	0.74%**	0.28%	0.57%*	0.06%	7.00%***	3.14%***
High CGQ	2.04%***	0.76%***	2.14%**	0.63%**	10.21%***	3.53%***
Low CGQ	0.07%	0.09%	-0.24%	-0.22%	5.35%***	2.75%***
High versus Low CGQ T-stat/z-statT-stat/z-stat	2.84**	2.71**	3.14***	2.49**	2.58**	1.44
Panel B: Sale						
Sweden	-0.17%	0.01%	-0.95%**	-0.52%**	-4.75%**	-5.21%***
Germany	-1.45%***	-1.34%***	-1.94%***	-1.83%***	-8.44%***	-8.81%***
USA	-0.24%*	0.07%	-0.62%***	-0.39%***	-3.75%***	-3.85%***
Full sample	-0.36%***	-0.12%	-0.81%***	-0.59%	-4.45%***	-4.49%***
High CGQ	-0.38%**	0.02%	-0.84%***	-0.50%***	-4.02%***	-3.52%***
Low CGQ	-0.31%	-0.44%*	-0.73%**	-0.92%***	-5.51%***	-7.18%***
High versus Low CGQ T-stat/z-stat	0.29	1.122	0.32	1.53	1.04	2.921***
T-stat/z-stat						

Table 5: Descriptive CAR after insider transactions
Note *p < 0.05; **p < 0.001;***p < 0.001
The table shows mean and median CARs in various windows. Day 0 is the transaction day. The Wilcoxon sign-rank test is used to test the significance of the median. The Wilcoxon rank-sum test is used to test the equality of medians.

for sales are somewhat less obvious than those for purchases. The overall average market is negatively significant over the three windows, with the market adjusting on average by -0.4%, -0.8% and -4.45%. For the three windows, the markets mainly react negatively for all countries as well as for the full sample. However, we find no significantly negative reaction (except for the median for the 101-day window) for high shareholder protection firms relative to low shareholderprotection firms. Therefore, we could argue that our results are consistent with the insider literature, which stipulates that sale transactions are less informative because an insider may sell for reasons related to liquidity and portfolio. In summary, Table 5 indicates that abnormal returns differ across firms with different shareholder protections.

Empirical results

Our main focus of this study is the effect of firm-level corporate governance on abnormal returns on insider transactions. In the regressions shown in Table 6, we also control for other characteristics, but because our research design involves 26 similar firms in each country, we find no need to control for certain factors such as firm size and market capitalisation, among others. We estimate the following regression model:

$$CAR_{ij} = \beta CGQ + \gamma Controlvariables$$

whereCAR_{ij} is the cumulative abnormal returns for transaction i in company j. CGQ represents firm-level shareholder protections, our main variable of research interest. Control variables in our regression include Ownership, Country, Insider position, and Transaction size. However, although we analyse similar firms, firm characteristics such as ownership concentration, insider position and transaction size could differ among the sample. Therefore, we control for these variables. Ownership concentration is measured as a dummy variable where 1 stands for concentration ownership while 2 stands for dispersed ownership. Insider position is measured on a scale in which 1=other, 2=Board member, 3=CEO, and 4=Major owner. Transaction size is measured on a scale in which 1=0-3,550 U.S. dollars, 2=3,550-14,000 U.S. dollars, 3=14,000-35,000 U.S. dollars, 4=35,000-140,000 U.S. dollars, and 5=140,000+ U.S. dollars. Table 6 shows the regressions for CARs over 6, 11 and 101 days. The impact of shareholder protections on abnormal returns is estimated using the firm-level CGQ index.

Panel A of Table 6 shows strong positive shareholder protection effects on purchases. In Column 1, after controlling for ownership concentration, country, insider position and transaction size, the 6-day CAR is positively significant with a p-value < 0.01 for CGQ, meaning that higher firm-level CGQ means larger abnormal returns. For the other windows CGQ is also significant with p-value < 0.01 for the 11-day and p-value 0.001 for the 101-day window. Notably, the country variable is not significant in any of the three windows indicating no significant difference across countries.

For sales in Panel B CGQ is only significant (p-value <0.001) for the longer window. This latter result could be in line with earlier research. For example, Bruno [25] show large difference in trading volume between insider purchase and sale around announcement day.

Conclusions

In this study, we extend the few studies [22,23] that have analysed insider trading and shareholder protection. Unlike these earlier studies, we use firm-level shareholder protection data. Our results show that firm-level shareholder protection has a significantly positive impact on abnormal returns on insider purchases, indicating that firm-level shareholder protection is more influential than country-level shareholder protection. This positive correlation supports the results obtained by Fidrmuc et al. [22] that information content is decisive in strengthening shareholder protection. We found support that the information content hypothesis is valid for explanation of abnormal return on insider trading, which is in line with earlier studies. This result is an indication that insider purchases in firms that have adopt strict corporate governance rules are viewed by the market as trustworthy leading to positive market reactions on insider trading.

We contribute to the extensive research on insider trading by proposing an important explanation of abnormal returns on insider trading. The novel contribution of our study is namely the examination of the relationship between firm-level shareholder protections and abnormal returns. Our positive results also shed some light on the agency cost problem in which insiders exploit superior information to gain profits from insider trades. Our results particularly indicate that stricter firm-level corporate governance might not mitigate these agency costs. The shortcomings of this research may result from our not capturing all of the companies in each exchange, but the sample used in this study should be sufficient to infer any differences that exist between countries.

	CAR (0.5)	CAR (0.10)	CAR (0.100)
	Panel A: Purchase		
CGQ	0.1160**	0.1503***	0.3171** (0.1234)
	-0.0392	-0.0445	
Ownership	-0.0104	-0.0129**	0.0134 (0.0182)
	-0.0058	-0.0066	
Country	-0.0026	0.0019	0.0112 (0.0114)
	-0.0036	-0.0041	
Insider position	0.0052	0.0100**	0.0310** (0.0117)
	-0.0037	-0.0042	
Transaction size	0.0001	-0.0009	-0.0246** (0.0070)
	-0.0022	-0.0025	
Constant	-0.0466	-.0769** (0.0279)	-0.1366 (0.0775)
	-0.0246		
Number of observations	2,312	2,312	2,312
R2	0.68%	0.87%	1.58%
	Panel B: Sale		
CGQ	0.0036	0.0171 (0.0182)	0.4664*** (0.0763)
	-0.0141		
Ownership	0.0054	0.0052 (0.0042)	-0.044** (0.0175)
	-0.0032		
Country	-0.0063**	-0.0046 (0.0029)	-0.0173 (0.0120)
	-0.0022		
Insider position	0.0039**	0.0046** (0.0019)	0.0543*** (0.0079)
	-0.0015		
Transaction size	-0.0003	-0.0008 (0.0011)	-0.0153*** (0.0046)
	-0.0009		
Constant	-0.009	-0.0008** (0.0011)	-0.2759*** (0.0510)
	-0.0094		
Number of observations	3,470	3,470	3,470
R2	0.56%	0.42%	3.22%

Table 6: The regressions for CARs over 6, 11 and 101 days
The impact of shareholder protection on abnormal returns is estimated using the firm-level CGQ index. The control variables are ownership, country, insider position and transaction size.

References

1. Padilla A, Brian G (2009) Insider Trading: Is There an Economist in the Room? The Journal of Private Enterprise 24:113-136.
2. Seyhun N (1986) Insiders' profits, costs of trading, and market efficiency. J Financ Econ 16: 189–212.
3. Jagolinzer A (2009) SEC Rule 10b5-1 and insiders' strategic trade. Management Science55: 224–239.
4. Ravina E and Paola S (2010) What do independent directors know? Evidence from their trading. Review of Financial Studies 23: 962-1003.
5. Manove M (1989) The harm from insider trading and informed speculation. Quarterly Journal of Economics 104: 823-845.
6. Ausubel L (1990) Insider trading in a rational expectations economy. American Economic Review 80: 1022–1041.
7. Fischer P (1992) Optimal contracting and insider trading restrictions. J Finance 47: 673–694.
8. Brudney V (1979) Insiders, outsiders, and the informational advantages under the Federal Securities laws. Harvard Law Review 93: 322–376.
9. Easterbrook F (1985) Insider trading as an agency problem. In: Pratt JW, Zeckhauser RJ Principals and Agents: The Structure of Business. Harvard Business School Press, Boston, USA.
10. Glosten L (1989) Insider trading, liquidity and the role of the monopolist specialist. J Bus 62: 211–235.
11. Maug E (2002) Insider trading legislation and corporate governance. European Economic Review 46: 1569-1597.
12. Cox James D (1986) Insider Trading and Contracting: A Critical Response to the Chicago School. Duke Law Journal.
13. Georgakopoulos NL (1993) Insider Trading as a Transactional Cost: A Market Microstructure Justification and Optimization of Insider Trading regulation. 26 Conn L Rev 1.
14. Kraakman R (1991) The Legal Theory of Insider Trading Regulation in the United States. In: Hopt, Klaus J. and Eddy Wymeersch, eds. European Insider dealing. London: Butterworths.
15. Carlton DW, Fischel DR (1983) The regulation of insider trading. Stanford Law Review 35: 857–895.
16. Dye RA (1984) Insider trading and incentives. J Bus 57: 295–313.
17. Manne HG (1966) Insider Trading and the Stock Market. Book Review, New York: Free Press, USA.
18. Beny LN (2005) Do Insider Trading Laws Matter? Some Preliminary Comparative Evidence. American Law & Economics Review7: 144-183.

19. Beny LN (2007) Insider Trading Laws and Stock Markets around the World: An Empirical Contribution to the Theoretical Law and Economics Debate. Journal of Corporation Law32: 237-300.

20. Durnev A, Kim E (2005) To Steal or Not to Steal: Firm Attributes, Legal Environment, and Valuation. J Finance 60: 1461–1493.

21. Bhattacharya U, Daouk H (2002) The World Price of Insider Trading. J Finance57:75-108.

22. Fidrmuca PJ, Adriana K, , Piotr K (2013) Why does shareholder protection matter for abnormal returns after reported insider purchases and sales? Journal of Banking & Finance 37: 1915–1935.

23. KasparDardas (2012) Identifying Profitable Insider Transactions. The Journal of Investing 21: 61-75.

24. Aggarwal R, Erel I, Stulz R, Williamson R (2008) Differences in Governance Practices between U.S. and Foreign Firms: Measurement, Causes, and Consequences. The Review of Financial Studies 22: 3131-3169.

25. Bruno V, Claessens S (2010) Corporate governance and regulation: Can there be too much of a good thing? Journal of Financial Intermediation, 19: 461–482.

26. Chhaochharia V, Laeven L (2009) Corporate governance norms and practices. J FinancIntermed 18: 405-431.

27. Levine R (2005) Finance and growth: theory and evidence. Handbook of Economic Growth 1:865–934.

28. Shleifer A, Vishny R (1997) A Survey of Corporate Governance. J Finance 52: 737–783.

29. Becht M, Bolton P, Roéll A (2003) Corporate Governance and Control. Handbook of the Economics of Finance. Amsterdam, Netherlands.

30. Brown P, Beekes W, Verhoeven P (2011) Corporate governance, accounting and finance: A review. Accounting and Finance 51: 96–172.

31. La Porta R, Lopez de S (1999) Corporate Ownership Around the World. J Finance 54: 471–517.

32. La Porta R, Lope -de-Silanes F, Shleifer A, Vishny RW (1998) Law and finance. J Polit Econ 106: 1113-1155.

33. Bebchuk LA, Cohen A (2005) The Costs of Entrenched Boards. J Financ Econ 78: 409-33.

34. Bebchuk LA, Cohen A, Ferrell A (2009) What matters in corporate governance? Review of Financial Studies 22: 783-827.

35. Brown LD, Caylor ML (2006) Corporate Governance and Firm Valuation. Journal of Accounting and Public Policy 25: 409–434.

36. Chhaochharia V, Grinstein Y (2007) Corporate governance and firm value: The impact of the 2002 governance rules. J Finance 62: 1789–1825.

37. Core J, Guay W, Rusticus T (2006) Does weak governance cause weak stock returns? An examination of firm operating performance and investors' expectations. J Finance 61: 655–687.

38. Dittmar A, Mahrt-Smith J (2007) Corporate governance and the value of cash holdings. J Financ Econ 83: 599–634.

39. Doidge C, Karolyi A, Stulz R (2007) Why Do Countries Matter so Much for Corporate Governance? J Financ Econ 86: 1-3.

40. Francis J, Khurana I, Pereira R (2005) Disclosure Incentives and Effects on Cost of Capital around the World. Accounting Review 80: 1125–1162.

41. Gompers P, Ishii J, Metrick A (2003) Corporate Governance and Equity Prices. Quarterly Journal of Economics 118: 107–55.

42. Hope OK (2003) Disclosure practices, enforcement of accounting standards, and analysts' forecast accuracy: An international study. J Accounting Res 41: 235-272.

43. Lang M, Lins K, Miller D (2004) Concentrated control, Analyst Following, and Valuation: Do Analysts Matter Most When Investors Are Protected Least? J Account Res 42: 589-623.

44. Barniv R, Myring M, Thomas W (2005) The Association between the Legal and Financial Reporting Environments and Forecast Performance of Individual Analysts. Contemporary Accounting Research 22: 727-758.

45. Chang J, Khanna T, Palepu K (2000) Analyst Activity around the World. HBS Unit, working paper.

46. C von Koch, Nilsson O, Eriksson K (2013) Does shareholder protection affect the performance of analysts as a gatekeeper? Journal of Management & Governance.

47. Beekes W, Brown P (2006) Do better-governed Australian firms make more informative disclosures? J Bus Financ Account 33: 422–450.

48. Heflin F, Subramanyam K, Zhang Y (2003) Regulation FD and the financial information environment: Early evidence. The Accounting Review 78:1-37.

49. Irani A, Karamanou I (2003) Regulation Fair Disclosure, analyst following, and analyst forecast dispersion. Accounting Horizons 17: 15-29.

50. Viral VA, Stewart CM, Raghuram R(2008)The Internal Governance of Firms, Journal of Finance, American Finance Association 66: 689-720.

51. Leland HE (1992) Insider trading: should it be prohibited? J Polit Econ 110: 859–887.

52. Bebchuk LA, Fried JM (2003) Executive compensation as an agency problem. J Econ Perspect 17: 71–92.

53. Piotroski JD, Roulstone DT (2004) The influence of analysts, institutional investors, and insiders on the incorporation of market, industry, and firm specific information into stock prices. Accounting Review 79: 1119–1151.

Using Historical Financial Statements to Separate Winning from Losing Value Stocks in Canada: Interlisted Vs. Non-Interlisted Stocks

George Athanassakos*

Ben Graham Chair in Value Investing, Richard Ivey School of Business,The University of Western Ontario, London, Ontario, Canada N6A 3K7.

Abstract

The purpose of this paper is two-fold. First, to determine whether there is value premium in our sample of Canadian non-interlisted and interlisted stocks for the period May 1, 1985-April 30, 2010. Second, to examine whether an additional screening to the first step of the value investing process can be employed to separate the good value stocks from the bad ones. For both non-interlisted and interlisted stocks, we document a consistently strong value premium over the sample period, which persists in both bull and bear markets, as well as in recessions and recoveries for non-interlisted stocks, but less so for interlisted stocks. We show that the value premium is not driven by a few outliers, but it is pervasive. Interlisted stocks have a higher value premium than non-interlisted stocks. The other difference between interlisted and non-interlisted firms is with regards to stock liquidity, debt to equity and market cap metrics, as well as to the fact that a typical size effect does not exist for interlisted stocks. We are able to construct a composite score indicator (SCORE), combining various fundamental and market metrics, which enables us to predict future stock returns and separate the winners from the losers among value stocks. Results are stronger for interlisted than non-interlisted stocks. It is not clear, however, whether the SCORE indicator performance is linked to risk as evidence is inconclusive.

Keywords: Financial Statement Analysis; Value; Growth; Price-to-Earnings; Risk; Mispricing

JEL Classification: G12, G14, M41.

Introduction

Value investors tend to prefer to invest in stocks that have low P/E or P/B ratio, while at the same time avoid stocks with high P/E or P/B values. Because of this, academics call the low P/E or P/B stocks value stocks and the high P/E or P/B stocks growth stocks. Thus defined value stocks (namely, low P/E or P/B stocks) outperform growth stocks (namely, high P/E or high P/B stocks). The so called "value premium" is documented around the globe [1-10].

However, there is more to being a value investor than just sorting stocks by P/E or P/B and investing in the low P/E or low P/B stocks. While it is true that value investors tend to prefer to invest in stocks that have low P/E or P/B, not all low P/E or P/B stocks are truly undervalued. Some low P/E or P/B stocks deserve to have low P/E or P/B values because they are bad stocks. In fact, on average, 40% of all value stocks in our sample had a negative return in the year following the sorting into value. That is why value investors proceed to value individually each stock to determine its intrinsic value and then arrive at their investment decision using the concept of the "margin of safety". This way they can separate the good from the bad value stocks. But this is a very time consuming exercise [11]. The question is: Can we apply an additional screening to the low P/E or P/B approach that can separate the good value stocks from the bad ones without having to go through the time consuming valuation exercise? And can we base this additional screening of value stocks on company historical financial statements and market related information?

Consequently, the purpose of this paper is two-fold. First, to determine whether there is a value premium in our sample of Canadian stocks for the period May 1, 1985-April 30, 2010. Second, to examine whether an additional screening to the low P/E value investing process can be employed to separate the good value stocks from the bad ones. In this regard, we will test not only whether this extra screening better predicts future stock returns by selecting the value stocks with superior performance, and avoiding those with inferior performance, but also whether it is extra risk that drives such outperformance.

Previous studies examining these questions have used P/B ratios to form value portfolios. For example, Piotrioski [12] measures a firm's investment attractiveness using a composite score of individual firm fundamental ratios of past performance, such as profitability, liquidity, capital structure and operating efficiency. He finds that among the low P/B (value) stocks those with the high composite score tend to outperform those with a low score. Mohanram [13], on the other hand, designs a composite score from fundamental signals that can differentiate winning from losing high P/B (growth) stocks. Bird [14] use a model of 23 accounting variables to measure financial strength and they show that their fundamental analysis can differentiate good from bad value stocks.

We will use P/E ratios as this is another key screening metric that value investors, and investors in general, use to isolate value stocks and in doing so we will carry out an out of sample test of the earlier findings. Additionally, we will use a different set of variables and make the separation of good from bad value stocks more intuitive and user friendly than previous studies. We will examine the Canadian markets as previous research focused on the US markets. There are many differences between the two markets to justify a separate examination of the Canadian market. For example, the Canadian stock market is

***Corresponding author:** George Athanassakos, Ben Graham Chair in Value Investing, Richard Ivey School of Business, The University of Western Ontario, London, Ontario, Canada N6A 3K7
E-mail: gathanassakos@ivey.uwo.ca

more regulated and includes less growth oriented sectors. In addition, the Toronto Stock Exchange (TSX) is dominated by resource, gold and energy stocks, which make up close to 50% of the exchange making the TSX less diversified and more exposed to the business cycle than the US market.

We will separate interlisted from non-interlisted Canadian stocks.[1] The reasons for this are the following. First, interlisted stocks tend to be larger, more glamorous and well known than non-interlisted stocks and are followed by more analysts [15], and we wish to keep our sample as homogeneous as possible. We would like to examine whether a value premium exists among non-glamorous and relatively smaller cap stocks as well as among glamorous and larger stocks. Second, there is evidence that the marginal trader for Canadian interlisted stocks is an American investor [16]. We wish to keep separate the stocks that are most likely to be traded by Canadians from those that are not. This will help us answer the following questions: (a) is a value premium observed in Canada because the marginal trader is the US investor and (b) is the value premium a purely US phenomenon or not. Finally, extant Canadian studies [9] have examined all Canadian stocks, interlisted and not, and they find a significant value premium in Canada. But the question is, if we separate the interlisted from the non-interlisted stocks, is the value premium in Canada driven primarily by one or the other group of stocks or is equally driven by both?

First, we will examine whether a value premium exists in our sample of Canadian interlisted and non-interlisted stocks, and then, whether the return of interlisted and non-interlisted value stocks, as defined by academics, can be improved upon by further screening these value stocks using company historical financial statement fundamental information and market metrics.

For both non-interlisted and interlisted stocks, we document a consistently strong value premium over the May 1, 1985-April 30, 2010 sample period, which persists in both bull and bear markets, as well as in recessions and recoveries for non-interlisted stocks, but less so for interlisted stocks. We show that the value premium is not driven by a few outliers, but it is pervasive as the overwhelming majority of stocks in the value portfolio have positive returns, and all business risk categories in our sample, on average, have positive value premiums. The value premium remains positive and statistically significant over time. Our results are consistent with those of other Canadian and US studies [9,10]. We can conclude from this that the value premium is not a purely US phenomenon and that the observed value premium in Canada is not only due to interlisted stocks, even though interlisted stocks have a higher value premium than non-interlisted stocks.

In terms of the attributes of non-interlisted and interlisted stocks, the evidence in this paper shows that, in general, non-interlisted and interlisted stocks have similar company fundamentals and market metrics. The area where there is a difference is with regards to stock liquidity, debt to equity and market cap metrics, as well as to the fact that a typical size effect does not exist for interlisted stocks. Interlisted firms are more liquid, larger and have more debt to equity ratio than non-interlisted firms. At the same time, larger cap interlisted stocks have higher returns than lower cap interlisted firms.

Finally, we construct a composite score indicator (SCORE), combining various fundamental and market metrics, which enables us to predict future stock returns and separate the winners from the losers among value stocks. Results are stronger for interlisted than non-interlisted stocks. It is not clear, however, whether the SCORE indicator performance is linked to risk as evidence is inconclusive.

The rest of the paper is structured as follows. Section 2 examines whether a value premium exists in our sample of Canadian interlisted and non-interlisted stocks, and presents the findings. Section 3 examines whether the return of interlisted and non-interlisted value stocks, as defined by academics, can be improved by further screening these value stocks using company historical financial statement fundamental information and market metrics and presents the findings. In this section, a composite score indicator is constructed and the indicator's performance, as well as its possible association to risk are tested. Each of the above two sections will also develop the research questions and discuss the data sources, sample selection and methodology. Section 4 concludes the paper and discusses the implications of findings and future research directions.

Is There a Value Premium in our Sample of Canadian Interlisted and Non-interlisted Stocks?

Research Question and Formation of Expectations

Value stocks should outperform growth stocks-the value premium: Based on previous research in Canada and around the globe [1-10], low P/E (value) stocks in our sample of interlisted and non-interlisted stocks should have higher return than corresponding growth stocks.

Data and methodology: Our sample includes all Canadian Interlisted and non-interlisted companies that traded on Canadian Stock Exchanges for the period 1984-2010. The reasons why we treat separately interlisted from non-interlisted stocks were detailed in the previous section.

The data are from COMPUSTAT from which earnings per share (E), stock prices and dividends paid are obtained, and from which trailing price to earnings (P/E), total returns are derived.[2] For the trailing P/E ratios, the price (P) is as of the end of April of year (t) and E is the fully diluted annual earnings per share for companies with fiscal year end in year (t-1), as reported in COMPUSTAT.[3] Annual (forward) total stock returns are calculated as the price change plus the dividend from May 1 of year (t) to April 30 of year (t+1) over the price in May 1 of year (t).

Industry coding is also from COMPUSTAT. We have grouped interlisted and non-interlisted companies into business risk categories based on the results reported in Athanassakos (1998). They are follows: Food and Staples retailing (GICS 3010), Media (GICS 2540), Utilities (GICS 5510), Retailing (GICS 2550), Telecommunications Services (GICS 5010), Health care Equipment and Services (GICS 3510) are classified as low business risk industries; Household & Personal Products (GICS 3030), Commercial Services & Supplies (GICS 2020), Consumer Services (GICS 2530), Consumer Durables & Apparel (GICS 2520), Banks (GICS 4010), Diversified Financials (GICS 4020), Insurance (GICS 4030) Capital Goods (GICS 2010) and Energy (GICS 1010) as medium business risk industries; and Software & Services (GICS 4510), Semiconductors & Semiconductor Equipment (GICS 4530), Transportation (GICS 2030), Automobiles & Components (GICS 2510), Real Estate/Construction (GICS 4040), Food Beverages and Tobacco (GICS 3020), Materials (GICS 1510) and Pharmaceuticals,

[1]The Toronto Stock Exchange refers to cross-listed stocks as interlisted.

[2]There is no survivorship bias in the COMPUSTAT data employed in this paper as dead/merged companies are included in our sample.

[3]All firms in our sample have reported financials for fiscal year (t-1) by April of year (t).

Biotechnology & Life Sciences Capital Goods (GICS 3520) as high business risk industries.[4]

To prevent problems arising from including negative P/E ratio firms, and eliminate likely data errors [17-19], we have excluded negative P/E ratio firms as well as firms with a P/E ratio that exceeds 500 times. Finally, to be included in our sample a stock had to have a price over $1 and to have reported financials in COMPUSTAT.

At the end of April of every year (t), starting in 1985, firms are ranked based on trailing P/E ratios from low to high and the ranked firms are divided into four groups of equal size. Quartile-1 (Q1) is the lowest P/E ratio portfolio or the value stocks, while Quartile-4 (Q4) is the highest P/E ratio portfolio or the growth stocks. This process is repeated for each year of our sample.

For each stock within each quartile, total returns are calculated for the following year (i.e., May year (t) to April year (t+1)) and equally weighted mean (and median) returns for each quartile are derived [3, 7, 17].

Non-overlapping forward annual stock returns, which are adjusted for stock splits and stock dividends, are thus obtained over the period May 1, 1985-April 30, 2010. After all aforementioned screenings, we end up with 7,981 cross sectional-time series (firm-year) observations belonging to a cumulative number of 1,262 unique companies. From those, 1043 unique companies (6479 firm-year observations) belong to the interlisted sub-sample and 219 to the non-interlisted (1502 firm-year observations) sub-sample.

Variable	Mean	Median	Minimum	Maximum
P/E	27.8343	15.72	0.06	487.5
RETURN	0.116	0.06	-0.96	2
CASH	0.060831	0.01	0	0.94
MARGIN	0.17785	0.12	-1.65	1.27
TURNOVER (x)	0.98229	0.76	-0.09	6.96
LIQUID	0.33849	0.1884	0	8.838
CURRENT (x)	2.69999	1.6	0	169.35
SIZE (CAD$ mil)	813.9	178.3	0.5	38614.5
DEBT	0.66599	0.38	0	9.56
REVG	0.43768	0.11	-3.91	180.13
EBITG	0.27370	0.11	-98.57	160.17

Panel 1: Total Sample/Non-Interlisted.

Variable	Mean	Median	Minimum	Maximum
P/E	35.5157	19.615	1.1	496.9
RETURN	0.14764	0.1	-0.92	1.22
CASH	0.094462	0.04	0	1.96
MARGIN	0.17442	0.15	-0.87	0.74
TURNOVER (x)	0.66644	0.5	0	0.95
LIQUID	0.77492	0.264	0	11.5968
CURRENT (x)	2.59487	1.665	0.13	62.81
SIZE (CAD$ mil)	6529.5	1995.4	21.7	86025.3
DEBT	1	0.44	0	8.7
REVG	0.80169	0.13	-0.98	70.34
EBITG	0.43512	0.11	-47.66	183.53

Panel 2: Total Sample/Interlisted.

Table 1: Descriptive Statistics

The table reports summary information for 6,479 firm-year observations of 1,043 non-interlisted firms that are only listed in Canada and 1502 firm-year observations of 219 interlisted in Canadian and US markets firms. All data are from COMPUSTAT and are available from 1984-2010. P/E is price as at April of year (t) over earnings as fiscal year end (t-1). RETURN is the annual return for the year following the sorting into portfolios by P/E. CASH is cash over revenues. MARGIN is EBIT over Revenues. TURNOVER is revenues over assets (times). EXTRA is the occurrence of reporting extraordinary charges and restarting historical financials in year (t-1) (yes=1, no=0). LIQUID is trading volume for the year prior to May of year (t) over shares outstanding as at April of year (t). CURRENT is the ratio of cash plus short term investments and accounts receivable to current liabilities (times). SIZE is market cap in millions of Canadian dollars determined by multiplying shares outstanding by price per share as at April of year (t). DEBT is short and long term debt to equity. REVG and EBITG are the annual growth rates of revenues, and EBIT, respectively for the fiscal year (t-1).

Empirical results

Summary statistics: Table 1, Panels 1, 2 report the summary statistics of key variables for the non-interlisted and interlisted firms included in our sample. We observe that interlisted stocks have higher P/E and higher overall returns than non-interlisted stocks over the sample period. Consistent with previous research, there are valuation benefits arising to a firm from interlisting.

The value and growth stocks returns over time and at different states of the world: Tables 2.1 and 2.2 report, respectively, the mean and median annual non-interlisted stock returns of P/E sorted quartiles and the value premium (Q1 minus Q4) per year, sub-period and total sample. Tables 3.1 and 3.2 report corresponding figures for interlisted stocks.

Overall, the mean annual value premium is 6.7% and the median 8%. The value premium is economically and statistically significant at traditional levels of significance for the total sample using both mean and median tests. For interlisted stocks, the mean and median annual value premiums are 10.8% and 10%, respectively.

Tables 2 and 3 also report the value premium for two sub-periods (May 1, 1985-April 30, 1997 and May 1, 1997-April 30, 2010). There are significantly positive mean and median value premiums in both sub-periods. The hypothesis that the mean and median value premiums are equal across sub-periods is rejected at traditional levels of significance. The value premium has increased significantly over time for the stocks in our sample.

Looking at the value premium per year in Tables 2 and 3, one can see that the non-interlisted stock value premium is positive irrespective of whether there is a bull market or bear market or there is a recession or recovery.[5] These findings are consistent with Kwag, Chan and Athanassakos [20, 8-10]. However, for interlisted stocks, we see that the mean value premium is mostly negative in bad economic states of the world, while the median is negative only half of the time in bad economic states over the past 25 years. Had we grouped all stocks in our sample together, we would have missed this differentiating finding, as the non-interlisted sample would have dominated that of the interlisted stocks.

Value and growth stocks returns across business risk categories: Tables 4.1 and 4.2 examine whether the documented value premium is driven only by a specific business risk category stocks or not. They report the mean and median annual value and growth stock returns per business risk category within which the companies in our sample belong for non-interlisted and interlisted stocks, respectively. Value

[4]The Global Industry Classification Standard (GICS) is collaboration between Standard & Poor's and Morgan Stanley Capital International. GICS is based upon a classification of economic sectors, which can be further sub-divided into a number of industry groups, industries and sub-industries" (COMPUSTAT (Global) Data). The four digit identification code used in this paper focuses on the 23 industry groups of the GICS system.

[5]The timing of recessions/recoveries and bear/bull markets is obtained from www.thedowtheory.com/ bear&recessions.htm. The timing of recessions from this database is consistent with NBER's business cycle dates. However, this database also makes available dates for bull and bear markets. The following years were flagged as bear market years: 1987, 1990, 2000, 2002 and 2008/09. The following years were flagged as recession years: 1990, 2001 and 2008.

Year	P/E Ratio Stored Quartiles			Total	Value Premium	
	Q1(Value)	Q2 & Q3	Q4(Growth)		Q1-Q4	
1985	0.28250	-0.02667	-0.07308	-0.00857	0.3556	
1986	0.36357	0.30267	0.34250	0.34000	0.0211	
1987	0.00800	-0.02389	-0.04357	-0.02703	0.0516	
1988	0.09000	0.10950	-0.08750	0.03024	0.1775	
1989	-0.05000	-0.05474	-0.07071	-0.05974	0.0207	
1990	-0.03200	0.17500	-0.01695	0.07694	-0.0151	
1991	0.03667	-0.03647	0.01000	-0.01219	0.0267	
1992	0.08400	-0.02231	0.29000	0.08640	-0.2060	
1993	0.26000	0.09158	0.11286	0.13182	0.1471	
1994	-0.00500	0.09889	-0.02750	0.03474	0.0225	
1995	0.13400	0.22905	0.39900	0.29261	-0.2650	
1996	0.07818	0.18550	-0.15143	0.02673	0.2296	
1997	0.30714	0.27629	0.20722	0.25917	0.0999	
1998	-0.23900	-0.15028	-0.13563	-0.16081	-0.1034	
1999	0.09889	0.05545	0.14700	0.09129	-0.0481	
2000	-0.06429	0.21400	-0.01947	0.11727	-0.0448	
2001	0.27875	0.16290	0.10600	0.15932	0.1728	
2002	0.02623	-0.05397	-0.11328	-0.04883	0.1395	
2003	0.40328	0.35462	0.38661	0.37352	0.0167	
2004	0.28191	0.23862	0.23673	0.24922	0.0452	
2005	0.38356	0.32774	0.32377	0.33867	0.0598	
2006	0.14234	0.09895	0.04111	0.09797	0.1012	
2007	-0.06309	-0.07236	-0.06247	-0.06792	-0.0006	
2008	-0.36270	-0.33436	-0.37672	-0.34987	0.0140	
2009	0.81426	0.38805	0.46239	0.49422	0.3519	Q1≠Q4 P-values
1985-2009	0.14219	0.1192	0.0757	0.1160	0.0665	0.0002
1985-1997	0.14849	0.1421	0.1152	0.1384	0.0333	0.0515
1998-2009	0.13699	0.1031	0.0484	0.0997	0.0886	0.0005

Table 2.1: Mean Annual Stock Returns to P/E Ratio (April, Trailing) Based Value and Growth Strategies by Year, Sub-period and State of the World: Non-Interlisted.

This Table reports mean annual returns of value, growth, other and total sample stocks for the period May 1, 1985-April 30, 2010. It also reports the percentage of value and growth stock returns within value and growth portfolios that had negative returns. Every year, starting in April 30, 1985, firms are ranked based on P/E ratios from low to high and the ranked firms are divided into four groups of equal size. Returns are then obtained for the following year starting in May 1, 1985. This Table reports the mean subsequent annual returns of prior April P/E sorted quartiles (from lowest (Q1) to highest (Q4)), respectively and the value premium (Q1-Q4) per year, sub-period (1985-1997 and 1998-2009) and total sample (1985-2009). P-values for the mean tests are based on the t-statistic for testing the null hypothesis that the mean returns of the value and growth strategies are equal. Return stands for the annual subsequent year returns of the sample stocks. P/E stands for the ratio of the price per share at the end of a given April divided by trailing earnings per share as at the end of fiscal year of the year before. Annual stock returns, price per share, and trailing EPS are from COMPUSTAT. The table reports summary information for 6,479 firm-year observations of 1,043 non-interlisted firms that are only listed in Canada.

beats growth for all business risk categories for both interlisted and non-interlisted stocks. Moreover, the value premium is pervasive as all business risk classes have a positive and statistically significant value premium.

Can the Return of Interlisted and Non-interlisted Value Stocks be Improved upon by Screening Stocks using Company Historical Financial Statement Fundamental Information and Market Metrics?

Research questions and formation of expectations

Stock price performance in relation to company historical financial statements and market related information-setting the basis for the composite indicator: On average, about 40% of the interlisted and non-interlisted value stocks in our sample had a negative return in the year following the sorting into value. As a result, there is no guarantee that choosing randomly stocks from a low P/E group will guarantee an investor a positive return. Can we then devise a further screening that will enable an investor to zero in on the positive return low P/E stocks and avoid investing in those stocks with negative returns? As per Athanassakos [21], we choose a number of company fundamental and market metrics to relate to a stock's performance and set the basis for constructing the composite indicator. They are: stock liquidity, firm size (market cap) and measures of profitability, efficiency and financial leverage/liquidity.

Stock liquidity: Prior research [22] has shown that low liquidity stocks are avoided by institutional investors who have too much money to invest in and low liquidity stocks do not provide enough depth to make investing worthwhile. In fact, many institutional investors are prevented from owning shares in less liquid and obscure stocks. Because of this, the stock of such companies may be undervalued. As a result, we would expect low liquidity stocks to outperform high liquidity stocks.

Many proxies for liquidity have been used in the literature. We will proxy stock liquidity with the ratio of trading volume (for the year prior to May of year (t)) to shares outstanding as at April of year (t) [23].

Firm size: Many institutional investors tend to avoid small stocks as they have too much money to manage and small cap stocks cannot absorb enough flow [22]. Moreover, smaller cap companies tend to be followed by fewer analysts [24]. Hence, smaller cap companies, followed by fewer analysts and owned by a smaller number of institutions, tend to be less in the public eye than larger companies. This leads to the possible underpricing of small stocks vis-à-vis larger stocks.

Year	P/E Ratio Stored Quartiles			Total	Value Premium	
	Q1(Value)	Q2 & Q3	Q4(Growth)		Q1-Q4	
1985	0.28250	-0.02667	-0.07308	-0.00857	0.3556	
1986	0.36357	0.30267	0.34250	0.34000	0.0211	
1987	0.00800	-0.02389	-0.04357	-0.02703	0.0516	
1988	0.09000	0.10950	-0.08750	0.03024	0.1775	
1989	-0.05000	-0.05474	-0.07071	-0.05974	0.0207	
1990	-0.03200	0.17500	-0.01695	0.07694	-0.0151	
1991	0.03667	-0.03647	0.01000	-0.01219	0.0267	
1992	0.08400	-0.02231	0.29000	0.08640	-0.2060	
1993	0.26000	0.09158	0.11286	0.13182	0.1471	
1994	-0.00500	0.09889	-0.02750	0.03474	0.0225	
1995	0.13400	0.22905	0.39900	0.29261	-0.2650	
1996	0.07818	0.18550	-0.15143	0.02673	0.2296	
1997	0.30714	0.27629	0.20722	0.25917	0.0999	
1998	-0.23900	-0.15028	-0.13563	-0.16081	-0.1034	
1999	0.09889	0.05545	0.14700	0.09129	-0.0481	
2000	-0.06429	0.21400	-0.01947	0.11727	-0.0448	
2001	0.27875	0.16290	0.10600	0.15932	0.1728	
2002	0.00333	-0.00914	-0.03833	-0.01678	0.0417	
2003	0.79300	0.37097	0.44423	0.46239	0.3488	
2004	0.40000	0.29410	0.13261	0.26474	0.2674	
2005	0.75167	0.49417	0.50167	0.53551	0.2500	
2006	0.35750	0.10405	0.10579	0.13391	0.2517	
2007	0.00091	0.10905	0.06591	0.08053	-0.0650	
2008	-0.42375	-0.44000	-0.38909	-0.42333	-0.0347	
2009	0.76714	0.76515	0.54864	0.69652	0.2185	Q1≠Q4 P-values
1985-2009	0.22894	0.1410	0.1210	0.1476	0.1079	0.0105
1985-1997	0.15136	0.1145	0.1059	0.1172	0.0455	0.0823
1998-2009	0.28265	0.1556	0.1324	0.1668	0.1503	0.0050

Table 2.2: Mean Annual Stock Returns to P/E Ratio (April, Trailing) Based Value and Growth Strategies by Year, Sub-period and State of the World: Interlisted.

This Table reports mean annual returns of value, growth, other and total sample stocks for the period May 1, 1985-April 30, 2010. It also reports the percentage of value and growth stock returns within value and growth portfolios that had negative returns. Every year, starting in April 30, 1985, firms are ranked based on P/E ratios from low to high and the ranked firms are divided into four groups of equal size. Returns are then obtained for the following year starting in May 1, 1985. This Table reports the mean subsequent annual returns of prior April P/E sorted quartiles (from lowest (Q1) to highest (Q4)), respectively and the value premium (Q1-Q4) per year, sub-period (1985-1997 and 1998-2009) and total sample (1985-2009). P-values for the mean tests are based on the t-statistic for testing the null hypothesis that the mean returns of the value and growth strategies are equal. Return stands for the annual subsequent year returns of the sample stocks. P/E stands for the ratio of the price per share at the end of a given April divided by trailing earnings per share as at the end of fiscal year of the year before. Annual stock returns, price per share, and trailing EPS are from COMPUSTAT. The table reports summary information for 1502 firm-year observations of 219 interlisted in Canadian and US markets firms.

Year	P/E Ratio Stored Quartiles			Total	Value Premium	
	Q1(Value)	Q2 & Q3	Q4(Growth)		Q1-Q4	
1985	0.280	0.350	0.070	0.320	0.2100	
1986	0.235	0.055	0.120	0.100	0.1150	
1987	-0.100	-0.090	-0.160	-0.110	0.0600	
1988	0.120	0.100	-0.060	0.090	0.1800	
1989	-0.070	0.000	-0.060	-0.020	-0.0100	
1990	0.060	0.090	-0.025	0.060	0.0850	
1991	0.040	0.020	-0.060	0.005	0.1000	
1992	0.110	0.070	0.270	0.100	-0.1600	
1993	0.190	0.070	0.135	0.140	0.0550	
1994	-0.005	-0.060	-0.030	-0.040	0.0250	
1995	0.150	0.120	0.130	0.125	0.0200	
1996	0.240	0.265	0.235	0.250	0.0050	
1997	0.290	0.295	0.145	0.260	0.1450	
1998	-0.115	-0.135	-0.260	-0.160	0.1450	
1999	0.010	-0.080	-0.005	-0.050	0.0150	
2000	0.000	0.215	0.000	0.140	0.0000	
2001	0.115	0.220	0.025	0.150	0.1300	
2002	0.000	-0.020	-0.120	-0.060	0.1200	
2003	0.265	0.300	0.250	0.280	0.0150	
2004	0.230	0.160	0.210	0.185	0.0200	
2005	0.190	0.230	0.240	0.230	-0.0500	
2006	0.070	0.070	-0.070	0.050	0.1400	
2007	-0.070	-0.080	-0.130	-0.090	0.0600	
2008	-0.375	-0.320	-0.425	-0.350	0.0500	
2009	0.740	0.360	0.435	0.440	0.3050	Q1≠Q4 P-values
1985-2009	0.0800	0.0700	0.0000	0.0600	0.0800	0.0001
1985-1997	0.1050	0.0800	0.0400	0.0800	0.0650	0.0078
1998-2009	0.0600	0.0600	-0.0300	0.0400	0.0900	0.0006

Table 3.1: Median Annual Stock Returns to P/E Ratio (April, Trailing) Based Value and Growth Strategies by Year, Sub-period and State of the World: Non-Interlisted.

This Table reports median annual returns of value, growth, other and total sample stocks for the period May 1, 1985-April 30, 2010. Every year, starting in April 30, 1985, firms are ranked based on P/E ratios from low to high and the ranked firms are divided into four groups of equal size. Returns are then obtained for the following year starting in May 1, 1985. This Table reports the median subsequent annual returns of prior April P/E sorted quartiles (from lowest (Q1) to highest (Q4)), respectively and the value premium (Q1-Q4) per year, sub-period (1985-1997 and 1998-2009) and total sample (1985-2009). P-values for the median tests are based on (the Brown-Mood) $\chi 2$ tests for testing the null hypothesis that the median returns of the value and growth strategies are equal. Return stands for the annual subsequent year returns of the sample stocks. P/E stands for the ratio of the price per share at the end of a given April divided by trailing earnings per share as at the end of fiscal year of the year before. Annual stock returns, price per share, and trailing EPS are from COMPUSTAT. The table reports summary information for 6,479 firm-year observations of 1,043 non-interlisted firms that are only listed in Canada.

As a result, we would expect smaller cap stocks to outperform larger cap stocks. Market cap is derived by multiplying price per share by shares outstanding at the end of April of year (t).

Profitability: Firm profitability at all levels of the income statement gives an investor confidence about the company's ability to generate not only current profits and growth, but also profitability and growth in the future, too. Piotroski [12] finds that value firms have poor historical earnings growth performance. It is possible that stocks with poor historical profitability growth performance may prompt investors to become overly pessimistic about the future profitability of such stocks leading to underpricing and better future stock performance. As a result, in this case, we should expect stocks with poor historical profitability growth to outperform those with better historical profitability growth.

We measure profitability growth characteristics by the year over year (i.e., year (t-2) to year (t-1)) annual EBIT and revenue growth rates.

Efficiency: A firm that manages well its balance sheet and income statement is said to be efficient. To measure how efficiently a firm manages its balance sheet, we will use asset turnover (Revenues/Assets). To measure how efficiently a company manages its income statement, we will use operating margin (EBIT/Revenues). Asset turnover along with operating margin are the two components of the before tax return on invested capital (ROIC). A firm that generates an ROIC that exceeds the cost of capital creates value. These are firms that value investors tend to favor.

As a result, we would expect stocks with better efficiency measures to outperform those that are less efficient.

Leverage & liquidity: The way a firm finances its assets and its ability to meet short term obligations play a very important role in firm's ability to survive and continue to operate as a going concern. Low liquidity can also be considered as a measure of financial distress if a company cannot meet short term obligations. Value investors, in general, tend to avoid consistently overleveraged or highly risky firms. We would expect better performing firms to have lower leverage and/or higher liquidity than inferior performance firms.

We measure leverage by the total debt to equity ratio, and liquidity by the current ratio (cash plus accounts receivable plus short term investments plus inventories over current liabilities) and cash to assets.

Composite score–A further screening for value stocks: The previously discussed company fundamentals and market metrics and their relationship to stock returns set the basis for the construction of a composite indicator which will be tested to see if it is able to separate good

Year	P/E Ratio Stored Quartiles			Total	Value Premium	
	Q1(Value)	Q2 & Q3	Q4(Growth)		Q1-Q4	
1985	0.340	-0.050	-0.120	-0.050	0.4600	
1986	0.295	0.280	0.285	0.280	0.0100	
1987	0.050	-0.015	0.095	0.030	-0.0450	
1988	0.000	0.070	-0.065	0.020	0.0650	
1989	-0.035	0.010	-0.095	-0.040	0.0600	
1990	-0.100	0.105	-0.030	0.055	-0.0700	
1991	0.060	-0.080	-0.125	-0.090	0.1850	
1992	0.100	-0.030	0.340	0.090	-0.2400	
1993	0.050	0.120	-0.020	0.050	0.0700	
1994	0.000	0.040	-0.100	-0.010	0.1000	
1995	0.010	0.130	0.255	0.185	-0.2450	
1996	0.070	0.165	-0.230	0.085	0.3000	
1997	0.220	0.220	0.130	0.200	0.0900	
1998	-0.265	-0.160	-0.185	-0.190	-0.0800	
1999	-0.020	-0.050	0.115	0.000	-0.1350	
2000	0.130	0.210	0.040	0.185	0.0900	
2001	0.105	0.130	-0.065	0.100	0.1700	
2002	0.035	0.030	-0.035	0.000	0.0700	
2003	0.760	0.390	0.325	0.390	0.4350	
2004	0.370	0.270	0.170	0.270	0.2000	
2005	0.600	0.420	0.395	0.425	0.2050	
2006	0.330	0.115	0.130	0.130	0.2000	
2007	0.000	0.100	-0.080	0.050	0.0800	
2008	-0.380	-0.450	-0.430	-0.430	0.0500	
2009	0.610	0.670	0.465	0.600	0.1450	Q1≠Q4 P-values
1985-2009	0.1500	0.1100	0.0500	0.1000	0.1000	0.0100
1985-1997	0.0900	0.0800	0.0200	0.0700	0.0700	0.0624
1998-2009	0.1900	0.1300	0.0800	0.1300	0.1100	0.0236

Table 3.2: Median Annual Stock Returns to P/E Ratio (April, Trailing) Based Value and Growth Strategies by Year, Sub-period and State of the World: Interlisted.

This Table reports median annual returns of value, growth, other and total sample stocks for the period May 1, 1985-April 30, 2010. Every year, starting in April 30, 1985, firms are ranked based on P/E ratios from low to high and the ranked firms are divided into four groups of equal size. Returns are then obtained for the following year starting in May 1, 1985. This Table reports the median subsequent annual returns of prior April P/E sorted quartiles (from lowest (Q1) to highest (Q4)), respectively and the value premium (Q1-Q4) per year, sub-period (1985-1997 and 1998-2009) and total sample (1985-2009). P-values for the median tests are based on (the Brown-Mood) $\chi 2$ tests for testing the null hypothesis that the median returns of the value and growth strategies are equal. Return stands for the annual subsequent year returns of the sample stocks. P/E stands for the ratio of the price per share at the end of a given April divided by trailing earnings per share as at the end of fiscal year of the year before. Annual stock returns, price per share, and trailing EPS are from COMPUSTAT. TThe table reports summary information for 1502 firm-year observations of 219 interlisted in Canadian and US markets firms.

value stocks from bad ones [21]. The methodology and determination of the composite score indicator will be detailed and discussed later. We would expect value stocks that have better composite indicator values to out-perform those with worse composite indicator values.

Data and methodology

Our sample includes firm financials for Canadian interlisted and non-interlisted firms for the period 1984 to 2008, obtained from COMPUSTAT. Firm fundamentals are derived from firm financials and are defined as follows: CASH is cash over assets. MARGIN is EBIT over Revenues. TURNOVER is revenues over assets (times). CURRENT is the ratio of cash plus short term investments and accounts receivable to current liabilities (times). DEBT is short and long term debt to equity. REVG and EBITG are the annual growth rates of revenues and EBIT, respectively for fiscal year (t-1). Market metrics, on the other hand, are for the period 1984 to 2009 and are defined as follows: LIQUID is trading volume for the year prior to May of year (t) as a percentage of shares outstanding as at April of year (t). SIZE is market cap in millions of Canadian dollars determined by multiplying shares outstanding by price per share as at April of year (t). We also construct other variables which we will use later. They are as follows: EXTRA is a binary variable signifying the occurrence of reporting extraordinary charges and restating historical financials in year (t-1) or not (yes=1, no=0).[6] BRISK is the industry code that captures an industry's business risk (1=low business risk, 2=medium business risk and 3=high business risk). BRISK combines the industry groups from COMPUSTAT with the business risk categories from Athanassakos [25], as discussed earlier.

Non-overlapping trailing company fundamentals and market metrics are obtained for the period 1984 to 2008 and 1985 to 2009, respectively. The number of observations and unique companies are as discussed earlier. Summary statistics of variables of interest (i.e., company fundamentals and market metrics) are calculated and uni(bi) variate analysis ensues that looks at the relationship of interlisted and non-interlisted value stock returns to company fundamentals, firm size and stock liquidity. Such relationships lead to the construction of the composite score indicator which will be detailed later. The composite score indicator's ability to forecast future interlisted and non-interlisted stock returns (does the composite indicator work equally well for both groups of stocks?) and differentiate between good and bad value stocks, as well as its possible association to risk are examined.

Empirical results

Summary statistics: The descriptive data in Panel 1 of Table 1 indicate important characteristics across the non-interlisted stock sample. The median operating margin and asset turnover for the firms in our sample are 12% and 0.76, respectively. The median growth rates of revenues and EBIT have been positive over the sample period. The median firm is not overleveraged as indicated by the debt to equity ratio and it is normally a smaller cap firm as indicated by the median market cap of CDN$178.3 million. It has maintained some cash on the balance sheet and sufficient liquidity. Finally, the median firm has traded about 19% of the shares outstanding over the previous year and has had an annual stock return of 6% which is quite different from the mean return of 11.6% indicating many positive outliers in the sample. The key difference for the interlisted firms as shown in Panel 2 of table 1 is that interlisted firms are bigger, have more debt and are more liquid than the interlisted firms of our sample.

Business Risk	OBS	Value(Q1) Mean	Value(Q1) Median	OBS	Growth(Q4) Mean	Growth(Q4) Median
Low	471	0.1419	0.1	264	0.0242	-0.03
Medium	628	0.1702	0.1	660	0.1093	0.04
High	561	0.1378	0.07	557	0.0811	-0.01

Table 4.1: Mean and Median Annual Returns for Value and Growth Stocks by Business Risk Group - Non-Interlisted: May 1, 1985-April 30, 2010.
(Mean and median returns for value stocks are statistically different from the corresponding returns for growth stocks at traditional levels of significance).

Business Risk	OBS	Value(Q1) Mean	Value(Q1) Median	OBS	Growth(Q4) Mean	Growth(Q4) Median
Low	92	0.1855	0.05	30	0.0719	-0.02
Medium	140	0.2794	0.185	131	0.1108	0.06
High	138	0.1872	0.13	242	0.1332	0.045

Table 4.2: Mean and Median Annual Returns for Value and Growth Stocks by Business Risk Group - Interlisted: May 1, 1985-April 30, 2010.
(Mean and median returns for value stocks are statistically different from the corresponding returns for growth stocks at traditional levels of significance).

Relationship between fundamentals/market metrics and stock returns: In this section, we will examine the relationship of non-interlisted and interlisted value stock returns to fundamental and market metrics. To this end, we sub-divide the lowest P/E sorted quartile, independently, into two groups (above and below median) by cash/assets (CASH), current ratio (CURRENT), asset turnover (TURNOVER), operating margin (MARGIN), revenue growth rate (REVG), EBIT growth rate (EBITG), stock liquidity (LIQUID), firm-size (SIZE) and debt to equity ratio (DEBT) and examine how the non-interlisted and interlisted stocks perform as we go from the below to above median values of the above variables. Tables 5.1 and 5.2 report the mean and median annual non-interlisted and interlisted stock returns for the value stocks that have CASH, CURRENT, TURNOVER, MARGIN, REVG, EBITG, LIQUID, SIZE and DEBT below and above these variables' median values.

Efficiency measures: Above median turnover stocks beat the below median turnover stocks for non-interlisted stocks. This is not true for interlisted firms. One would have expected the opposite, unless the interlisted firms in our sample had undertaken significant new investments which lowered their asset turnover while making their operations more efficient, leading to higher returns or unless there is reversion to the mean and those firms that did extremely well in the past revert to the mean in the future. That is, it is possible that historical outperformance as far as these metrics are concerned leads to future underperformance, assuming reversion to the mean, and so it is possible that previously less efficient firms outperform in the future previously more efficient firms. At the same time, high EBIT margin firms outperform low EBIT margin firms for both non interlisted and interlisted stocks. This is as expected.

Profitability growth measures (EBIT and revenue growth rates): Below median revenue growth rate firms outperform those that are above median for both non-interlisted and interlisted firms – consistent with expectations. Below median EBIT growth rate firms, however, underperform those that are above median both for non-interlisted and interlisted stocks. Rather than reversion to the mean, we may have here a momentum effect of EBIT growth whereby good past performance leads to further good performance in the future.

Liquidity and leverage measures: Stocks with low liquidity measures outperform those with high liquidity measures. This is

[6]Good quality companies and managers tend to avoid aggressive revenue recognition, which may lead to frequent restatement of financials. A firm that restates its historical financials or frequently incurs non-recurring charges may imply that either the manager does not understand the business well or there are conflicts that affect his/her performance. Investors put less trust in firms that restate their financials frequently and/or incur non-recurring charges and consider them riskier.

	Value(Q1)	
	Mean	Median
TURNOVER		
Below Median	0.1399	0.09
Above Median	0.144	0.1
EBITG		
Below Median	**0.1295**	0.08
Above Median	**0.1552**	0.09
MARGIN		
Below Median	0.1365	**0.06**
Above Median	0.1485	**0.1**
REVG		
Below Median	**0.1513**	**0.1**
Above Median	**0.1305**	**0.06**
CURRENT		
Below Median	**0.1631**	**0.1**
Above Median	**0.114**	**0.06**
CASH		
Below Median	**0.1519**	**0.1**
Above Median	**0.1264**	**0.05**
DEBT		
Below Median	0.1458	0.09
Above Median	0.1386	0.08
LIQUID		
Below Median	**0.1603**	**0.09**
Above Median	**0.129**	**0.07**
SIZE		
Below Median	**0.1547**	**0.1**
Above Median	**0.0869**	**0.01**

Table 5.1: Mean and Median Annual Returns for Stocks with Key Financial Metrics which are Above or Below their Contemporaneous Median Values for Value Stocks– Non-Interlisted: May 1, 1985-April 30, 2010.

(Above and below median returns are statistically different from each other at traditional levels of singificance in cases wise returns are bolded).

Mean and median returns in this table are the mean and median returns of all contemporaneous results over the sample period. TURNOVER is the asset turnover (revenues/assets), EBITG is the annual growth rate of EBIT, REVG is the annual growth rate of revenues, LIQUID is stock trading liquidity (volume/shares outstanding), SIZE is firm size (price per share times shares outstanding). DEBT is short and long term debt to equity. MARGIN is EBIT/Revenues. CURRENT is the ratio of cash plus short term investments and accounts receivable to current liabilities (times). CASH is cash/assets.

consistent for both non-interlisted and interlisted stocks, but it is against our expectations. On the other hand, low leverage non-interlisted stocks outperform the high leverage stocks, as we had expected. However, this is not the case for interlisted stocks.

Stock liquidity: Stocks with below median stock liquidity beat those that have above median stock liquidity for both interlisted and non-interlisted stocks, as expected.

Firm size: As expected, non-interlisted small cap stocks beat large cap stocks. However, against expectations, this is not the case for interlisted stocks. This finding is surprising and may indicate that the size effect does not exist within large market cap stocks such as the interlisted stocks whose median market cap is 10 times that of the non-interlisted stocks. The benefit of separating interlisted from non-interlisted stocks is apparent.

Composite score indicator: To form the composite score indicator, we employ the following methodology.[7] We first obtain the contemporaneous medians for all metrics examined in Tables 5.1 and 5.2 separately for the non-interlisted and interlisted value firms in our sample. We assign binary values (0 or 1) to the sample non-interlisted firms based on where a stock's SIZE, LIQUID, EBITG, REVG, CURRENT, CASH, TURNOVER, DEBT and MARGIN lie vis-à-vis their median values. For example, in Table 5.1, we see that SIZE, LIQUID,

	Value(Q1)	
	Mean	Median
TURNOVER		
Below Median	**0.3222**	**0.23**
Above Median	**0.1824**	**0.125**
EBITG		
Below Median	**0.1546**	0.09
Above Median	**0.2896**	0.1
MARGIN		
Below Median	**0.189**	0.14
Above Median	**0.2714**	0.155
REVG		
Below Median	0.2346	0.155
Above Median	0.2227	0.13
CURRENT RATIO		
Below Median	**0.289**	**0.19**
Above Median	**0.1458**	**0.05**
CASH		
Below Median	**0.2452**	**0.16**
Above Median	**0.1915**	**0.11**
DEBT		
Below Median	**0.1575**	0.13
Above Median	**0.2922**	0.16
LIQUID		
Below Median	0.2368	0.15
Above Median	0.2243	0.145
SIZE		
Below Median	**0.1918**	**0.12**
Above Median	**0.3483**	**0.29**

Table 5.2: Mean and Median Annual Returns for Stocks with Key Financial Metrics which are Above or Below their Contemporaneous Median Values for Value Stocks – Interlisted: May 1, 1985-April 30, 2010.

(Above and below median returns are statistically different from each other at traditional levels of singificance in cases wise returns are bolded).

Mean and median returns in this table are the mean and median returns of all contemporaneous results over the sample period. TURNOVER is the asset turnover (revenues/assets), EBITG is the annual growth rate of EBIT, REVG is the annual growth rate of revenues, LIQUID is stock trading liquidity (volume/shares outstanding), SIZE is firm size (price per share times shares outstanding). DEBT is short and long term debt to equity. MARGIN is EBIT/Revenues. CURRENT is the ratio of cash plus short term investments and accounts receivable to current liabilities (times). CASH is cash/assets.

SCORE	OBS	Value(Q1)	
		Mean	Median
Low	61	0.1613	0.17
1	608	0.1275	0.07
2	129	0.2107	0.14
3	83	0.25	0.2
4	67	0.0828	0
5	59	0.1769	0.12
6	77	0.1913	0.16
7	78	0.1518	0.1
8	213	0.1282	0.04
High	285	0.0094	-0.035
P-values [SCOREs (0-3) ≠ SCORES (6-9)]:		0.002	0.001

Table 6.1: Mean and Median Annual Returns of Stocks Based on the Composite Score for Value and Total Sample Stocks-Non-Interlisted: May 1, 1985-April 30, 2010.

SCORE is a composite indicator of a number of fundamental and market firm characteristics.

SCORE	OBS	Value(Q1)	
		Mean	Median
Low	8	0.3032	0.22
1	14	0.45	0.31
2	17	0.4156	0.29
3	20	0.2953	0.11
4	80	0.3098	0.21
5	60	0.1395	0.05
6	117	0.1817	0.13
7	22	0.1742	0.1
8	20	0.03	0.16
High	12	0.01	-0.015
P-values [SCOREs (0-3) ≠ SCORES (6-9)]:		0.015	0.040

Table 6.2: Mean and Median Annual Returns of Stocks Based on the Composite Score for Value and Total Sample Stocks-Interlisted: May 1, 1985-April 30, 2010.

SCORE is a composite indicator of a number of fundamental and market firm characteristics.

[7]The methodology for constructing the composite indicator is consistent with Mohanram [13]. However, unlike Mohanram [13], rather than using contemporaneous medians for each fundamental or market metric within value firms in the same industry as benchmarks for assigning a good or bad signal for a specific firm-related fundamental or market metric, we use contemporaneous medians for the fundamental and market metrics within value firms irrespective of the industry – but separate the interlisted from the non-interlisted stocks. This is because (a) good stocks in a homogeneous sample, in general, should have certain positive characteristics independent of the industry they belong to, and (b) truly comparable companies are difficult to find, particularly a significantly large number of such companies, and this may bias values (signals) given to a firm. Moreover, value investors abstract from industry P/E metrics when they search for firms to invest in.

SCORE	Value(Q1)-Mean								Value(Q1)-Median							
	OBS	P/E	LIQUID	CURRENT	SIZE	DEBT	EXTRA	BRISK	OBS	P/E	LIQUID	CURRENT	SIZE	DEBT	EXTRA	BRISK
Low	61	9.5	0.14	1.45	137.7	0.82	0	1.97	61	10	0.07	1.1	74.8	0.6	0	2
1	608	7.8	0.18	2.86	85.2	0.63	0	2.09	608	8.1	0.08	1.65	40.2	0.34	0	2
2	129	7.8	0.27	1.93	105.7	0.9	0	2.2	129	8.2	0.11	1.44	90.4	0.47	0	2
3	83	7.3	0.29	1.94	204.2	0.57	0	2.28	83	7.6	0.18	1.68	188.1	0.31	0	2
4	67	7.5	0.35	1.93	275.2	0.6	0	2.3	67	7.7	0.19	1.69	154.1	0.31	0	2
5	59	7.2	0.19	1.92	253.5	0.69	0.08	2.33	59	7.9	0.12	1.79	160.2	0.49	0	3
6	77	7.2	0.34	2.42	1074	0.57	0	2.29	77	7.6	0.24	1.69	284	0.35	0	2
7	78	7.7	0.49	2.31	751.2	0.72	0.1	2.23	78	7.9	0.33	1.79	312.5	0.36	0	2
8	213	7.7	0.4	2.44	613.7	0.77	0.65	2.22	213	7.8	0.19	1.55	181.3	0.51	1	2
High	285	7.9	0.5	2.21	699.9	0.95	0.88	2.31	285	8.4	0.3	1.71	239.5	0.46	1	2

Table 7.1: Mean and Median Risk Related Variables by the Composite Score for Value Stocks-Non-Interlisted: May 1, 1985-April 30, 2010.
EXTRA is the occurrence of reporting extraordinary charges and restarting historical financials in year (t-1) (yes=1, no=0). LIQUID is trading volume for the year prior to May of year (t) as a percentage of shares outstanding. CURRENT is the ratio of cash plus short term investments and accounts receivable to current liabilities (times). SIZE is market cap in millions of Canadian dollars determined by multiplying shares outstanding by price per share as at April of year (t). BRISK is the industry code that captures an industry's business risk (1=low business risk, 2=medium business risk and 3=high business risk). DEBT is short and long term debt to equity and SCORE is a composite indicator of a number of fundamental and market firm characteristics.

SCORE	Value(Q1)-Mean								Value(Q1)-Median							
	OBS	P/E	LIQUID	CURRENT	SIZE	DEBT	EXTRA	BRISK	OBS	P/E	LIQUID	CURRENT	SIZE	DEBT	EXTRA	BRISK
Low	8	7.5	1.01	1.45	2912	0.58	0.5	2	8	9.1	0.13	1.31	963	0.45	1	2
1	14	7.3	1.16	1.64	11382	0.75	0.7	2	14	9.1	0.11	1.63	2912	0.61	1	2
2	17	6.9	1.31	1.78	10321	1.68	0.8	2.4	17	6.7	0.53	1.54	5077	0.66	0	2
3	20	7.5	0.83	2.63	4541	0.72	0.4	2.4	20	7.7	0.38	1.63	3777	0.49	0	2.5
4	80	8.2	0.84	2.18	1772	0.72	0.4	2.3	80	9	0.38	1.82	2096	0.47	0	2
5	60	9.1	0.42	1.86	2253	0.79	0.3	2.4	60	9	0.8	1.45	750	0.58	0	2
6	117	8.3	0.37	2.79	349	0.82	0.4	2.3	117	9.1	0.16	1.62	204	0.53	0	2.5
7	22	6.2	0.16	6.72	1121	0.42	0.1	2.3	22	7.6	0.02	1.82	349	0.23	0	2
8	20	7.6	0.15	2.69	1099	0.57	0.1	2.6	20	8.6	0.15	2.74	346	0.68	0	3
High	12	8.6	0.15	1.09	989	1.74	0	2	12	8.6	0.15	1.09	989	1.74	0	2

Table 7.2: Mean and Median Risk Related Variables by the Composite Score for Value Stocks-Interlisted: May 1, 1985-April 30, 2010.
EXTRA is the occurrence of reporting extraordinary charges and restarting historical financials in year (t-1) (yes=1, no=0). LIQUID is trading volume for the year prior to May of year (t) as a percentage of shares outstanding. CURRENT is the ratio of cash plus short term investments and accounts receivable to current liabilities (times). SIZE is market cap in millions of Canadian dollars determined by multiplying shares outstanding by price per share as at April of year (t). BRISK is the industry code that captures an industry's business risk (1=low business risk, 2=medium business risk and 3=high business risk). DEBT is short and long term debt to equity and SCORE is a composite indicator of a number of fundamental and market firm characteristics.

REVG, CURRENT, DEBT and CASH are negatively related to future performance, while TURNOVER, EBITG and MARGIN are positively related.[8] As a result, if a firm has SIZE, LIQUID, REVG, CURRENT, DEBT and CASH below their respective contemporaneous medians, we assign to the firm the value of zero. A firm with EBITG, TURNOVER and MARGIN values that are above their respective contemporaneous medians also receives the value of zero. Otherwise, values are equal to one. A similar process is followed for the interlisted stocks in our sample. We assign binary values to the sample interlisted firms based on where a stock's SIZE, LIQUID, EBITG and REVG, CURRENT, CASH, TURNOVER, MARGIN and DEBT lie vis-à-vis their median values. For example, in Table 5.2, we see that LIQUID, TURNOVER, REVG, CURRENT and CASH are negatively related to future performance, while EBITG, SIZE, DEBT and MARGIN are positively related. As a result, if a firm has LIQUID, TURNOVER, REVG, CURRENT and CASH below their respective contemporaneous medians, we assign to the firm the value of zero. A firm with EBITG, SIZE, DEBT and MARGIN that are above their respective contemporaneous medians also receives the value of zero. Otherwise, values are equal to one. This way a value (non-interlisted or interlisted) firm receives a signal for each of the fundamental and market metrics.

The sum of the above firm-specific values (signals) for the fundamental and market metrics constitutes the composite indicator (SCORE) of each firm. We rank all value stocks by the SCORE indicator and form ten value portfolios. The way the indicator is constructed implies that the lower the SCORE the better it is. We should expect, consistent with our previous evidence, that the lower the SCORE, the better the performance of a value portfolio and vice versa.

Table 6.1 relates the composite (SCORE) indicator to forward annual non-interlisted value stock returns. Table 6.2 shows the same but for interlisted firms. There is a negative relationship between the SCORE indicator and annual stock returns for both non-interlisted and interlisted value stocks. The lowest SCORE indicator non-interlisted portfolio has a mean annual return of 16.1%, whereas the highest SCORE indicator portfolio has a mean annual return of 0.009%. For interlisted stocks, the lowest SCORE indicator portfolio has a mean annual return of 30.3%, whereas the highest SCORE indicator portfolio has a mean annual return of 0.01%. The median annual returns for both interlisted and non-interlisted value stocks are consistent with the mean values.[9]

While the overall sample mean and median annual non-interlisted value stock returns over May 1, 1985-April 30, 2010 are 14.2% and 8% (See Tables 2.1 and 3.1), respectively, value stocks with SCORE values of 0 to 3 have a mean annual return of 15.5% and a median annual return of 10%. - value stocks with SCORE values of 6 to 9 have a mean annual return of 8.5% and a median return of 2.8%. Similarly, whereas the overall sample mean and median annual interlisted value stock returns over May 1, 1985-April 30, 2010 are 22.9% and 15% (See Tables 2.2 and 3.2), respectively, value stocks with SCORE values of 0 to 3 have

[8]Mean and median returns reported in Tables 5-1 and 5-2 are the mean and median returns of all contemporaneous results over the sample period, and so what is reported in these tables may not reflect actual values in any given year.

[9]We also regressed SCORE against forward returns for interlisted and non-interlisted stocks in order to more formally examine the relationships documented in Tables 6.1 and 6.2. The coefficient of SCORE (and t-statistic) for non-interlisted stocks is -0.009 (2.71) and for interlisted stocks -0.0187 (2.13). These findings confirm the negative relationship between SCORE and forward returns, as well as the stronger relationship of SCORE to interlisted stock returns.

a mean annual return of 36.7% and a median annual return of about 22% - value stocks with SCORE values of 6 to 9 have a mean annual return of 15% and a median return of 11.9%. As shown in Tables 6.1 and 6.2, mean and median returns of stocks with SCORE values of 0 to 3 are statistically different from those with SCORE values of 6 to 9 at traditional levels of significance.[10]

Does the composite SCORE indicator proxy for risk, with lower SCORE indicating higher risk, which justifies the higher return of the low SCORE portfolios?

In Tables 7.1 and 7.2 a number of risk related metrics, such as stock liquidity (LIQUID), current ratio (CURRENT), debt-to-equity (DEBT), market cap (SIZE), occurrence of reporting extraordinary items (EXTRA) and stock business risk category (BRISK), are related to the SCORE indicator. We see that for the non-interlisted stocks, while the low SCORE portfolios tend to include less liquid and smaller cap firms, they also tend to include stocks that report less frequently extraordinary items than the high SCORE portfolios. The findings for the interlisted stocks, on the other hand, show that the low SCORE portfolios have lower risk than the higher ones in terms of larger market cap and higher stock liquidity, although they seem to report more frequently extraordinary items.[11] At the same time, the betas across the ten SCORE portfolios (from low to high) for non-interlisted stocks are: 0.389, 0.53, 0.809, 0.654, 0.822, 1.2, 0.86, 0.91, 0.656 and 0.551. The corresponding numbers for interlisted stocks are: 0.74, 0.86, 0.66, 1.23, 1.08, 0.57, 1.05, 1.0, 0.68, and 0.90. As a result, it is not clear that SCORE sorted portfolio performance is linked to risk (at least the sources of risk examined above) as there are no consistent and systematic differences in the aforementioned variables between the low and high SCORE portfolios.

Conclusions

For both non-interlisted and interlisted stocks, we document a consistently strong value premium over the May 1, 1985-April 30, 2010 sample period, which persists in both bull and bear markets, as well as in recessions and recoveries for non-interlisted stocks, but less so for interlisted stocks. Our results are consistent with those of other Canadian and US studies. We can conclude from this that the value premium is not a purely US phenomenon and that the observed value premium in Canada is not only due to interlisted stocks.

Moreover, the evidence in this paper shows that, in general, non-interlisted and interlisted stocks have similar company fundamentals and market metrics. The area where there is a difference is with regards to stock liquidity, debt to equity and market cap metrics, as well as to the fact that a typical size effect does not exist for interlisted stocks. Interlisted firms are more liquid, larger and have more debt to equity ratio than non-interlisted firms. At the same time, larger cap interlisted stocks have higher returns than lower cap interlisted firms.

We were able to construct a composite score indicator (SCORE) which enabled us to predict future stock returns and separate the winners from the losers among value stocks. Results were stronger for interlisted than non-interlisted stocks. It is not clear, however, whether the SCORE indicator performance is linked to risk as evidence is inconclusive in this regard. Future research should explore this issue further. Finally, future research should also examine whether the findings reported in this study can be replicated to a sample of US and global stocks.

References

1. Basu S (1977) Investment Performance of Common Stocks in Relation to Their Price-Earnings Ratios: A Test of the Efficient Market Hypothesis. J Financ 32: 663-682.
2. Chan LKC, Hamao Y, Lakonishok J (1991) Fundamentals and Stock Returns in Japan. J Financ 46: 1739-1764.
3. Fama EF, French KR (1992) The Cross Section of Expected Stock Returns. J Financ 47: 427-465.
4. Fama EF, French KR (1993) Common risk factors in the returns on stocks and bonds. J Financ Econ 33: 3-56.
5. Fama EF, French KR (1995) Size and Book-to-Market Factors in Earnings and Returns. J Financ 50: 131-155.
6. Fama EF, French KR (1996) Multifactor Explanations of Asset Pricing Anomalies. J Financ 51: 55-84.
7. Lakonishok J, Shleifer A, Vishny RW (1994) Contrarian Investment, Extrapolation and Risk. J Financ 49: 1541-1578.
8. Chan LKC, Lakonishok J (2004) Value and Growth Investing: Review and Update. Financial Analysts' Journal 60: 71-86.
9. Athanassakos G (2009) Value versus growth stock returns and the value premium: The Canadian experience 1985-2005. Can J Adm Sci 26: 109-121.
10. Athanassakos G (2011) The Performance, Pervasiveness and Determinants of Value Premium in Different US Exchanges: 1985-2006. Journal of Investment Management 9.
11. Athanassakos G (2011) Do Value Investors Add Value? Journal of Investing 20: 86-100.
12. Piotroski JD (2000) Value Investing: The Use of Historical Financial Statement Information to Separate Winners from Losers. J Accounting Res 38: 1-41.
13. Mohanram SP (2005) Separating Winners from Losers among Low Book-to-Market Stocks Using Financial Statement Analysis. Review of Accounting Studies 10: 133-170.
14. Bird R, Casavecchia L (2007) Sentiment and Financial Health Indicators for Value and Growth Stocks: The European Experience. The European Journal of Finance 13: 769-793.
15. Athanassakos G, Ackert L, Naydenova B, Tafkov I (2010) Determinants of Investor Demand for Cross-Listed Firms. Financial Markets, Institutions and Instruments 19: 245-267.
16. Booth L, Johnston DJ (1984) The Ex-Dividend Day Behavior of Canadian Stock Prices: Tax Changes and Clientele Effect. J Financ 39: 457-476.
17. La Porta R, Lakonishok J, Schleifer A, Vishny R (1997) Good News for Value Stocks: Further Evidence on Market Efficiency. J Financ 52: 859-873.
18. Griffin JM, Lemmon ML (2002) Book-to-Market Equity, Distress Risk, and Stock Returns. J Financ 57: 2317-2336.
19. Cohen RB, Polk C, Vuolteenaho T (2003) The Value Spread, J Finance 58: 609-642.
20. Kwag SW, Lee SW (2006) Value Investing and the Business Cycle. Journal of Financial Planning Article 7: 1-10.
21. Athanassakos G (2012) Separativs Winners from Losers Among Value and Growth Stocks in Canada. Working Paper, Western University.
22. Greenwald BCN, Kahn J, Sonkin PD, Van Biema M (2004) Value Investing: From Graham to Buffett and Beyond. Wiley Finance, John Wiley & Sons, Inc., Hoboken, N.J.
23. Datar VT, Naik NY, Radcliffe R (1998) Liquidity and stock returns: An alternative test. Journal of Financial Markets 1: 203-219.
24. Ackert LF, Athanassakos G (2003) A Simultaneous Equation Analysis of Analysts' Forecast Bias, Analyst Following and Institutional Ownership. Journal of Business, Finance and Accounting 30: 1017-1042.
25. Athanassakos G (1998) Estimating the Cost of Equity and Equity Risk-Premia of Canadian Firms. Multinational Finance Journal 1: 229-254.

[10]Return differences reflect cross sectional differences as opposed to time series differences as the findings for these SCORE portfolios are spread across time and so differences in returns between these portfolios are not driven by market returns.

[11]The remaining risk-proxying variables, for both non-interlisted and interlisted stocks, show no real differences between the low and high SCORE portfolios.

Statistical Methods for Estimating House Price Index

Ashish Garg*
Masters in Financial Engineering - UCLA, PhD - Philadelphia University, USA

Abstract

House Price Index (HPI) is the key barometer of house prices measured from the aggregated house sales transactions data. HPI provides summary of the housing market that is used to track the movement in the house prices through time and analyze the performance of housing market. It is one of the most closely monitored economic indicators in the United States. In US, HPIs are estimated and published at various levels of geographic region including US census divisions, states, Metropolitan Statistical Area (MSA), Core Based Statistical Area (CBSA), zip code. The most popular indices published in US are FHFA HPI, Standard & Poor's Case-Shiller Indices, Nahb.

Keywords: Statistical methods; House price index; Housing market

Introduction

Houses have set of different hedonic characteristics like number of bedrooms, number of bathrooms, square footage, school district, location, indicated condition, modernized, garage. Further, there are different types of properties: single family house, condonium, cooperative unit. The characteristics of the units sold may vary from period to period, resulting in change in representation of the population in the sample set used in estimating the appreciation or depreciation in prices. For example, at one period if the population represents high-end houses and in next period, it represents low-end houses, the changes in sales price as a measure for house price movement would give an indication of house price depreciation, though in reality, the house prices might have appreciated if the population sample set has been kept standard. A naive statistical approach of simple moving average of house prices does not provide the true measure of house price movement due to above-mentioned reasons. The numbers of studies have been done to solve this problem and it narrowed down to two methodologies that are widely used: 1) Hedonic regression, 2) Repeat Sales Method.

In Hedonic regression approach, first introduced by Griliches, Ball, Rosen [1-3], the differences in the characteristics of units in various samples are statistically controlled. The sales price is regressed on a set of variables that describe the unit characteristics like number of rooms, square feet of interior space, lot size, quality of construction, condition. The house price indexes are constructed in number of ways by using the sensitivity of coefficients from the hedonic regression. First, the estimated equations from each period can be used to predict the value of a standard unit in each period. The characteristics of the unit do not change over the estimating period. This is similar to constructing a basket of goods for Consumer Price Index calculation. Alternatively, dummy variables are introduced in the equation to capture change in price over time while controlling for characteristics. In this alternative way, the prices for different characteristics are implicitly not allowed to change with time whereas in the first one, individual characteristic gets its own price and changes with time. The hedonic approach requires a large quantity of data on individual units sold including their characteristics.

In Repeat Sales Method, developed by Bailey, Muth, and Nourse [4], the data is restricted to the properties that have actually sold more than once during the estimation period. The method has the major advantage of isolating actual increases in the price of housing without requiring detailed information about the characteristics of individual properties. The groups of studies have shown that controlling the population to repeat sales gives the more accurate measure of changes in house prices. This approach does not require the measurement of the quality but requires that quality does not change over time. Much research have been further done to improve the indices, most notable by Case and Shiller [5,6] where they extended the method to incorporate heteroscedastic error due to gap time between sales and called it weighted repeat sales method (WRS). Due to limitation to using properties that have been sold more than once, only small percentage of the total sales data is usable for this approach. Though, repeat sales method is widely used in research studies and commercially as well, it has received lot of criticism too that it only provides information about a very specific type of home and may not apply to the entire housing market – England et al, Meese and Wallace [7,8].

A hybrid model has been proposed by Case and Quigley [9] that combined repeat sales methodology with hedonic regression so that all the sales transaction data could be made usable and the issues with repeat sales method could be addressed to some extent. Clapp and Giacotto [10] developed an assessed value method by constructing a modified repeat sales method which incorporated assessed values of homes as a hedonic variable coupled with actual sales. Knight, Dombrow, and Sirmans [11] proposed another variant of a hybrid index in which the hedonic coefficients were allowed to vary over time.

Survey of Prominent US House Price Indices

Freddie Mac and Fannie Mae are government sponsored enterprises (GSEs) chartered by Congress to provide a secondary market in conventional mortgages and increase lending for home ownership. Federal Housing Finance Agency (FHFA) is the regulatory agency responsible for oversight of these GSEs. FHFA publishes HPI based on weighted repeat sales methodology on monthly and quarterly basis. The mortgage data includes single family properties whose mortgages have been purchased or securitized by Fannie Mae or Freddie Mac since January 1975. The HPI includes house price figures for the nine

***Corresponding author:** Ashish Garg, Masters in Financial Engineering - UCLA, PhD - Philadelphia University, USA, E-mail: ashish.philly@gmail.com

Census Bureau divisions, for the 50 states and the District of Columbia, and for Metropolitan Statistical Areas (MSAs) and Divisions (Figure 1).

The standard and Poor's Case-Shiller house price indices are based on repeat sales methodology. There are multiple indices from Case-Shiller including National home price index, a 20 city composite index, a 10 city composite index, and 20 individual metro area indices. The index includes only single-family, detached residences and excludes new construction. There are futures and options available for investment community based on Case-Shiller index. This index was first developed by Karl Case and Robert Shiller is now considered as industry's standard (Figure 2).

Nahb Housing Market Index is reported by the National Association of Home Builders. It is based on a monthly survey of home builders. They are asked to rate current sales of single-family homes and sales expectations for the next six months and to rate traffic of prospective buyers. Scores for responses to each component are used to calculate a seasonally adjusted overall index. This concept tracks sentiment among participants in the housing industry. A reading above 50 indicates more builders view conditions as good than poor. Contrary to previous two indices discussed, this index is based on qualitative methodology (Figure 3).

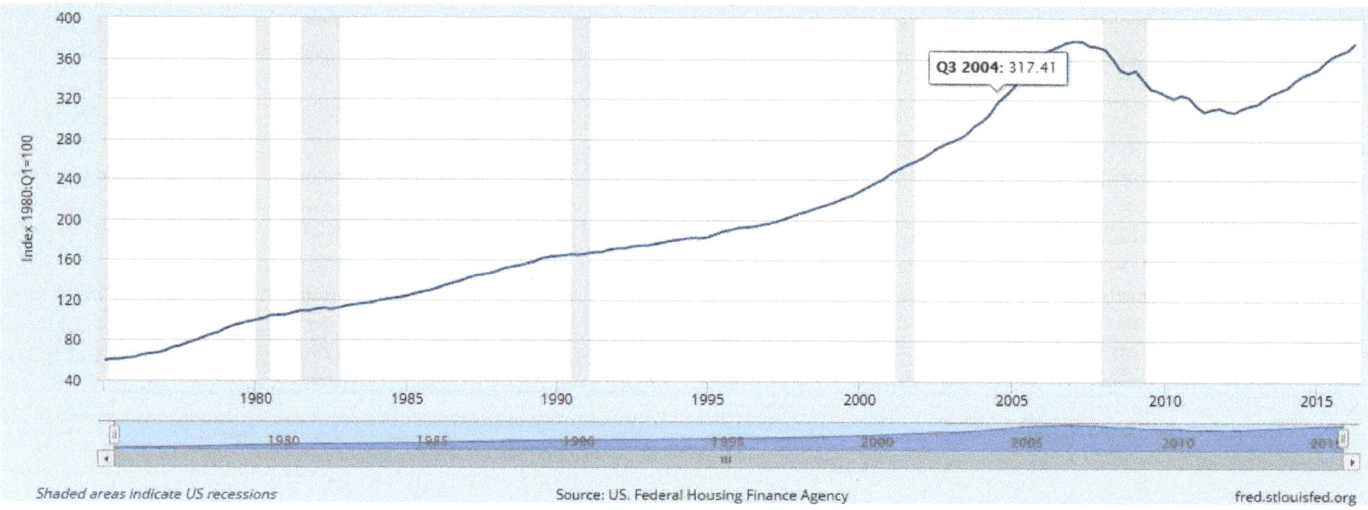

Figure 1: House price figures.

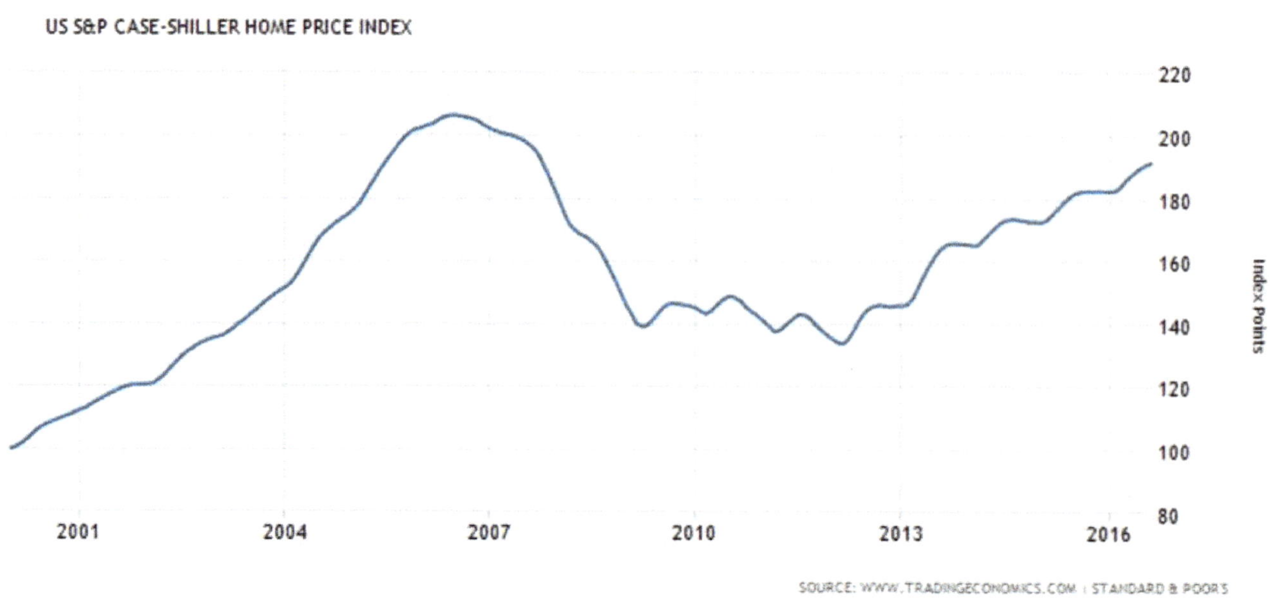

Figure 2: Case-Shiller Home price index.

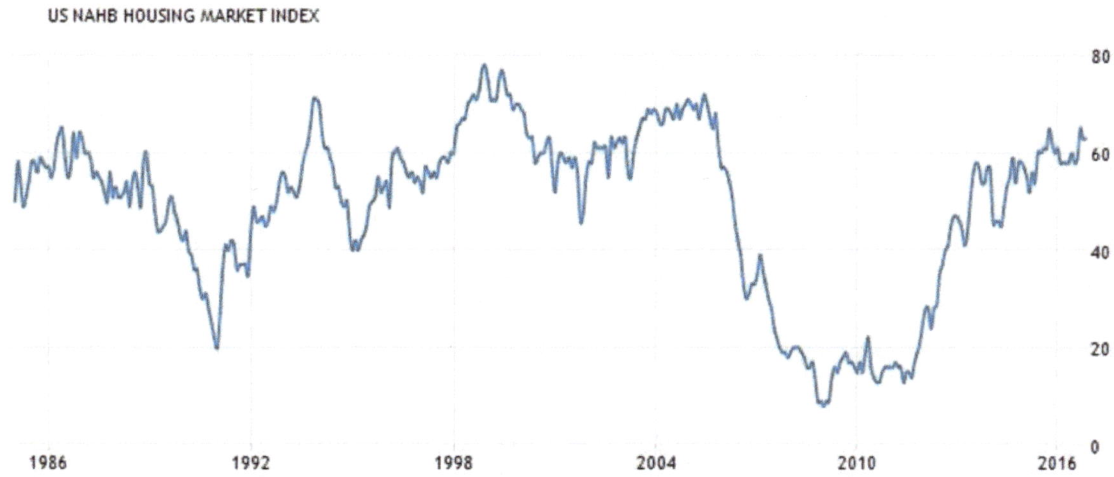

Figure 3: Hosuing market index.

Conclusion

House price index has found its application widely in mortgage prepayment and default modeling. Prepayment defines the ability of the borrower to pay early and default indicates inability of borrower to pay its scheduled payments of principal and interest. These models are extensively used in valuation and risk analysis of mortgage backed securities, pooled mortgages. The house price index is forecasted using econometric models, artificial neural network models, and time series models like auto regression. Some of the significant macro-economic variables used in modeling and forecasting HPI are interest rate, oil price shock, currency movement, business cycle, legislative and regulatory policy, inflation.

References

1. Griliches Z (1971) Price Indexes and Quality Change. Harvard, Cambridge, Massachusetts.
2. Michael JB (1973) Recent empirical work on the determinants of relative house prices. Urban studies 10: 213-233.
3. Sherwin R (1974) Hedonic prices and implicit markets: product differentiation in pure competition. Journal of political economy 82: 34-55.
4. Bailey MJ, Muth RF, Nourse HO (1963) A regression method for real estate price index construction. Journal of the American Statistical Association 58: 933-942.
5. Karl EC, Shiller RJ (1987) Prices of single family homes since 1970: New indexes for four cities. National bureau of economic research, Cambridge, USA pp: 1-53.
6. Karl EC, Shiller RJ (1988) The efficiency of the market for single-family homes.
7. Peter E, Quigley JM, Redfearn CL (1999) The choice of methodology for computing housing price indexes: comparisons of temporal aggregation and sample definition. The journal of real estate finance and economics 19: 91-112.
8. Nancy EW, Meese RA (1997) The construction of residential housing price indices: a comparison of repeat-sales, hedonic-regression, and hybrid approaches. The Journal of Real Estate Finance and Economics 14: 51-73.
9. Bradford C, Quigley JM (1991) The dynamics of real estate prices. The Review of Economics and Statistics 73: 50-58.
10. John MC, Giaccotto C (1992) Estimating price indices for residential property: a comparison of repeat sales and assessed value methods. Journal of the American Statistical Association 87: 300-306.
11. John RK, Dombrow J, Sirmans CF (1995) A varying parameters approach to constructing house price indexes. Real Estate Economics 23: 187-205.

The Regulatory Effect on the Performance of Financial Analysts: Time Series from Two Different Legal Systems

Christopher von Koch, Ola Nilsson* and Karin Jonnergård
School of Business and Economics, Linnaeus University, Sweden

Abstract

The focus of this paper is the relationship between regulatory settings and financial analysts' performance, which is examined by studying the level of shareholder protection and the performance of financial analysts in two countries with different legal origins. By using a newly constructed index to measure shareholder protection, we are able to analyze how changes in shareholder protection over time can affect analysts' performance. By comparing two countries with different legal traditions (the United Kingdom (UK) and Sweden), we are also able to assess whether the underlying legal origin is an influential factor. The results show that increased shareholder protection improves forecast accuracy in both the UK and Sweden, supporting the idea that stronger shareholder protection regulations improve analysts' performance whether the legal context is rooted in common law or Scandinavian civil law tradition. The findings also indicate that strengthened shareholder protection decreases forecast dispersion in Sweden and forecast bias in the UK, further supporting the idea that stronger shareholder protection improves analysts' performance even though the results differed across legal contexts. We did, however, find a substitution effect in both countries: Strengthened shareholder protection makes analysts' services less valuable to investors, thus leading to a reduction in the number of analysts. Our main conclusion is that changes in shareholder protection affect the performance of analysts irrespective of the country's legal origin, i.e. common law or Scandinavian civil law. However, legal origin seems to have an impact on the magnitude of analysts' performance based on changes in shareholder protection.

Keywords: Shareholder protection; Financial analysts; Regulatory changes; Forecast accuracy; Legal origin

Introduction

Schipper [1] and Revsine et al. [2] argue that analysts are considered among the most influential users of financial reports and among the most important information intermediaries between firms and investors. In light of their information-processing ability and access to resources, they are typically viewed as sophisticated users of accounting information and less likely to misunderstand the implications of such information [1,3]. Managers are also less likely to issue fraudulent financial reports when analysts can inspect those reports. A consequence of this conception is market participants regard inefficient information processing by analysts as strong evidence of overall market inefficiency. This has led to a stream of research focusing on analysts and the importance of the regulatory settings when it comes to analysts' role, behavior and performance [4-12]. Several studies have used the level of legal protection of shareholders as a variable, and a number of these have shown that it has an impact on analysts' performance. This variable has also been connected to a discussion of a differentiation between countries based on their legal origingrounded in the legal origin theory advanced by La Porta, et al. [13]. Many researchers suggest that analysts in common-law countries play a more important role and perform better than analysts in civil-law countries. Their arguments are based on studies analyzing the relationship between different aspects of analysts' performance and a country's level of legal protection [4,5,14,15].

A common denominator in most prior studies highlighting the impact of shareholder protection is the use of either "Legal Enforcement" or the anti-director rights (LLSV) index from La Porta, et al. [13] as a proxy for the level of investor protection in a country and, in some cases, as a way to categorize a country as either a strong investor protection country or a weak investor protection country. Both Legal Enforcement and the LLSV are based on cross-sectional data, which makes them relevant for classifying countries. Previous studies using these indexes, however, are lacking in one important aspect because they do not take into consideration the fact that shareholder protection regulations change over time in most countries [16-21].The validity of the legal origin theory has also been questioned lately by several scholars and the idea that historical roots will exert powerful impact on today's market is far from obvious [22-26]

In this study we: 1) overcome the earlier shortcoming using a static index by using times series analyses of shareholder protection to investigate the relationship between the level of shareholder protection and analysts' performance, and 2) challenge the legal origin hypothesis by looking at two countries (the UK and Sweden) with a similar pattern of shareholder protection regulation development but different legal origins as expressed in the legal origin theory. Our main conclusion is that strengthened shareholder protection improves analysts' ability to reduce information asymmetry, a deduction based on significant results showing that strengthened shareholder protection improves forecast accuracy in both countries. We do, however, find some differences between the countries in terms of the effect of strengthened shareholder protection on analysts' performance. For Sweden increased shareholder protection decreased forecast dispersion, whereas in the UK it decreased forecast bias. An interpretation of this could be that strengthened shareholder protection has different impacts on analysts working within different legal traditions. In addition, we

***Corresponding author:** Ola Nilsson, School of Business and Economics, Linnaeus University, Nygatan 18B, 392 34 Kalmar, Sweden
E-mail: ola.nilsson@lnu.se

found a substitution effect in both Sweden and the UK: Strengthened shareholder protection makes analysts' services less valuable, leading to a reduction in the number of analysts following the firms. In other words, as analysts' performance increases due to stronger shareholder protection, their monitoring role, i.e. monitoring firms by interpreting public information and gathering private information, becomes less beneficial; thus, the substitution effect renders them less useful to investors. However, in light of the decrease in information asymmetry, it seems obvious that investors' need to use analysts' services would decline. Overall our results indicate that legal origin matters. Legal origin seems to have an impact on the magnitude of analysts' performance based on changes in shareholder protection. We find significantly different impact on changes in shareholder protection between UK and Sweden concerning analyst's performance.

This study makes notable contributions to the existing literature. First, it adds to the limited international research on financial analysts' role by using a newly constructed index to study changes in shareholder protection over time within a given context. This is an important contribution because earlier empirical studies in the field largely used the static anti-directors rights LLSV or the "Legal Enforcement" [13] index when examining analysts' forecasts over several years. Our study also contributes to more nuanced results when it comes to the impact of shareholder protection and the influence of a countries legal environment.

The remainder of this paper is organized as follows: First we present the theoretical foundations for our hypotheses and look at prior studies analyzing the relationship between shareholder protection indexes and analysts' behavior/performance. We next provide a background to the distinctions between the countries' legal contexts and follow this with a more thorough discussion of the common-law and the Scandinavian-law contexts and their characteristics and differentiations vis-à-vis legal and institutional settings, especially distinctions in the regulations concerning shareholder protection. We then explain the research design and methodology. This is followed by a presentation of the results and, finally, some concluding thoughts.

Earlier Research and Theory Development

Within accounting research there is significant focus on the importance that legal and institutional settings have for reducing information asymmetry. For example, changes in both legislation and the fundamental institutional environment have been shown to be linked to accounting quality. Several contributions within the international accounting literature show that accounting quality is higher in countries with a common-law origin than in countries with a code-law origin [17,18,20]. In one stream of research the difference has been linked to enforcement and its role for the users of accounting information. For example, Francis, et al. [27] and Hope [7] found that common-law countries have stronger enforcement of accounting standards than do code-law countries, and Hope [7] argues that strong enforcement of accounting standards encourages (or forces) managers to follow the accounting rules that are in place (thereby reducing analysts' "accounting uncertainty"). In addition, strong shareholder mechanisms both address and facilitate the possibility of litigation against managers and auditors [28]. Based on their examination of the impact of the mandatory introduction of International Financial Reporting Standards (IFRS) in Europe, Byard, et al. [29] support the notion that the legal system and the enforcement mechanisms in a given country affect the quality of the accounting reports that analysts use to generate forecasts. They found that analysts' forecast errors and forecast dispersion were affected only in countries that had both strong enforcement regimes and domestic accounting standards that differed significantly from IFRS as a starting point.

These studies highlight the relationship between a market's regulatory setting and its efficiency and also emphasize analysts' performance as a measure of reducing information asymmetry. Thus, we have reason to expect that changes in regulation designed to strengthen investor protection will lead to greater reduced information asymmetry; furthermore, it seems reasonable to analyze countries with different legal origins.

Hypothesis

Analysts' performance can be assessed by looking at several different variables. In this paper we choose four variables related to the discussion about information asymmetry. In order to make a forecast, an analyst processes a lot of information from the firm; the degree of accuracy is therefore highly related to the degree of asymmetry of that information. Thus, forecast accuracy, which is the most used variable for measuring analysts' performance [3], is selected as our first performance variable. Since the literature also suggests that forecast dispersion could be seen as a measure of information asymmetry [30], forecast dispersion is our second variable. Earlier studies also suggest a positive relationship between our first variable, forecast accuracy, and the number of analysts following a firm [4,11]. Our third performance variable is therefore the number of analysts. Our fourth variable is forecast bias. Empirical studies suggest that analysts have an incentive to issue optimistic forecasts so as to improve their relationship with management; their motivation is to be in a position to obtain private information when the benefits of doing so are greatest, namely, when earnings are unpredictable [31]. Bias can therefore be seen as a conscious way through which analysts increase information asymmetry. Below we examine these variables more closely within the context of different legal origins and use them to generate four hypotheses that will enable us to assess analysts' performance both within each country and across the two.

Analysts' forecast accuracy: Several studies use analysts' forecast accuracy to examine analysts' performance and its relationship to the legal and institutional settings. For example, Barniv et al. [5], Basu et al. [32], Ashbaugh et al. [6], and Hope [7,8] offer evidence that the accuracy of analysts' earnings forecasts varies around the world and that such variation relates positively to disclosure practices and investor protection. Barniv et al. [5] found that analysts in common-law countries outperform their peers in civil-law countries and therefore suggest an association between legal and financial reporting environments and analysts′ forecast behaviour. Analysts may also have greater incentives to forecast accurately in well-developed capital markets (strong shareholder protection countries), where investors may exhibit greater demand for earnings forecasts [5]. Chang et al. [4] studied the extent and accuracy of analysts' activity across 47 countries around the world and found forecast accuracy to be lower in civil-law countries than in common-law countries. They also found differences between common-law and civil-law countries when it comes to both the presence of analysts and their performance.

In a sample of 22 countries, Hope [7] investigated the relationship between analysts' earnings forecast accuracy and the extent of annual report disclosure as well as the relationship between forecast accuracy and the degree of enforcement of accounting standards. He suggests that in countries with strong shareholder protection, analysts perform better when accounting standards are routinely enforced and their predictions are more accurate. And, finally, Lang et al. [12] find that the relationship between firm value and the interaction of analyst coverage and concentrated ownership is more positive in countries with weak shareholder protection than in those with strong shareholder protection. What is especially interesting is that both Hope [7] and Lang et al. [12] emphasize shareholder protection as a means of differentiating countries and note that this differentiation has an effect on the quality of analysts' forecast performance.

In summary, previous studies suggest that institutional differences among countries in terms of shareholder protection may influence analysts' forecast accuracy. Therefore, we propose our first performance hypothesis as follows:

H 1: There is a positive relationship between analysts' earnings forecast accuracy and the level of shareholder protection.

Analysts' forecast dispersion: Forecast dispersion (measured as the standard deviation in analysts' forecasts), a signal of the extent of analysts' disagreement about a firm's upcoming earnings, can be used as a proxy for investor uncertainty prior to the release of key information [3]. According to Krishnaswami and Subramaniam [30], this dispersion is a measure of information asymmetry. They claim that when information asymmetry between a firm and its market is high, it is difficult for the market to evaluate or predict the firm's performance. Lang and Lundholm [33] provide evidence for the relationship between disclosure and decreased information asymmetry. Firms with more informative disclosure policies have a larger analyst following, more accurate earnings forecasts, less dispersion among those forecasts, and less volatility in forecast revisions. Firms that provide firm-specific information, in particular, have more accurate earnings forecasts and less forecast dispersion. Based on this we assume that if public information is analysts' primary source of facts and figures, there should be less dispersion because that information is available to all. We therefore state the following as our second hypothesis:

H 2: There is a negative relationship between the dispersion of analysts' earnings forecasts and the level of shareholder protection.

Number of analysts following a firm: Analyst services have both a demand and a supply side. On the one hand, expanded disclosure due to strengthened corporate governance, e.g., more refined segment disclosure, potentially enables analysts to create valuable new information and, hence, increases the demand for their services. On the other hand, disclosure could preempt analysts' ability to distribute managers' private information to investors, leading to a decline in demand for their services [8,34]. The net effect of these forces is theoretically ambiguous.

Lang et al. [33] argue on the basis of Bhushan's [35] model that the number of analysts following a firm depends on whether the analysts are *information intermediaries or information providers.* If they are information intermediaries, the principle flow of information goes from the firm through the analysts to the investors. An increase in information means that the analysts have more information to sell, thus leading to a higher demand for their services. In contrast, if analysts are seen as providers of information that competes with information given by firms directly to investors, increased information stemming from strengthened shareholder protection would be a substitute for analysts' services, leading to a decline in the number of analysts in a given context.

According to Knyazeva [36], the number of analysts following a firm may serve as a replacement for other corporate governance mechanisms. Empirical studies relating shareholder protection to the number of analysts seem to support this substitution effect. Chang et al. [4] found that the number of analysts is lower in common-law countries than in civil-law countries, which suggests that analyst coverage may be more important in countries with weak shareholder protection than in those with strong shareholder protection. Sun [11] also supports this notion of a substitution effect, arguing that analysts have a much more important role in countries with weak shareholder protection. In light of these more recent empirical studies, we test the following hypothesis:

H 3: There is a negative relationship between the number of analysts following a firm and the level of shareholder protection.

Analysts′ forecast bias: Another stream of literature seeks to describe explanations for relative optimism or pessimism among analysts. These explanations fall into two broad categories: 1) strategic optimism to improve relationships with management and 2) potential biases caused by incentives.

Empirical evidence shows that earnings forecasts tend to be biased. In the 1980s and '90s, analysts showed excessive optimism, a positive forecasting bias due perhaps to the available information [37]. Since 2000, there seems to have been a shift toward pessimism in the U.S. [38]. This shift can be explained by legislative changes that not only place limitations on the relationship between investment units and research units in investment banks, but also restrict the flow of private information from management to analysts. One might therefore reasonably expect strengthened shareholder protection to have the same impact on analysts' bias: a gradual change from positive to negative.

Empirical studies before 2000 [31] argue that analysts have an increased incentive to issue optimistic forecasts to improve their relationship with management and thereby gain access to private information when the benefits of doing so are greatest (when earnings are unpredictable). Das et al. [31] found evidence consistent with this argument, noting that forecast error and measures of predictability are negatively correlated. However, Eames, Glover and Kennedy [39] replicated Francis and Philbrick's [27] study and found that the relationship between recommendation optimism and forecast optimism was reversed when actual earnings were included in the equation. Lim [40] argues that analysts may trade off positive bias for improved forecast accuracy resulting from access to better information. He finds, further, that both firm and analyst characteristics correspond to forecast optimism. Firm size and the number of analysts following a firm are negatively related to optimism, whereas target-specific uncertainty is positively related to optimism. In other words, the demand for private information is a proxy for optimism.

Balboa et al. [41] indicate that strong shareholder protection countries exhibit bias in stock recommendations due to the dispersed ownership, but not in earnings forecasts. In a context with shifting shareholder protection, we would first expect to see a higher demand for private information and thus a positive bias on the part of analysts, but as corporate governance rules strengthen we would anticipate a negative bias. However, these biases will mainly be expressed in stock recommendations. Since we are examining bias in earnings forecasts, we therefore state our fourth, and last, hypothesis as follows:

H 4: There is a negative relationship between the bias of analysts' earnings forecasts and the level of shareholder protection.

Legal Context

We are using data from two countries - the United Kingdom (UK) and Sweden - representing two different legal origins according to the legal origin theory. In this theory national variation of corporate governance law has its roots in the historical origin of the legal system of each country. The differentiation between common and civil law is the initial basis for the theory. Common law originated in England in the Middle Ages and became the legal tradition of many countries around the world that were at one time colonies of the British Empire. One may therefore view the UK as the model country for the common-law tradition. Sweden, in contrast, belongs to the Scandinavian legal system, which derives from the civil-law tradition.

Codification of the legal system in Sweden occurred in the 19th century, influenced largely by the German legal tradition, and the early Companies Act was more or less a translation of the corresponding German legislation. The legal systems in Sweden and the other Scandinavian countries have since developed along similar paths and in a direction that departs in some ways from other legal systems. La Porta et al. [13] define the Scandinavian legal tradition as a specific civil-law tradition distinguishable from other civil-law traditions such as the German and French civil-law traditions. They contend that characteristic features of the Scandinavian legal system are very strong law enforcement and greater investor protection than in other civil-law systems. In the case of Sweden, they found a score of 3 out of 5 on the anti-director rights index and legal enforcement indexes that were amongst the highest in the world. The UK, by comparison, is characterized by very high shareholder protection (5 out of 5 on the anti-directors index) and relatively strong law enforcement[1] [13]. The main differences between the legal contexts of Sweden and the UK appear in the juridical processes involved in developing and enforcing the laws, as the Swedish system is based on codified law and the UK system on case law. Figure 1 shows the development of shareholder protection in the UK and Sweden over 19 years, based on the SPI-index (see section 4.3 for a detailed description). The figure pinpoints the problem of using a static index like the LLSV; for example, the level of shareholder protection in Sweden during the last several years is almost as high as the level for the UK in 1987. It is also important to bear in mind that using the "Legal Enforcement" variable from La Porta et al. [13], as Sun [11] did, resulted in Sweden showing stronger investor protection than the UK, i.e. achieving a score of 10.00 as compared to the UK's 9.22[2].

In Figure 1, shareholder protection strengthened considerably in both countries over the study period. One factor behind Sweden's development is the deregulation of Swedish financial markets that occurred in the mid-1980s. This deregulation was succeeded by changes in regulations affecting shareholder protection. In addition,

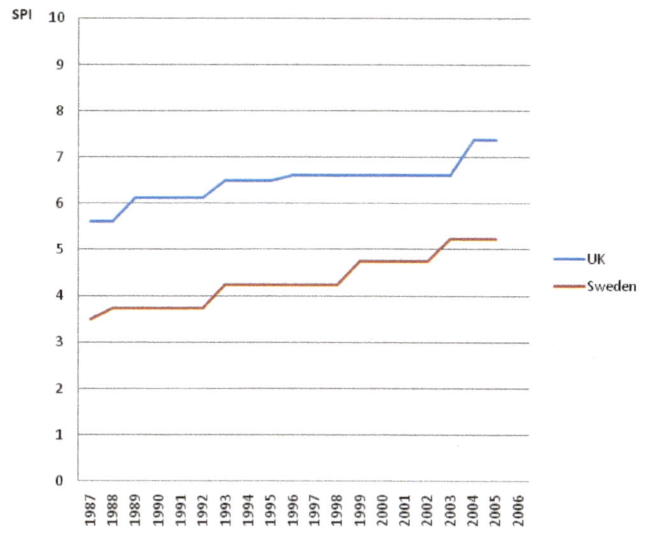

Figure 1: Shareholder protection in UK and Sweden (yearly observations)

Sweden's entry into the European Common Market necessitated changes to the Swedish Companies Act, with successive revisions taking effect in 1998 and 2006. The UK also experienced a changing legal framework during this time period, with new regulations for the financial services industry imposed in 2000 and a new Companies Act in 2006. In other areas such as accounting and auditing, the EU has issued new regulations, implying that today both Sweden and the UK apply International Standards for Financial Reporting (IFRS) as well as auditing (ISA). Similar efforts at harmonization have been carried out for issues related to the financial markets.

Another bundle of regulations developed and dispersed during the last 20 years relates to corporate governance codes. The idea of a code was initiated by the Cadbury Commission in the UK in 1992. The commission had been set up by the accountancy profession, the Financial Reporting Council and the London Stock Exchange as a response to financial scandals that took place during the 1980s [42-44]. Following the Cadbury Code was voluntary, but it became part of the listing requirement of the London Stock Exchange. Several other committees were subsequently established and issued related recommendations, notably the Greenbury Committee in 1995, the Hampel Committee in 1998, and the Turnbull Committee in 1999, when all of the recommendations were assembled into what became the Combined Code [42].

The different committees provided responses to different problems, namely, accountability and control (Cadbury Commission), managers' remuneration (Greenbury Committee) and internal control (Turnbull Committee). However, the idea of corporate governance codes spread very quickly around the world [45,46]. In Sweden a governmental task group initiated a corporate governance code of conduct in the early 2000s in response to corporate scandals that occurred at the end of the 1990s. A code was implemented in 2004 and became a part of the listing criteria for the Stockholm Stock Exchange (SSE). Further development of the Code and its enforcement were put in the hands of a new organization, with a majority of members from the business society. In this way both the Swedish and the UK codes of conduct can be viewed as part of the self-regulation of the business.

In summary, the legal traditions of Sweden and the UK have

[1]The 10-point legal enforcement index showed Sweden at 10 for "efficiency of juridical system," "rule of the law," and "risk for corruption". For "risk for expropriation" the index was 9.40 and for "risk for contract repudiation" 9.58; the accounting standards were rated at 83. For the UK the indexes were 10 for "efficiency of judicial system," 8.57 for "rule of the law," 9.10 for "risk for corruption", 9.71 for "risk for expropriation", and 9.63 for "risk for contract repudiation"; the accounting standards were rated at 78 [13]

[2]The "Legal Enforcement" index is measured as the mean score across three legal variables: (1) the efficiency of the judicial system, (2) an assessment of the rule of law, and (3) the corruption index. All three variables range from 0–10.

different origins, and, based on the categorization of La Porta et al. [13], the UK has a higher anti-director rights index whereas Sweden has somewhat higher indexes of law enforcement. We also note that the different legal traditions imply differences in the juridical processes applied in the countries. Over the last 20 years, however, membership in the European Common Market has meant some similar regulatory changes for both countries. In addition, the UK has been leading in the development of corporate governance codes, which have spread to most of the world, including Sweden. Thus, despite their different legal traditions, recent developments in shareholder protection regulations have been similar in both Sweden and the UK.

Data and Sample

Data sources and sample construction

Analysts' forecast data were obtained from the Institutional Brokers Estimate System (I/B/E/S)[3] [47]. I/B/E/S [47] has data on Swedish and UK firms dating to 1987. For this study, we compiled sample firm years from all Swedish and UK firms listed on I/B/E/S [47] from 1987 to 2005, achieving a total sample of 95,020 forecasts for Earnings Per Share (EPS) in the UK and 14,175 forecasts for EPS in Sweden[4].

Analysts usually forecast the EPS of a particular fiscal year several times before the actual figures are released. The frequency of the forecasts differs depending on the analyst. I/B/E/S [47] collects forecast data from individual analysts around the world once a month and uses those data to calculate statistics such as the mean, median, standard deviation, etc. Only the final estimates are included in the monthly calculation. Thus, I/B/E/S [47] provides calculated statistics of analysts' forecasts of EPS once a month.

In this study, we use the final calculated mean of an analyst's forecasts of EPS before the actual EPS is released. For example, the forecast statistics of Ericsson B[5] for the fiscal year end December 31, 2005, were calculated once a month from May 2005 to March 2006. Hence, we use the mean forecast calculated in March 2005 as the forecast data for actual EPS on December 31, 2005. The mean forecast can therefore consist of several individual forecasts from analysts - some firms have around 50 analysts making predictions on their future EPS. Our final sample comprises 16,592 mean EPS forecasts in the UK and 2,827 mean EPS forecasts in Sweden.

Dependent variables, selection and measurement

In each of our models the dependent variable is based on a performance measurement noted earlier. Accordingly, we use four dependent variables to measure analysts' impact on information asymmetry: forecast accuracy, standard deviation of forecasts, number of analysts following the firm, and forecast bias. The data obtained from the I/B/E/S [47] Database are applied to these variables.

Following Lang and Lundholm [33], the first dependent variable, forecast accuracy, is calculated as the negative of the absolute value of the actual earnings minus the analyst's earnings forecast, scaled by the stock price at the beginning of the year, and forecasted EPSt is the mean analyst forecast of the earnings per share in period *t*.

$$Forecast\ Bias = \frac{-\left(Actual\ EPS_t - Forecasted\ EPS_t\right)}{Beginning\ of\ the\ fiscal\ year\ stock\ price}$$

The second dependent variable, standard deviation of forecasts, is the inter-analyst standard deviation of forecasts scaled by the stock price in the beginning of the year, also in line with Lang et al. [33]. The third dependent variable is the number of analysts who are following the company. This is determined simply by a count of analysts who are providing an earnings forecast for the company, again in line with Lang et al. [33].

We apply Francis et al. [27] method to measure the fourth dependent variable, forecast bias. This variable is calculated as the negative of the actual earnings minus the analyst's earnings forecast, scaled by stock price in the beginning of the year, and forecasted EPSt is the mean analyst forecast of the earnings per share in period t.

The forecast measures are scaled with the stock price to make cross-company comparisons possible. Forecast accuracy is defined as the negative of the scaled absolute forecast error. In other words, more accurate forecasts are represented by higher values, i.e. a lower forecast error. Forecast bias is defined as the negative of the scaled forecast error. In the event the analyst has overestimated the company's EPS, the result is a positive value, and in the event the analyst has underestimated the company's EPS, the result is a negative value.

The shareholder protection variable

The variables in our shareholder protection index (SPI) are chosen and defined in a way that aims to remedy several shortcomings of the LLSV. The differences concern notably the sources of the SPI. This index with a maximum value of 10 was developed by the Corporate Governance Research Program at the Centre for Business Research, University of Cambridge, UK and the dataset is fully accessible via www.cbr.cam.ac.uk. Armour et al. [22] include not only positive law, but also rules stemming from self-regulation, such as corporate governance and takeover codes, where they are binding for (listed) companies. The SPI also differs from the LLSV in that it is not based on binary variables, but allows for intermediary scores between 0 and 1 where appropriate. Moreover, the SPI, unlike the LLSV, is sensitive to "default rules" in the sense of rules that apply in certain circumstances depending on the involved actors' choices. Such laws, although not strictly binding, are not necessarily coded 0. The SPI also explicitly acknowledges the importance of coding for functionally equivalent instruments in different countries. Finally, it is constructed as a longitudinal measure for quantifying the legal SPI of a given country for each year [22,48,49].

Control variables, selection and measurement

The five control variables in this study were selected on the basis of prior research into factors that normally affect the accuracy of analysts' forecasts [33]. They are: market value, trading volume, earnings

[3] The benefit of using I/B/ES has been discussed by Ramnath, Rock, and Shane [3]. They find, contrary to Philbrick [27] that actual EPS data from Value Line and I/B/E/S [47] are comparable, but I/B/E/S consensus forecasts are more accurate and are a better proxy for the market's earnings expectations. The superiority of I/B/E/S [47] consensus forecasts can be traced to two attributes: 1) the ability to provide forecasts that are closer to the earnings announcement date (Value Line publishes only one forecast per quarter, while the I/B/E/S [47] consensus is updated monthly), and 2) the advantage of being able to aggregate across forecasts from multiple analysts (Value Line forecasts are issued by a single analyst, whereas the I/B/E/S consensus is based on forecasts contributed by multiple analysts). Bradshaw [54] uses First Call as his source for analyst data. First Call and I/B/E/S [47] differ in that First Call includes consensus data for a month only if the consensus was revised during the month. I/B/E/S [47] is more comprehensive in that it includes all months, including those with no changes in the consensus.

[4] The sample includes both active and inactive firms for which analysts have made forecasts during the study period. Analysts make forecasts far from all listed firms what does this mean? For example, for our study period I/B/E/S [47] has forecast data for 468 firms listed on Stockholm Stock Exchange (SSE) and 1,925 firms listed on London Stock Exchange. These firms comprise our sample.

[5] In Sweden it is common to have dual-class shares with different voting rights. For example, an owner of an A-share in Ericsson has ten times more votes than an owner of a B-share.

surprise, loss, and standard deviation of return on equity (std ROE).

Market value is the company's market value at the beginning of the fiscal year. Trading volume refers to the company's daily trading volume in the first month of the fiscal year. Earnings surprise, which is the variation in a firm's results from one year to another, is calculated as the absolute value of a given year's earnings per share minus the previous year's earnings per share, scaled by the share price at the beginning of the fiscal year. EPS_t is the earnings per share in period $_t$ (a given year), and EPS_t-1 is the earnings per share in period $_t$-1 (the previous year).

$$Earnings\ Surprise = \frac{|EPS_t - EPS_{t-1}|}{Beginning\ of\ fiscal\ year\ stock\ price}$$

According to Lang et al. [33], earnings surprise controls for the fact that forecast characteristics are likely to be affected by major events, such as a firm's introduction of a new product. In these circumstances realized earnings are most apt to deviate from expected earnings, and there are likely to be significant revisions in analysts' forecasts.

Loss is a dummy variable that takes the value of 1 if the company reported a loss and zero otherwise. Standard deviation of return on equity is the standard deviation of the company's return on equity over the previous three years.

Models

Because we have a time-series shareholder protection index, we are able to examine how shareholder protection affects analysts over time in the UK and Sweden, both separately and collectively. We have two models for testing each performance hypothesis. Models 1 and D1 test the first performance hypothesis to determine if a positive relationship exists between analysts' forecast accuracy and the SPI index. Model 1 regresses forecast accuracy on each country's individual SPI value and the control variables, as shown in the following model:

$$ForecastAccuracy_{it} = \alpha + \beta_1 SPI_t + \beta_2 MarketValue_{it} + \beta_3 TradingVolume_{it} + \beta_4 Loss_{it} + \beta_5 EarningsSurprise_{it} + \beta_6 StdDevROE_{it} + \varepsilon_{it} \quad (1)$$

In Model D1, below, we insert the country as a dummy variable to test the sample as well as compare the effects of legal origin.

$$ForecastAccuracy_{it} = \alpha + \beta_1 SPI_t + \beta_2 MarketValue_{it} + \beta_3 TradingVolume_{it} + \beta_4 Loss_{it} + \beta_5 EarningsSurprise_{it} + \beta_6 StdDevROE_{it} + \beta_7 Land_t + \beta_8 D * SPI_{it} + \beta_9 D * MarketValue_{it} + \beta_{10} TradingVolume + \beta_{11} D * Loss_{it} + \beta_{12} D * EarningsSurprise_{it} + \beta_{13} D * StdDevRov\ \varepsilon_{it} \quad (D1)$$

The model pairs set out below follow the same principle. Models 2 and D2 test the second hypothesis and determine if there is a negative relationship between the shareholder protection and forecast dispersion by regressing the standard deviation of forecasts on the SPI value and the control variables.

$$ForecastDispertion_{it} = \alpha + \beta_1 SPI_t + \beta_2 MarketValue_{it} + \beta_3 TradingVolume_{it} + \beta_4 Loss_{it} + \beta_5 EarningsSurprise_{it} + \beta_6 StdDevROE_{it} + \varepsilon_{it} \quad (2)$$

$$ForecastDispertion_{it} = \alpha + \beta_1 SPI_t + \beta_2 MarketValue_{it} + \beta_3 TradingVolume_{it} + \beta_4 Loss_{it} + \beta_5 EarningsSurprise_{it} + \beta_6 StdDevROE_{it} + \beta_7 Land_t + \beta_8 D * SPI_{it} + \beta_9 D * MarketValue_{it} + \beta_{10} TradingVolume + \beta_{11} D * Loss_{it} + \beta_{12} D * EarningsSurprise_{it} + \beta_{13} D * StdDevROE \varepsilon_{it} \quad (D2)$$

Models 3 and D3 test the third hypothesis to determine if whether a relationship exists between shareholder protection and the number of analysts following a firm. These models regress the number of analysts on the SPI index value and the control variables.

$$Number\ of\ Analysts_{it} = \alpha + \beta_1 SPI_t + \beta_2 MarketValue_{it} + \beta_3 TradingVolume_{it} + \beta_4 Loss_{it} + \beta_5 EarningsSurprise_{it} + \beta_6 StdDevROE_{it} + \varepsilon_{it} \quad (3)$$

$$Number\ of\ Analysts_{it} = \alpha + \beta_1 SPI_t + \beta_2 MarketValue_{it} + \beta_3 TradingVolume_{it} + \beta_4 Loss_{it} + \beta_5 EarningsSurprise_{it} + \beta_6 StdDevROE_{it} + \beta_7 Land_t + \beta_8 D * SPI_{it} + \beta_9 D * MarketValue_{it} + \beta_{10} TradingVolume + \beta_{11} D * Loss_{it} + \beta_{12} D * EarningsSurprise_{it} + \beta_{13} D * StdDevROE\ \varepsilon_{it} \quad (D3)$$

The fourth and final models test the final hypothesis by regressing forecast bias on the SPI value and the control variables to determine if a relationship exists between shareholder protection and forecast bias.

$$Forecast\ Bias_{it} = \alpha + \beta_1 SPI_t + \beta_2 MarketValue_{it} + \beta_3 TradingVolume_{it} + \beta_4 Loss_{it} + \beta_5 EarningsSurprise_{it} + \beta_6 StdDevROE_{it} + \varepsilon_{it} \quad (4)$$

$$Forecast\ Bias_{it} = \alpha + \beta_1 SPI_t + \beta_2 MarketValue_{it} + \beta_3 TradingVolume_{it} + \beta_4 Loss_{it} + \beta_5 EarningsSurprise_{it} + \beta_6 StdDevROE_{it} + \beta_7 Land_t + \beta_8 D * SPI_{it} + \beta_9 D * MarketValue_{it} + \beta_{10} TradingVolume + \beta_{11} D * Loss_{it} + \beta_{12} D * EarningsSurprise_{it} + \beta_{13} D * StdDevROE\ \varepsilon_{it} \quad (D4)$$

Our study uses unbalanced panel data in which both cross-sectional and time-series dependence are present. To address these forms of dependence, a number of advances have been made in the econometrics literature there the use of cluster-robust standard errors is an important one. It is common practice in many studies to use cluster-robust standard errors, with clustering either along a cross-sectional dimension (e.g., analyst, firm, industry, or country) or along a time-series dimension [50]. All our regression analyses use cluster-robust standard errors to avoid overstating t-statistics due to multiple observations of the same firm (different fiscal years) within the dataset [50,51].

Note in the models above, analyst following is not used as an explanatory variable. In reality, the number of analysts following a firm is likely to vary with a number of factors. Consistent with this presumption, significant variation in analyst following has been found in both within [33] and across-country studies [32] causing endogenous problem. This is especially important when analyst following is used as a conditioning variable to test whether the role of legal origin varies with the information environment. Since we do not use the variable as such we do not test for endogeneity problem. Also there could be an endogenous relationship between several performance variables and analyst coverage. This endogenous relationship may exist because analysts are more likely to select companies with high earnings quality than companies with low earnings quality. By not using analyst following in the same model as the performance variable (market value, trading volume, earnings surprise, loss, and standard deviation of return on equity) we might mitigate this endogeneity problem. However while prior evidence shows that both analyst following and the properties of the analysts' forecast are affected by shareholder protection, the results should be interpreted with care as most research in this area has not taken into account the potentially endogenous nature of a firm's shareholder protection and analyst following.

Results

Table 1 gives an overview of the sample, showing the number of forecasts and forecast accuracy by year over the sample period. The two other performance variables, forecast dispersions and forecast bias, are omitted due to lack of space. The table also shows the average number of forecasts per firm, the average forecast accuracy, and the standard deviation of forecast accuracy. The second and the fourth column in Table 1 show the number of mean forecast for UK and Sweden. The trend in the two countries is similar with a peak of forecast during the dot-com bubble in the late 1990^{th,} indicating that the market for financial analysts was the greatest during that period. However, the decline in forecast in Sweden since that period is sharper than UK

	UK		Sweden		UK		Sweden	
Year	Number of mean forecasts	Avg # forecasts per firm	Number of mean forecasts	Forecasts per firm	Accuracy mean	Accuracy std	Accuracy mean	Accuracy std
1987	636	5.50	70	1.93	-0.037	0.234	-0.071	0.128
1988	781	6.34	75	1.67	-0.026	0.083	-0.059	0.095
1989	879	6.43	78	1.90	-0.028	0.120	-0.040	0.060
1990	803	5.92	76	2.33	-0.033	0.082	-0.040	0.045
1991	743	5.75	76	3.53	-0.063	0.160	-0.122	0.176
1992	786	6.34	92	5.13	-0.092	0.792	-0.154	0.187
1993	813	6.77	128	4.16	-0.093	0.431	-0.411	1.340
1994	835	6.82	126	5.08	-0.029	0.115	-0.068	0.092
1995	868	6.66	156	5.74	-0.027	0.074	-0.054	0.083
1996	895	6.20	198	5.85	-0.026	0.076	-0.073	0.100
1997	1 018	6.11	198	6.48	-0.026	0.101	-0.055	0.071
1998	1 077	5.55	227	5.51	-0.028	0.069	-0.041	0.061
1999	1 080	6.21	227	6.64	-0.046	0.125	-0.089	0.195
2000	1012	6.05	256	5.60	-0.047	0.163	-0.069	0.112
2001	935	2.72	230	5.22	-0.044	0.111	-0.090	0.206
2002	920	4.18	170	4.28	-0.060	0.309	-0.117	0.291
2003	822	4.59	162	4.00	-0.075	0.226	-0.097	0.159
2004	808	5.09	143	5.73	-0.048	0.234	-0.077	0.346
2005	881	5.80	139	5.35	-0.059	0.876	-0.074	0.384
87-05	16 592	5.72	2.827	5.01	-0.046	0.324	-0.094	0.359

Table 1: Descriptive statistics 1987-2005

probably due to relatively more dot-com firms in Sweden than UK. Column three and five show the average forecast per firm in each country over the sample period. The average number of forecasts per firm is similar for each country over the sample period, 5.72 in the UK and 5.01 in Sweden, meaning that on average slightly more than five analysts are following a firm. The trend between the two countries exhibits here some differences.

The average forecast per firm is much more stable in UK with an average around little bit less than six forecasts per firm over the entire sample period but with a sharp decline just after the dot-com period. The average forecast per firm in Sweden has during the same period been much more volatile, varying from 1.93 to 6.64 forecast per firm in average. These latter numbers are indicating that financial houses changes their coverage of specific firms more easily in Sweden than UK. The last four columns show forecast accuracy and accuracy standard deviation for the two countries. The overall standard deviation of forecast accuracy for each country is also similar, 0.324 for the UK and 0.359 for Sweden. However, the forecast accuracy mean is much lower in the UK (-0.046) than in Sweden (-0.094), indicating that analysts in the UK perform better than analysts in Sweden. It is worth noting that forecast accuracy in Sweden was very low in 1993, when the country experienced bank and real estate crises. Over the sample period the trend in accuracy mean and accuracy standard deviation are similar for the two countries with variation in the two numbers from one year to another which can be due to the business cycle which we control for in our models with for example earnings surprise and standard deviation of ROE.

Table 2 and 3 present descriptive Statistics Pertaining to the Dependent, SPI and control variables in the four models for Sweden and the UK, respectively. These tables show that the mean firm in Sweden has an analyst forecast error that is 9.4 percent (4.6 percent in the UK) of its share price, a standard deviation of forecasts (forecast dispersion) equal to 2 percent of its share price (2 percent in the UK as well), 5.01 analysts following it (5.72 in the UK), and a forecast bias of 0.1 percent (1.4 percent in the UK). The mean sample firm has market value of SEK 6.4 billion (GBP 1.8 billion), and the mean of its average daily trading volume is 12 million shares (in the UK 50 million shares). Around 20 percent of the sample firm years show negative earnings (9 percent in the UK), and the earning surprise is 9 percent of the share price (7 percent in the UK).

The tables also show the Pearson correlations between the variables. Our main independent variable of interest, Shareholder protection, correlates significantly and positively with forecast accuracy and the number of analysts and negatively with forecast dispersion and forecast bias in Sweden (Table 2), with the first three correlations significant? at 0.001 and forecast bias at 0.05. However, the coefficients are quite low, indicating weak relations with our four dependent variables. The strong significance combined with weak correlations indicates that the relationship between shareholder protection and the performance of analysts in Sweden clearly exist but the impact of shareholder protection is not overwhelming: lower forecast error, less forecast dispersion, a higher number of analysts, and less bias. In the UK (Table 3), however, the only dependent variable significantly correlated with shareholder protection is the number of analysts, and the relationship is negatively with a very low coefficient (0.04) which indicates but not fully convincing relation between shareholder protection and the number of analyst. To sum up, the bivariate analysis concerning the relationship between our main variable of interest and our four dependent variables do not indicate a strong relationship in neither of our two countries.

For our control variables the bivariate analyses in Table 2 and 3 shows that both forecast accuracy and forecast dispersion are highly correlated with earnings surprise both in Sweden and in the UK. This suggests that analysts are less accurate, meaning that there is more dispersion and volatility in their forecasts, when the company's earnings have undergone a significant change from the previous year. The number of analysts is, of course, most highly correlated with market value and trading volume, as there are more analysts following larger firms. Forecast bias, in both UK and Sweden, is most highly correlated with the dummy variable loss, suggesting that analysts display less bias

Variable	Mean	S.D	1	2	3	4	5	6	7	8	9	10
1 Forecast accuracy	-.094	.32	1.00									
2 Forecast dispersion	.02	0.07	-.51***									
3 Number of analysts	5.01	6.391	-.18***	-.04*								
4 Forecast bias	.001	0.33	.07***	-.08***	-.03							
5 Shareholder protection	4.67	.87678	.14***	-.16***	.19***	-.04*						
6 Market value (million SEK)	6,446	28,465	.30***	-.24***	.72***	.08***	.14***					
7 Trading volume (thousands)	12,442	51,533	.15***	-.05**	.61***	.07***	.23***	.66***				
8 Loss	.19	.395	-.37***	.23***	-.10***	-.45***	.03	-.25***	-.10***			
9 Earnings surprise	.089	.21	-.50***	.46***	-.12***	-.04*	-.13***	-.26***	-.11***	.26***		
10 Std ROE	18.49	55.92	-.41***	.26***	-.19***	-.11***	.06***	-.33***	-.05**	.37***	.25***	1.00

Pearson correlations
Note *p<.05;**p<.01;***p<.001

Table 2: Correlation Matrix – Sweden

Variable	Mean	S.D	1	2	3	4	5	6	7	8	9	10
1 Forecast accuracy	-.046	.32	1.00									
2 Forecast dispersion	0.02	0.07	-.30***									
3 Number of analysts	5.72	6.391	.05***	-.03**								
4 Forecast bias	.014	0.33	-.81***	.27***	-.02*							
5 Shareholder protection	6.65	.3972	-.01	-.00	-.04***	-.00						
6 Market value (million GBP)	1793	6996	.02*	-.01	.36***	.00	.05***					
7 Trading volume (thousands)	49.985	295.959	.01	-.01	.24***	.00	.02*	.64***				
8 Loss	.09	.292	-.21***	.06***	-.16***	-.18***	.11***	-.05***	-.04***			
9 Earnings surprise	.067	.21	-.64***	.82***	-.05***	.46***	.00	-.02*	-.01	.16***		
10 Std ROE	.23	1.67	-.04***	.07***	-.05***	.00	.03***	-.01	-.00	.12***	.06***	1.00

Pearson correlations
Note *p<.05;**p<.01;***p<.001

Table 3: Correlation Matrix - UK

for firms with negative earnings. From the tables can be seen that the control variables seems to impact the four dependent variables in a similar manner in the two countries.

The regression results for analysts' performance are reported in Table 4. Panel A in Table 4 shows the results for the two countries individually while Panel B provides the results for the interaction variables for the entire sample. In other words, Panel A provides the results for Model 1 to Model 4, whereas Panel B shows the results for interaction variables in Model D1 to Model D4. Models 1 and D1 show the estimated strength of the positive relationship between forecast accuracy and shareholder protection that was predicted by Hypothesis 1. Models 2 and D2 indicate the estimated strength of the negative relationship between analysts' forecast dispersion and shareholder protection predicted by Hypothesis 2. In models 3 and D3 we see the estimated magnitude of the association between shareholder protection and the number of analysts following a firm, as predicted by Hypothesis 3. Finally, models 4 and D4 provide the estimated strength of the link between analysts' forecast bias and shareholder protection, as predicted by Hypothesis 4. Moreover, multicollinearity diagnostic statistics (variance inflation factor, VIF) confirm that no multicollinearity problem is affecting the variables assumed to be determinants in the first four models.

Moreover the F-statics show that models D1 to D4 are highly significant and R-squared values (we report both within and between R-squared values for models D1 to D4) for most of the 12 models are reasonable high.

The results in Table 4 for Model 1 show that the coefficient of shareholder protection is positive and significant for both Sweden ($t=4.36$, $p<.001$) and the UK ($t=2.47$, $p<.05$). Hypothesis 1 is therefore supported by the fact that stronger shareholder protection seems to improve analysts' forecast accuracy in both countries individually. Nor did we find any statistical evidence suggesting that shareholder protection affects forecast accuracy differently depending on the legal context (Panel B Table 4, variable D*SPI). Also, the coefficient of earnings surprise is very high in Model 1 for Sweden, which indicates that the variation in earnings of the firms that the analysts follow strongly affects their forecast error. In the UK firms' profit/loss affects forecast accuracy. Model 2 supports Hypothesis 2 by showing a negative and significant coefficient of shareholder protection ($t=-3.97$, $p<.001$) and forecast dispersion in Sweden. Although this relationship was found not to be significant in the UK, it was significant for the sample overall (not shown in the table). Results for Sweden as well for the entire sample also indicate that in an environment with stronger shareholder protection there is less uncertainty among analysts about a firm's future earnings, which could be another way of saying that information asymmetry decreases when shareholder protection

Variable	Forecast accuracy Model 1		Forecast dispersion Model 2		Number of analysts Model 3		Forecast bias Model 4	
	Sweden	UK	Sweden	UK	Sweden	UK	Sweden	UK
Panel A:								
Shareholder protection	0.017***	0.016*	-0.010***	0.002	-0.548*	-3.917***	-0.006	-0.027***
	(4.36)	(2.47)	(-3.97)	(1.37)	(-2.22)	(-19.12)	(-1.11)	(-4.88)
Market value	0.000	0.000	0.000	0.000	0.043***	0.000***	0.000	0.000
	(0.02)	(0.83)	(-1.70)	(-0.60)	(3.28)	(4.07)	(-0.71)	(1.49)
Trading volume	0.000*	-0.000	0.000	0.000	0.039***	0.000	0.000	0.000
	(2.20)	(-0.50)	(0.35)	(0.71)	(6.38)	(-0.03)	(-0.23)	(-0.95)
Loss	-0.020	-0.114*	0.027**	0.006	-1.638***	-3.411***	-0.220***	0.121*
	(-0.52)	(-2.15)	(2.99)	(0.29)	(-3.64)	(-12.84)	(-5.34)	(2.43)
Earnings surprise	-0.441***	-0.374	0.089	0.214*	-1.748*	-0.514*	0.120	0.276***
	(-6.49)	(-1.39)	(1.42)	(2.37)	(-2.42)	(-2.45)	(0.80)	(1.10)
Std ROE	-0.004	-0.002	0.001*	0.002	-.022**	-0.125	0.003	-0.005
	(-1.63)	(-0.96)	(2.21)	(1.85)	(-3.12)	(-0.87)	(1.32)	(-1.46)
Constant	-0.079***	-0.115*	0.053***	-0.012	8.637***	33.990***	0.027	0.166***
	(-4.15)	(-2.43)	(4.38)	(-0.99)	(6.00)	(24.08)	(0.89)	(4.24)
N	2,053	6,999	2,053	5,997	2,053	6,999	2,053	6,999
R-squared	0.20	0.341	0.14	0.466	0.36	0.224	0.09	0.196
Maximum VIF	1.75	1.83	1.73	1.83	1.75	1.83	1.75	1.83
Mean VIF	1.29	1.30	1.32	1.31	1.29	1.30	1.29	1.30

Panel B				
	Model D1	Model D2	Model D3	Model D4
D*SPI	0.001	-0.012***	3.370***	0.021**
	(0.16)	(-4.43)	(15.21)	(2.40)
D*MV	-0.000	0.000	-0.000***	-0.000
	(-0.84)	(0.32)	(-5.96)	(-1.64)
D*VO	0.000	0.000	0.000***	-0.000
	(2.21)	(0.34)	(3.73)	(-0.11)
D*PL	0.094	0.022	1.773***	-0.342***
	(1.35)	(1.05)	(5.24)	(-5.10)
D*ES	-0.067	-0.125	-1.233**	-0.156
	(-0.21)	(-1.17)	(-2.21)	(-0.51)
D*ROE	-0.002	-0.002	0.103	0.007
	(-0.51)	(-1.30)	(0.75)	(1.8)
F-statistics	424.15***	405.79***	57.80***	142.04***
R-squared (within)	0.31	0.41	0.26	0.17
R-squared (between)	0.41	0.28	0.08	0.16

Note *p<.05;**p<.01;*** p<.001

Table 4: Multiple Regressions for Effects of Shareholder Protection on Analysts' Performance

increases. Model D2 (variable D*SPI) shows significant difference between the two legal contexts in terms of the effect of shareholder protection on forecast dispersion, which can be interpreted as there is significantly less uncertainty among analysts in Sweden about a firm's future earnings than UK with stronger shareholder protection.

Model 3 in Table 4 shows that shareholder protection is negatively associated with the number of analysts following firms in each country (Sweden: t=-2.22, p<.05; UK: t=-19.12, p<.001), and this result holds for the entire sample. As suggested by Model 3 in Panel A and D3 in Panel B, the need for analysts is less when shareholders have more protection. Moreover, the variable D*SPI is significant (t=15.21, p<.001), indicating that strengthened shareholder protection has a greater substitution effect in UK than in the Sweden. This finding supports the substitution effect described in earlier studies and thus supports Hypothesis 3. It also suggests that there is reason to assume that this substitution effect is influenced by legal origin. Model 3 shows, as well, that in both countries market value is significantly and positively associated with the number of analysts, whereas loss and earnings surprise have significant negative associations. These results indicate that the market for analysts depends on several factors. When shareholder protection is strengthened, the market for analysts' services declines; however, that market increases with firms' market value. Also, the demand for analysts increases when there is more variability in earnings or profitability.

As shown in Model 4, the shareholder protection variable does not have a significant impact on forecast bias in Sweden. It does, however, in the UK (t=-4.88, p<.001) and for the sample as a whole. The D*SPI variable indicates significant difference between the two countries, meaning that forecast bias decreases with strengthened shareholder protection in the UK and overall, and there is significantly greater effect in UK than Sweden.

Conclusion

Our overall aim in this study was to analyze the relationship between regulatory settings and financial analysts' performance. We did this by investigating whether strengthened shareholder protection has any effect on analysts' performance and if this potential effect differs between countries with different legal traditions. Using four performance measures, we found support for the positive effect of increased shareholder protection on analysts' performance, which is in line with earlier studies [4,9]. We found that in both the UK and Sweden forecast error decreases with stronger shareholder protection; forecast dispersion also decreases in Sweden and forecast bias in the UK. In line with these results showing improved analyst performance, the demand for analysts' service decreased in both countries during the sample period. Our analyses also show that over the aggregate sample, all four performance measures were improved by strengthened shareholder protection. The investigation into whether strengthened shareholder protection has a greater impact on analysts' performance within a specific legal environment doesn't show uniform results, but gives some support of a stronger effect of changes in UK than Sweden. We found, for example that there a significant stronger effect in UK for number of analysts following firms and forecast bias but the opposite when it comes to forecast dispersion. There was no significant difference between the countries concerning forecast accuracy. However, overall we conclude that it seems that legal origin matters but affects the performance differently. Improvement in shareholder protection has greater impact on forecast dispersion in Sweden than UK, while improvement in shareholder protection has greater impact on the number of analysts and forecast bias in UK than in Sweden. In short, the interaction between the impact of shareholder protection and the type of legal environment in which the country functions, often assumed as important in prior studies can be supported by our study.

This study makes notable contributions to the existing literature. First, it adds to the limited international research on financial analysts' role by using a newly constructed index to study changes in shareholder protection over time within a given context. This is an important contribution because earlier empirical studies in the field largely used the static anti-directors rights LLSV or the "Legal Enforcement" [33] index when examining analysts' forecasts over several years. Those indexes do not take into account the fact that shareholder protection has dramatically changed in many countries during the past 10–15 years [20,52,53].

Our study also contribute to a more nuanced results concerning the interaction between the impact of shareholder protection and the type of legal environment in which the country functions.

The study also highlights the relationship between institutional changes and analysts' role. The findings are especially important for policy makers since they show the effects of institutional changes on information asymmetry. Furthermore, the study is important for market participants such as investors in that it emphasizes the effectiveness of analysts' role.

References

1. Schipper K (1991) Analysts' Forecasts. Accounting Horizons 5: 105–121.
2. Revsine L, Collins DW, Johnson W B (2004) Financial Reporting and Analysis (2ndedn) Prentice Hall, Upper Saddle River, New Jersey.
3. Ramnath S, Rock S, Shane P (2008) The financial analyst forecasting literature: A taxonomy with suggestions for further research. Int J Forecasting 24: 34-75.
4. Chang J, Khanna T, Palepu K (2000) Analyst Activity around the World. Harvard Business Strategy Unit, working paper 1-61.
5. Barniv R, Myring M, Thomas W (2005) The Association between the Legal and Financial Reporting Environments and Forecast Performance of Individual Analysts. CAR 22: 727-758.
6. Ashbaugh H, Pincus M (2001) Domestic accounting standards, international accounting standards and the predictability of earnings. JAR 39: 417-434.
7. Hope O (2003a) Disclosure practices, enforcement of accounting standards, and analysts' forecast accuracy: An international study. Journal of Accounting Research, 41: 235-272.
8. Hope O (2003b) Accounting policy disclosures and analysts' forecasts. CAR 20: 295-321.
9. Barniv R, Myring M (2006) An international analysis of historical and forecasted earnings in accounting-based valuation models. JBFA 33: 1087-1109.
10. DeFond M, Hung M, Trezevant R (2007) Investor protection and the information content of annual earnings announcements: International evidence. J Account Econ 43: 37-67.
11. Sun J (2009) Governance Role of Analyst Coverage and Investor Protection. FAJ 65: 1-13.
12. Lang M, Lins K, Miller D (2004) Concentrated control, Analyst Following, and Valuation: Do Analysts Matter Most When Investors Are Protected Least? JAR 42: 589-623.
13. La Porta R, Lopez-de-Silanes F, Shleifer A, Vishny R (1998) Law and finance. J Polit Econ 106: 1113-1155.
14. Bhat G, Hope O, Kang T (2006) Does corporate governance transparency affect the accuracy of analyst forecasts? Accounting & Finance 46: 715-732.
15. Coffee J C (2006) Gatekeepers. Oxford University Press.
16. Alford A, Jones J, Leftwich R, Zmijewski M (1993). The relative informativeness of accounting disclosures in different countries. JAR 31: 183-223.
17. Ali A, Hwang L, Trombley M (2003) Residual-income-based valuation predicts future stock returns: Evidence on mispricing vs. risk explanations. The Accounting Review 78: 377-397.
18. Ball R, Kothari S, Robin A (2000). J Account Econ 29: 1-51.
19. Hung M (2000) Accounting standards and value relevance of earnings: An international analysis. J Account Econ 30: 401-420.
20. Leuz C, Nanda D, Wysocki P (2003) Investor protection and earnings management: An international comparison. J Financ Econ 69: 505–527.
21. Hail L, Leuz C (2006) International differences in the cost of equity capital: Do legal institutions and securities regulation matter? JAR 44: 485-531.
22. Armour J, Deakin S, Sarkar P, Siems M, Singh A (2009) Shareholder protection and stock market development: an empirical test of the legal origins hypothesis. J Empirical Legal Stud 6: 343-380.
23. Acemoglu D, Johnson S (2005) Unbundling Institutions. J Polit Econ 113: 949-995.
24. Gourevitch P, Shinn J (2005) Political Power and Corporate Control: The New Politics of Corporate Governance. Princeton: Princeton University Press, USA
25. Rajan RG, Zingales L (2003) The Great Reversals: The Politics of Financial Development in the Twentieth Century. J Financ Econ 69:5-50.
26. Pistor K, Xu C (2005) Governing Stock Markets in Transition Economies: Lessons from China. American Law and Economics Review 7:184-210.
27. Francis J, Philbrick D (1993) Analysts' decisions as products of a multi-task environment. JAR 31: 216-230.
28. Soderstrom N, Sun K (2007) IFRS Adoption and Accounting Quality: A Review. European Accounting Review 16: 675-702.
29. Byard D, Li Y, Yu Y (2011) The Effect of Mandatory IFRS Adoption on Financial Analysts' Information Environment. Journal of Accounting Research 49: 69-96.
30. Krishnaswami S, Subramaniam V (1999) Information Asymmetry, Valuation, and the Corporate Spin-off Decision. Journal of Financial Economics 53: 73-112.
31. Das S, Levine CB, Sivaramakrishnan K (1998) Earnings Predictability and Bias in Analysts' Earnings Forecasts. The Accounting Review 73: 277-295.
32. Basu S, Hwang L, Jan C (1998) International variation in accounting measurement rules and analysts' earnings forecast errors. Journal of Business

Finance & Accounting 25: 1207-1247.

33. Lang MH, Lundholm RJ (1996) Corporate Disclosure Policy and Analyst Behavior. The Accounting Review 71: 467-492.
34. Healy R, Palepu K (2001) Information Assymmetry, Corporate Disclosure-and the Capital Markets: A Review of the Empirical Disclosure Literature. Journal of Accounting and Economics 31: 405-440.
35. Bhushan R (1989) Firm characteristics and analyst following. Journal of Accounting and Economics, 11: 255-274.
36. Knyazeva D (2007) Corporate Governance, Analyst Following, and Firm Behavior. Working paper, New York University.
37. Kothari S (2001) Capital market research in accounting. Journal of Accounting and Economics 31: 105-231.
38. Kadan O, Madureira L, Wang R, Zach T (2009) Conflicts of Interest and Stock Recommendations: The Effects of the Global Settlement and Related Regulations. Rev Financ Stud 22: 4189-4217.
39. Eames M, Glover S, Kennedy J (2002) The association between trading recommendations and broker-analysts' earnings forecasts. Journal of Accounting Research 40: 85-104.
40. Lim T (2001) Rationality and analysts' forecast bias. Journal of Finance 51: 369-385.
41. Balboa M, Gomez-Sala JC, Lopez-Espinosa G (2009) The value of adjusting the bias in recommendations: International evidence. European Financial Management 15: 208-230.
42. Spira LF (2001) Enterprise and accountability: striking a balance. Management Decision 39: 739-748.
43. Dewing IP, Russell PO (2000) Cadbury and beyond: Perceptions on establishing a permanent body for corporate governance regulation. The British Accounting Review 32: 355-374.
44. Dewing IP, Russell P O (2004) Regulation of UK Corporate Governance: lessons from accounting, audit and financial services. Corporate Governance: An International Review 12: 107-115.
45. Aguilera R, Cuervo-Cazurra A (2004) Codes of good governance worldwide: What is the Trigger? Organization Studies 25: 415-443.
46. Aguilera R, Cuervo-Cazurra A (2008) Codes of good governance Corporate Governance: An International Review 17: 376-387.
47. Ramnath S, Rock S, Shane P (2005) Value Line and I/B/E/S earnings forecasts. International Journal of Forecasting 21: 185-198.
48. Lele P, Siems M (2007) Shareholder protection: a leximetric approach. Journal of Corporate Law Studies 7: 17-50.
49. Schnyder G (2008) Does social democracy matters? Corporate governance reforms in Switzerland and Sweden (1985-2005). CBR Working paper 370.
50. Gow I, Ormazabal G, Taylor D (2010) Correcting for Cross-Sectional and Time-Series Dependence in Accounting Research. Accounting Review 85: 483-512.
51. Petersen M (2009) Estimating Standard Errors in Finance Panel Data Sets: Comparing Approaches. Review of Financial Studies 22: 435-480.
52. DeFond M, Hung M (2007) Investor protection and analysts' cash flow forecasts around the world. Review of Accounting Studies 12: 377-419.
53. Hope OK, Kang T, Thomas WB, Yoo YK (2009) Impact of excess auditor remuneration on cost of equity capital around the world. Journal of Accounting, Auditing and Finance 24: 177-210.
54. Bradshaw MT (2004) How Do Analysts Use Their Earnings Forecasts in Generating Stock Recommendations. Accounting Review 79: 25-50.

The Determinants of Currency Hedging in Indian IT Firms

Raghavendra RH[1]* and Velmurugan PS[2]

[1]Research Scholar, Department of Commerce School of Management, Pondicherry University, Pondicherry-605 014, India
[2]Fulbright Post doctoral Fellow and Assistant Professor, Department of Commerce School of Management, Pondicherry University, Pondicherry, India

Abstract

This paper explores the factors which determine the usage of currency derivatives by Indian IT companies. It has taken a total of 18 large IT firms in India. Those have disclosed the currency derivative data in their financial reports from 2011 to 2013; this study uses cross-sectional panel data and applies a multiple regression model. For this reason, the firm-specific features such as financial distress cost, underinvestment cost, multinationality, firm size, Taxation and Liquidity are regressed against the notional amount of currency derivatives reported for hedging activities. Finally result found that Size (Total assets) and Underinvestment (PE ratio) is the major determinant factors of the currency derivative usage in large Indian IT firms.

Keywords: Hedging; Financial distress; Under investment; Derivatives; Size; Multinationality

Introduction

IT firms in India use to involve in hedging activity to protect themselves against of exposures like volatility in interest rates, commodity prices and foreign exchange rates. In order to overcome this exposure some instruments used for hedging are financial derivatives. The costs of financial distress, underinvestment, and taxes are some of the reasons put forward to explain the widespread use of hedging activities [1].

To minimize foreign exchange risk, firms can involve in either currency hedging or operational hedging or both to reduce their exchange rate exposure. According to corporate risk management, by lowering the volatility of cash flows, the cost of firms' financial distress can be reduced and firm's value can be increased. In the perspective of managers' reputations, managers can prefer to conduct risk management activities to express their strategies. All these arguments prove the theory of Modigliani and Miller with regard to the worthlessness of firm value and risk management activities. Financial derivatives instruments to hedge against exchange rate risk would support firms to mitigate their risk and also benefitted by a reduction in a firm's exposure to financial risk and market imperfections, leading to value creation for shareholders. However, derivatives are risky instruments that might bring huge losses to a firm. Several previous studies have attempted to find if firms behave according to the principles established in the theories of optimal hedging. One of the main difficulties has been obtaining the necessary information. Prior 1990's, hedging information was considered to be an important element of the firm's competitive strategy, and, thus, it was considered confidential. The increasing demands on firms for expose of information, partly due to changes in accounting and business regulations made it possible in developed countries for this type of information to become a part of the financial reports of large firms.

Recent, and ongoing, huge losses on derivatives transactions announced by Indian IT firms. Feeling the heat of the global economic recession, Apart from that, derivative contracts backfiring during the past year was one of the main reasons. Therefore, the ensuing fears for systemic risk highlight the need for focused research on firms risk management activity and derivative practices.

Literature Review

Katie Hundman analyzed of the determinants of financial derivative usage in Commercial banks, the sample of the study was banks with assets over $500 million. By using regression model estimates the determinants of derivative use by commercial banks based on pooled time series, cross sectional quarterly data for 38 banks for the period 1995 to 1997. The result found that larger banks tend to use derivatives to a greater extent than smaller banks and those banks with a greater proportion of credit risk are more likely to use derivatives. Interest rate exposure, Capitalization, Credit risk, Profitability, Bank size among these variables, it is found that no relationship between bank profitability and derivative use.

Niclas Hagelin examined on the determinants factors of Swedish firms' hedging decisions. The study used data on firm characteristics include accounting data, stock price data and data on ownership structure from companies' annual reports of 1997-98. By using Logit regression tests he found that firms hedge transaction exposure with currency derivatives to increase firm value by reducing indirect costs of financial distress or alleviating the underinvestment problem.

Talat Afza and Atia Alam [2] aimed to determine the factors affecting firms hedging policies of both foreign currency and interest rate derivative instruments of 105 non-financial firms listed on Karachi Stock Exchange for the period of 2004-2008. By using Logit regression model on firm's decision to use hedging instruments. The result found the negative effect of financial distress, taxes, underinvestment and managerial risk aversion. Though, inconsistent with the theory, interest coverage ratio demonstrated positive effect on firms hedging policies.

Charumathi [3] explored the factors which determine the usage of derivatives by large Indian non-financial companies. By taking 49 companies in 2007, 68 companies in 2008, 56 companies in 2009, the derivative data in their annual reports, used cross sectional panel data for three years from 2007 to 2009 and applied a multiple regression

***Corresponding author:** Raghavendra RH, Research Scholar, Department of Commerce School of Management, Pondicherry University, Pondicherry-605 014, India, E-mail: raghavpondiuni@gmail.com

model. Those variables are financial distress cost, underinvestment cost, multinationality, economies of scale, firm size and agency variables are regressed against reported notional amount of derivatives. Finally found that size is the major determinant of the derivative usage by large Indian non-financial companies.

Naveed et al. examined the determinants the factors affecting the firm's decision on derivative usage in risk management practices by using the 75 Pakistani non-financial firms listed in Karachi Stock Exchange for the period of 2007 to 2011. By using regression model, they pooled variables like derivative usage as dependent variable and dividend per share, quick ratio, debt, Price to earnings ratio, Ratio of market to book value of equity, foreign purchase, EBDIT, depreciation and tax, market value of firm, size as independent variable. Finally result found that that there is a strong relationship between the derivatives usage and firm's foreign purchase, growth options, liquidity and size.

Research gap

Above mentioned detailed reviews are concentrating about determinants of currency hedging in corporate firms in developed countries, not many studies have been attempted on the determinants of derivative usage in IT firms and Studies about Indian IT firms are nil. Though Charumathi [3] studied the determinants of derivative usage by large Indian non-financial Firms, failed to concentrate on export oriented IT firms. However, there are no studies on the determinants of derivative usage in IT firms in India. So the present study intends to fill this gap.

Objectives of the study

This research initiates to model the factors which determine the usage of currency derivatives by major IT firms in India.

Research Methodology

Data

The data has been collected from firms annual reports, which are available on the NSE website or concerned IT firms' websites. In India there is no regulation to disclose the derivative aspects by any companies, so there are not many IT firms which have disclosed the details of derivative usage in their annual reports. To understand the extent of derivatives used by the firms, they need to use any one of the derivative instruments like forward, option, future, and currency swaps, and the notional values have to be disclosed.

Sample

The sample is arranged by studying the annual reports of 18 large IT firms which are highly involved in currency hedging activity. (Highly involved, Moderately involved and Not involved IT firms are categorized in the level of currency hedging activity during survey to collect a research data from primary sources, Out of the 103 firms that responded to the survey, 54 respondent state that they use derivatives moderately involved and 24 firms represented as highly involved in currency hedging activity) Those selected IT firms are listed in the National Stock Exchange (NSE), data has been collected for the financial years of 2011 to 2013. The rationale behind selecting the highly involved IT firms are, Smith and Stulz [1] argue that when the ownership structure is more concentrated, the motivation to hedge increases as the owners are less likely to hold well-diversified portfolios. Since the manager of the firm often handles the hedging activity, his/her risk aversion can be an important factor for managing risk. In order to capture this relationship, this study will focus on highly involved firms. Out of 24 IT firms highly involved in hedging activity, only 18 firms' met our criteria of data on derivatives and other variables are taken in to consideration.

Dependent variables

Notional value of currency derivative: Nominal or notional amounts outstanding are known as the gross nominal or notional value of all deals concluded and not yet settled on the reporting date. For contracts with variable nominal or notional principal amounts, the basis for reporting is the nominal or notional principal amounts at the time of reporting.

The dependent variable is the extent of derivative as in the study by Allayannis and Ofek [4], hence the total notional value of currency derivatives like Forward, option, Future and swaps are used by IT firms in India.

There are many reasons to why we use notional amount as a measure of derivative usage. The group of Thirty states that "Activity in OTC derivatives can be measured in two ways: by the notional principal contracts, either the amount outstanding at a particular period (e.g., annually or quarterly), and by the number of transactions. These measures provide a rough, but nevertheless useful, measure of the level of activity in derivatives, both in the aggregate and at the individual firm level", only the notional principal amounts outstanding at end of the year are publicly available for Indian IT firms.

Independent variables

The proxies discussed above in Table 1, constitutes independent variables of the present study.

Financial distress costs

Risk management can minimize the costs associated with financial

Author	Variables affecting the decision to hedge with derivatives
Stephen R. Goldberg et al.	Taxes Investment opportunities Size Multinationality
Mian	Taxation Size
Geczy et al.	Size Degree of exposure
Allayannis Ofek	Size R&D expences Degree of exposure
Hagelin	Underinvestment
Luis A. Otero González	Liquidity Earnings per share Size (log value)
Epharaim Clark and Amrit judge	Financial distress Underinvestment Tax
Andrew Marshall et al.	Financial distress Size Underinvestment Tax Multinationality Liquidity
B. Charumathi and Hima Bindu Kota	Financial distress Underinvestment Multinationality Size

Table 1a: Some of the studies based on the variables affecting the decision to hedge with derivatives.

Si no	Factors		Proxy variables
1	**Financial Distress**	DRatio (Debt ratio)	Total debt divided by the book value of assets
		DER (Debt-equity ratio)	Ratio of long-term debt to shareholders' equity
2	**Under Investment/ Investment opportunities**	PE (Price-Earnings Ratio)	Ratio of Price per share to the annual earnings per share
		RDEXP(R&D Expenses/sales)	Ratio of R& D expenses to total sales
		EPS (Earning per share)	The portion of a company's profit allocated to each outstanding share of common stock
3	**Multinationality**	FE (Foreign exchange sales/ total sales)	Ratio of foreign exchange sales to total sales
4	**Size**	REV (Revenue)	Natural logarithm of the total revenue
		TotAsset (Total Asset)	Natural logarithm of the total assets
5	**Taxation**	Taxes	Total tax paid
6	**Liquidity**	Current ratio	Current Asset divided by Current liability

Table 1b: variables considered for the present study.

distress. By minimizing the chance of financial distress, an optimal debt-ratio can be easily obtained. Many previous studies like, Nance et al. [5]; Akshay madhava [6]; Geczy et al. [7]; and Briggs [8] looked on whether economic theories for optimal hedging can determine derivatives usage by firms. Two of these studies found a positive relation between hedging and leverage while the remaining two failed to find connection. Mayers and Smith argue that hedging activity can reduce the probability of the firm encounters in financial distress by minimizing the variance of firm value, and also reduces the expected costs of financial distress [9]. The enormity of this cost reduction is a positive function of probability that a firm can encounter financial distress if it does not hedge and the costs the firm incurs if it does not encounter financial distress. Nance et al. [5] recognized the hypothesis that the likelihood of bankruptcy increases along with leverage (book value of Debt divided by book value of Capital). To proxy for financial distress costs, we used two variables those are Debt Ratio (DRATIO) and Debt–Equity Ratio (DER). Debt Ratio is defined as total debt divided by the book value of assets. Debt–Equity Ratio is a measure of a firms' financial leverage calculated by dividing the total liabilities by stockholders' equity.

Underinvestment costs/investment opportunities

A company with high growth opportunities suffers from a larger underinvestment and is more prone to use derivatives to hedge. Myers characterizes firm's prospective investment opportunities as options and with fixed claims in the capital structure, taking a Net Present Value (NPV) project in certain states reduces shareholders' wealth. Accordingly shareholders have incentive to forego some positive NPV projects. Hedging can help to control by restricting the states in which the firm would default on bond payment. Hence, companies with more growth options in their investment opportunity set to undertake a hedging program aimed at minimizing variance in value. Adverse FX movements can reduce firms' ability to undertake positive net present value investments. The possibility of having to forego positive net present value investments is referred to as underinvestment. Since hedging can reduce the probability of adverse FX movements it can add value. Following Allayannis and Ofek [4] it is argued that a firm with more growth opportunities would face higher underinvestment costs and have a greater incentive to hedge.

We used three measures to underinvestment/investment opportunities. To proxy for the three variables: PE Ratio (PE) is the first measure, second measure is the R&D Expenses/Sales (RDEXP) and Earning Per Share (EPS) is the third measure.

Multinationality

Present study samples are exposed to foreign exchange risk. However, it could be argued that companies with higher levels of multinational operation have greater foreign exchange risk exposure and thus receive more benefits from hedging. Goldberg et al. and others found that foreign sales in explaining the foreign exchange derivative usage. Allayannis and Ofek [4], used the ratio of foreign sales to total sales as a measure of Multinationality.

For multinationality, we used a proxy as: Foreign Sales divided by Total Sales (FE). We predict a positive relationship between multinationality and derivative usage.

Size

To proxy for size, we use two variables: Revenue (natural logarithm of the total revenue) (REV) and Size (SIZE) that is measured by the value of total asset (natural logarithm of the total asset). There are several reasons how the size of the firm can affect the incentive to hedge. Financial distress can lead to situations where the firm faces direct legal cost. For smaller firms, this cost might be a higher portion of the market value of the firm which implies that these firms are more likely to hedge. Additionally, small firms are likely to have fewer natural hedging alternatives. These firms might have a smaller product range, thereby making them more exposed to volatility in demand. This is an additional argument as to why one can expect that smaller firms in fact should use more derivatives than larger firms. However, several studies argue that large firms are more likely to have the resources to warrant the use of derivatives compared to smaller firms [10]. This is based on an economy of scale argument, meaning that larger firms are more likely to employ managers with the specialized information to set up a derivatives program. Moreover, large firms often have more developed risk management systems than smaller firms. Finally, the market for trading derivatives includes a portion of transaction cost. By once again looking at economies of scale, it can be argued that this cost is easier to bear for larger firms [11].

Taxation

Smith and Stulz [1] showed that hedging could reduce expected tax payments when firms were subject to a progressive tax system. Therefore, a greater convexity in the tax function should lead to a greater likelihood of hedging.

Liquidity

If small firms are financially constrained they can reduce the probability of default by carrying more liquid assets. It has been suggested that there would be less hedging if Firms can also reduce the probability of default by investing in more liquid assets; therefore, we construct a currency ratio. Also more liquid firms have greater flexibility in meeting cash flow needs and thus they have less need to use FX hedging instruments. To proxy for economies of liquidity, we use one variable: current ratio i.e., Current asset is divided by the Current liability.

Model used

The linear multiple regression models developed for estimate the factors which determine the derivative usage by selected IT firms in India:

To explore the determinants factors' influence on currency derivative usage and the significance of that influence, we have used a multiple linear regression model. In this model dependent variable takes the notional value of firms which use derivatives. Independent variable takes the value for firms which used as factors. In order to find an analysis of identifiable factors considerably affecting the motivation of companies to use currency derivatives, we constructed a multiple linear regression model describing this relationship. The decision to use logistic regression as a probability model is determined by the type of the dependent variable. In this study, we use multi logistic regression including the use of derivatives as a dependent variable and certain factors as an independent variable. The first step was to identify the main components which may have a significant impact on the usage of currency derivatives. It has been determined on the basis of risk management theory and previous studies. In order to verify the hypotheses, we find that the use of currency derivatives may be related to the financial distress, underinvestment costs/investment opportunities, multinationality, company's size, taxation and liquidity. In this way we can formulate the first theoretical model describing the problem:

$$TOTDER = \beta_0 + \beta_1\, DRATIO + \beta_2\, DER + \beta_3\, PE + \beta_4\, \mathrm{RDEXP} + \beta_5\, EPS + \beta_6\, FE + \beta_7 REV + \beta_8$$

$$TOASSET + \beta_9\, TAXATION + \beta_{10}\, CURR + \varepsilon_i$$

Where TOTDER refers to notional amount of total derivatives of a firm, DRATIO refers to Debt ratio of a firm, DER refers to Debt Equity Ratio of a firm, PE refers to Profit earnings ratio of a firm, RDEXP refers to ratio of Research and Development Expenditure to total sales, EPS refers to Earning Per Share of a firm, FE refers to ratio of foreign exchange sales to total sales, REV refers to Natural logarithm of the total revenue, TOASSET refers to Natural logarithm of the total assets, TAXATION refers to Total tax paid and CURR refers to Current Asset divided by Current liability. The multiple logistic regression models that we estimate for the period of 2011 to 2013 [12]. By using this equation and the multiple logistic regression procedure, we try to answer the question about the influence of various factors known from theory and other empirical studies.

Hypotheses

To achieve the objectives, the study tested the following null hypotheses:

H_0: There is no relationship between Currency derivative usage and

H_{01a} : Debt Ratio as a proxy for financial distress,

H_{01b} : Debt equity ratio as a proxy for financial distress,

H_{01c} : PE ratio as a proxy for under-investment,

H_{01d} : R & D Expenses/sales as a proxy for under-investment,

H_{01e} : EPS as a proxy for under-investment,

H_{01f} : Revenue as a proxy for size,

H_{01g} : Total asset as a proxy for size,

H_{01h} : Foreign sales/total sales as a proxy for multinationality,

H_{01i} : Tax paid as a proxy for Taxation,

H_{01j} : Current ratio as a proxy for Liquidity.

Research Methodology and Data

As mentioned, no study has been taken on the determinants factors of currency derivative usage by IT firms in India. The methodology used for this study is empirical in nature unlike other previous studies on derivative usage. Though, the tools used are similar to that of majority of the financial empirical studies, specifically, multiple linear regression models [13]. Regarding the data, this study used the notional value of currency derivatives as a dependent variable and certain factors as independent variable which is disclosed in the annual reports of the particular IT firms in India.

Data Analysis

The Table 2 shows the summary of descriptive statistics for the variables chosen for the study. The result indicated that the mean values of currency derivative (notional amount of total currency derivatives of a firm) are 35736000000 and its standard deviation value is 164603000000, this indicates that our sample supports that larger companies are more likely to use currency derivatives [14]. Mean value of Revenue (Natural logarithm of the total revenue) is 24.1388 and its Std deviation is 1.70887 respectively and about Total assets (Natural logarithm of the total assets of firm) mean value is 24.1116 and its Standard deviation value is 1.70570. Debt ratio of the firms mean value is 0.235 and its standard deviation value is 0.83711 only, about Debt equity ratios mean value is 0.1298 and its standard deviation value is 0.17927 respectively [15]. PE ratio (Profit earnings ratio of a firm) mean value is 0.3287 and its std deviation value is 0.55220 only, RD exp (Research and Development Expenditure to total sales) mean value is 0.0123 and its standard deviation value is 0.03081only, EPS (Earning Per Share of a firm) mean value is 36.7813 and its std deviation value is 42.08994. FE to sales (Percentage of foreign sales to the total sales of a firm) mean value is 0.6891 and its standard deviation value is 0.17334 only. Tax paid mean value is 5.0126E9 and its std deviation value is 9.50808E9 only and liquidity (Current asset is divided by current liability) mean value is 2.1356 and its std deviation value is 1.05171 respectively [16].

	Mean	Standard Deviation	N
Derivative	3.5736E10	1.64603E11	54
Revenue	24.1388	1.70887	54
Total assets	24.1116	1.70570	54
Debt ratio	.2385	.83711	54
Debt equity ratio	.1298	.17927	54
PE ratio	.3287	.55220	54
RD exp	.0123	.03081	54
EPS	36.7813	42.08994	54
FE to sales	.6891	.17334	54
Tax paid	5.0126E9	9.50808E9	54
Current ratio	2.1356	1.05171	54

Note: Results computed by using SPSS 16.0

Table 2: Descriptive Statistics.

Model	R	R Square	Adjusted R Square	Std. Error of the Estimate	Durbin-Watson
2	.677[b]	.458	.437	1.23527E11	1.847

b. Predictors: (Constant), PE ratio, Total assets
c. Dependent Variable: Total derivative/factors
Note: Results computed by using SPSS 16.0

Table 3: Model Summary.

Model		Sum of Squares	df	Mean Square	F	Sig.
2	Regression	6.578E23	2	3.289E23	21.554	.000[b]
	Residual	7.782E23	51	1.526E22		
	Total	1.436E24	53			

b. Predictors: (Constant), PE ratio, Total assets
c. Dependent Variable: Total derivative/factors Note: Results computed by using SPSS 16.0

Table 4: ANOVA.

Model		Unstandardized Coefficients		Standardized Coefficients	t	Sig.	Collinearity Statistics	
		B	Std. Error	Beta			Tolerance	VIF
2	(Constant)	1.192E12	3.243E11		3.677	.001		
	PEratio	-2.616E11	4.037E10	.878	6.480	.000	.579	1.726
	Totalassets	-4.441E10	1.307E10	.460	3.398	.001	.579	1.726

a. Predictors in the Model: (Constant) PE ratio, Total assets
b. Dependent Variable: Totalderivatives/factors
Note: Results computed by using SPSS 16.0

Table 5a: Coefficients.

The Table 3 shows the model summary of the multiple linear regressions for the sample firms. The R-Squre of the model equals .458 percent and adjusted R-square model equals .437 per cent. This means that only 43.7 per cent of the changes in the dependent variable (TOTDER) are due to the variations of the independent variables used in this model. The result of Adjusted R^2 is relatively similar to those reported in other studies such as Allayannis and Ofek [4]. It is not surprising that the power of the multiple logitistic regression is low. Present studies sample size is small relative to other studies. We use 11 variables, while there are 54 observations only.

Table 4 shows the result of ANOVA, by using the analysis of variance, it is found that F-test of the model is equal to 21.554 and it is significant at the 1 per cent level of significance.

From Table 5a, we estimate the above model using logistic regression by pooling all firm-year observations in SPSS.16.0, to establish the factors which had the greatest influence on financial derivatives use in the evaluated firms. For that purpose, the selected dependent variable was "financial derivatives use" and the independent variables were the ten identified factors. It is clear that two of the ten independent variables were significant that there is a positive relationship between the usages of currency derivatives [17]. (a) PE (Profit earnings ratio proxy of Underinvestment) ratio is positive and also significant at the .001 level of significance; It is because IT firms are required to hold a certain percentage of investment on the riskiness of their asset, this result may indicate that IT firms with greater tendencies towards risk are more likely to use derivatives. (b) Total asset (Proxy for Size) is positive and significant at the .000 level; it indicates that selected larger IT firms tend to use currency derivatives to a greater extent than other IT firms. IT firms hold more capital relative to assets also tend to be more frequent users of derivatives according to this model. This result supporting the theoretical predictions that due to economies of scale, larger IT firms are more likely to hedge. This result supports some of the findings for large financial or non-financial firms [4]. Result found that null hypotheses of H_{01c} and H_{01g} are rejected. Hence there is a relationship between derivative usage and PE ratio as a proxy for under-investment and Total asset as a proxy for size.

Total model effect is: TOTDER= $\beta0 + \beta3$ PE + $\beta8$ TOASSET+ εi

=0.1192-0.02616-0.0441

Accordingly, the result was that the influencing variables for the model that presented significant relationship with the dependent variable were: (a) PE ratio (Underinvestment) (b) Total asset (Size).

The most interesting findings, in Table 5b, that there is a positive relationship between the use of derivatives and; (a) Research and Development exp (b) Foreign sales to total sales (c) Taxation; and (d) Current ratio;. The coefficient of these variables, namely, 0.215, 0.314, 0.724, and 0.419 respectively are positive but not significant at both the 1 per cent and 5 per cent confidence levels. Hence, the null hypotheses $H_{01d,}$ $H_{01h,}$ H_{01i} and H_{01j} are accepted. So, there is no relationship between derivative usage and R&D exp, FE, Taxation and Current ratio. There is a negative relationship between the use of derivates and (a) Revenue; (b) Debt ratio; (c) Debt equity ratio and (d) EPS. The coefficient of these variables, namely, -897, -1.499, -1.306 and -1.424 respectively are negative but not significant at both the 1 per cent and 5 per cent confidence levels. Hence, the null hypotheses $H_{01f,}$ $H_{01a,}$ H_{01b} and H_{01e} are accepted. So there is no relationship between derivative usage and Revenue, Debt ratio, Debt equity ratio and EPS. According to the results of model 1, financial distress costs (the proxy is DRatio, Debtequity ratio) do not affect the hedging likelihood but this significant finding is consistent with a number of prior studies of larger firms and generally there is support avoidance of financial distress as one of the key objectives of foreign exchange hedging in Nguyen and Faff [18] and El-Masry and Ahmed [19] studies. There is no evidence from the linear regressions in line with the underinvestment (PE ratio, R&D exp, and EPS) for IT firms. It could be that since small firms generally have higher growth than larger firms, the impact of the decision to hedge on this growth is not as considerable as in large firms. It is also possible that this proxy does not fully capture a strong relation between investment opportunity and the foreign exchange hedging decision.

It is fond that there is no support for the taxation hypothesis can be an indication that the influence of the tax is not a determining factor for derivative usage by IT firms in India. There is also no support for some of the other determinants of hedging, including Multinationality (FORSALES), liquidity (Current Ratio). Further, as our sample firms have a high level of liquidity (Current Ratio), this argument might not be as important in the decision to hedge in comparison to larger IT firms [20]. Hence, that there is no statistical significant relationship between derivative usage by IT firms in India and the Liquidity (current ratio). Likewise several cases the direction of the relationship is inconsistent with the previous studies.

The values of variance inflation factor (VIF) for all the independent variables have also been checked and none of the independent variable indicates any occurrence of a serious multi co linearity problem.

The above Table 5c contains the residuals statistics which comprises the unstandardized predicted and residuals values along with the standardized predicted and residuals values. Standardized values have a mean of 0 and a standard deviation of 1. It means that residuals are normally distributed and there are no outliers of influential data points in the present study.

Model		Beta In	t	Sig.	Partial Correlation	Collinearity Statistics		
						Tolerance	VIF	Minimum Tolerance
2	Revenue	-.233b	-.897	.374	-.126	.158	6.322	.150
	Debt ratio	-.156b	-1.499	.140	-.207	.958	1.044	.555
	Debt equity ratio	-.136b	-1.306	.198	-.182	.973	1.028	.571
	RD exp	.023b	.215	.830	.030	.946	1.057	.550
	EPS	-.158b	-1.424	.161	-.197	.841	1.189	.529
	FE to sales	.033b	.314	.755	.044	.969	1.032	.562
	Tax paid	.109b	.724	.472	.102	.474	2.109	.295
	Current ratio	.044b	.419	.677	.059	.979	1.022	.569

C. Dependent Variable: Total derivatives/factors
Note: Results computed by using SPSS16.0

Table 5b: Excluded variables.

	Minimum	Maximum	Mean	Std. Deviation	N
Predicted Value	-2.4292E11	5.7565E11	3.5736E10	1.11406E11	54
Residual	-2.33945E11	6.37096E11	-.00048	1.21174E11	54
Std. Predicted Value	-2.501	4.846	.000	1.000	54
Std. Residual	-1.894	5.158	.000	.981	54

a. Dependent Variable: Total derivatives/factors
Note: Results computed by using SPSS 16.0

Table 5c: Residuals Statistics.

	Current ratio	Revenue	RD exp	FE to sales	Debt ratio	PE ratio	Debt equity ratio	Tax paid	EPS	Total assets
Current ratio	1.000									
Revenue	-.068	1.000								
RD exp	-.097	.174	1.000							
FE to sales	-.271	.137	.004	1.000						
Debt ratio	.422	-.037	.210	-.376	1.000					
PE ratio	-.005	.173	-.035	.131	.035	1.000				
Debt equity ratio	.364	-.288	-.469	-.060	-.085	-.181	1.000			
Tax paid	-.221	-.193	.045	-.088	.210	-.380	.248	1.000		
EPS	-.419	.004	-.120	.192	-.753	.091	-.104	-.382	1.000	
Total assets	.219	-.679	-.188	-.035	.121	.366	.034	-.362	-.028	1.000

Table 6: Correlation Matrix.

Variables	Relationship	Sig. at 1% & 5%	Hypothesis	H_0 Accepted/ Rejected
DRATIO	Negative	No	H_{01a}	Accepted
DER	Negative	No	H_{01b}	Accepted
PE Ratio	Positive	Yes	H_{01c}	Rejected
RDEXP	Positive	No	H_{01d}	Accepted
EPS	Negative	No	H_{01e}	Accepted
FE sales	Positive	No	H_{01f}	Accepted
Revenue	Negative	No	H_{01g}	Accepted
Total assets	Positive	Yes	H_{01h}	Rejected
Taxation	Positive	No	H_{01i}	Accepted
Current ratio	Positive	No	H_{01j}	Accepted

Table 7: Results when Derivative is tested by null hypotheses.

In the above Table 6, we estimated the Pearson correlation coefficients in order to find out whether there is a linear correlation between the dependent and the independent variables, and if so, how they correlate with each other between dependent and independent variable of the study.

We found that larger IT firms in India have significantly higher use of currency derivatives. This mainly suggests only the large IT firms are capable of engaging in currency derivatives trading due to economies of scale in establishing and at the same time maintaining the expertise (Table 7). Consistent with the concept that larger IT firms have economies of scale in setting up a hedging programme, thus we found a positive and significant relationship between firm size, underinvestment and usage of currency derivatives. The same result found in the previous studies by Ameer [21], Charumathi and Kota [4], Géczy et al. [7], Goldberg et al. [22], Nance et al. [5], Nguyen and Faff [18], Shu and Chen [23], Nance and Smith [24].

The arguments on financial distress, Taxation and Liquidity for hedging failed to provide realistic evidences in predicting a IT firm's currency derivative usage Davies et al. [25], Ali Fatemi and Glaum [26], Nguyen and Faff [18] and Shu and Chen [23] also reported similar results.

Conclusion

In the present study, we explored the major determinants of derivative usage by IT firms annual reports for the period of 2011 to 2013. The present study is important due to huge mark-to market losses undergone by Indian IT firms and an imperative need to study the currency derivative usage. The theoretical rationale for hedging includes financial distress costs, underinvestment, Taxation, Liquidity, size related issues and alternative approaches for hedging. The empirical evidence shows that the determinant of IT firm's currency derivative use is firm size (Total assets) and underinvestment (PE ratio) which suggests that only large IT companies are able to afford currency derivatives. The financial distress hypothesis, underinvestment,

Taxation and Liquidity and rationale for alternate methods of hedging failed to provide convincing evidences in predicting a IT firm's currency derivatives usage [27-29].

Finally, an interesting issue for scope of further research would be to conduct the same studies in other corporate firms in India, or testing with different variables other than the present studies independent variable to the same firms also analyze alternative time periods.

References

1. Smith CW, Stulz RM (1985) The determinants of firms' hedging policies. J Financ Quant Anal 20: 391-405.
2. A Alam TA (2011) Determinants of corporate hedging policies: A case of foreign exchange and interest rate derivative usage. Afr J Bus Manage 5: 5792-5797.
3. Charumathi B, Kota HB (2012) On the determinants of derivative usage by large Indian companies. J Account Financ 25: 54-88.
4. Allayannis G (2001) The use of foreign currency derivatives and firm market value. The review of financial studies spring 14: 243-276.
5. Nance D, Smith CW, Smithson CW (1993) On the determinants of corporate hedging. J Financ 48: 267-284
6. Akshay madhava Y.S, MD (2008) The study of impact of currency fluctuation on the Indian IT sector 1-12.
7. Géczy C, Minton BA, Schrand C (1997) Why firms use currency derivatives. The Journal of Finance 52: 1323-1354.
8. Briggs P (2005) Currency hedging by exporters and importers. Reserve Bank of New Zealand: Bulletin 67: 17-27.
9. Marshall A (2013) The determinants of foreign exchange hedging in Alternative Investment Market firms. Euro J Financ 19: 89-111.
10. A Muller, Verschoor WF (2006) Foreign exchange risk exposure: Survey and suggestions. Journal of Multi Financial Management 16: 385-410.
11. Skok AB, Igor L (2012) The evolution of the use of derivatives in Slovenian non-financial companies. Contemporary Studies in Economic and Financial Analysis 94: 399-427.
12. Brown GW (2001) Managing foreign exchange risk with derivatives. J Financ Eco, 60; 401-448.
13. Ephraim Clark AJ (2008) The Determinants of Foreign Currency Hedging: Does Foreign Currency Debt Induce a Bias? European Financial Management 14: 445-469.
14. Lee-Lee C, Chang XJ (2014) Determinants of corporate foreign exchange risk hedging. J Manage Financ 40: 176-188.
15. Antti Hakkarainen, Nathan J (1998) The foreign exchange exposure management practices of finnish industrial firms. J int firnanc manage and account 1: 34-57.
16. Martin G (2002) The Determinants of Selective Exchange Risk Management ---Evidence From German Non-Financial Corporations. J Appl Corp Financ 14: 108-121.
17. Kapitsinas SK (2009) Derivatives Usage in Risk Management by Non-Financial Firms: Evidence from Greece. paper is part of the author's thesis, 1-51.
18. Nguyen H, Faff R (2002) On the determinants of derivative usage by Australian companies. Aust J Manage 27: 1-24
19. El-Masry, Ahmed A (2006) Derivatives use and risk management practices by UK nonfinancial companies. J Manage Financ 32: 137-159.
20. Clifford MS, Stulz RM (1985) The determinants of firms heding policies. J finance and quantit analysis 20: 391-405.
21. Ameer R (2010) Determinants of corporate hedging practices in Malaysia. International Business Research 3: 120-130
22. Goldberg SR, Godwin JH, Kim MS, Tritschler CA (1998) On the determinants of corporate usage of financial derivatives. J Int Financ Manag Account 9: 132-166.
23. Shu Pei-Gi, Chen Hsuan-Chi (2003) The determinants of derivatives use: Evidence from non-financial firms in Taiwan. Review of Pacific Basin Financial Markets and Policies 6: 473-500.
24. Nance DR, Smith CW (1993) On the determinant of corporate hedging. J Financ 48: 267-284.
25. Davies D, Eckberg C, Marshall A (2006) The determinants of Norwegian exporters' foreign exchange risk management. Euro J Financ 12: 217-240.
26. Ali Fatemi, Glaum M (2000) Risk Management Practices of German Firms. J Manage Financ 26: 1-17.
27. Singh A, Upneja A (2007) Extend of Hedging in the US lodging industry. J Hospitality Manag 26: 764-776.
28. Dick D, Eckberg C (2006) The determinants of Norwegian exporters foreign exchange risk management. Euro J Financ 12: 217-240.
29. El-Masry AA (2006) Derivatives use and risk management practices by UK nonfinancial companies. J Managel Financ. 32: 137-159.V Ashutosh, Kumar S (2010) Development of Financial Derivatives Market in India- A Case Study. Int Res J Financ Eco 37: 15-29.

Productivity Change in Microfinance Institutions in Sarrc Region: A Malmquist Productivity Index Approach

Kiran Bibi* and Sir Habib Ahmad

Department of BusinessAdministration (finance), Foundation University, New lalazar, Rawalpindi, Pakistan

Abstract

Microfinance Institutions (MFIs) play vital role in developing countries. This study is dedicated to inspect the productivity change in microfinance Institutions (MFIs) in the SAARC region. A panel of 85 MFIs with five diamond information status from 2003 to 2011 with annual frequency is investigated in the analysis. Inputs and outputs used in the study are selected on the basis of double bottom line objective of MIF; s. the methodology which we adopt is Malmquist index through DEA software. The study will be helpful to find that whether the MFIs of SAARC countries effectively manage cost efficiency, technical efficiency and scale efficiency? Also the study will guide the MFIs to remove the deficiency (If any) in the above said forms of efficiencies. Also the total productivity change with respect time and country is investigated in the analysis. On average a positive TFP growth of MFIs in the SAARC region is documented except from 2005 to 2006 and 2007 to 2009. The efficiency of these MFIs will be helpful for completion of the financial sector and will improve the overall competence and growth. The study will be helpful for both welfarist and institutionalisms to achieve their objectives. We found many article related to measure the productivity change in different region but there is limited articles and research work related on SARRC region. This study has been carried out to find either Micro finance institutions are working efficiently or not.

Keywords: Productivity change; Malmquist productivity index; Technological change; Technical Change; SAARC region

Introduction

Microfinance organizations (MFIs) are considered important especially for developing countries. They give a variety of monetary (financial) facilities to the world low income family units and entrepreneur persons. This not only fills the gap in the financial sector but also provide credit access to the ignored segment of society. MFIs two fold objective of welfare and sustainability [1], which revolve around two approaches or paradigms first is institutionist paradigms and other one is welfarist paradigms. The "institutionist paradigm", which encourage MFIs to produce enough returns to cover their operational and financial expenses (sustainability) and on other side welfarist paradigm which stick to the objective of poverty reduction and depth of outreach and attaining financial sustainability [2]. In the same context, [3] argues that MFIs need to generate high profit, but at the same time, they are required to balance the social objectives of reaching low-income entrepreneurs with generating an effective return for their investors.

Microfinance has three types of sources formal institutions such as rural banks and co-operatives, semi-formal institutions, such as nongovernment organizations (NGOs) and informal sources such as money lenders and shopkeepers. Microfinance provides two types of services "financial services" and "non-financial services". Financial services include saving, microcredit, money transfer, micro insurance etc. Non-financial services include training, counseling, education, health etc. In both type of microfinance the common object is the creation of employment opportunities for the poor people and also indicts decrease poverty. Microfinance has come to be regarded as an important vehicle to reduce the incidence of poverty. An increasing proportion of the poverty in many developing countries needy people receive lone from microfinance institutions (MFI, s).

Many significant studies are conducted by different researchers to estimate the performance of MFIs in different region, in recent years some studies are conducted by [4-15].

However according to our knowledge very limited literature is available to investigate the productivity change in micro finance insinuation in SARRC countries but as a whole SARRC region we never found any single study so far, so this study is aims to fill this gap by investigating the productivity change in MFI, s of SAARC region during the time period of 2003 to 20011 by applying Malmquist index and aiming that it is valuable contribution to literature in areas of MFIs.

The remaining paper is arranged in following pattern In Section 2 gives brief Overview of origin of microfinance industry in SAARC region, Section 3 consist of literature review, Section 4 describe the data and methodology, Section 5 presents results and discussions. Finally, Section 6 ends up with conclusions.

Overview of origin of microfinance industry in SAARC region

The birth of 'modern' micro-finance in developing countries is said to have occurred in the mid-1970s by Muhammad Yunus, who developed it as a way to get rid of poverty in his home country Bangladesh. In 1983, he Founded Grameen Bank, the first institution which introduced this concept and started to Operate in the micro finance business in the proper sense. The Grameen Bank project, which translates literally as "Village Bank", was born, and today works in over eighty-thousand villages with more than six million borrowers. In 2006 both Yunus and Grameen were awarded the Nobel Peace Prize for their

***Corresponding author:** Kiran Bibi, Department of Business Administration (finance), Foundation University, new lalazar, Rawalpindi, Pakistan
E-mail: Kiranbb_89@yahoo.com

work with the poor. Although there have been many other organizations engaged on offering loans and saving opportunities to needy people before, Grameen Bank is known for successfully implementing the system of group lending. In particular, it has proposed a number of indicators to measure the impact of poverty elimination methods. These consider primarily basic needs similar to the definition of the International Labor Organization in 1976 and the financial situation of the poor. Together, Yunus and Grameen Bank were awarded with Nobel Peace Prize in 2006 for their efforts through Microcredit to create economic and social development from below" [16].

The idea of micro finance institutions meets the two bottom line concept requirements. They provide access to capital on smallest scales, and ideally act as social businesses realizing economic behavior improved by social preferences. They enable poor people to engage in productive economic activities and thus contribute to development in low income population but still to measure the performance of MFIs is very critical in order to provide continuous financial and social support to the poor. Despite social goals attempted by the MFIs, the self-sustainability objective is to exit from the permanent subsidies recipient group [17]. This objective can be achieved through good performance practice, critical to ensure nonstop operations of MFIs in providing services.

The performance of MFIs is therefore very critical in order to provide continuous financial and social support to the poor. Despite social goals strived by the MFIs, the self-sustainability objective is key to exit from the permanent subsidies recipient group [17]. This objective can be achieved through good performance practice, critical to ensure continual operations of MFIs in providing services.

Literature Review

Based on a longitudinal and geographical wide study from 1995-2010 by Goswami [17], introduced a new conceptual model of performance assessment for MFIs. Eight dimensions of performance (efficiency, productivity, sustainability, social, institutional characteristics, outreach governance and financial) are proposed to be the more holistic view of MFIs performance [18]. Our study will focus two dimensions suggested by Goswami [17], which are productivity and efficiency. Efficiency analysis will provide information specifically related to use of resources and magnitude of wastes while Productivity analysis will provide information specifically relate to a vital performance indicator which help the institutions to restructure its operations by calculating its cost of output. This paper looks at efficiencies of MFI, s in South Asia Traditionally, to evaluate the performance of MFI,s there are different method which provide information but that is not as much use full because its provide only partial measures of efficiency and remaining partial efficiency may be ambiguous When we describe conclusion on the overall efficiency of MFIs. Here is some of literature related to topic [8].

Uses borrower per staff and saver per staff to check efficiency level and recommended that in MFI, s high productivity level of the staff help in achieving MFI, s double bottom line objective.

Farrington [19] identifies a number of accounting variables to reflect the efficiency of MFIs. These accounting variables are administrative expense ratio, number of loans per loan officer and loan officers to total staff, portfolio size, loan size, lending methodology, source of funds and salary structure as the efficiency drivers and hence as the measurements for MFI efficiency.

By utilizing cost per borrower and cost per saver as a measure of effectiveness [20] find that formal micro finance institution have greater efficiency then semi formal MFI,s in African and in formal MFI,s, cooperative MFIs are the least effective. Also, [20] differentiate on the basis of efficiently cost management (cost for every borrower and expense for every saver.) Africa is the most beneficial MFI, s region then different areas.

Examine the efficiency of micro financial institution in Africa Asia and Latin America by using production approach and result revile that non-governmental MFI,s are working most efficiently than others to achieve dual objective. On the other way, bank micro finance institutions also outperforming efficiently under intermediate approach. So in financial intermediaries banks have access to the local market. Most probably in future bank also performs as a non-governmental micro finance institution [21].

Using both production and intermediation approach. So by status show that NGOs and NBFIs were the best performers in both production and intermediation efficiency. The findings of this study is different from findings in most of efficiency studies in MFIs which report the presence of higher inefficiency in both production and intermediation efficiency [22] measure the Efficiency and Sustainability of Micro Finance Institutions in South Asia and concluded that When the scale efficiency were superior than the pure efficiency its indicate that most of inefficiencies are either due to improper allocation of input resources or operation at inappropriate scale opposite to most empirical results which indicate that most of inefficiencies in MFIs were technical in nature [21,23].

Ahmad [23] Use combination of input and output and result indicate that MFI, s is specialized (technical) in nature which is essential requirement for any micro money related establishment achievement.

Which revealed that the classical ratio analysis is not efficient like DEA efficiency, by examining the performance and productivity changes of MFBs, the study noticed a steady growth in the operations of the MFBs but there are lots of opportunities for progress? The performance indicators of the MFBs shows that return on assets (ROA) and return on equity (ROE) of the MFIs were beneficial indictor for any MFI but at high interest rates [24]. The Malmquist productivity index showed variation in the technical and technological changes as the MFIs had more distinct changes in their technical productivity changes than their technological productivity changes. It was revealed that the MFBs experienced technological productivity decline. Overall, the MFBs had alternating progress and deterioration all over forms of the constituents of their Total Factor Productivity Changes but had the best tendency in their scale efficiency change [2].

Tahrim [25] investigate the efficiency and productivity change of microfinance institutions by data envelopment approach (DEA) with dynamic malmquist productivity index (MPI) and concluded that technological change have strong impact on the productivity change which eventually improve the efficiency.

Using the malmquist productivity index (MPI) to calculate the productivity of MFI, s and result of study indicated that MFI, s have practiced an augmentation of pure technical efficiency (advancement in management practices) instead of a change in ideal size. So in order to meet double bottom line objective they need to seek a technological advancement [10].

Ahmed [26] Examines the specialized productivity level of microfinance establishments and result demonstrates that there few microfinance foundations are working effectively and its show experience (Age) of the microfinance institution is very important determinants to measure efficiency. Additionally mean efficiency of microfinance establishments are low which demonstrates that microfinance foundations can build their output by the same measure of inputs and Innovation.

Siti Nurzahira [27] Examine the effectiveness of microfinance organization by Using a nonparametric methodology which empowers to recognize technical efficacy along with pure and scale efficiencies. Result shows that the Technical efficiency of the microfinance institutions is moderately higher than the other counterpart. Then again, amid this study pure technical efficiency is lower than the scale efficiency that shows the microfinance institution has been inefficient in controlling their expenses as opposed to working at the wrong scale...

Ines Ben Abdelkader [12] Assess the execution of microfinance organizations by applying non parametric DEA methods. The assessed results demonstrate that efficacy level in most of countries decreased during the study period and it indicated that the efficiency level in NGO, s are greater than Nonbank financial institutions NBFIs.

As indicated by assess the general proficiency by utilizing Data envelopment analysis (DEA). All of these efficiencies (Technical, Pure Efficiency and Scale Efficiency) are build by diverse models on basis of size as well as location And result conclude that the geographical locations have significant differences in their efficiency. And an interesting face is observed that the efficiency of banks is closely associated with size of the banks.

Moreover Eric Fosuoteng Abayie [13] use stochastic frontier approach to measure the economic effectiveness of microfinance organization and logical that the main source of inefficiencies in the microfinance division are because of the variety in management practices and specialized limits (both in training and portfolio quality). We additionally require an adaptable approach that will take into account all micro finance foundations to have the capacity to get deposits from clients.

In the same way, Oteng-Abayie [28] applied a Cobb–Douglas Stochastic frontier model for Ghana MFIs for the period from2007 to 2010. They found an average economic efficiency of average; And identify some of key significant determinants of economic efficiency which are cost per borrower and age and saving are key indicator of outreach and productivity.

Ahmad [23] use the DEA efficiency analysis and consider 25 MFIs, that is functioning in Pakistan, India and Bangladesh which is part of SAARC region on efficiency scores and result concluded that most of inefficiency is technical in nature so MFI, s related to these three SARRC nation should enhance the managerial expertises and technology utilized as a part of offering service in order to improve their efficiency level.

Similarly, Ferdousi [9] Findings exposed that among the three countries, MFIs in Bangladesh are enjoying comparatively greater economies of scale. On the other hand average source of inefficiency was purely technical in nature than to the scale inefficiency for all the countries. Therefore, improved management skills are required in order to ensure the efficiently utilization of available input resources to enhance increased outreach and performance of MFIs. However, size of MFI, s are also vital factor for determination MFIs efficiency. Secondly MFIs return on assets (ROA) should be positive, otherwise it becomes inefficient.

The assessment of effectiveness of MFI, s in the Mediterranean nations [7] utilizing Malmquist productivity index approach. The determination of inputs and output are on the premise of the dual objectives concept of MFIs achieving self-sufficiency by taking care of its expenses and arriving at numerous poor customers (outreach). The result demonstrated that MFIs have encountered mainly an addition of pure technical efficiency (improvement in management practices) Instead of a change in ideal size. Overall, an essential strategic implication for the micro finance industry is that they need innovative progress to meet the double objective reaching the poor people and financial sustainability.

Mamiza Haq [21] Examine cost efficiency of MFI, s in Africa, Asia and Latin America with both production and intermediate approaches. So result shows that under production approach non-governmental institute are more efficient and under intermediate approach banks MFI, s are more efficient and it is possible in long run banks may performing as non- governmental microfinance institution in lone run.

Furthermore idea that the impact of subsides relies on upon their intensity [29]. On one hand, the subsides play very important role to increase MFI,s efficiency, by providing the liquidity to develop the human and physical infrastructure. This effect dominant at lower levels of subsidy intensity which in turn lend to uphold the "smart subsidies" idea, that take into account the intensity and magnitude of the subsidies.

The most notable researches conducted on MFIs and Non-Bank Financial Institutions (NBFIs) productivities are by [30,31] and using the Malmquist productivity index approach and suggesting that pure technical efficiency has largely contributed to MFI and NBFI technical efficiency progress.

Data and Methodology

MFIs in the SAARC region are investigated in the study. In SAARC region most of the countries are developing where the poor is in need of microfinance. Also the idea of microfinance is originated from SAARC region which makes it a more localized concept. So the selection of SAARC region will be sagacious criteria for sample selection. The MFIs level variables are gathered from MIX data base, a nongovernmental association whose objective is to advance the exchange of information on the microfinance sector around the world. This database gathers data on 85 MFI, s working according to international standards from six countries of SAARC (Afghanistan, Bangladesh, India, Nepal, Pakistan and Sri Lanka). The most recent information for the selected MFI, s dates from 2003 to 2011.

The Malmquist productivity index

In the academic financial literature, there are number of different methods like Fisher index, Tornqvist index and the Malmquist Index are adopt to compute the productivity changes but The Total Factor Productivity (TFP) Index is commonly used to evaluate the productivity and efficiency level.

Lovell [32] Identify that the Malmquist index has three fundamental benefits as compare to the other index. Firstly, the institutionist paradigm approach (profit maximization, or the cost minimization, assumption) is not compulsory. Secondly, information related to input and output prices are not required. Finally, in this index researcher use panel data, it allows the decomposition of productivity changes into two components firstly technical efficiency change, and secondly technical change. Its main disadvantage is it's required to compute the distance functions.

However, the Data Envelopment Analysis (DEA) technique can overcome this problem efficiently. Due to following three basic reasons, we have selected the malmquist productivity index (MPI) to examine productivity change in SAARC MFIs and also estimation the productivity change of decision making units (MFI, s examined) between two time periods.

Selection variables

Production function basic purpose is to indicate the maximum amount of output firm can deliver from by use a defined set of inputs efficiently and other applicable variables that may clarify the amount of output produced. We adopt, output-oriented Malmquist Productivity Change Index, which emphasize on the equi-proportionate increase of input and output [33]. This methodology is select on the basis of dual objective which is depth to outreach and financial stability by offering loan to the poor people and collect revenue from the lender which not only fulfil their social objective as well their organizational objective (financial stability). Additionally they not only take up an imperfect economic environment as the markets for MFIs but also developed as the conventional banking sector and these MFI, s have limited resources (money, human resource) which they spend on commercial banks to generate revenue from shareholders [34].

On the basis of literature and Pattern (which we followed of [24] and [1] we select two input and two output.

Results and Discussion

By following the Malmquist total factor of productivity (FTP) change index has been calculated [33]. The basic rule that is followed for evaluation is if the total factor of productivity index is more than one it means micro finance institution are working efficiently But if the value of TFP is less than one that means efficiency is declining during the study period.

The Table 1 and Figure 1 of Malmquist Index Summary of Annual Means and chart of TFP shows that overall, microfinance industry has reported general productivity regress during the study period despite the fact that all the SAARC MFI,s have positive TFP development except for the year 2005-2006, 2007-2008, 2008-2009. Furthermore, the result shows that the average technical efficiency annual rate is 3.9% while there is alarming indication for technological change so attention is required.

Furthermore, Table 2 of malmquist index summary of firm means result demonstrate that 65 out of 85 MFI,s (around 76%) has indicated change in specialized productivity changes. Interestingly, just 21 out of 85(25%) MFI,s have indicated change in innovative (technological) change and study recommended that there has been a decline in the execution of the best rehearsing micro fund organizations and overall only 45 out of 85 microfinance institutions shows positive total factor of productivity index (TFP) growth. Now If the technical efficiency change is decompose into pure technical efficiency and scale efficiency result illustrate that during study time frame, pure technical efficiency increased by 0.7% while scale efficiency Contributed on average 0.11% increase and subsequently recommended that amid the study period the SAARC MFI,s have encountered predominantly an augmentation of pure technical efficiency improvement in management practices) instead of change in optimum size (scale efficiency change).

Conclusion

The present study was conducted to examine productivity change in south Asian MFIs over the period of 2003–2011 using the Malmquist productivity index and a balanced panel dataset of 198 observations from 85 MFIs. The selection of inputs and outputs is selected according to the dual objectives of MFIs: achieving self-sufficiency by covering its costs and reaching many poor clients (outreach). Therefore, we specify number of employees, and operating expenses as inputs and gross loan portfolio and as number of loans outstanding. The exact discoveries of the study demonstrate that the microfinance business has reported general productivity regress in the study period despite the fact that all the SAARC MFI,s have positive TFP development except for the year 2005-2006, 2007-2008, 2008-2009.

Furthermore, our study indicates that the main wellspring of total factor of productivity TFP development for the MFI,s was ascribed to the technical efficiency change (3.9 percent increment) as the result demonstrate that 65 out of 85 MFI,s (around 76%) has indicated change in specialized productivity changes. Interestingly, just 21 out of 85(25%) MFI, s has indicated change in innovative (technological) change and study recommended that there has been a Decline in the execution of the best rehearsing micro fund organizations. furthermore the result demonstrated that pure technical efficiency by 3.1 percent

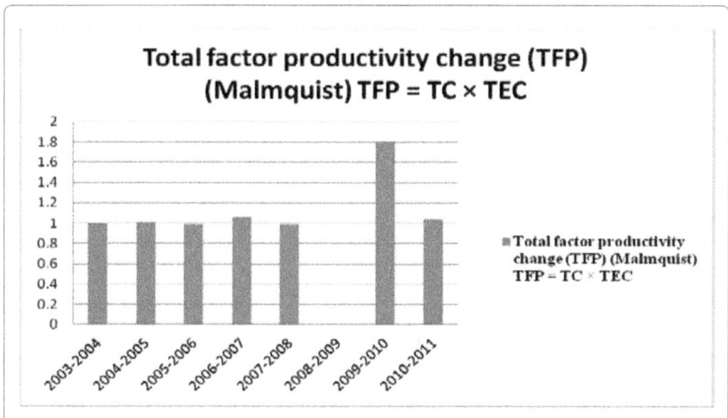

Figure 1: Total Factor of Productivity.

Years	Technical efficiency change TEC=TE×SE	Technological change (TC)	Pure technical efficiency Change TE)	Scale efficiency change (SE)	Total factor productivity change TFP = TC × TEC
2003-2004	1.046	0.962	0.915	1.143	1.006
2004-2005	1.134	0.891	1.194	0.950	1.010
2005-2006	1.120	0.886	1.056	1.060	0.992
2006-2007	0.815	1.303	0.876	0.930	1.062
2007-2008	1.103	0.900	1.107	0.996	0.992
2008-2009	0.794	0.000	0.861	0.922	0.000
2009-2010	1.2784	1.809	1.195	1.0694	1.809
2010-2011	1.125	0.922	1.111	1.013	1.038
Mean	1.039	0.000	1.031	1.008	0.000

Table 1: Malmquist Index Summary of Annual Means.

Firms	Technical efficiency change	Technological change (TC)	Pure technical efficiency Change (TE)	Scale efficiency change (SE)	Total factor productivity change TFP=TC×TEC
1.	0.986	0.908	1.000	0.986	0.895
2.	0.866	0.971	0.834	1.038	0.840
3.	1.084	0.926	1.119	0.969	1.004
4.	1.019	0.943	1.048	0.972	0.961
5.	1.087	0.929	1.096	0.992	1.011
6.	1.042	0.923	1.045	0.996	0.962
7.	1.019	0..919	1.007	1.011	0.936
8.	1.114	1.040	1.164	0.957	1.158
9.	1.055	0.969	1.054	1.001	1.022
10.	1.075	1.012	0.991	1.085	1.089
11.	0.992	1.014	1.000	0.992	1.006
12.	1.069	0.966	1.100	0.972	1.033
13.	1.037	0.884	1.034	1.003	0.917
14.	1.059	0.926	1.076	0.984	0.981
15.	0.840	0.920	0.908	0.926	0.773
16.	1.083	0.943	1.051	1.031	1.022
17.	1.026	1.004	1.008	1.017	1.030
18.	0.945	0.988	0.942	1.003	0.934
19.	0.994	0.915	0.925	1.075	0.910
20.	1.105	0.963	1.172	0.943	1.064
21.	1.187	1.019	1.228	0.967	1.210
22.	1.016	1.015	1.000	1.016	1.032
23.	1.049	0.989	0.999	1.050	1.038
24.	1.076	0.996	1.146	0.938	1.072
25.	0.927	0.968	0.919	1.009	0.897
26.	1.041	0.989	0.991	1.051	1.030
27.	0.986	1.022	0.954	1.033	1.007
28.	1.055	0.901	1.060	0.996	0.951
29.	0.993	0.965	0.906	1.029	0.900
30.	0.982	0.965	0.967	1.015	0.947
31.	1.022	0.941	1.012	1.010	0.962
32.	0.991	0.945	0.984	1.007	0.936
33.	1.114	1.035	1.060	1.051	1.153
34.	0.975	0.999	0.961	1.014	0.974
35.	0.978	0.965	0.979	1.000	0.944
36.	1.078	0.959	1.092	0.987	1.034
37.	1.000	0.964	1.000	1.000	0.964
38.	1.034	0.963	1.103	0.938	0.996
39.	1.075	1.001	1.111	0.968	1.077
40.	1.159	1.025	1.110	1.044	1.188
41.	1.041	0.949	1.000	1.041	0.989
42.	1.128	1.008	1.215	0.928	1.137
43.	1.033	0.987	1.029	1.003	1.020
44.	0.973	0.991	1.001	0.972	0.964
45.	1.008	0.910	1.004	1.005	0.917
46.	1.046	0.967	1.026	1.020	1.012
47.	1.077	1.027	1.111	0.969	1.106
48.	1.105	0.970	1.121	0.986	1.072
49.	1.000	0.915	1.000	1.000	0.915
50.	1.012	0.999	0.995	1.016	1.010
51.	1.109	0.949	1.000	1.109	1.053
52.	0.987	0.954	0.983	1.005	0.942
53.	1.103	0.980	1.122	0.983	1.080
54.	1.110	1.017	1.112	0.998	1.129
55.	1.010	0.911	1.014	0.997	0.920
56.	1.046	0.991	1.040	1.005	1.036
57.	1.043	0.995	1.069	0.976	1.037
58.	0.998	0.923	0.968	1.031	0.921
59.	1.003	1.017	0.978	1.026	1.019

60.	1.042	0.969	1.000	1.042	1.009
61.	1.028	NaN	1.050	0.979	NaN
62.	1.091	0.964	1.018	1.072	1.053
63.	1.023	0.935	1.014	1.008	0.956
64.	1.043	1.008	1.064	0.980	1.051
65.	1.046	0.978	1.070	0.978	1.023
66.	1.020	1.013	1.000	1.020	1.033
67.	1.433	1.036	1.419	1.010	1.485
68.	1.013	0.974	1.000	1.012	0.986
69.	1.147	1.011	1.156	0.992	1.160
70.	0.987	0.949	1.038	0.951	0.937
71.	1.026	1.003	0.997	1.029	1.029
72.	1.030	0.956	1.027	1.003	0.984
73.	1.105	0.965	1.073	1.030	1.066
74.	0.952	0.962	0.939	1.014	0.916
75.	1.089	0.976	0.971	1.121	1.062
76.	0.962	0.940	0.960	1.002	0.904
77.	1.003	0.974	0.974	1.030	0.977
78.	0.991	0.900	0.964	1.027	0.891
79.	1.151	0.947	1.100	1.046	1.090
80.	1.067	1.001	1.039	1.026	1.067
81.	1.044	0.953	1.038	1.005	0.995
82.	1.018	0.952	0.893	1.140	0.969
83.	1.098	0.988	1.080	1.017	1.085
84.	1.022	1.013	0.982	1.041	1.035
85.	1.044	0.947	1.032	1.012	0.989
Mean	1.039	NaN	1.031	1.008	NaN
	65/85	21/85	59/85	55/85	45/85

Table 2: Malmquist index summary of firm means.

while scale effectiveness helped generally 0.8 percent expansion and subsequently recommended that amid the study period the SAARC MFI,s have encountered mostly an augmentation of unadulterated specialized productivity (change in administration hones) instead of a change in ideal size(scale productivity change). For the most part, a paramount ramification for the SAARC micro money industry is that they have to seek after a mechanical advancement to meet the double bottom line objective of reaching many poor people and budgetary maintainable quality.

Our discovery lends solid backing to past studies directed by many scientists and purposing that [2,10,11,31,34]. Generally, a vital implication for the SAARC micro finance industry is that they have to increase technological progress to meet the dual objectives of reaching many poor people to reduce the poverty elevation as well to contribute the economy by providing loan to needy people to start up their entrepreneurial activity which is welfarist side and financial sustainability which is survival of any MFIs.

Acknowledgment

This research paper is made possible through the help and support from everyone, including: parents, teachers, family, friends, and in essence, all sentient beings. Especially, please allow me to dedicate my acknowledgment of gratitude toward the following significant advisors and contributors.

References

1. Bassem BS (2014) Total factor productivity change of MENA microfinance institutions A Malmquist productivity index approach, Science Direct Economic Modeling 1-8.
2. Musa A, Olasupo CA (2014) Performance and Productivity Changes of Microfinance Banks in South-West, Nigeria. Int J Inno Educ Res 43-51.
3. Otero M (1998) Types of owners for microfinance institutions. Ownership, Competition and Control of Microfinance.
4. Ahmad, Masood T (2010) Technical Efficiency of Microfinance Institutions in India- A Stochastic Frontier Approach, 1-21.
5. Lafourcade AJ, J I (2005) Overview of the Outreach and Financial Performance of Microfinance Institutions in Africa. 1-20.
6. Annim SK (2010) Microfinance efficiency trade-offs and complementarities 1-32.
7. Bassem BS (2008) Efficiency of Microfinance Institutions in the Mediterranean: An Application of DEA 343-352.
8. Baumann T (2005) Pro poor microcredit in South Africa: cost efficiency and productivity 95-118.
9. Ferdousi F (2013) Performance of Microfinance Institutions in Asia DEA based efficiency analysis 91-94.
10. Gebremichael BZ (2012) Total Factor Productivity Change of Ethiopian Microfinance, Euro J Bus Manage, 1-11.
11. Hidenobu O, Poleng C (2014) Operational Efficiency and TFP Change of Major Cambodian Financial Institutions 1-22.
12. Abdelkader IB, Hathroubi S (2014) Microfinance Institutions' Efficiency in the MENA Region: Research, J Financ Account 1-13.
13. Jayamaha A (2009) Efficiency of Small Financial Institutions in Sri Lanka, J Emerging Trends in Ecoand Manage Sci 1-12.
14. Sanchez MK (2009) Efficiency Analysis of Microfinance Institutions in Developing Countries 1-22.
15. Kipesha EF (2012) Efficiency of Microfinance Institutions in East Africa: A Data Envelopment Analysis, Euro J Bus Manage 1-12.
16. Yaron J (1994) What Makes Rural Finance Institutions Successful? The World Bank Research Observer 9: 49-70.
17. Goswami R (2013) A scientometric analysis of literature on performance assessment of microfinance institutions (1995-2010). Int J Com Manage 148-174.
18. Tahrim IM (2014) Efficiency and Productivity Analysis of Microfinance

Institutions in Cambodia: A DEA Approach. Proceedings of Eurasia Business Research Conference 1-20.

19. Farrington (2000) Efficiency in microfinance institutes. Micro Bank Bull 8-23.

20. Lafourcade AL (2005) Overview of the Outreach and Financial Performance of Microfinance Institutions in Africa. 1-22.

21. Haq M, Skully M, Pathan S (2010) Efficiency of Microfinance Institutions: A Data Envelopment Analysis. Pakistan Institute of Development Economics (PIDE) 1-13.

22. KipeshaEF (2012) Efficiency of Microfinance Institutions in East Africa: A Data Envelopment Analysis. Euro J Bus Manage 1-12.

23. Ahmad AQ (2006) Efficiency and Sustainability of Micro Finance. Pakistan Institute of Development Economics (PIDE) 1-37.

24. Begona GN, Carlos SC, Cecillo MM (2007) Microfinance institutions and efficiency, Elsevier 131-142.

25. Tahrim IM (2013) Efficiency Analysis of Microfinance Institutions in ASEAN: A DEA Approach. Business Management Dynamics 13-23.

26. Ahmad TM (2010) Munich Personal RePEc Archive, 1-21.

27. Oteng-Abayie EA (2011) The measurement and determinants of economic efficiency of microfinance institutions in Ghana: a stochastic frontier approach. Elsevier Science 1-18.

28. Balkenhol (2007) Microfinance and public policy. Outreach, performance and efficiency. Palgrave Edition.

29. Gebremichael BR (2007) Total factor productivity change of ethiopian microfinance institutions (MFIs): a malmquist productivity index approach (MPI), Elsevier Science 105-114.

30. Sufian F (2007) Total factor productivity change in non-bank financial institutions: Evidence from Malaysia applying a malmquist productivity index (MPI). Elsevier Science 177-186.

31. Lovell CAK, Grifell-Tatjé E (1996) Deregulation and productivity decline: the case of Spanish savings banks. European Economic Review 40: 1281-1303.

32. Fare RG (1994) Productivity growth, technical progress, and efficiency change in industrialized countries. American Economic Review 66-83.

33. Ahmad N (2010) Efficiency and productivity of microfinance: incorporating the role of subsidies.

34. Krishnasamy G, Ridzwa AH (2004) Malaysian post-merger banks productivity:application of Malmquist productivity index. Managerial Finance 30: 63-74.

The Relevance of Freight Rates in Forecasting Cargo Port Volume: A Study of the Guangzhou, China Port

Jeffrey E Jarrett[1]*, Huanxin Zhang[2] and Xia Pan[2]

[1]*Department of Management Science, University of Rhode Island*
[2]*Lingnan College, Sun Yat-sen University, China*

Abstract

We study historical data of the cargo going through the Guangzhou (GZ) port and related research the relationships between cargo shipments through the GZ port and its relation to domestic and international shipping prices (rates).In turn, we develop a regression based forecasting model based on the data of the GZ cargo port. The second task is to introduce the GZ port, the international dry bulk shipping market; the Chinese coast bulk freight index (CCBFI); and the Baltic dry index (BDI) which reflect domestic and international freight rates respectively. The third task is to make use of the data of the GZ cargo port, CCBFI and BDI from January 2004 to February 2010. The developed model establishes a multi-linear regression to relate the impact of the previous month BDI and CCBFI on the current GZ port cargo and determine the magnitude of the effect. Second, we establish a time series-regression forecasting model. This requires us to observe and consider including historical data of BDI, CCBFI and GZ cargo and come to a conclusion that relates the impact of BDI and CCBFI on the GZ cargo port. Finally, by developing a two parameter exponentially weighted moving average (EWMA), we obtain forecast with high predictive accuracy.

Keywords: Port handling capacity; Dry bulk freight rates; EWMA; CCBFI; BDI

Introduction

In this paper, we analyze the data of the GZ cargo port cargo, CCBFI and BDI from January 2004 to February 2010 by using a variety of models. There are two main research purposes. First, through data analysis, we study the relationships between Guangzhou cargo port and domestic and international shipping prices. Second, by establishing a Guangzhou cargo port cargo forecasting model, we obtain an accurate prediction of the magnitude of the activity of the Guangzhou cargo port cargo

The GZ Port is a window of foreign trade for this region of the People's Republic of China (PRC). The cargo port is a weathervane of the international trade activity level of the port and its regional environment. Through the forecast of the cargo port activity, we, in addition, also determine the trends of international trade in the Pearl River Delta. For the long term, predicting the cargo port activity with great accuracy is of great importance in designing a reasonable and scientific port layout; the basic scale of investment, business strategy; and developing strategies for integrated transport planning.

Previous research

The cargo port activity is statistically a time series with random fluctuations which is affected by political, economic and natural and other factors. Cargo port activity forecasting systems are complex. There is not a universal technique applied for this system up to now. More commonly, we use linear regression, nonlinear regression, and time series prediction method, logistic function fitting method, exponential curve fitting method, gray system prediction method and elastic coefficient method and many other methods to solve this system.

Currently, the researches on the port throughput forecast focus on three areas [1,2].

First, making local improvements on the existing prediction methods, so we can obtain the prediction result which is closer to the true value. By adjusting the inflection point of the Logistic curve, researching the methods of blur compensation and estimation of optimism and pessimism on production trends including Logistic curve prediction methods.

Second, some experts predict the cargo port handling activity by referring to methods from other applications including the use of econometrics, control theory and related methods. Others have produced dynamic PHQDF models to predict the cargo port activity, which systematically combines the historical trend of cargo activity, the socio-economic development of the hinterland, politics, policy, and psychological and technical factors. The example tests show that the model has higher prediction precision and better prediction results than the models suggested above.

Third, have the raw data processed. And through selecting appropriate explanatory variables from a plurality of explanatory variables, we may obtain better forecast results. Regression models to predict the cargo port activity are not uncommon. As results often indicate, when one utilizes mathematical models to predict, the most critical aspect is that the accuracy of the model, relationship of the response variable and predictor's variables and the quality of data is most important. The complexity of the model, especially in the case of only having small amounts of historical data is of lesser importance. Some examples of forecasting port activity include Wang [3], Xu et al. [4], Hui et al. [5], Yuan and Xie [6], Chen et al. [7], Lam et al. [8] Sun and Wang [9] Sun and Zheng [1]. In each application, they use very large amounts of data to predict port capacity, tonnage and other measures of activity.

***Corresponding author:** Jeffrey E Jarrett, Department of Management Science, University of Rhode Island, USA
E-mail: jeffreyejarrett@gmail.com

In this paper, by using large amounts of historical data and establishing multi-linear regression model and time series regression model, we study the impact of the domestic and international shipping freight on the current GZ cargo port activity the In addition. We construct a two parameter exponentially weighted moving average model (EWMA), we develop a better model for forecasting activity for the major port in the PRC.

GZ Port and Dry Bulk Shipping Market; Overview

According to the Harbor Law of the PRC, a port refers to a region consisting of landside area and waters and with the functions as ships entering and leaving, mooring, berthing, passengers leaving and entering the ship, cargo handling, storage and other functions containing the corresponding terminal facilities. Ports are the assembly point and hub of the water and land transportation, and also they are collecting and distributing centers of the industrial and agricultural products and the import and export goods. The port is a natural interface linking the hinterland with maritime transport, and as a result, ports are a special node of international logistics.

According to the locations, ports can be divided into the estuary ports, harbors and river ports. Estuary ports are located in estuaries or the segments of tidal estuaries and can also serve for both seagoing vessels and riverboats. Large cities are the basis for convenient transportation. The inland waterways are often extend to the vast economic hinterland, undertaking a lot of goods traffic. As a result, many of the ports around the world are built near the estuary, such as the Ports of Rotterdam, London, New York, Leningrad, and Shanghai. Estuary ports are characterized by terminal facilities arranged along the river bank, the distance between the port and the sea is short and do not need to build breakwaters. Besides, if the length of shoreline is not enough, you can add the excavated basin. GZ Port belongs to the estuary port grouping.

Harbors are located on the coast or in the bay or lagoon, but also some are built on the deep sea which is far from the coast. The ports located in the open sea shore or in the bay lacking of natural reserve ports are usually required to build the considerable size breakwater, such as the Port of Dalian, Qingdao Port, and the Port of Lianyungang, the Port of Keelung, the Port of Genoa and others. The single point or multi-point mooring docks served berthing for supertankers and ore ships belong to the harbors off the coast having no screenings, such as Marsa el Brega (Libya), the Port of Sidon (Lebanon) and others. In addition, there are also large seaports rely entirely on natural cover, such as the ports of Tokyo, Hong Kong, and Sydney.

River ports are located on the natural rivers or canals, including lake harbors and reservoir ports. Lake harbors and reservoir ports have broad surface and sometimes large waves. Therefore, there are many similarities with the harbors, for example, they often need to build breakwaters. The ports built on the Kuibyshev, Tsimlyansk and other large reservoirs in Russia, St. Louis, Memphis and Philadelphia in the United States and the small ports built on the Hongze Lake in the PRC belong to the river port group.

Ports, especially the coastal ports, make a good connection between hinterland and overseas transportation. With economic development as a goal and international division of labor, these ports play an important role in the development of the hinterlands in many aspects. A Port is a junction point of sea and land transportation where a combination of the waterway transport, road transport and rail transport merge. These ports achieve the ability of multimodal transport. Goods coming from other countries or regions will be transported by road transport to inland areas. Also, a Port is an industrial base designed to reduce transportation costs of raw materials or finished products, many manufacturing companies including steel industries, petrochemical industries, shipbuilding industries and other heavy industries have chosen to set up factories in the surrounding area of the port to carry out industrial activities. In addition, the enterprises processing imported materials then exporting also tend to set the plant at the bonded area around the port. The Port is an integral part of the "Supply Chain," from raw materials to end user products.

The Port is an integrated logistics center with the purpose of building international logistics nodes. The ports carry out activities including not only the traditional logistics warehousing and transport operations but also customs clearance, freight forwarding, shipping agency, buyer groupage, distribution processing, container leasing and other activities.

Excellent ports provide cities with a window for external development, in which a city makes full use of its own superior resources in the international division of labor to gain profit from the international trade and promote urban development. Developing cities with their harbor and port development is not a new idea, but is a mature method for creating wealth and the movement of goods and services.

Port handling capacity refers to the total amounts of goods imported and exported to the port by water transport and after handling operation in a certain time. The unit of the dry bulk cargo throughput is ton. The unit of container port is TEU (Twenty-foot equivalent units). Port handling capacity is the important quantity index of the results of the operating activities reflects of the port and the size of the port. The flow structure, quantitative structure and physical classification structure of the port handling capacity are the most direct expression of status, role and impact at the international and regional water transport chain, but also a statistical measure of national, regional and urban construction and development.

Factors that affect the port handling capacity are complex and can roughly divided into two parts; one is objective regional factors, such as the size of the hinterland, the level of production development, export-oriented economic development and the quantity of import and export commodities. The other portion refers to its own conditions for constructing harbors which include natural conditions and socio-economic factors. When we obtain the above conditions the, the level of labor organization and management, the quantities of handling machinery, technical level, ship type, vehicle type, hydrological and meteorological conditions, seasonal characteristics of the industrial and agricultural production, the balance of ships and vehicles travel to the port, as well as the varieties and quantities of goods through the port handling are all likely to become important factors affecting the port handling capacity. The most direct and critical factor is the size of the ability of berth, that is, the maximum tonnage limit of the port for berthing ships.

GZ Port development

GZ Port is located in the Pearl River estuary and the center of the Pearl River Delta where the export-oriented economy is most active for PRC China. It is near the South China Sea, adjacent to Hong Kong and Macao. The East River, West River and North River flow into the sea at this point. Through the water system of the Pearl River, the GZ Port communicates with major cities in the Pearl River Delta, i.e.,

Figure 1: Geographical location map of GZ Port.

Hong Kong and Macau, and meeting the southwest of PRC by the West River. Through the seaward channel of the Ling ding Sea, the GZ Port can communicate with coastal harbors in the PRC and the harbors all over the world. The geographical location of GZ is shown in Figure 1.

GZ Port has a long history and is an important port for ancient Chinese foreign trade, one of starting points of "Marine Silk Road". In Tang-Song period, "Guangzhou Marine Silk Road" is the world's longest ocean routes. In Qing Dynasty, GZ Port became the only external port and the largest foreign trade port. Since China carried out reform and open policy, the rapid socio-economic development make GZ Port an important hub of integrated transport system and an important foreign trade port in southern China. It is one of China's container shipping transport arteries and the largest bulk cargo (energy, raw materials, etc.) transshipment port and container transportation trunk port in southern China.

GZ Port is divided into the Inner Harbor, Huangpu Port, Xinsha Port, Nansha Port and the Pearl River estuary. The inner harbors based on the original eight inland waterways of GZ mainly offer energy, raw materials, food, bulk cargo and container handling and passenger transport services for the region of GZ and the Pearl River Delta. The Huangpu Port mainly undertake the coastal and offshore, container transportation and the bulk cargo transport including food, coal, chemical fertilizer, refined oil. The Xinsha Port focuses on container, coal, ore, petrochemical, food, chemical fertilizer and other materials transport. Both the Nansha Port and the Pearl River Estuary water area are the integrated ports, the work area of Shazai Island focuses on the Ro-Ro and general cargo transportation, the main work of Xiaohu operation area is the energy, liquid chemical transportation, Lu Wan operation area mainly works for general cargo transportation, Nansha operation area dominated by foreign trade container transportation develops the bonded function, logistics function, commerce function and other functions, and develops and undertakes large bulk cargo transportation combining harbor industry.

GZ Port has a number of advanced facilities such as the large containers and the specialized deepwater docks for coal, grain, oil and chemical, as well as the largest ro-ro ship pier in the south region of China. As of 2008, Guangzhou Port has 631 quay berths of all kinds, 88 anchorages, 23 buoys, 59 big tonnage berths; and the maximum tonnage is 300,000 tons.

GZ as a transportation hub in southern China has developed waterways, rail and road transport. There are crisscrossing waterways in the Pearl River Delta. Shipping resources are in excellent condition. The harbor district has five special railway lines where Beijing-Guangzhou, Beijing-Kowloon, Guangzhou-Shenzhen, Guangzhou-Zhanjiang and Guangzhou-Meizhou-Shantou railway intersect. Highways extend in all directions. Highways of each port connect with expressways, highways and national highways. "Nansha Port Express" through to the Nansha harbor district. On the basis of the sound infrastructure of land and water transportation, the hinterland of GZ Port not only cover the Pearl River Delta which heart was Canton but also extend to the Pan-Pearl River Delta region, which make the circulation of goods more substantial.

Entering the 21st century, on the basis of sustained and rapid economic growth of the hinterland, GZ Port developed rapidly. Beginning in 2004, for three consecutive years, the growth of the cargo throughput of the GZ port is at the speed of 50 million tons per year. In 2009, cargo throughput of GZ Port is 364 million tons, ranked fourth in the country and the container throughput is 11.2 million TEUs, ranked third in the country and sixth in the world. Two main indicators are among the world's top ten ports. At present, GZ Port connects with more than 350 ports in more than 80 countries and regions around the world and more than 100 domestic ports. GZ port cargo in the last 10 years is shown in Figure 2.

Dry bulk shipping market and major freight index

Narrow shipping markets refer to all kinds of shipping exchanges such as the London Shipping Exchange, Baltic Exchange, Shanghai Shipping Exchange and others. Generalized shipping market refers to the trading relationships of the shipping industry. Transaction object is shipping products, namely all the services that is offered by shipping enterprises for the shipping market to meet the needs of the displacement of people and goods to and connect with shipping tools and equipment. According to the shape and packaging of goods, the transported goods across oceans are classified as three categories including liquid cargo, dry bulk and general cargo by maritime sector. Liquid cargoes include oil, refined oil, liquefied gas, liquid chemicals and other liquid cargo. Dry bulk includes a variety of primary commodities, raw materials. On the basis of the size of bulk transport, bulk cargo is divided into two types as large bulk cargo and minor bulk cargo. The large bulk cargoes mainly include coal, metal ores and grain. Minor bulk cargoes include steel, wood, chemical fertilizer, cement, etc. General cargoes mainly include mechanical and electrical equipment,

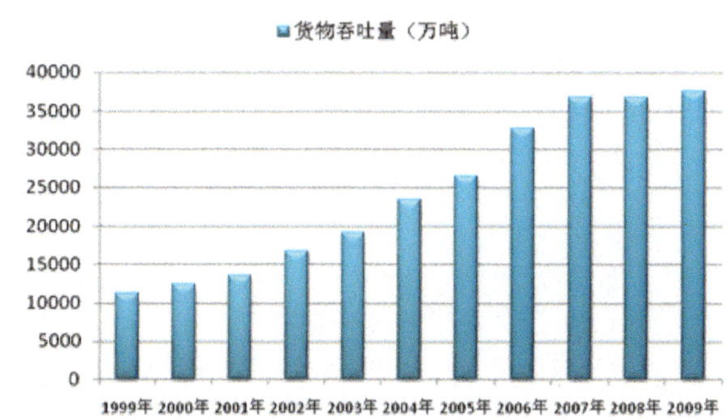

Figure 2: Histogram of the Guangzhou port cargo from 1999 to 2009..

chemicals, pharmaceuticals and other light industrial products, farm products and pasture products, fishery products and so on. Dry bulk shipping market refers to the trading relationships of all the services that are offered by shipping enterprises for the shipping market to meet the needs of the displacement of dry bulk cargoes among different countries and regions and connect with shipping tools and equipment.

The Relation between Supply and Demand in Dry Bulk Shipping Markets

Dry bulk shipping markets include two main elements, the demand for dry bulk shipping and dry bulk shipping capacity. Demand for dry bulk shipping refers to the quantity of dry bulk cargoes transported by sea among countries and regions at a certain period of time, which is a demand factor of the shipping market. Dry bulk shipping capacity refers to the total transport capacity of dry bulk carriers including Handymax bulk carriers, Panamax, Capsize bulk carriers and the Lake bulk carriers in the current dry bulk shipping market, which is a supply factor of the shipping market.

In the dry bulk shipping market, if dry bulk shipping capacity cannot meet the demand for dry bulk shipping, dry bulk shipping freight rates will rise. Meanwhile, if dry bulk shipping capacity significantly exceeds demand for dry bulk shipping, dry bulk shipping freight rates will decline. In addition, commodity price changes result in changes in supply and demand. Holding other factors constant, price rise leads to reduced demand and prices fall leads to increased demand. Similarly, price rise causes increased supply and price fall leads to reduced supply. Specific performance in the dry bulk shipping market, the rise in dry bulk freight rates will lead to a decline in demand for dry bulk shipping, while the fall in freight rates will promote the rise in demand for dry bulk shipping. In contrast, the rise in dry bulk freight rates will lead to the rise in dry bulk shipping capacity, while the decline in freight rates will promote a decline in dry bulk shipping capacity.

Price fluctuations by adjusting supply and demand, so that tends to balance, but in the shipping market, because demand for shipping derived resistance, potential, and long life cycle marine, construction costs are high, long construction period and other reasons, often entice shipping bullwhip effect occurred in the market, resulting in the shipping market supply and demand imbalance.

For Chinese ports, being able to reflect the dry bulk shipping market there are two tariff indexes, respectively, to reflect the international shipping market, the Baltic Dry Freight Index, as well as dry bulk shipping market reflecting domestic freight China coastal (bulk) freight index.

Baltic Dry Index (BDI) [2-10], is an index of economic activity in the shipping industry, including dry bulk shipping industry, trading volume changes, known as the international trend of the overall dry bulk market barometer. BDI is composite index being composed of Capsize, Panamax and Handysize vessels, each occupying third of the weight of the index. It was weighted according to the spot freight of twelve major routes to reflect the current market price. Therefore, the change of shipping price will result in a change in the index. For the index to be fair its manager, the Baltic Exchange, has very strict rules on calculating this freight index. These rules include:

(1) The selection of routes requires geographical balance, the route reflects the trade of both the Atlantic and Pacific, as well as the inter-oceanic trade (Maintaining the balance of round-trip routes). The weight of each route does not exceed 20%.

(2) The routes including in the calculation of the index have a certain turnover, or important relevant routes. Seasonal routes are not considered.

(3) There is a reasonable amount of accurate transaction reports. The routes potential or actual rented or controlled by one or a few charterers are not considered.

(4) 20 brokerage firms which are internationally renowned, reputable, representative, consisting of three groups, each responsible for calculating the day of the ship freight index.

China Coastal Bulk Freight Index (abbr. CCBFI) as a "barometer" of the coastal shipping market, reflects the trends of price movements of coastal shipping market without delay and help shipping companies, shippers, trade enterprises, ports, agents and other related businesses gain market information and grasp the market dynamics.

(1) The base period. China coastal bulk freight index takes January 2000 as the base period. The base index is 1000 points.

(2) Sample route selection. Based on the importance of the selection, it takes top five kinds of goods in our coastal port cargo throughput as samples of goods of coastal freight index, including coal, crude oil, refined oil, metal ores and grain. Based on the volume size, taking regional coverage and future trends of routes into consideration, it selects 21 samples of domestic coastal routes.

(3) Tariff information collection. Currently, there are 27 major incoming units to provide tariff information.

(4)Release mode. Shanghai Shipping Exchange prepares and publishes China Coastal Bulk Freight Index, sub-indices and the index of 21 routes every Wednesday.

GZ Cargo Port Forecasting Models

This section utilizes three models to predict GZ port cargo activity by making use of the collected historical data of the GZ cargo port freightage and domestic and overseas dry bulk freight. First, taking the last BDI and CCBFI as the explanatory (predictor) variables and the current GZ port activity as response variable, we build a multi-linear regression model to study the relationship of these two indices on the GZ port activity. In turn, we introduce the time series of GZ cargo port to build a model to predict the GZ port activity, test the validity of the model and estimate the influence of dry bulk freight activity. Finally, using the historical data of GZ port activity, we aim at building a forecasting model having predictive accuracy by making use of the two-parameter exponential smoothing method. The multi-linear by OLS regression results is the following;

$$Y_{t+1} = \beta_0 + \beta_1 X_{1t} + \beta_2 X_{2t}$$

Where,

$$Y_{t+1} = 2626.134 + 0.0366 X_{1t} - 0.044 X_{2t}$$

$Y_{t+1=}$period ahead prediction of GZ cargo port activity,

X_{1t} =BDI, the mean monthly value

X_{2t} =CCFBI (mid-monthly value)

Table 1 contains the output of EVIEWS® (multi-linear regression software). [For complete discussion of Regression modeling see Fahrmeir, Kneib, Leib and Marx, 2013]. Observe the coefficient of determination, R^2 =0.0196 and the adjusted coefficient, $\bar{R}^2 = -0.0088$. These coefficients indicate that the regression of port activity is largely

Variable	Coefficient	Std. Error	t-Statistic	Prob.
β_0	2626.134	349.2942	7.518401	0.0000
X_{1t}	2626.134	0.047248	0.774825	0.4411
X_{2t}	-0.043952	0.300456	-0.146285	0.8841
R-squared	0.019585	Mean dependent var		2718.985
Adjusted R-squared	-0.008833	S.D. dependent var		547.8405
Durbin-Watson stat	0.349792	Prob (F-statistic)		0.505416

Table 1: Output of the multiple regression analysis.

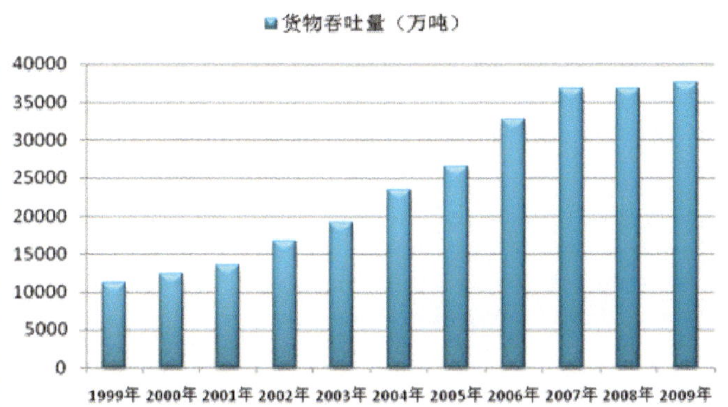

Figure 3: The residuals, actuals and fitted values are shown in one scatterplot.

unexplained by the multi-linear regression on the variation in the two freight indexes, BDI and CCBFI. In addition, significance tests would not reject the hypothesis that there is no relation between the response variable and the two predictors, BDI and CCBFI.

In addition, Table 1 indicates that tests for the significance of the individual predictors result in not rejecting the hypotheses that each predictor taken individually is related to the response variable. The p-values for both t-tests are large, that is, $p - value > \alpha$.

The output is shown in Table 1 based on 73 sets of corresponding data.

The residuals indicate that there may be a trend in their values. This appears corroborated by comparison of the actuals and fitted values. Hence, one may conclude that improvements can and will be made to the forecasting model.

In summary, the previous monthly mean values of BDI and the mid-monthly values of CCBFI may influence the current GZ port handling capacity. However, other factors not included in the multi-linear regression probably influence the GZ port handling capacity. These factors may have a time dimension.

In the linear regression model, we failed to take into account that international dry bulk shipping prices and domestic coastal bulk shipping price as influencing factors.Shipping rates for both international and domestic cargo due tend to increase over time especially for the shipping industry because rates are reflected in long term contract between the shippers and haulers. One method is to include a surrogate variable for time. Hence, by including a time series component in the forecasting model perhaps will improve our forecasting model (Figure 3).

In the next section, we consider the use of combinations of time series and regression analysis model.

Autoregressive forecasting model

An objective of time series methods is to discover a pattern in the historical data, develop a forecasting model and then extrapolate the pattern into the future. Time series method is often used to provide predictions of future by taking advantage of the chronological data. Autoregressive prediction model refers to the establishment of a regression equation for prediction by making use of the existing association in the individual observations of an historical time series. Regression and time series model refers to the model combining of the time series analysis and regression analysis and taking the influence of the time series and other factors on the time series into account. In this application the modeler selects the predictor variables and may express the model as follows:

$$Z_t = \alpha X_t + \beta Y_t + \eta_0 + \eta_1 Z_{(t-1)} + \eta_2 Z_{(t-2)} + \eta_3 Z_{(t-3)} + \cdots + \eta_n Z_{(t-n)}$$

On the basis of the 74 sets of data in Appendix 1, we make use of time series analysis and eliminating several sets of data in January 2004, we analyze the residual values including the monthly mean value of BDI, the mid-monthly value of CCBFI and the monthly cargo handling capacity of the GZ port.

We use Z_t to identify the response variable of the GZ port cargo handling capacity, X_{t-2}, X_{t-2}, X_{t-3} ... to identify the monthly mean value of BDI of each period and , Y_{t-2}, Y_{t-3} ... to identify the mid-monthly value of CCBFI of each period. In turn, the multiplicative autoregressive model is expressed as follows:

$$Z_t = \alpha_1 X_{(t-1)} + \alpha_2 X_{(t-2)} + \alpha_3 X_{(t-3)} + \cdots + \alpha_j X_{(t-j)} + \beta_1 Y_{(t-1)}$$
$$+ \beta_2 Y_{(t-2)} + \beta_3 Y_{(t-3)} + \cdots + \beta_m Y_{(t-m)} + \eta_1 Z_{(t-1)} + \eta_2 Z_{(t-2)} + \eta_3 Z_{(t-3)} + \cdots \eta_n Z_{(t-n)} + \phi$$

Variable	Coefficient	Std. Error	t-Statistic	Prob.
ϕ	757.0150	319.8731	2.366611	0.0214
$X_{(t-1)}$	0.020419	0.028933	0.705738	0.4833
$Y_{(t-1)}$	0.042297	0.251350	0.168278	0.8670
$Y_{(t-2)}$	-0.253484	0.220607	-1.149029	0.2554
$Z_{(t-1)}$	0.561794	0.139947	4.014328	0.0002
$Z_{(t-2)}$	-0.020117	0.166008	-0.121181	0.9040
$Z_{(t-3)}$	-0.041358	0.16967	-0.247700	0.8053
$Z_{(t-4)}$	0.074706	0.166727	0.448077	0.6558
$Z_{(t-5)}$	0.099610	0.169451	0.587841	0.5590
$Z_{(t-6)}$	0.161814	0.141661	1.142267	0.2582
R-squared	0.644852	Mean dependent var		2813.638
Adjusted R-squared	0.587775	S.D. dependent var		479.5500
Durbin-Watson stat	1.884267	Prob(F-statistic)		0.000000

Table 2: Output of analysis on regression-time series forecasting model.

Where $j,m,n<t \quad j,m,n \in Z$.

For changing values of j,m,n, we present the outputs of $\bar{R}^2$ in Appendix 2. $\bar{R}^2$ is maximum value when $j=1, m=2, n=6$.

When $j=1, m=2, n=6$, the value of $\bar{R}^2$ get to maximum $\bar{R}^2=0.588$. The outputs are shown in Table 2.

The regression equation is

$$Z_t = 0.0204X_{(t-1)} + 0.0423Y_{(t-1)} - 0.2535Y_{(t-2)} + 0.5618Z_{(t-1)} - 0.0201Z_{(t-2)} \\ -0.0414Z_{(t-3)} + 0.0747Z_{(t-4)} + 0.0996Z_{(t-5)} + 0.1618Z_{(t-6)} + 757.015$$

[For greater information of multi-linear regression time series modeling [11].

The multiple coefficient of determination $R^2=0.645$. The adjusted multiple coefficient of determination $\bar{R}^2=0.588$. The Durbin-Watson Statistic is 1.884 indicating that there is no evidence of autocorrelation in the residuals. The F-test for overall regression indicates that for the regression, taken together the predictor variables are related to the response variable. Further, the scatterplots of the residuals, actual and fitted values are all shown in Figure 4.

We observe that there is no trend or pattern in the scatter of the residual which corroborates the results of the Durbin-Watson statistic. Also, the patterns in the fits and actual observations indicate that the forecast contain a much smaller amount of error (magnitude of residuals) than in the first multi-linear regression model.Application of the forecasting model. Hence in Table 3, we observe the implementation of the model in predicting cargo handling capacity.

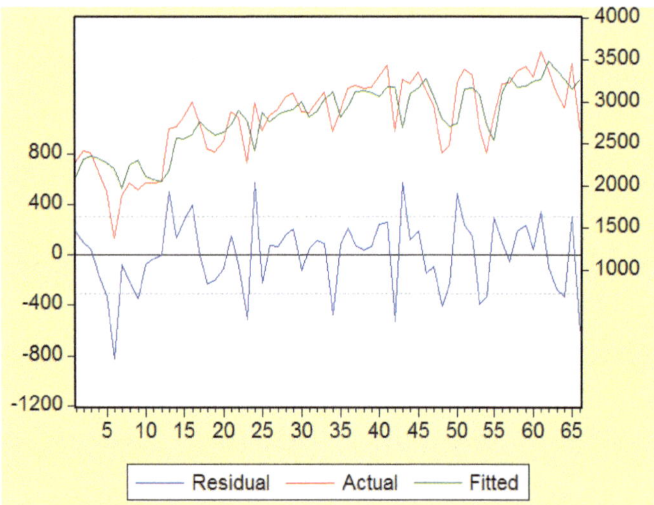

Figure 4: Scatterplots of residuals, fits and actual values.

月份	BDI	CCBFI	Volume in 10k tons)
2009年9月	—	—	3616.29
2009年10月	—	—	3388.27
2009年11月	—	—	3097.17
2009年12月	—	—	2938.37
2010年1月	—	1678.61	3469
2010年2月	2677.85	1255.95	2662

Table 3: Partial Data Table of BDI, CCBFI and cargo handling capability in 2009.

To forecast, we substitute the values of BDI, CCBFI and cargo handling capability into the fitted regression as follows:

$$Z_t = 0.0204X_{(t-1)} + 0.0423Y_{(t-1)} - 0.2535Y_{(t-2)} + 0.5618Z_{(t-1)} - 0.0201Z_{(t-2)} \\ -0.0414Z_{(t-3)} + 0.0747Z_{(t-4)} + 0.0996Z_{(t-5)} + 0.1618Z_{(t-6)} + 757.015$$

From the results, we know that the GZ port cargo handling capability is almost 28,975,500 tons. From statistics of the Guangzhou Port Authority (GPA), we find the actual value of the GZ cargo was 31.98 million tons in March 2010 and the percentage error is 9.39%.

From the results, we conclude that there is little relationship among the Guangzhou cargo port handling capacity, the international dry bulk shipping freight rates and coastal dry bulk shipping freight rates. However, there is better relationship between cargo handling capacity and its own historical data.

Based on the observation of the international shipping market and taking the analysis of the actual situation in GZ port into consideration, we can conclude that the dry bulk shipping freight rates have little effects on the GZ cargo port handling capacity. The possible factors that lead to this conclusion are as follows:

First, in international trade, with cargo ships becoming larger in scale and the rapid development of information technology, the proportion the transportation costs account for a much smaller percentage of cargo value. In the United States, transport costs of shipping account for 4% in 1997 whereas the proportion around 8% in 1974. By 2007 this percentage dropped 100% in three decades [12].

Second, there is little flexibility in transport costs for the majority of GZ Port's cargo strategic supplies such as grain, energy and raw materials. The import and export goods of the four main harbor districts of GZ port are mostly grain, coal, petroleum, iron ore and other necessities of life and the production or industrial raw materials. Regardless of the level of transport costs, these import and export goods cannot at present change radically.

In view of this conclusion, we will remove BDI and CCBFI from our forecasting model and include the time series of GZ port handling capacity to predict.

Two parameter exponentially weighted moving average (EWMA forecasting model)

EWMA models assume smoothing parameters weight previous observations of the variable to be predicted [12,13].

The simple exponential smoothing is to "smooth out" the irregular fluctuations in the time series, which is adjusted for the stationary time series, i.e. the time series without trend, cyclical and seasonal component. Two parameter EWMA models should be employed when a trend component exists in a time series. Two parameter models improve forecasting results by adjusting the single EWMA by including and adding the trend component in the model. The equations for two parameter EWMA forecasting are given by the following equations.

$$F_t = \alpha Y_t + (1-\alpha)(F_{t-1} + R_{t-1})$$

$$R_t = \beta(F_t - F_{t-1}) + (1-\beta)R_{t-1}$$

Where,

$F_t = forecast\ of\ the\ time\ series\ for\ period\ t+1$

$Y_t = actual\ value\ of\ the\ time\ series\ in\ period\ t$

$F_{t\text{-}1} = forecast\ of\ the\ time\ series\ for\ period\ t\text{-}1$

$R_t = the\ best\ estimate\ of\ the\ trend\ at\ time\ t$

$\alpha = smoothing\ constant(0 \le \alpha \le 1)$

$\beta = the\ trend\ smoothing\ factor(0 \le \beta \le 1)$

Although any value of α and β between 0 and 1 are acceptable, however they yield different results. Often forecasters choose the mean squared error [12] and/or the mean absolute deviation (as a measure of forecast accuracy. The smaller the MSE or MAD value is, the better is the forecast accuracy. Figure 5 below shows the scatterplot of the linear trend in the GZ port handling capacity.

The GZ port handling capability indicates a linear growth in the port capacity. Hence, the two parameter EWMA model appears useful in the prediction of the port capacity. According to the time series combined by 74 sets of data of the GZ port cargo capacity from January 2004 to February 2010, we do predict an accurate short-term multi-period ahead model.

For different values of α and β, the associated and calculated values of **MAD** and **MSE** are shown in Appendix 3. If $\alpha = 0.9, \beta = 0.1$; **MAD** and MSE are at minimum values, $MAD = 24.56209$, and $MSE = 1067.885$; or at the optimal prediction accuracy for the sampled data. If one draws the fits and actual values on a single plot as shown in Figure 6, the two plots are nearly coincident, indicating that the prediction model has great accuracy.

On the basis of the two parameter exponential smoothing prediction formula for period *t+i*; $\hat{F}_{t+i} = F_t + iR_t \quad 0 < \alpha \le 1$, and according to the data of the actual and smoothed values, and the

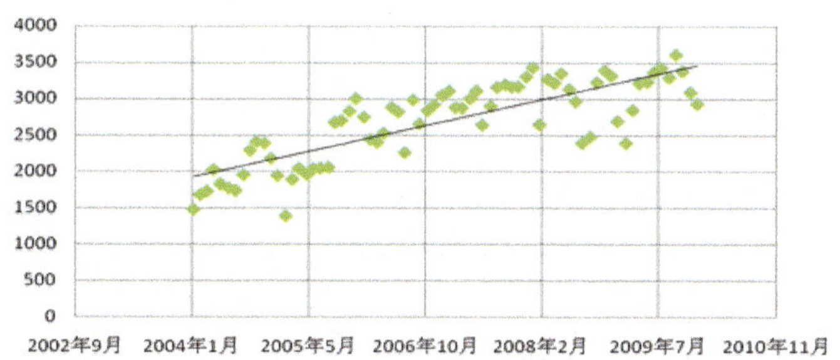

Figure 5: Trend chart of the GZ port handling capability from 2004 to 2009.

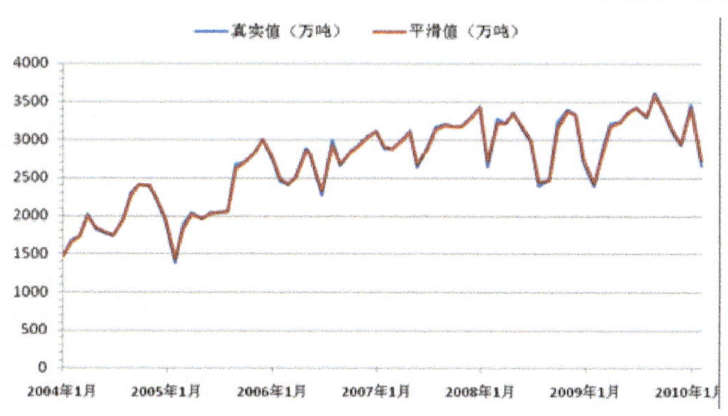

Figure 6: Chart of smoothing values of the GZ cargo port cargo capacity.

Month	Actual value	Smoothing value	Trend term	predicted value	Average of predicted value (Ten thousand tons)
May. 2009	3241.72	3237.717	27.47169	3512.434	3406.823
Jun. 2009	3373.94	3363.065	37.25929	3698.398	3395.088
Jul. 2009	3434.15	3430.767	40.30361	3753.196	3357.175
Aug. 2009	3299.92	3317.035	24.90002	3491.335	3300.6
Sept.2009	3616.29	3588.855	49.59196	3886.406	3268.811
Oct. 2009	3388.27	3413.288	27.07608	3548.668	3145.292
Nov. 2009	3097.17	3131.489	-3.81136	3116.244	3044.448
Dec. 2009	2938.37	2957.301	-20.8491	2894.754	3020.516
Jan. 2010	3469	3415.745	27.08026	3469.906	3083.397
Feb. 2010	2662	2740.083	-43.194	2696.889	2696.889
Mean value					3171.904

Table 4: Partial data table of the Guangzhou port cargo throughput in March 2010.

trend terms of the GZ port capacity from May 2009 to February 2010 (Schedule D) respectively, we forecast the GZ port capacity in March 2010 and draw the predicted results based on the data of each month. On this basis, we calculate the mean values of the predicted results over the past 10 months, 9 months, 8 months ... and 1 month respectively. Finally, we calculate the average of 10 mean values and make it the final predictions of the GZ port capacity in March 2010. Calculating the arithmetic mean of the mean values is equivalent to placing different weights on different months, the closer the months is to predict the greater are the weights. By this method, the predicting outcomes of the GZ port capacity in March 2010 are shown in Table 4.

According to the above method, we can draw the conclusion that the GZ cargo is 31,719,040 tons in March 2010. From the statistics of GZ Port Authority, we know that the actual cargo capacity of the GZ port is 31.98 million tons in March 2010 and the error is 0.816%, achieving very high prediction accuracy.

In the same way, we can predict that the Guangzhou port capacity is 32,579,840 tons in April 2010. From the statistics of Guangzhou Port Authority, we know that the actual value of the Guangzhou cargo is 34.44 million tons in April 2010 and the error of the prediction is 5.40%.

Tests on the prediction of the GZ port in March 2010 and April 2010, we can conclude that the two parameter EWMA model has greater prediction accuracy for the Guangzhou port than the other methods employed before, and ,hence, the best choice the forecasting models studied for short-term prediction on the samples data.

Comparison between the GZ cargo port capacity and dry bulk freight

In the last section, we make use of three mathematical models in turn to establish the forecast model for the GZ cargo port. Based on the multi-linear regression forecasting model and regression and time series forecasting model, taking the values of CCBFI and BDI reflecting the domestic and international dry bulk freight as predictors, we obtained the relationship of the two indexes to GZ cargo handling capacity. In turn we estimated the magnitude of the relations the coastal dry bulk freight and international shipping dry bulk freight affect the GZ cargo port handling capacity.

In the multiple linear regression model, taking the BDI and CCBFI for last period as variables for prediction, we study effects which the dry

Variable	Coefficient	Std. Error	t-Statistic	Prob.
X_{2t}	0.036609	0.047248	0.774825	0.4411
X_{2t}	-0.043952	0.300456	-0.146285	0.8841

Table 5: Partial data table of the operational report of the multiple regression model.

Variable	Coefficient	Std. Error	t-Statistic	Prob.
$X_{(t-1)}$	0.020419	0.028933	0.705738	0.4833
$Y_{(t-1)}$	0.042297	0.251350	0.168278	0.8670
$Y_{(t-2)}$	-0.253484	0.220607	-1.149029	0.2554

Table 6: Part of operational data.

bulk freight for last period have on the GZ port cargo throughput. The part of the operational report after running EViews® is shown in Table 5, where X_{1t} and X_{2t} denote the values of BDI and CCBFI for period t respectively and Y_{t+1} represents the Guangzhou port cargo throughput for period t +1.

If the significance value, $\alpha = 0.05$ the $p-$value corresponding to the coefficient of X_{1t} for the t test is, suggests that X_{1t} have on Y_{t+1} are not related. Meanwhile the $p-$value corresponding to the coefficient of X_{2t} for the t test is $p-$value=0.884>α, also suggests that X_{2t} and Y_{t+1} are not related. Therefore, we may conclude from the multiple linear regression analysis that the international dry bulk freight and coastal dry bulk freight for last period have little relation to the GZ port cargo activity.

In the analysis of regression and time series model, we can take the values of BDI, CCBFI and the GZ port cargo throughput in the past several periods as variables to predict, and study the effects the domestic and international dry bulk freights in the past several periods have on the Guangzhou port cargo throughput. We select periods have the best goodness of fit. The part of the operational report (using EViews® software) was shown in Table 6.

Where

$X_{(t-1)} = value\ of\ BDI\ for\ period\ t-1$

$Y_{(t-1)} = value\ of\ CCBFI\ for\ period\ t-1$

$Y_{(t-2)} = value\ of\ CCBFI\ for\ period\ t-2$

$Z_t = value\ of\ the\ Guangzhou\ port\ cargo\ throughput\ in\ period\ t$

If $\alpha = 0.05$, the $p-$value corresponding to the coefficient of $X_{(t-1)}$ for the t test is $Y_{(t-1)}$, which suggests that $Y_{(t-1)}$ and Z_t are not related. Similarly, the $p-$value corresponding to the coefficient of $Y_{(t-1)}$ for the t test is $p-$value=0.867>α, indicating that $Y_{(t-1)}$ and Z_t are not related. The $p-$value corresponding to the coefficient of $Y_{(t-2)}$ for the t test is $p-$value=0.2554>α, which suggests that $Y_{(t-2)}$ and Z_t are not related. Therefore, we may conclude that the international dry bulk freight and coastal dry bulk freight in the past several periods have little effects on the GZ cargo port handling capacity.

Since the coefficient estimates for the multi-linear regression and the time series regression cannot reject the null hypothesis that they are zero, or the past several periods that the domestic and international dry bulk freight rates in all have little effects on the cargo activity of the GZ port and cannot afford a significant role.

Implications and Summary

When making development strategies and policies Guangzhou port, we must give sufficient consideration to the conclusion that the international and domestic dry bulk freight rates have little effect on estimatingGZ cargo port capacity. Thus, despite the changing environment in the international shipping market, we see little effect of the activity in the GZ port development. The GZ port can continue to develop on the basis of improving its own port facilities. If the port meets the growing demand for cargo handling capacity, then growth will occur. Port conditions include waterway facilities, berthing facilities and harbor management level. Waterway is the lifeline of the port. The ship channel depth is related directly to whether the ship can reach the harbor. The port channel of the GZ port is 115 kilometers, which easily get accumulation of silt, we must attach great importance to deepening sea routes and improving port conditions. Wharfs, especially the size and number of berths, are important factors in determining the port handling capacity. GZ Port must pay attention to the construction of new berths and increasing port handling capacity so as to meet the growing demand for cargo throughput. Port management level affects not only the utilization efficiency and economic efficiency of the port, but also affects the level of service and the images of port companies which cannot be ignored similarly.

Opening up new routes and friendly ports is a means of broaden services scope at home and increasing supplies. Therefore, it is an integral part of development strategies of the port. On the one hand, we can open up new routes having development potential through the cooperation with shipping companies (Appendix 4).

For the purpose of forecasting handling capacity, in this study we determined that good and accurate prediction is warranted for future planning. In turn, the results of our study indicate that a simple two parameter EWMA model may prove extremely accurate, easy-to-use and an important model in predicting future needs. Conclusion

At first, in this paper we use 74 sets of data of the Guangzhou cargo port, BDI and CCBFI from January 2004 to February 2010 to establish the multiple linear regression model. The analysis on the regression results shows that the BDI and CCBFI have little effects on the GZ port cargo throughput for next period. According to the preliminary judgment, there are two reasons for this result. One is the lag on the effects that the dry bulk shipping freight have on the GZ port cargo throughput and another is the effects of other factors [13,14].

Then, according to the above analysis, we introduce the data of the BDI, CCBFI and the time series of the GZ cargo port in the past several periods and analyze the effects the above three kinds of series have on the GZ cargo port by making use of the regression and time series model. We conclude that dry bulk freight rates in international shipping market and the Chinese coastal shipping market have little effects on the GZ cargo port, while the time series is of great help for us to predict the GZ cargo port. In addition, the prediction accuracy of the model is not large [15].

In addition, two parameter EWMA requires use of only the historical time series of the GZ port for the purpose of forecasting. By example tests on the Guangzhou port cargo in March 2010 and

April 2010, we can conclude that the two parameter EWMA resulted in the best forecasts. Future modeling should consider ARIMA and Multivariate ARIMA models. The second set of these models may aid in long-term forecasting. Further, these models should be considered in the light of studies of the practice of forecasting [19-21].

References

1. Sun YG, Zheng G (2007) Research on Forecast of Port Throughput Capacity Based on Grey Theory. China Water Transport 5: 160-162.
2. Bakshia G, Panayotov G, Skoulakis G (2011) The Baltic Dry Index as a Predictor of Global Stock Returns, Commodity Returns and Global Economic Activity.
3. Wang C (2006) Port Handling Capacity Forecasting Based on Unascertained Number Regressive Model Communication Standardization.
4. Xu CY, Yan Y, Zhang P (2006) Prediction Model of Port Throughput Based on System Dynamics. Port andWaterway Engineering 32: 26-29.
5. Hui E, Seabrooke W, WoongK (2004) Forecasting Cargo Throughput for the Port of Hong Kong: Error Correction Model Approach. Journal of Urban Planning and Development 130: 195-203.
6. Yuan E, XieY (2007) On Ports Throughput Probability Forecasting Model Port and Waterway Engineering 33: 1028-1031.
7. Chen N, Zhu M, Yu (2005) Comparing Two Forecast Models of Ports Handling Capacity. Journal of Wuhan University of Technology 27: 77-79.
8. Lam WHK, Pan LP, Seabrooke W, Hui ECM (2004) Forecasts and Reliability Analysis of Port Cargo Throughput in Hong Kong. Journal of Urban Planning and Development 130: I33-144.
9. Sun L, Wang Z (2007) Studying the Probability Distribution of the port handling capacity in the port. Proceedings of SSMSSD 6: 1869-1873.
10. Pindyck RS, Rubinfeld DL (2010) Econometric Model and Economic Forecasts (4thedn.) McGraw-Hill.
11. Hummels D (2007) Transportation Costs and International Trade in the Second Era of Globalization. Journal of Economic Perspectives 135-136.
12. Jarrett J (1991) Business Forecasting Methods. 2nd Basil Blackwell, Oxford.
13. Brockwell PJ, Davis RA (2006) Time Series; Theory and Methods. Springer.
14. Anderson DR, Sweeney DJ (2006) Statistics for Business and Economics. China Machine Press.
15. Chase RB, Jacobs ER (2008) Operations Management for Competitive Advantage. China Machine Press 477-481.
16. Cheng LK, Wong YL (1997) Port Facilities and Container Handling Services: The Hong Kong Economic Policy Studies. City University of Hong Kong Press.
17. Yang S, Guan K (2005) Application of Spreadsheet to Forecasting Port Throughput. Wuhan Journal of University of Technology (Transportation Science and Engineering).
18. Sun L (2010) The research on a double forecasting model of port cargo throughput. World Journal of Modeling and Simulation 6: 57-62.
19. Fahrmeir L, Kneib T, Lang S, Marx B (2013) Regression Models, Methods and Applications. Springer.
20. Holt CC (1957) Forecasting Trends and Seasonal by Exponentially Weighted Averages. International Journal of Forecasting 20: 5-10.
21. Yuan E, Xie Y (2007) On Ports Throughput Probability Forecasting Model Port and Waterway. Engineering 33: 1028-1031.

Permissions

All chapters in this book were first published in JBFA, by OMICS International; hereby published with permission under the Creative Commons Attribution License or equivalent. Every chapter published in this book has been scrutinized by our experts. Their significance has been extensively debated. The topics covered herein carry significant findings which will fuel the growth of the discipline. They may even be implemented as practical applications or may be referred to as a beginning point for another development.

The contributors of this book come from diverse backgrounds, making this book a truly international effort. This book will bring forth new frontiers with its revolutionizing research information and detailed analysis of the nascent developments around the world.

We would like to thank all the contributing authors for lending their expertise to make the book truly unique. They have played a crucial role in the development of this book. Without their invaluable contributions this book wouldn't have been possible. They have made vital efforts to compile up to date information on the varied aspects of this subject to make this book a valuable addition to the collection of many professionals and students.

This book was conceptualized with the vision of imparting up-to-date information and advanced data in this field. To ensure the same, a matchless editorial board was set up. Every individual on the board went through rigorous rounds of assessment to prove their worth. After which they invested a large part of their time researching and compiling the most relevant data for our readers.

The editorial board has been involved in producing this book since its inception. They have spent rigorous hours researching and exploring the diverse topics which have resulted in the successful publishing of this book. They have passed on their knowledge of decades through this book. To expedite this challenging task, the publisher supported the team at every step. A small team of assistant editors was also appointed to further simplify the editing procedure and attain best results for the readers.

Apart from the editorial board, the designing team has also invested a significant amount of their time in understanding the subject and creating the most relevant covers. They scrutinized every image to scout for the most suitable representation of the subject and create an appropriate cover for the book.

The publishing team has been an ardent support to the editorial, designing and production team. Their endless efforts to recruit the best for this project, has resulted in the accomplishment of this book. They are a veteran in the field of academics and their pool of knowledge is as vast as their experience in printing. Their expertise and guidance has proved useful at every step. Their uncompromising quality standards have made this book an exceptional effort. Their encouragement from time to time has been an inspiration for everyone.

The publisher and the editorial board hope that this book will prove to be a valuable piece of knowledge for researchers, students, practitioners and scholars across the globe.

List of Contributors

Preuss B
Department of International Management and Economics, Copenhagen Business School, Denmark

Wei-Lung Huang
Assistant Professor, Department of Finance, China University of Science and Technology, Taiwan

Yan-Kai Fu
Assistant Professor, Department of Business Administration, China University of Science and Technology, Taiwan

G Martin Izzo
Fulbright Scholar, Visiting Associate Professor, Department of Marketing, King Abdulaziz University, Saudi Arabia

Shaza W Ezzi
Assistant Professor, Department of Marketing, King Abdulaziz University, Saudi Arabia

Sharda Haryani
M.Sc, (Ph.D pursuing), Prestige Institute of Management and Research, Indore, Madhya Pradesh, India

Bharti Motwani
MBA, PhD, Prestige Institute of Management and Research, Indore, Madhya Pradesh, India

Sukhjeet Kaur Matharu
MBA, MPhil, PhD, Prestige Institute of Management and Research, Indore, Madhya Pradesh, India

Tavana MA
Assistant Professor of Political Science, University of Yazd, Iran

Umme Aymon Janifa
Department of Aquaculture, Faculty of Fisheries, Bangladesh Agricultural University, Mymensingh-2202, Bangladesh

Md. Imran Omar
Agricultural Economics Division, Bangladesh Agricultural Research Institute, Joydevpur, Gazipur 1701, Bangladesh

Sabur SA and Moniruzzaman M
Department of Agribusiness and Marketing, Faculty of Agricultural Economics and Rural Sociology, Bangladesh Agricultural University, Mymensingh-2202, Bangladesh

Haque Md.S
Department of Agricultural Economics, Faculty of Agricultural Economics and Rural Sociology, Bangladesh Agricultural University, Mymensingh-2202, Bangladesh

Abam EN
Department of Hospitality Management, Catholic University Institute of Buea, Cameroon

Chaher Alzaman and Molham Chikhalsouk
Business and Engineering Management Department, Higher Colleges of Technology, UAE

Elsadig Musa Ahmed
Faculty of Business, Multimedia University, Cyberjaya, Malaysia

Anwar Ammar
Faculty of Management, Multimedia University, Cyberjaya, Malaysia

Selvaraj N
Saraswathi Narayanan College, Madurai, Tamilnadu, India

Doan Van Dinh
College of Economics and Trade Management of Hunan University, China and Faculty of Finance and Banking of the Industrial University of Ho Chi Minh City, Vietnam

Guangming Gong
Business school Hunan University in China

Natesa Prasad
Economics & Finance, College of Business, University of Bahrain, Bahrain

Babatolu Ayorinde
Department of Accounting, Federal University of Agriculture, Abeokuta, Ogun State, Nigeria

Oyewo Babajide
Department of Accounting, University of Lagos, Nigeria

Hossain SA
Teaching Assistant, London college of business management and Information technology, UK

Hassan N
Department of Statistics, University of Peshawar, KPK, Pakistan

Hassan T
Department of Economics, University of Malakand, KPK, Pakistan

George Athanassakos
Ben Graham Chair in Value Investing, Richard Ivey School of Business, The University of Western Ontario, London, Ontario, N6A 3K7 Canada

Robin H Luo
School of Economics and Finance, Wuhan University, China

Maniam Kaliannan and Samuel Narh Adjovu
School of Business, University of Nottingham Malaysia

Saeed MS and Zahid N
Glasgow Caledonian University, Glasgow Business School, Glasgow, UK

Novatorov EV
Department of Management, Higher School of Economics, National Research University, Russia

Ljupco Davcev
Faculty of Economics, Goce Delcev University, Stip, FYROM

Nikolas Hourvouliades
American College of Thessaloniki, Greece

Christopher von Koch, Ola Nilsson, MicaelJönsson, Jeff Andersson, Karin Jonnergård and Erik Matthiesen
School of Business and Economics, Linnaeus University, Sweden

Ashish Garg
Masters in Financial Engineering - UCLA, PhD - Philadelphia University, USA

Raghavendra RH
Research Scholar, Department of Commerce School of Management, Pondicherry University, Pondicherry-605 014, India

Velmurugan PS
Fulbright Post doctoral Fellow and Assistant Professor, Department of Commerce School of Management, Pondicherry University, Pondicherry, India

Kiran Bibi and Sir Habib Ahmad
Department of Business Administration (finance), Foundation University, New lalazar, Rawalpindi, Pakistan

Jeffrey E Jarrett
Department of Management Science, University of Rhode Island

Huanxin Zhang and Xia Pan
Lingnan College, Sun Yat-sen University, China

Index